# COREL
# WordPerfect Suite 8
## INTEGRATED COURSE

**Mary Alice Eisch,** Appleton, Wisconsin
**Susan K. Baumann,** Coralville, Iowa
**John Blake,** Chicago, Illinois

**JOIN US ON THE INTERNET**
WWW: http://www.thomson.com
EMAIL: findit@kiosk.thomson.com    A service of I(T)P®

**South-Western Educational Publishing**
*an International Thomson Publishing company* I(T)P®

Cincinnati • Albany, NY • Belmont, CA • Bonn • Boston • Detroit • Johannesburg • London • Madrid
Melbourne • Mexico City • New York • Paris • Singapore • Tokyo • Toronto • Washington

WQ75AA ISBN: 0-538-68527-1
WQ75A8H881 ISBN: 0-538-68528-X

2                                                                                            98
Printed in the United States of America


I(T)P®
International Thomson Publishing

South-Western Educational Publishing is a division of International Thomson Publishing Inc. The ITP logo is a registered trademark used herein under License by South-Western Educational Publishing.

Corel, Paradox, Quattro, and WordPerfect are registered trademarks and Presentations is a trademark of Corel Corporation or Corel Corporation Limited in Canada, the United States and/or other countries. Windows is a registered trademark of Microsoft Corporation. IBM is a registered trademark of International Business Machines Corporation. Paradox, Quattro Pro, Presentations, WordPerfect, and Windows, together with the names of all other products mentioned herein, are used for identification purposes only and may be trademarks or registered trademarks of their respective owners.


Some screen shots for this text were created using Collage Complete, a product of Inner Media, Inc., Hollis, New Hampshire.

| | |
|---|---|
| *Managing Editor:* | Carol Volz |
| *Project Manager:* | Anne Noschang |
| *Consulting Editor:* | Judith Voiers |
| *Contributing Author:* | Kathy Krueger |
| *Content Reviewers:* | Sue Ehrfurth, Meredith Flynn |
| *Cover and Internal Design:* | Grannan Graphic Design, Ltd. |
| *Cover Illustration:* | Grannan Graphic Design, Ltd. |
| *Design Coordinator:* | Mike Broussard |
| *Production Services:* | Electro-Publishing |

# *How to Use this Book*

What makes a good applications text? Sound pedagogy and the most current, complete materials. That is what you will find in the new Corel Word Perfect Suite 8 series. Not only will you find a colorful, inviting layout, but also many features to enhance learning.

**SCANS** (Secretary's Commission on Achieving Necessary Skills) — The U.S. Department of Labor has identified the school-to-careers competencies. The five workplace competencies (resources, interpersonal skills, information, systems, and technology) and foundation skills (basic skills, thinking skills, and personal qualities) are identified in the exercises throughout the text. More information on SCANS can be found on the *Electronic Instructor.*

**Notes** — These boxes provide necessary information to assist you in completing the exercises.

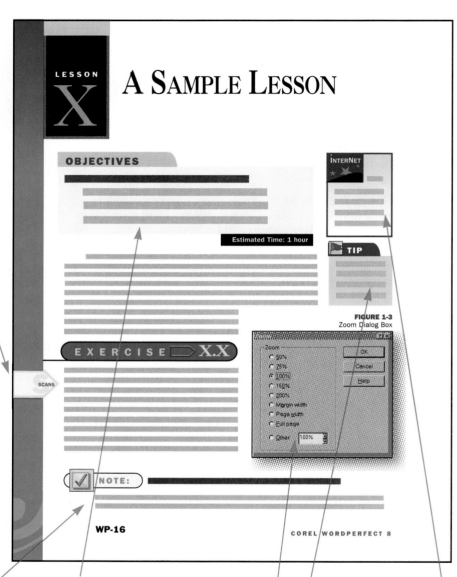

**Objectives** — Objectives are listed at the beginning of each lesson, along with a suggested time for completion of the lesson. This allows you to look ahead to what you will be learning and to pace your work.

**Enhanced Screen Shots** — Screen shots now come to life on each page with color and depth.

**Tips** — These boxes provide enrichment information about features of the software.

**Internet** — Internet terminology and useful Internet information is provided in these boxes located throughout the text.

# How to Use this Book

**Summary** — At the end of each lesson you will find a summary to prepare you to complete the end-of-lesson activities.

**Lesson Review Questions** — Review material at the end of each lesson enables you to prepare for assessment of the content presented.

**Lesson Project** — End-of-lesson hands-on application of what has been learned in the lesson allows you to actually apply the techniques covered.

**Critical Thinking Activity** — Each lesson gives you an opportunity to apply creative analysis to situations presented.

*Summary*

LESSON X REVIEW QUESTIONS

LESSON X PROJECT

CRITICAL THINKING ACTIVITY

Lesson X A Sample Lesson

**WP-17**

# PREFACE

## *To the User*

Congratulations on choosing to learn Corel® WordPerfect® Suite 8. At the end of the course, you should be an expert in the use of the suite to prepare documents, perform calculations, prepare presentations, and keep track of data of all types.

## Organization of the Text

Take a few minutes to page through this text. You will see that it is divided into sections for each of the software applications in the suite. Each section begins with a listing of the lessons in the section and the estimated time for completion of those lessons. Positioned between the separate applications are integration sections. These sections give you an opportunity to use the features learned in one application and to integrate those with applications previously learned.

In each of the application sections, the lessons contain explanatory material about Corel WordPerfect Suite 8 features and tools, along with short exercises in which you will practice using those features and tools. At the beginning of each lesson is an introduction and a list of lesson objectives so you can see at a glance what you will be learning in the lesson. Each lesson ends with a summary, review questions, a hands-on project, and a critical thinking activity.

It is important that you proceed through the lessons in order. Do not skip around, or you will miss important information about Corel WordPerfect Suite 8 tools. As you work through a lesson, read the information provided in the paragraphs carefully to get the background information for each of the tools. The exercises that provide practice in the use of the tools are printed in a different font face and have numbered steps that lead you through the use of the feature. Follow the steps carefully so you get the expected results with each exercise. Develop the habit of reading through an exercise before you begin it so you have an idea of the purpose of the exercise.

A suggested time is provided at the beginning of each lesson to give you a target time frame for the completion of the lesson. As indicated, this time is just an estimate. The time it will take for you to learn the content of a lesson will depend on the following variables:

- Is this your first computer class?

- Have you had previous experience with Windows?

- Have you had previous training in word processing, the use of spreadsheets, preparing presentations, or working with a database?

- Are you learning in an independent setting or in an instructor-led classroom?

Obviously, if you've had extensive computer training, you will progress through the lessons more quickly than you would if this were your first computer class. If you are working in an individualized, self-paced classroom, work carefully and methodically so you don't miss any important information. See how well you can complete the exercises without help from your instructor.

At the back of the text is a set of Quick Reference cards. The cards contain alphabetical listings of features learned in each application, together with information about how to choose the features from menus or how to access the features from the keyboard. In addition, the lesson number which covers each feature is listed, in case you wish to refer back to the lesson to review the use of the feature.

## Other Resources

A set of prerecorded files is available to save keying time as you progress through the lessons. These documents are saved in what's referred to in the text as the student **Datafile** folder. When you need to open a prerecorded file, your exercise instructions will clearly specify that the file is in the student **Datafile** folder. (These files are available on the *Electronic Instructor* CD-ROM or in the text/data disk package, ISBN 0-538-68528-X.) Check with your instructor about the location of the student **Datafile** files.

A Progress Record for each segment of your training is located at the end of the text, just before the Quick Reference. The Progress Record lists the work your instructor will evaluate as you progress through the lessons. Check with your instructor to find out how you should use the Progress Record.

The reference material for Corel WordPerfect Suite 8 comes on CD-ROM. This reference may or may not be available in your classroom. Ask your instructor whether or not you may use the CD containing the reference.

## Before You Begin

If you have never before used a computer, study Appendix A before beginning Lesson 1. In that appendix, you will find information about the sophisticated piece of equipment on which you will be working as you learn the application programs in Corel WordPerfect Suite 8. This introduction to the equipment should make you feel more comfortable with the hardware that you will be using.

Before beginning Lesson 1 of the WordPerfect segment, you should also work through the Getting Started section at the beginning of the text. This section provides a brief introduction to the Windows 95 environment and shows you the important parts of the working windows in the suite. It also teaches you how to start and exit from Corel WordPerfect Suite 8 applications, as well as how to create and save text. You are also expected to know the information found in the following appendices:

- Appendix B introduces the Windows 95 environment. If you have not had an introduction to this operating system under which Corel WordPerfect Suite 8 runs, take the time to read through it.

- Appendix C is an introduction to file management. You'll learn more about file management in some of your lessons.

Once you are comfortable with all of the material in the Getting Started section as well as Appendices A, B, and C, you will be ready to begin your work with WordPerfect Lesson 1.

If you work hard and concentrate as you progress through the material in this text, you are sure to complete the course with a good understanding of what Corel WordPerfect Suite 8 is and how it can help you do your work. Happy learning!

## *To the Instructor*

An *Electronic Instructor* is available to provide you with a variety of instructional materials to be used in the classroom. This *Electronic Instructor* includes a CD-ROM and a printed instructor's manual. On the CD-ROM you will find lesson plans, scheduling charts, evaluation materials, the prerecorded **Datafile** files, solution files, SCANS materials, figures in the text that may be used to prepare transparencies, and much more. You'll have all the materials you need in one convenient location. The materials on the CD-ROM may be copied onto your hard drive or onto the network server. The printed manual shows solutions to the hands-on exercises and suggested lesson plans to help you guide users as they learn Corel WordPerfect Suite 8.

## *Acknowledgments*

Many thanks to Judy Voiers for her guidance, inspiration, good sense, and seemingly unlimited time resources as the consulting editor on this project. Thanks, too, to Anne Noschang for holding it all together, even when the going got tough.

*Mary Alice Eisch, Sue Baumann, and John Blake*

# TABLE OF CONTENTS

## GETTING STARTED ✓

## COREL® WORDPERFECT® 8

## COREL® QUATTRO® PRO 8

# NEW FEATURES

**Corel WordPerfect 8 includes the following new features:**

- The Power Bar has been replaced with a series of context-sensitive Property Bars to provide the tools needed for the current application.

- The Status Bar has been replaced with the Application Bar which shows, in addition to the usual Status Bar information, the names of all open documents.

- A large number of context-sensitive Toolbars have been added.

- QuickTasks, templates, and Coaches have been combined into a feature called PerfectExpert projects that WordPerfect remembers from one use to another.

- The PerfectExpert panel provides button access to designing and formatting tools for completion of projects.

- The Address Book has been improved, making it possible for you to enter business and home information about your contacts.

- HTML support has been improved to help with the preparation of Web documents.

- A drawing layer has been added that enables you to draw graphics directly into your text, group the objects, and specify the order of the graphics layers.

- TextArt can now be displayed in either 2-D or 3-D format.

- Tools have been regrouped into the menus in a more logical manner.

- The Bullets & Numbering feature now contains full Outline flexibility for creation and editing of outlines.

- The Prompt-As-You-Go feature helps you with spelling and grammatical errors and provides help with finding the correct word (thesaurus).

- The Abbreviations feature is now called QuickWords and has expanded capabilities, allowing you to automate the insertion of frequently used, formatted text.

- The Tables tool includes features that make it easy to split cells and columns and add formatting to your tables.

- The Clipart Scrapbook enables you to drag the desired image into your document. Tens of thousands of graphics images are available on the Corel WordPerfect Suite 8 CD-ROM.

**Corel Quattro Pro 8 includes the following new features:**

- The Power Bar has been replaced with context-sensitive Property Bars to provide the tools needed for the current application.

- The Status Bar has been replaced with the Application Bar, which shows, in addition to the usual Status Bar information, the names of all open notebooks.

- Some menu options have been regrouped in a more logical manner.

- Templates, Experts, and QuickTasks have been replaced with more than 65 PerfectExpert projects that are simpler and more flexible.

- The PerfectExpert panel provides button access to designing and formatting tools for completion of projects.

- Hot keys are shown in QuickTips.

- Page view allows spreadsheets to be displayed as they will appear when printed, including margins, headers, and footers.

- Spreadsheets can be edited while in Page view.

- Multiple font types and sizes can be used in cells.

- The QuickFormat feature allows you to copy and paste the formatting of one cell to another cell.

- The QuickFilter instantly removes irrelevant data to let you focus on key information.

- The Formula Composer can be accessed by simply clicking a Toolbar button.

## Corel Presentations 8 includes the following new features:

- The Status Bar has been replaced with the Application Bar, which shows, in addition to the usual Status Bar information, the names of all open documents.

- The Custom Audiences™ feature enables you to create different versions of the same slide show by allowing you to skip designated slides while making a presentation.

- Intel MMX™ Technology Support speeds up transitions between slides and redraws the screen faster and more accurately.

- Navigation Tabs make it easy to switch between slides.

- Predesigned slide shows, called PerfectExpert™ projects, save you the time of choosing a master and slide layouts, and provide you with prompts on what type of information belongs in each slide.

- The Power Bar has been replaced with a series of context-sensitive Property Bars to provide the tools needed for the current application.

- The Clipart Scrapbook enables you to drag the desired image into your slide show. Tens of thousands of graphic images are available on the Corel WordPerfect Suite 8 CD-ROM.

- The View Tabs enable you to switch easily between the Slide Editor, Slide Sorter, and Slide Outliner views.

# START-UP CHECKLIST

## HARDWARE

### Minimum Configuration

✓ PC using 486 processor operating at 66 Mhz

✓ 8 Mb RAM

✓ Hard disk with at least 106 Mb free disk space

✓ VGA monitor with graphics adaptor

✓ Mouse or alternative pointing device

✓ Printer

### Recommended Configuration

✓ PC using 486 or Pentium processor operating at 66 Mhz or faster

✓ 16 Mb RAM or more

✓ Hard disk with at least 205 Mb free disk space

✓ CD-ROM drive, 4x or faster

✓ VGA monitor with graphics adaptor

✓ Mouse or alternative pointing device

✓ Printer

## SOFTWARE

✓ Microsoft Windows 95 or Windows NT 4.0

✓ Corel WordPerfect Suite 8 Professional

# PET PARADISE

Congratulations! You have been hired as an office employee for Pet Paradise, a pet shop in Austin, Texas. Polly and Paul Paradeis are the owners of the shop, and they have a second shop named Pet Paradise II in a different area of Austin. Most of your work will be for Polly. She understands that you will be learning Corel WordPerfect Suite 8 as you begin your work with the company.

The addresses, phone numbers, and managers of the shops are as follows:

| | |
|---|---|
| Pet Paradise | Pet Paradise II |
| 9001 Parkway Boulevard | 7922 Pendleton Way |
| Austin, TX 78711 | Austin, TX 78745 |
| Phone: 512-555-5455 | Phone: 512-555-8712 |
| Fax: 512-555-5422 | Fax: 512-555-8713 |
| Manager: Alma Alvaro | Manager: Daniel LaPierre |

# GETTING STARTED

Corel® WordPerfect® Suite 8 applications are tied together by a common user interface. In this section we will look at that interface using Corel WordPerfect 8. When you work with Quattro Pro 8, Presentations 8, and Paradox, you'll discover that the parts of the window are familiar.

In the same way, starting and exiting the applications, as well as file management, are the same for all applications of the suite.

**NOTE:**

If this is your first experience with a computer, Appendix A contains important information to make you comfortable with the hardware and the mouse.

Also, if you have never before worked with Windows 95, you should explore Appendix B before beginning this section. It provides a valuable introduction to Windows 95 and the desktop.

## *Starting Applications*

You may start any of the Corel Word-Perfect Suite 8 applications in a number of ways:

- Click the Start button and choose Corel WordPerfect Suite 8 from the section at the top. Then choose the desired application from the pop-out menu.

- Click the icon on the Desktop Application Director (DAD), probably at the bottom of your window. (See Figure GS-1.)

- Click the appropriate icon on the desktop (if a shortcut has been created).

**FIGURE GS-1**
The Corel WordPerfect Suite 8 DAD Bar

Corel PerfectExpert

Corel Presentations 8

Corel Quattro Pro 8

Corel WordPerfect 8

CorelCENTRAL

Netscape Communicator

Corel Paradox 8

Corel WEB SiteBuilder

# EXERCISE ⟩ GS.1

1. With the Windows 95 desktop showing, start Corel WordPerfect 8 using any method.

2. Look at the WordPerfect window. Find the parts that are identified in Figure GS-2, including the insertion point.

3. Move your mouse around in the window. What does the mouse pointer look like? Key your first name. Note that it begins at the vertical and horizontal guidelines.

4. Press **Enter** several times. Watch the *Ln* indicator on the Application Bar at the lower right corner of the window. This indicator measures your distance from the top of the window in inches. Press the space bar several times. Watch the *Pos* indicator measure your distance in inches from the left edge of the page.

5. Look at the Title Bar at the top of the window. When you began to key, the message changed from *Corel WordPerfect - Document 1 (Unmodified)* to *Corel WordPerfect - Document 1.*

6. Press **Backspace** until the insertion point is a double space below your name. Key your complete name and press **Enter** twice. Key your name one more time and press **Enter** twice again.

7. Look at the *Ln* indicator. You should be at approximately 2.18" from the top of the page. Leave the text in the window as you explore the parts of the WordPerfect window.

**FIGURE GS-2**
The Corel WordPerfect 8 Working Window

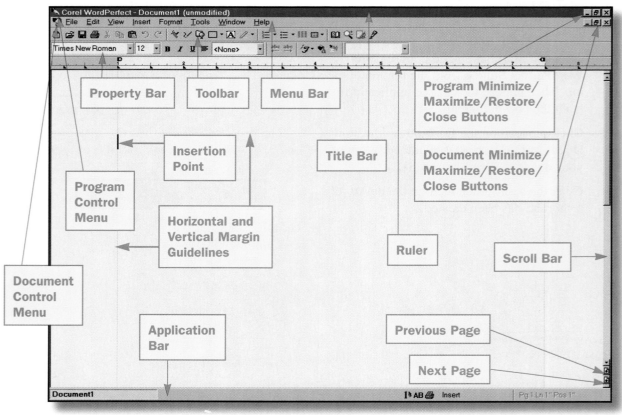

# *Window Parts*

**TIP**

When you read about a *default*, that means the feature looks or works the way it did when the software was installed. It contains the factory settings.

WordPerfect has created shortcuts making many useful tools available by a click of the mouse when pointing to a tool on one of the bars. (Many don't look like buttons until you point to them with the mouse pointer.) These tools are in a variety of places on the window. Let's look at those tools, beginning with the Application Bar.

## Application Bar

The Application Bar shows at the bottom of the window, above the Windows 95 taskbar. Figure GS-3 illustrates the default Application Bar. It lists the open files. As you learned in Exercise GS.1, it also reports the location of your insertion point on the page.

**FIGURE GS-3**
Application Bar

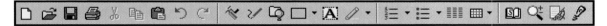

Look for the large *I* with an arrow beside it. If the button with the *I* appears to be depressed, click once to deselect it. This button is for the Shadow Cursor, which you'll learn about later. You should also see *AB* (caps lock), the picture of a printer, and the word *Insert*. If you see *Typeover*, press the Insert key on your keyboard.

## Toolbar

Each Corel WordPerfect Suite application has a Toolbar, which provides buttons for frequently used tools. Corel WordPerfect 8 comes with more than a dozen Toolbars; the default Toolbar is illustrated in Figure GS-4.

WordPerfect switches to the appropriate Toolbar depending on your work.

**FIGURE GS-4**
WordPerfect 8 Toolbar

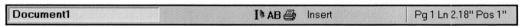

You can choose other Toolbars and display several at once. You can also edit the Toolbars that come with WordPerfect or create your own Toolbar. You'll learn that later.

## Property Bar

The tools on the Property Bar also change depending on what you're doing. The default WordPerfect Property Bar is illustrated in Figure GS-5.

**FIGURE GS-5**
Default Property Bar

All three of these bars are located in the same position in each of the major Corel WordPerfect Suite 8 applications. If you point to a button on any of those bars, a Quick Tip appears, telling you the function of the button. Let's work briefly with these tools.

# EXERCISE ▷ GS.2

1. With the three lines of names showing in the window and your insertion point a double space below the third, point to the **AB** button on the Application Bar. Hold the pointer on the button a few seconds and read the Quick Tip.

2. Click to select the **AB** button. The button will remain depressed. Key your name and press **Enter** twice. It should appear in all capital letters. Click the **AB** button again to deselect Caps.

3. Look at the Property Bar. At the left is the default font face. What is that font name? Point to the name of the font face and hold the pointer there while you read the Quick Tip.

4. Click the arrow beside the font name and move the mouse pointer slowly down through the list. Look at the sample for each font. Choose any font and key your name again. Press **Enter** twice.

5. Find the original font in the drop-down list and choose it.

6. Find the button near the right of the Toolbar that looks like a magnifying glass with a + and – beside it. Hold the pointer there and read the Quick Tip.

7. Click that button and choose **50%**. Click it again and choose **200%**. Finally, return to **100%**.

8. Key your name again. Then find the button on the Toolbar that looks like a blue arrow curved to the left. Read the Quick Tip and then click the button. Undo has taken the name away. Click the button to the right of it (Redo) to replace your name. Keep your file open as you read on.

The buttons used in the previous exercise are buttons that appear on those same bars in most of the Suite applications. You can browse through the buttons using the Quick Tips to learn what each button does.

The buttons on the bars are shortcuts to features that can be selected from menus. Since not all menu items have shortcuts, you need to learn to use the menus and the dialog boxes that are accessed from the menus. In addition, by right clicking (clicking the right mouse button), you can display a QuickMenu that offers more shortcuts.

## Menus

The Menu Bar is just above the Toolbar. The WordPerfect Menu Bar is illustrated in Figure GS-6. The menus available vary from application to application. In WordPerfect, the menus provide all of the tools needed to create, edit, and format files, in addition to a large number of specialized tools to make your work easier. Let's learn about menus.

**FIGURE GS-6**
Corel WordPerfect 8 Menu Bar

File   Edit   View   Insert   Format   Tools   Window   Help

SCANS

1. Open the **Edit** menu and compare it to the menu illustrated in Figure GS-7. Note the information at the right of the menu choices. If those keystroke shortcuts aren't displayed on your menu, you'll learn to display them in Exercise GS.5.

2. Look at the items in gray. Those items are not available at this time. When text is selected, more choices are available.

3. Look at the items followed by three dots. If you choose one of them, a dialog box will be opened.

4. Look at the items followed by an arrow (▶). When you choose one of these items, a submenu appears. To see a submenu, move the highlight to **Select**.

5. Use your mouse to click **Repeat Next Action**. Look at the little dialog box. Click **Cancel** to close the dialog box.

**FIGURE GS-7**
WordPerfect Edit Menu

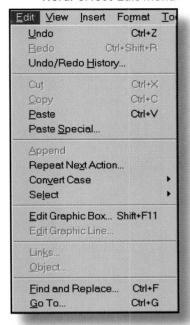

## Dialog Boxes

Like menus, dialog boxes group tools to make them easy to find. While some dialog boxes look complex because they contain many parts, most dialog boxes present choices in a logical manner. Let's explore a dialog box that you'll use frequently in your work with WordPerfect.

 **TIP**

When making choices with round buttons, only one button may be chosen at a time.

Figure GS-8 illustrates the dialog box used for page setup. In this box you:

- click a tab at the top to choose a different major category.

- choose a different size of paper by simply clicking the desired size in the white box.

- change from *portrait* to *landscape* orientation (which way the paper is turned) using the round buttons.

- create a new paper size or edit the selected size using the buttons at the right.

- click the Help button to learn more about the available settings.

- accept any choices made by clicking OK.

- cancel any choices made and close the dialog box by clicking Cancel.

Let's open a menu, choose the Page Setup dialog box, and explore this menu.

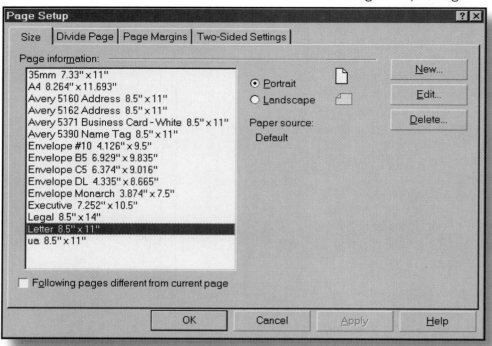

# EXERCISE ⇨ GS.4

**SCANS**

1. Open the **Format** menu and choose **Page**. Then choose **Page Setup**. The dialog box illustrated in Figure GS-8 should appear.

2. Change from Portrait to Landscape and then back to Portrait again. Look at the tiny illustrations beside the buttons.

3. Click the **Page Margins** tab at the top and look at the choices available in the dialog box. Figure GS-9 illustrates the Page Margins portion of the Page Setup dialog box.

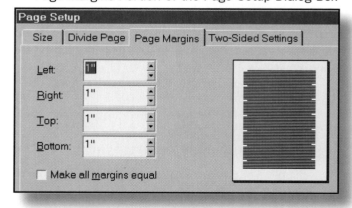

4. Note that the setting in the text box for the Left margin is highlighted (in blue). When a dialog box choice is highlighted, you can simply begin to key the replacement value. The

(continued on next page)

original value will automatically be deleted. Key **2** to set the left margin at 2" and press **Tab**.

5. Key **2** for the right margin. Look at the illustration in the dialog box. It shows a sample page with 2-inch side margins.

6. Point to the *2"* setting for the left margin and double click to highlight it. Use the "elevator buttons" at the side of the text box to change the margin back to **1"**. (You'll have to click the down arrow ten times. This is not a very efficient method!)

7. Finally, click **Cancel** to cancel all settings and return to your document window.

## QuickMenus

Another way to make choices when using the mouse is with a QuickMenu. Right click to display a QuickMenu. The features available in the QuickMenu will depend on where the pointer is when you right click. The available features will also depend on the current application. A different QuickMenu will appear, for example, if you have text selected.

Figure GS-10 illustrates the QuickMenu that will appear now if you point near your name and right click. You can choose features from the QuickMenu just like from one of the other menus.

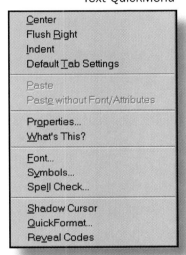

**FIGURE GS-10**
Text QuickMenu

## Function Keys

Many features can be chosen using function keys—those keys across the top of the keyboard identified with *F* and a numeral. While you'll probably use your mouse for most choices, using the function keys keeps your hands on the keyboard and is useful for some features. In the WordPerfect lessons, when a feature may be chosen with a function key combination more easily than from a menu, your instructions will include that information.

# *Changing Defaults*

As you'll learn throughout your training, many decisions were made by the developers of the software regarding what is best for most users. Usually, those decisions are fine.

In the next exercise you will go to the Settings dialog box to see where you can make changes. **With your instructor's permission**, you may change a couple of settings. One is to display the keyboard shortcuts in your menus. Another is to change the number of minutes between automatic backup.

Ask your instructor if you should make any changes in Exercise GS.5. If so, complete the exercise. If not, look at the dialog boxes in the exercise, but don't make any changes. (If you are working on a network, it may not accept any changes you make in this lesson.)

## EXERCISE ▷ GS.5  (Optional, with instructor's approval)

1. Open the **Tools** menu and choose **Settings** (at the bottom). A dialog box with icons will appear.

2. Double click to choose **Environment** and click the **Interface** tab. At the left are three items regarding what will be displayed in the menus. If *Display shortcut keys* doesn't have a check mark, click to choose that option. Click **OK** to leave this dialog box.

3. In the Settings dialog box choose **Files**. Look at the choices. It is here that you tell WordPerfect to save your files with the *.wpd* extension. It is here that you can also set the time for automatic backup. The default is 10 minutes.

4. Change to 5 minutes and click **OK**. Close the Settings dialog box to return to your document window.

5. Open the **Edit** menu and look to see if the shortcuts are now listed at the right of some choices (Ctrl+ and a letter or other character).

## Exiting Applications

You may exit a Corel WordPerfect Suite 8 application in the following ways:

- Open the File menu and choose Exit.
- Double click the icon at the left of the title bar in the upper left corner.
- Click the *X* in the upper right corner of the window.

Because you have text in the window, you will be asked if you would like to save the file. We'll practice exiting without saving. Then we'll create some more text and save the file.

## EXERCISE ▷ GS.6

1. Open the **File** menu and choose **Exit**. At the *Save Changes* question, choose **No**.

2. When you are back at the Windows 95 desktop, use one of the methods you learned about earlier and start WordPerfect again.

3. Key the following sentence: **This is my first document to be saved.**

4. Keep the sentence in the window as you read on.

## Saving a File

To save a file, you must know two things—where you will save it and what it will be named. If you haven't learned about naming and saving computer files, you should study Appendix C before continuing with this section. The appendix provides very important information regarding file management.

**Location of Files**. For these learning materials, it is assumed that you will be saving your work on a diskette in Drive A. When instructions about file location are given, *a:\* or *3¹/₂ Floppy (A:)* will be used as the location for your files. Ask your instructor where you should save your work. If you are to save your work on the hard drive of your computer or in a network location, your instructor will help you the first time you save a file. In that case, each time you see references to Drive A, you will be expected to make the appropriate adjustments so your files are saved in the correct location.

**Naming Files**. For these learning materials, your file names will have three parts. The first part is some information about the content of the file. The second part tells the lesson and exercise where the file was created. The third part contains your reference initials so your files don't get mixed up with those of other students. For example, you will be told to save a file about insurance created in Lesson 4, Exercise 5 as **insurance 4-5 xxx**. (The *xxx* should always be replaced with your initials.)

You can save a file in one of the following ways:

- Open the File menu and choose Save.

- Click the Save button on the Toolbar.

- Press Ctrl+S.

- If you wish to close the file and save it, open the File menu and choose Close.

If the file has not yet been saved, you will be asked whether or not you wish to save the file. If you answer *Yes*, the Save As dialog box will be displayed, where you will choose the location for the file and name the file. Let's learn about the Save As dialog box as you save your short file.

## EXERCISE ▭⟹ GS.7

**SCANS**

**1.** Open the **File** menu and choose **Close**. At the question about saving, click the **Yes** button or key **Y**. The Save As dialog box will appear, looking like Figure GS-11.

**2.** Above the large white box is a white *Save in* text box. If it doesn't show the location where your files are to be saved, click the small black arrow at the right end of the box and choose the desired location from the list in the drop-down menu (see Figure GS-12). You may need to use the scroll bar to locate the desired folder.

**FIGURE GS-11**
Save As Dialog Box

Save As - My Documents

File  Edit  View  Tools  Favorites  Help

Save in: My Documents

Corel User Files

File name: *.wpd                    Save

File type: WordPerfect 6/7/8   Last modified: Any Time    Close

Password protect    Find    Advanced...    New Search

1 object(s)    90.4KB

3. Below the large white box is a *File name* text box, with *.wpd* highlighted. Key **practice GS-7 xxx** to name your file. (If *.wpd* isn't highlighted, double click to select it before keying the file name.)

4. Finally, click the **Save** button to save the file. The file will remain in the window. Look at the Title Bar. The name of the file should be showing there. Look at the Application Bar. The file name will be there, too.

5. Click to position the insertion point after the *t* of *first* in the sentence in your window. Use **Backspace** to remove the word and replace it with **second**.

**FIGURE GS-12**
Save In Drop-Down List in the Save File Dialog Box

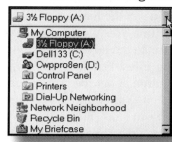

6. Click at the end of the sentence and press **Enter** twice. Key your name. Keep the file open in the window as you learn about Save As.

# Save As

In your WordPerfect training you will often save a file with a different name. To do this choose Save As from the File menu. In the Save As dialog box choose the location for your new file, and either change the old name or key a new name.

EXERCISE ▷ GS.8

SCANS

1. Open the **File** menu and choose **Save As**. The old name of the file will be showing in the *File name* text box.

2. Click beside the *7* and change it to an **8** so **practice GS-8 xxx** is displayed. Click the **Save** button.

3. Change the word *second* to **third**. This time, simply add an **a**, making the file name **practice GS-8a xxx**. Click the **Save** button. You now have three files.

4. Open the **File** menu again and choose **Close** to close the file.

# The Open File Dialog Box

You may open a file in one of the following four ways. Each method uses the Open File dialog box which looks much like the Save As dialog box.

■ Click the Open button on the Toolbar.

■ Open the File menu and choose Open.

■ Press Ctrl+O.

■ Press F4.

In addition to all of those methods, another choice exists if the file you wish to open is one of the last nine files you saved. The names of the last nine files accessed are listed at the bottom of the File menu. If the file you want appears in that list, you can choose it there.

Let's learn about features of the Open File and Save As dialog boxes.

## View Options

Look at the Open File dialog box in Figure GS-13. The following options have been chosen:

- The Menu Bar is displayed. (A button at the far right of the *Look in* box controls this option.)

- The Status Bar is displayed at the bottom of the box, telling how many objects (files) are displayed in the folder, how much space they take (in terms of bytes or kilobytes), and how much room remains on the disk. (This option may need to be chosen in the View menu.)

- The Toolbar is displayed below the Menu Bar, with List selected.

- Files are listed alphabetically by name.

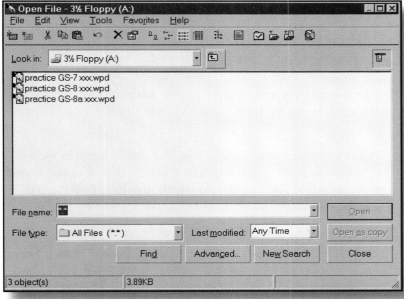

**FIGURE GS-13**
Open File Dialog Box

Six options are available for viewing your list of files. The choices begin with the ninth button from the left on the Toolbar. The choices are Large Icons, Small Icons, List, Details, Tree View, and Preview. We'll look at those shortly.

In addition, you can arrange your list of files alphabetically by name, size, date, or type of file. The default is to list the files by name. Let's explore all these choices.

## EXERCISE ⟹ GS.9

1. Use one of the four methods above to open the Open File dialog box. If *3¹/₂ Floppy (A:)* isn't selected, click the little down arrow beside the *Look in* box and choose *3¹/₂ Floppy (A:)*. (You may need to use the scroll bar to find it.)

2. Compare your list of files with the list in Figure GS-13. It should be similar. If your dialog box doesn't display a Menu Bar, click the Menu toggle button at the right.

3. Find the six buttons on the Toolbar that are illustrated in Figure GS-14.
   a. Click the first one and look at the *large icons*.

**b.** Click the second one and look at the *small icons*.

**c.** Click the third one and look at the *list*.

**d.** Click the fourth one and look at the *details*. With this button, you can see when a file was created and how large it is. Keep *details* chosen.

**e.** Click the fifth button. This shows the Tree View. Click it again to turn it off.

**f.** Point to **practice GS-7 xxx** and click once to highlight it. Click the sixth button and look at the *preview* of the file. Click the *preview* button again to deselect it.

**4.** Open the **View** menu and choose **Arrange Icons**. Choose **by Date**. Note that the most recent file is now at the top. Use the same procedure to arrange the icons **by Name**.

**5.** Point to **practice GS-7 xxx** and double click to open the file. (You could have also clicked once to select the file and then clicked the Open button.) It's that easy to open a file.

**6.** Close the file. Display the Open File dialog box again and read on.

**FIGURE GS-14**
View Buttons on Open
File Dialog Box Toolbar

At the bottom of the dialog box, \*.\* should show in the *File name* text box, indicating that you'd like all files with all extensions listed. Below that, a folder should indicate that you want all types of files. At the right, you can choose which revision of the file you'd like. If your settings look like those in Figure GS-13, they are exactly right.

## QuickFinder

QuickFinder is a tool used to search for files by name or unique content. QuickFinder can catalog all files on your computer so that it can find files in a hurry (Fast Search). We will not use Fast Search in this course. Let's try a short exercise with QuickFinder on the three short files you created.

## E X E R C I S E  GS.10

SCANS

**1.** With your three practice files showing in the dialog box, click to position your insertion point in the *File name* text box.

**2.** Key your first name and click the **Find** button near the bottom of the dialog box. WordPerfect should list only the last two files, since they are the ones that contain your name.

**3.** Click the **Back** button to return to the full list. Point to your name and click once to select it. Key the word **first**. Then click the **Find** button. Only the first file should be listed. Click **Back** again and keep the Open File dialog box open as you learn about Favorites.

## Favorites

It is time consuming to use the drop-down menu by the *Look in* box to change to Drive A every time you want to open a file. An easier way is to assign the location of your files to the Favorites list. Favorites is an easily customizable list that can be used to identify the folder to which your files are saved.

As before, the next exercise assumes that you are saving your work on a diskette in Drive A. If you are saving your work in a different location, please substitute the location for your work whenever reference is made to *3¹/₂ Floppy (A:)*.

## EXERCISE ▷ GS.11

1. With the Open File dialog box still displayed, click the **Favorites** button and look at the list of favorites. If it hasn't been changed, you might see folders for graphics, macros, and personal files.

2. Look for *3¹/₂ Floppy (A:)*. If it is there, continue with this exercise. If it is not there, skip to Step 4.

3. Position the highlight on *3¹/₂ Floppy (A:)* and press **Delete** on the keyboard. At the prompt asking if you would like to delete *3¹/₂* floppy to the Recycle Bin, answer **Yes**. (You are only deleting a shortcut!)

## Folders

As in a drawer of paper documents or files, folders help group computer files so you can find them more easily. Folders may be created in either the Open File dialog box or the Save As dialog box. Once a folder is created, you can copy, move, or save files into the folder.

4. Click the down arrow beside the *Look in* text box. Use the scroll bar, if necessary, to find the *3¹/₂ Floppy (A:)* location. Click to highlight it.

5. With the *3¹/₂ Floppy (A:)* location highlighted, click the **Add to Favorites** button. (It is just to the right of the Favorites button.) Answer **Yes** at the question about the **\*.\*** filter. You want all files listed. Keep the Open File dialog box displayed.

### 🚩 TIP

When you copy a file from one place to another, you end up with two copies—one in the old location and one in the new location. When you move a file, the only copy of it is in the new location.

## EXERCISE ▷ GS.12

*right click*

1. With the Open File dialog box showing, open the **File** menu. Choose **New** and choose **Folder**. A New Folder icon will appear in your list of files, with a box around the words *New Folder*.

2. Key **learn** and press **Enter**. Close the Open File dialog box and open it again so the folder is moved to the top of the list. Your file list will look much like Figure GS-15, with the folder at the top of the list.

3. Click **practice GS-7 xxx** once to highlight it. Then point to it again and press and hold the left mouse button. Move the mouse slightly. When the pointer turns into a circle with a line through it, drag the highlighted file to the **learn** folder. Release the mouse button and the file will be moved.

**FIGURE GS-15**
File List

> learn
> practice GS-7 xxx.wpd
> practice GS-8 xxx.wpd
> practice GS-8a xxx.wpd

4. Point to the **learn** folder and double click to open it. Is the **GS-7** file in the folder? Now click the button to the right of the *Look in* box above the list to go back one level of folders. This returns you to your original list. Only two files will show with the folder.

5. Double click the **learn** folder again and click

the **GS-7** file once to select it. Open the **File** menu and choose **Move to Folder**. Click the **Go Back** button again to return to the main list in Drive A. Click the **Move** button in the dialog box. Your file should be moved back to the main list. Return to the main list to check it. Keep the Open File dialog box displayed.

## Selecting Files

In Exercise GS.12 you moved one file. To copy the file instead of moving it, hold the Ctrl key while you drag the file to the other folder. Sometimes you might want to work with several files at a time. Select several consecutive files by clicking to highlight the first file. Then hold the Shift key while you click the final file. All files in between will be selected.

You can select several files that are not consecutive by holding the Ctrl key while you click the files to be selected. Let's practice selecting files. Then we'll copy them to the **learn** folder. Finally, we'll delete the folder and all of the files. You won't need them again.

### EXERCISE ⬜▷ GS.13

1. With the Open File dialog box showing, click once to select the **GS-7** file. Press and hold the **Shift** key while you click once on the **GS-8a** file. Release the Shift key. All three files should now be selected.

2. Click away from the files to deselect them.

3. Again, click once to select the **GS-7** file. Press and hold the **Ctrl** key while you click once on the **GS-8a** file. Release Ctrl. Only those two files are selected.

4. Press and hold the **Ctrl** key while you point to either of the selected files and drag to copy the two of them to the **learn** folder. Check to see if copies of the files are in the folder.

5. Click the **Favorites** button and double click $3^1/2$ *Floppy (A:|)*. Click once to highlight the remaining file. Open the **File** menu and choose **Rename**. Key your first name as the new name of the file.

6. Browse through the buttons on the Toolbar and look at the menus to see what they include. (The Undo button will not bring back a file you have deleted!)

7. Delete the file you just renamed. Do this by highlighting it and either choosing Delete from the File menu or pressing the Delete button on the keyboard.

8. Use the other procedure to delete the **learn** folder and its contents. Then close the Open File dialog box.

# Help

**W**hen working with any computer program, you are bound to need help periodically. Your best resource is the Help facility. Help looks the same in most programs running under Windows 95. You may access help from the Help menu (see Figure GS-16) or by pressing F1. The Help Topics choice displays the WordPerfect Help dialog box (see Figure GS-17).

**FIGURE GS-16**
Help Menu

**FIGURE GS-17**
WordPerfect Help Dialog Box

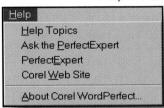

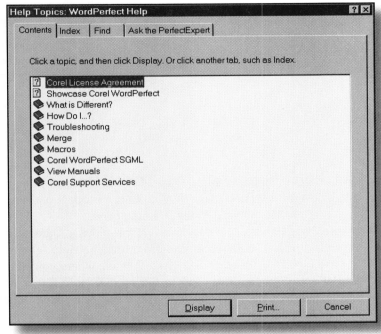

Note the tabs near the top of the dialog box. *Contents* lists major topics. At the right, *Ask the PerfectExpert* makes a good attempt to find the appropriate Help section if you key a question. *Find* enables you to search for a help by specific word or phrase.

The *Index* section is arranged alphabetically by category. Here you can key the name of the feature. The more you key, the closer Word-Perfect will get to the topic you're seeking. When the topic is listed, click Display to go to that category. Let's practice by reviewing how to exit a Corel WordPerfect Suite application.

## EXERCISE ⟹ GS.14

SCANS

1. Open the **Help** menu and click the **Index** tab. Key **exit** and look at the four choices.

2. Choose **Corel WordPerfect**. The Help window in Figure GS-18 will appear. Read the Help information.

3. Point to the *About Close and Exit* icon at the bottom. Note that the pointer turns into a hand. Click that icon.

4. Read about closing and exiting. Then click the **Back** button at the top of the dialog box to return to the Exit box.

5. Click the **Help Topics** button at the top of the box to return to the list of Help topics.

(continued on next page)

6. Use the scroll bar to go to the bottom of the Help topics. What is the last major topic in the list? It should be *zooming*.

7. Click the **Cancel** button at the bottom right to close the dialog box. Click the **X** to close Corel WordPerfect Help.

**FIGURE GS-18**
WordPerfect Help Topics Dialog Box

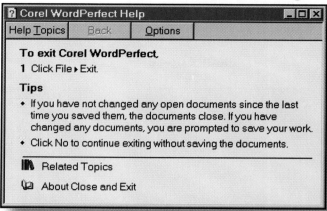

The Help menu (see Figure GS-16) contains some other ways to get help. *PerfectExpert* leads you through several common tasks. If you have a modem and an Internet connection, *Corel Web Site* will take you to the Corel WordPerfect 8 home page.

Finally, *About Corel WordPerfect* provides program information about your registered serial number and release numbers of the program. The Help feature is packed full of important information. What's more, it is *context-sensitive*; that is, when you are using a feature and you access Help, WordPerfect will often take you to the special Help topics related to the feature with which you are working. You'll want to spend some time exploring Help when you've learned more about the Corel WordPerfect Suite 8 applications.

# COREL®
# WORDPERFECT® 8

**Estimated Time: 22 hours**

# CREATING DOCUMENTS

## OBJECTIVES

**Upon completion of this lesson, you will be able to:**

- Create, print, and save a document.

- Vary the appearance of the text in the document.

- View a document a number of ways.

- Work with the codes that control the formatting of your document.

- Move the insertion point within the document.

- Enter the date automatically.

- Insert a file into an existing document.

- Identify the document with the Path and Filename code.

- Create and print a letter, complete with an envelope.

**⏱ Estimated Time: 1¹/₂ hours**

Before beginning Lesson 1, it is important that you are familiar with your computer and the operating system, as well as the basics with regard to managing files. Appendices A, B, and C will provide that important information. Read them!

In addition, the Getting Started section of the text provides an overview of what you can expect to see as you work with Corel® WordPerfect® Suite 8. It will introduce you to starting the Suite applications, opening, saving, and closing files, and the working window parts. The material in the Getting Started section is critical to your work with the Suite applications. If you haven't already studied that section and completed the exercises in it, do that now, before you begin this lesson.

## Creating Text

To create documents in a word processing program, simply key the text to be included. If the text is in paragraph format, key continuously, letting WordPerfect wrap the text to the next line when a line is filled. Do NOT press Enter until you have finished the paragraph. Let's begin by keying a simple paragraph.

**TIP**

In the printing and publishing business, the preferred practice is to put only one space following the punctuation at the end of a sentence. In personal and business documents, two spaces should be used for increased readability.

## EXERCISE ▷ WP1.1

1. Start WordPerfect. In a new document window key the text in Figure 1-1 as follows:
   a. Press the **Tab** key to indent the beginning of the paragraph.
   b. If you feel an error when you make it, use **Backspace** to delete the error and fix it.
   c. Press the **space bar** twice at the end of each sentence.
   d. Otherwise don't worry about errors. Some words with errors will be underlined in red. You'll learn about that feature later.

2. At the end of the paragraph, press **Enter** twice.

3. Open the **File** menu and choose **Save**. Change to the folder where you will keep your work and name the file **pp 1-1 xxx**, substituting your initials for *xxx*.

4. Keep the file open in the window as you read on.

**FIGURE 1-1**
Text for Exercise WP1.1

This is my first exposure to Corel WordPerfect Suite 8 as I begin work at Pet Paradise in Austin, Texas. The other employees at Pet Paradise have been using WordPerfect for a number of years and assure me that I will enjoy it as much as they do. I am looking forward to learning how to use WordPerfect, Quattro Pro, Presentations, and Paradox. I will also enjoy learning how to put all of the pieces of the Suite together.

## Text Appearance

You can change the appearance of text by changing the font face, font size, or font color. In addition, the use of bold, underline, and italic gives variety to the text appearance. All of these choices may be made from the Property Bar that appears just above your text. Look at the default Property Bar and use the mouse pointer to point to the buttons, looking at the Quick Tips for each button.

You can apply changes to the appearance of the text as you key, or you can select the text and format it after it has been keyed. In Exercise WP1.2 you'll apply the format as you key. In Lesson 2 you'll learn to select text for formatting.

## EXERCISE ▷ WP1.2

1. With your insertion point a double space below the paragraph, open the **File** menu and choose **Save As**. Save the file as **pp 1-2 xxx**, again substituting your initials for the *xxx*.

2. Click the **Bold** button on the Property Bar. Note that it looks like the button is depressed. Key your name. At the end of your name, click the **Bold** button again to deselect that option, and press **Enter** twice.

(continued on next page)

**3.** Using the same procedure but with the **Italic** button, key your name in italic followed by a double space.

**4.** Click the arrow beside the **Font Face** button and move your mouse pointer over some of the available font faces. Look at the sample at the right of the list. Choose a different font face and key your name again.

**5.** Before pressing Enter, click the **QuickFonts** button on the Property Bar and choose the default font (what you were using before you changed fonts). Press **Enter** twice.

**6.** Click the arrow beside the **Font Size** button and change to **20** pt. Choose **Bold**. Key your name. Change back to the original font size and turn Bold off. Press **Enter** twice.

**7.** Key your name one more time, using any combination of fonts, font sizes, or appearance choices you wish. (Even though your printer probably can't print it, try a different font color. That button is farther to the right on the Property Bar.)

**8.** Save the file again with the same name. Keep it open in the window.

# *Viewing a Document*

WordPerfect's View menu provides several ways to view your documents. These choices include the following:

- **Page.** This is the default setting. The document is shown with margins and full formatting.

- **Draft.** This setting shows side margins, but only shows a line separating pages and no top or bottom margins. If you have headers, footers, or footnotes, they are not displayed in Draft view.

- **Two Pages.** This choice shows a miniature of two pages, side by side. All formatting is included.

- **Zoom.** When you choose Zoom from the View menu, the dialog box illustrated in Figure 1-2 is displayed. You can choose any Zoom option from 25% to 400%. The default Toolbar also includes a Zoom button. The icon looks like a magnifying glass. Can you find it?

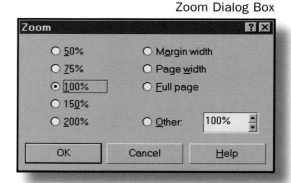

**FIGURE 1-2**
Zoom Dialog Box

It is a good idea to use Zoom or Two Pages to preview your document before printing so you can see how it will look on the page. Let's look at the document in a variety of ways. Then we'll learn to print.

**INTERNET** The Internet is a telecommunications system that connects many different networks of computers. The Internet is often called a "network of networks."

# EXERCISE ⟶ WP1.3

1. Open the **View** menu and choose **Draft**. Note that the text moves to the top of the window, and the top margin is not displayed.

2. Open the **View** menu and choose **Two Pages**. Obviously you don't need two pages to look at your document this way.

3. Return to **Page** view.

4. Open the **Zoom** menu and choose **200%**. Use the scroll bar at the right to move to the top of the document. Is the top margin visible?

5. Use the **Zoom** button on the Toolbar to Zoom to **Full Page**. This is probably the best choice to check document placement before printing.

6. Now Zoom to **100%** and read on.

# Printing

You can print your documents in a variety of ways. If they are showing in the window, you may choose any of the following methods to open the Print dialog box:

■ Click the Print button on the Toolbar.

■ Open the File menu and choose Print.

■ Click the Print button on the Application Bar.

■ Press F5 or Ctrl+P.

Study Figure 1-3. Look at the tabs at the top (below the Title Bar). For most printing, you'll use the *Print* tab. We'll explore the other tabs as they are needed.

Look at the setting for the *Current printer*. The printer illustrated in this figure is probably different from the printer attached to your computer. Have your instructor show you where your work will be printed and check the make and model of the printer you are to use. The setting in the dialog box MUST match the printer, or you will get pages of garbage when you try to print.

In the next section of the dialog box note that you have several choices regarding how much of the document to print. If you have a multiple-page document and need to print only one page, it is time-consuming and wasteful to print more than the *Current page*.

At the right you can tell WordPerfect how many copies of the document you'd like printed. For your work in this training, you'll print only one copy. Sometimes you may need to print several. In most cases, it's less expensive to print one copy and take it to a copy machine for multiple copies than it is to make multiple copies on the printer.

The *Status* button at the bottom lets you look at your document in the print queue (the documents sent to the printer from your computer). This is where you'd go to cancel a print job if you change your mind after sending the document to the printer. Most of the time, the computer will be faster than you are, and the document will already be sent before you can cancel it.

**FIGURE 1-3**
Print Dialog Box

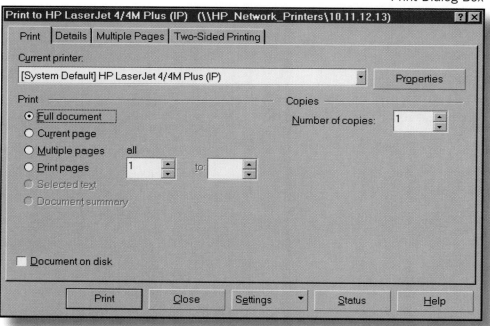

## EXERCISE ⇨ WP1.4

1. Use one of the methods above to display the Print dialog box. Check to make sure the printer listed matches the printer you are to use. If it doesn't, click the arrow beside the *Printer* text box and choose the correct printer.

2. Click the **Print** button at the bottom of the dialog box or press **Enter** to send the document to the printer. (You can press Enter because the button you want—in this case Print—is enclosed in a heavy black line. That is the default choice.)

3. Retrieve your printed copy from the printer. After showing it to your instructor, you can take it home and put it on your refrigerator as your first Corel WordPerfect Suite 8 document!

4. Keep the document open in the window as you read on.

## *Reveal Codes*

One of the features that sets WordPerfect apart from other word processing programs is Reveal Codes. Each time you add formatting to a document, a code is hidden in the document. WordPerfect shows that code in a special codes window where you can see it. Codes help you edit the formatting or check on the type of formatting used. You can reveal your codes by:

■ choosing Reveal Codes from the View menu.

■ right clicking to display the QuickMenu and choosing Reveal Codes.

■ pressing Alt+F3.

■ dragging the Reveal Codes window open using the small gray buttons on the scroll bar (one is above the up arrow at the top and one is below the down arrow at the bottom)

When your codes are revealed, you will see two copies of the text in the window—one without codes at the top and a gray one at the bottom with codes. Both copies have an insertion point, but it looks different. Let's look at the codes in your document.

## EXERCISE ▷ WP1.5

1. Point with your mouse at the end of the final keying of your name and click the right mouse button to display the QuickMenu.

2. Choose **Reveal Codes** from the bottom of the menu. Find the red box in the Reveal Codes window. That red box is your insertion point.

3. Look at the codes at the beginning of the final keying of your name. You should see a code for each of the appearance options you choose— Bold, Italic, Underline, font face, font size, or font color.

4. Use the left arrow key on your keyboard to move the insertion point to the left, past the codes and the words. Watch the codes as you do this. When the insertion point is at the left of a code, the code sometimes expands to provide more information.

5. Explore the codes in your document:
   a. Use the up arrow key to move back through your document until you come to the occurrence of your name that is enclosed in [Bold] codes.
   b. Notice the [HRt] codes. Those are *Hard Returns*, and one is entered each time you press the Enter key. Because you pressed Enter twice after each name, you should see two [HRt] codes between each name.
   c. Press the up arrow key to move the insertion point into the paragraph. Note that each line that wrapped automatically ends with a [SRt] code. Those are *Soft Returns*, and one is entered each time WordPerfect automatically begins a new line.
   d. Move the insertion point down to the first occurrence of your name.

6. Point to one of the [Bold] codes with the mouse pointer, and drag the code up and out of the Reveal Codes window. Note that both [Bold] codes are gone from the Reveal Codes window, and the formatting is removed from the name in the normal viewing window.

7. Using your mouse, point to the line that divides the Reveal Codes window from the rest of your window. When the pointer becomes an arrow that points both up and down, press the left mouse button and drag that "border" down and off the page to close the Reveal Codes window.

8. Practice each of the other methods of revealing and hiding your codes that are listed prior to this exercise. Then close the Reveal Codes window. Keep the document open in the window as you read on.

**W P - 7**

# *Moving the Insertion Point*

In the next lesson you will learn a number of ways of editing a document. In order to edit, you need to be efficient at moving around in the document. There are a number of ways to move the insertion point within a document. You can do it with the mouse or you can use the keyboard. (Both methods work well—which you use will depend on where you hands are positioned.)

## Moving the Insertion Point from the Keyboard

Besides the arrow keys, which you've already used, the keyboard has a number of keys dedicated to moving the insertion point. Figure 1-4 lists those keys or keystroke combinations and tells how each is used.

**FIGURE 1-4**
Keystrokes for Moving the Insertion Point

| | | | |
|---|---|---|---|
| End | moves to the end of the line | Ctrl+G | Go To enables you to move to a specific page. |
| Home | moves to the beginning of the line | Ctrl+→ | moves one word to the right |
| Page Up | moves to the top of the window | Ctrl+← | moves one word to the left |
| | | Ctrl+↑ | moves up one paragraph |
| Page Down | moves to the bottom of the window | Ctrl+↓ | moves down one paragraph |
| | | Alt+Page Up | moves to the first line on the previous page |
| Ctrl+Home | moves to the beginning of the document | Alt+Page Down | moves to the first line on the next page |
| Ctrl+End | moves to the end of the document | | |

When you use keystroke combinations, like those in Figure 1-4 where the Ctrl or Alt key is displayed together with a plus sign (+) and another key, hold the Ctrl or Alt key while you press the other key in the combination. You'll get very good at some of these, like Ctrl+Home and Ctrl+End! Let's practice on your short document. Then you will access a longer document that has been saved for you in the student **Datafile** folder. If you don't know where the presaved documents are stored, ask your instructor before you begin.

## E X E R C I S E ⟹ WP1.6

1. Use your right thumb to press and hold the **Ctrl** key at the right of your keyboard. While you are holding that key, use a finger on that hand to press the **Home** button. Your insertion point should be moved to the beginning of the document.

2. Use the same procedure for **Ctrl+End** to move the insertion point to the end of the document.

3. Practice the Ctrl+arrow key combinations.

4. Close your document without saving it again. Go to your Open File dialog box and locate the student **Datafile** folder. Open **welcome**.

5. Use **Save As** to save the file as **welcome 1-6 xxx**. (Did you remember to put your initials in place of *xxx*?)

6. With the insertion point at the beginning of the document, choose **Font Size** from the Property Bar and change to **16 pt**.

7. Move your insertion point in your document as follows:
   a. Press **Ctrl+End** to move to the end of the document. Look at the position section of the Application Bar. It should report that you are on *Pg 2*.
   b. Press **Ctrl+Home** to move to the beginning of the document.
   c. Press **Alt+Page Down** to move to the beginning of the second page.
   d. Return to the top of the first page with either **Alt+Page Up** or **Ctrl+Home**.
   e. Use **Page Down** to move through the document a windowful at a time. (This is great for proofreading.)

8. Practice some of the other combinations. Then keep the document open as you read on.

## Moving the Insertion Point with the Mouse

When your hands aren't on the keyboard for keying, you may prefer to move in the document using the mouse. Click to position the mouse anywhere in your document.

In addition, the scroll bar provides a number of options for moving around in a document—many that are similar to those you just practiced. Look at the scroll bar at the right side of your window. When the scroll box is at the top of the scroll bar, you are looking at the beginning of the document. When the scroll box is at the bottom of the scroll bar, you are looking at the end of the document—no matter how long the document is. A shorter document will have a larger scroll box. A long document will have a very small scroll box. You can:

- click the down arrow at the bottom of the scroll bar to move the document in the window one line at a time.

- go the opposite way with the up arrow at the top of the scroll bar.

- drag the scroll box up or down to move greater distances quickly.

- click above the scroll box to move backwards through your document a windowful at a time.

- click below the scroll box to move forward by a windowful.

- click the page turn buttons at the bottom of the scroll bar to move a page at a time—forward or backward.

 NOTE:

When you use the scroll bar to move through a document, the insertion point doesn't move. When you move in a document with the keyboard, the insertion point goes with you.

1. If you are not at the top of the document, drag the scroll box to the top of the bar and click to position your insertion point at the beginning of the first line.

2. For practice, click to position the insertion point between the words *Pet* and *Paradise* in the first line of the document. Then click to position it after the year in the first paragraph.

3. Click below the scroll box to move forward a windowful. (Again, this is good for proofreading!) Continue to click below the scroll box until you are below the text on the second page.

4. Touch the right arrow key once. Because the insertion point was still at the beginning of the document, your insertion point simply moved past the first character following the date.

5. Click on the scroll bar below the scroll box. Your page should move up in the window so you are looking at the middle of the first page. Click the same place again. You should see the bottom of the first page and the top of the second.

6. Click the scroll bar below the scroll box once more. Where is your insertion point?

7. Return to the beginning of the document. Reveal your codes. Find the Font Size code and drag it out of your document. Close Reveal Codes.

8. Zoom to **Full Page** and look at the document. Because the font size is smaller, the entire document fits on one page.

9. Close the document without saving again.

# Date

Your computer keeps track of the current date. WordPerfect enables you to take advantage of that fact by automatically inserting the date whenever you request it. The date can be inserted in one of two ways. It can be entered as:

**FIGURE 1-5**
Date/Time Dialog Box

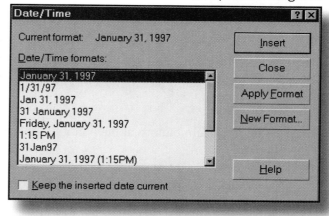

- **Text.** A date entered as text won't change. Insert the current date as text at the insertion point by pressing Ctrl+D.

- **A code.** Enter a date code by pressing Ctrl+Shift+D. When the date is entered as a code, each time that document is opened or printed, the date changes to the current date.

If you prefer, you can insert the date by opening the Insert menu and choosing Date/Time. A variety of formats are available, as illustrated in Figure 1-5. Look at the check box at the bottom of the dialog box. When you click to place an *x* in that box, the date will be entered as a code, and it will update each time you open the document.

Let's add the date to a previous document.

## EXERCISE ⟩ WP1.8

1. Open the **File** menu and choose **Open** to display the Open File dialog box.

**TIP**

Press **Ctrl+O** or click the **Open** button on the Toolbar to display the Open File dialog box.

2. Go to your solution files and choose **pp 1-2 xxx**. Open that file. Use **Save As** to save the file as **pp 1-8 xxx**.

3. With the insertion point at the beginning of the document, press **Enter** twice to move the text down. Then press the up arrow twice so your insertion point is a double space above the paragraph.

4. Key the date (e.g., January 5, 1998) and press **Enter** twice. (The paragraph will move down two more line spaces.)

5. Enter the date text by pressing **Ctrl+D**. Press **Enter** twice.

6. Open the **Insert** menu and choose **Date/Time**. Compare your dialog box with Figure 1-5.

7. Click the check box at the bottom of the dialog box to tell WordPerfect to **Keep the inserted date current** (*Automatic update* in some dialog boxes). Then click **Insert** or press **Enter** to close the dialog box.

8. Reveal your codes and look at them. Move the insertion point to the left of the [Date] code. It should show the current date. Note that only the final date has a code. The others are text.

9. Keep the document open in the window as you read on.

## Insert a File

WordPerfect makes it easy for you to join two documents together. Simply position the insertion point in one document at the location where you would like the other document to be inserted. Then choose File from the Insert menu, locate the desired file, and insert it. Let's add a short pre-saved paragraph to your document.

**QuickSteps**

**Insert File**
1. Position the insertion point.
2. Open the Insert menu and choose File.
3. Locate the file to insert.

## EXERCISE ⟩ WP1.9

1. With **pp 1-8 xxx** showing in the window, use **Save As** to save the file as **pp 1-9 xxx**.

2. Click to position the insertion point at the end of the last line of the paragraph, following the word *together*.

3. Press **Enter** twice. Your insertion point will be positioned halfway between the end of the paragraph and the first keying of your name.

(continued on next page)

4. Open the **Insert** menu and choose **File**. Go to the student **Datafile** folder and choose **intro**. Double click to insert it into your document or click once to highlight it and click **Insert**. The paragraph should be added at the location of the insertion point.

5. Save your file again as **pp 1-9 xxx** and keep it open as you read on.

# Path and Filename Code

In the classroom as well as on the job, it is a good idea to identify documents so that if you want to work with them again, you'll be able to find them. One way WordPerfect helps you to identify your documents is with the Path and Filename code. Let's learn how to insert that code as you add it to your current document.

**QuickSteps**

**Path and Filename**
1. Position the insertion point.
2. Open the Insert menu and choose Other.
3. Choose Path and Filename.

1. With **pp 1-9 xxx** showing in the window, use **Save As** to save the file as **pp 1-10 xxx**.

2. Press **Ctrl+End** to move the insertion point to the bottom of the document. Position the insertion point a double space below the last name. (Use Enter if you need to add line spaces.)

3. Open the **Insert** menu and choose **Other**. Then choose **Path and Filename**. The name of the

document should appear, accompanied by the drive or folder where the document is saved.

4. Reveal your codes and move the insertion point to the left of the [Filename] code. Note that the code expands to show the information included in it.

5. Print the document and close it, saving it again as **pp 1-10 xxx** when you close it.

# Create a Letter

Now that you know how to create text, insert the date, save a document, and print it, let's create a letter to be printed on Pet Paradise letterhead and sent to a customer changing a grooming appointment. Follow along carefully. You'll get to key some of the letter. Part of it has been keyed and saved for you.

## EXERCISE ▷ WP1.11

1. Beginning in a new document window, watch the right side of the Application Bar as you press **Enter**. When your insertion point is somewhere near **Ln 2"**, insert the date as text.

2. Following the date, press **Enter** four times and key the name, address, and greeting in Figure 1-6. Following the greeting, press **Enter** twice.

3. Use **Insert** to insert **resched** from the student **Datafile** folder. Move your insertion point to the bottom of the document.

4. Press **Enter** four times and key your name. Save the document as **Buster 1-11 xxx**.

5. Press **Enter** twice and insert the Path and Filename code. Print the letter, and keep it open in the window.

**FIGURE 1-6**
Opening Lines for Letter

```
Barb Nelson
9832 Oak Street
Austin, TX 78736

Dear Barb:
```

# *Envelope*

W̲ordPerfect makes the preparation of envelopes easy. With a letter showing in the window, choose Envelope from the Format menu, and WordPerfect will copy the name and address of the letter recipient onto the envelope. It also offers some options— whether or not you want to include a return address, or whether you want a POSTNET bar code, as well as some other options. In the next exercise we'll prepare an envelope for Ms. Nelson's letter. Before you begin the exercise, check with your instructor to see if you can print envelopes on the classroom printer. Your instructor may wish to give you special instructions.

**QuickSteps**

**Create an Envelope**
1. With the letter showing, open the Format menu.
2. Choose Envelope.
3. Set the options.

## EXERCISE ▷ WP1.12

1. With the letter showing in the window, open the **Format** menu and choose **Envelope**. Notice that Barb's name and address show in the proper position on the envelope. Your dialog box should look much like Figure 1-7.

2. At the left, be sure the *Print return address* check box is NOT selected. (Pet Paradise has preprinted envelopes.)

3. Look for the *POSTNET Bar Code* box below the *Mailing addresses* box at the right. If it is not there, click the **Options** button and choose to put the bar code BELOW the address. Click **OK**.

(continued on next page)

**WP-13**

**4.** Be sure your printer is ready to print your envelope. Then click the **Print Envelope** button.

**5.** Retrieve your envelope from the printer and close the document without saving it again.

**FIGURE 1-7**
Envelope Dialog Box

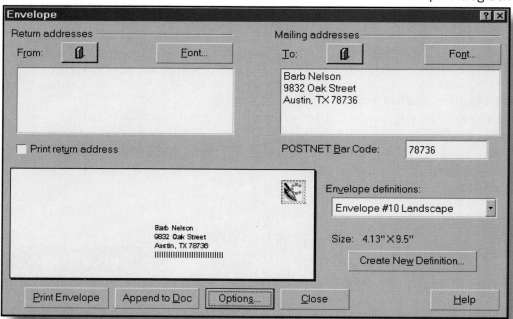

# *Summary*

This lesson contains a variety of topics—all aimed at getting you started with WordPerfect. You learned that:

■  when creating text in paragraphs, you should press Enter only at the end of the paragraph.

■  you can use Bold, Italic, and Underline, as well as font face, font size, and font color to add interest to your documents.

■  you can view your document in a variety of ways, including looking at the codes that format the document.

■  both the keyboard and the mouse offer a variety of ways to move the insertion point.

■  WordPerfect will help you enter the date both as text and as a code.

■  the Path and Filename code identifies the name and location of a document.

■  WordPerfect helps you create envelopes.

## LESSON 1 REVIEW QUESTIONS

### MULTIPLE CHOICE

**Circle the best answer to each of the following statements.**

1. Which key combination moves your insertion point most quickly to the beginning of a multiple-page document?
   A. Page Down
   B. Ctrl+End
   C. Ctrl+Home
   D. Alt+Page Up

2. Which view of the document shows the document without top and bottom margins?
   A. Zoom
   B. Draft
   C. Page
   D. Two Pages

3. Which "bar" contains the tools for changing the appearance of your text?
   A. Menu Bar
   B. Toolbar
   C. Property Bar
   D. Application Bar

4. When you click above or below the scroll box on the scroll bar, your text moves
   A. a line at a time.
   B. a paragraph at a time.
   C. a windowful at a time.
   D. a page at a time.

5. Which menu did you use to enter the date, insert a file, and add the Path and Filename code to your document?
   A. File
   B. View
   C. Insert
   D. Help

6. You can choose Reveal Codes from all of the following sources EXCEPT
   A. the QuickMenu.
   B. the View menu.
   C. buttons on the scroll bar.
   D. buttons on the Property Bar.

(continued on next page)

# WRITTEN QUESTIONS

**Write your answers to the following questions.**

7. Briefly describe the procedure for finishing one line and beginning the next when you are keying paragraph material.

8. What happens to the insertion point when you move around in your document using the scroll bar?

9. Describe the difference between entering the date as text and entering the date as a code.

10. Briefly describe the procedure for combining the open file with a file saved on the disk.

## LESSON 1 PROJECT

SCANS

A friend called and asked you about your training on WordPerfect. You haven't had much time to learn yet, but you want to give your friend some information about the program. Key a letter to that friend, including some information you found in an advertisement. Follow these steps.

1. Begin in a new document window. Position the date text about **2"** from the top of the page.

2. Press **Enter** four times and key the name and address of a friend. (You may make up the address if you'd like.) Press **Enter** twice (a double space) and key the greeting followed by another double space.

**FIGURE 1-8**
Text for Lesson 1 Project

```
I am just beginning my training with the first application in Corel
WordPerfect Suite 8. The application is WordPerfect, and I am learning
to create letters like this one. I am looking forward to learning to
use Quattro Pro, Presentations, Paradox, and CorelCENTRAL.
```

3. Press **Tab** once and key the text in Figure 1-8 as the first paragraph of your letter. Each time you key the name of one of the Suite applications, use Bold as shown in the figure. Press **Enter** twice following the paragraph.

4. Insert **corel2** from the student **Datafile** folder as the second paragraph. Leave a double space and insert **corel4** from the student **Datafile** folder as the third paragraph.

5. Double-space below the third paragraph, key **Sincerely,** and press **Enter** four times to leave room for the signature above your name.

6. Save the letter as **Corel proj1 xxx.** Insert the Path and Filename code a double space below your name.

7.  Prepare an envelope with the POSTNET bar code. Print both the letter and the envelope.

8.  Close the file, saving it again with the same name.

## CRITICAL THINKING ACTIVITY

You are working in WordPerfect and viewing a document created by a coworker that seems to have a change of font face in the middle of the document. You want the entire document to be formatted with the font used at the beginning. How can you fix the problem?

# EDITING TEXT

## OBJECTIVES

**Upon completion of this lesson, you will be able to:**

■ Insert and delete text.

■ Use Typeover to replace text.

■ Select blocks of text of any size.

■ Use Delete, Undo, Redo, and Undelete.

■ Highlight text with the Highlight feature.

■ Use Cut, Copy, Paste, and Drag and Drop to edit text.

■ Open a new blank document.

■ Use QuickFormat to format related text parts.

■ Work more efficiently using QuickCorrect.

■ Insert symbols and special characters into your text.

■ Edit text using proofreaders' marks.

🕐 **Estimated Time: 1$\frac{1}{2}$ hours**

When using word processing software, a good rule to go by is "never rekey." Rekeying takes time and provides an opportunity to introduce errors into text that has already been proofread. You should become adept at correcting your work and, whenever possible, reusing text that has already been keyed. In this lesson you will learn a variety of ways of correcting text, as well as several ways to take text from one document into another document. You'll also learn additional shortcuts for formatting your work and using special symbols.

## *Inserting and Deleting Text*

To insert text into text that has already been keyed, simply click to position the insertion point and key the new text.

Text can be deleted with either the Backspace key or the Delete key. Figure 2-1 illustrates several delete keystrokes available in WordPerfect. Let's practice.

FIGURE 2-1
Deletion Tools

Lesson ② Editing Text

**Backspace** removes text to the left of the insertion point, one character or space at a time. Hold down this key to delete several characters quickly. The text to the right of the insertion point will shift to the left to close up the space as you press the Backspace key.

**Del** and **Delete** are used to delete characters following the insertion point. Again, if you hold the key down, characters will be deleted as they scroll in from the right.

**Ctrl+Backspace** deletes the word in which the insertion point is located. If you hold the Ctrl key and press Backspace several times, you will delete several consecutive words.

**Ctrl+Delete** deletes from the insertion point to the end of the line.

## E X E R C I S E ⟹ WP2.1

1. Beginning in a new document window, go to the student **Datafile** folder and open **return**. Save the file as **return 2-1 xxx**.

2. Use **Ctrl+Home** to go to the bottom of the document. Insert the Path and Filename code a double space below the last line.

3. Edit the document as follows:
   a. Position the insertion point at the beginning of the first occurrence of the word *pet* in the first line. Key **precious** and space once.
   b. Position the insertion point at the left of the next *pet* and key **Pet Come Home** followed by a space.
   c. Change *then* in the last line of the first paragraph to **the** and add **chip is**.

4. Save the document again with the same name.

5. Practice all of the methods of deleting text listed in Figure 2-1. Don't worry about destroying the document.

6. When you are comfortable with deleting text, close the document without saving it again.

## *Typeover*

Typeover enables you to key new text over existing text. Turn Typeover on by pressing the Insert key. When Typeover is on, the word *Typeover* appears on the Application Bar, just before the position information. Always use Typeover for a specific purpose. Then turn it off again. WordPerfect does strange things when Typeover is left on.

1. Go to your solution files and open **return 2-1 xxx**. Use **Save As** to save the file as **return 2-2 xxx**.

2. Position the insertion point at the beginning of the word *system* at the beginning of the last sentence. Press the **Insert** key on the keyboard to turn on Typeover.

3. Key **Network** over *system*. Note that it replaces letter for letter, and *network* is one letter longer than *system*. Turn Typeover off and add the needed space.

4. Use the same procedure to key **Network** over *system* at the end of the preceding sentence. Turn Typeover off so you can add the period and correct the spacing, if necessary.

5. Save the document again with the same name. Print a copy of it and keep it open in the window.

**TIP**

Are you remembering to click in the name of the file prompted at the bottom of the Save As dialog box and are you changing the name instead of rekeying the entire name?

## Selecting Text

In Lesson 1 you learned to format text as you go. Text can also be formatted after it is keyed. To format existing text, the text to be formatted must be selected. WordPerfect provides you with a variety of methods for selecting text.

■ Position the mouse pointer at the beginning of the text to select, press and hold the left mouse button, and drag the pointer to the end of the desired text.

■ Click to position the insertion point at one end of the text to select, press F8, and use the arrow keys to extend the selection to the desired ending point.

■ Click to position the insertion point at one end of the text to select, and hold the Shift key while you click at the other end of the text.

■ Open the Edit menu, choose Select, and then choose All to select all of the text in a document.

If you make a mistake and select too much text or the incorrect text, click anywhere in your text to deselect the text and begin again.

In addition to the methods above, the following QuickSelect methods are available:

■ **Word**. Select a word by pointing to it and double clicking.

■ **Sentence**. Select a sentence by pointing to it and triple clicking.

■ **Sentence**. Point in the left margin opposite the sentence and click once.

■ **Paragraph**. Select a paragraph by pointing to it and quadruple clicking.

■ **Paragraph**. Point in the left margin opposite the paragraph and click twice.

Let's practice selecting text.

1. With **return 2-2 xxx** showing in the window, use **Save As** to save the file as **return 2-3 xxx**.

2. Use your mouse to point to the word *unique* in the second line and double click to select it. Press **Ctrl+I** to italicize the word.

3. For practice, point to the same word and triple click to select the entire sentence. Point anywhere in the text and click once to deselect the text.

4. Open the **Edit** menu and choose **Select**. Then choose **All**. The entire document should be selected. Click the Font Size arrow and change the document to **16** pt. Click once to deselect the text.

5. Drag across *Pet Come Home* in the first paragraph to select it, and format it with bold.

6. Point in the left margin beside the title. Your insertion point will look like a fat white arrow pointing to the right. Click once to select the title. Click the **Bold** button on the Property Bar.

7. Practice each of the selection methods listed before this exercise. Practice deselecting text after you have selected it.

8. Print the document. Then keep the document open as you read on.

# *Delete, Undo, Redo, and Undelete*

Once text is selected, you can change its appearance with the tools you learned about in Lesson 1. You can also delete the text by simply pressing the Delete key or the Backspace key on the keyboard. If you should change your mind after deleting text, several features are available to restore the text.

**Undo** (Undo from the Edit menu or the Toolbar, or Ctrl+Z). Undo reverses the last change you made to the document. It should be used immediately.

**Redo** (Redo from the Edit menu or the Toolbar, or Ctrl+Shift+R). Redo reverses the last Undo action. To see a history of edits using Undo and Redo, choose Undo/Redo History from the Edit menu. WordPerfect displays a list of up to 300 edits in a document.

**Undelete** (Ctrl+Shift+Z). If you incorrectly delete text, the deletion is not automatically lost. WordPerfect remembers the last three deletions. Undelete enables you to display the deletions one at a time and to restore the proper one at the location of the insertion point.

1. With **return 2-3 xxx** showing in the window, select the first sentence. Press the **Delete** key on the keyboard to delete the sentence.

2. Point to the curvy blue arrow buttons on the Toolbar and use the Quick Tips to locate Undo.

Use **Undo** to replace the sentence in your document.

3. Use **Redo** to take the sentence out again. Then put it back with **Undo**.

(continued on next page)

4. Select the word *unique* in the second sentence. Delete it. Then press **Ctrl+Shift+Z** and click **Restore** to put the word back into place again. Fix the spacing.

5. Select *unique* again and delete it. Move the insertion point to the blank line between paragraphs. Press **Ctrl+Shift+Z** and click

**Restore** to undelete the word at that location.

6. Select *chip* and press **Ctrl+K** to change the word to uppercase. Use **Undo** to change it back.

7. Keep the document open as you read on.

# Highlight

Another kind of formatting that can be applied to selected text is Highlight. You can also turn on Highlight and drag the mouse pointer over the text to be highlighted. Highlight puts a transparent bar of color over the selected text. The user can choose whether the highlighting will show or not. With shared documents, each user can have a different color of highlighting.

E X E R C I S E ⟶ WP2.5

1. With **return 2-3 xxx** showing in the window, click the **Highlight** button on the Toolbar.

2. Use the mouse to drag across *Animal Help Network* in the second paragraph to highlight it. Does the highlighting show?

3. Open the **Tools** menu and choose **Highlight**. The *Print/Show* option should have a check mark at the left. (If your highlighting didn't show, it probably wasn't selected.)

4. Click the **Highlight** button again to turn Highlight off. Select the title of the document

and click the **Highlight** button to highlight those three words.

5. Click the arrow beside the Highlight button and look at the colors. Leave the setting at yellow. Close the dialog box and close the document without saving it again.

**TIP**

When selecting text that continues to the next line, begin with the first letter of text and drag down one line—then to the left until only the desired text is selected.

# Cut, Copy, Paste, and Drag and Drop

Selected text can also be copied or moved from one location to another with Cut, Copy, and Paste, as well as Drag and Drop. Let's look at these features.

## Cut

As you know, you can cut selected text with Delete or Backspace. When you do this, it goes into the Delete holding space—the place that holds the last three deletions. Those deletions can be restored, if you wish, with Undelete.

The Windows Clipboard is a temporary storage area that holds only one thing at a time. You can cut text to the Clipboard in the following ways:

- By using the Ctrl+X shortcut.

- By clicking the Cut button (scissors icon) on the Toolbar.

- By choosing Cut from the Edit menu or the QuickMenu.

When you cut text to the Windows Clipboard, it remains there until you cut or copy something else or until you close WordPerfect. Usually when you cut text, your intention is to move the insertion point to a different location where you will choose to paste the text.

## Paste

Paste is used to place text that is on the Clipboard back into your document. You can paste from the Clipboard in the following ways:

- By pressing Ctrl+V.

- By clicking the Paste button (clipboard icon) on the Toolbar.

- By choosing Paste from the Edit menu or the QuickMenu.

Before you paste, you must position the insertion point where you want the text to be pasted. Cutting and pasting is a great way to move text from one location to another.

## Copy

Copy is like Cut except that the text you copy to the Clipboard will also remain in its original position in the document. You might use Copy to copy a phrase, sentence, or paragraph to a different location in a document. Or you might copy a block of text onto the Clipboard so it can be used in a different document. Like Cut and Paste, Copy can be selected in the following ways:

- By pressing Ctrl+C.

- By clicking the Copy button (two "pages" icon) on the Toolbar.

- By choosing Copy from the Edit menu or the QuickMenu.

## EXERCISE ⟹ WP2.6

1. Open **return 2-3 xxx** and use **Save As** to save the file as **return 2-6 xxx**.

2. Point in the left margin opposite the second paragraph and double click to select that paragraph. Press **Ctrl+C** to copy the paragraph to the Clipboard.

3. Press **Ctrl+End** to move the insertion point to the bottom of the document. Add returns, if necessary, to position the insertion point a double space below the Path and Filename code. Press **Ctrl+V** to paste the paragraph there. (You should now have TWO copies of paragraph 2.)

(continued on next page)

**4.** Select the second paragraph again and press **Ctrl+X** to cut the paragraph to the Clipboard.

**5.** Move the insertion point to the beginning of the first paragraph. Choose **Paste** from the Toolbar.

**6.** Keep your messed-up document showing in the window as you read on.

## Drag and Drop

Drag and Drop can be used to move or copy text. The procedure is to select the text to be moved or copied and then drag it to the new location. (If you use Copy, a copy of the text will remain in the old position. With move, the text is deleted from the old location.) The procedure for both is the same except when you use Copy, you must hold the Ctrl key while you drag the text.

**1.** With a very messy **return 2-6 xxx** showing in the window, select the *Protect your precious pet . . .* paragraph. Point to the selected text and press and hold the left mouse button. Move the mouse slightly. The move icon should look like an arrow with a page on the tail.

**2.** Continue to hold the left mouse button while you drag the pointer out of the selected text. The pointer will be accompanied by a flashing vertical line. Position that flashing vertical line so it's at the beginning of the last sentence in the paragraph above.

**3.** Release the mouse button and your paragraph should be dropped in the new position.

**4.** Select any three words in your document. This time, hold the **Ctrl** key while you point to the selected text and press the mouse button. The pointer should now look like it has two pages.

**5.** Move the mouse slightly and look at the pointer. Drag it to a new location. Check to see if you moved a COPY of the text—the original text should remain in its original location.

**6.** Now that you have the basics, practice copying and moving words, sentences, phrases, or paragraphs until you are comfortable with them. Then close the document without saving it.

# *New Blank Document*

While you will normally work on one document at a time, Windows 95 makes it possible for you to have as many as nine documents open at a time. Sometimes when you are working in one document, you want to begin another document—to take notes during a phone call, to save a section of text that eventually will be inserted in a different place, or to begin a new document that suddenly takes priority over the current document.

You can keep the current document open and begin a new blank document by clicking the New Blank Document button on the Toolbar. In the next exercise you'll open the familiar **welcome 2-3** document, create a new blank document, and actually drag some text from one document to another using the document name on the Application Bar.

**EXERCISE ▷ WP2.8**

**1.** Beginning in a new document window, go to the student **Datafile** folder and open **welcome**. Use **Save As** to save the file as **welcome 2-8 xxx**. Insert the Path and Filename code a double space below the last line of the document.

**2.** Briefly look through the layout of the document. (We'll do some formatting on this document soon.)

**3.** Click the **New Blank Document** button on the Toolbar. (It is the first button on the default Toolbar.)

**4.** Look at the Application Bar. Two documents should be listed—**welcome 2-8 xxx** and **Document2**. The **Document2** button should appear to be depressed because that is the open file.

**5.** For practice, open the **File** menu and choose **Close** to close the document. Repeat Step 3 to open a new document.

**6.** Click the **welcome 2-8 xxx** button on the Application Bar to switch back to that

🚩 **TIP**

To select text that begins at the margin, begin selecting in the middle of the first word. WordPerfect will highlight the entire word, and you don't have to worry about accidentally grabbing the margin guideline.

document. Select the title and first paragraph of the document.

**7.** Drag the selected text to the **Document2** button on the Application Bar. Keep holding the mouse button until WordPerfect switches to **Document2**. Then drag the text up and into the **Document2** window. When the text is in the desired location, release the mouse button.

**8.** Select the text in **Document2** and drag it back to **welcome 2-8 xxx**, this time moving the pointer to the top of **welcome 2-8 xxx** before releasing the mouse button. The text should return to its original position.

**9.** Change back to **Document2** and close the document without saving it.

 **NOTE:**

If you release the mouse button while the pointer is still over the Application Bar, you'll get an error message and the text will remain in the original window.

 **INTERNET** The Internet is not a single network, but a super network made up of more than 50,000 smaller networks.

# QuickFormat

Now that you're good at selecting, cutting, copying, etc., let's look at some other formatting tools. Sometimes you want the same format applied to several places in your documents. It can be time-consuming to select each piece of text to be formatted and apply all of the desired formats to each.

WordPerfect offers a feature called QuickFormat which enables you to copy the format from one part of a document to several other parts. This feature ties the parts together with a *style*. If you change your mind after using QuickFormat to format the parts, you only need to change one of the parts, and the others will change automatically. Let's practice on the **welcome** document.

**QuickSteps**

**QuickFormat**
1. Position the insertion point in the formatted sample.
2. Click the QuickFormat button on the Toolbar.
3. Choose Character or Heading.
4. Apply the format in the other locations.

## EXERCISE ➡ WP2.9

1. With **welcome 2-8 xxx** showing in the window, use **Save As** to save the file as **welcome 2-9 xxx**.

2. Select the first side heading (*Boarding*). Press **F9** to open the Font dialog box (or choose it from the Format menu). It should look like Figure 2-2. Note that it combines Font face, Font size, and Text color with a variety of Appearance and other attributes.

3. Scroll through the *Font face* list and choose **Arial**. Change the *Font size* to **14** pt.

**FIGURE 2-2**
Font Dialog Box

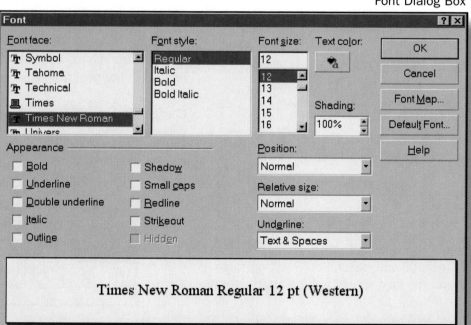

**4.** In the *Appearance* section, choose **Bold** and **Small caps**. Change the *Text color* to one of the **red** choices. Click **OK** to close the dialog box.

**5.** Back in your document window, click away from the heading so you can see how it looks. Then click once in the heading to position your insertion point anywhere in the heading.

**6.** Choose the **QuickFormat** tool from the Toolbar. A dialog box will ask if you want to format a heading or characters. Choose **Headings** and click **OK**. Your insertion point will look like a paint roller.

**7.** Click **Pet Store** and **Grooming** to apply the format to those headings. Then click the **QuickFormat** button again to deselect the tool.

**8.** Reveal your codes and look at the [Para Style: Auto QuickFormat] codes that were inserted into your document when the headings were formatted.

**9.** Save the document again with the same name and read on.

You have the option of formatting headings or characters. The difference is that headings are surrounded by hard returns, while characters are buried within the text. With character formatting, you must paint the format onto the text to be formatted. We'll try that in the next exercise. In addition, we'll change the format of one of the side headings to see if all side heading formats will change as promised.

## E X E R C I S E ⇨ WP2.10

**1.** With **welcome 2-9 xxx** showing in the window, use **Save As** to save the file as **welcome 2-10 xxx**.

**2.** Select *Pet Bath*, format it with bold and italic, and change the font size to **13** pt. Keep the text selected.

**3.** Click away from the text to see how it looks. Then select *Pet Bath* again. (This step is necessary.)

**4.** Click the **QuickFormat** button on the Toolbar. Note that this time, *Selected characters* is highlighted because you had text selected when you made the choice. Click **OK** because this text is not a heading. Your insertion point now looks like a paintbrush.

> **TIP**
>
> When formatting text that is followed by a punctuation mark, do NOT format the punctuation mark.

**5.** Carefully paint the format onto the following paragraph headings: *Training* and *Tours*. (If you make a mistake, click Undo and try again.)

**6.** Turn QuickFormat off and reveal your codes. Look at the [Char Style: Auto QuickFormat] codes.

**7.** Click to position the insertion point in the middle of any of the three paragraph headings. Click **Italic** on the Property Bar to deselect that attribute. Italic should be removed from all three paragraph headings.

(continued on next page)

8. Click in one of the red side headings. Return to the Font dialog box and change the text from *red* to **green**. All three side headings should be changed.

9. Save your document again as **welcome 2-10 xxx**. Print it and close it.

The styles created when you use QuickFormat are saved with the current document. They cannot be retrieved for future documents. In a later lesson you'll learn to create styles that can be saved and reused.

# *QuickCorrect*

QuickCorrect is a customizable feature that corrects some of your errors as you key. Simple words in which you might make an error when keying and commonly misspelled words are included in the dozens of words in QuickCorrect. Let's see what QuickCorrect can do.

**QuickSteps**

**Add QuickCorrect Entry**
1. Choose QuickCorrect from the Tools menu.
2. Key the unique abbreviation in the Replace box.
3. Key the expanded word(s) in the With box.
4. Click Add Entry.

## EXERCISE WP2.11

1. Beginning in a new document window, key (complete with errors) the following phrase: **THe dog adn cat are in teh barn.** Watch the errors as they are automatically fixed.

2. If your errors weren't fixed, a setting needs to be changed in the QuickCorrect dialog box.

3. Either way, open the **Tools** menu and choose **QuickCorrect**. A large dialog box will list all of the errors (at the left) and what will replace them (at the right). Scroll through the list and look at some of the items.

4. At the bottom of the box, be sure the box beside *Replace words as you type* is selected. (This is what makes QuickCorrect work.)

5. With your insertion point in the *Replace* text box at the top, key **cp**. Tab to the *With text* box and key **Corel WordPerfect Suite 8**. Click the **Add Entry** button and then **OK** to return to your document window.

6. Key **cp** and space once. The letters should expand to the entire name of your Suite.

7. Return to the QuickCorrect dialog box. Scroll through the list until you find the one you just entered. Click to highlight it and click the **Delete Entry** button. (You'll need to confirm the deletion.)

8. Click the **Format-As-You-Go** tab and keep that dialog box selected as you read on.

You needed to delete the entry so it wouldn't be in the way for other students. On the job you will find it useful to add entries to this list. You can include your initials that will expand to your entire name. You could do the same for your boss or the name of your company. In the classroom you probably shouldn't add entries to QuickCorrect.

The two capital letters at the beginning of the sentence are not included in the QuickCorrect list but were corrected in your little exercise. As you can see, fixing sloppy capitalization is one of the features in the *Format-As-You-Go* section of the QuickCorrect dialog box.

**FIGURE 2-3**
QuickCorrect Dialog Box

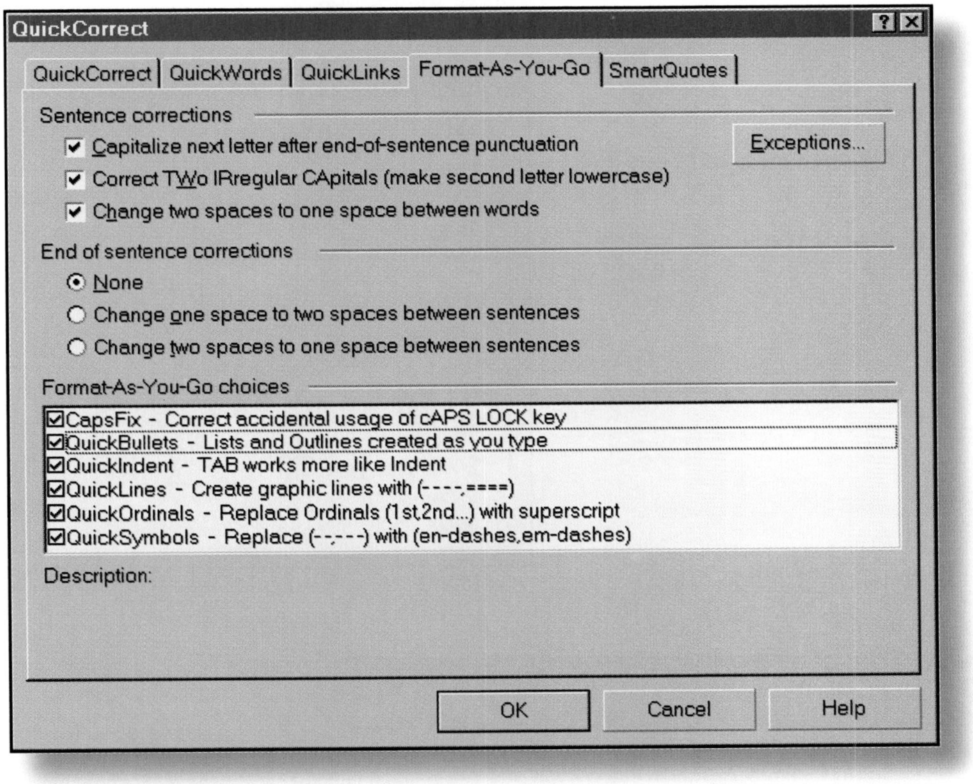

Spend a moment studying this dialog box. It will affect your work greatly. The settings you see here are the default settings. For some special projects, you may wish to deselect some of the features. When you leave the computer, come to this dialog box and reset the features you've deselected so they are selected for the next student. When you're finished, close the dialog box with OK.

# *Special Characters*

WordPerfect doesn't limit you to the characters that show on the keyboard keys. Hundreds of other characters are available to help you key other languages, mathematical symbols, iconic symbols, bullets, check boxes, superscripts and subscripts, and dashes like those used by printers. Let's learn to access these characters.

## Symbols

WordPerfect has 15 sets of symbols. Each symbol is referenced by a set number and a symbol number within the set. Figure 2-4 illustrates, for example, a few of the bullets that are available and the set numbers for those bullets.

Check boxes are used for choices. The 4,38 check box might be used like this:

☐ Yes or  ☐ No

☐ Male or  ☐ Female

All of these and more come from the Symbols dialog box (see Figure 2-5) that can be accessed in one of the following ways:

- Press Ctrl+W.

- Display the Insert menu and choose Symbol.

- Display the QuickMenu and choose Symbols.

**FIGURE 2-4**
Sample Bullets

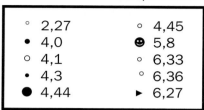

| | |
|---|---|
| ° 2,27 | ° 4,45 |
| • 4,0 | ☻ 5,8 |
| ° 4,1 | ° 6,33 |
| • 4,3 | ° 6,36 |
| ● 4,44 | ► 6,27 |

**FIGURE 2-5**
Symbols Dialog Box

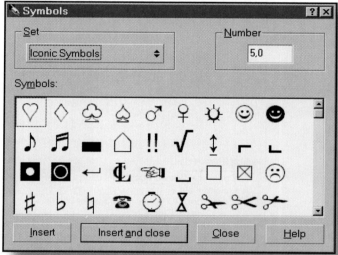

## EXERCISE ⟹ WP2.12

1.  Close the dialog box and close the open document without saving it. Beginning in a new document window, press **Ctrl+W** to display the Symbols dialog box.

2.  Click the button in the *Set* section of the dialog box and look at the names of the sets. Spend a brief time browsing through the sets. Use **Insert** at the bottom of the dialog box to insert a couple of check boxes, bullets, and other symbols or icons.

3.  Sometimes a symbol needs to be larger. Select one or two of the symbols you just inserted and change the font size to **20** pt.

4.  Go to the Typographic Symbols set and scroll through the list until you come to the row with $^3/_8$ and $^5/_8$. Click **Insert** to put $^3/_8$ in your document window.

5.  Keep the Symbols dialog box displayed. Click in your document window and press Enter to move your insertion point a double space below your practice.

6.  Key the sentences in Figure 2-6. The numbers of the sets and symbols are listed in parentheses at the end of each sentence to help you find the symbols.

7. When you finish, position the insertion point a double space below the last line of text and key **Corel WordPerfect Suite 8**. Put a registered symbol (®) after *Corel* and another after *WordPerfect*. (Use the Typographic set.) This is the way Corel would like the Suite listed.

8. Save your exercise as **char 2-12 xxx**. Position the insertion point a double space below the final line and insert the Path and Filename code. Keep the document open in the window as you read on.

**FIGURE 2-6**
Text for Exercise WP2.12

```
The cake was baked in a 350° oven. (6,36)
It might cost $1.70 or more to buy £ of British money. (4,11)
"¿Dónde está su niña?" (4,8) (1,59) (1,27) (1,57)
```

A number of shortcuts are available to save you from hunting for the appropriate symbol. You may have noticed in the QuickCorrect dialog box that you can key *(* and then *r* for a ® symbol or *(* and *c* for ©. You can do a variety of other shortcuts with *Ctrl+W*. After you press Ctrl+W, key *r* and then *o* and press Enter for the registered symbol or *c* and then *o* for the copyright symbol. This works for some foreign characters, too. Pressing Ctrl+W, *a,* and then an apostrophe gives you *á* or *a,* and then pressing quotation marks gives you *ä.*

## Hyphens and Space Codes

Occasionally you will need special codes to make your lines wrap the way you want. Here is a brief description of some codes you can use to help you work:

■ **Hyphen.** A normal hyphen is used for words like *self-confidence* and *full-time.* If the word falls at the end of the line, WordPerfect will divide the word.

■ **Hyphen Character.** A hyphen character should be used to join two words that are NOT to be divided at the end of the line. Examples are the hyphen in a telephone or Social Security number or the minus character in a formula. Key a hyphen character by holding Ctrl while pressing the hyphen key.

■ **Dash.** In typography, dashes are known as *en dashes* or *em dashes*, and both are longer than a hyphen. Where a hyphen joins two closely related words, a dash provides a break in thought or a pause. Key an *em dash* by pressing the hyphen key three times. WordPerfect will convert it to a dash from the symbol set. A dash never has a space before it or following it.

■ **Hard Space.** A hard space tells WordPerfect not to divide at the end of the line. For example, when a date like *January 5, 2001* comes at the end of the line, keyboarding rules tell you the only place that date can be divided is after the comma. Key a hard space by holding the Ctrl key while you press the space bar.

## Superscripts and Subscripts

WordPerfect has a great equation feature that you'll learn about in Lesson 8. Occasionally you might need a number to be raised above the line. This choice can be made from the Font dialog box. When we finish with the equation in Exercise WP2.13, we'll "square" some of the numbers in the equation using superscript.

## EXERCISE ▷ WP2.13

**SCANS**

1. With **char 2-12 xxx** showing in the window, use **Save As** to save the file as **char 2-13 xxx**. Move your insertion point to a double space below the Path and Filename code.

2. Key the silly sentence in Figure 2-7 as follows:
   a. For each dash, key three hyphens and continue keying.
   b. In the equation, for each space, hold the Ctrl key while you press the space bar.
   c. In the equation, hold the Ctrl key while you key the minus sign.
   d. In the date, press Ctrl+Space Bar between *January* and *9*.

3. When you finish, look at your work. The entire equation should be on one line. The date should not be divided after the month. Reveal your codes and move your insertion point back through the equation. Look at the miscellaneous codes inserted by WordPerfect to format the sentence.

4. Key a **2** just to the right of the *a* in the equation. Select the *2* and open the Font dialog box.

5. Click the arrow for the drop-down menu in the *Position* section. Choose **Superscript**. Click **OK** to close the dialog box. Look at the *2*. It should be raised above the *a* and a little smaller. Look at the superscript code.

6. Add a raised *3* following the *x* in the equation using the same method.

7. Print your document. Then close it, saving it again with the same name.

**FIGURE 2-7**
Text for Exercise WP2.13

> The scientists discovered that the best formula—the one that will solve your problem—is a + b - c =  x + y.  This spectacular formula was discovered in Butte des Morts, Ohio, on January 9, 1936.

If you change the position of text as you are keying a document, you'll need to get past the ending code to continue with your document. You can do that by pressing the End key or the right arrow key.

## Proofreaders' Marks

Figure 2-8 illustrates some of the most frequently used proofreaders' marks. Study the marks. Then follow the steps in Exercise WP2.14 to create and edit a document.

**FIGURE 2-8**
Proofreaders' Marks

| Change | Mark | Example | Result |
| --- | --- | --- | --- |
| Capitalize | ≡ | Pet paradise | Pet Paradise |
| Close up | ⌒ | Pet Para dise | Pet Paradise |
| Delete | ℐ | Pet pet Paradise | Pet Paradise |
| Insert | ∧ | Pet Pardise | Pet Paradise |
| Insert comma | ⌄ | dogs cats and mice | dogs, cats, and mice |
| Insert space | # | PetParadise | Pet Paradise |
| Insert period | ⊙ | The dogs barked | The dogs barked. |
| Lowercase | /lc | mice and Ferrets | mice and ferrets |

**WP-32**

**COREL WORDPERFECT 8**

# EXERCISE ▷ WP2.14

1. Beginning in a new document window, go to the student **Datafile** folder and open **sale memo**. Use **Save As** to save the file as **sale memo 2-14 xxx**.

2. Position your insertion point a double space below Polly's name and insert the Path and Filename code.

3. Study the corrections in the document illustrated in Figure 2-9. Then make those corrections using delete, backspace, and insert. After keying **15th**, in the final paragraph, space once to get the *th* to format. Then remove the extra space. Work quickly and carefully.

4. When you finish, save your document again as **sale memo 2-14 xxx**. Print it and close it.

**FIGURE 2-9**
Corrections for **sale memo 2-14 xxx**

Subject: Next ~~Week's~~ Month's Specials

This is just to let you know that an advertisement will be included in the *Austin Times* next week, listing the following specials:

Free: 5-lb. bag Nutty Dog Food with the purchase of a 40-lb. bag of Nutty Nibbles
Free: 3 cans Jupiter catfood with the purchase of any size bag of Nina's dry cat food
Free: 1-lb. bag of Nutty Treats with the purchase of 20-lb. bag of Nutty Nibbles
Free: birdseed scoop with purchase of any ~~Kaytee~~ Kaytie bird seed

$1 off the Dog Lover's brand grooming tools
$1 off Cat Lover's brand grooming tools
$2 off Itch Control tablets

10% off all brands of cat litter
10% off all new ferret accessories
10% off all Dog Tab and Cat Tab nutritional supplements /lc
10% off ~~Karver's~~ Carver's Reptile Ranch
10% off all ~~Karver's~~ Carver's aquariums
15% off all cat furniture
20% off all chew toys

The sale will last for two weeks beginning on the ~~first~~ 15th of next month. Please check your supplies of these items and let me know if you need to replenish your stock so you won't be short during the sale.
Polly

# Summary

In this lesson you learned a variety of skills. Most of them had to do with editing your text, but some involved formatting the text. You learned that:

- you can insert text by simply keying.

- you can delete text in a variety of ways.

- Typeover can be used to key new text over existing text.

- there are many ways to select text, and you can select blocks of text of varying sizes.

- when you delete text, it isn't necessarily lost—Undo, Redo, and Undelete might be of help in restoring the text.

- you can cut, copy, and move text in a number of ways.

- if you want to begin a new document, you can open a new blank document using a button on the Toolbar.

- QuickFormat may be used to format and tie sections of your text together with a style.

- QuickCorrect helps speed up your work by fixing errors and replacing specified keystrokes with words or phrases.

- WordPerfect enables you to enter a vast array of special characters and symbols in your documents.

## LESSON 2 REVIEW QUESTIONS

### MATCHING

**Write the letter of the term in Column 2 that best matches the description in Column 1.**

| Column 1 | Column 2 |
|---|---|
| _____ 1. Used to retrieve material that has been cut or copied to the Clipboard. | **A.** Cut |
| _____ 2. Used to put a copy of the selected text on the Windows Clipboard. | **B.** Copy |
| | **C.** Paste |
| _____ 3. Used to reverse the last change made to your document. | **D.** Undelete |
| _____ 4. Used to key new text in the place of existing text. | **E.** Undo |
| _____ 5. Used to remove selected text from the document and put it on the Windows Clipboard. | **F.** Redo |
| | **G.** Typeover |

## FILL IN THE BLANKS

**Complete each of the following statements by writing your answer in the blank provided.**

6. With Drag and Drop, you can drag text from one document to another document button on the _____ Bar.

7. You can select a _____ by pointing in the left margin and double clicking.

8. The feature that enables you to quickly apply the same format to several document parts is called _____.

9. If you wish to bold, italicize, or change the font face or font size of text that has already been keyed, you must first _____ the text.

10. When working with windows, you may have as many as _____ documents open at one time.

## LESSON 2 PROJECT

SCANS

### PROJECT 2A

The **welcome** document is only partially formatted. Let's finish it.

1. Open **welcome 2-10 xxx**. Use **Save As** to save the file as **welcome proj2a xxx**.

2. Remove all formatting from the three side headings that are formatted in color.

3. Position the insertion point after *Boarding* and key a period and a space. Press **Delete** until the text of the first line of the boarding period is on the same line. (The heading should run into the paragraph like *Pet Bath* near the bottom of the document.)

4. Repeat the procedure with the other two side headings.

5. Select one of the formatted headings near the bottom and use QuickFormat to format the three headings at the top.

6. Save the document again with the same name and print it. Keep it open.

### PROJECT 2B

A customer is interested only in boarding and grooming services. Create a new document by dragging parts of the old one to a new document window.

(continued on next page)

1. Click the **New Blank Document** button on the Toolbar. Save the empty document window as **welcome proj2b xxx**.

2. Return to **welcome proj2a xxx** and select the title and the first three paragraphs. Hold the **Ctrl** key to copy, and drag the selected text to the Application Bar and into the new window.

3. Do the same with the grooming information. Make any necessary adjustments to spacing so the document is attractive.

4. Position the Path and Filename code a double space below the final paragraph. Save the document again with the same name, print it, and close it. Close **welcome proj2a xxx** without saving it again.

## PROJECT 2C

Key the text in Figure 2-10. Insert the symbols as shown, including the em dash in the second sentence. Put a hard space before the *8* each time it is included so no matter how the paragraph is formatted, the *8* won't be on a line by itself. When you finish, save the document as **suite proj2c xxx**, add the Path and Filename code as always, print the file, and close it, saving it again.

**FIGURE 2-10**
Text for Project 2C

```
With Corel® WordPerfect® Suite 8, you won't have to wait for the
software to get your work done. Each program is turbocharged for
streamlined performance—especially in program startup, operating files,
saving files, and redrawing the screen.  What's more, in Corel®
Presentations® 8, you can tap into Intel's MMX™ technology to slash
graphic redraw time and accelerate transitions.
```

## CRITICAL THINKING ACTIVITY

SCANS

You are working on the rough draft of a document that will be shared electronically with several coworkers. You'd like to emphasize several areas in the document to one coworker and several other areas in the document to another coworker. How might you use your skills from Lesson 2 to do this?

# FORMATTING TEXT

## OBJECTIVES

**Upon completion of this lesson, you will be able to:**

- Discuss the default template.

- Adjust line spacing in your documents.

- Use Justification to give text a different appearance.

- Use Center and Flush Right to format text.

- Format text with the Shadow Cursor.

- Format text by changing the margins.

- Work with WordPerfect tabs.

- Use Indent, Hanging Indent, and Double Indent to format paragraphs.

- Format text with outlining, bullets, and numbering.

- Format your work with text columns.

**⏱ Estimated Time: 1$^1$/$_2$ hours**

When WordPerfect is installed on your computer, certain decisions have been made about the appearance of your work. The settings for those decisions are stored in what's called the *default template*. (You'll learn about other templates in a later lesson.)

The default template specifies many, many settings. You don't even care about most of them. But some of them should be of interest to you—especially because they are so easily changed. Some of those settings include one-inch margins on all sides of the page, left justification, single spacing, and tab stops set at each half inch.

While the default settings work for most documents, they can be easily changed so your documents will look exactly as you'd like. Here are some general formatting guidelines:

- Formatting changes that affect an entire document should be inserted at the beginning of the document.

- Formatting changes affect the text forward from the point where the change is made. The text prior to the change is not affected.

- Formatting changes remain in effect until another change to the same format is made. Then only the text following the change is affected.

■ Formatting codes become a permanent part of the document template and are saved with the document. When you close a document, you are returned to the default template.

# Line Spacing

Most text is single-spaced. If you want to double-space your text, change the line spacing setting. Do NOT press Enter twice at the ends of lines in paragraphs. To change line spacing, open the Format menu, choose Line, and then choose Spacing. Line spacing can be set in tenths of an inch. Let's practice.

## EXERCISE ⇨ WP3.1

1. Open **welcome proj2a xxx** from your file of solutions. Use **Save As** to save the file as **welcome 3-1 xxx**.

2. Open the **Format** menu and choose **Line**. Look at the options available. Then choose **Spacing**. The Line Spacing dialog box will appear (see Figure 3-1).

3. Note that *1.0* for single spacing is highlighted. Key **2** and click **OK** to set double spacing.

4. Look through your document. Line spacing throughout the document is doubled, including the places between paragraphs where the document originally had a blank line.

5. Return to the Line Spacing dialog box and change to **1.5** spacing. Look at your document. Then go to the beginning of the document, reveal your codes, and delete the [Ln Spacing] code.

**FIGURE 3-1**
Line Spacing Dialog Box

6. Position the insertion point at the beginning of the *Pet Store* section and change to double spacing. Then position the insertion point at the blank space before *Grooming* and change to single spacing.

7. Save your document again as **welcome 3-1 xxx**. Keep it open.

# Justification

Justification is used to give your documents a different look. WordPerfect offers five kinds of justification.

■ **Left** justification (Ctrl+L) is the default, where the text is all aligned at the left margin and is ragged at the right.

■ **Full** justification (Ctrl+J) evens the lines at both the left and right margins.

- **Right** justification (Ctrl+R) aligns all lines at the right, and the left edge is ragged.

- **Center** justification (Ctrl+E) centers all lines.

- **All** justification stretches each line to the margins, regardless of how long the line is. (There is no keyboard shortcut for All justification.)

You can choose Justification from the Format menu. An easier way is to use the Justification button on the Property Bar (see Figure 3-2). Let's practice on the document you have in the window. Look at how each change affects the document following the insertion of the code.

**FIGURE 3-2**
Justification

---

E X E R C I S E ⟹ **WP3.2**

1. With **welcome 3-1 xxx** open in the window, use **Save As** to save the file as **welcome 3-2 xxx**.

2. With the insertion point at the beginning of the first paragraph, click the **Justification** button on the Property Bar and choose **Right**. Watch how the entire document shifts to the right.

3. Position the insertion point at the beginning of the next paragraph. Choose **Center** justification.

4. Use **Full** justification for the *We follow . . .* paragraph.

5. Select the double-spaced paragraph and format it with **All** justification. Note that the paragraphs following the *Pet Store* paragraph are still formatted with Full justification. That's because you formatted only the selected paragraph.

6. Save the document again as **welcome 3-2 xxx** and keep it open in the window.

## *Center and Flush Right*

Often you want to format only a line or two of the document. Instead of changing justification, you can center a line at a time:

- with Shift+F7.

- by choosing Center from the QuickMenu.

- by choosing Format, Line, and Center.

Flush Right can be chosen from the same places, though the keyboard command is Alt+F7. These commands may be given before you key the text or after. If you give them after you've keyed (as you did with changes to the justification), you must position the insertion point at the beginning of the text to be formatted when you give the command.

## EXERCISE ⟹ WP3.3

1. With **welcome 3-2 xxx** showing in the window, use **Save As** to save the document as **welcome 3-3 xxx**.

2. Add hard returns, if necessary, to position the insertion point a double space below the Path and Filename code. Use **Shift+F7** (Center) to move your insertion point to the center and key your name.

3. Press **Enter** twice. (Enter ends the Center command.)

4. Use **Alt+F7** to move your insertion point to the right margin (Flush Right). Key your name again. Press **Enter** twice. Keep the document open.

5. Save the document again with the same name and keep it open.

# Dot Leaders

Dot leaders are used to lead your attention from one side of the page to the other. You can insert them when you use Flush Right by giving the Flush Right command twice. We'll try it, and then we will add more formatting to the document.

## EXERCISE ⟹ WP3.4

1. With **welcome 3-3 xxx** showing in the window, save it as **welcome 3-4 xxx**.

2. With the insertion point at the left margin, a double space below your second name, key your name again.

3. Position the insertion point at the left of your name and press **Alt+F7** to flush right the name. Without moving the insertion point, give the flush right command again. All of the space between the left margin and the name should be filled with periods.

4. Position the insertion point at the left of the title of the document and give the Center command. Select the title, format it with bold, and change the font size to **20** pt.

5. Press **Home** twice to move the insertion point to the left margin, before all codes (You know you're before all codes because you can see on the Property Bar that Bold is deselected, and the Font Size button reads 12 pt.)

6. Press **Enter** until the title is approximately 2" from the top of the paper. Add one more return between the title and the first paragraph.

7. Save the document again as **welcome 3-4 xxx**. Keep it open.

 **INTERNET** The Internet reaches schools in more than 140 countries around the world. Through email and other connections, you learn about students in other countries and foreign students can learn about you.

# *Shadow Cursor*

Another way to key something at the center or the right of the page is with the *Shadow Cursor*. You learned briefly about the Shadow Cursor in the Getting Started section, and you were told to deselect that option. You will probably select the Shadow Cursor for specific tasks and turn it off again when you finish.

When selected, the Shadow Cursor enables you to click and key anywhere in the window. You don't have to use hard returns, tabs, or spaces to reach a certain point. In addition, the feature enables you to click and center or click and flush right. Let's learn by working with the Shadow Cursor.

## EXERCISE ⟩ WP3.5

1. Click the **New Blank Document** button on the Toolbar to go to a new document window.

2. Click the **Shadow Cursor** button on the Application Bar at the bottom of the window to choose the Shadow Cursor.

3. Move your mouse pointer around in the empty window. Notice the following:
   a. When the pointer is about a half inch from the left margin, it is accompanied by a gray arrow pointing to the right.
   b. When the pointer is near the center of the window, it has arrows pointing in both directions.
   c. When the pointer is near the right margin, it has an arrow pointing to the left.

4. About an inch below the top margin guide, point to the center (when the arrows point to both the left and right). Click and key your name. It should be centered.

5. About a half inch below that, click near the right margin and key your name. It will end flush with the right margin.

6. About a half inch below the second name, click about two inches from the left margin. Key your name again.

7. Reveal your codes. Note that even though you never pressed the Enter key, the space from the top margin to your final name is filled with [HRt] codes. Look at the [Left Tab] codes as well as the [Hd Center on Marg] and [Hd Flush Right] codes.

8. Turn off the Shadow Cursor. Open the **Edit** menu and choose **Select** and then **All**.

9. Press **Ctrl+X** to delete the text. Close the document without saving. Position the insertion point at the bottom of **welcome 3-4 xxx** and paste the practice from the other document at that point. Your name will be scattered all around the bottom of the document.

10. Save the document again with the same name. Print it and close it.

# Margins

While WordPerfect provides you with a number of ways to set margins, the easiest is to move the margin guidelines to the desired locations. The tool to use looks like an intersection with arrows. When you use that tool to move the margins, a box will appear, displaying the size of the margin in increments of a sixteenth of an inch.

## EXERCISE ➤ WP3.6

1. Open **welcome proj2a xxx** again. Use **Save As** to save it as **welcome 3-6 xxx**.

2. Point to the top margin. When the cross-hair tool appears, drag the margin down until the little box reports *2"*.

3. Point to the left margin, either above the top margin or even with the first line of text. When the cross-hair tool appears, drag the margin to the right until the little box reports *2"*.

4. Adjust the right margin so it also gives you a 2-inch margin. Your text is now quite long and narrow.

5. Beside the second paragraph, move the left margin to the left about a half inch (to *1.5"*). Adjust the right margin to the right the same distance.

6. Position the insertion point beside the third paragraph. Open the **Format** menu and choose **Margins**. The Margins portion of the Page Setup dialog box should appear (see Figure 3-3). Change the Left and Right margins to **1** inch. Click **OK** to close the dialog box. The top part of your document should now look kind of like a pyramid!

7. Reveal your codes. Remove all margin set codes, so the margins are at the default 1-inch settings. Save and close the file.

**FIGURE 3-3**
Margins Portion of the Page Setup Dialog Box

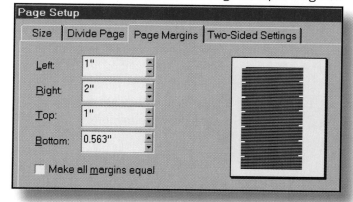

# The Ruler

The Ruler can also be used for margins. In addition, it offers a couple of indent features. Look at the top of the window. Is your Ruler displayed? If not, open the View menu and choose Ruler so you can see it as you learn about it. Figure 3-4 shows an enlarged version of the left end of the Ruler. Note the following:

■ The top part (above the numerals) is for setting margins.

**FIGURE 3-4**
Left End of the Ruler

- The heavy black part above the 1 is for setting the left margin.

- The two little triangles beside the margin marker are for indents. The top one can be set to automatically indent the first line of a paragraph. The bottom one can be set to indent the entire paragraph.

- The middle part of the scale is marked in eighths of an inch.

- The bottom part is for setting tabs. The triangles at each half inch are Left tabs.

The right portion of the Ruler is illustrated in Figure 3-5. It has a margin marker and only one indent triangle. The triangle is for indenting the right side of a paragraph. Let's experiment.

**FIGURE 3-5**
Right End of Ruler

## EXERCISE ▷ WP3.7

1. Open **welcome proj2b xxx**. Save the file as **welcome 3-7 xxx**. Change to **Full** justification.

2. Position your insertion point at the beginning of the first paragraph. With your mouse pointer, grab the tiny top triangle and drag it to **1.5"**. All paragraphs should now be indented by that amount.

3. Drag the same triangle to the left one notch, so the paragraphs are indented by **1.38"**.

4. Position the insertion point at the beginning of the second paragraph. Grab the bottom triangle at the left and move it to the third mark (1.38"). All of the following paragraphs will be formatted.

5. You wanted only the one paragraph indented. Click **Undo**. Then select the paragraph and indent it again. While it is still selected, indent the paragraph the same amount on the right (to 7.13"). Deselect the text.

6. Reveal your codes and look at the codes. Then save your document again with the same name. Print it and keep it open.

# *Tabs*

As you know, default tab stops are set at half-inch intervals. You can change tab stops in the Tab Set dialog box or on the Ruler. To change one or two tabs, the Ruler is probably quicker. If you want to set evenly spaced tabs, the Tab Set dialog box is probably faster.

## EXERCISE ▷ WP3.8

1. With **welcome 3-7 xxx** showing in the window, save it as **welcome 3-8 xxx**. With your codes revealed, drag all of the codes you entered in Exercise WP3.7, except the justification code, out of the document. (All lines will be justified at both the right and left margins.)

2. With the Ruler displayed, position the insertion point at the beginning of the first paragraph. Point to the tab stop (the triangle) at *1.5"* and drag it to the left (to the 1.38" marker).

(continued on next page)

3. Press **Tab** to indent the paragraph. Use Tab to indent all of the remaining paragraphs. Return your insertion point to the beginning of the first paragraph.

4. Look at the left margin of your document, opposite the first paragraph. Look at the blue marker there telling you that a tab set code is at that location.

5. Click the blue marker. A temporary tab ruler should appear. Drag the tab stop at 1.38" off the temporary ruler. Your paragraphs will all be indented one inch.

6. Point to the tab portion of the normal Ruler at $1^1/_2$" and click to put the tab stop back into place.

7. Close the document, saving it again with the same name.

You can see how easy it is to move, delete, and add tab stops on the ruler. Tabs can also be used to create columns of text. You can begin by guessing at the locations for the tabs, or you can begin with them set at even intervals. To set tabs evenly, use the Tab Set dialog box. You can display that box in one of the following ways:

■ Choose Format, Line, and Tab Set.

■ Point to one of the tab triangles and double click.

■ Point to the tab portion of the Ruler and right click. Choose Tab Set.

**FIGURE 3-6**
Tab Set Dialog Box

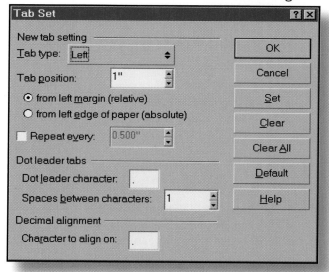

Look at the Tab Set dialog box (see Figure 3-6). Notice the buttons at the right. *Clear all* and *Default* are useful. To set individual tabs, key the location in the *Tab Position* box and click Set. If you choose *Repeat every*, you get to choose the distance between the tabs. The drop-down menu at the top provides one way to change the types of tabs. We'll look at that soon.

## EXERCISE ➡ WP3.9

1. Beginning in a new document window, use one of the methods above to open the Tab Set dialog box.

2. Click **Clear All** to clear all tabs. (Check your Ruler—all of the triangles should be gone.) Click the **Repeat every** check box. In the box to the right, key **1.6**. Click **OK**.

3. Back in your document window, key the text in Figure 3-7. Begin at the left margin, and tab as you work across the columns. Press **Enter** at the end of each line.

4. When you finish, check your work. Save the document as **dog stuff 3-9 xxx**. Add the Path and Filename code a double space below the text and save the file again.

**FIGURE 3-7**
Text for Exercise WP3.9

| | | | |
|---|---|---|---|
| Rawhide Bones | Biscuits | Leads | Collars |
| Bark Control Collars | Dog Chow | Pet Gate | Dog Food |
| Training Guides | Pet Beds | Coats | Sweaters |
| Nail Trimmers | Doggy Treats | Dog House | Puppy Chow |

After keying the text, you can adjust column placement. Remember that you must have your insertion point above the text to be formatted.

## EXERCISE ➡ WP3.10

1. With **dog stuff 3-9 xxx** showing in the window, save the file as **dog stuff 3-10 xxx**. Position your insertion point at the beginning of the first item in the list.

2. Use the mouse pointer to drag the tab stops as follows:
   a. Drag the first tab to **2.75"** on the Ruler.

   b. Drag the second tab to **4.25"** on the Ruler.
   c. Drag the third tab to **5.75"** on the Ruler.

3. If the columns still aren't quite evenly spaced, make any additional adjustments. Print your document and close it, saving it again with the same name.

## Tab Types

WordPerfect gives you the option of four kinds of tabs. In addition, you can tell WordPerfect to put dot leaders between the columns. Look at Figure 3-8. It uses each kind of tab, and the tab markers on the Ruler have different shapes:

- **Left.** The Left tab is set at 1.5" for the kinds of pets.

- **Center.** The names of the pets are centered on the Center tab set at 2.75".

- **Decimal.** The tab at 4" is a Decimal tab. The prices of the pets align with the decimal point at the location of the tab stop.

- **Right.** Text backs up from a Right tab (at 5.25"). Note that the ages of the pets end at the location of the tab stop.

**FIGURE 3-8**
Sample Tabs

| | | | |
|---|---|---|---|
| Scottie | Fritz. . . . . . . . . | $45.00 | 6 months |
| Pug | Patricia . . . . . . | $275.00 | 8 weeks |
| Lab | Hildegaard . . . . . . | $30.00 | 6 weeks |

You noticed that you can change the types of tabs in the Tab Set dialog box. You can set different kinds of tabs using the Ruler, too.

## EXERCISE ▭▷ WP3.11

1. Beginning in a new document window, be sure the Ruler is displayed. Point to the tab portion of the Ruler and right click. The Tab QuickMenu will appear, looking like Figure 3-9.

2. Click the **Clear All Tabs** choice in the menu. Click your Ruler at **1$^1$/$_2$"** to set a Left tab at that position.

3. Point to the Ruler and right click. Choose a Center tab (from near the top of the list). Click your Ruler at **2$^3$/$_4$"** to set a Center tab stop there.

4. Point to the Ruler and right click. Choose a Decimal tab from the bottom of the list of types. That Decimal tab will have dot leaders leading up to it. (See the difference in the tab symbol—it has dots. So does the descriptive word.)

5. Set a Decimal tab stop with dot leaders at **4"** on the scale. Change to a Right tab and set it at **5$^1$/$_4$"**.

6. Tab once and key **Scottie**. Tab again and key **Fritz**. Continue in the same manner and key the entire exercise illustrated in Figure 3-8. Save the document as **prices 3-11 xxx**. Insert the Path and Filename code a double space below the list.

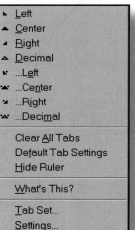

**FIGURE 3-9**
Tab QuickMenu

Left
Center
Right
Decimal
...Left
...Center
...Right
...Decimal

Clear All Tabs
Default Tab Settings
Hide Ruler

What's This?

Tab Set...
Settings...

7. Position your insertion point at the beginning of the first line. Beginning with the tab stop at the right, drag to adjust each tab marker so the list is centered on the page and the columns are somewhat evenly spaced.

8. When the list looks good, save it, print it, and close it.

The tabs for Figure 3-8 were purposely set close together for the illustration. When you prepare a list like this in real life, you can begin with roughly estimated placements, knowing that you can come back and adjust the settings when the text is keyed.

Also, note that WordPerfect remembers the last kind of tab you set. If you were to set a new tab stop right now, it would be a Right tab because that's what you used last. Now is a good time to point to the Ruler, right click, and change back to a Left tab, since that's what you'll use most often.

## Underline Tabs

You can tell WordPerfect to underline when you tab. This is great for forms. If you are underlining to the end of the line, Flush Right saves lots of time. Let's create a short, two-line form to practice this useful feature.

**EXERCISE** ⟹ **WP3.12**

1. Beginning in a new document window, open the **Font** menu and click the arrow beside the *Underline* box (lower right). Choose **Text & Tabs**. Close the dialog box.

2. Back in your document window, key **Name**. Space once, turn on **Underline**, and press **Tab** eight times. Turn Underline off.

3. Space once, key **Phone**, space once, turn on **Underline**, and press **Alt+F7** to complete the line to the right margin. Turn Underline off.

4. Press **Enter** twice, key **Address**, space once, turn on **Underline**, and press **Alt+F7** to extend the line across the page.

5. Save your short practice as **form 3-12 xxx**. Insert the Path and Filename code a double space below the *Address* line. Print the practice and close it.

# *Indent Features*

As you know, Tab is used to indent the first line of a paragraph. You also know that you can adjust the Ruler to indent an entire paragraph—from only the left or from both sides. When you use the Ruler, the text will remain indented until you readjust the triangles on the scale.

You can also indent whole paragraphs with a few keystrokes. When you indent from the keyboard, the feature is ended when you press Enter. Indent comes in three flavors and includes a shortcut:

- **Indent** causes the lines of the paragraph to begin at the first tab setting. Choose Indent by pressing F7.

- **Hanging Indent** causes the first line of the paragraph to begin at the margin and the remaining lines to begin at the first tab setting. Use Ctrl+F7 for this.

- **Double Indent** causes the lines of the paragraph to be indented from the right as well as the left. Choose Double Indent by pressing Ctrl+Shift+F7.

- **QuickIndent.** QuickIndent provides a shortcut for indented paragraphs and hanging indent. If you press Tab at the beginning of any line of a paragraph after the first line, QuickIndent will indent the remaining lines.

All four of these features can be chosen from a menu. To do so, open the Format menu, and choose Paragraph. The indent choices are listed at the bottom of the menu. Any of these features can be used to format the text as you go, or you can come back later and insert them. A code is placed in your document for each occurrence. That code can be removed if you want the paragraphs to be normal.

## EXERCISE ➡ WP3.13

1. Open **welcome proj2b xxx** again. Save it as **welcome 3-13 xxx**.

2. Position the insertion point at the beginning of the first paragraph. Use **Double Indent** (Ctrl+Shift+F7) to format that paragraph.

3. Position the insertion point at the beginning of the second paragraph. Use **Hanging Indent** (Ctrl+F7) on that paragraph. Do the same with the fourth paragraph.

4. Format the third paragraph with **Indent**. Note that you can see the indents at the left easily. Ragged right kind of covers up the formatting at the right.

5. Return your insertion point to the beginning and choose **Full** justification.

6. Look at the codes for each style of indent. Position your insertion point at the beginning of the *Grooming* paragraph.

7. Reveal your codes and remove the [Hd Left Ind] and [Hd Back Tab] codes to return the paragraph to the margin.

8. Click to position the insertion point at the beginning of the second line of that paragraph and press **Tab**. QuickIndent reformatted the paragraph.

9. Print your practice, save it again with the same name, and close it.

# Outline/Bullets & Numbering

WordPerfect uses the Indent feature together with the Outline/Bullets & Numbering feature to help you in creating lists. Bulleted lists and numbered lists usually are indented with Indent following the bullet or numeral. Not only will WordPerfect convert a tab to an indent following a bullet or numeral, it will also insert the next bullet or numeral when you press Enter. When you are done with the list, you can deselect the option by backspacing to remove the unwanted bullet or numeral.

## EXERCISE ➡ WP3.14

1. Beginning in a new document window, key **1.** and press **Tab**. Key the information for the first item in Figure 3-10. Press **Enter** twice. The numeral should be in place and your insertion point should be at the tab stop.

2. Key the text for the second item. Press **Enter** twice and backspace to delete the numeral. The list is finished.

3. Key your name at the left margin (just to have some text). Press **Enter** twice.

4. Key an asterisk (*) at the left margin and press **Tab**. The asterisk will change to a bullet. Select the text in the first item at the top of the document (from the *Y* of *Your* to the period after *command*).

5. Hold the **Ctrl** key (to copy) while you drag that text to the line with the bullet. With your insertion point at the end of the bulleted item, press **Enter** twice.

6. Select and copy the text in the second item to the line with the second bullet.

7. After the final item, press **Enter** twice again. Backspace to remove the bullet.

8. Return to the beginning of the document and key **Beginner Training** followed by a double space. Save the document as **bullets 3-14 xxx**. Insert the Path and Filename code. Print the practice and save it again as you close it.

**FIGURE 3-10**
Text for Exercise WP3.14

```
Beginner Training

1.  Your dog will learn how to respond to your first command to "SIT,"
    go "DOWN," "STAND," and "STAY" in each of those positions until
    you release it or give it another command.

2.  Your dog will learn to come immediately when called and sit at
    your feet, waiting for your next command. It will also learn to
    walk with you in the "HEEL" position at your side on a loose leash
    and sit when you stop walking.
```

In Exercise WP3.14 all of the bullets and numerals were keyed at the left margin. They work just as well if you tab before entering the first bullet or numeral. In addition, you can use other kinds of numbering. Roman numerals or letters (a, b, c) all work if you key a period after the numeral or letter. You can also use a wide variety of characters for bullets—check boxes, check marks, arrows, or any available symbol will work. What's more, you can edit the list by changing the items around or changing the kind of listing.

If you lose a numeral, position the insertion point at the end of the previous item and press Enter. Then press Delete until the item is properly aligned beside the numeral.

## EXERCISE ▷ WP3.15

1. Beginning in a new document window, key the list in Figure 3-11. When you finish, save the list as **list 3-15 xxx**. Press **Enter** twice at the bottom and insert the Path and Filename code.

2. Select the list. Open the **Insert** menu and choose **Outline/Bullets & Numbering**.

3. Click the **Bullets** tab and click the style with stars. Then click **OK** to apply that style.

(continued on next page)

**FIGURE 3-11**
Text for Exercise WP3.15

```
Small animals
Tropical fish
Favorite breeds of birds
Dog and cat supplies
Quality brands of food
```

4. If the list is not still selected, select it again and return to the same dialog box. Choose Roman numerals and click **OK**. Select it again, return to the dialog box, and choose one of the numbering styles that begins with *1* and has several indent levels. Click **OK**.

5. Point in the left margin opposite *Dog and cat supplies*. Click twice to select the line and the hard return.

6. Point to the selected line and drag it up to the top of the list. When the floating black line is at the left of the first item, release the mouse button. Your list should renumber.

7. Position the insertion point at the left of *Favorite*. Backspace once to delete the number. Oops! That was an error. Position the insertion point after *fish*, press **Enter** (to insert the numeral), and press **Delete** to bring the Favorites line up into position.

8. Keep the document open as you read on.

When you are in a list, the Property Bar changes to provide tools to help with your list. Look at the Outline Property Bar (see Figure 3-12). The special tools are between the Underline button and the Prompt-As-You-Go box. Look at them in your window. When you move your insertion point out of the list, the normal Property Bar tools will appear.

**FIGURE 3-12**
Outline Property Bar

Outlines in WordPerfect have families. When an item has second- or third-level items, that entire group is called a *family*. One of the tools you'll use in Exercise WP3. 16 will hide or show the family. You can also choose how many levels will be displayed.

## EXERCISE ⟹ WP3.16

1. With **list 3-15 xxx** showing in the window, save the file as **list 3-16 xxx**. Position the insertion point at the beginning of the second item.

2. Click the **Demote** button to make that item a second-level item. Position the insertion point at the beginning of the third item in the list. Click the **Demote** button twice.

3. Position the insertion point at the beginning of the fifth item. Click the **Demote** button once.

4. Point to the **Show levels** tool (just to the left of Prompt-As-You-Go). Click it and choose **Two**. Can you guess why the fish disappeared? Return to the same button and choose **One**. Now how many items remain?

5. Display **Four** levels. Position the insertion point in the first item. Click the **Hide Family** button. Only the first-level family remains. Click the **Show Family** button to return all levels.

6. Position the insertion point in the third-level item (*Tropical fish*). Click the **Move Up** button. Click it again.

Now click the **Move Down** button twice to return the fish to their original location.

7. Can you figure out how to "promote" all items to be first-level items? Do that. Then print the document and close it, saving it with the same name.

You may have noticed that the default Toolbar contains two buttons for Outline/Bullets & Numbering. You may practice with them at your leisure. This is a powerful tool in WordPerfect.

# Columns

Wordperfect helps you create Newspaper-style columns, where the text fills the first column and snakes to the next, as well as Balanced newspaper columns, where both columns end evenly at the bottom. Let's learn about the Columns feature.

## EXERCISE ▷ WP3.17

1. Open **welcome proj2a xxx**. Use Save As to save the file as **welcome 3-17 xxx**. Position the insertion point at the beginning of the first paragraph.

2. Click the **Columns** button on the Toolbar and choose **2 Columns**. Zoom to **Full Page** and look at your columns. Change to **3 Columns** and then **4 Columns**. Finally, return to **2 Columns**. These are newspaper columns.

3. Without moving the insertion point, click the **Columns** button again and choose **Format**.

Look at the various choices in the dialog box. Then choose **Balanced newspaper** and click **OK**.

4. Point to the space between columns (the *gutter*), and drag it to the right until your columns are **4"** and **2"** wide. Drag the guideline at the left of the second column to the left until the column at the right is **2¹/4"** wide. (The left column is still **4"** wide.)

5. Keep the document open. Zoom to **Full Page** as you read on.

The default gutter between columns is a half inch wide. When you adjust your column guidelines, WordPerfect automatically adjusts the text in the columns so they end evenly.

You may have noticed that the Path and Filename code was included in the right column. That's a little irregular. The Columns format begins at the location of the insertion point when it is begun and continues until it encounters another Columns code. You can either select the text to be in columns before choosing the feature, or you can enter an ending code in the desired location.

**WP-51**

# EXERCISE ▷ WP3.18

1. With **welcome 3-17 xxx** showing, save it as **welcome 3-18 xxx**. Reveal your codes at the beginning of the first paragraph and remove the [Col Def] code.

2. Select paragraphs 2-7. Open the **Format** menu and choose **Columns** to open the same dialog box. (The shortcut button is easier, isn't it?) Choose **2 Balanced newspaper** columns and click **OK**.

3. Save your document again with the same name. Print it and close it.

**NOTE:**

You are getting very good at working with dialog boxes. You know by now that to close a dialog box and accept your choices, you simply click OK or Close. For the remainder of your lessons, you may not receive that instruction. It is assumed that you will make the requested changes to the dialog box and return to your document for the next instruction.

## Summary

This lesson contains a vast number of tools for changing the look of your paragraphs. You learned that:

■ WordPerfect default settings help you do your work without making any changes.

■ line spacing enables you to spread your work out vertically.

■ justification gives paragraphs a different look.

■ Center and Flush Right are normally used on one or two lines at a time.

■ dot leaders join text at the left with text at the right.

■ the Shadow Cursor enables you to key anywhere on the page.

■ margins and tabs are easy to change, either with the Ruler or with the dialog box.

■ a variety of indent formats enables you to stress paragraphs in different ways.

■ you can easily add lists to your documents with the Outline/Bullets & Numbering feature.

■ text columns are easy to insert, adjust, and remove.

Each dialog box that you used in this lesson contains a number of additional options to give you more choices about how your work will look. As you need these tools on the job, you will want to spend a little time exploring some of the other options.

## LESSON 3 REVIEW QUESTIONS

### FILL IN THE BLANKS

**Complete each of the following statements by writing your answer in the blank provided.**

1.  The settings that automatically give you 1-inch margins and single spacing are stored in the _____ template.

2.  The justification setting that causes text to extend to the margins on all lines of the paragraph except the last is _____ justification.

3.  The bar you can use to change tab and margin settings is the _____ .

4.  When the first line of text begins at the left margin and the remaining lines are indented, that format is called _____ .

5.  The kind of text columns that end evenly at the bottom are called _____ columns.

### TRUE/FALSE

**Circle the T if the statement is true. Circle the F if it is false.**

**T  F**    6. To insert dot leaders, you must give the Center command twice.

**T  F**    7. When you use double spacing, all lines of text are separated by two blank lines.

**T  F**    8. The Shadow Cursor may be chosen from the Application Bar.

**T  F**    9. When keystrokes are used to set an indent format, that format is turned off when you press Enter.

**T  F**    10. Most of the formatting features in this lesson can be chosen from the menu system or from one of the on-screen bars.

## LESSON 3 PROJECT

SCANS

1.  Go to the student **Datafile** folder and open **fund**. Use **Save As** to save the file as **fund proj3 xxx**.

2.  Format the document as follows:
    a.  Center the title. And enough hard returns so the title is about **2"** from the top of the page.
    b.  Format the title with 24-pt. bold.
    c.  Beginning with the first paragraph, change to **Full** justification.

(continued on next page)

**d.** Use the Ruler to set the first line indent at **1.38"**.

**e.** Make the entire document double-spaced except the second paragraph. Remove the extra blank lines between paragraphs.

**f.** Format the second paragraph with **Double Indent**.

**g.** Select the three lines that begin with *express* and use **Outline/Bullets & Numbering** to format those lines with check mark bullets.

**h.** Add the three items in Figure 3-13. (Be sure they have check marks, too.)

**FIGURE 3-13**
Text for Step 1h of Lesson 3 Project

```
show appreciation for the love and comfort that animals provide us
celebrate a pet's, owner's, or friend's birthday
give a gift of love to an owner who loves and values animals
```

**i.** Rearrange the checked items so they are in the following order:
  ✓ *give a gift...*
  ✓ *celebrate...*
  ✓ *express appreciation...*
  ✓ *show appreciation...*
  ✓ *express joy...*
  ✓ *express sympathy...*

**j.** Insert the Path and Filename code a double space below the last line of the document. Position it at the left margin. (Can you figure out a way to do this?)

**3.** Save the document again with the same name. Then print it and close it.

## CRITICAL THINKING ACTIVITY

SCANS

You started to key a list using bullets and expected the second bullet to appear when you pressed Enter. The bullet didn't appear. What is your problem and how will you fix it?

# PAGE FORMATTING

LESSON

4

## OBJECTIVES

**Upon completion of this lesson, you will be able to:**

- Format multiple-page documents with headers and footers.

- Use Suppress to prevent headers, footers, or numbers from appearing on certain pages.

- Control the end of pages with Widow/Orphan and Block Protect.

- Use Page Numbering to identify pages.

- Use soft and hard page breaks.

- Format documents with footnotes and endnotes.

- Center the text on a page from top to bottom.

- Use Delay Codes to start the formatting at the desired location.

- Use Make It Fit to fit the text on the designated number of pages.

- Use Divide Page to make several logical pages fit on one piece of paper.

- Change the orientation of type on a page.

- Use Default Font and Current Document Style for full-document formatting.

- Print using several print options.

- Create labels with the WordPerfect Labels feature.

**⏱ Estimated Time: 2 hours**

In Lesson 3 you learned about formatting text by paragraph or by selected blocks of text. This lesson deals with page formatting—in most cases, formatting that is used with multiple-page documents.

# *Headers and Footers*

Headers and footers are text at the top or bottom of a page that tie the document together. When headers and footers are used in reports, they usually contain the name of the document. They may also include page numbering, although pages can be numbered without using headers and footers.

You may have as many as two headers and two footers in a document. The extra ones are for facing pages if you print a document on both sides of the page. Headers or footers are automatically separated from the text on the page by a blank line. They take space from the document on the page, and do not extend into the margin. If you want them closer to the top or bottom of the page, you must adjust the margins. You can use most kinds of formatting in your headers or footers.

In addition to reports, headers are used for letters. When a header is used for a multiple-page letter, it usually contains the name of the person to receive the letter as well as the date the letter was prepared. Let's begin with a letter.

## E X E R C I S E ⟹ WP4.1

1. Beginning in a new document window, insert today's date about 2 inches from the top of the page. Press **Enter** four times. Save your letter as **obedience 4-1 xxx**.

2. Key the inside address in Figure 4-1 and add an appropriate greeting a double space below the address. Following the greeting, press **Enter** twice.

**FIGURE 4-1**
Address for Exercise WP4.1

```
Kris Reynolds
223 Olive Street
Austin, TX 78713
```

3. Go to the student **Datafile** folder and insert **obedience**. Look through the letter. It has an awful page break. Return to the top and press **Enter** three more times between the date and mailing address.

4. Position your insertion point at the beginning of the document. Open the **Insert** menu and choose **Header/Footer**. The Headers/Footers dialog box will appear (see Figure 4-2).

**FIGURE 4-2**
Headers/Footers Dialog Box

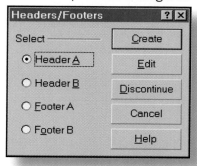

5. Header A is chosen. That's great. Click **Create** Your insertion point will be enclosed in a box at the top of the letter. This is the header area. Several new tools should appear on the Property Bar (see Figure 4-3).

**FIGURE 4-3**
Header/Footer Tools

6. Key the full name of the person to receive the letter and press **Enter**.

7. Key **Page** and space once. Search through the new tools on the Property Bar until you find the Page Numbering button. Click it and choose **Page Number**. Press **Enter**.

8. Enter today's date. Note the tool at the right of the Property Bar that looks like a file folder.

Click it to close the Header/Footer Property Bar and move your insertion point out of the header area.

9. Save your document again. Open the **View** menu and switch to **Two Pages** view. Keep your document open.

You were told to end your header by clicking the Close button. You could have simply clicked to position your insertion point anywhere outside of the header area. Many Property Bars have a Close button, so you'll be using it often.

# *Suppress*

Look at both pages of the letter. The second page looks good. The first page looks awful. Few documents include the header on the first page. Besides, if this letter was printed on a company letterhead, the header would print right over the letterhead information.

The solution to this problem is to suppress the header on the first page. When you use Suppress, it affects only the page on which the insertion point is located when the command is given. You can use Suppress as often as you wish in a document. You'll get to try Suppress on this document in a moment.

**QuickSteps**

**Suppress**
1. Position the insertion point at the top of the document.
2. Open the Format menu and choose Page.
3. Choose Suppress and specify the feature to suppress.

# *Widow/Orphan*

When you remove the header from the first page of the letter, it is likely that one line of a paragraph will be at the top of the second page. A single line of a paragraph at either the top or bottom of a page looks bad. One of the rules of good document production is to always have at least two lines of a paragraph on a page if the paragraph must be split.

The Widow/Orphan tool takes care of that for you. You insert the code once, at the top of the document, and WordPerfect will protect your entire document. It does this by moving enough text to the next page so one line never stands alone.

**QuickSteps**

**Widow/Orphan**
1. Position the insertion point at the top of the document.
2. Open the Format menu and choose Keep Text Together.
3. Choose Widow/Orphan.

**INTERNET**

The Internet can be found on all seven continents, including Antarctica. A host at the South Pole sends out scientific and weather information.

**WP-57**

1. With **obedience 4-1 xxx** showing in Two Pages view in the window, save it as **obedience 4-2 xxx**. Position your insertion point at the top of the first page of the letter (but NOT in the header area).

2. Open the **Format** menu, choose **Page**, and choose **Suppress**. Click **Header A** and then click **OK**. The header should disappear from the first page.

3. Does your letter have one line of a paragraph on the second page? Open the **Format** menu and choose **Keep Text Together**. In the Keep Text Together dialog box (see Figure 4-4), you should see three choices.

4. Click **Widow/Orphan** to select it. (You'll learn about the other tools later.) Click **OK**.

5. Position the insertion point a double space below the last line of the letter and key

**FIGURE 4-4**
Keep Text Together Dialog Box

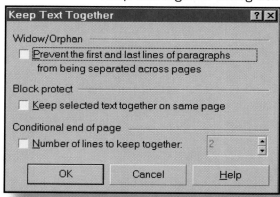

**Sincerely,**. Press **Enter** four times and key **Polly Paradeis**.

6. Press **Enter** twice and add the Path and Filename code. Save the letter again and print it. Close the document.

# Page Numbering

As mentioned earlier, you can tell WordPerfect to number your pages without using a header or footer. WordPerfect is always counting your pages, but it doesn't print the numbers unless you request them. A variety of formats are available for page numbering, and you can begin numbering with any number. We'll add page numbering to a new document. Then we'll do some basic formatting of the document.

 **QuickSteps**

**Page Numbering**
1. Position the insertion point where you want page numbering to begin.
2. Choose Page from the Format menu.
3. Choose Numbering and set the preferences.

**SCANS**

1. Beginning in a new document window, go to the student **Datafile** folder and open **ethics**. Use **Save As** to save the file as **ethics 4-3 xxx**.

2. Open the **Format** menu, choose **Page**, and choose **Numbering**. The Select Page Numbering Format dialog box will be displayed showing the default settings (see Figure 4-5).

3. Click the arrow beside the *Position* box and look at the choices you have for the location of the page number. Choose **Bottom Right**.

4. Below that, look at the formats available. (You can customize formats, if you wish.) Choose the default setting (*1*) and click **OK** to return to your document. Look at the page numbers. (You have to use the scroll bar to see the page number at the bottom of the final page.)

5. Return to the top of the document. Center the title approximately **2"** from the top of the page, and format it with bold, 20-pt. Arial. Beginning with the first paragraph, set **Full** justification.

6. Change the indent format of the indented paragraph to **Double Indent**. Change the first tab stop to **1.38"** and the second to **1.75"**.

7. Choose the **Widow/Orphan** feature. Press **Ctrl+Home** and look at your document with **Two Pages** view.

8. Save the document again with the same name and keep it open.

**FIGURE 4-5**
Select Page Numbering Format Dialog Box

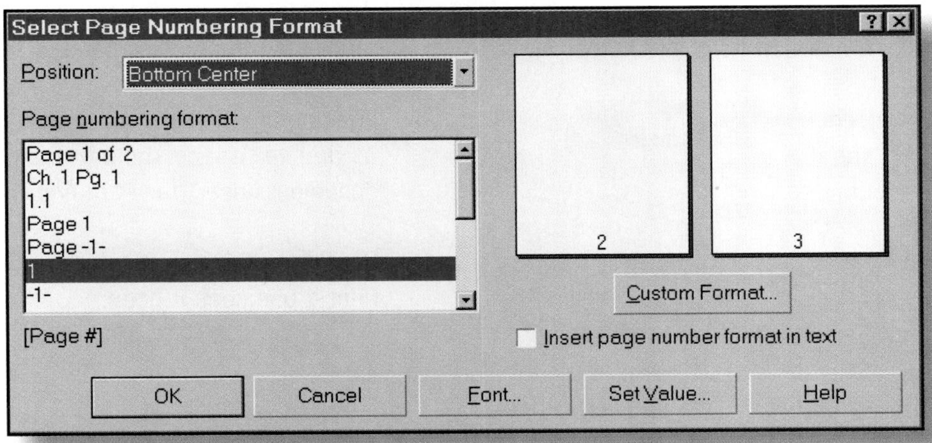

## *Page Breaks*

$A$s you know, when the page is full, WordPerfect spills the text over to the next page. This is known as a *soft page break*, and the only way you can change the location of that soft page break is to change the amount of text on the page.

You can manually begin a new page with a *hard page break*. To do this, press Ctrl+Enter or choose New Page from the bottom of the Insert menu. When you insert a hard page break, the page break always stays in the same place unless you remove it. We'll work with page breaks and then practice with footers.

SCANS

1. With **ethics 4-3 xxx** open in the window, save the document as **ethics 4-4 xxx**. If you can read the text, stay in Two Pages view.

2. Position the insertion point at the beginning of the second paragraph below the indented paragraph (*Integrity is the key . . .*).

3. Press **Ctrl+Enter** to begin a new page. Do the same at the beginning of the *In addition . . .* paragraph. Your document is now three pages long. Return to **Page** view.

4. Position your insertion point at the beginning of the first page. Reveal your codes and remove the [Pg Num Pos] code. Can you guess what that code does?

**TIP**

You can reveal your codes only in Page or Draft view.

5. Give your document a footer. In that footer,
   a. key the name of the document at the left.
   b. use **Flush Right** and key the word **Page**.

Space once and insert the page number (from the Property Bar).
   c. click outside of the footer space to exit the footer edit mode.

6. Position your insertion point just below the final paragraph on the first page. Reveal your codes and find the [HPg] code. Delete it to join the first page and the second page.

7. Follow the same procedure to join the third page to the second page. Look through your document. Do the footers look good? Do any problems with spacing need to be corrected?

8. Position the insertion point at the left margin, a double space below the end of the document. Insert the Path and Filename code.

9. Save the document again as **ethics 4-4 xxx**. Print it and keep it open.

# *Footnotes and Endnotes*

In technical writing, footnotes and endnotes identify the sources of the information used and to provide additional information for the reader. Footnotes are usually numbered consecutively, and each footnote appears at the bottom of the page where the reference appears.

Endnotes provide the same kind of information as footnotes. Endnotes, however, are usually on a page by themselves at the end of a document. For both footnotes and endnotes, numbering is automatic. If you delete text that contains a footnote or endnote, the rest of the notes will be renumbered automatically. The same is true if you add a note. Footnotes and endnotes can be entered as the document is keyed, or they can be added afterwards.

**QuickSteps**

**Footnotes and Endnotes**
1. Position your insertion point where you want the reference number.
2. Open the insert menu; choose Footnote/Endnote.
3. Specify Footnote or Endnote and click Create.
4. Key the text of the footnote and click the close button.

# EXERCISE ⟹ WP4.5

1. Click the **New Blank Document** button on the Toolbar to open a new window.

2. Key the text in Figure 4-6. When you come to the superscripted numeral, open the **Insert** menu and choose **Footnote/Endnote**.

3. Look at the choices. With **Footnote Number** chosen, click **Create**. Look at the new tools on the Property Bar.

4. Without spacing after the numeral, key the information for the first footnote. It will be at the bottom of the page. When you finish, click the **Close** button at the right of the Property Bar. Your insertion point will be returned to the paragraph.

5. Key up to the next footnote. Repeat the procedure for the second footnote.

6. Zoom to **Full Page** to look at your document. Note the position of the footnotes and the spacing and formatting of the footnotes.

7. Save the file as **footnotes 4-5 xxx**. Insert the Path and Filename code a double space below the last line of text at the top. Print the file and save it again.

8. Return to **100%**. Delete the first footnote number in the paragraph at the top of the page. Look at the other footnote number. Look at the footnote at the bottom. Click **Undo** to put the footnote back in again.

9. Click in the second footnote. Try to move the insertion point using the keyboard. (You can't move up or down. You're in a special editing window.) Change the page number to **122**.

10. Close the document without saving it again.

**FIGURE 4-6**
Text for Exercise WP4.5

```
This is a paragraph that contains a footnote.   The first footnote
number is here.¹  This is the text for the second footnote.²  This is
the end of the text.
_____

    ¹Sara Stewdent, Practice Footnotes, (Winneconne: Main Street Press,
199x), p. 55.
    ²Sara Stewdent, Practice Footnotes, (Winneconne: Main Street Press,
199x), p. 102.
```

Now let's take your knowledge of footnotes to the **ethics 4-4 xxx** document.

**TIP**

Headers, footers, page numbering, footnotes, and endnotes do not show in Draft view.

# EXERCISE → WP4.6

1.  With the **ethics 4-4 xxx** document showing, save it as **ethics 4-6 xxx**.

2.  Position the insertion point at the end of the double indented paragraph. Insert Footnote 1 from Figure 4-7.

3.  Position the insertion point at the end of the first bulleted list. Insert Footnote 2. Put the third footnote at the end of the last word in the second bulleted list.

4.  Zoom to **75%** and look through your document. With footnotes, the footer looks awful. Click into either of the footers and select the text, complete with the page number code. Copy it to the Clipboard.

5.  Go to the beginning of the document. Find the [Footer A] code and drag it out of the document.

6.  Insert Header A. In the header editing space, paste the text from the footer. (You just saved keying the text again!)

7.  Give the document a new footer. The footer should include only the Path and Filename code—flush with the right margin. Format that information with 8-pt. Arial. Delete the Path and Filename code following the final bullet.

8.  Click below the header space and suppress the header on the first page. Look through the document. It should look better. Save it again with the same name.

9.  Print the document and keep it open.

**FIGURE 4-7**
Footnotes for **ethics 4-6 xxx**

[1]Susan Bailey, "Morals in the Workplace," *Magical Management*, June, 199x, p. 23.
[2]Michaela Seitz, "Can We Build Integrity?" *Workplace Wildness*, Volume XXI, February, 199x, p. 42.
[3]Jacob Steiner, "Motto for Success," *Magical Management*, May, 199x, p. 16.

Look at the footnotes in **ethics 4-6 xxx**. These are footnotes for references from magazines. Compare the arrangement of information with the footnotes from **footnotes 4-5 xxx**. That layout is correct for footnotes from a book. Now let's remove all three footnotes from this document and insert them again as endnotes. The notes will go in the same places, and they will use the same references.

**WP-62**                                                      COREL WORDPERFECT 8

## EXERCISE ▷ WP4.7

SCANS

1. With **ethics 4-6 xxx** showing in the window, save it as **ethics 4-7 xxx**. Go through the document and delete each footnote number to delete the footnotes. (Make a mental note of the locations. You will be placing the endnote reference numbers in the same places.)

2. Position the insertion point for the first endnote. Open the **Insert** menu and choose **Footnote/Endnote**. In the dialog box choose **Endnote** and click **Create**. Your insertion point will be positioned to the right of a *1.*, immediately below the final line of the document. That's OK.

3. Press **F7** for indent and key the text for the first endnote from Figure 4-7. Use the same procedure to insert the other two endnotes.

4. With your insertion point just to the right of the final endnote number in the text, press **Ctrl+Enter** for a hard page break.

5. Press **Backspace** twice to get rid of the bullet for the list and return the insertion point to the left margin. Press **Enter** until the insertion point is approximately **2"** from the top of the page.

6. Center and Bold **ENDNOTES**. Press **Enter** twice. Look through the document. Does everything look right?

7. Let's print only the endnotes page. Position the insertion point somewhere on the endnotes page. Choose **Print** from the Toolbar. Click **Current page**. Send the page to the printer.

8. Save your document again as **ethics 4-7 xxx**. Keep it open.

## *Center Page*

The Center Page command is used to tell WordPerfect to center the text on the page vertically. Some people use it for letters. In this lesson we will use it for a title page on the report you have been formatting. Assume you are one of the employees of Pet Paradise, and your boss has asked you to help her get the report ready for a management class she has been taking.

**QuickSteps**

**Center Page**
1. Open the Format menu and choose Page.
2. Choose Center and set the options.

## EXERCISE ▷ WP4.8

SCANS

1. With **ethics 4-7 xxx** open, save it as **ethics 4-8 xxx**. Position the insertion point at the beginning of the first paragraph. Change to double spacing.

2. Change each of the following sections to single spacing. When you finish, each of the single-spaced sections should be preceded and followed by one blank line.
   a. The double indented paragraph.

(continued on next page)

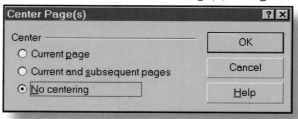

**FIGURE 4-8**
Center Page(s) Dialog Box

b. The first bulleted list.

c. The second bulleted list.

d. The beginning of the endnotes page, above the title.

 **TIP**

For the indented paragraph and bulleted lists, you only need to insert one line spacing code if you select the text and then choose single spacing.

3. Press **Ctrl+Home** twice to position your insertion point above all codes at the top of the first page. Press **Ctrl+Enter** to add a new page there. Press **Page Up** to go to the title page.

4. Open the **Format** menu, choose **Page**, and choose **Center**. In the Center Page(s) dialog box (see Figure 4-8), choose **Current page**.

5. Choose **Center** justification and key the title page information in Figure 4-9. Add extra returns between the parts so the information is attractively placed on the page. Provide your information in the areas with parentheses.

6. Press **Alt+Page Down** to move your insertion point to the beginning of the first page of text. Note that the insertion point is still at the center of the page. Change to **Full** justification. Look through your document. Especially look at the page numbers.

7. Press **Ctrl+Home** twice to return to the beginning of the title page. Open the **Format** menu and choose **Page**. Then choose **Delay Codes**. (Follow along blindly here. An explanation will follow the exercise.)

8. In the Delay Codes dialog box, pages to skip will be prompted at *1*. Click **OK** to open the Styles Editor. Note the following:

a. The buttons on the Feature Bar just above the white portion of the window.

b. The codes section at the bottom that will show your codes as you enter them.

9. Open the **Format** menu, choose **Page**, and choose **Numbering**. Since your page numbers are in the header, set the *Position* section at **No page numbering**.

10. Click the **Set Value** button. It should report *1*. That is correct. Click **OK** twice to close two dialog boxes. Click the **Close** button on the Styles Editor Feature Bar.

**FIGURE 4-9**
Title Page Information for Exercise WP4.8

Integrity, the Common Thread

by
(Student name)

(Current date)
The Basics of Ethical Management
(Your school name)

**11.** Look through your document. Are the page numbers right—with a *2* on the second page of text? Are the endnotes on page 4? If the page number on the endnotes page is *5*, repeat Steps 7-10 and check again.

**12.** Save the document again with the same name. Keep it open.

# Delay Codes

I t is generally a good idea to have the codes that format an entire document at the beginning of the document. Then the Delay Codes feature can be used to tell WordPerfect where to begin a particular feature, like page 1. If it wasn't already at the top of the first page of text, the header code, for example, could have been located in the Delay Codes section. In Exercise WP4.8 it worked well to get the page numbering corrected. You'll work again with Delay Codes later.

**QuickSteps**

**Delay Codes**
1. Choose Page and Delay Codes from the Format menu.
2. Set number of pages to delay.
3. Insert codes to delay.

In addition, you needed to tell WordPerfect not to number the pages using the Page Numbering feature, because the page numbers were already included in the header. Let's look at a different feature.

# Make It Fit

M ake It Fit will either condense your text to get it on fewer pages than it would normally take, or expand your work to fill a specified number of pages. The default setting changes only the font size and line spacing to accomplish the desired goal. If you change the defaults, WordPerfect can also consider margins. We'll take a portion of the **ethics 4-8 xxx** document to try Make It Fit.

**QuickSteps**

**Make it Fit**
1. Choose Make It Fit from the Format menu.
2. Set desired number of pages.

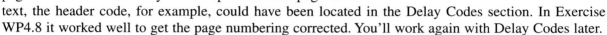

**EXERCISE ⟹ WP4.9**

**SCANS**

**1.** Position your insertion point in the upper left corner of the first page of text of **ethics 4-8 xxx**. Then press **F8** to turn on Select.

**2.** Press **Page Down** and use the down arrow key until you have selected all of the first page and the first paragraph on the second page. Press **Ctrl+C** to copy that text to the Windows Clipboard.

**3.** Click the **New Blank Document** button to go to a new window. Paste the text into that window. Save the short document as **fit 4-9 xxx**. Press **Ctrl+End**. You should have a small amount of text on the second page.

**4.** Press **Enter** and insert the Path and Filename code a double space below the last line of the document.

**5.** Open the **Format** menu and choose **Make It Fit**. The dialog box should look like Figure 4-10. Be sure only *Line spacing* and *Font size* are checked. Be sure the desired number of pages is *1* page. Click **Make It Fit**.

**6.** After a moment, your document will be on one page. Look at the Font Size in the Property Bar. It is probably less than the original 12 pt.

(continued on next page)

**7.** Go to the Line Spacing dialog box and check the setting. It is probably less than 2 (double spacing).

**8.** Print the one-page document. Then close it, saving it again as you close it. Save and close **ethics 4-8 xxx**.

**FIGURE 4-10**
Make It Fit Dialog Box

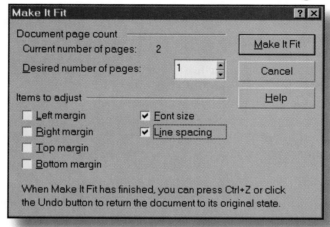

Make It Fit doesn't do anything that you couldn't do by adjusting font size or line spacing. But it's a lot easier to let the computer do the work for you!

# *Block Protect*

**A**nother feature that is useful in multiple-page documents is Block Protect. Like Widow/Orphan, it helps control page endings. However, while Widow/Orphan may be inserted at the beginning of the document to control the entire document, block Protect must be used at the bottom of each page where it is needed. The procedure is to select text that should be "protected" (kept together) and then choose Block Protect from the Keep Text Together dialog box. We'll use a contrived document to practice.

**QuickSteps**

**Block Protect**
1. Select the text to keep together.
2. Display the QuickMenu and choose Block Protect.

SCANS

**1.** Beginning in a new document window, go to the student **Datafile** folder and open **ethics-2**. Save the file as **ethics 4-10 xxx**.

**2.** Look at the page break between pages 1 and 2. A listing like this one would probably read better if it was all on one page.

3. Beginning with the bullet at the bottom of the first page, use the mouse to select all of the first bulleted item and a portion of the second one.

4. Open the **Format** menu and choose **Keep Text Together**. Click to choose **Block Protect** and then click **OK**. The bulleted item from the bottom of the first page should move to the second page.

5. Insert the Path and Filename code at the left margin, a double space below the list. Print the exercise and close it, saving it again with the same name.

It is important at this point to understand that you could have accomplished the same thing by inserting a hard page break before that first bulleted item. The problem with that method is that if you come back later to edit the document and the list moves to a different position on the page, the hard page break is still in the document and might cause a half page or more to be empty. With Block Protect, the code just hides in the text and doesn't do anything unless the protected text comes at the end of the page.

Now we'll format your long ethics document into a booklet. This involves a number of Word-Perfect features. Follow along carefully.

# Divide Page

You can divide a physical page (the normal sheet of paper) into a number of logical pages. Each logical page is considered a page by WordPerfect, so you can number them. For a booklet, you must divide a physical page into two logical pages. The Divide Page feature is part of Page Setup. We'll try it shortly.

# Orientation

Orientation has to do with which way a page is turned. The normal orientation is *portrait*, where the short edge is at the top. The other choice is *landscape*, where the long edge is at the top. A change in orientation is also made in the Page Setup dialog box.

## E X E R C I S E ▷ WP4.11

**SCANS**

1. Open **ethics 4-8 xxx** and save it as **ethics 4-11 xxx**. Position the insertion point at the beginning of the title page.

2. First, you've been asked to use a sans serif font for the report. Change to **Arial**. Position the insertion point below the title and change to **10** pt.

3. Open the **Format** menu and choose **Page**. Then choose **Page Setup**. Look at the variety of sizes of documents available. Just to the right of that, click to choose **Landscape**.

4. Click the **Divide Page** tab. Note that the illustration is in landscape orientation because you chose that in the previous step. Change Columns to **2**. Note the illustration.

(continued on next page)

**5.** Click the **Page Margins** tab and set all four margins at **0.5"**. Click **OK**.

**6.** Zoom to **Full Page** and look at your document. It has some things wrong with it—for instance, the headers still have one-inch margins. Also,

the headers and endnotes are still formatted with the serif font.

**7.** Save the document again with the same name. Keep it open as you read on.

# Default Font and Current Document Style

When you change such formats as the font or the margins of a document, those changes affect only the body of the document. The formatting does NOT extend to the special parts of the document such as headers, footers, footnotes, endnotes, and page numbering. All of those parts can be formatted separately. A better way is to put font changes for the entire document in the Default Font or all formatting in the Current Document Style. Let's reformat the document.

## E X E R C I S E ⟹ WP4.12

**SCANS**

**1.** With **ethics 4-11 xxx** showing in the window, save the file as **ethics 4-12 xxx**. Return to the top of the document. Remove all four margin set codes and any font codes.

**2.** With the insertion point still at the top of the document, open the **File** menu and choose **Document**. Then choose **Default Font**. The Document Default Font dialog box will appear, looking like Figure 4-11.

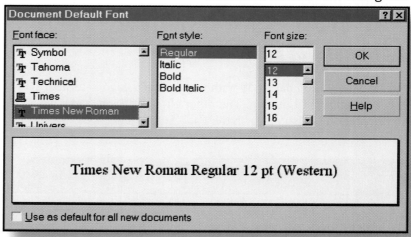

**FIGURE 4-11**
Document Default Font Dialog Box

**3.** Change the Font face to **Arial** and the Font size to **10**.

**4.** Look at the check box at the bottom. That should NOT be checked. If it is, the change you're now making will be a "permanent" setting for WordPerfect. Click **OK**.

**5.** Return to the **File** menu. Choose **Document** and then **Current Document Style** to display the Styles Editor (see Figure 4-12).

**6.** Choose **Margins** from the **Format** menu in the dialog box and set all four margins at **0.5"**. Close the Margins dialog box and the Styles Editor to return to your document.

7. Look through the document. Are the headers properly formatted? What about the endnotes and the footer containing the Path and Filename code?

8. Save the document again with the same name. Keep it open.

**FIGURE 4-12**
Styles Editor Dialog Box

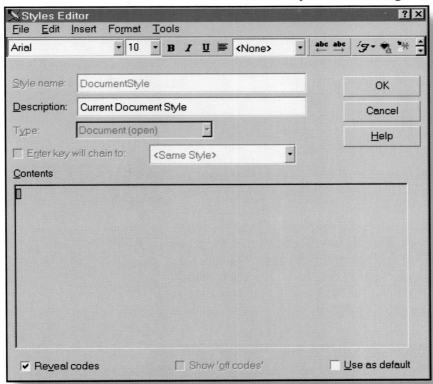

Since this document will be printed as a booklet, the inside of the cover should be blank. That means you need a blank page between the title page and the first page of text. You can add that page simply by positioning the insertion point at the top of the first page of text and inserting a hard page break. It will goof up your numbering, and you will then need to fix the Delay Codes code—so it skips two pages.

## EXERCISE  WP4.13

SCANS

1. With **ethics 4-12 xxx** in your window, save it as **ethics 4-13 xxx**. Reveal your codes and position your insertion point just to the right of or below the [HPg] code separating the title page from the first page of text. Press **Ctrl+Enter** to add another hard page break.

2. Return to the top of the title page. Choose **Format**, **Page**, and **Delay Codes**. This time, delay **2** pages.

(continued on next page)

3. In the editor, open the **Format** menu, choose **Page**, and choose **Numbering**. Set the *Position* section at **No page numbering** and the *Set Value* section at **1**. Return to your document window.

4. Check the page numbering at the top of the second page of text. It should be *page 2*.

5. The header looks too much like the rest of the text. Select the entire header on that page and change the font size to **8** pt. and format it with italic.

6. Check through the document. If you find problems, fix them. When it looks good, save it again as **ethics 4-13 xxx**. Keep it open.

# Booklet Printing

As you know from working on this document, the pages are in chronological order. When you print a booklet, you want the pages rearranged so they can be folded for a booklet. WordPerfect rearranges the pages if you choose the correct printing option. Because WordPerfect thinks the pages should be printed on both sides of the page, you will be prompted to reinsert the pages. For this practice, do that. If you were making a booklet for duplication, you would insert clean paper at the prompt.

**QuickSteps**

**Booklet Printing**
1. Divide and format the pages.
2. Choose print and Two-Sided Printing.
3. Insert pages into printer as directed.

## EXERCISE WP4.14

1. With **ethics 4-13 xxx** showing in the window, choose **Print**. In the Print dialog box click the **Two-Sided Printing** tab.

2. Off to the right is a *Print as booklet* check box. Select **Print as booklet**. Then click **Print**.

3. WordPerfect will immediately prompt you to reinsert page 1. When the page has printed, put it in the bypass on your printer. (It is probably the same place you put envelopes to print them.) Then click **OK** at the prompt.

4. Repeat the process for page 2. Fold your pages in half and assemble them into a booklet.

5. Close your document again without saving it. (WordPerfect doesn't remember you want it printed as a booklet.)

Look at your booklet. The footer that includes the Path and Filename code looks funny on all pages. You could insert the footer command on the top of the last page of the document. Then it would appear only on that page. Or you could suppress it on some of the pages where it looks so bad. As you work with these formats, you will get good at making adjustments so your documents look great.

SCANS

# Labels

When you divided the page for the booklet, you were using a powerful tool that enables you to divide the page into any number of segments for particular purposes. One of those uses is labels. WordPerfect, however, has done all of the formatting for labels by adding a labels feature. When you choose the feature, you may select from dozens of labels, name badges, disk labels, business cards, and rolodex card forms that match the labels available commercially. Let's use Labels to create name tags for some of the employees of Pet Paradise.

## EXERCISE ⟳ WP4.15

1. Beginning in a new document window, open the **Format** menu and choose **Labels**. Click the **Laser printed labels** button at the top.

2. Look through the list to find **Avery 5390**. Click once to highlight it. Then select it. You should see the label size in your window, on a gray background.

3. Open the **Format** menu, choose **Page**, and then choose **Center**. Choose to center the current and subsequent pages.

4. Back in your document window, choose **Center** justification, **Arial**, and **25** pt. Key **Alma Alvaro**, **Manager**, and press **Ctrl+Enter**. Key **Daniel LaPierre**, **Manager**. Press **Ctrl+Enter** again.

5. Create a label for **Lisa Pérez** and **Annabelle Vu**. (They don't need titles.)

6. Save your file as **labels 4-15 xxx**. On the fifth label insert your Path and Filename code. Format it with 8 pt.

7. To print the labels, you'll need to feed a sheet of paper into the bypass on your printer because WordPerfect is expecting you to feed a sheet of labels. Print and close the document.

If you need to prepare labels for your work, it is best to go to your local office products store and purchase the labels that will work for you. Then choose the correct format from the WordPerfect list of label formats.

# Summary

As promised at the beginning of this lesson, you acquired many skills in the manipulation of a long document. You learned that:

■ you can tie longer documents together with headers and footers and tell WordPerfect not to display that information on some pages.

■ Widow/Orphan and Block Protect work in different ways to control page endings.

■ WordPerfect will print page numbers in a variety of locations on your pages.

- hard page breaks can be added to your document or deleted, while soft page breaks occur when a page is full.

- footnotes and endnotes are used for references within the text.

- you can give a page equal top and bottom margins with the Center Page command.

- Delay Codes helps you begin formatting wherever you want it.

- Make It Fit can help you squeeze or expand a page for the desired number of pages.

- a page can be divided into a number of logical pages that are equal in size.

- most printers will rotate the print so you can use landscape orientation.

- Default Font and Current Document Style can be used to format all parts of a document.

- you can print a page at a time, and WordPerfect will arrange your text into booklet format, if you request it.

- the WordPerfect Labels feature enables you to prepare perfect labels easily.

## LESSON 4 REVIEW QUESTIONS

### MULTIPLE CHOICE

**Circle the best answer to each of the following statements.**

1. Which of the following commands puts a hard page break into your document?
   **A.** Ctrl+Home
   **B.** Alt+Page Down
   **C.** Ctrl+Enter
   **D.** Alt+Enter

2. Which feature puts the same text at the top of each page?
   **A.** Footnote
   **B.** Header
   **C.** Endnote
   **D.** Footer

3. Which feature prevents single-line paragraphs at the tops and bottoms of the pages in an entire document?
   **A.** Block Protect
   **B.** Divide Page
   **C.** Delay Codes
   **D.** Widow/Orphan

4. Which feature prevents a header or footer from being displayed on a specific page?
   - **A.** Block Protect
   - **B.** Suppress
   - **C.** Delay Codes
   - **D.** Divide Page

5. Which feature enables you to split a page into a number of smaller pages of equal size?
   - **A.** Divide Page
   - **B.** Block Protect
   - **C.** Suppress
   - **D.** Delay Codes

## WRITTEN QUESTIONS

**Write your answers to the following questions.**

6. What choice must you make in the Print dialog box to print only the page on which the insertion point is located?

7. Besides using the Page Numbering feature, what other feature enables you to print the page numbers?

8. What is the name of the feature that will squeeze or expand your text to make it fit on the prescribed number of pages?

9. What happens to the text on the page when you use the Center Page command?

10. What is the orientation of a page when the long edge is at the top? What about when the long edge is at the left?

## LESSON 4 PROJECT

SCANS

We'll reformat a document prepared in an earlier lesson. See how much you can do without looking back in the lesson.

1. Open **welcome proj2a xxx**. Use **Save As** to save the file as **welcome proj4 xxx**.

2. The document will be used as an informational handout to be held at both stores next Sunday from 2-6 p.m. Reformat the document as follows:
   - **a.** Center the title about **2"** from the top of the page and make it pretty.
   - **b.** Set line spacing at double for the entire document. Go through the document and take out the extra line spaces between paragraphs.
   - **c.** Indent each paragraph with **Tab**.
   - **d.** Use the **Widow/Orphan** feature to control page endings.

(continued on next page)

   **e.**   Give the document a header or a footer. You decide what text should be included in it.

   **f.**   Include page numbering—either in the header or footer or separately.

**3.**   Prepare a title page for the document. It should include the addresses of both stores, the date of the open house, and the time of the open house. The store addresses are as follows:

| | |
|---|---|
| Pet Paradise | Pet Paradise II |
| 9001 Parkway Boulevard | 7922 Pendleton Way |
| Austin, TX 78711 | Austin, TX 78745 |
| Phone: 512-555-5455 | Phone: 512-555-8712 |
| Manager: Alma Alvaro | Manager: Daniel LaPierre |

The owners of the stores are Paul and Polly Paradeis. Make the title page pretty.

**4.**   Use **Delay Codes** so the page numbering begins on the first page of text.

**5.**   If you wish, you may format the document for booklet printing and print it in that manner.

**6.**   When you finish, save the document again as **welcome proj4 xxx** and close it.

## CRITICAL THINKING ACTIVITY

SCANS

     You've received a document with odd margins and a peculiar font face. The document has a header, but the margin on the header is different from the margin of the document, and so is the font face and size. What's wrong with the document, and what could you do to fix it?

# SPECIAL TOOLS

## OBJECTIVES

**Upon completion of this lesson, you will be able to:**

■ Use the WordPerfect Spell Checker and Spell-As-You-Go to help with spelling.

■ Use Prompt-As-You-Go for suggestions as you key.

■ Use the Thesaurus and Grammatik for help with your writing.

■ Use Properties for information about a document.

■ Find unique text and use Replace, if needed, to replace that text.

■ Simplify your keying with QuickWords.

■ Use Bookmarks, QuickMarks, and Go To for moving around quickly in a document.

■ Use Advance to position text in a certain location.

■ Simplify your work with macros.

■ Create a customized Toolbar.

🕐 **Estimated Time: 1¹/₂ hours**

## *Prompt-As-You-Go*

When you are keying text, several things are happening. First, WordPerfect is checking each word you key against a large internal dictionary. If it doesn't find the word in the dictionary, the word is underlined in red. (You've seen plenty of underlined words so far in your training.) In addition to the word being underlined in red, words not found in the dictionary will show in red in the Prompt-As-You-Go box until the insertion point moves out of the word. The Prompt-As-You-Go box is at the right of the Property Bar.

WordPerfect is also checking your grammar as you key. If the Prompt-As-You-Go box shows a word in blue, it is telling you that WordPerfect has identified a grammatical error.

The third thing that happens is that some words are displayed in the Prompt-As-You-Go box in black. When a word shows in black, that means WordPerfect has prepared for you a list of synonyms (words that mean the same) for the word in which the insertion point is located.

1. Beginning in a new document window, go to the student **Datafile** folder and open **psych**. Save the file as **psych 5-1 xxx**. Key your entire name a double space below the last line of the paragraph.

2. Press **Enter** twice and key your name again. Then double-space and insert the Path and Filename code. Save the file again with the same name.

3. Look at the words underlined in red. Click in *treeted* at the right of the first line. Look at the red word in the Prompt-As-You-Go box. Click the arrow beside the box and click once to choose the correct spelling of the word.

4. Use the same procedure to fix *manged*.

5. Position your insertion point in *experience*, just below *treated*. This time, instead of using Prompt-As-You-Go, right click. The same list of choices will appear as you would have seen with Prompt-As-You-Go. Choose the correct word.

6. Point to *propery* at the beginning of the second line and right click. Choose the correct word.

7. Click to position the insertion point in the word *private* in the last sentence. Look at the Prompt-As-You-Go box. The word *private* should appear there in black.

8. Click the arrow to see a list of possible substitute words. These words come from the Thesaurus. Choose any one that looks good to you. The new word should be positioned in your text, and the list will be closed.

9. Practice making corrections to words underlined in red. Use the Thesaurus in the Prompt-As-You-Go box to replace some words. Then close the document without saving it again.

# Spell Checker

Prompt-As-You-Go is fine for correcting the spelling of words as they occur or if you have only a few of them in your document. If you have lots of errors to be corrected, however, the Spell Checker can do it more quickly. You don't need to position the insertion point in a word to correct it with the Spell-As-You-Go feature. Simply point to the word and right click for a list of choices.

**QuickSteps**

**Spell Checker**
1. Click the Spell Check button on the Toolbar.
2. Fix or skip highlighted words.

**INTERNET** At the beginning, the Internet was a not-for-profit network. Now, many commercial businesses are moving onto the Net in order to advertise, provide technical information, and take orders.

# E X E R C I S E ⟹ WP5.2

1. Open **psych 5-1 xxx** from your solutions file. Save the file as **psych 5-2 xxx**. Look at the paragraph. Note that the word *psychology* is misspelled three times. Watch to see what the Spell Checker does with that word.

2. Open the **Tools** menu and choose **Spell Check**. Look at the dialog box that appears. Note that it has a tab for Spell Checker, one for Grammatik, and a third for Thesaurus.

**TIP**

The default Toolbar has a Spell Check button. It looks like a book with a red *S*.

3. The Spell Checker probably stopped at *treeted* and the dialog box looks like Figure 5-1. The correct word is prompted. Click the **Replace** button.

4. *The Spell Checker will move to manged* and is prompting the correct word. Click **Replace** again.

5. Continue through the document, correcting the words. If the correct word isn't prompted, choose the correct word from the *Replacements* list and then click the **Replace** button.

6. The Spell Checker will skip your name if all parts of it are common. Common names are in the WordPerfect dictionary. If it stops for your name the first time, tell WordPerfect to **Skip All** so it doesn't highlight it again.

7. When you finish, WordPerfect will ask if you would like to close the Spell Checker. Click **No** to keep the dialog box displayed. Save your document again with the same name.

**FIGURE 5-1**
Spell Checker Dialog Box

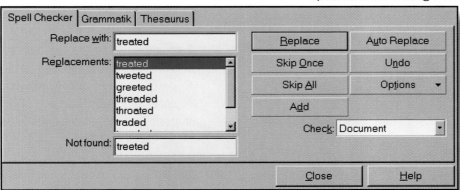

Spell Checker offers other choices. For example, if the correct word doesn't appear in the *Replacements* text box, you can either key the correct word in the *Replace with* box or click into the document and key the correct word there. If you key directly into the document, you must click the *Resume* button to continue.

You won't use it in the classroom, but the *Add* button enables you to add words you use frequently that aren't in the dictionary. Examples might be your name, the name of your boss or business associate, or your company's name.

The *Auto Replace* button can be used to add words you regularly misspell to the QuickCorrect list. You shouldn't use this feature in the classroom, either.

The *Options* button gives you some choices about what will be highlighted when you use the Spell Checker. Figure 5-2 shows those options and which are set by default. Click the Options button and compare Figure 5-2 with your list.

Below Options, you can see that the default is to check the entire document. Click the arrow beside that choice to see the other choices.

**FIGURE 5-2**
Spell Checker Options

User Word Lists...
Main Word Lists...
Language...

✔ Auto start
Beep on misspelled
Recheck all text

Check words with numbers
✔ Check duplicate words
✔ Check irregular capitalization
Prompt before auto replacement
✔ Show phonetic suggestions

# *Thesaurus*

You learned how the Thesaurus works in the Prompt-As-You-Go box in Exercise WP5.2. Let's see how the Thesaurus in this dialog box is different.

## EXERCISE ⟹ WP5.3

1. With **psych 5-2 xxx** still showing in the window and the Spell Checker dialog box displayed, click the **Thesaurus** tab in the dialog box.

2. Click to position the insertion point in the word *private* and click the **Look Up** button in the dialog box. At the left is a list of synonyms. Scroll all the way through the list to see the list of antonyms (words that mean the opposite).

3. Scroll back through the list and find the word *personal*. Double click to choose it. That word should appear at the top of the middle list, and

a whole list of synonyms and antonyms for *personal* will appear. Double click the word *exclusive* to see a list for that word.

4. Find *individual* in the list and double click to choose it. As you can see, you could go on forever. Choose any word you wish as a replacement for *private* and click the **Replace** button. The Thesaurus will close. Click **Yes** to close the Spell Checker.

5. Save the document again with the same name and keep it open.

# *Grammatik*

The other tool in the dialog box you just closed is the grammar checker. It checks your document for poor grammar, long sentences, style flaws, punctuation errors, etc. Even if you have a good command of the English language, Grammatik can help you improve the way you write. Let's use Grammatik on **psych 5-2 xxx**. You can use a variety of styles for checking, ranging from Quick Check (which is very lax) to Very Strict or Student Composition (which is a compromise).

# EXERCISE ▷ WP5.4

1. With **psych 5-2 xxx** showing in the window, use **Save As** to save the file as **psych 5-4 xxx**. Open the **Tools** menu and choose **Grammatik**.

 **TIP**

Note that Spell Check, Thesaurus, and Grammatik are all in the Tools menu. Grammatik is the second tab when you have the Spell Checker open.

2. If Grammatik goes directly to the word *possible* in the sixth line, reset it for stricter checking as follows:
   a. Click the **Options** button, choose **Checking Styles**, and then choose **Student Composition**.
   b. Click **Select** to return to the Grammatik dialog box.
   c. Click **Close** to end the session. Then open the **Tools** menu again and choose **Grammatik**.

3. The entire first line should be selected. Look at the information in the dialog box. It doesn't like the passive voice, and offers two possibilities for changing the sentence in the *Replacements* box.

4. Move the highlight to the second possibility. Read the new sentence in the *New Sentence* box, and click **Replace** to replace the sentence. Choose the second possibility for the second error.

5. Continue through the document, either skipping the suggestions or making corrections as you see fit.

6. When you finish, close Grammatik and print your document. Save it again with the same name and keep it open.

If you looked at the text surrounding the items highlighted by Grammatik, the suggested corrections didn't fit. A total rework of the paragraph is sometimes necessary after Grammatik has finished with it. Use this feature for suggestions, but be careful that your text still says what you want it to say when you finish.

## Properties

WordPerfect keeps track of information about your documents for you. This information falls into two categories:

- **Summary**. You can create a summary of a document that identifies the person who created the document and a description of the content. The summary is saved with the document but does not display or print with the document. You can view the summary in the Properties dialog box when the document is open, or you can view the summary from the Windows Explorer. You can print summary information or save it as a separate file.

- **Information**. WordPerfect provides statistical information about the document (e.g., the number of sentences or words contained in it).

Let's create a document summary for our short document and look at the statistical information.

## EXERCISE ⟹ WP5.5

1. With **psych 5-4 xxx** showing in the window, open the **File** menu and choose **Properties**. Fill in the text boxes using the information in Figure 5-3. (Use Tab to move from box to box. The dates will appear automatically.)

2. When you finish, click the **Options** button. Save your summary as a new document with the name **summary 5-5 xxx**.

3. Click the **Options** button again and print the summary.

4. Click the **Information** tab at the top of the dialog box. Look at the number of words in the paragraph, the number of sentences, the average sentence length, etc. Sometimes that information is very useful.

5. Close the dialog box. Then close the document, saving it again with the same name. (If you don't save it, the summary won't be saved with it.)

**FIGURE 5-3**
Information for Exercise WP5.5

**Descriptive name**: Behavioral Consultants for Pets
**Descriptive type**: pet behavior
**Author**: (Your name)
**Typist**: (Your name)
**Subject**: Working with disturbed pets
**Account**: None
**Keywords**: ethology, psychology
**Abstract**: Your pet can have a private session with a psychologist or professional trainer to help with behavioral problems.

## *Find and Replace*

The Find and Replace feature enables you to look through the open file to locate specific words, phrases, or codes. It will also replace one piece of text with another.

Find and Replace normally works forward through your document. So you'll usually have the insertion point at the top of the document when beginning. The menus in the Find and Replace dialog box offer you many choices—one of which allows you to search backwards, if you wish. Let's experiment with Find and Replace, using three different methods of choosing the feature.

**QuickSteps**

**Find and Replace**
1. Open the Edit menu and choose Find.
2. Key the unique text to find.
3. If desired, key the replacement text.

## EXERCISE ⟹ WP5.6

1. Beginning in a new document window, go to the student **Datafile** folder and open **fund**. Save the file as **fund 5-6 xxx**.

2. Open the **Edit** menu and choose **Find and Replace**. The Find and Replace dialog box should look like Figure 5-4.

3. In the *Find* text box key **Fund**. Click the **Find Next** button. WordPerfect will stop at the first occurrence of *Fund*. Click **Find Next** again.

4. Continue going through the document, stopping at each *Fund*, and clicking **Find Next** to go on. Respond to the dialog box when it tells you that it is finished.

**5.** Click outside of the Find and Replace dialog box in your document. Press **Ctrl+Home** to return the insertion point to the top of the document.

**6.** Click in the *Replace with* text box and key **Endowment**. Click **Find Next**. When it stops at *Fund*, click **Replace** to replace that word with *Endowment*. Continue through the document until all occurrences have been replaced.

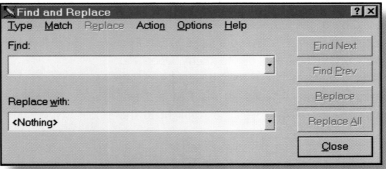

**FIGURE 5-4**
Find and Replace Dialog Box

**7.** Close the dialog box. Keep the document open.

In Exercise WP5.6 you reserved the right to give permission for each replacement, so you could look at the surrounding text to see if the replacement was appropriate. WordPerfect will also replace all occurrences without asking your permission. That's what the Replace All button does.

The dialog box contains other options. The Match menu, for example, offers the following options:

■ **Whole Word**. With this option, WordPerfect will not find the specified text if it is part of another word. (An example might be the *fund* in *refund*.)

■ **Case**. The default for Find is not case-sensitive. In other words, whether the word had an initial capital letter would not make a difference.

■ **Font**. This choice enables you to choose a font code or appearance attribute.

■ **Codes**. This choice provides a long list of codes for which you may search.

**EXERCISE WP5.7**

**1.** With **fund 5-6 xxx** showing in the window, return the insertion point to the top of the document. Press **Ctrl+F** to open the Find and Replace dialog box.

**2.** In the *Find* text box key **Endowment**. In the *Replace with* text box key **Fund**.

**3.** Click the **Replace All** button. WordPerfect should report that 7 occurrences were found.

**4.** Click outside of the Find and Replace dialog box and return the insertion point to the top of

the document. In the dialog box, replace *Endowment* with a period and two spaces. In the *Replace with* text box key a period and one space. Click **Replace All**. This time there are 6 occurrences.

**TIP**

This is a quick way to prepare text for a printer. It replaces the two spaces following ending punctuation with one space.

(continued on next page)

**5.** Return to the top of the document again. Select the period and two spaces in the *Find text* dialog box and delete them. Open the **Match** menu of the Find and Replace dialog box and choose **Codes**. In the Codes dialog box key **hrt**. This moves the highlight to the [HRt] code.

**6.** Double click the code twice to put two [HRt] codes in the *Find* text box. Delete the period

and one space in the *Replace with* text box and insert one [HRt] code. Then click **Replace All**.

**7.** Look at the document. All of the blank lines are gone except one near the end. If you reveal your codes, you'll see that the ending outline code is between the two hard return codes.

**8.** Close your document without saving it again.

Find looks for EXACTLY what you request. When the search turned up something different than two hard return codes in a row, that instance didn't count. Computers don't think, so if you ask for something different from what you want, you may be surprised with the results!

Searching for codes is a useful tool. Sometimes you may need to find a font face code, a Suppress code, or a Block Protect code. WordPerfect will find it for you in a jiffy.

# QuickWords

QuickWords may be used for abbreviations that expand into the complete text when you key the QuickWord and then press the space bar, Enter, or Tab. QuickWords work much like QuickCorrect. QuickWords, however, can contain formatting such as Bold, Italic, Underline, and font changes.

## EXERCISE ⟹ WP5.8

**1.** Beginning in a new document window, key your entire name. Select the name and format it with bold, italic, and **24-pt. Arial**.

**2.** Below your name, key your address using 10-pt. Arial (no Bold or Italic).

**3.** Select the entire name and address. Then open the **Tools** menu and choose **QuickWords**. The dialog box illustrated in Figure 5-5 will appear.

**4.** In the QuickWords portion of the QuickCorrect dialog box, key the characters that you will use

for an abbreviation for your name. If your initials are unique characters, like *dk* for *Donald R. Knowles*, use them.

**5.** Click **Add Entry**, which closes the dialog box.

**6.** Back in your document window, move your insertion point to a double space below your formatted name. Key the abbreviation and press the **space bar**. Watch your name and address appear, complete with formatting.

**7.** Close your document without saving it.

**FIGURE 5-5**
QuickWords Portion of the QuickCorrect Dialog Box

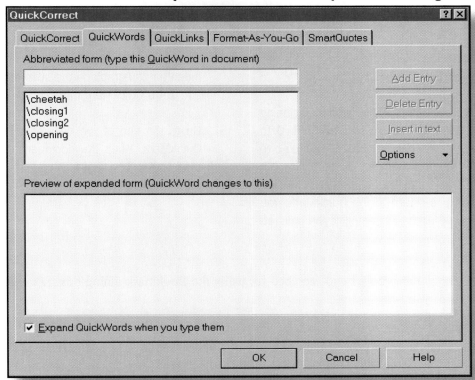

As you discovered in Exercise WP5.8, you aren't limited to one or two words with QuickWords. In fact, you aren't even limited to a single line, as you are with QuickCorrect. You can create as many QuickWords as you wish, and you can use them as often as they are needed. When a QuickWord is no longer needed, you can use Delete to remove it from the list.

# QuickMark and Bookmark

WordPerfect enables you to move quickly from one location in your document to another using two similar tools—QuickMarks and Bookmarks.

QuickMarks don't have names. A document may contain only one QuickMark. If you set a new one, the old one disappears. You might use a QuickMark in a lengthy document to mark your place while you go to a different place to check something or get additional information. After finding the information, use the QuickMark to return quickly to the original location.

**QuickSteps**

**QuickMark**
1. Set a QuickMark with Ctrl+Shift+Q.
2. Return to the QuickMark with Ctrl+Q.

SCANS

1. Beginning in a new document window, open **ethics 4-12 xxx**. Press **Ctrl+G** for Go To, key **3**, and press **Enter** to go to page 3.

2. Position your insertion point at the beginning of the bulleted list and press **Ctrl+Shift+Q** to set a QuickMark. Then press **Ctrl+End** to go to the end of the document.

3. Press **Ctrl+Q** to return to the QuickMark. You should now be at the beginning of the bulleted list.

4. Go to the beginning of the document and test **Ctrl+Q** again. Return to the single-spaced, indented paragraph on the second page of text and set a QuickMark there.

5. Go to the end of the document and test the QuickMark. Keep the document open as you read on.

QuickMarks can also be set and searched for using the Bookmark dialog box. It's much easier to use the keyboard keystrokes.

## Bookmark

Bookmarks are named. You may have as many bookmarks in a document as you wish. Like QuickMarks, Bookmarks mark certain locations so you can return quickly to those locations. You can set a Bookmark by selecting text for the Bookmark and choosing Create in the Bookmark dialog box. The Bookmark will be named using the text you had selected. Sometimes you may prefer to select the text and give the Bookmark a different name.

When you tell WordPerfect to search for a bookmark, you can tell it to automatically select that text. Then you can copy the selected text to the Windows Clipboard for insertion in a different location.

**QuickSteps**

**Bookmark**
1. Open the Tools menu and choose Bookmark.
2. Name the Bookmark.
3. To find the Bookmark, return to the dialog box and choose the name of the Bookmark.

SCANS

1. With **ethics 4-12 xxx** showing in the window, select the word *children* the first time it appears in the first paragraph.

2. Open the **Tools** menu and choose **Bookmark**. Look at the Bookmark dialog box. Then click **Create** (see Figure 5-6). The selected word will be prompted.

**FIGURE 5-6**
Create Bookmark Dialog Box

3. Click **OK**. You'll be returned to your document. Look at the Bookmark codes in Reveal Codes. Move your insertion point to the left of the first code. The name of the bookmark will be displayed.

4. Follow the steps above to mark the following words:
   a. *culture* near the end of the first paragraph
   b. *Golden Rule* near the end of the second paragraph
   c. *integrity* at the beginning of the last paragraph on page 2

   d. *work environment* near the top of page 3 (key YOUR name to name this Bookmark)

5. Open the **Tools** menu and choose **Bookmark**. Double click **children** in the Bookmark list. Did you go to *children* in the text? Return to the dialog box and double click your name. Try **Golden Rule**.

6. Close the document without saving it again.

This short exercise demonstrates how Bookmarks can be used. If you have a passage of text a coworker should read, select it and mark it with that person's name. The possibilities are endless.

# *Advance*

Advance enables you to position your text anywhere on the page, measured in inches from either the top or the side of the page. You can do much the same thing with the Shadow Cursor, but you don't have the measurements with that tool. We'll learn about Advance here. Then we'll put it to work later.

## EXERCISE ⇨ WP5.11

1. Beginning in a new document window, open the **Format** menu. Choose **Typesetting** and then **Advance**. The Advance dialog box (see Figure 5-7) should appear.

2. Look at the options. In the *Horizontal position* section choose **From left edge of page**. Key **4.25"** in the *Horizontal distance* box.

3. In the *Vertical position* section click **From top of page**. Key **5.5"** in the *Vertical distance* box. Click **OK**.

(continued on next page)

**FIGURE 5-7**
Advance Dialog Box

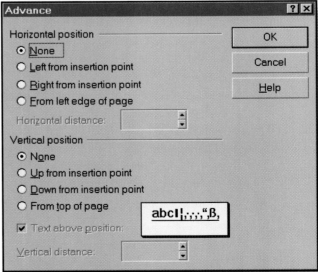

4. Key **Pet Paradise** and Zoom to **Full Page**. The words should begin at the exact center of the page.

5. Save the document as **advance 5-11 xxx**. Give it a footer that contains the Path and Filename code and save again.

6. Print your document and fold it in half in both directions. Does the shop name begin at the center of the page? Close the document without saving it.

# Macros

In most jobs there are some sets of keystrokes that are repetitive. You key the same thing over and over and wish for some way to streamline the task. WordPerfect has provided you with a number of those features—QuickCorrect and QuickWords do certain jobs very well. Another way is to create a *macro*, which saves a series of keystrokes. Once the macro is created, you can play it whenever you need those keystrokes.

## Settings

In the Getting Started section you learned that most default settings don't need to be changed. If you are in a classroom, however, you need to fix one of the settings so you can save your macros with your work (so they don't get mixed up with those from other students) and WordPerfect will still be able to find them when you need them. We'll make that setting.

## EXERCISE ▷ WP5.12

SCANS

1. Beginning in a new document window, open the **Tools** menu and choose **Settings**. The dialog box illustrated in Figure 5-8 will appear.

2. Double click **Files** to open the Files Settings dialog box. Click the **Merge/Macro** tab (see Figure 5-9).

3. Look at the *Supplemental macro folder* text box. It should say *a:\*. (Customize that information if your files are stored in a different place.) If it doesn't, key that information in that text box.

4. When your dialog box looks like Figure 5-9, click **OK** to close the dialog box and click **Close** to return to your document window.

**FIGURE 5-8**
Settings Dialog Box

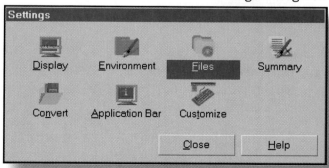

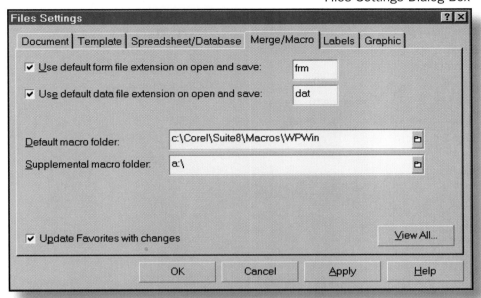

**FIGURE 5-9**
Files Settings Dialog Box

If you have problems with Exercise WP5.12, be sure to have your instructor help you. It is important that these settings be correct.

## Record and Play a Macro

Recording a macro is kind of like recording a song on a tape player. You tell the machine to record, and then you play what needs to be recorded. Finally, you turn the machine off.

## EXERCISE ⟶ WP5.13

**SCANS**

1. Beginning in a new document window, open the **Tools** menu and choose **Macro**. Click **Record** to open the Record Macro dialog box. (It looks much like your Open File dialog box.)

2. Key **a:\close** as the name of your macro and press **Enter**. Move your mouse. The insertion point should look like a circle with a line through it. 🚫

3. Look at the Macro Feature Bar that's just below the Property Bar. It should look like Figure 5-10.

4. Key the information in Figure 5-11. Double-space between the closing and the company name. Press **Enter** five times following the company name.

**FIGURE 5-10**
Macro Feature Bar

(continued on next page)

5. Press **Enter** twice at the end of the macro so the insertion point is in position for possible Enclosure notations.

6. When you finish, open the **Tools** menu, choose **Macro**, and deselect **Record** to end the recording of the macro.

7. Press **Enter** twice and test the macro by choosing **Tools**, **Macro**, and **Play**. Then key **close** and press **Enter**. The closing lines should appear in your window.

8. Keep the window open to give you some text for the next exercise.

**FIGURE 5-11**
Text for **close** Macro

```
Sincerely,

PET PARADISE




Polly Paradeis
```

**TIP**

Look at the macros in the Play Macro dialog box. Some of them are quite interesting. For example, note the **Footend** macro that converts footnotes to endnotes. Others might be files other students accidentally saved to that folder. You can tell by clicking the Details button and looking at the dates of the macros.

Let's create another quick macro that will help with all of your lessons. This macro will be a footer that contains the Path and Filename code.

EXERCISE ⟹ **WP5.14**

1. Save the practice document as **doc** so the file has a name. Open the **Tools** menu and choose **Macro** and **Record**.

2. Key **a:\pf** to name the macro (*pf* for Path and Filename) and save it with your files. Click **Record** or press **Enter**.

3. In the document window create a footer that contains the Path and Filename code. Align the

information at the right with **Flush Right**. Format the code with **8-pt. Arial**. Close the Footer Property Bar.

4. Open the **Tools** menu, choose **Macro**, and deselect **Record**. Use the scroll bar to check the footer at the bottom of the document. Then close the practice document without saving it.

## Edit a Macro

You've just discovered that you put too much space in the closing lines macro. Macros are easy to edit. They look much like regular documents.

# EXERCISE ➔ WP5.15

**SCANS**

1. Beginning in a new document window, go to the Open File dialog box and open **close** as a regular document. It will look like Figure 5-12. Delete one of the *HardReturn( )* codes following the company name. Delete the empty blank line, too.

2. Click the **Save & Compile** button on the Macro Feature Bar. (WordPerfect will check to make sure everything is correct.)

3. Click the **Options** button on the Macro Feature Bar and choose **Close Macro**.

4. In a new WordPerfect window test your revised macro. If it looks good, close the document and read on. If it has a problem, fix that problem before continuing.

**FIGURE 5-12**
**close** Macro in Editing Window

```
Application (WordPerfect;
"WordPerfect"; Default!; "EN")
Type (Text: "Sincerely,")
HardReturn ()
HardReturn ()
Type (Text: "PET PARADISE")
HardReturn ()
HardReturn ()
HardReturn ()
HardReturn ()
HardReturn ()
Type (Text: "Polly Paradeis")
HardReturn ()
HardReturn ()
```

## Macro with Pause

You can set up a macro to stop for you to enter information. We'll create a fax cover sheet for Pet Paradise, complete with pauses for you to enter information. As you create the macro, note that you must use the keyboard for some tasks. When creating macros, you don't have complete use of the mouse. Work carefully when you create macros. Remember that everything is being recorded.

# EXERCISE ➔ WP5.16

**SCANS**

1. Beginning in a new document window, create a macro named **a:\pet fax**. Key the beginning of the macro shown in Figures 5-13 and 5-14 using this helpful information:
   a. The phone numbers are on the first two lines of the return address, positioned with **Flush Right**.
   b. Switch to **20 pt**. for the words *FAX TRANSMITTAL*. Switch back to **12 pt**. following the words.

**FIGURE 5-13**
Beginning of Fax Form in Exercise WP5.16

PET PARADISE                  Phone: 512-555-5455
9001 Parkway Boulevard        Fax: 512-555-5422
Austin, TX 78711

## FAX TRANSMITTAL

(continued on next page)

**2.** Key **Date:** followed by two spaces with the space bar. Press **Ctrl+Shift+D** to insert the date code. Press **Enter** twice.

**3.** Key **To:**, as illustrated in Figure 5-14. Press the **space bar** twice and click the **Pause** button on the Macro Feature Bar. Click the **Pause** button again.

**TIP**

To pause and restart the recording of the macro, you must always click the Pause button twice.

**4.** Follow the same procedure to enter the information in Figure 5-14 for the rest of the macro. Space twice after each colon and add a Pause code. Press **Enter** twice between each of the lines and at the end.

**5.** When you finish, look your work over and make any needed corrections. Then end the recording of the macro. Close the document window without saving.

**6.** Play the **pet fax** macro. The date should be entered automatically. Send it to **Daniel LaPierre** at **512-555-8713**. It is from **Alma** at **512-555-5422**. The number of pages should be **3**.

**FIGURE 5-14**
More of the Exercise WP5.16 Form

```
Date:

To:

At Fax Number:

From:

At Fax Number:

Number of pages (including this page):
```

**FIGURE 5-15**
Note for Exercise WP5.16 Fax

```
Attached is the information you
requested about flea dip for our
customers' pets.

Alma
```

**7.** Key the brief note in Figure 5-15 on the cover sheet. Then save the page as **fax 5-16 xxx**.

**8.** Play your **pf** macro to identify the page. Print it and close it, saving it again as you close it.

# Personalized Toolbar

The default Toolbar can be edited. On the job you might do that but not in the classroom. Instead, we'll learn about the Toolbar by creating a new one. We'll include some features that aren't readily available.

EXERCISE WP5.17

SCANS

1. Beginning in a new document window, point to the Toolbar with the mouse pointer and right click. Look at the list of Toolbars available. Remember that they change according to the work you are doing.

2. Click **Settings** at the bottom of the list. Then click **Create** and key **practice** to create a Toolbar named *practice*. Click **OK** to reveal the Toolbar Editor dialog box (see Figure 5-16). A new, empty Toolbar will be displayed.

3. See the *Feature categories* box. Note that the features listed are from the File menu. Double click **Close All** so you can close all open documents with the click of a button on the Toolbar. Check the Toolbar to see what the button looks like.

4. Change the *Feature categories* box to **Edit** and point to **Case Toggle**. Double click to add that button so you can switch to uppercase or lowercase. Look at the button on the new Toolbar.

5. Click the **Macros** tab at the top. Click the **Add Macro** button. Locate your **a:\pf** macro and add it to the Toolbar, complete with filepath.

6. On the Toolbar grab the Macro button (it looks like a tiny tape) and drag it to the left so it's the first button.

7. In the lower right corner of the dialog box grab a separator and drag it to the Toolbar. Position it just to the right of the **pf** macro button.

8. Drag the **Case Toggle** button off the Toolbar. (See the tiny garbage can?)

9. Since this was only practice, click **Cancel** to close the dialog box. In the Customize Settings dialog box, be sure the highlight is on **WordPerfect 8** and click **Delete** to delete the *practice* Toolbar.

10. Close the dialog box with the *WordPerfect 8* Toolbar chosen.

**FIGURE 5-16**
Toolbar Editor Dialog Box

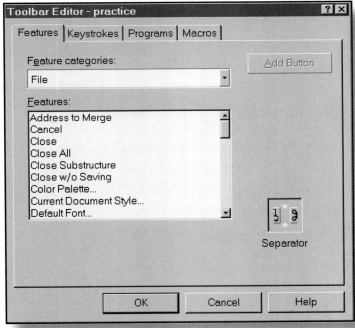

For the classroom, you'll probably use the default WordPerfect 8 Toolbar. On the job you will no doubt create one that contains the tools you use most. You'll enjoy looking through the available tools. The list contains some really interesting ones!

# Summary

This lesson contains a bit of this and a bit of that. All of the features covered are great tools to help you with your work. You learned that:

- Prompt-As-You-Go helps you with your spelling, your grammar, and choosing the correct word.
- the Spell Checker is best when used at the completion of a document.
- Grammatik makes suggestions about your writing style.
- you can create a document summary, and WordPerfect will count the words, paragraphs, and sentences in your document.
- Find and Replace can be used to exchange one piece of text with another.
- QuickWords enable you to key short versions of text that expand.
- Bookmarks and QuickMarks help you move around in a document.
- Advance enables you to specify exactly where text will begin.
- you can record your keystrokes and save them in a macro for instant replay.
- it is easy to customize a Toolbar with the tools you use most.

## LESSON 5 REVIEW QUESTIONS

### TRUE/FALSE

**Circle the T if the statement is true. Circle the F if it is false.**

**T   F**   1.   Prompt-As-You-Go shows a word in black if the word is misspelled.

**T   F**   2.   The Spell Checker is part of a three-tab dialog box that also contains Grammatik and Bookmarks.

**T   F**   3.   Advance is a feature that tracks cash you receive before the trip.

**T   F**   4.   Prompt-As-You-Go shows a word in blue if the sentence isn't grammatically correct.

**T   F**   5.   The Properties dialog box contains a Document Summary feature.

### FILL IN THE BLANKS

**Complete each of the following statements by writing your answer in the blank provided.**

6.   The feature that quickly locates a unique string of characters is known as _____ .

7.   The feature that enables you to give selected text a name so you can return to it quickly is known as a _____ .

8. The mouse pointer looks like a circle with a line through it when you are recording a
_____ .

9. The _____ contains a feature the enables you to add names or unusual words to the WordPerfect dictionary.

10. The _____ feature provides a list of synonyms from which you may choose.

## LESSON 5 PROJECT

SCANS

### PROJECT 5A

1. Beginning in a new document window, use **Advance** to tell WordPerfect to begin **2"** from the top of the page. Use **Ctrl+D** to insert the date. Press **Enter** four times.

2. Key the address in Figure 5-17, double-space, key a suitable greeting, and double-space again.

**FIGURE 5-17**
Address for Project 5A

```
Phyllis Linc
84 Riverview Drive
Rollingwood, TX 78746
```

3. Insert **obedience** from the student **Datafile** folder. Move your insertion point to the end and play the **close** macro to add the closing.

4. Give the document a header that includes the proper information for a two-page letter. Fix the header so it shows only on the second page.

5. Use **Block Protect** to keep the entire schedule together on one page.

6. Save the file as **obedience proj5 xxx**. Position the insertion point at the top of the second page and play your **pf** macro. (The footer code formats forward from where it is inserted, so only the second page of the letter has the footer.)

7. Create an envelope to go with your letter. Print both the letter and the envelope. Then close the file, saving it again with the same name.

### PROJECT 5B

You are about halfway through your training, and you've accumulated lots of solutions files. Many of them were interim saves. You didn't print them, and they won't be needed again. Let's delete some files and move the rest of them into a folder where they will be out of your way. Remember that you've done this. If you are asked in a later lesson to open a file from an earlier lesson and you can't find it in your solutions list, look for the file in the **lessons 1-5** folder.

You can delete scattered files all at one time by holding the Ctrl key while you click to select them. Some of the files listed here to be deleted may not be included in your list because you forgot to save them. That's OK.

1. Go to your Open File dialog box.

2. Hold **Ctrl** while you click to select each of the files listed in Figure 5-18. When they are all selected, press the **Delete** key on the keyboard and confirm that you DO want to delete these files.

3. Still in your Open File dialog box, open the **File** menu and choose **New**. Key **lessons 1-5** as the name for a new folder.

4. Select the files listed in Figure 5-19 to be moved to that folder.

5. When the files are all selected, point to one of the highlighted files and drag your insertion point to the **lessons 1-5** folder. When that folder changes color, release the mouse pointer to move the files into that folder.

6. Check your remaining list. You may have some renegade files that don't belong. The macros (with the *.wcm* extensions) should remain in the main folder. You may delete any other files that are left.

**FIGURE 5-18**
Files to Delete

| | |
|---|---|
| char 2-12 | psych 5-1 |
| doc | psych 5-2 |
| dog stuff 3-9 | return 2-1 |
| ethics 4-11 | return 2-6 |
| ethics 4-12 | welcome 1-6 |
| ethics 4-3 | welcome 2-8 |
| ethics 4-8 | welcome 2-9 |
| fund 5-6 | welcome 3-1 |
| list 3-15 | welcome 3-17 |
| obedience 4-1 | welcome 3-2 |
| pp 1-1 | welcome 3-3 |
| pp 1-8 | welcome 3-6 |
| pp 1-9 | welcome 3-8 |

**FIGURE 5-19**
Files to Move to the **lessons 1-5** Folder

| | | | |
|---|---|---|---|
| advance 5-11 | ethics 4-7 | pp 1-10 | welcome 3-13 |
| bullets 3-14 | fax 5-16 | pp 1-2 | welcome 3-18 |
| Buster 1-11 | fit 4-9 | prices 3-11 | welcome 3-4 |
| char 2-13 | footnotes 4-5 | psych 5-4 | welcome 3-7 |
| Corel proj1 | form 3-12 | return 2-2 | welcome proj2a |
| dog stuff 3-10 | fund proj3 | return 2-3 | welcome proj2b |
| ethics 4-10 | labels 4-15 | sale memo 2-14 | welcome proj4 |
| ethics 4-13 | list 3-16 | suite proj2c | |
| ethics 4-4 | obedience 4-2 | summary 5-5 | |
| ethics 4-6 | obedience proj5 | welcome 2-10 | |

## CRITICAL THINKING ACTIVITY

SCANS

You created a macro a couple of days ago and you need to use it now. You can remember the name of the macro, but it doesn't work and you can't seem to find it on one of your disks. You don't recall exactly how you saved the macro. Where might you look to find the elusive macro?

# TABLES

**Upon completion of this lesson, you will be able to:**

- Discuss table terminology.
- Create a WordPerfect table.
- Format the table.
- Calculate in a table.
- Use SpeedFormat to format your tables.
- Use floating cells to reference table cells.
- Create forms using tables.

**⏱ Estimated Time: 2 hours**

WordPerfect tables can be used for a variety of applications. A table provides quick columns for normal columnar information, and the columns are easy to adjust. As you work through these lessons, most exercises are dependent on the exercise before. Work carefully and thoughtfully so that when you finish, you know what you did and why.

## Table Terminology

Before beginning, you should be familiar with table terms. Most of these terms are the same as those used for work with spreadsheets—partly because a WordPerfect table works much like a spreadsheet.

- **Spreadsheet**. A spreadsheet is a grid made up of columns and rows that contain data and/or formulas.

- **Columns**. Vertical collections of information are called columns and are labeled with letters (e.g., A, B, C).

- **Rows**. Information is arranged horizontally into rows. Rows are labeled with numbers.

- **Cells**. The point at which a row meets a column is called a *cell*. The *address* of a cell is identified by the column and row. For example, the cell where Column B meets Row 3 is called Cell B3. This information is reported on the Application Bar.

# Create a Table

If you open the Insert menu and choose Table, a dialog box will ask how many columns and rows you want. An easier way to create a table is to use the Table tool on the Toolbar. We'll start with a very simple table.

## EXERCISE ⟩ WP6.1

**1.** Point to the **Table QuickCreate** button on the Toolbar and drag the pointer until the table is 3 columns wide and 2 rows high (see Figure 6-1).

**2.** When you achieve the right size, release the mouse button. Your table should appear, looking much like Figure 6-2, although it will extend from margin to margin. If you don't get it right on the first try, click **Undo** and start again.

**3.** Your insertion point will be in the first cell. Keep your new table open while you learn to move around.

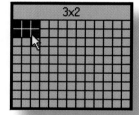

**FIGURE 6-1**
Table Grid

**FIGURE 6-2**
3 x 2 Table

When you key, move your insertion point in the table using the following keystrokes:

- **Tab** moves your insertion point to the next cell, even at the end of a row. When used in the final cell, it adds a new row to the table.

- **Shift+Tab** moves your insertion point to the previous cell.

- **Home, Home** moves your insertion point to the first cell in the row.

- **End, End** moves your insertion point to the last cell in the row.

Look at Figure 6-3. The table in your window is purposely not large enough. In the next exercises you will learn a couple of ways to increase the size of a table. When you finish preparing and formatting your first table, it will look much like the one in the figure.

> **TIP**
>
> Do NOT press Enter when working in a table unless you purposely want to add another line to a cell.

**INTERNET** The communications structure of the Internet is the global telephone system, which is a network of networks working together. By using the phone system, the Internet has worldwide coverage and significant potential for growth.

**FIGURE 6-3**
Finished Table

| FAVORITE PRODUCTS FOR DOGS | | | |
|---|---|---|---|
| Rawhide Bones | Biscuits | Nail Trimmers | Leads & Collars |
| Dog Chow | Puppy Chow | Dog Gates | Training Guides |
| Pet Beds | Coats | Sweaters | Dog Houses |

## EXERCISE ⟹ WP6.2

1. With your insertion point positioned in the first cell of the table, save the document as **bones 6-2 xxx**. Play your **pf** macro to identify the table and save it again.

2. Position the insertion point in Cell A1. (Check the location on the Application Bar.) Key **Rawhide Bones** and press **Tab**. Key **Biscuits** and press **Tab**. Key **Nail Trimmers** and press **Tab**. Your insertion point should be at the beginning of the second row in Cell A2.

3. Skip all of the items in the fourth column for now and key the rest of the items into your table. Note that when you press **Tab** after keying *Dog Gates*, another row is added to your table.

4. When you finish, click in the Biscuits cell. Look near the right on the Application Bar. Note that you are in Cell B1. What is the address of the *Sweaters* cell? It should report Cell C3.

5. Save the table again with the same name and keep it open as you read on.

## Table Formatting Tools

Formatting tools for a table come from several sources. When your insertion point is in the table, the *Property Bar* contains a number of formatting tools. One of those tools is a *Drop-Down Menu* that contains a variety of formatting tools. The third source for tools is the *Tables QuickMenu*. In addition, the tools on the Property Bar change depending on whether or not you have cells selected. In the first few exercises you will be told where to go for a formatting tool. Then you'll be on your own.

## EXERCISE ⟹ WP6.3

1. With **bones 6-2 xxx** showing in the window, save it as **bones 6-3 xxx**.

2. Position your insertion point somewhere in the last column. Point to the table and right click to display the Tables QuickMenu. Compare Figure 6-4 with your QuickMenu.

(continued on next page)

3. Click away from the QuickMenu but still within the table. Click the **Table** button on the Property Bar. Compare the choices in that menu with Figure 6-4. As you can see, the choices are similar.

4. With your insertion point in the last column, display the QuickMenu and choose **Insert**. Click the **Columns** button, leave the setting at **1**, and click **After**. Click **OK**.

5. Look at your table. The column at the right (Column D) is divided into two columns, and the text is scrunched. Begin in the *Dog Chow* cell. When the pointer becomes a fat arrow, drag across all four cells in that row to select them. (The cells will be black.)

6. Open the **Table** menu on the Property Bar and choose **Equal Column Widths**. Your cells should even up. Key the information for Column D.

7. Position the insertion point somewhere in Row 1 and right click. Choose **Insert** and insert one row above the location of the insertion point. Point to the first cell in that row and drag across, selecting all cells in the row.

8. Display the QuickMenu and choose **Join Cells**. Give the **Center** command and key the title. Save the table with the same name and read on.

**FIGURE 6-4**
Table QuickMenu

Paste
Paste without Font/Attributes

Format...
Numeric Format...
SpeedFormat...
Borders/Fill...

Insert...
Delete...
Size Column to Fit
Split Cell...

QuickSum
Calculate
QuickFormat...
Chart

Row/Column Indicators
Formula Toolbar
Table Tools

What's This?

**TIP**

When you have text selected and you right click to display the QuickMenu, you must point at the selected text when you right click. If you point elsewhere in the table or out of the table, the text will be deselected and you may get a different QuickMenu.

As you can see, it is easy to add columns and rows. It is also easy to join cells. When you joined the cells in Exercise WP6.3, you dragged across the cells to select them. If you have a steady hand when pointing to either the top or left cell margin, your mouse pointer will turn into a fat white arrow and you can select cells as follows:

⇦ Click **once** to select the cell.
⇦ Click **twice** to select the row.
⇧ Click **once** to select the cell.
⇧ Click **twice** to select the column.
   With either arrow, click **three** times to select the table.

We'll practice these selection methods shortly.

It doesn't matter if you select cells by dragging the mouse pointer or by clicking. Whichever method you use, work efficiently.

You can size the cells of the table by grabbing one of the lines and dragging it to the desired position. In the next exercise we'll make the table a little tighter around the cells. Then we'll center it horizontally on the page.

## EXERCISE ⟹ WP6.4

1. With **bones 6-3 xxx** open, save it as **bones 6-4 xxx**. Practice selecting cells as follows:
   a. Point to the top of Cell D2. When the fat white arrow appears, double click to select the column. Click in the table to deselect the column.
   b. Point to the left edge of the same cell. Double click to select the row.
   c. Point to the top of Cell B2. Triple click to select the entire table.

2. Point to the right border of Column D. When the pointer looks like an intersection, grab the border and drag it to the left until the little box tells you that the column is **0.5"** wide. (The text will be long and skinny.)

3. Select all of Row 2 and click the **Tables** button on the Property Bar. Choose **Equal Column Widths**. Your columns should now be even, and the table will be off center on the page. Deselect the row.

4. With the insertion point in the table, use the QuickMenu to choose **Format**. Click the **Table** tab. In the lower left corner of the dialog box is *Table position on page*. Click the arrow and choose **Center** from the drop-down menu. Click **OK**.

5. Select the entire table to put a border around it. Use the QuickMenu to choose **Borders/Fill**. Look at the dialog box (see Figure 6-5).

6. Click the button beside **Outside** and look at the choices. At the bottom, you can choose a style by name. In this case choose the second style in the second row and click **OK**.

7. Back in your document window, you should see a heavy double line around the outside of your table. Select all of Row 2.

8. Return to the Properties for Table Borders/Fill dialog box and choose the button beside **Top**. Choose the second button in the first row and click **OK**.

9. To change the height of Row 1, position the insertion point anywhere in Row 1. Go to the Format dialog box and choose the **Row** tab. In the upper right corner click the **Fixed** button for *Row height*. Change the amount in the box to **0.5"** to make the cell a half inch high.

10. Click the **Cell** tab and change *Align cell contents: Vertical* to **Center**. Click **OK**.

11. With the insertion point still in Row 1, go to the Borders/Fill dialog box and click the button beside **Fill** (upper right). Choose the third Fill button in the first row—**10%**—to make the row stand out from the rest of the table.

12. Return to your table. Check to see if it looks like Figure 6-2. If not, see if you can fix it on your own. When it looks good, print it and close it, saving it again as **bones 6-4 xxx**.

**FIGURE 6-5**
Properties for Table Borders/Fill Dialog Box

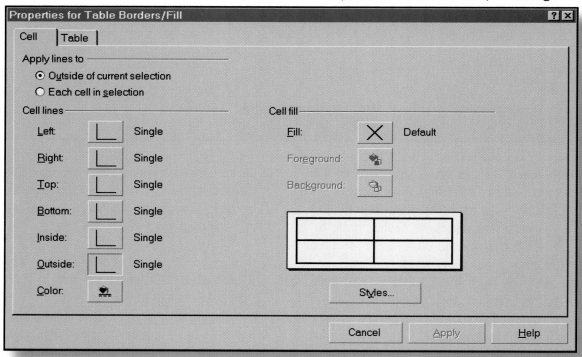

You just finished your first table. It was a simple table, but you learned all the basics of working with tables. To review, you created the table, keyed text into it, added a column, added a row, joined the cells in a row, made the columns equal widths, adjusted the size of the table, centered the table between the margins, adjusted cell lines—on the outside of the table and inside, adjusted the height of a row, centered the text vertically in that row, and added fill. You used the Toolbar, the QuickMenu, the Table menu on the Property Bar, and you worked with a variety of dialog boxes. Remember how to do all of those things. You'll need those skills in the remaining exercises of the lesson.

When you choose *Format* from either the Table menu on the Property Bar or the QuickMenu, the dialog box illustrated in Figure 6-6 appears. Study this dialog box. Note that it has four tabs—Cell, Column, Row, and Table. When you click one of these tabs, a different dialog box appears. These will be referred to as the "Cell Format dialog box," the "Column Format dialog box," etc., in the following exercises.

**FIGURE 6-6**
Properties for Table Format Dialog Box

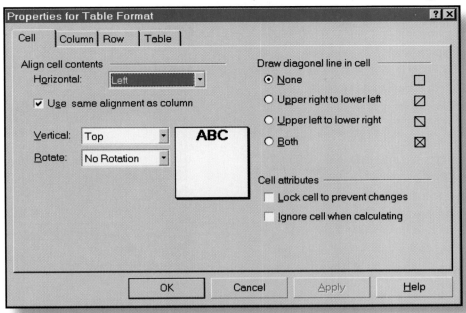

# *Tables with Calculations*

WordPerfect contains many of the tools available in spreadsheets for calculations in a table. Let's improve a table that was already keyed for you and learn to do calculations.

## EXERCISE ⇨ WP6.5

**SCANS**

1. Beginning in a new document window, go to the student **Datafile** folder and open **grooming**. Save the file as **groom 6-5 xxx**. Press **Ctrl+Home** twice to move the insertion point out of the table and play your **pf** macro.

2. Add a row at the top of the table. Join the cells. Center and key this two-line title:

   **Grooming Receipts**
   **Week of September 22**

3. Beginning with Cell B2 (Monday), select Cell B2 and the remainder of Row 2. Click the **QuickFill** button on  the Tables Toolbar to fill in the remaining days of the week.

4. Add a row at the bottom of the table. Key **Totals** in Cell A8.

5. Choose the **QuickSplit Column** button on the Property Bar and "draw" a line at the right of *Friday* down to the bottom of the column, creating a new column in Rows 2-8 (see Figure 6-7). Click the QuickSplit Column button again to deselect it.

(continued on next page)

**6.** Grab the line between Columns A and B and drag it to the left so Column A is **1"** wide. Skipping Column A, select the rest of the cells in any row (Columns B through G) and click the **Equal Columns** button on the Tables Toolbar.

**7.** If *Wednesday* wraps, select the cell containing *Wednesday* and click the **Size Column To Fit** button on the Tables Toolbar. The column should adjust just enough to fit *Wednesday*.

**8.** Select Row 3. Go to the Cell Format dialog box and set Vertical alignment at **Bottom**. Do the same with Row 5.

**9.** Select all of Row 2, go to the Cell Format dialog box and set Horizontal alignment at **Center**. Key **Totals** in Cell G2.

**10.** Save the table again with the same name. Keep it open as you read on.

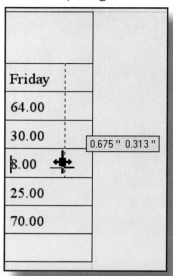

**FIGURE 6-7**
Splitting a Column

You can format numbers in a variety of ways. For this table, we'll use a *Currency* setting because we're working with money. As you use the program for other kinds of tables, you may experiment with other settings. The default is *General*. We'll also align the numbers and total them. For the totals at the right, we'll use QuickSum, beginning at the bottom and working up the table. WordPerfect's preference is to add the numbers above the insertion point. If there are no numbers above the insertion point, it will add across.

# E X E R C I S E ⬜▷ WP6.6

**1.** With **groom 6-5 xxx** open, save the file as **groom 6-6 xxx**. Select all of the number cells, including the Totals column and the Totals row.

**TIP**

The easiest way to select this odd range of cells is to begin with the mouse pointer in Cell B3 and drag diagonally to Cell G8.

**2.** Choose **Numeric Format** from the QuickMenu. Be sure the **Cell** tab is selected. Take a good look at the dialog box and then choose **Currency**. Click **OK**.

**3.** With the block of text still selected, go to the Cell Format dialog box and set Horizontal alignment at **Decimal Align**.

**4.** Position the insertion point in Cell B8. Display the QuickMenu and choose **Formula Toolbar** (see Figure 6-8). Click the **QuickSum** button to add the Monday figures.

**5.** With the insertion point still in Cell B8, click the **Copy Formula** button on the Formula Toolbar (see Figure 6-9). Choose **Right** and key **5** times. (Cell G8 will contain only zeros.)

**6.** Position the insertion point in Cell G7. Click the **QuickSum** button to add across. Working up the column, total each of the rows.

**7.** Click to position the insertion point in Cell G8 and click the **Calculate** button on the Formula Toolbar.

**8.** With the insertion point in the table, display the QuickMenu and choose **SpeedFormat**. Go through the list at the left, choosing sample formats and looking at the samples at the right to see how they look. Near the bottom of the list, highlight **Fancy Fills**. Click the **Apply** button. Your finished table should look much like Figure 6-10.

**9.** Then save the file again as **groom 6-6 xxx**, print it, and close it.

**FIGURE 6-8**
Tables Formula Toolbar

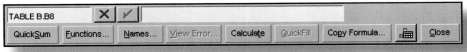

**FIGURE 6-9**
Copy Formula Dialog Box

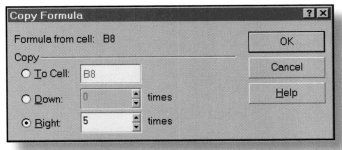

**W P - 1 0 3**

**FIGURE 6-10**
Completed **grooming 6-6** Table

### Grooming Receipts
### Week of September 22

| Service | Monday | Tuesday | Wednesday | Thursday | Friday | Totals |
|---|---|---|---|---|---|---|
| Complete Grooming | $64.00 | $96.00 | $32.00 | $128.00 | $64.00 | $384.00 |
| Bathing | $30.00 | $45.00 | $60.00 | $15.00 | $30.00 | $180.00 |
| Toenail Clipping | $8.00 | $0.00 | $16.00 | $4.00 | $8.00 | $36.00 |
| Brush Out | $12.50 | $25.00 | $37.50 | $12.50 | $25.00 | $112.50 |
| Flea Dip | $50.00 | $30.00 | $10.00 | $60.00 | $70.00 | $220.00 |
| Totals | $164.50 | $196.00 | $155.50 | $219.50 | $197.00 | $932.50 |

If you look at your finished table, you will see that the formatting added with SpeedFormat is all formatting you could have added to the table. When you're familiar with the SpeedFormat formats, you may find that WordPerfect can do what you want more quickly than you can do it.

## Table Formulas

QuickSum is a great way to add columns or rows. Some tables, however, need different kinds of formulas. Figure 6-11 lists four common symbols for formulas on computers. We'll work with some short nonsense tables so you can learn to work with formulas.

**FIGURE 6-11**
Calculation Tools

| | |
|---|---|
| * | Multiply |
| / | Divide |
| + | Add |
| – | Subtract |

### EXERCISE ▷ WP6.7

SCANS

1. Beginning in a new document window, go to the student **Datafile** folder and open **boarders**. Use **Save As** to save the file as **board 6-7 xxx** and play your **pf** macro.

2. Think about the formula needed for Column D of Exhibit 1. It should be Column B multiplied by Column C, and that product multiplied by 3 (for three days). Display the Formula Toolbar.

3. Position your insertion point in Cell D2. Then click in the box to the right of the blue check mark on the Formula Toolbar.

4. Click the **Functions** button on the Formula Toolbar and key **product** to find the multiplication formula [PRODUCT (List)]. Double click to choose it.

5. Look at the formula in the box on the Formula Toolbar. Note that the word *List* appears between the parentheses. WordPerfect is waiting for you to list the cells to be inserted. Drag across Cells B2 and C2. The range of cells should show between the parentheses (B2:C2).

You may either key a range of cells or drag across that range with your mouse pointer to enter the range in the *List* portion of your formulas.

6. Position the insertion point to the right of the closing parenthesis, and key **\*3** to multiply times the number of days.

7. When the formula looks good, click the blue check mark to put the formula into your table. The total of *75* should appear in Cell D2. Copy the formula down three times.

8. Mentally check the numbers. Are they correct? If so, save the file. Keep it open.

Exhibit 2 is looking for some averages. That function also is available in the Function list.

## EXERCISE ▷ WP6.8

**SCANS**

1. Save **board 6-7 xxx** as **board 6-8 xxx**. Position your insertion point in Cell F2. Then click in the formula box beside the blue check mark.

2. Click the **Functions** button on the Formula Toolbar and key **ave**. When the highlight stops on *AVE(List)*, double click it to put the formula on the Toolbar.

3. Drag across the numbers in Row 2 to insert the list of numbers in the formula. Check the cells listed. If they are correct, click the blue check mark to complete the calculation. Copy the formula down three times.

4. Since you can't divide a dog or cat into fractions, select the cells in Column F and go to the Numeric Format dialog box. Change the format to **Fixed** and the number of decimal places to **0**.

5. Add a row at the bottom of Exhibit 2 for Totals. Add Column B using QuickSum. Check that total. It should be *17*, but it's *18* because the 1 from 1ˢᵗ in the column heading is included.

6. Select all of Row 1. Return to the Numeric Format dialog box and change the format to **Text**. Back in your document, position the insertion point in Cell B6 and click the **Calculate** button on the Formula Toolbar.

7. Copy the formula to the **Right**, **4** times. Save the document and keep it open.

Now let's review the formatting of number columns and learn how to get white letters on a black background.

1. Save **board 6-8 xxx** as **board 6-9 xxx**. Select all of the number cells in Exhibit 2 and open the Cell Format dialog box. Set Horizontal alignment at **Center**.

2. Select all of the number cells in Column B of Exhibit 1. Set them for **Currency** and **Decimal Align**. Do the same with the number cells of Column D.

3. Select the number cells of Column C of Exhibit 1 and set the Horizontal alignment at **Center**.

4. Select Row 1 of Exhibit 1 and set Horizontal alignment at **Center**. Go to the Borders/Fill dialog box and set the fill at **100%** (the last button in the second row). When you return to your document, the row will appear to have disappeared.

5. Open the Font dialog box and change the text color to **White**. Return to your document and click away from the row you are formatting. Your row should now be formatted with *reverse type*. Format Row 1 of Exhibit 2 the same way.

6. Check your work over carefully. If it looks good, save it again and keep it open.

## *Floating Cell*

WordPerfect enables you to create a tiny, one-cell table in a document containing a table. The one-cell table is used to reference information in the normal table, and is referred to as a *floating cell*. Look at Figure 6-12. The number in the sentence below the table is a floating cell, and that number will change if the amount in the referenced cell is amended.

Let's create a floating cell that references Cell F6 in Exhibit 2. Then we'll see how easy it is to change information in a table that has been calculated.

**FIGURE 6-12**
Sample Table with Floating Cell

| Shop | 4th Quarter Profits |
|---|---|
| Pet Paradise | $10,500 |
| Pet Paradise II | $8,275 |
| Total | $18,775 |

The total fourth-quarter profits from both shops amount to $18,775.

# EXERCISE ⟩ WP6.10

**1.** Save **board 6-9 xxx** as **board 6-10 xxx**. Position the insertion point a double space below Exhibit 2.

**2.** Key the following sentence:

**Exhibit 2 shows that the average number of pets boarded per week is \*\*.**

When you come to the asterisks, insert a floating cell as follows:

**a.** Open the **Insert** menu and choose **Table**. The Create Table dialog box will appear, looking much like Figure 6-13. Click **Floating cell** and then click **Create**.

**b.** Reveal your codes to be sure your insertion point is between the floating cell codes.

**c.** Click in the box to the right of the blue check mark on the Formula Toolbar.

**d.** Click in Cell F6 of Exhibit 2 (the last cell in the final column). Click the blue check mark to insert the reference in your floating cell.

 **NOTE:**

The number in the floating cell isn't a whole number. This is tricky to fix, because when you select that *21.5* and right click, you don't get the right QuickMenu. What's more, the Tables Property Bar tools aren't showing, so you can't choose Numeric Format from any available location.

**e.** Point to your normal Toolbar and right click to display the list of Toolbars. Choose **Tables**. (The Tables Property Bar will now appear below your Toolbar.)

**f.** With the insertion point between the floating cell codes, click the **Table** button on the Tables Toolbar and choose

**FIGURE 6-13**
Create Table Dialog Box

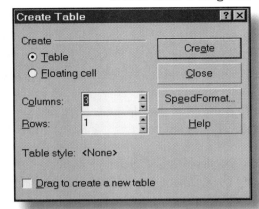

**Numeric Format**. Change the number type to **Fixed** and the decimal places to **0**.

**g.** Reverse Step 2e to hide the Tables Toolbar.

**h.** Finish the sentence following the floating cell by pressing the **End** key to get past the floating cell codes, and key a period.

**i.** Save your document.

**3.** You just learned that you have incorrect information in Exhibit 2. The number of cats boarded the first weekend should have been 14. Click in the table and change *4* to **14**.

**4.** Click the **Calculate** button on the Formula Toolbar to recalculate the table. Note that the Cats total changes, as well as the final average and the number in the floating cell.

**5.** Save your document again as **board 6-10 xxx**. Print it and close it.

 **TIP**

If the Formula Toolbar isn't displayed when you want to recalculate, you can also choose Calculate from the QuickMenu.

# *Forms*

$W$ordPerfect tables can also be used to prepare office forms. In the next exercise you'll review your tables knowledge by preparing a quarter-page phone message form for use in the pet shop office. Follow along carefully.

## EXERCISE ⟹ WP6.11

1.  Beginning in a new document window, go to the Page Setup dialog box and make the following settings:
    a.  Change to **Landscape** orientation.
    b.  Divide the page into **2** columns and **2** rows. Return to your document window.

2.  Go to **Current Document Style** and change all four margins to **0.3"**. Save your document as **message 6-11 xxx**.

3.  Create a table consisting of 2 columns and 12 rows. The table will not all fit on one page. Select the entire table. Then open the Row Format dialog box and set Row Height at

**Fixed**. Change Row Height to **0.3"** to make the table fit on the quarter page.

4.  Look at Figure 6-14. See how quickly you can duplicate this form in your window following these suggestions:
    a.  Use a 10-pt. sans serif font for the text.
    b.  Join cells where necessary. In the first row the cell containing *Urgent* was created using the QuickSplit Column feature.
    c.  Use symbol 4,38 for the check boxes.
    d.  Use **Right Align** for the six cells in the middle that have check boxes.

**FIGURE 6-14**
Table for Exercise WP6.11

| For | URGENT ☐ |
|---|---|
| Date | Time |
| **WHILE YOU WERE OUT** | |
| M | Phone |
| Of | |
| Telephoned ☐ | Please Call ☐ |
| Came To See You ☐ | Will Call Again ☐ |
| Returned Your Call ☐ | Wants To See You ☐ |
| Message | |
| | |
| | |
| Signed: | C:\Suite\Lesson 6.wpd |

e. Use **Reverse Text** for the *While You Were Out* line.

5. After *Signed* in the last row, use **Flush Right** for the Path and Filename code. Format it with an 8-pt. font size.

6. When you finish, save the file again. Then open the **Edit** menu and choose **Select** and **All**. Copy the selected text to the Windows Clipboard.

7. Position your insertion point in the second quarter page and paste the table there. Paste it in each of the remaining quarter pages.

8. Zoom to Full Page and look at your document. It should look much like Figure 6-15.

9. Print your four message forms and close the document without saving it again.

 **TIP**

When a document contains a table that extends to the bottom of the page, the document will appear to have a second page. If it contains no text or codes, it won't print.

**FIGURE 6-15**
Quarter-Page Memo Forms

| For | | URGENT ☐ |
|---|---|---|
| Date | Time | |
| WHILE YOU WERE OUT | | |
| M | Phone | |
| Of | | |
| Telephoned ☐ | | Please Call ☐ |
| Came To See You ☐ | | Will Call Again ☐ |
| Returned Your Call ☐ | | Wants To See You ☐ |
| Message | | |
| | | |
| Signed: C:\Suite\Electronic Instructor\Solutions\lessons 6-10\message 6-11 xxx.wpd | | |

When you create a form of this kind, it is much easier to repair a single form than each of the forms on the page. Therefore, when you save the form, do it before duplicating the form in case the form later needs editing. Now your printed copy can be taken to the paper cutter and made into real message slips.

This little exercise should have given you an idea of what you can do with forms. Don't be afraid to experiment. You have the table skills to create some really fantastic forms.

## *More Tables Features*

Many tables features won't be practiced in this lesson, but several of them deserve mention:

- If you have a multiple-page form and want the same header section to be continued on each page of the form, select the header rows on the first page. In the Row Format dialog box click the Header Row check box.

- Also in the Row Format dialog box the Row Margins are set at 0.083" for the top and 0.04" for the bottom. When you want vertical spacing to be a little tighter, you can change that top margin to match the bottom one. In fact, you have lots of control over the height of the rows in this dialog box.

- You can use a table to create an organizational chart. Create a table with lots of cells. Key in the information, and set all of the lines that shouldn't show to None.

- You can have several formulas in a table. For example, you can use multiplication to figure the extensions in an invoice. Then after the totals column is added up, insert a formula that figures the sales tax and another to combine the subtotal with the amount of the tax.

- You cannot key text beside a table, even if the table doesn't extend to the margins. If you want to key text beside the table, put your table in a graphics text box. You'll learn to create graphics boxes in Lesson 8.

- Near the bottom of the Tables QuickMenu is a Table Tools choice. This choice opens a dialog box that contains many table formatting tools. You can keep this dialog box open as you format your tables.

- In the Create Table dialog box, you may have noticed the check mark at the bottom giving you the option to Drag to create a new table. When you choose this option, the table is automatically placed in a graphics box and can be surrounded by text.

Let's try one more quick exercise to practice a few of these powerful features.

# EXERCISE ▷ WP6.12

1. Beginning in a new WordPerfect window, go to the student **Datafile** folder and open **forests**. Look through the document and note that the table extends to a second page.

2. Grab the side margins above the table and make each margin a little smaller—approximately **0.8"** will work.

3. Position your insertion point in the table and click the QuickSplit Column button on the Tables Property Bar to choose that tool. (This is tricky—work carefully!)

4. Beginning in the *68%* cell for Alabama, create a new column between the percentage and the *Montana* cell. You must begin in the *68%* column and end in the *32%* column for Missouri. That goes across a page break, but if you drag the tool below the bottom of the window, the text will move up.

5. Adjust the column sizes as necessary so the column in the middle is **0.126"** wide and none of the text in any of the cells wraps to a second line. (If you have great difficulty with this, select the entire table and change the text of the table to 11 pt.)

Now that you have the middle column in your table, let's remove the lines in that middle column so it looks like a gutter between text columns. Then we'll add a row for column heads, format it, and tell WordPerfect to make it a header row.

# EXERCISE ▷ WP6.13

1. Save the document as **forests 6-13 xxx**. Go to the top of the second page and play your **pf** macro.

2. With your insertion point in the table, display the QuickMenu and choose **Table Tools**. The Table Tools dialog box will look like Figure 6-16. Point to the blue title bar and move it off to the side so it's out of the way.

3. Select that narrow column in the middle of the table. Using the Tools dialog box, Change Top, Bottom, and Inside lines to None (X).

4. Use the **Insert/Delete** button to insert a row at the top of the table. For each half of the table, center these column headings:

   **State**      **State Tree**      %

5. With the insertion point in the first row, click the **Format** button in the dialog box and choose the **Row** tab. Click the check box for **Header Row**.

6. Select the first three cells in Row 1, and click the **Fill** button. Format those cells with **10%** fill. Do the same with the last three cells in Row 1.

7. Look at the header row at the top of the second page. It should be exactly like the header row on the first page.

8. Check your work for accuracy. Make sure the Path and Filename code are at the bottom of the second page. Then print the document and close it, saving it again as you close it.

# *Summary*

This lesson on tables has been quick and filled with features and tools to use in the preparation of tables. You learned that:

- the terminology for tables is similar to the terminology for spreadsheets.
- tables can be of any size.
- tables can be formatted in a wide variety of ways.
- tables can contain formulas so that the numbers are automatically calculated.
- tables can be used to prepare forms.
- a floating cell can be created outside of a table to reference a cell in a table.

**FIGURE 6-16**
Table Tools
Dialog Box

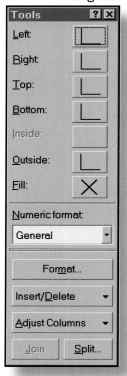

## LESSON 6 REVIEW QUESTIONS

### MATCHING

**Write the letter of the term in Column 2 that best matches the description in Column 1.**

| Column 1 | Column 2 |
|---|---|
| _____ 1. Center an entire table between the margins. | **A.** Cell Format dialog box |
| _____ 2. Set Row Height at a fixed size. | **B.** Column Format dialog box |
| _____ 3. Set Horizontal alignment of selected cells. | **C.** Row Format dialog box |
| _____ 4. Set Vertical alignment of selected cells. | **D.** Table Format dialog box |
| _____ 5. Set the format of a selected group of numbers at Currency. | **E.** Numeric Format dialog box |
| | **F.** Speed Format dialog box |

## TRUE/FALSE

**Circle the T if the statement is true. Circle the F if it is false.**

**T  F**    **6.** SpeedFormat can be used to apply a predetermined format to your tables.

**T  F**    **7.** The Tables Toolbar, the Tables QuickMenu, and the Application Bar can all be used to make choices for formatting your tables.

**T  F**    **8.** The Formula Toolbar contains the tools you need to enter formulas into your tables.

**T  F**    **9.** You should proofread your numbers in your tables carefully because once the table has been calculated, the numbers can't be changed.

**T  F**    **10.** A floating cell is a numeral in a paragraph that is boxed with a double line.

## LESSON 6 PROJECT

SCANS

Figure 6-17 illustrates the beginning of a daily time sheet for the Pet Paradise hourly workers. Create a similar time sheet that's formatted two-to-a-page on paper turned to landscape orientation. Add extra rows until the page is filled. Save the file as **time proj6 xxx**. Put the Path and Filename code in the lower right corner, formatted with a very small font. (You may need to join two cells to make it fit.)

When you finish, save the first form. Then copy the form to the second half of the paper. Print the form and close it.

**FIGURE 6-17**
Table for Lesson 6 Project

| Employee: | | | | | |
|---|---|---|---|---|---|
| Department: | | | Date: | | |
| Company: | Pet Paradise | Pet Paradise II | Total Hours: | | |
| Job No. | Kind of Work | Began | Finished | | Hours |
| | | | | | |

# CRITICAL THINKING ACTIVITY

You have prepared a table to record the number of minutes you spend each week studying. Across the top of the table, you have named your eight columns—Days, 8 a.m., 9 a.m., etc., up to 10 p.m. Down the side you have labeled the days of the week. At the bottom, you've inserted another row to total the number of minutes per week per class you've spent studying. Since you have a class scheduled during the 8 a.m. time frame, you know the total in that column will be zero. However, when you clicked the QuickSum button, an 8 was inserted into the cell. What would cause that to happen and how would you fix it?

# MERGE, SORT, EXTRACT

## OBJECTIVES

**Upon completion of this lesson, you will be able to:**

- Discuss the terminology connected with Merge and Sort.
- Prepare and edit data files in either text format or table format.
- Prepare and edit form documents.
- Merge data files with form documents.
- Create envelopes during a merge.
- Use Merge to prepare lists and tables.
- Troubleshoot a merge when something doesn't work.
- Work with keyboard merge.
- Use Sort, Extract, and Select Records.

**⏱ Estimated Time: 3 hours**

Simplified, Merge is the process of combining a document to go to several people with the list of names and addresses of the people to receive the document. Dozens of variations exist in this procedure. We'll work with the basics in this lesson and discuss some of the additional options.

# *Merge Terminology*

Every merge requires a *form document* that contains text and codes. This document contains standard text that will be included in each completed document. It may be combined with a data source (such as an address list), with information keyed on the keyboard, or a combination of these. Following are the terms:

- **Merge Codes**. WordPerfect has dozens of codes that tell WordPerfect what to do in a merge. Most common are FIELD, ENDFIELD, and ENDRECORD.

- **Record**. A record is one complete entry in the list or data source. In a list of names and addresses, all of the information about one person is a record. An ENDRECORD code and hard page break always identify the end of a record.

- **Field**. A field is one piece of data in a record. Each of the following could be a field: Name, Street Address, City, State, ZIP, Telephone, or Fax. There is no limit to the number of lines in a field. Dividing records into more fields with smaller chunks of information makes your data files more versatile. An ENDFIELD code marks the end of a field. Look at Figure 7-1. Notice how this record has been divided into ten fields.

- **Form Document**. This document is sometimes called a form file or a shell document. It contains the standard text for all documents in the completed merge.

- **Data Source**. The data source for merge in WordPerfect may be a file created in WordPerfect or a different program or information from the Address Book. The data source is made up of a list containing records. When the data source is created in WordPerfect, we'll call that source a *data file*. In WordPerfect the number of records in a data file is unlimited. Each record may consist of as many as 255 fields. Let's create a data file.

**FIGURE 7-1**
Sample Record

```
AntonioENDFIELD
HernándezENDFIELD
9211 Main StreetENDFIELD
AustinENDFIELD
TXENDFIELD
78762ENDFIELD
(512) 555-3114ENDFIELD
cat, BurmeseENDFIELD
BellaENDFIELD
6-96ENDFIELD
ENDRECORD
```

# Data File

**W**e'll begin with a text file with named fields. It is a list of Pet Paradise customers and some information about their pets, including whether or not the pets are ever groomed or boarded at Pet Paradise.

**QuickSteps**

**Create Data File**
1. Choose Merge from the Tools menu.
2. Choose Create Data.
3. Name the fields.
4. Key the data.

**EXERCISE ⟹ WP7.1**

SCANS

1. Beginning in an open window, open the **Tools** menu and choose **Merge**. The opening Merge dialog box gives you a choice of creating data, creating a form document, or merging.

2. Choose **Create Data** to display the Create Data File dialog box (see Figure 7-2). Key **first name** and press **Enter**. Key **last name** and press **Enter**. Continue keying the rest of the field names in Figure 7-3. When you finish, click **OK** to display the Quick Data Entry dialog box (see Figure 7-4).

**FIGURE 7-2**
Create Data File Dialog Box

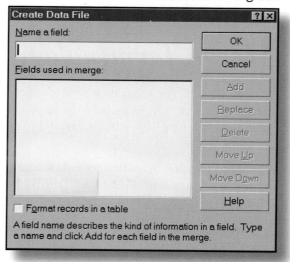

**FIGURE 7-3**
Field Names

```
first name
last name
street
city
state
ZIP code
phone
pet type
pet name
birth date
grooming
boarding
```

**FIGURE 7-4**
Quick Data Entry Dialog Box

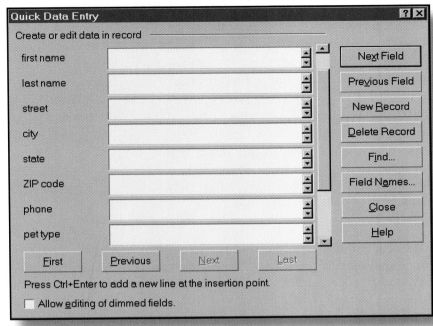

3. Key the information about Norris Christensen from Figure 7-5 into the dialog box, pressing **Enter** or **Tab** at the end of each piece of information. The field names will continue to scroll up when you get to the bottom. At the *grooming* field, just press **Enter**.

4. When you finish with Norris, press **Enter** and the information in the dialog box will be entered into your document. The Quick Data Entry box will be ready for Adam. Note that Adam's street address is two lines. To enter the second line in the same field, press **Ctrl+Enter** after the apartment number.

**FIGURE 7-5**
Data File Information for Exercise WP7.1

```
first name:   Norris              Adam
last name:    Christensen         Hart
street:       4215 Main Street    Apt. 134-C
                                  6219 Hunter Way
city:         Austin              Austin
state:        TX                  TX
ZIP code:     78716               78713
phone:        (512) 555-3115      (512) 555-3022
pet type:     spaniel, springer   Dachshund
pet name:     Max                 Gordon
birth date:   5-94                8-95
grooming:                         x
boarding:     x                   x
```

5. After finishing with Adam, return to Figure 7-1 and key the information for Antonio. Be sure to include the accent in his name. Antonio brings Bella for boarding but never grooming.

(continued on next page)

**6.** When you finish with the third record, click the **Close** button on the dialog box. At the prompt to save, key **a:\cust 7-1 xxx**. (You can key right over the *\*.dat* to name your file. WordPerfect will add the *.dat* extension because it knows this is a data file.)

**7.** Look at your data file. The records should look much like Figure 7-1. Each record should have 12 ENDFIELD codes and one ENDRECORD code.

**8.** Click anywhere in the file. Look at your Application Bar toward the right. It tells you the name of the field. This is handy when you edit.

**9.** Look at the Merge Bar above your document. It contains tools you'll be using often. Keep the file open in the window as you read on.

Each record must have the same number of fields. And the same type of information must be in the same field of each record. In other words, the sixth field of each record in this data file MUST contain the ZIP code number. A field does not have to contain information, but the ENDFIELD code must still be present. If a field contains two lines of information (like Adam's street address), that's OK as long as only one ENDFIELD code marks the end of the field. If a field contains the wrong information, your merge will not work.

# *Form Documents*

$\mathrm{F}$orm documents can be different types of documents—letters, lists, labels, forms, etc. For practice in this lesson we'll use a simple invitation to an open house at the Pet Paradise shops.

**QuickSteps**

**Create Form Document**
1. Choose Merge from the Tools menu.
2. Choose Create Document.
3. Identify the Associated Data File.
4. Enter the FIELD codes and key the text.

SCANS

**1.** With the **cust 7-1 xxx** data file showing in the window, click the **Go to Form** button on the Merge Bar. WordPerfect will tell you that there is no associated form document. Click **Create**.

**2.** Use **Advance** to tell WordPerfect to begin about **2"** from the top of the page. Click the **Date** button on the Merge Bar and press **Enter** four times.

**3.** Click the **Insert Field** button on the Merge Bar to open the Insert Field Name or Number dialog box. Double click *first name* to put that code in your document and space once with the space bar. Double click *last name*.

**4.** Press **Enter** and continue entering fields as illustrated in Figure 7-6, remembering to insert spaces and punctuation as shown. Following the greeting, press **Enter** twice. Close the Insert Field dialog box.

5. Use **Insert** and **File** to insert **open** from the student **Datafile** folder. Move your insertion point to a double space below the last paragraph and play your **close** macro to enter the closing lines.

6. Save the file as **open 7-2 xxx**. (You can key right over *\*.frm*. WordPerfect will add the *.frm* extension to your file anyhow because it knows this is a form document.) Keep it open.

**FIGURE 7-6**
Fields for Exercise WP7.2 Form Document

```
FIELD(first name) FIELD(last name)
FIELD(street)
FIELD(city), FIELD(state)
FIELD(ZIP code)

Dear FIELD(first name):
```

Now that the data file and the form document are ready, you can perform the merge. Both files happen to be in your window, so WordPerfect is pretty sure what you want to merge. On the other hand, they could be files saved on your disk. You have an opportunity during the merge to identify the files to be merged.

When the merge is completed, the three letters will be displayed in yet a different WordPerfect window, each on a separate page. The insertion point will be at the bottom of the final letter.

EXERCISE WP7.3

**SCANS**

1. With **open 7-2 xxx** showing in your window, click the **Merge** button on the Merge Bar. Look at the Perform Merge dialog box (see Figure 7-7).
   a. It prompts that the form document is the current document.
   b. It knows what the data source is because you started there when you created the form document.
   c. It reports that the merged documents (Output) will be in a new document window.

2. Click the **Merge** button to begin the merge. Almost immediately, your three letters will appear. Look through the letters.

3. Save the final merged letters as **open 7-3 xxx**. Move the insertion point to the top of the document and play your **pf** macro. Then print the letters and close them.

**FIGURE 7-7**
Perform Merge Dialog Box

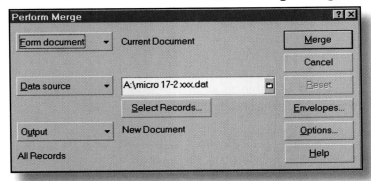

4. Close the form document, saving again if asked.

**TIP**

On the job you probably won't save merged documents. If you have the form document and data file, you don't need to waste disk space with completed merges.

## Edit a Data File

It is easy to make changes to a data file after it has been prepared. Let's repair one of the records and add one more record to the file.

### EXERCISE ⟹ WP7.4

1. With **cust 7-1 xxx** showing in the window, save the file as **cust 7-4 xxx**. In the first record change *Christensen* to **Christianson**.

2. Move the insertion point to the bottom of the file and click the **Quick Entry** button on the Merge Bar. Add the customer in Figure 7-8. Remember how to deal with the two-line street address? Taylor doesn't come for grooming or boarding.

3. When you have finished adding the information, respond affirmatively to the question about saving the file again.

4. Close the document without saving it again.

**FIGURE 7-8**
Exercise WP7.4 Addition

```
Lucas
Jacobs
Suite 1450
800 Kings Ridge Ct.
Austin
TX
78763
(512) 555-3225
cat
Taylor
4-94
```

# Envelopes

You can prepare an envelope as part of a merge. Choose the envelope option in the Perform Merge dialog box. In the next exercise you will also merge files that are not open in the window.

### EXERCISE ⟹ WP7.5

1. Beginning in a new document window, open the **Tools** menu and choose **Merge**. Then click the **Perform Merge** button.

2. WordPerfect will remember the last data source, and it's not correct. You need to identify both files.
   a. Click the file folder button beside the *Form document* text box and select **open 7-2 xxx**.

   b. Click the file folder button beside the *Data source* text box and select **cust 7-4 xxx**.

3. When both files are identified, click the **Envelopes** button. Study Figure 7-9. Note that the information for the merge has already been supplied in the upper right corner. Note also that a bar code has been added. (Yours will be blank.)

a. Click the **Field** button at the bottom of the dialog box. In the Insert Field Name or Number dialog box double click to insert **first name**. Space once and insert **last name**.

b. Continue entering the FIELD codes so they look like an address.

c. If the *POSTNET Bar Code* text box isn't showing below the *Mailing addresses* text box, click the **Options** button and choose the option that puts the POSTNET bar code **below** the address.

d. Click in the *POSTNET Bar Code* text box and click the **Field** button again. Select the **ZIP code** field.

e. Check for return address. The check box at the left should not be selected, since we'll assume that Pet Paradise has preprinted envelopes.

4. When everything in the Envelope dialog box is correct, click **OK**. Back in the Perform Merge dialog box click **Merge**.

5. When the merge is completed, your insertion point is still at the bottom of the letters. The envelopes follow. Scroll down and look through the envelopes.

6. Print only the envelope for the letter to Norris Christianson. Save your merge as **open 7-5 xxx** and close it.

**FIGURE 7-9**
Envelope Dialog Box

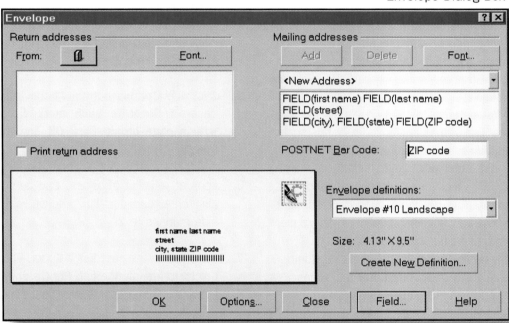

# *Labels*

The procedure for merging to labels is exactly like the procedure for the letter. Choose your label definition from the Labels dialog box and insert the merge codes. Then complete the merge and insert your labels to be printed.

# *Lists*

Sometimes you want to prepare a list of people in a data file. You can't print the data file, because each record is on a separate page—you'd get a page for each person in the file, and the data wouldn't be arranged in a very desirable manner. Let's make a list of our four customers.

## EXERCISE ⟹ WP7.6

1. Beginning in a new document window, open the **Tools** menu and choose **Merge**. Click the **Create Document** button.

2. WordPerfect will ask you to identify the data source to associate with the form document. Click the little file beside the box and identify **cust 7-4 xxx**.

3. When you click **OK**, you will be taken to a new document window with the Merge Bar at the top. Click **Insert Field** and prepare a form document that looks like Figure 7-10. Format it as follows:
   a. After entering the ZIP code field on the last line of the mailing address, flush right and insert the phone number code.
   b. Press **Enter** twice and insert the *pet type* code. Give the **Center** command and insert the *pet name* code. Flush right again and key **Birth Date:**, space once, and insert the *birth date* code.
   c. Close the Insert Field Name and Number dialog box and press **Enter** four times.

 **TIP**

You may have noticed that when you need a data file, WordPerfect lists only the files with a *.dat* extension. When you need a form document, WordPerfect lists only the *.frm* files.

4. When the form looks good, save it as **cust form 7-6 xxx**. Click the **Merge** button on the Merge Bar. In the Perform Merge dialog box click the **Reset** button so the Envelopes feature is deselected.

5. Click the **Options** button. At the top click to deselect **Separate each merged document with a page break**. Click **OK** and then click **Merge**.

6. Look at your list of owners and pets. It looks kind of spread out. For practice, change the side margins to **2"**.

7. Save the file as **cust list 7-6 xxx**. Play your **pf** macro to identify the list. Print it and close it. Close the form document without saving it.

**FIGURE 7-10**
Format for **cust form 7-6**

```
FIELD(first name) FIELD(last name)
FIELD(street)
FIELD(city), FIELD(state) FIELD(ZIP code)                    FIELD(phone)

FIELD(pet type)          FIELD(pet name)        Birth Date: FIELD(birth date)
```

# *Table Data File*

The data file can also be prepared in the form of a table. Some users prefer that method because the information is spread across the page rather than in a column at the left. Let's create a short data file in table format and use it for a merge.

## EXERCISE ⟹ WP7.7

1. Beginning in a new document window, open the **Tools** menu and choose **Merge**. Click **Create Data**.

2. In the Create Data File dialog box click the **Format records in a table** check box at the bottom. Then key the field names in Figure 7-3, just as you did in Exercise 7.1. After keying the last field name, click **OK** to display the Quick Data Entry dialog box.

3. Enter the information for Norris and Adam from Figure 7-5. Pay attention to the following:
   a. Spell *Christianson* correctly.
   b. Just press **Enter** for Max because he doesn't require grooming.
   c. Remember to press **Ctrl+Enter** for Adam's two-line street address. (Note the tiny scroll bars in that box so you can look at both lines, if you wish.)

4. When you finish, click the **Close** button and save your list as **cust 7-7 xxx**. Look at your table. It looks TERRIBLE. It will still work, but for the sake of cosmetics, let's format it a little.
   a. With your insertion point a the top of the page, go to **Page Setup** and change to **Landscape** orientation. Also, change the margins to **0.5"** on the left and right.
   b. Back in your document window, you'll notice that the table is still sized for portrait orientation. Open the Table Format dialog box. In the *Table Position* section in the lower left corner, display the drop-down menu and choose **Full**.

5. Proofread your work. (Don't worry about tight cells.) Then save the file again.

6. Click the **Merge** button on the Merge Bar. In the Perform Merge dialog box identify **cust form 7-6 xxx** as the form document. WordPerfect will remember that last time you used that form document, you used **cust list 7-4 xxx**. Change to **cust 7-7 xxx.dat**.

7. Note that the Reset button isn't grayed. (It is remembering your last option.) Click the **Options** button to be sure the list of customers will be on one page. Then complete the merge.

8. Save your completed merge as **cust list 7-7 xxx**. Identify it with your **pf** macro. Print it and close it, saving it again as you close it. Close the data file.

**INTERNET** Hypermedia means using hypertext links to connect different types of media. Examples of different media are animation, graphics, pictures, sound, text, and video.

# *Merging into a Table*

You can also use a form document that is in table format. When you merge into a table, you must use a number of different codes that keep the merge going until all records have been entered. You'll learn to use these codes in Exercise WP7.8.

## EXERCISE ⟹ WP7.8

1. Beginning in a new document window, open the **Tools** menu and choose **Merge**. Then choose **Create Document**. At the Associate prompt, enter **cust 7-4 xxx**.

2. When the Merge Bar appears at the top of the window, create a table that is 4 columns by 2 rows. Your finished table will look like Figure 7-11.

   a. After keying the column headings, position your insertion point in Column A2. Click the **Merge Codes** button on the Merge Bar.

   **TIP**

   If two dialog boxes are on top of one another, remember that you can point to the Title Bar and drag any dialog box to a different location.

   b. Key **lab** to move to the *Label (label)* code. At the prompt, key **top**.

   c. Click the **Insert Field** button and insert the rest of the codes up to the *NEXTRECORD* code in the Boarding column. Click in the Insert Merge Codes dialog box and key **nextr** to move to the *NEXTRECORD* code and insert it. Press **Tab** to add the final row.

   d. Get the *GO(label)* code from the Insert Merge Codes dialog box. Key **top** as the label again. Close both dialog boxes.

   e. Check your work and compare it to Figure 7-11. Don't worry about the size of columns and the fact that the codes don't fit very well within the columns.

3. Save the table form as **cust form 7-8 xxx**. With your insertion point at the top, play the **pf** macro to identify the form.

4. Click the **Merge** button on the Merge Bar. In the Perform Merge dialog box, click the **Reset** button unless it is grayed. You don't need any options for this merge.

5. Complete the merge. Save the completed merge as **cust table 7-8 xxx**. Print it and close it. Close the form file.

**TIP**

It doesn't matter what you use for a *label* in the merge codes, but they must match. When WordPerfect comes to the GO code, it looks for the matching label and begins the merge again.

**FIGURE 7-11**
Form for **cust form 7-8**

| Customer | Pet | Grooming | Boarding |
|---|---|---|---|
| LABEL(top)FIELD(first name) FIELD(last name) FIELD(street) FIELD(city), FIELD(state) FIELD(ZIP code) | FIELD(pet type) FIELD(pet name) FIELD(birth date) | FIELD(grooming) | FIELD(boarding) NEXTRECORD |
| GO(top) | | | |

# Troubleshooting a Merge

Always check through a completed merge before printing. If you find something wrong on all letters, you can bet it's a problem with the form document. If something is wrong on only one letter, you probably made a mistake in the data file.

When you still can't find the problem, open both the data file and the form document. Tile your windows so you can see both documents at once. Make sure the FIELD codes match. Be sure the correct information is in each field of the data file.

After making a correction to either the form document or the data file, be sure to save those documents again before performing the merge. You should have some good ideas about how form documents and data files can be merged.

# Keyboard Merge

Form documents can also be merged with text from the keyboard—in other words, the merge stops for you to enter information. This kind of merge is useful when you use the same form document over and over but only need one or two documents prepared each time you use it. Let's prepare a keyboard merge document and then use it in a merge.

## EXERCISE ⟹ WP7.9

1. Beginning in a new document window, save the file as **refer form 7-9 xxx**. Play your **pf** macro.

2. Open the **Tools** menu and choose **Merge**. Then choose **Create Document**. At the *Associate* prompt, click **No association**.

3. Key the text in Figure 7-12. Begin by clicking the **DATE** button on the Merge Bar. Double-space. For each KEYBOARD code, follow this procedure:

a. Click the **KEYBOARD** button on the Merge Bar.

b. At the prompt, key the information enclosed in the parentheses.

c. After keying the prompt, click **OK** and continue keying the paragraph.

(continued on next page)

**FIGURE 7-12**
Text for Exercise WP7.9

```
DATE

KEYBOARD(owner) brought KEYBOARD(pet name) to the shop today for
KEYBOARD(service performed). The employee working with KEYBOARD(pet
name) thinks that your pet may have a problem with KEYBOARD(problem).
Please make an appointment with your local veterinarian for a checkup
for KEYBOARD(pet name).

Polly Paradeis
PET PARADISE
```

**4.** When you finish keying the paragraph, save it again with the same name.

**5.** Click the **Merge** button on the Merge Bar and then **Merge** again. WordPerfect will insert the date and stop at the first KEYBOARD code.

**6.** Look at the prompt at the bottom of the window. It is asking for the name of the owner. Key **Adam Hart** and press **Alt+Enter** to continue the merge.

**7.** Continue through the document, inserting the correct information from Figure 7-13 about Gordon's problem and pressing **Alt+Enter** after entering each piece of information. After inserting the final information, press **Alt+Enter** again to end the merge. Save the finished referral as **gordon 7-9 xxx**. Print it and close it. Close the form document.

That's enough merge. Let's look at Sort.

**8.** Beginning in a new document window, go to the Perform Merge dialog box and choose **Merge**. Identify **refer 7-9 xxx** as the form document. (It isn't saved with a *.frm* extension, so you'll have to list your files with *.* to find the file.) You don't need a data source. Begin the merge.

**9.** Complete the merge as in Steps 6 and 7 for Bella (see Figure 7-13). Don't forget the accent in the owner's name.

**10.** Save the finished referral as **bella 7-9 xxx**. Print it and close it.

**FIGURE 7-13**
Information for Keyboard Merge

| Referral 1 | Referral 2 |
|---|---|
| Adam Hart | Antonio Hernández |
| Gordon | Bella |
| nail clipping | boarding |
| periodontal disease | an ear infection |

# Sort, Extract, and Select Records

The four records in the data file you prepared in this lesson don't present much of a problem. When you do a larger merge, however, the post office prefers that the letters be sorted in ZIP code order. You can hand sort the letters after they are printed (it could be a huge job), or you can sort the records before printing. In fact, you can sort your records in a number of ways, as well as extract certain records to be included in the merge. Let's begin by learning about Sort.

**QuickSteps**

**Sort**
1. Open the file to be sorted.
2. Open the Tools menu and choose Sort.
3. Define the sort and complete it.

## Sort

The Sort dialog box enables you to set up *keys* that specify where the data is that's to be sorted and how it should be sorted. If you set several keys, WordPerfect will sort the data for the first key and then sort again for the second key. For example, you can sort by ZIP code and then alphabetically by last name within the ZIP code groups. You can even add a third key to sort by first name within the last name groups.

All text is sorted with an *Alpha* sort. So are numbers that have an equal number of digits (like telephone numbers and Social Security numbers). Numbers that vary in size (such as amounts of

Lesson 7 Merge, Sort, and Extract

money) are sorted with a *Numeric* sort. In addition, you can specify that the resulting list be in *ascending* (getting bigger or arranged A-Z) or *descending* (getting smaller or arranged Z-A) order.

You can sort lines, paragraphs, merge data files, and paragraphs. We'll begin with a simple Line sort.

## EXERCISE WP7.10

**SCANS**

1. Beginning in a new document window, key the names in Figure 7-14 in a list at the left margin. Save the finished list as **sort 7-10 xxx**. Play your **pf** macro.

2. Open the **Tools** menu and choose **Sort** to display the Sort dialog box (see Figure 7-15). Look at the following features:
   a. The file to sort is the Current Document. You could sort a file on a disk.
   b. The completed sort will replace the Current Document. You could tell WordPerfect to save the completed sort on a disk.
   c. WordPerfect knows from the file that it will be a Line sort.

3. Do you see *<User Defined Sort>* in the list? If so, choose it and click **Edit**. If not, click **New** to display the New Sort dialog box (see Figure 7-16).

**FIGURE 7-14**
Names for Exercise WP7.10

```
Barb Jean Nelson
Norris Christianson
Adam Hart
Lucas Jacobs
Maureen O'Malley
Carlos Christianson
Andreas Graf
May Day
Vin Robinson
Megan O'Malley
Sara Anne Anderson
Antonio Hernández
```

(continued on next page)

**FIGURE 7-15**
Sort Dialog Box

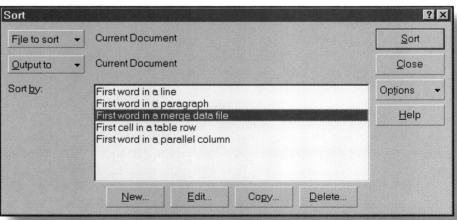

**WP-127**

4. Look at the box and note the following:
   a. You are sorting by Line.
   b. The sort type is Alpha, and it is in Ascending order.
   c. It will sort by Field 1 (in this case, the first column) and Word 1 (the first name of the customer).

5. Click **OK** and then **Sort**. Look at your sorted list. Are the people in order by first name?

6. Now let's sort it by last name. Open the **Tools** menu, choose **Sort**, highlight *<User Defined Sort>*, and click **Edit**. (Use that procedure throughout these sort exercises.)

7. Change *Word* from *1* to **-1**. (Click to the left of the *1* and key a hyphen.) Click **OK** and then **Sort** to complete the sort.

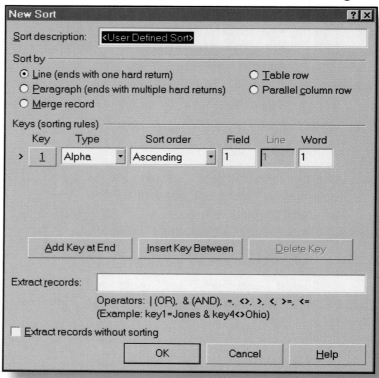

**FIGURE 7-16**
New Sort Dialog Box

8. Are the first names of the Christiansons in alphabetic order? The O'Malleys are not correct. Let's add a second key to sort by first name. Return to the Edit Sort dialog box and click the **Add Key at End** button. Look at the setting for Key 2. (It points to the location of the first name.)

9. Complete the sort. Are Megan and Maureen in alphabetic order? Print your sorted file and save it again.

The *minus 1* (-1) setting in Step 7 works because it tells WordPerfect to count from the right. You had to do this to sort your people by last name. You couldn't sort by *word 2* because some of them had middle names. The *minus 1* setting works well for ZIP codes, when they occur on the same line as the city and state, because some cities have two or three words in their names.

Let's take line sort one step further. We'll give each of these people some money in a second column and sort these people according to how much money they have.

# EXERCISE ▷ WP7.11

1. With **sort 7-10 xxx** showing, save it as **sort 7-11 xxx**. Display your Ruler (if it isn't already showing) and remove the tab stops between 1" and 3". Set a Decimal tab stop (no dot leaders) at $3^1/4$".

2. Position your insertion point after *Anderson* and tab once. Key a money number that's somewhere between $5 and $500. Use whole dollars, including the dollar sign. Don't include the decimal point.

3. Press the down arrow key and repeat the process for Carlos. Continue until each person has an amount of money. Save the file again.

4. Go to the Edit Sort dialog box and change *Key 1* to **Numeric**, **Descending**, **Field 2**, and **Word 1**. Click somewhere in Key 2 and click the **Delete** button to remove it.

5. Complete the sort. Your person with the largest amount should be at the top. The one with the least should be at the bottom. Do you know what you did?

6. Resort the list with the smallest amount of money at the top. Save the file again with the same name. Print it and close it.

Now let's try a sort with your Pet Paradise customers. You'll join the four customers from earlier in the lesson with a list of customers that was prepared for you and saved in the student **Datafile** folder. This file contains the merge records you worked with in the Merge section of this lesson. Because each field contains only one piece of information, you'll always be working with *Word 1*. Each ENDFIELD code marks the end of the field. So the name of the pet, for example, is always in Field 9.

# EXERCISE ▷ WP7.12

1. Open **cust 7-4 xxx**. Resave the file as **cust 7-12 xxx**. Position the insertion point at the bottom of the file and use **Insert, File** to go to the student **Datafile** folder and insert **customers.dat**.

2. Carefully remove the *Field Names* section (including one hard page break) at the top of the inserted file so your document has only the required hard page break between Lucas Jacobs and Carlos Christianson. Save the file again.

3. Go to the Sort dialog box, choose **<User Defined Sort>** and click **Edit**. At the top of the Edit Sort dialog box, choose **Merge record**.

4. Change *Key 1* to **Alpha**, **Ascending**, and **Field 9** to sort the customers by the name of the pet. Complete the sort. Check through the list. Is Carlos' pet, Andre, at the top and Lu-yin's pet, Ying, at the bottom?

5. On your own, sort the customers by last name.

6. Sort the list by ZIP code number. (Put that in *Key 1*). Add a *Key 2* and set that to sort by last name. Save the sorted file again with the same name.

(continued on next page)

7. Click the **Merge** button on the Merge Bar and merge this file with **cust form 7-8 xxx**. (Be sure to change the data source after inserting the name of the form document. WordPerfect remembers the old data file.)

8. Your merged table should be six pages long. Look through the pages. Note that the column headings are on the first page only. Let's fix that.

   a. Position the insertion point in the header row.

   b. Go to the Row Format dialog box.

   c. Click the **Header row** check box. Return to your document and save it as **customers 7-12 xxx**.

9. Press **Ctrl+G** and then **5** to go to page 5. Print that page only and close the document. Keep **cust 7-12 xxx** open in the window.

## Extract

You can separate out certain records for a merge. When you do this, the larger list is destroyed, and only the specified records remain in the window. IT IS IMPORTANT THAT YOU GIVE THE SMALLER LIST A DIFFERENT NAME so you don't save the short list over the master list.

Extract takes place in the Edit Sort dialog box. You begin by setting up the field to be used in one of the keys. Then you key a formula in the bottom of the box to tell WordPerfect what you want extracted. Let's try it.

EXERCISE ⟹ WP7.13

SCANS

1. With **cust 7-12 xxx** open in the window, save the file as **cust 7-13 xxx**. Go to the Edit Sort dialog box.

2. Set *Key 1* to alphabetize the owners by last name. Set *Key 2* for Field 11 (grooming). In the *Extract records* box at the bottom, key

   **key 2 = x**

   (If the dog gets groomed at Pet Paradise, an *x* appears in Field 11.)

3. Complete the sort. Check your list. Winnie the poodle should be the last record in the list, and the list is now only 27 records long instead of 66.

4. Close the file without saving it and open **cust 7-13 xxx** again. Leave *Key 1* set to alphabetize the owners. Set *Key 2* to identify the pet type.

5. In the *Extract* box at the bottom, key

   **key 2 = terrier**

   Complete the sort. Look through the list. Now you have only five terrier owners listed. Save the extracted file as **cust terrier 7-13 xxx**.

6. Merge the file with **cust form 7-8 xxx**. Save the file as **terrier 7-13 xxx**. Print it and close all files.

# Select Records

You can specify certain records to be used in a merge in one more way. This method doesn't have anything to do with Sort, and it doesn't destroy your original list. The name of the feature is *Select Records* and it is chosen in the Perform Merge dialog box. Let's use this method to separate out all cat, gerbil, and hamster owners.

## EXERCISE ⟹ WP7.14

**SCANS**

1. Open **cust 7-13 xxx**. Go to the Perform Merge dialog box and prepare to merge the file with **cust form 7-8 xxx**. Before merging, click the **Select Records** button below the *Data Source* box.

2. In the Select Records dialog box click the **Mark records** button. The Select Records dialog box will now look like Figure 7-17.

3. Click the arrow beside the *First field to display* text box and choose **pet type**. Then click the **Update Record List** button. The list will be redisplayed with the pet type at the left.

4. Go through the list and check the box at the left for all cats, hamsters, and gerbils.

5. Complete the merge. Your final document should have approximately 20 customers. Save the table as **small pets 7-14 xxx**. Print it and close all documents.

**FIGURE 7-17**
Select Records Dialog Box

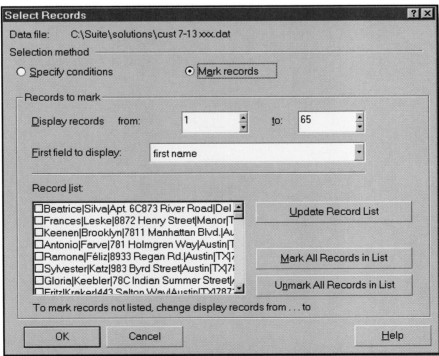

WP-131

# Summary

This lesson has included lots of tools for working with data files and form documents. For each tool you practiced, there are probably four or five variations—for some even more. Dozens of merge codes, for example, can be accessed from the Merge Bar. In addition, you can customize Sort, Extract, and Select Records in a number of ways.

It is important to note that you should have a fair idea of what you are going to do with a data file before you create it. For example, if the terriers hadn't been entered the way they were in the *pet type* field, you wouldn't have been able to extract that group of dogs.

WordPerfect data files are a flat database. You may have an opportunity to learn to use Paradox or Access. These programs are relational databases. There is a vast difference between a flat database and a relational database in terms of flexibility.

Following is a brief reminder of what you learned in this lesson. You learned that:

- special terminology applies to working with Merge.

- WordPerfect has customized dialog boxes that make entry of data easy.

- data files can easily be edited after they have been created.

- data files can be in table format.

- form documents are often letters, but they can also be tables, lists, and labels as well as other formats.

- envelopes can also be prepared as part of a merge.

- if you merge into a table, you need special merge codes.

- keyboard merge is useful when you're preparing only a couple of standard text documents.

- Sort easily rearranges your data file so your merged documents are in order when you print them.

- Extract is used to separate certain records from the larger list.

- Select Records can be used as part of a merge to specify which records should be included in the merge.

# LESSON 7 REVIEW QUESTIONS

## MATCHING

**Write the letter of the term in Column 2 that best matches the description in Column 1.**

| Column 1 | | Column 2 |
|---|---|---|
| _____ 1. | A document that contains records. | **A.** Data file |
| _____ 2. | The process of combining a form document with a data source. | **B.** Form document |
| | | **C.** Sort |
| _____ 3. | The process of specifying records to be used in a merge during the merge process. | **D.** Select Records |
| _____ 4. | The process of sorting out certain records and discarding those not meeting the criteria. | **E.** Extract |
| | | **F.** Merge |
| _____ 5. | The process of combining a form document with information entered during the merge. | **G.** Keyboard merge |

## FILL IN THE BLANKS

**Complete each of the following statements by writing your answer in the blank provided.**

6. The kind of code that marks the end of a field in a data file is an _____ code.

7. The kind of code used in a form document that indicates which piece of information should be inserted at a certain location is a _____ code.

8. Merge and sort are chosen from the _____ menu.

9. If you want the POSTNET bar code to appear on envelopes created in a merge, you must select the option and insert the appropriate _____ in the Envelope dialog box.

10. If you want all records merged onto one page, you must click the _____ button in the Perform Merge dialog box and tell WordPerfect not to separate each merged document with a page break.

## LESSON 7 PROJECT

Create a four-column table with the following column headings: **Cat Owner**, **Phone Number**, **Cat's Name**, **Date of Birth**. Make it a form document to be merged with **cust 7-12 xxx** and save it as **form proj7 xxx**.

Sort **cust 7-12 xxx** so the owners of CATS ONLY are in alphabetic order. Save the shortened data file as **data proj7 xxx**. After the merge, save the table as **cats proj7 xxx** and play your **pf** macro. Format the document attractively, giving it a title which includes the following information before printing the document and closing it.

Cat Customers
Pet Paradise and Pet Paradise II
(Current date)

## CRITICAL THINKING ACTIVITY

You have just completed a merge between a letter (form document) and a mailing list of customers. As you proofread the merged documents, you notice that the names in the inside address run together on each of the letters. What is the first thing you should check, and how would you fix this problem?

# WORKING WITH GRAPHICS

## OBJECTIVES

**Upon completion of this lesson, you will be able to:**

- Insert images and format graphics boxes.

- Use Text boxes for special text in your documents.

- Bend your words with TextArt.

- Add drop caps to your documents.

- Work with lines and other shapes.

- Decorate your documents with borders and fill.

- Decorate documents with watermarks.

- Create charts and graphs.

- Create equations with the WordPerfect Equation Editor.

- Use the WordPerfect Draw Picture program.

🕐 **Estimated Time: 3½ hours**

Corel WordPerfect Suite 8 offers you a complete smorgasbord of graphics tools to decorate and format your documents. Many of those tools are mentioned in the objectives. Others will creep into your learning as you work through this lesson. We'll begin by inserting a graphics image into a graphics box.

## *Graphics Boxes*

Literally hundreds of graphics images ship with the WordPerfect program on the CD. If you are in a classroom and the CD isn't available, you'll discover that about 50 good images are transferred to your hard drive when the program is loaded. In addition, a few WordPerfect graphics images have been saved in the student **Datafile** folder for your use—some from earlier versions of the program and some from the Corel WordPerfect Suite 8 CD.

**QuickSteps**

**Insert Image**
1. Position the insertion point.
2. Open the Insert menu and choose Graphics.
3. Choose Clipart.
4. Drag the image into your document.

When you insert an image into your document, it goes into a graphics box. That box can be sized, moved, rotated, or given a caption. You can also specify how you want the text to wrap around it, what style box you'd like it to be, and how you'd like it attached to your text. In short, you can make the graphics image fit into your document exactly as you want it to fit. Let's insert an image and learn to work with graphics boxes.

## E·X·E·R·C·I·S·E ▷ WP8.1

1.  Open the **Insert** menu and choose **Graphics**. Choose **Clipart**. When the Scrapbook appears, click on the yellow arrow with four points and drag it into your window. Align it with the margin guides in the upper right corner before releasing the mouse button. Click the **X** in the upper right corner to close the Scrapbook.

2.  Point to the graphics box and click once to select it. It will be surrounded by black *sizing handles*. Click away from the box to deselect it. Then click to select it again.

 **TIP**

When you size a graphics box using a corner handle, the height/width ratio is not affected. When you use a handle on the middle of a side, the box will be contorted.

3.  Grab the handle in the lower left corner and drag it so the box is about twice its original size.

4.  Grab the middle handle at the left and drag it to the right so the box is long and narrow. Then grab the bottom center handle and drag it up

 **TIP**

Image boxes are always 1.5" wide when they are inserted into your document. You can adjust that size as you format the box.

so the box is approximately the size it was when you began.

5.  Point to the selected box. Your mouse pointer should look like this image—a four-headed arrow. This is the *Move* tool. Drag the box to the upper left corner and align it inside the margin guidelines.

6.  With the box selected, press **Ctrl+C** to copy it to the Windows Clipboard. Deselect the box. Press **Ctrl+V** to put another copy of the box in your window. Drag that box to the upper right corner. Look at the two [Box] codes in Reveal Codes.

7.  Click away from the image to deselect it. Save your document as **arrow 8-1 xxx**. Play your **pf** macro to identify the file, and keep it open in the window.

# Editing Graphics Boxes

**FIGURE 8-1**
Graphics Property Bar

**FIGURE 8-2**
Graphics QuickMenu

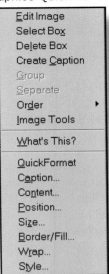

The same three sources of editing tools are available for graphics boxes as you had for editing tables. The Property Bar (see Figure 8-1) contains a number of tools, along with the Graphics menu that drops down from the Property Bar when you click the button at the left. The Graphics QuickMenu contains many of the same tools (see Figure 8-2). Remember that the Property Bar contains shortcuts for the tools in the other sources. When you are on the job, you may want to edit the Property Bar or Toolbar so it contains the tools you use often. In the exercises of this lesson try to use all three sources so you can decide which you prefer. Let's look at graphics box styles.

## E X E R C I S E ▭▷ WP8.2

1. With **arrow 8-1 xxx** showing in the window, save the file as **arrow 8-2 xxx**.

2. Select the image at the right. Display the QuickMenu and choose **Style**. Look at the Box Style dialog box. It displays quite a range of styles—some of which are not appropriate for a graphics image.

3. Choose **Text Box**. Back in your document window, you'll see that the selected box is now enclosed. Try the following box styles: Button, Watermark, and Sticky note text. Return to the Image style.

4. Keeping the box at the right selected, choose **Size** from either the Graphics drop-down menu or the QuickMenu to display the Box Size dialog box.

5. Change the settings in your box so they match the settings in Figure 8-3. (Unless you want a lot of empty space in the box, it is best to set

**FIGURE 8-3**
Box Size Dialog Box

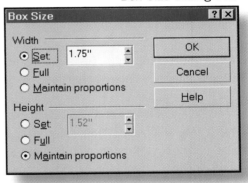

either width or height and let WordPerfect maintain proportions in the other setting.)

6. Add a caption to your box by displaying the QuickMenu and choosing **Create Caption**. WordPerfect will display *Figure 2* because this is your second box. Backspace once and key the new caption: **Which Way to Go?**

(continued on next page)

**7.** Click out of the caption, on the image, and choose **Caption** from the lower part of the QuickMenu. At the left of the dialog box, change Side of box to **Left**, Position to **Center,** and at the bottom, change Rotate caption to **90 degrees**.

**8.** Move the caption back to the bottom, aligned at the right of the box. Turn off the rotation.

**9.** Back in your document window, deselect the image and save the document again as **arrow 8-2 xxx**. Play your **pf** macro.

WordPerfect will wrap text around your image in a variety of ways. The default is for the text to respect the entire box, not just the image in the box. We'll play with the options shortly.

The default for Image boxes is that the Position is set so the box is anchored to the page. That means that the box will stay in the same position on the page, no matter what you do with the text. That's not always desirable. Sometimes you want the image to stay with a certain paragraph. We'll look at the difference between those two settings in the next exercise.

# EXERCISE ⟹ WP8.3

**1.** Save **arrow 8-2 xxx** as **arrow 8-3 xxx**. Select the image at the left and press the **Delete** key to delete that extra image.

**2.** Choose **Insert** and **File**. Go to the student **Datafile** folder and choose **graphics**.

**3.** Select the arrow image at the right and display the QuickMenu. Choose **Wrap**. In the Wrap Text dialog box choose **Contour** and **Largest side**. Back in your document window, look at how the text fits around the image.

**4.** Drag the image down along the right margin. Then adjust it so the top of the image is even with the beginning of the second paragraph. Deselect the image and change justification to **Full**. See how the text wraps around the image. Deselect the image.

**5.** Move the insertion point to the top of the document. Press **Enter** three times. Note that the image doesn't move. Backspace three times to remove those hard returns.

**6.** Select the image and display the Graphics drop-down menu from the Property Bar. Choose **Position**. At the top of the dialog box, click the arrow beside the *Attach box to* text box and change to **Paragraph**. Back in your document window, move the image slightly. Do you see the "pushpin" that shows where the image is anchored?

**7.** Position the insertion point at the top of the document and press **Enter** three times again. Note that the image moves with the paragraph.

**8.** Save your document again as **arrow 8-3 xxx**. Print it and keep it open. Read about *Graphics Images* in the document you have open in the window.

You must be getting tired of that image. Let's work with a different one for a while. We'll learn about a whole new set of tools.

# EXERCISE ⟹ WP8.4

1. With **arrow 8-3 xxx** showing in the window, use **Save As** to save it as **rose 8-4 xxx**. Select the image and press **Delete** to remove it from your document.

2. Choose **Insert**, **Graphics**, and **Clipart** and scroll through the list until you come to the **rose2** image. Drag it into your document, again with the box at the right margin and the top of the box aligned with the top of the second paragraph. Set Position so the box is anchored to the paragraph.

3. Display the QuickMenu and choose **Content**. At the bottom left, click the check box that tells WordPerfect to preserve the image width/height ratio.

4. With the graphics box selected, display the QuickMenu and choose **Image Tools** (see Figure 8-4). Point to the Title Bar of the palette and drag it to the center of your window where you can see it better.

5. Click the **Flip** button to make the image "face" the text on the page. Click the **Rotate** button. (Now the box has rotate handles as well as sizing handles.)

6. Grab the rotate handle in the upper left corner and drag the box into the text until the back petal of the rose sticks out of the box about a quarter inch. Release the mouse button.

7. Click the **Move** button on the palette and use the Move tool to move the rose over in the box so the entire image shows again (but at a different angle).

8. Experiment with Contrast, Brightness, and Fill. Then set those back at their original settings (the center choice for Contrast and Bright-ness and the first setting for Fill).

9. Close the Image Tools palette and set Wrap at **Contour** and **Both sides**. Save your document again as **rose 8-4 xxx**. Print it and keep it open.

**FIGURE 8-4**
Image Tools Palette

You can crop an image to get a particular view. The cropped area must be square. When you crop an image, the entire image is still there, in case you want to retrieve it. If you reset all attributes in the Image Tools palette, the image will return to its original form.

In the next exercise we'll also change the text to columns. Long words in narrow columns leave big spaces. Hyphenation is a WordPerfect tool that helps fill the lines. WordPerfect divides some of the words at the end of the line. Sometimes it needs your help. Use the word division rules in Figure 8-5 as a guide.

**QuickSteps**

**Hyphenation**
1. Open the tools menu and choose Language.
2. Click the Hyphenation on check box.
3. If necessary, help WordPerfect with hyphenation.

1. Save **rose 8-4 xxx** as **rose 8-5a xxx**. Display the Image Tools palette and move it so you can see it.

2. Click the Zoom button. It looks like a magnifying glass. Choose the magnifying glass in the pop-out menu. Using this crop tool, draw an elastic box around the bloom of the rose, including the first leaf only. When you release the mouse button, the rest of the rose disappears.

3. Use the Rotate tool to turn the rose so the back petal and the stem are in a vertical line with each other. Move the rose so that the vertical line snuggles up to the right margin.

4. Set Wrap at **Largest Side**. Make any other adjustments to make the rose look good and print it.

5. Position your insertion point at the beginning of the first paragraph and change to two Balanced newspaper columns.

6. Move the rose so the top of the box is even with the beginning of the *Graphics Images* section, in the middle of the page.

**FIGURE 8-5**
Word Division Rules

**WORD DIVISION RULES**

Divide words only between syllables.
Carry at least three letters to the next line.
Avoid dividing the last word on a page or in a paragraph.
Avoid dividing words with fewer than six letters.
Avoid dividing proper nouns.
Avoid dividing more than two lines in a row.

7. Use Hyphenation to close up the text as follows:
   a. Open the **Tools** menu, choose **Language**, and choose **Hyphenation**.
   b. At the top of the Hyphenation dialog box, click the check box that turns Hyphenation on.
   c. Return to your document. WordPerfect may ask for help with some of the hyphens. The dialog box is simple to use. Don't be afraid to skip words that shouldn't be divided. Use the rules in Figure 8-5 as a guide.

8. Save the file, this time as **rose 8-5b xxx**. Print it and close it.

**TIP**

Some lines may still be spread out. Position your insertion point at the end of a spread line. Press Delete to delete the space. When the line wraps more tightly, put the space back in again.

Now let's quickly look at the Border/Fill option. You have already worked with borders and fill, so most of this will be review.

# EXERCISE ⟩ WP8.6

1. Open **rose 8-4 xxx**. Save it as **rose 8-6 xxx**. Select the rose image and display the Image Tools palette.

2. Click the **Reset Attributes** button at the bottom. Then flip the rose again so it faces the page. Close the Image Tools palette.

3. With the rose selected, choose **Border/Fill** from either menu. You'll work with all three tabs to make your rose look like Figure 8-6.

**FIGURE 8-6**
Exercise WP8.6 Rose

4. With the **Border** tab selected, move the scroll bar for border styles to the top and choose the fourth border in the first row. Click the **Fill** tab and set **10%** fill.

5. Click the **Advanced** tab.
   a. Change the Corner radius to **0.200"**.
   b. In the *Drop shadow* area, change Color to **Black**.
   c. For Width, choose the third line thickness in the left column.
   d. At the left, click the button beside *Inside* spacing. Again, choose the third line thickness in the left column.

6. Save your document again as **rose 8-6 xxx**. Print it and close it.

# Text Boxes

You can put a Text box into your document by choosing that feature from the Insert menu. Text boxes are used for tips, notes, or "pull quotes," like you see in newspaper or magazine articles.

Working with Text boxes is a little different than working with graphics boxes. When you key in a Text box, you are in the edit mode, and dashed lines appear around the box. You can size the box as usual in the edit mode. You cannot format the box in the edit mode.

To format the box, you must click outside of the box to exit from the edit mode. Then point to one of the box borders. When an arrow appears, click once to apply the sizing handles. The box can be edited when the sizing handles are showing. Let's put a pull quote in a document and format it.

# EXERCISE ⟩ WP8.7

1. Beginning in a new document window, go to the student **Datafile** folder and open **graphics**. Save the file as **text box 8-7 xxx**. Play your **pf** macro.

2. Position your insertion point in the space above the paragraph about *Text Boxes*. Read that paragraph.

(continued on next page)

**3.** Select the last sentence of the paragraph about *Copyrights* (just above *Text Boxes*). Copy the sentence to the Windows Clipboard. Click at the beginning of the paragraph.

**4.** Open the **Insert** menu and choose **Text Box**. The box will appear with a dashed border around it. Paste the sentence from the Clipboard into the box. Click outside of the box to exit from the edit mode.

**5.** Point to one of the edges of the box. When the mouse pointer turns into a white arrow, click once to give the box sizing handles. (It should not have the dashed border.)

**6.** Set the size of the box so it is **1.8"** wide. Height should be set to maintain proportions. Change the border of the box so the text is enclosed in heavy top and bottom lines (no lines at the sides of the box).

**7.** Position the box beside the paragraph about copyrighting. Save the file, print it, and close it.

Text boxes are always 3.25" wide when they are created. You can make them any size when you format them.

# TextArt 8

Another kind of graphics box is the TextArt 8 feature. This feature is used for decorative text on special kinds of documents. We'll use it on a serious document—just for practice.

**TextArt**
1. Choose Graphics from the Insert menu.
2. Choose TextArt.
3. Key the text to be formatted.
4. Set options.

**1.** Beginning in a new document window, open **graphics** from the student **Datafile** folder again. Save it as **art 8-8 xxx**. Play your **pf** macro.

**2.** Select the title of the document and cut it with **Ctrl+X**.

**3.** Open the **Insert** menu and choose **Graphics**. Then choose **TextArt**. When the dialog box appears, press **Ctrl+v** to paste the title into the *Type here* text box (see Figure 8-7). Look at the area above the dialog box. Your TextArt is previewed there.

**4.** Click the **More** button to look at the available shapes for your TextArt. Try a few of them. When you finish, choose the one that is boxed in red in Figure 8-7.

**5.** Explore some of the other options in the General and 2D Options dialog boxes. (Unless a special custom install was used when your software was loaded, the 3D options will not be available.)

**6.** Choose a color, an outline style, and a shadow color of your choice. Then close the TextArt dialog box.

7. If the Image box containing your TextArt isn't centered between the margins, center it and check to be sure your document is lovely. Make whatever adjustments are necessary to fit the document on one page.

8. Print your document. Then close it, saving it again as you close it.

**FIGURE 8-7**
Corel TextArt 8.0 Dialog Box

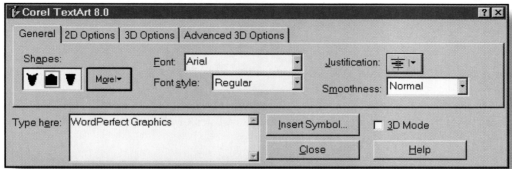

# *Drop Cap*

Drop caps, those fancy letters at the beginning of articles in magazines and newspapers, can be formatted in a variety of ways, using the tools on the Drop Cap Property Bar.

## QuickSteps

**Drop Cap**
1. Position the insertion point at the beginning of the paragraph.
2. Open the Format menu and choose Paragraph.
3. Choose Drop Cap and select the format.

## EXERCISE ⟹ WP8.9

1. Open **text box 8-7 xxx**. Save it as **drop cap 8-9 xxx**. Read about drop caps in the last paragraph of the document.

2. Position the insertion point beside the first paragraph and delete the tab that indents the paragraph. Open the **Format** menu and choose **Paragraph**. Then choose **Drop Cap**.

3. Look at the lovely large letter. Look at the Drop Cap Property Bar tools (see Figure 8-8). Explore the options on each of those six tools. Then format your drop cap as follows:
   a. For *Style*, choose the first style in the third row of styles.

**FIGURE 8-8**
Drop Cap Property
Bar Tools

b. For *Size*, set your drop cap to be **4** lines high.
c. For *Position*, don't make a change. That was set when you chose the style.
d. For *Font*, choose a sans serif font. Make it green.

(continued on next page)

**e.** For *Border/Fill*, choose the seventh border in the first row. Change fill to **10%**.

**f.** For *Options*, experiment with some of the options. Then return to **1** character and only the *Wrap . . .* option chosen.

**4.** Save your document again with the same name. Print it and close it.

# Lines and Shapes

Lines are primarily used to decorate your documents. In the past, WordPerfect only allowed you to insert horizontal or vertical lines. Now you can insert lines of all shapes, and they can go right over the text. Let's begin with horizontal and vertical lines.

E X E R C I S E ⟹ **WP8.10**

**1.** Beginning in a new document window, press **Ctrl+F11**. You just inserted a horizontal line that extends from margin to margin at the location of the insertion point. Press **Ctrl+Shift+F11**. You now have a vertical line.

**2.** Point to the horizontal line. When your pointer becomes an arrow, click once to select it. When the handles appear, press **Delete** to delete the line.

**3.** Point to the vertical line and double click to open the Edit Graphics Line dialog box. Change the settings of the line as follows:

   **a.** Change the Color to **Olive** green. (Point to a color with the mouse pointer and hold it until the name appears.)

   **b.** Change the Line thickness to the first choice in the second column.

   **c.** Set the Length at **10"**.

   **d.** Change Horizontal to **Set** and key **0.25"** for the setting. (You just set the line to be positioned a quarter inch from the left edge of the paper.)

   **e.** Change Vertical to **Set** and key **0.5"** for the setting. Click **OK**. (You just set the line

**FIGURE 8-9**
Shape Pop-Out Menu

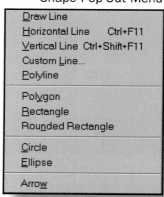

to begin a half inch from the top of the paper.)

**4.** Open the **Insert** menu, choose **Shape** (see Figure 8-9), and choose **Custom Line** to return to the dialog box to create another line.

   **a.** At the top, click **Vertical**.

   **b.** Change the Color to **Grape** and Line thickness to the fourth choice in the first column.

   **c.** Set Length at **9.5"**.

d. Change Horizontal to **Set** and key **0.5"** for the setting.

e. Change Vertical to **Set** and key **0.75"** for the setting.

5. Create one more vertical line that is pink, the second thickness choice in the first column,

and **9"** long. Set Horizontal at **0.75"** and Vertical at **1"**.

6. Look at the lovely lines at the left of your page. If you have a color printer, this could be the start of a letterhead. Save the file as **lines 8-10 xxx**. Play the **pf** macro and print the page. Save and close the document.

Lines can be drawn in a variety of shapes. Let's practice. Then we'll put the lines to work.

## E X E R C I S E ⇨ WP8.11

1. Beginning in a new document window, open the **Insert** menu and choose **Shape** again. Study the choices. Draw Line, and all of the choices below Custom Line give you free reign in drawing lines in your documents. Try each of them as follows:

   a. Choose **Polyline**. In your document window click and release the mouse button. Use the mouse to draw a line. Click each time you want a corner. When you finish, double click to end the line. Deselect the shape.

   b. Choose **Polygon**. Click once to begin. Move the mouse and click each time you want a corner. Double click to end the polygon.

   c. Choose **Rectangle**. Press and hold the mouse while you draw the shape you want. Do the same with **Rounded Rectangle**.

   d. Choose **Circle** and then **Ellipse**. Follow the same procedure as for Rectangle.

   e. Choose **Arrow**. Press and hold the mouse while you create an arrow the length and thickness you'd like. If you go to the right of the starting point, the arrow points to the left. If you go to the left of the starting point, the arrow points to the right.

2. Select any one of the images and drag it so it's partly covering another image. Keep it selected and display the QuickMenu. Choose **Order** and change which image is on top of the other one.

3. With an image selected, look at the Property Bar (see Figure 8-10). Look at the Quick Tip for each of the tools on the Property Bar. Then practice with them on your various shapes.

4. Save the document as **shapes 8-11 xxx**. Play your **pf** macro. Print it, save it again, and close it.

5. Go to the student **Datafile** folder and open **joining**. Save the file as **joining 8-11 xxx** and play your **pf** macro. This is a little test.

6. Choose **Draw Line** from the **Shapes** menu and draw a line from *Ctrl+B* to the feature you access with that command. Continue until you have drawn lines to match all of the commands with all of the features.

7. When you finish, save the file again. Print it and close it.

**FIGURE 8-10**
Graphics Shape Property Bar

# *Borders and Fill*

You worked with borders and fill when you learned about tables and graphics boxes. Those two features are applied in much the same way when you use them for paragraphs, columns, and pages.

**QuickSteps**

**Borders/Fill**
1. Open the Format menu.
2. Choose Paragraph, Page, or Column.
3. Set the border and fill parameters.

## EXERCISE ⟹ WP8.12

1. Beginning in a new document window, open **graphics2** from the student **Datafile** folder. Save the file as **graphics 8-12 xxx**. Play your **pf** macro.

2. Read the first two paragraphs—about Lines and about Borders and Fill.

3. Select the first paragraph. Open the **Format** menu, choose **Paragraph**, and choose **Border/Fill**. Choose a border style for your paragraph and a fill style.

4. Select the next two paragraphs. Go to **Border/Fill** and choose a different style of border. Click the **Advanced** tab and tell WordPerfect to make the space inside of the border larger.
   a. Did you figure out how to do that without help?
   b. Did you notice that the border pushed farther into the margin space—that the margins of the paragraph stayed the same?

5. Select the next two paragraphs. Go to the Column Format dialog box and set **2 Balanced newspaper** columns. Still in that dialog box, click the **Border/Fill** button and scroll to the bottom of the list.

6. Choose the border style that consists of a vertical line in the middle of the page. Click **OK** until you return to your document.

7. Open the **Format** menu, choose **Page**, and choose **Border/Fill**. Look at the *Border type* box at the top. If it says *Fancy*, click the arrow beside the box and choose **Line**. Choose a border style for the page. Zoom to **Full Page** to look at your page with its borders. Return to **100%**.

8. Save the document again as **graphics 8-12 xxx**. Print it and close it.

Fancy page borders are fun. WordPerfect offers a wide variety of borders for different circumstances. Some are appropriate for certificates. Others are appropriate for flyers or handbills. Study Figure 8-11. This flyer uses one of the fancy borders.

**EXERCISE** ⟹ **WP8.13**

1. Beginning in a new document window, save the empty file as **flyer 8-13 xxx**.

2. Go to the fancy page borders. Find the border in Figure 8-11 and insert it into your document. Zoom to **50%** so you can see most of the page as you work.

3. Using **Enter** to position your text vertically and **Center** to position your text horizontally, create a similar flyer. Use a variety of large fonts and make the document lovely.

4. When you finish, save the document again with the same name. Print it and close it.

**FIGURE 8-11**
Text for Exercise WP8.13

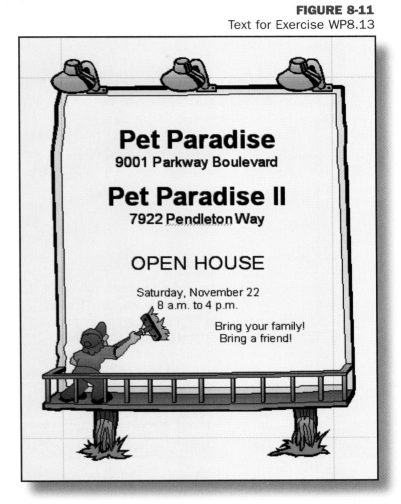

# *Combining Graphics*

In Exercise 8.13 you had to fiddle around on the page with hard returns and Center to get the text where you wanted it to be. Sometimes that procedure is awkward, especially when the text shouldn't be in the center of the page. You can combine Text boxes with graphics images to achieve a different look for your documents. Let's create yet another advertisement for the open house.

1. Beginning in a new document window, open the **Insert** menu, choose **Graphics**, and choose **Clipart**.

2. Drag the first image in the Scrapbook (**dogholdi**) into your document. Set the size at **Full**. Click in the margin to deselect the image.

3. Create a Text box. Before keying anything, drag the Text box onto the paper being held by the dog. Size the Text box so it is almost as large as the dog's paper, just below the horizontal lines on the paper.

4. Fit the important information about the open house into the Text box and format it attractively.

5. When the flyer looks good, save it as **dog 8-14 xxx**. Play your **pf** macro, print the document, and close it.

# Watermarks

Watermarks are in the background behind the text. A watermark is a graphics image, but it is managed like a header or footer. It will appear on every page of a document unless you tell WordPerfect to discontinue it. After choosing a watermark, you can select the image from any of your sources of images and edit it before returning to your document.

**QuickSteps**

**Watermarks**
1. Choose Watermark from the Insert menu.
2. Locate the desired image.
3. Set the Watermark parameters.

1. Beginning in a new document window, go to the student **Datafile** folder and open **graphics2**. Save the file as **graphics 8-15 xxx**. Play your **pf** macro and read the paragraph about watermarks.

2. Open the **Insert** menu and choose **Watermark**. In the Watermark dialog box look at the available options. Then click **Create**. (Watermark A is OK. You could have different watermarks on opposing pages.)

3. You will be taken to a window that looks like Page Zoom Full. Preview the tools on the

**FIGURE 8-12**
Watermark Property Bar Tools

Property Bar by looking at the Quick Tip for each button (see Figure 8-12).

4. Open your normal **Insert** menu, choose **Graphics**, and choose **Clipart**. Find the *Not Negotiable* watermark image (**watrm229**) near the bottom of the list. Drag the image into your document window.

**5.** Close the Scrapbook. If the image isn't centered within the margins, drag it so it is. Click in a margin to deselect the image. Click the **Close** button on the Property Bar to return to your document.

**6.** Look at the watermark behind the text. Print your document and close it, saving it again.

# *Chart*

The Chart feature in Corel WordPerfect Suite 8 is tied a little more closely to the Quattro Pro program or the Presentations program, since both of those programs deal with displaying data. Let's create a quick chart using the grooming figures from Lesson 6.

## EXERCISE ⟩ WP8.16

**1.** Beginning in a new document window, open **groom 6-6 xxx**. Save the file as **groom 8-16 xxx**.

**2.** Select the entire table section of the document, excluding the Totals column at the right and the Totals row at the bottom. (Begin with *Service* and end with *$70.00*.)

**3.** Open the **Insert** menu, choose **Graphics**, and choose **Chart**. After a moment a chart will appear containing the data in your table. Study the chart. It needs some work. Make the following changes:
   **a.** Point to the *$140.00* at the top of the Y axis. Right click and choose **Primary Y Axis Properties**. Change the font size to **16** pt.
   **b.** Use the same procedure to change the X axis labels (Monday) to **16** pt.
   **c.** Double click the title and key **Grooming Receipts**.
   **d.** Open the **Chart** menu, choose **Subtitle**, and key **Week of September 22**.
   **e.** Point to the legend area at the bottom. Right click and choose **Legend Properties**. Choose the appropriate tab (you can figure it out) and change the font size to **18** pt.

**4.** Click outside of the chart to exit the edit mode. Then click outside of the chart to deselect it.

**5.** Return to the beginning of the document. Reveal your codes and find the [Tbl Def] code. Delete it. At the prompt, tell WordPerfect you wish to delete the entire table.

**6.** Your chart is now like a graphics box. Select it and display the QuickMenu and choose **Content**. Click the box that tells WordPerfect to preserve the width/height ratio.

**7.** Go to the Size dialog box and set the width at **Full**. Set height at **Maintain Proportions**.

**8.** Point to the chart and double click to enter the editor. Open the **Chart** menu and choose **Gallery**. Spend a minute or two looking at the different kinds of charts you can prepare using this tool. Then click **Cancel** to return to your document.

**9.** Save your chart again as **groom 8-16 xxx**. Print it and close it.

Oodles of options are available with charts—you can key the data into the data sheet that appears when you start a chart without first selecting data. You can create a wide variety of chart types. If you need charts in your work, this brief introduction will give you the basics you need to explore this option on your own.

# *Equations*

The Equation Editor in Corel WordPerfect Suite 8 enables you to build complex equations. It doesn't calculate solutions, but it does enable you to create graphical representations of equations. The Editor is based on a series of more than 100 templates into which you insert the data to create the equation.

**QuickSteps**

**Equations**
1. Position the insertion point.
2. Choose Equation from the Insert menu.
3. Create the equation using the templates.

When your equation is finished, it is entered into your document as a graphics box. The default setting for the box is an Inline Equation. If you wish to have the equation on a line by itself, simply change the box style to Equation. Let's learn by creating some equations, beginning with one that doesn't involve the use of any of the templates.

## E X E R C I S E  WP8.17

**SCANS**

1. Beginning in a new document window, save the file as **equation 8-17 xxx** and play your **pf** macro.

2. Open the **Insert** menu and choose **Equation**. The Equation Editor will open (see Figure 8-13). Each of the buttons at the top contains a number of templates. Browse through a few of them and look at the templates. Information can be entered in each gray box.

3. Key **a+b=c**. The equation will appear in the white area. Open the **File** menu and choose **Exit and Return to . . . .** Your equation should appear with sizing handles. Deselect the graphics box and press **Enter** twice.

4. Open the **Insert** menu and choose **Equation** to return to the Equation Editor. Key **a+** and choose the second button in the second row of buttons. Choose the first template on that button.

**FIGURE 8-13**
Equation Editor

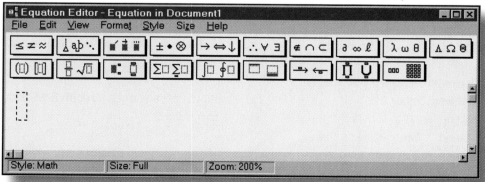

**5.** Position your insertion point in the top box and key **b**. Click to position your insertion point in the bottom box and key **d**. Click to the right of the box and key **=c**. Return to your document window.

**6.** Point to the equation you just completed and double click to return to the Equation Editor. Click to position the insertion point just to the right of the *b*. Choose the third button on the second row and choose the first template. Key **2** in the box.

**7.** Position the insertion point to the right of the *d* and choose the same template. This time, key **3** in the box. Return to your document. Your equation should look like Figure 8-14.

**FIGURE 8-14**
Second Equation

$$a + \frac{b^2}{d^3} = c$$

**8.** Figure 8-15 illustrates a third equation. Can you create it on your own? Here is a little help:

**a.** The entire first part of the equation is prepared using the fraction template you used for the *b over d* section of the second equation.

**b.** The brackets come from the first set of templates on the second row. The square bracket is the second button in the set.

**c.** If the equation looks messy, open the **View** menu and choose **Redraw**.

**9.** In your document with the equation selected, display the Graphics QuickMenu. Choose **Style**. Change to **Equation** so the equation is centered between the margins. (Note that the graphics box extends from margin to margin.)

**10.** Save the document again as **equation 8-17 xxx**. Print it and close it.

**FIGURE 8-15**
Third Equation

$$\frac{a + \left[x^2 y\right] + b}{d} = c^2$$

**NOTE:**

The Equation Editor for WordPerfect versions 5.1 though 7 is also installed with WordPerfect 8. If you wish to use the earlier Editor, choose Tools, Settings, Environment, and the Graphics tab. Make your choice there.

## *Draw Picture*

The WordPerfect Draw Picture program (part of Presentations 8) goes beyond the simple Shapes choice in Graphics. Draw Picture can be used to create actual pictures—if you have artistic talent. It can also be used to combine graphics images and save them as single images so they can be used repeatedly.

A letterhead was prepared for you using the Draw Picture program. You'll learn about Draw Picture by printing that letterhead and seeing if you can use the same tools to create a different style letterhead for Pet Paradise.

1. Beginning in a new document window, open the **Insert** menu and choose **Graphics**. Then choose **From File**. Change folders to the student **Datafile** folder. (Change *.* to *.wpg so only the *.wpg* files are listed.)

2. Locate **letterhead.wpg** and double click to insert it into your document. Change the size to **8"** wide. Drag the letterhead image up so it's about a half inch from the top of the page.

3. Deselect the image and save the entire file as **top 8-18 xxx**. Play your **pf** macro and print the page. Close it, saving it again with the same name.

The letterhead image actually contains four separate parts—two animal images, a circle drawn and colored in the Draw Picture program, and a Text box. They stay together as one image because they were combined in the Draw Picture program and then saved as a single image. In the next exercises you will look at some additional images and try some of the Draw Picture tools.

1. Beginning in a new document window, save your empty document as **draw 8-19 xxx**. Play your **pf** macro.

2. Choose **Insert**, **Graphics**, and **From File**. List only the *.wpg* files.

3. Click the **Preview** button on the dialog box Property Bar. (It's just to the left of the Favorites button.)

4. Point to one of the cats and wait a moment until it is previewed in your window. Look at each of the cats and dogs. Double click **cat2** to put it in your document.

5. Back in your document window, size the cat so it is **4"** wide (maintain height proportions). Point to the cat and double click to enter the Draw Picture mode.

6. Using the sizing handles, drag the side of the box so it extends from the left margin to the right margin. Open the **Edit** menu and choose

 **TIP**

When you are in Draw Picture mode, be careful not to click outside of the Draw Picture box until you are finished. If you do, you'll have to double click the image to re-enter Draw Picture. That takes time on some computers.

**Select Objects**. Drag the cat to the right margin.

7. Point to the image and double click. When your mouse pointer is an arrow, point to the cat's tail and click to select it. Press **Delete** to remove the tail.

8. One piece at a time, delete all parts of the cat. Then click the **Undo** button on the Toolbar as many times as necessary to put the cat back together.

9. Point to an ear and click to select the head. Use a sizing handle to make the orange part of the head a little bigger. Select the green center

of the head and enlarge it to fill the orange portion.

10. Delete the cat's second rib. Click the first rib to select it and press **Ctrl+C** to copy it to the Clipboard. Click away from the rib to deselect it. Press **Ctrl+V** to make a copy of that rib. (They're on top of one another.) Drag the second rib over so the cat has two identical ribs.

11. If you wish, choose **Rotate** from the QuickMenu to rotate one of the ribs so they are parallel.

12. Click outside of the Draw Picture box to exit Draw Picture mode. Deselect the image and save the document again as **draw 8-19 xxx**. Keep it open.

As the name implies, you can actually *draw* in the Draw Picture program. Much of what you do there is similar to what you did with the Shapes portion of the Graphics tools. In addition, you can add text to your drawing.

## E X E R C I S E ⟩ WP8.20

1. Point to your cat and double click to enter Draw Picture mode again. Enlarge the box containing the cat and move the cat to the lower right corner so about an inch of space surrounds the cat at the left and top.

2. Click the arrow part of the **Closed Object Tools** button on the Toolbar (it looks like a rectangle) and choose the second tool in the second row. Try your hand at drawing a cartoon-like bubble.

3. With the bubble selected, click the **Foreground Fill Color** button and change to a different color for the bubble. (White is OK, too.)

4. Click the **Fill Pattern** button (just to the left of *Foreground Fill Color*), and choose a pattern that appeals to you.

5. Click the **Text tool** on the Toolbar. (It has a large A on it.) Change to a smaller font size. Draw a box in the bubble and key **Feed me!**

(continued on next page)

**FIGURE 8-16**
Draw Image

**6.** When you finish, your cat MAY look like Figure 8-16. Click outside of the Draw Picture box to exit from Draw Picture mode.

**7.** Open the **File** menu and choose **Save As**. Because the cat image is still selected, you have a choice of whether you want to save the entire file or just the image. Choose **Selected Image**.

**8.** Save the image with your solutions as **cat 8-20 xxx**. It will save with a *.wpg* extension like other WordPerfect images. Deselect the image.

**9.** Print the file and close it, saving it again as a document.

In each case you entered the Draw Picture program by double clicking an image. You can begin with an empty drawing by choosing Insert, Graphics, and Draw Picture. As you can see, a person could spend hours fiddling with images and trying options in the Draw Picture portion of Corel WordPerfect Suite 8. For now, it's time to move on.

# *Summary*

In this lesson you explored nearly a dozen of the graphics tools that are part of Corel WordPerfect Suite 8. Some were covered in more depth than others, but you should have a good idea of what you can do with graphics in this program. You learned that:

- you have a wide selection of graphics images that can be used in WordPerfect, and those images can be sized, rotated, and manipulated in a number of ways.

- text boxes enable you to separate text from the rest of the document and box it.

- with TextArt, you can bend text and change it in a wide variety of ways.

- Drop Cap simply adds a large letter to the beginning of any paragraph.

- graphics lines (rules) can take any shape with the Shapes feature of Graphics.

- borders and fill can be used on paragraphs, columns, and pages.

- watermarks are shaded images behind the text of your document.

- WordPerfect will help you prepare a variety of kinds of charts and graphs.

- the Equation Editor enables you to put professionally prepared equations into your documents.

- you can create any kind of graphics image using the Corel WordPerfect Suite 8 Draw Program.

**INTERNET** The federal government has plans to link schools, government agencies, colleges, and universities to a network that will be much faster than the current Internet. This new network is called the National Research and Education Network (NREN).

## LESSON 8 REVIEW QUESTIONS

### MATCHING

**Write the letter of the term in Column 2 that matches the description in Column 1.**

**Column 1**

_____ **1.** Puts a shaded image behind the text on the page.

_____ **2.** Is used to shape the letters of words and format them to make them fancy.

_____ **3.** A large letter at the beginning of a paragraph.

_____ **4.** The choice that enables you to draw lines right into your text.

_____ **5.** A graphics box that contains words.

**Column 2**

**A.** Graphics images

**B.** Text box

**C.** TextArt 8

**D.** Drop cap

**E.** Shapes

**F.** Watermarks

**G.** Equations

### TRUE/FALSE

**Circle the T if the statement is true. Circle the F if it is false.**

**T   F   6.** You must go to the Position dialog box to make the choice that preserves the width/height ratio of an image.

**T   F   7.** You can rotate the contents of a Text box so the words are sideways or upside down on the page.

**T   F   8.** The Drop Cap feature is chosen from the Font dialog box.

**T   F   9.** To prepare equations using WordPerfect, you must go to the Draw Picture dialog box and draw the equation.

**T   F   10.** If you wish to apply a border to one paragraph in a document, you must first select that paragraph.

## LESSON 8 PROJECT

SCANS

Using any three of the tools you learned about in this lesson, prepare a one-page flyer advertising the company open house. Be sure to include some graphics images and rules. (The dog and cat image on the company letterhead is saved in your student **Datafile** folder as **logo.wpg**, if you want to use that image.) When you finish, save the project as **flyer proj8 xxx**, play your **pf** macro, and print the document.

## CRITICAL THINKING ACTIVITY

SCANS

You are working with three images that are to be overlapped in your document. When you get the images where you want them to be, the one that ought to be on the bottom is covering parts of both of the other images. What can be done to solve the problem?

# PRODUCTIVITY TOOLS

## OBJECTIVES

**Upon completion of this lesson, you will be able to:**

■ Map your keyboard to make special characters more readily available.

■ Work with the WordPerfect Address Book.

■ Use PerfectExpert to create and format documents.

■ Create, edit, and use styles.

■ Design and create a Web page using the WordPerfect Internet Publisher.

**🕐 Estimated Time: 3¹/₂ hours**

A variety of powerful productivity tools have been developed to help you with particular kinds of tasks. For example, the Address Book may be used to keep frequently used addresses, phone numbers, e-mail addresses, etc., together in one place. This lesson contains quite a number of tools. We'll begin with the creation of a specialized keyboard.

## *Keyboard Mapping*

Since you learned about WordPerfect symbols, you've needed some of those symbols periodically. In some offices you use special symbols often, so it would be useful to have those symbols on your keyboard. WordPerfect enables you to map the keyboard so it contains those frequently used keys. When you have done that, you can switch to the customized keyboard whenever it is needed. You can have several customized keyboards—one for Spanish, another for French, etc. We'll begin this lesson by creating a German keyboard, mapping only ä, Ä, ö, Ö, ü, and Ü.

# EXERCISE ⟹ WP9.1

1. Beginning in a new document window, open the **Tools** menu and choose **Settings**. Double click the **Customize** icon and click the **Keyboards** tab. *<<WPWIN 8 Keyboard>>* should be highlighted.

2. Click **Create**. Key **German** for the name of your keyboard and click **OK** to display a large dialog box with all keystroke assignments at the left and tab choices at the right. Click the **Keystrokes** tab.

3. Scroll through the list of assignments at the left until you come to **A+Alt**. Click to highlight that assignment. Then click in the large white box on the right. Press **Ctrl+W** for symbols and key **a** and then ". Insert the selected symbol and close the dialog box.

4. Click the **Assign Keystrokes to Key** button below the box. The assignment should appear in the box at the left.

5. Move the highlight to the **A+Alt+Shift** combination. Click in the large white box at the right and delete the previous character. Adjust the procedure in Steps 3 and 4 to assign the uppercase **Ä** character.

6. Follow the same procedure to assign the symbols as follows:

   | ö | O+Alt | ü | U+Alt |
   |---|-------|---|-------|
   | Ö | O+Alt+Shift | Ü | U+Alt+Shift |

7. When all are assigned, click **OK**, **Select**, and **Close** to return to your working window with the German keyboard chosen.

**TIP**

Since not all foreign language characters have keystroke shortcuts, you may need to locate the character in the multinational set and choose it.

With the keyboard chosen, you can try it. A coworker has started a letter to a family in Germany who is moving to Austin and wants to purchase an Irish Setter when they arrive. You need your German keyboard to complete the letter.

# EXERCISE ⟹ WP9.2

1. Beginning in a new document window, go to the student **Datafile** folder and open **travel**. Save the file as **travel 9-2 xxx**. Play your **pf** macro.

2. Move your insertion point to the bottom of the letter. With your German keyboard selected, key the text in Figure 9-1. When you come to the first foreign character (ä), press **Alt+A** to insert the character. Use the assigned keystrokes for each foreign character.

3. When the letter is completed, prepare an envelope. Print your letter and envelope and close the file, saving it again.

4. Open the **Tools** menu and choose **Settings**. Double click the **Customize** icon and click the **Keyboards** tab. With your highlight on the German keyboard, click the **Delete** button so your keyboard isn't in the way for other students.

**5.** Select *<<WPWIN 8 Keyboard>>* and return to your document window.

**FIGURE 9-1**
Text for Exercise WP9.2

So bald Sie in ihren neuem Heim eingezogen sind und es Ihnen zeitmässig passt, rufen Sie uns bitte an somit wir einen Termin festlegen wenn sie mit Oliver bekannt werden können.

Wir danken Ihnen für ihre interesse an unserem Geschäft und verbleiben Ihr


Polly Paradeis

# *Address Book*

As mentioned at the beginning of the lesson, the Address Book can be used like a phone book and information center for all your printed address needs. The Address Book can store names and addresses, phone numbers, e-mail addresses, and more. You can also dial the phone from the Address Book if your computer has a modem and is connected to a phone line.

You may have multiple Address Books, and you may keep both business and personal information in the Address Book. An Address Book exists for Pet Paradise employees, but more names need to be added.

## EXERCISE ▷ WP9.3

SCANS

**1.** Beginning in a new document window, open the **Tools** menu and choose **Address Book**. The dialog box illustrated in Figure 9-2 will appear. The default dialog box has the two tabs illustrated. If others are using your computer, you might see other tabs.

**2.** With the **My Addresses** tab chosen, click the **Add** button and choose **Person**. Enter your name and address. If you wish to protect your privacy, you may use bogus information. To enter the telephone numbers, click the **Phone Numbers** tab.

**3.** When you finish, click **OK** to return to the Address Book.

**FIGURE 9-2**
Corel Address Book

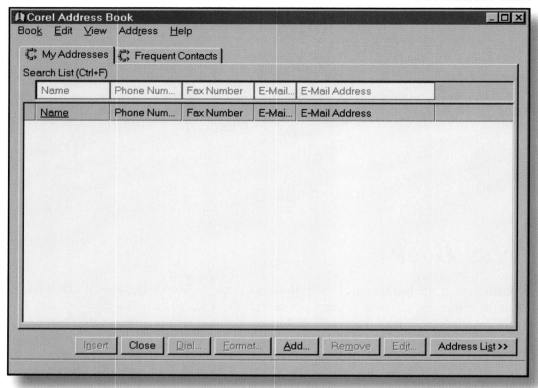

## Import and Export Books

A book in the Address Book feature is different from a file. When you create a book, it will stay in the Address Book dialog box until you do something with it, even if you close the Address Book or turn the computer off. Consequently, when you are not using the computer, your Address Book might still be available. In the classroom it's not a very good idea to have your Address Book where others can fiddle with it. So you will learn to export your book to your solutions file. You should probably do that and delete from the Address Book each time you leave the computer.

When you wish to use the Address Book again, you can *import* it. Before importing, you must create a new book and import into that book. Otherwise, the imported file will be mixed in with the names in whichever tab is chosen.

To save you some keying, most of the Pet Paradise employees have been entered into a book called **Employees**. That book is in the student **Datafile** folder. We'll import the **Employees.abx** book and add some newer employee names.

# EXERCISE ⟩ WP9.4

**SCANS**

1. Still in the Address Book dialog box, open the **Book** menu and choose **New**. In the New Properties dialog box key **Employees** to name the book. When you press **Enter,** the new book will appear.

2. With the **Employees** book displayed, open the **Book** menu and choose **Import**. Click **Next**. Use **Browse** to go to your student **Datafile** folder and find **Employees.abx**. Choose that file and click **Finish** (if necessary) to import the **Employees** Address Book.

3. Click the **Add** button at the bottom, and add the three people in Figure 9-3 to the **Employees** Address Book.
   a. Use **Tab** or click with the mouse to move through the dialog box. Key the information in the appropriate boxes. Some boxes will be empty.
   b. To enter the phone numbers, click the **Phone Numbers** tab and then click in the appropriate text box.
   c. To enter the odd information, such as date of birth, Social Security number, etc., click the **Custom** tab. Some of the blanks will be empty there, and you'll need to scroll to find all of the blanks.
   d. After entering each person, click the **New** button and confirm saving of the information.
   e. There is no way to enter special characters in the Address Book, so when you get to Reynaldo, key everything but his last name. Click **OK** and close the Address Book. Key the name with the tilde in a normal document window. Then copy the name to the Windows Clipboard, return to the Address Book, choose to **Edit** Reynaldo's information, and paste the name into the appropriate box.

   f. After the final person, click **OK** to return to the Address Book dialog box.

4. Open the **Book** menu and choose **Export**. Follow the prompts to save the book with your files as **employees.abx**.

5. Keep the Address Book open as you read on.

**FIGURE 9-3**
New Employees

```
Robert Greene
353 Buttermilk Circle
Austin, TX 78762
Phone: 512-555-1012
Birth: 8-4-81
Hire: 5-30-96
SS#: 636-02-4837
Status: Part Time
Pay: 7.50

Reynaldo Nuñoz
4815 North Butner Street
Austin, TX 78714
Phone: 512-555-1345
Birth: 5-5-71
Hire: 6-1-95
SS#: 648-61-0934
Status: Full Time
Pay: 11.00

George Young
947 East Juniper Street
Rollingwood, TX 78746
Phone: 512-555-9367
Birth: 7-12-80
Hire: 9-1-97
SS#: 634-47-3915
Status: Part Time
Pay: 7.50
```

## Customizing

The custom fields you used in Exercise 9.3 were added for the employees. To add custom fields, open the Edit menu in the Address Book and choose Custom Fields. Once they have been added, they are available for all books in the Address Book.

You also have choices regarding which fields show in the main window. Instead of e-mail information, for example, you might want to show addresses.

1. With the Address Book open and the **Employees** book showing, open the **Edit** menu and choose **Columns**. Then choose **More Columns**.

2. The dialog box that appears lists ALL columns at the left and the columns to display at the right. You would like *Name, Social Security #, Hire Date, Pay Rate,* and *Address* to show. Use **Add** and **Remove**, if necessary, to remove the unwanted columns and add the wanted columns.

3. If necessary, grab the line between the first two gray column headings and drag it to the right to size the column—so all employees' names are complete. Also, if necessary, size the Address Book dialog box so you can see all of the employees at one time.

4. Keep the Address Book open.

**TIP**

Size dialog boxes by grabbing the outside edge with the mouse pointer. When the double-headed arrow appears, drag to the desired size. Not all dialog boxes can be sized.

## Sorting the Entries

WordPerfect automatically alphabetizes the first word in the Name column. You can tell WordPerfect to display the last name first so names are alphabetized by last name. This choice is made from the View menu, Name Format.

You can also tell WordPerfect to rearrange the entries according to the information in the columns. For example, you could sort the employees by how much they are paid per hour. Computers are quirky in this regard. They look at the first figure in the number, so 15 is considered a smaller number than 9. (That's why you had to choose *Numeric* sort in Lesson 7 when you sorted by amounts of money.)

**INTERNET**

HyperText Markup Language, or HTML, is a set of computer commands. HTML is used to create World Wide Web documents that can be viewed by a browser program.

1. Open the **View** menu and choose **Name Format**. If it isn't already chosen, choose **Last, First**.

2. Back in your Address Book, note that your employees are sorted by last name. Now open the **Edit** menu, choose **Columns**, and choose **Sort**. Change the Column Sort dialog box (see Figure 9-4) so WordPerfect will sort the employees by **Pay Rate** and in **Descending sort** order.

3. Click **OK**. Note that the employees that earn more than $10 are listed at the bottom.

4. Finally, return your list to the original order—sort by **Last Name** in **Ascending sort** order.

5. Point to Albert Hapner in the list and double click. It is that easy to get a name and address from the Address Book into your document. Close the document without saving.

**FIGURE 9-4**
Column Sort Dialog Box

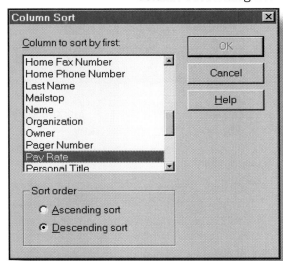

6. Export the **employees.abx** Address Book to your disk again. Then open the **Book** menu and choose **Delete**. Follow the prompts to remove it from your computer. If you need it, you can import it again.

## Using the Address Book

The Address Book is very useful—you can use it for reference. You can also use the Address Book to merge with a form document. When you use the Address Book for a merge, choose Address Book as the data source. You can even select certain records (entries) in the Address Book to use in the merge by selecting the Address Book as the data source when you create a form document.

# *PerfectExpert*

Corel WordPerfect Suite 8 provides you with a list of predefined projects to help you with your work. From any of the core Corel Suite applications (except Corel Paradox), you can choose File and then New to get a list of projects. Projects are divided into categories. You can add your own projects, including documents, templates, and macros. Once you open a project, the PerfectExpert panel appears on the left side of the document window for your use in finishing the document.

Some of the PerfectExpert projects aren't installed when you do a standard install, so even though they appear in the list, you may not be able to run them without the Corel WordPerfect Suite program CD. Let's create a monthly calendar for Polly as we learn about PerfectExpert.

**NOTE:**

The Professional version of Corel WordPerfect Suite 8 varies slightly from the non-professional version. Depending on the version you are running you may need to choose the commands in brackets in Step 5 of Exercise WP9.7.

## EXERCISE ⟹ WP9.7

1. Beginning in a new document window, open the **File** menu and choose **New**. Be sure [Corel WordPerfect 8] is showing in the box at the top of the list.

2. Scroll down the list until you find **Calendar, Monthly**. Double click to choose that project.

3. You'll need to wait until the Calendar Information dialog box appears (see Figure 9-5). If it contains all of the desired information for a calendar for next month, click **Finished**.

4. Your calendar is ready to format. Look at the PerfectExpert panel at the left. This panel is context-sensitive. Because you are currently in a table, it shows the tools for formatting a table.

5. Click anywhere in the calendar. Then click the **Change Table Look** [Change Table Format] button and choose **Striped Horizontal** [Row Fill Columns]. Click to position the insertion point just to the top right of the numeral for the first Tuesday of the month. Key **7:30 a.m. Staff Meeting**. Let the text wrap as it will.

6. Schedule 7:30 staff meetings for every Tuesday morning in the month. Add other appointments to the calendar as follows:

    10 a.m. Pet Paradise II (1$^{st}$ and 3$^{rd}$ Wednesdays)

    Noon - Lunch with Paul (every Friday)

    7:30 a.m. Manager Meeting (1$^{st}$ Thursday)

    Noon - Lunch with Renée Gutierrez (3$^{rd}$ Thursday)

7. Insert **logo.wpg** from the student **Datafile** folder in one of the empty boxes at either the top or bottom of the calendar.

8. Save your calendar as **calendar 9-7 xxx**. Insert the Path and Filename code in the lower right corner. Print the calendar. Then save it again and close it.

When you closed your calendar document, most likely PerfectExpert stayed displayed at the left of your window. Look at it. Now it doesn't have anything to do with tables. Instead, it provides tools for a normal document. If you had a graphics image selected, different tools would be provided. You can display PerfectExpert at any time by choosing it from

**FIGURE 9-5**
Calendar Information Dialog Box

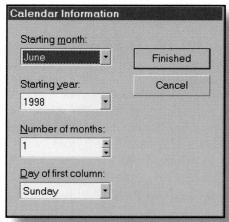

the Help menu. You can close it by clicking the blue *X* in the upper right corner of the panel. Let's explore PerfectExpert briefly.

## EXERCISE ⟹ WP9.8

**1.** With the PerfectExpert panel displayed at the left of your empty document window, click the **Edit and Proofread** button. Look at the tools displayed.

**2.** Click the **Collaborate** button and look at the tools. Click the **House** button. That returns you to the beginning PerfectExpert panel.

**3.** Click the blue **X** in the upper right corner of the panel to close it.

If you looked closely at the tools available in the PerfectExpert panel, you discovered a very important fact—few if any tools were included that you didn't already know how to use. You are so good at WordPerfect that you don't need those extra helps, although they might come in handy on certain types of projects. Let's look at another special tool that is useful when you need the same format for a number of documents.

## *Styles*

$S$tyles are used for formats that recur. If you want a document or a portion of a document to have a consistent appearance and you don't want the hassle of recreating it each time you prepare the document, styles are for you.

Pet Paradise distributes a quarterly newsletter. It is important that it look the same each time it is prepared so the customers recognize it. You can accomplish that quickly and accurately with styles. In the next few exercises we'll prepare a style document that contains two styles—one for the masthead and one for the article titles.

## EXERCISE ⟹ WP9.9

**1.** Beginning in a new document window, open the **Format** menu and choose **Styles**. You'll see listed some styles that are part of every document. Click **Create** to create a new style and display the Styles Editor (see Figure 9-6).

**2.** This dialog box should look familiar from when you worked with Current Document Style. In the *Style name* text box at the top key **Article Title**. Press **Tab**.

**3.** In the *Description* text box key **Title of Newsletter Articles**. Leave the *Type* box set at *Paragraph*. Click in the box at the bottom, next to the red rectangle that represents your insertion point.

**4.** Change the font size to **20** pt. Click **OK** to close the dialog box and return to the Style List.

(continued on next page)

**5.** Close the Style List. Click the arrow beside the **Styles** box on the Property Bar. Your *Article Title* style should be displayed in the list.

FIGURE 9-6
Styles Editor

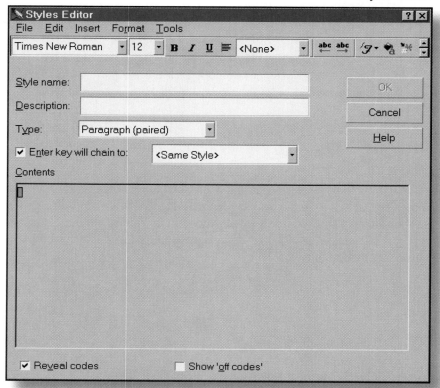

Working in the Styles Editor is difficult for complicated formats. You have the choice of looking at the codes or looking at the text you are creating, but the space is so small, and the display area doesn't have scroll bars. Sometimes you're better off to create the style out of the Styles Editor and paste it into place when define the style. We'll do that in the next exercise. The style you'll create will be the masthead for the newsletter. When you finish with the masthead, it will look much like Figure 9-7.

FIGURE 9-7
Newsletter Masthead

# EXERCISE ⟹ WP9.10

1. Change all four margins to **0.75"** and the font to **Arial 50** pt. Key **Pet Quarterly** and press **Enter**.

2. Change to **20** pt. and key **Pet Paradise**. Tab twice and key **Pet Paradise II**.

3. Change to **13** pt. and key the addresses as shown in the figure. Use **11** pt. for the telephone number. Press **Enter** twice and press **Ctrl+F11** for a horizontal line. Press **Enter**.

4. Key **Spring, 199x**, press **Enter**, and insert another horizontal line. Double click the line to go to the Edit Line dialog box and choose a greater thickness than the default.

5. Press **Enter** twice. Format the body of the newsletter as follows:
   a. Set an additional tab stop $1/4$" from the left margin for paragraphs.
   b. Change to two columns and select the **Widow/Orphan** feature.
   c. Set the font at **12-pt. Times New Roman**.
   d. Set **Full** justification.

6. Insert **logo.wpg** from the student **Datafile** folder. Size the logo so it's **3"** wide (maintain height proportions). Move the image into the upper right corner. Extend it into the top and right margins and make necessary adjustments so none of the address lines wrap.

7. Click to position the insertion point in the first column. Open the **Edit** menu and choose **Select** and **All**. Copy the entire masthead to the Windows Clipboard.

8. Open the **Format** menu, choose **Styles**, and then choose **Create**. In the Styles Editor, position your insertion point in the *Contents* box and paste the masthead from the Clipboard.

9. Name the style **Masthead** and key **Masthead for Quarterly Newsletter** in the *Description* text box. In the *Type* box choose **Document (open)** so the remainder of the newsletter is formatted with the chosen formats.

10. Click **OK**. Keep the Style List displayed as you read on.

It is important to think about the *Type* of style. An open style formats the entire document. Paragraph style is used for a section of the document that ends with a hard return. As you work more with styles, the difference will become obvious to you.

The styles you created may be used for the current document, but they will be lost when you close the document unless you save them. Once they are saved, they can be retrieved to be used each time the newsletter is created.

1. Click the **Options** button and choose **Save As**. Key **a:\newsletter styles** to name your newsletter style and tell WordPerfect where to save it. Complete the procedure, close the Style List, and close your document window without saving the document.

2. Beginning in a new document window, save the file as **Spring News 9-11 xxx**. Open the **Format** menu and choose **Styles**. In the Style List choose **Options** and then **Retrieve**.

3. Click the folder button and locate your **newsletter** style to retrieve. In the dialog box asking what you want to retrieve, click **User Styles** and then **OK**. (Your *Masthead* and *Article Title* styles should both be in the Style List.)

4. Study Figure 9-8. Your completed newsletter will resemble those two pages.

5. Point to **Masthead** and double click to choose it. The masthead should appear in your window, and your insertion point should be in the first column. Insert the following articles from the student **Datafile** folder, separating each with a double space: **teeth** (Entitle it *Your Pet's Teeth*), **flv**, **fund**, **ticks**, and **refer**.

6. You may arrange the articles in any order. Put a blank line before and after each title. With the insertion point in one of the titles, open the **Styles** drop-down menu on the Property Bar and choose the **Article Title** style to format the title. Follow the same procedure to format all article titles.

7. In the **fund** article, remove the blank lines between paragraphs and indent each paragraph. Key an asterisk and press **Tab** to insert a bullet before *express sympathy . . . .* Add bullets before the next two items.

**FIGURE 9-8**
Sample Newsletter

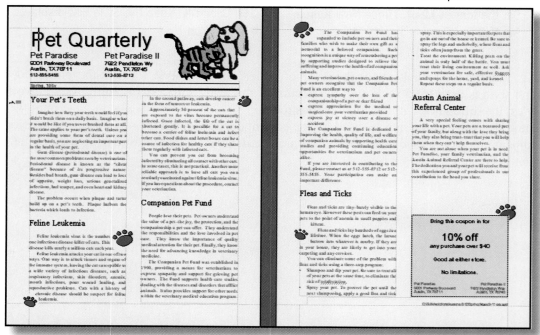

8. In the space at the end of the final column create a coupon using a Text box as follows:
   a. Extend the coupon the width of the column.
   b. Enclose it in a dotted line border (for clipping, of course), and add 10% fill.
   c. Use **Center** for the information above the addresses.
   d. Use **Left** justification and **Flush Right** for the addresses at the bottom.
   e. The text for the coupon is illustrated in Figure 9-9.
   f. Vary the font size to emphasize important information (like 10% off). Make the coupon attractive. Perhaps you could decorate the coupon with the store logo.

9. If you wish to use it, a **paw.wpg** image is on the student **Datafile** disk. You can vary the size, brightness, and rotation and have paw prints all over your newsletter. Or you can go to the Draw program and create some other kind of decoration.

10. Find a place somewhere on your newsletter to hide the Path and Filename code. Check the newsletter over and do any tweeking necessary. (You may wish to use Hyphenation.) When you finish, print the newsletter, save it, and close it.

**FIGURE 9-9**
Coupon Text

```
Bring this coupon in for
         10% off
any purchase over $40
Good at either store.
   No limitations.

   Pet Paradise
9001 Parkway Boulevard
Austin, TX 78711


 Pet Paradise II
7922 Pendleton Way
Austin, TX 78745
```

You've created the styles and saved them in a style document. Then you retrieved the styles and used them to create a newsletter. Any style can be edited by highlighting the style to edit and clicking the Edit button in the Style List. If you edit styles, be sure to save them again after editing.

# Internet Publisher

Most documents published on the Internet are written in HyperText Markup Language (HTML). The Corel WordPerfect Internet Publisher automatically converts WordPerfect formatting into HTML format, so you don't need to know HTML to create Web documents. You can create a Web document using the Corel WordPerfect Internet Publisher, or you can format an existing document as a Web document. If you convert, Corel WordPerfect codes that have no HTML equivalents are modified or deleted.

We'll begin by creating the first three of five pages for a Pet Paradise home page. Then we'll link the pages.

# EXERCISE ⟹ WP9.12

**1.** Beginning in a new document window, open the **File** menu and choose **New**. Be sure **Corel WordPerfect 8** is selected in the box at the top of the list. Then choose **[WordPerfect Web Document]** from near the top. Click **Create**.

**2.** A gray window will appear with the Perfect-Expert panel at the left. Look at the Toolbar and the Property Bar (see Figure 9-10).

**3.** Click the **Justification** button on the Power Bar and choose **Center** justification. Change to the **Arial** font face.

**4.** Click the **Font/Size** button on the Property Bar and choose **Heading 1**. Key **Pet Paradise**.

**5.** Press **Enter**, click the **Font/Size** button, choose **heading 4**, and key **One-stop shopping for all of your pet needs**. Press **Enter**.

**6.** Click the **Extras** button on the PerfectExpert panel and add a horizontal line. Press **Enter** and change to Left justification.

**7.** Click the **Font/Size** button, choose **Bullet List**, and key the following four items in the list: **Grooming, Boarding, Obedience training, Pets and pet supplies**.

**8.** Press **Enter** and backspace to delete the bullet. Key **Serving you from two convenient Austin locations:**.

**9.** Press **Enter** and change to **Right** justification. Key the text in Figure 9-11 on three separate lines.

**10.** Insert the **logo.wpd** graphics image in the upper right corner. Size it to about **3"** and change the position to **Paragraph** so you can adjust its position.

**11.** Click the **Change Background** button on the PerfectExpert panel and choose a background that appeals to you and isn't too hard to read. Save your first Web page with your solutions as **web1 xxx (a:\web1 xxx)**.

**FIGURE 9-10**
Internet Publisher Toolbar and Property Bar

**FIGURE 9-11**
Text for Step 9 of Exercise WP9.12

```
29001 Parkway Boulevard (call 512-555-5455)
7922 Pendleton Way (call 512-555-8712)
6 a.m. to 9 p.m. daily
```

## Animated Graphics

Animated graphics add fun to your Web pages. If you have access to the World Wide Web, you have access to dozens of animated graphics. When you put an animated graphic into your document, it won't move unless you have a Web browser. You can access the browser by choosing the Finish button on the PerfectExpert panel. This doesn't dial you into the Internet, but it opens the browser window so you can see your graphics in action. If you don't have a browser, your animated image will just sit there. Five animated graphics are in the student **Datafile** folder for you: **cateyes.gif**, **whats_new.gif**, **kitten.gif**, **newmove.gif**, and **dogrun.gif**. You can use them as you wish. When you use a *.gif* graphic, it does not become part of the document. Instead, a link is created between the location of the graphic on disk and the document where you are using it. Keep that in mind when you take your Web pages to a different computer.

Now let's create two more Web pages and utilize some of the tools on the Toolbar and Property Bar. We'll also use a different method of starting the page and insert an animated graphics image.

## EXERCISE ⟹ WP9.13

1. Open the **File** menu and choose **Internet Publisher**. Then click **New Web Document** and **Select**. Click the **PerfectExpert** button on the Toolbar.

2. Change to **Heading 1** and key **Grooming**. At the right of that, insert **dogrun.gif** from the student **Datafile** folder. It is a tiny dog that may run in a Web browser. Deselect the image.

3. Insert a horizontal line and include the text in Figure 9-12. You may include the Pet Paradise logo on the page if you like.

4. Use **Center** justification for **Contents Page** at the bottom. When you finish, save the page as **web2 xxx**.

5. Click the **Change View** button on the Toolbar to see what your document would look like as a WordPerfect document. Then close the file without saving it again.

**FIGURE 9-12**
Text for **web2 xxx**

---

Pet Paradise has long been known for quality grooming. We offer trimming to breed standards or to your request. With every grooming, your pet receives additional services:

• Nail trimming
• Ear cleaning
• Bathing and fluff drying

After 15 years of experience, we feel confident that we can please you. In fact, our grooming is satisfaction guaranteed.

                    Contents Page

---

(continued on next page)

**6.** Create **web3 xxx**. Entitle it **Boarding** and make it look much like **web2 xxx**. For this one, include the text in Figure 9-13. You may choose any of the graphics images in your student **Datafile** folder. Perhaps you have a different source of graphics.

**7.** When you finish, save your document and close all documents.

**FIGURE 9-13**
Text for **web3 xxx**

We specialize in providing the healthiest, most comfortable environment for your pet.

Services:
• Personal playtime
• Personal belongings
• Individualized feeding program
• Proper diet
• Special medications
• Monitoring

Our boarding fees are comparable with other quality boarding facilities. We accept cash, checks, MasterCard and Visa. Owners who pick up their pets before noon will not be charged for that day.

Contents Page

This home page needs two more pages—*Pets and pet supplies* and *Obedience training*. Instead of working with those now, we'll link the pages you've already created so they work the way they would work if they were on the Web.

## Hypertext Link

To link the pages, they must always be in the same location. In other words, the link you create will only be good as long as WordPerfect can find your files. We'll link them in both directions. Follow along.

EXERCISE ▷ **WP9.14**

SCANS

**1.** Open **web1 xxx**. Click the **PerfectExpert** button on the Toolbar to display the PerfectExpert panel.

**2.** Select *Grooming*. Click the **Add a Hyperlink** button on the PerfectExpert panel.

**3.** Click the file folder button beside the *Document* text box and locate **web2 xxx**. Select that file and click **OK**. When you return to your Web page, *Grooming* should be displayed in a contrasting color, indicating that it has a hypertext link.

4. Repeat the process in Steps 2 and 3 to link *Boarding* to **web3 xxx**. Save **web1 xxx** again and close it.

5. Open **web2 xxx**. Select *Contents Page* at the bottom. Create a hyperlink that links those words with **web 1 xxx**. Save **web2 xxx** and close it. Repeat the process with **web3**, linking *Contents Page* with **web1**. Close **web3**, saving again.

6. Open **web1 xxx**. Click **Grooming**. It should take you directly to **web2 xxx**. Click **Contents Page** at the bottom of **web2 xxx**. You should be returned to **web1 xxx**.

7. Close all files without saving again. Open your list of solutions. Click **web1 xxx** to highlight it. Hold **Shift** while you click **web3 xxx**. Open the **File** menu in the Open File dialog box and choose **Print** to send all three files to the printer.

As you can see, creating a Web page using the WordPerfect Internet Publisher is not difficult. WordPerfect has taken the pain of HTML formatting out of the task. As the Internet becomes a more important part of our communications system, you are certain to find this feature useful.

# Summary

This short lesson includes some valuable tools for the serious WordPerfect user. You learned that:

- the WordPerfect Address Book is a powerful tool that enables you to keep track of the critical information about all of your contacts.

- PerfectExpert provides yet another tool to guide you through the job of creating and formatting documents.

- styles can be used to give consistency to repeated tasks.

- WordPerfect has provided you with a number of preformatted templates. You can create your own templates, if you wish.

- WordPerfect's Internet Publisher takes the pain out of preparing a Web document.

## LESSON 9 REVIEW QUESTIONS

### FILL IN THE BLANKS

**Complete each of the following statements by writing your answer(s) in the blank(s) provided.**

1. When you wish to create a new keyboard, you must open the _____ menu and choose _____.

2. To save an Address Book on a disk, you must open the _____ menu in the Address Book dialog box and choose _____.

(continued on next page)

3. To retrieve an Address Book from a disk, you must open the _____ menu in the Address Book and choose _____.

4. The programming language used for documents on the Internet is _____.

## WRITTEN QUESTIONS

**Write your answers to the following questions.**

5. Why do you need to save the styles you prepare before closing a document that uses the styles?

6. Why did you delete your German keyboard when you had finished the letter?

7. What must you first do in the Address Book before importing a new Address Book from a disk?

8. What can you do if the entries in the Address Book don't show the field of information you'd like displayed?

9. What is PerfectExpert?

10. Open the Help topics and key **PerfectExpert**. Go to the section about *Add a project*. How and where are predefined projects stored?

## LESSON 9 PROJECT

SCANS

Listed below are several projects from which you may choose. Read through all of the parts of each project so you can choose one that is truly meaningful to you.

## PROJECT 9A

### Address Book

1. Create an Address Book containing names and addresses of a group to which you belong or your friends and relatives. Add custom fields, if necessary. Enter at least 15 entries.

2. When you have the information in the Address Book, sort the entries by last name.

3. Create a form document similar to **cust form 7-6 xxx** (see Figure 7-11) that includes FIELD codes for all of the information about the people in your Address Book. Merge the form document with the Address Book so each page is filled with entries. Save the merged document and identify it with your **pf** macro. Print the file.

4. Export your Address Book to your disk and delete it from the computer.

## PROJECT 9B

**Keyboard Mapping**

1.  Create a custom keyboard for special characters in a language that you have learned. Name the keyboard with YOUR name.

2.  Key a letter or translate any two paragraphs from your solution files or from this textbook into that language, using the mapped keyboard.

3.  Save the completed translation and identify it with the **pf** macro. Print the file.

4.  Ask your instructor if you should delete the custom keyboard or if you may leave it on the computer for possible future use.

## PROJECT 9C

**Styles**

1.  Create at least two styles for a newsletter or other kind of document that requires formatting that you would like to prepare on a regular basis.

2.  Prepare a copy of the document using the styles. On the back of the document, list the names of the styles and briefly describe what each style does.

3.  Give your styles names and save them on your disk to be reused in a future document.

## CRITICAL THINKING ACTIVITY

SCANS

You have recently gone on-line and have access to the Internet. One of the services you are using frequently is e-mail. What WordPerfect feature could be used to enhance your use of e-mail?

# LONG DOCUMENT TOOLS

## OBJECTIVES

**Upon completion of this lesson, you will be able to:**

- Mark the text for a table of contents and generate the table.

- Work with hypertext references.

- Create a concordance file.

- Generate an index.

- Work with line numbering in your documents.

- Discuss the preparation of a table of authorities.

- Discuss the generation of lists and the use of Cross-Reference.

- Create, expand, and condense a master document.

- Determine the differences between two documents with the Compare Document feature.

- Mark text for editing with Redline and Strikeout.

- Insert a comment into your document.

⏱ **Estimated Time: 2 hours**

You learned in Lesson 4 that WordPerfect features such as headers, footers, and page numbering tie multiple-page documents together and give them continuity. Those tools are good for multiple-page documents of any length.

WordPerfect also has some additional features that help you keep track of VERY large documents—documents that could be hundreds of pages long. Let's learn about some of them.

# *Table of Contents*

A table of contents is a listing of the major topics in a document, along with the page numbers where those topics begin. The table of contents always appears at the beginning of a document, and the topics are listed in the order in which they are included in the document.

Take a moment now and look at the table of contents at the beginning of this book—the one from which you are reading. Note that the table of contents in this book consists of two levels—Level 1 lists the lessons, and Level 2 lists the main sections within the lessons.

In order for WordPerfect to know what to include in the table of contents, you must *mark the text*. Marking the text includes selecting the word or words to be in the table of contents and coding that text, including the level number for the text. In a long document, coding all of the text for the table of contents may seem to be a time-consuming and tedious job. The benefit comes when you edit the document and move sections of text around. WordPerfect will still be able to generate an accurate table of contents.

## EXERCISE WP10.1

1. Beginning in a new document window, go to the student **Datafile** folder and open **toc**. Save the file as **contents 10-1 xxx** and play your **pf** macro.

2. Select the first side heading (*Boarding*). Open the **Tools** menu and choose **Reference**. Then choose **Table of Contents**. The Table of Contents Feature Bar will appear at the top of your working window (see Figure 10-1).

3. Click the **Mark 1** button to mark the selected text as a Level 1 heading for the table of contents.

4. Select the next side heading—*Pet Store*. Mark the text in the same way.

5. Continue through the document, marking each of the remaining four side headings for Level 1. Save the document again and keep it open as you read on.

**FIGURE 10-1**
Table of Contents Feature Bar

Now let's add a page at the beginning of the document for the table of contents.

1. Save **contents 10-1 xxx** as **contents 10-2 xxx**. Press **Ctrl+Home** twice to move your insertion point above all codes on the first page.

2. Add a hard page break and move your insertion point to the new first page. Use **Advance** to tell WordPerfect to begin **2.5"** from the top of the page. Center **Table of Contents** and format the text with bold and a font size of 16 pt.

3. Press **Enter** three times. Click the **Define** button on the Table of Contents Feature Bar. Look at the dialog box. Note that if you change the number of levels at the top, WordPerfect gives you a choice regarding how those levels will be formatted.

4. Everything in this dialog box is fine. Click **OK**. A *<< Table of Contents will generate here >>* code will be inserted where the table of contents is to begin.

5. Click the **Generate** button on the Feature Bar. Note that a variety of lists will be generated, providing the text is marked for those lists. Deselect the check boxes of both options. Then click **OK**.

6. Look at your completed table of contents. Note that the page numbers are wrong—they begin with page 2. The first page of text should be page 1. Do you remember what code you used in Lesson 4 to solve a problem such as this?

7. If you said *Delay Codes*, you were right. Position your insertion point at the top of the table of contents page. Go to **Delay Codes**, tell WordPerfect to delay one page and leave page numbering at bottom center, but set the Value at **1**.

8. Return to your document and generate the table of contents again. Does the numbering begin with page 1? It should. If not, work your way through Delay Codes again. Think!

9. Print only the table of contents page. Save the document again as **contents 10-2 xxx**, and keep it open.

# *Hypertext Links*

One of the options available when you generate your table of contents is to build hypertext links from the page number in the table of contents to the topic in the document. When you do this, the page numbers in the table of contents will be in a contrasting color, telling you they are hypertext links. If you click one of those page numbers, WordPerfect will take you directly to the location of that topic.

**INTERNET** A Uniform Resource Locator (URL) is an address code for finding hypertext or hypermedia documents on World Wide Web (WWW) servers around the world. URLs can be accessed by WWW browsers.

## EXERCISE ⟹ WP10.3

**1.** With **contents 10-2 xxx** open, save the file as **contents 10-3 xxx**. Click the **Generate** button on the Table of Contents Feature Bar. Click the check box for **Build hypertext links**. Then click **OK**.

**2.** When the table of contents has generated, click the page number for *Tours*. Did WordPerfect take you to the *Tours* section?

**3.** Select the *Tours* side heading and the short paragraph following it. Move that entire section of text to page 1, just above *Boarding*.

**4.** Generate your table of contents again, this time without hypertext links. Check the page numbers. Did WordPerfect adjust the numbers for the new location of the document parts?

**5.** Print the table of contents page only. Then save the document again as **contents 10-3 xxx**. Keep it open.

### TIP

When you move text that has been formatted with QuickFormat, you sometimes get into trouble with the formatting. When that happens, remove all of the formatting from the affected area and, if necessary, use QuickFormat to reformat the side heading.

# *Line Numbering*

When a long document is going to be discussed in an office, it is often helpful to have the lines numbered. WordPerfect will put line numbers in the left margin of a document. When the document has been discussed and the numbers are no longer needed, it is simple to remove the [Ln Num] code from the document to deselect the option.

### QuickSteps

**Line Numbering**
1. Position the insertion point at the beginning of the document.
2. Choose Line from the Format menu.
3. Choose Numbering.
4. Set options and click the check box.

1. With **contents 10-3 xxx** open in the window, save the document as **numbers 10-4 xxx**. Position your insertion point at the beginning of the first page of text.

2. Open the **Format** menu, choose **Line**, and choose **Numbering**. The dialog box should look much like Figure 10-2.

3. In the upper left corner, click the check box for **Turn line numbering on**. Look at the other options. The default settings are fine. Click **OK**.

4. Back in your document, note that numbering starts on each page. That is one of the settings in the dialog box. (If you want continuous numbering, you would deselect that option.)

5. Note that every line is numbered up to the double spacing code. Then only the lines with text are numbered.

**FIGURE 10-2**
Line Numbering Dialog Box

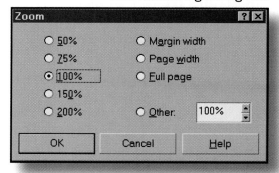

TIP

Depending on the size of your monitor, you may not be able to see items in the margins. Use Zoom when this occurs.

6. Go to page 2. Print that page. Close your document, saving it again as **numbers 10-4 xxx**.

# *Index*

An index is an alphabetic listing of words and terms together with the page numbers on which those words and terms are mentioned. Turn to the index at the back of this textbook and look at the entries. Note that some could be considered *headings* and others could be considered *subheadings*. In this lesson you will work only with headings.

Like the table of contents, an index may be generated after the text has been marked. Marking text for an index is much more tedious than for a table of contents, because an index lists the page number for each time the word or phrase is mentioned in the text.

Because marking the text for an index is so difficult, WordPerfect has provided a better way. You can prepare a list of the words and terms you want to appear in the index, alphabetize the list, save it, and tell WordPerfect to use that list to find the references and create your index. The list of terms for an index is called a *concordance file*. Let's begin by preparing the concordance file. Then we'll format the index page and generate the index.

EXERCISE ⟹ **WP10.5**

1. Beginning in a new document window, key the words in Figure 10-3 in a single list at the left margin. Use **Sort** to alphabetize the list and save it with your files as **concord**. (You can use any name you wish.) Close the file.

**FIGURE 10-3**
Concordance Terms

| | |
|---|---|
| training | obedience |
| bath | atrium |
| classes | toy |
| satisfaction | pet store |
| boarding | tours |
| grooming | breeds |
| convenience | health |
| feeding | visit |
| kennel | |

2. Open **contents 10-3 xxx**. Save the file as **index 10-5 xxx**.

3. Create a new page at the end of the document. Use **Advance** to position the insertion point about **1.5"** from the top of the page. Change to single spacing. Center **INDEX** in Bold, capital letters. Press **Enter** three times.

4. Open the **Tools** menu and choose **Reference**. Then choose **Index**. The Index Feature Bar will appear (see Figure 10-4).

5. Note the section at the left where you can designate the headings and subheadings. For now, click the **Define** button.

6. Click the folder button beside the *Concordance file* box at the bottom of the dialog box. Identify your **concord** document as the concordance file.

**TIP**

Even though you know the name of the concordance file needed in this situation, it is better to go to the Select File dialog box. When you do that, you are certain that the file path and spelling of the document name are both correct.

7. Click the arrow beside the *Position* box and choose the last style (*Text, #*). Then click **OK**. *<< Index will generate here >>* will be inserted in your document.

8. Click the **Generate** button on the Feature Bar. Click **OK** in the Generate dialog box. Your index should appear, listing the words from your concordance file along with the page numbers where those words are mentioned.

9. Print only the index page. Then save your file again as **index 10-5 xxx**. Close it.

**FIGURE 10-4**
Index Feature Bar

# *Table of Authorities*

A table of authorities is a legal document that lists all references cited in a legal document and identifies the position of each reference in a document by page number. The references might be to other cases, statutes, laws, or other sources. The completed table of authorities resembles a table of contents.

Figure 10-5 illustrates a possible table of authorities. Note that the references are divided into sections by type. A case or statute might be referred to several times in a legal document. The entire case or statute should appear only once in the table of authorities. So when you are marking the text, you must specify that the first time a reference is mentioned, it is called a *full form* reference. When the reference is marked the second and following times, it is marked as a *short form* reference. Only the page numbers are listed for short form references.

**FIGURE 10-5**
Sample Table of Authorities

---

**TABLE OF AUTHORITIES**

**CASES**

Becton Dickinson & Co. v. C.R. Bard, Inc., 922 F.2d 792, 795-96
(Fed.Cir. 990) . . . . . . . . . . . . . . . . . . . . . . . . . . . . . . . . . . . . . . . . . . . 2, 7

Johnston v. IVAC Corp., 885 F.2d 1574, 1577, 12 USPQ2d 1382, 184
(Fed.Cir. 1989) . . . . . . . . . . . . . . . . . . . . . . . . . . . . . . . . . . . . . . . . . . 2, 4

**STATUTES**

15 U.S.C. § 1125(a) (1982) . . . . . . . . . . . . . . . . . . . . . . . . . . . . . . . . . . 1

Lanham Act § 43(a) . . . . . . . . . . . . . . . . . . . . . . . . . . . . . . . . . . . . . . 1, 3

---

You will not prepare a table of authorities in this practice. If you should need this feature, Help will give you the information you need to mark your text and prepare the table.

# *Lists and Cross-Reference*

You may have noticed some other items in the *Reference* portion of the Tools menu. In addition to tables of contents and authorities, WordPerfect will keep track of other kinds of lists for you. For example, you can mark figures, illustrations, and graphics boxes to be listed at the beginning or end of a document. The procedure is the same—mark the item, define the location for the list, and generate the list. Help for this feature is included under *generate*.

The Cross-Reference feature also deserves mention. You can include hypertext links between parts of a document with Cross-Reference. The hypertext link you used with your table of contents was a one-way link. The hypertext link you used for your Web pages was a two-way link. You can use two-way links in regular documents, too. This feature isn't used much for documents that are to be printed. It is a great help when you are studying a document on the computer and you want to go to a figure, for example, to study it and then jump back to your original location. The Help utility provides specific instructions for setting up Cross-Reference links, in case you wish to explore this topic on your own.

# Master Document

When working with very long documents, you can break them into smaller parts called *subdocuments*. When you are ready to apply consecutive page numbering or generate a table of contents, you will create a *master document* which contains codes naming the documents to be included. To display the entire document, the subdocuments must be *expanded*. (You have the choice of expanding some or all of the subdocuments.) You may edit the subdocuments when the master document is expanded.

Before saving the master document, you should *condense* it so space isn't wasted on your disk with duplicate copies of the subdocuments. At the time you condense, you have the option of saving all or none of the subdocuments. You can then save the condensed master document, which simply contains the codes.

It's really not as complicated as it sounds. Let's prepare the files for a master document exercise. Then we'll work with a master document.

## EXERCISE ⟹ WP10.6

1. Beginning in a new document window, go to the student **Datafile** folder. Click to select **corel1**. Hold the **Shift** key while you click **corel6**. Click the **Open** button.

2. All six files should open into your window. Use **Save As** to save each of the files with your solutions. When you save them, put a space between *corel* and the numeral so you know you're working with the files from your folder or disk.

3. When each file has been saved with your work with the new name, close all six files and read on.

## EXERCISE ⟹ WP10.7

1. Beginning in a new document window, create a title page. Use the following features:
   a. Use the **Center Page** command to center your text vertically.
   b. Use **Center** to center each of the lines in Figure 10-6.
   c. After inserting each ® symbol, select the symbol, go to the Font dialog box, and choose **Superscript** to raise the symbols and make them a little smaller.

(continued on next page)

**d.** Format the title page so it has a professional appearance.

**2.** Save your title page as **master 10-7 xxx**. Play your **pf** macro and save the file again.

**3.** Add a hard page break at the bottom of the page. Open the **File** menu, choose **Document**, and choose **Subdocument**. WordPerfect will take you to the Include Subdocument dialog box, which looks like the Open File dialog box.

**4.** Go to your solutions and choose **corel 1**. When you are returned to your document, the page will look empty. That's OK. After inserting the file, press **Ctrl+Enter** for a hard page break.

**5.** Follow Steps 3 and 4 to insert the remaining *corel* files (**corel 2** through **corel 6**), with hard page breaks between each of them.

**6.** Go to the top of any of the pages and find the subdocument icon in the left margin. Click the icon to see the subdocument comment.

**7.** Open the **View** menu and change to **Draft** view. Here you can see the subdocument codes and the hard page breaks. Your window will look much like Figure 10-7.

**8.** Save the file again as **master 10-7 xxx**. Change back to **Page** view and keep the document open.

**FIGURE 10-7**
Subdocuments

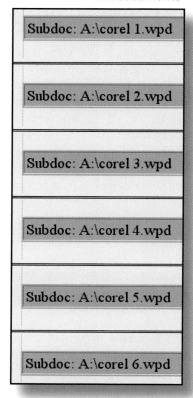

**FIGURE 10-6**
Text for Title Page

```
Corel® WordPerfect® Suite 8

A great way to do your work!

             By
       Student Name

       Current Date
```

Now that the master document has been created, you can expand the master document to see all files.

# EXERCISE ➤ WP10.8

1. With **master 10-7 xxx** open, save the file as **master 10-8 xxx**. Open the **File** menu, choose **Document**, and choose **Expand Master**. A dialog box will give you the opportunity to deselect files you don't want to open. Click **OK**.

2. Position your insertion point at the beginning of the first paragraph of **corel 1**.

3. Change to **Full** justification.

4. Go to the last page. In the first line, insert the words **World Wide** just to the left of *Web*.

5. Go to the **corel 2** page and insert a header. It should say **Corel WordPerfect Suite 8** at the left and the page number at the right. Format the entire header with italic.

6. Did you notice that the page number on the second page of text was *3*? Go to the title page and use **Delay Codes** to fix that problem. Look through your document to make sure the page numbers are correct.

### TIP

When you put the header on the second page, you don't have to worry about Suppress because the header will format forward from where it is inserted. However, most users prefer to have all of the codes together on the first page of a document.

7. Open the **File** menu, choose **Document**, and choose **Condense Master**. The dialog box in Figure 10-8 will appear, asking if you wish to save and condense all files. Click **OK**.

8. Save your master document again as **master 10-8 xxx**. Close the file.

**FIGURE 10-8**
Condense/Save Subdocument Dialog Box

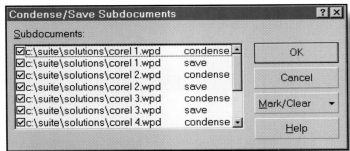

If you try to save an expanded master document before condensing, WordPerfect will ask if you'd like the document condensed and the subdocuments saved. When you respond affirmatively, the document will be condensed and everything will be saved. All that will remain will be the parts that belong to the master document itself—the title page, table of contents, pages with subdocument codes, and index.

If any of your subdocuments are more than a page in length (and in real life they would always be lengthy documents), the condensed master document only shows one page per subdocument. In other words, the index of a condensed master document might be on page 6, but in the expanded master document the index might be on page 632. On the other hand, you don't have to have a master document expanded to generate the table of contents or index. WordPerfect can go out to the files on the disk to find the information needed to generate.

# Compare Document

WordPerfect will compare a document you have open in the window with a document on disk to see what differences exist between the two documents. When it does this, it will show new text in red and deleted text in Strikeout (with a line through the words). Let's try it.

## EXERCISE ⟹ WP10.9

1. Go to your **lessons 1-5** folder and locate **sale memo 2-14 xxx**. Open the file and save it as **sale memo 10-9 xxx**. Play your **pf** macro.

2. Open the **File** menu and choose **Document**. Near the bottom is the **Add Compare Markings** choice. Choose it to reveal the Add Compare Markings dialog box.

3. The document to which you'd like the current document compared needs to be selected in the text box at the top. Click the arrow beside the box and go to the student **Datafile** folder. Choose **sale memo**.

4. Be sure that the documents will be compared by *word*. Then click **OK**. Your document will appear with red text (the new material) and Strikeout text (the old material).

5. Save the file again with the same name. Print it to see how Redline and Strikeout look when printed. Close the document.

# Redline and Strikeout

The Redline and Strikeout you saw in Exercise WP10.8 can be added to a document manually. You might do this when you are looking for approvals of edits to a document. Begin with an original document and make corrections, adding Redline to text to be added and Strikeout to text to be deleted (so other people know exactly what changes you are proposing). After the document is discussed, one step will remove all Strikeout text and all Redline markings. Let's try this feature.

**TIP**

When working with Redline and Strikeout, display the Legal Toolbar. It saves you from having to go to the Font dialog box to choose Redline and Strikeout.

# EXERCISE ⟶ WP10.10

1. Beginning in a new document window, go to the student **Datafile** folder and open **teeth**. Save the file as **teeth 10-10 xxx**. Play your **pf** macro and save it again.

2. Look at Figure 10-9. It shows the same document with added text in red (Redline) and text to be removed with a line drawn through it (Strikeout).

3. Point to the Toolbar and right click. From the list of available Toolbars, choose **Legal**. Look at the Redline and Strikeout buttons. They are a little difficult to distinguish. Redline is at the left. Strikeout is at the right.

4. Select *furry* in the first line. With the word selected, click the **Strikeout** button on the Legal Toolbar. Position your insertion point at the left of the word *feel*. Click the **Redline** button on the Legal Toolbar and key **look and**.

5. Continue through the document, marking the appropriate text with Strikeout and Redline.

6. When you finish, save your file again.

7. Now we'll assume all of your changes have been approved except the two in the final line. Reveal your codes and remove the word *can*, along with the [Redln] and [StkOut] codes.

8. Open the **File** menu, choose **Document**, and choose **Remove Compare Markings**. The first option should be chosen. Click **OK**.

9. Compare your document again with Figure 10-9. Did WordPerfect do a good job of fixing your text? Save the file one more time. Then print it and close it. Deselect the Legal Toolbar.

**FIGURE 10-9**
Text with Redline and Strikeout

Imagine how ~~furry~~ your teeth would look and feel if you didn't brush them ~~on a daily basis~~routinely.  Imagine what it would be like if you never brushed them~~ at all~~.  The same applies to your pet's teeth. Unless you are regularly providing some form of dental care~~ on a regular basis~~, you are neglecting an important part in the health of your pet.

Gum disease (periodontal disease) is one of the most common problems seen by veterinarians.  Periodontal disease is known as the "silent disease" because of its progressive nature.  Besides bad breath, gum disease can lead to loss of appetite, weight loss, serious generalized infections, ~~bad temper,~~ and even heart and kidney disease.

The problem occurs when plaque and tartar are allowed to build up on a pet's teeth.  Plaque harbors the bacteria which can lead~~s~~ to infection.

# Comment

When you were working in Page view with the master document, you may remember that an icon appeared in the left margin opposite the subdocument codes. WordPerfect uses the left margin for a variety of codes. For example, one of the outlining edit features includes numerals in the left margin. Another example is the Tab Bar icon that shows you where you have tab set changes.

WordPerfect allows you to put a nonprinting comment into a document. When a document has a comment, a comment icon appears in the left margin. Comments are used to remind yourself or someone else of something that must be done. If you wish, the comment can be changed to text. Usually it is just a reminder.

## E X E R C I S E ▷ WP10.11

1. Beginning in a new document window, open **master 10-8 xxx**. Save the file as **comment 10-11 xxx**.

2. With your insertion point at the beginning of the text on the title page, open the **Insert** menu and choose **Comment**. Choose **Create**. You will be taken to a special comment window, complete with special tools on the Property Bar. Check out the tools.

3. Key the text in Figure 10-10. When you finish, click the **Close** button at the far right of the Property Bar.

4. Back in your document window, look at the icon in the left margin. Point to the icon and click to read the comment. Change to **Draft** view to see the comment.

5. Change back to **Page** view. Close the document, saving it again as **comment 10-11 xxx**.

**FIGURE 10-10**
Text for Title Page

```
This is a master document. It
must be expanded before you can
work on the text.
```

# Summary

This lesson contains a strange but useful group of features: comments, comparing documents, master documents, tables of contents and authorities. While these features are certainly not used by every user of WordPerfect, for those who need them, they are valuable tools. You learned quite a few tricks. You learned that:

■ WordPerfect provides a tool that makes it easy for you to mark text for a table of contents.

■ when you generate your tables of contents, you can tell WordPerfect to make the page numbers hypertext links.

■ a concordance file is a great help in creating an index.

■ WordPerfect will number your lines for making it easy to locate specific text when discussing a document with others.

- you can create lists, Cross-References, and tables of authorities to help readers of your documents.

- the master document is a shell that contains the names of a number of subdocuments.

- Compare Document helps identify the differences between documents.

- Redline and Strikeout can be used to mark text that is to be deleted or added.

- document comments serve as reminders to help you with your work.

## LESSON 10 REVIEW QUESTIONS

### FILL IN THE BLANKS

**Complete each of the following statements by writing your answer in the blank provided.**

1. The file that contains the words to be included in an index is known as a _____ file.

2. The _____ Property Bar contains the tools needed to mark text for a table of contents.

3. When you are generating a table of contents, you can create a _____ link that will jump you to a different area of the document.

4. When you wish to work on the individual subdocuments of a master document, you must first _____ the master document.

5. Master Document tools and Compare tools are chosen from the _____ menu.

### WRITTEN QUESTIONS

**Write your answers to the following questions.**

6. Briefly describe the difference between a table of contents and a table of authorities.

7. What are some of the ways that an index is different from a table of contents?

8. What tool can you use to make marking text with Redline and Strikeout less cumbersome?

9. Why might you choose to use line numbering in a document?

10. How do you tell WordPerfect that you'd like the numbers in a table of contents to be hypertext links?

SCANS

## PROJECT 10A

Open **master 10-8 xxx**. Save it as **master proj10 xxx**. Add a table of contents and index to this document as follows:

1.  Expand all subdocuments of the master document.

2.  Mark the text for a table of contents. Use Level 1 for all markings. For the first page, use the second line of the title. For the remaining pages, use the bold heading at the beginning of each paragraph.

3.  Insert a page between the title page and the first page of text. Format it for the table of contents. Define the table of contents on that page.

4.  At the top of the title page, redo the Delay Codes code so it waits two pages before beginning page numbering.

5.  Select at least ten words from the paragraphs to include in a concordance file for the index. Create and alphabetize that list. Save the concordance file as **proj concord**.

6.  Create a page at the end of the document for an index. Change to single spacing. Format the page and define the index, being sure to include the name of the concordance file in the definition dialog box.

7.  Generate both the table of contents and the index. Do not use hypertext links. Print the table of contents page and the index page. Condense the master document, saving all subdocuments.

8.  Close the master document, saving it again as **master proj10 xxx** as you close it.

## PROJECT 10B

Since you are finished with this phase of your training, you need to make room on your disk for the next work. In this exercise you will create a **lessons 6-10** folder and move the files you'll keep. Then you'll delete the remaining files.

1.  Display your Open File dialog box with your practice files showing. Open the **File** menu and click **New**. Name the new folder **lessons 6-10**.

2.  Hold the **Ctrl** key while you select the files in Figure 10-11. Drag them to the **lessons 6-10** folder. (When the folder turns blue, you have the correct one selected and you can release the mouse button.)

3. Then sort through the remaining files. Keep macros (with *.wcm* extensions), styles (with *.sty* extensions), and any other files you might have created in projects that you'd like to keep. Select and delete the remaining files.

**FIGURE 10-11**
Move to **lessons 6-10**

| | | | |
|---|---|---|---|
| arrow 8-3 | corel 5 | master 10-8 | sort 7-11 |
| board 6-10 | corel 6 | master proj10 | Spring News 9-11 |
| bones 6-4 | cust form 7-6 | message 6-11 | terrier 7-13 |
| concord | cust form 7-8 | newsletter styles | web1 |
| corel 1 | data proj7 | open 7-2 | web2 |
| corel 2 | groom 6-6 | proj concord | web3 |
| corel 3 | index 10-5 | refer form 7-9 | |
| corel 4 | lines 8-10 | rose 8-6 | |

## CRITICAL THINKING ACTIVITY

SCANS

You have just finished marking your text for the table of contents, added a new page with a title, and defined your table of contents. You click OK and return to your document. A code appears in your document, but your table of contents does not appear. What is wrong?

# INTRODUCTION TO INTEGRATION

## OBJECTIVES

**Upon completion of Integration 1, you will be able to:**

■ Integrate parts of WordPerfect documents.

■ Discuss ways of integrating text with other suite applications.

■ Integrate WordPerfect features to prepare marketing documents.

*Estimated Time: 3 hours*

# *Introduction*

Corel WordPerfect Suite 8 is a collection of applications that are designed to work together—they are integrated. Each of the applications has many capabilities. Sometimes the capabilities in an application overlap the same capabilities in a different application. For example, in WordPerfect, you learned to create a table and perform calculations in that table. You learned that a spreadsheet program, such as Quattro Pro, has even greater calculation capabilities. In the same way, you learned to create a database (the data file) in WordPerfect. Paradox is a relational database that does the same and much more.

After you have learned to use Quattro Pro, you will learn how WordPerfect and Quattro Pro can be integrated so you can use spreadsheets in your word processing documents. After you've learned Presentations and Paradox, you'll integrate those programs with WordPerfect and Quattro Pro. You'll be pleased to learn that moving from one application to another is easy. It is also easy to move data and text between applications. In this section you'll have an opportunity to integrate the skills you acquired in the WordPerfect lessons to create some great documents.

## Disk Storage

If you have been saving your work on a disk in Drive A, you should either delete all files (except the **pf** macro) from your WordPerfect training or use a new disk for the integration activities. If you use a new disk, copy the **pf** macro to that disk so it is available to identify your work. Either way, label the disk **Integration 1**. You will need several disks for your integration sections.

# *Theme*

Paul and Polly Paradeis of Pet Paradise and Pet Paradise II have just announced to their employees that the empty half of the Pet Paradise building has been rented by Paul's brother, Glen. Glen has just graduated from veterinary college and is opening a veterinary clinic in Austin. He will specialize in companion animals—mostly dogs and cats. Paul and Polly have agreed to help Glen get started. In addition to helping with the location for the clinic, they will share the names of their customers who have dogs and cats.

Many things must be done to start a veterinary practice. In addition to outfitting the clinic, forms must be designed and advertising is imperative. Your boss, Polly, has offered your services to use your WordPerfect skills to design forms, including letterheads, business cards, and some advertising pieces. In doing so, you'll be integrating your WordPerfect skills with more WordPerfect skills, putting the tools together to create the forms.

# Letterhead

We'll begin with a letterhead style document, containing two styles for clinic letters. When you finish, the letterhead will look much like the miniature in Figure INT1-1.

**FIGURE INT1-1**
Clinic Letterhead

## EXERCISE ▷ INT1.1

SCANS

1. Start WordPerfect. Beginning in a new document window, change the top margin to **0.75"**. Play your **pf** macro to put the Path and Filename code in a footer. (Because the document hasn't been saved, an empty footer box will appear at the bottom of the document.)

2. Go to TextArt to insert the company name.
   a. Key **Parkway Animal Clinic**.
   b. Choose the first shape—square.
   c. Choose a bold sans serif font.

   d. Choose **Center** justification.
   e. Click the **2D Options** tab and choose **Text Color**. Choose a medium gray text color— the ninth choice from the left is a good one.
   f. Set the outline color at **black** and choose the first outline (thin).
   g. Deselect any pattern or shadow and click **Close**.

3. With the TextArt object chosen, resize the height of the object at **0.5"**.

4. Press **Enter** and insert a horizontal line.
   a. Move the line above the TextArt object.
   b. Create another horizontal line and leave it below the TextArt object.
   c. Adjust these lines so they are an equal distance from the top and bottom of the TextArt object.

5. Press **Enter** to position the insertion point below the second line to insert the address.
   a. Change the font to the same bold font face you used for the clinic name.
   b. Change to **16** pt. and **dark gray**.

c. Center the following address on one line, putting a space, symbol 5,1, and a space between address parts as shown:
   **9003 Parkway Boulevard** ◇ **Austin, TX 78711** ◇ **512-555-6886**

6. Press **Enter** two times and change to **12-pt. Times New Roman**. Change the text color to **black**. Your letterhead should look much like Figure INT1-1.

7. Keep the document open in the window.

Now that the letterhead is created, we'll select the entire letterhead and copy it to the Styles Editor. Since the letterhead will be used for a variety of documents, it doesn't include the date. Whenever you use the letterhead for a letter, be sure to include the date at least four line spaces above the mailing address.

## E X E R C I S E ⟫ INT1.2

1. Press **Ctrl+A** to select everything in the open window. Use **Ctrl+C** to copy it to the Windows Clipboard.

2. Open the **Format** menu and choose **Styles**. Then click **Create**.

3. Click in the Styles Editor *Contents* text box and press **Ctrl+V** to paste all text and formatting.

4. Position your insertion point in the *Style name* text box and key **Vet Letterhead**. In the *Description* text box key **Letterhead for Parkway Animal Clinic**.

5. Change *Type* to **Document (open)**. Click **OK** to close the dialog box.

6. Back in the Style List dialog box click **Create**. For *Style name*, key **Letter Closing**. For *Description,* key **Closing lines**. Change the *Type* to **Document (open)**.

7. Position your insertion point in the *Contents* text box and press **Enter** twice. Key **Sincerely,** and press **Enter** four more times.

8. Key **Glen Paradeis, D.V.M.** and press **Enter** two more times (in case you need to add an enclosure notation).

9. Click **OK** to return to the Style List dialog box.

10. Click **Options** and choose **Save As**. Click the folder beside the text box and locate the folder or disk where you are saving your work. Name the style **Vet Letterhead xxx** and save it.

11. Close the Style List dialog box and close the document.

Now that the letterhead style is completed, let's send a letter to Polly and Paul at the Pet Paradise shop thanking them for their help. In the first step of Exercise INT1.3 you will be retrieving the style document so you can use the letterhead and closing styles. PAY ATTENTION to this procedure. You will be using it often as you go through the integration segments.

## EXERCISE ⟹ INT1.3

1. Open the **Format** menu and choose **Styles**. Click **Options** and choose **Retrieve**. Choose the **Vet Letterhead** document and confirm that you would like to overwrite the files. Choose the **Letterhead** style.

2. Save the emerging letter as **P&P 1-3 xxx**.

3. Insert the date and key the following mailing address:

   **Polly & Paul Paradeis**
   **Pet Paradise**
   **9001 Parkway Boulevard**
   **Austin, TX 78711**

4. Key an appropriate greeting and double-space. Then go to the student **Datafile** folder and insert **P&P**.

5. Following the last paragraph, open the Style drop-down menu on the Property Bar and choose **Letter Closing**. Check your work and create an envelope.

6. Print the letter and the envelope. Close the document, saving it again.

## Business Card

Now let's create a business card that matches the letterhead you created. You'll use the WordPerfect Labels feature for the cards, which will be printed on Avery #5377 gray business card stock.

## EXERCISE ⟹ INT1.4

1. Beginning in a new document window, open the **Format** menu and choose **Labels**. Click the **Laser printed** button at the top of the dialog box.

2. Search through the label formats (they are listed in numeric order) and locate Avery #5377. Click once to highlight the format.

3. Look at the illustration and the information at the right where WordPerfect tells you the sizes of the cards. Then choose **Select**.

4. In your document window you will see only one card surrounded by a gray background.

5. Using TextArt and gray text, create a card that looks like Figure INT1-2. When you finish, save the document as **card 1-4 xxx**.

With the single card showing in the window, let's use Merge to duplicate the card for printing.

Parkway Animal Clinic

9003 Parkway Boulevard ◇ Austin, TX 78711

Dr. Glen Paradeis, D.V.M.

512-555-6886 | M, W, Th, F  8 a.m. to 6 p.m.
Tu 8 a.m. to 8 p.m., Sat, 8 to 11 a.m.

## E X E R C I S E ⟹ INT1.5

**SCANS**

**1.** Open the **Tools** menu and choose **Merge**. Click **Perform Merge**.

**2.** In the Perform Merge dialog box click the **Options** button and change the number of copies to **9**. Click **OK**.

**3.** Back in the Perform Merge dialog box click **Merge**. (One card will be blank. That's OK.)

**4.** With your insertion point at the end of the final card, press **Ctrl+Enter** to move your insertion point to the blank card. Insert the Path and Filename code to identify your document.

**5.** Save the completed business cards as **bus-card 1-5 xxx**, print it, and close both documents.

# Advertisement

Dr. Paradeis has decided that he needs to place advertisements in the local newspapers. He has asked if you would design an ad for his business. A suggested advertisement is illustrated in Figure INT1-3. Let's create the ad.

## E X E R C I S E ⟹ INT1.6

**SCANS**

**1.** Beginning in a new document window, save the empty document as **ad-copy 1-6 xxx**.

**2.** Go to the Page Setup dialog box and set all four margins at **0"**. (Remember that WordPerfect will adjust the margins to whatever the no-print zone is on your printer.)

**3.** Divide the page into two columns and three rows. Return to the document window.

(continued on next page)

4. Create a single-cell table at the top and fill the cell with **100%** fill. Change text color to **white.** Use a 20-pt. sans serif font face, and key the information in the bar at the top of the figure.

5. Use TextArt for the clinic name. Size it to about **0.5"** high.

6. Continue with the information in the figure, using a sans serif font face for all of the text. Size it so it fits.

a. The address and hours section at the bottom were prepared using a three-cell table.

b. The first and last cells were filled with 100% fill. The cell in the middle had the top and bottom lines set to None.

7. When your advertisement looks good, press **Ctrl+Enter** to move to the next logical page and insert the Path and Filename code.

8. Print the advertisement. Then close the document, saving it again.

**FIGURE INT1-3**
Ad Copy for Exercise INT1.6

# *Brochure*

Paul and Polly at Pet Paradise have suggested that Dr. Paradeis develop some brochures advertising his new veterinary practice. They have offered to hand out brochures at both of their pet shop locations. They also suggested that Dr. Paradeis might want to mail some of the brochures out to customers on the Pet Paradise mailing lists.

A sample 6-panel brochure has been prepared. Figure INT1-4 shows one side of the page, and Figure INT1-5 shows the other side. When completed, the brochure can be folded into thirds for mailing and distribution.

1. Study Figures INT1-4 and INT1-5. These figures show the information to be included in the panels.

2. Begin as follows:

   a. Go to Page Setup and divide the page into three columns.

   b. Change to **Landscape** orientation.

   c. Change all four margins to **0.5"**.

   d. Go to Document Default Font and set it at Arial or a similar sans serif font. (You may vary the point sizes of the font in each section as needed.)

3. Save the emerging brochure as **brochure xxx**.

4. As you are working on the brochure, save often so you won't lose lots of work if you run into problems. In that way you won't lose lots of work if you run into some kind of problem.

**FIGURE INT1-4**
One Side of 6-Panel Brochure

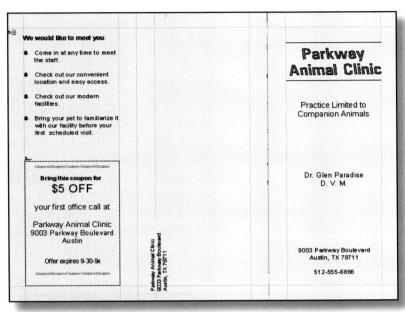

**FIGURE INT1-5**
One Side of 6-Panel Brochure

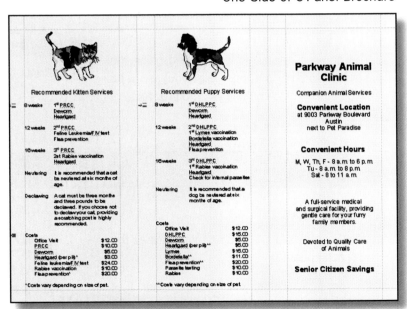

# EXERCISE ▷ INT1.8

*Panel 1, Figure INT1-6*
This panel contains the following features:

1. The bullets are from the Iconic Symbols set. Choose any style bullet you'd like.

2. The coupon is a Text box. Set the border of the box to a dotted line so it LOOKS like a coupon.

3. The little scissors is from the Iconic Symbols set.
   a. Create a Text box to contain the scissors so you can move it wherever you want it.
   b. Within the Text box, insert Symbol 5,33.
   c. Enlarge the symbol so it's at least 25 pt.
   d. Change the size of the box so it's just large enough for the scissors.

e. Change the box to an Image box to remove border (or change the border to None).
f. Position the scissors so it's near the border of the coupon.

4. When you have all of the required parts in the panel, size the text so it is attractive.

5. Press **Ctrl+Enter** to go to Panel 2.

6. Save your work.

*Panel 2*
All that is on Panel 2 is a Text box that is rotated 90 degrees. The box contains the name and address of the clinic and is positioned in normal return address position. Press **Ctrl+Enter** to go to Panel 3.

# EXERCISE ▷ INT1.9

*Panel 3, Figure INT1-7*
This panel is the "cover" of the brochure. It contains the following components:

1. The name of the clinic is prepared using the same TextArt settings as you've used throughout—black outline around gray text.

2. The horizontal lines should be above and below the name of the clinic.

3. Use **Enter** to space the text out attractively.

4. Press **Ctrl+Enter** to go to Panel 4.

# EXERCISE ▷ INT1.10

*Panel 4, Figure INT1-8*
This panel contains a lot of information. It has the following components:

1. The cat is in the student **Datafile** folder. It is simply **cat.wpg**.

2. Set a tab for the list of kitten services.

3. In the *Costs* area, set a regular tab for the service and a decimal tab for the costs.

4. Use a sans serif font that makes the text look good and fits it all on one page. You may vary the size of the figure or add hard returns for spacing.

5. Are you remembering to save often?

**We would like to meet you:**

✳ Come in at any time to meet the staff.

✳ Check out our convenient location and easy access.

✳ Check out our modern facilities.

✳ Bring your pet to familiarize with our facility before your first scheduled visit.

✂

Coupon-Coupon-Coupon-Coupon-Coupon

**Bring this coupon for**

# $5 OFF

your first office call at

**Parkway Animal Clinic**
**9003 Parkway Boulevard**
**Austin**

Offer expires 9-30-9x

Coupon-Coupon-Coupon-Coupon-Coupon

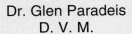

# Parkway Animal Clinic

Practice Limited to Companion Animals

Dr. Glen Paradeis
D. V. M.

9003 Parkway Boulevard
Austin, TX 78711

Recommended Kitten Services

| | |
|---|---|
| 8 weeks | 1st PRCC<br>Deworm<br>Heartgard |
| 12 weeks | 2nd PRCC<br>Feline Leukemia/FIV test<br>Flea prevention |
| 16 weeks | 3rd PRCC<br>1st Rabies vaccination<br>Heartgard |
| Neutering | It is recommended that a cat be neutered at six months of age. |
| Declawing | A cat must be three months and three pounds to be declawed. If you choose not to declaw your cat, providing a scratching post is highly recommended. |

Costs

| | |
|---|---|
| Office Visit | $12.00 |
| PRCC | $10.00 |
| Deworm | $5.00 |
| Heartgard (per pill)* | $3.00 |
| Feline Leukemia/FIV test | $24.00 |
| Rabies vaccination | $10.00 |
| Flea prevention* | $20.00 |

*Costs vary depending on size of pet.

SCANS

*Panel 5, Figure INT1-9*

Panel 5 is similar to Panel 4. The image is **dog.wpg,** and you'll have to flip it so it is facing the cat.

SCANS

*Panel 6, Figure INT1-10*

This panel contains important information about the clinic. Be sure that the address and hours are above the top of the coupon on the reverse side so when the customers cut the coupon out, they will still have that critical information.

SCANS

Finish the brochure.

1. Find a place somewhere for the Path and Filename code. Make it very small so it doesn't detract from the brochure.

2. Save the brochure a final time. Then print one page only (Current Page). Put the page in the printer bypass to print the second page on the back of the sheet.

3. Check your work. Make any necessary changes, save, and print the document before closing it.

Recommended Puppy Services

| | |
|---|---|
| 8 weeks | 1st DHLPPC<br>Deworm<br>Heartgard |
| 12 weeks | 2nd DHLPPC<br>1st Lymes vaccination<br>Bordetella vaccination<br>Heartgard<br>Flea prevention |
| 16 weeks | 3rd DHLPPC<br>1st Rabies vaccination<br>Heartgard<br>Check for internal<br>parasites |
| Neutering | It is recommended that a<br>dog be neutered at six<br>months of age. |

Costs
| | |
|---|---|
| Office Visit | $12.00 |
| DHLPPC | $15.00 |
| Deworm | $5.00 |
| Heartgard (per pill)** | $5.00 |
| Lymes | $15.00 |
| Bordetella** | $11.00 |
| Flea prevention** | $20.00 |
| Parasite testing | $10.00 |
| Rabies | $10.00 |

**Costs vary depending on size of pet.

# Parkway Animal Clinic

Companion Animal Services

## Convenient Location
at 9003 Parkway Boulevard
Austin
next to Pet Paradise

## Convenient Hours

M, W, Th, F - 8 a.m. to 6 p.m.
Tu - 8 a.m. to 8 p.m.
Sat - 8 to 11 a.m.

A full-service medical
and surgical facility, providing
gentle care for your furry
family members.

Devoted to Quality Care
of Animals

## Senior Citizen Savings

# *Labels*

Now let's prepare mailing labels for the brochure. We'll use the customer list from Pet Paradise, but we'll need to separate out the cat and dog owners from the rest of the customers.

## EXERCISE ⟹ INT1.14

1. Go to the student **Datafile** folder and open **customers.dat**. Save the file as **cust 1-14 xxx**. (This is the complete list of customers that you worked with in WordPerfect Lesson 7.)

2. Go through the list and delete all of the Pet Paradise customers who have animals other than cats or dogs. Delete from one ENDRECORD code to the next, including the hard page break that separates the records. Figure INT1-11 illustrates an easy way to select the text to be deleted. When you finish, you will still have nearly 60 customers with cats and dogs.

3. Save the revised list again as **cust 1-14 xxx.dat** and sort the customers by last name. Save the list again.

4. Click the **Go to Form** button on the Merge Bar and click **Create** in the Associate dialog box.

5. Choose **Format**, **Labels**, and click the **Laser printed** button. Select Avery #5160 or #5260 labels (3 rows of 10 per page).

6. Choose **Format**, **Page**, and **Center** to center the Current and subsequent pages.

7. Click the **Insert Field** button and insert the FIELD codes to put the addresses on the labels. The codes are larger than the names, so they probably won't fit on one label (see Figure INT1-12).

**FIGURE INT1-11**
Selecting a Record to Delete It

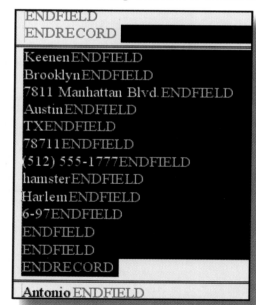

**8.** Save the form document as **30-labels xxx** and complete the merge. Click the **Reset** button in the Perform Merge dialog box. WordPerfect probably remembers that you merged nine copies of the business card.

**9.** With your insertion point at the end of the final address, press **Ctrl+Enter** to go to the next label and insert the Path and Filename code.

**10.** Look through your labels. If the four-line addresses don't fit on the label, change the font size slightly.

**11.** Save the file as **mailing 1-14 xxx**. Print the completed labels and close all files, saving again as you close.

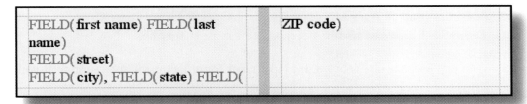

Now that the customer labels have been prepared and the brochures have been printed, it is an easy task to put the labels on the brochures for mailing.

# *Summary*

You've done a fine job of preparing marketing documents for Dr. Paradeis. You have combined your knowledge of WordPerfect features to prepare a wide variety of documents. You've integrated the following skills:

- creating and using a style.
- preparing business cards using the Labels feature and Merge.
- using TextArt 8, WordPerfect Symbols, and WordPerfect lines.
- using different font faces, font sizes, and font colors.
- using tables, including reverse video and table formatting for the advertisement.
- using Divide Page and setting margins for the brochure.
- using Text boxes and adjusting the size and border of the boxes.
- using graphics boxes and formatting images.
- editing a data file and preparing a form document for labels.
- identifying all of your work with the Path and Filename code.

## TRUE / FALSE

**Circle the T if the statement is true.  Circle the F if it is false.**

**T F** **1.** You must use Divide Page to set up a page for business cards or labels.

**T F** **2.** You can save formatting time by changing the font of an entire document with Document Default Font.

**T F** **3.** TextArt 8 may only be used in documents that are the full 8½- by 11-inch page size.

**T F** **4.** If you want to rotate text in a box, you must use a Text box.

**T F** **5.** You can prepare labels by setting up a label form document and merging it with a data file.

## WRITTEN QUESTIONS

**Write your answers to the following questions.**

**6.** What two things must you do with a table cell to get the reverse video effect?

**7.** What three features did you use in the Page Setup dialog box to prepare your window for a 6-panel brochure?

**8.** When you have set up several logical pages using the Divide Page feature, how do you move the insertion point to the next logical page?

**9.** If you wish to edit the letterhead you created for Dr. Paradeis, how could you do that?

**10.** Why did you need to put the scissors in a graphics box when you inserted it to "clip the coupon"?

# INTEGRATION 1 PROJECT

SCANS

This project will be an opportunity for you to review Cut, Copy, Move, and Paste, along with Drag and Drop. These skills are important in all of the work that you do with WordPerfect, but they are especially important when you combine applications.

At the end of your Quattro Pro training, you will be integrating Quattro Pro and WordPerfect. You will use all of these skills, along with a new one called *Paste Special*. Let's practice.

1. Beginning in a new document window, go to the student **Datafile** folder and hold **Ctrl** while you click **Anne**, **David**, and **Judy**. Click **Open** to open these three tiny practice documents.

2. Save each of them in your solutions folder. Add your initials to each, so you're saving **Anne xxx**, **David xxx**, and **Judy xxx**. Keep all three documents open.

3. Choose **David xxx** from the Application Bar and select the second paragraph. (Point in the left margin and click twice to select the sentence and the following blank line.)

4. Press **Ctrl+X** to cut the paragraph. Remember that it is now on the Windows Clipboard.

5. Go to **Judy xxx** and position the insertion point a double space below the second paragraph. Press **Ctrl+V** to paste the paragraph there.

6. Return to **David xxx** and paste again in its original location. (The paragraph was still on the Clipboard, and you've now pasted it in two places.)

7. Go to **Anne xxx** and select the first paragraph. Press **Ctrl+C** to copy it to the Clipboard. Go to **Judy xxx**, position the insertion point a double space below the last paragraph, and paste the paragraph there.

8. Still in **Judy xxx**, select the fourth paragraph and drag it down to the **Anne xxx.wpd** name on the Application Bar. Still holding the mouse button, drag it into the **Anne xxx** document window when it appears, and position it at the beginning of the page—before the first paragraph. Add a hard return, if necessary, to separate the paragraphs.

9. With that *Anne* sentence still selected, hold the **Ctrl** key while you drag it via the Application Bar to the top of the **David xxx** document. Return to **Anne xxx** and see if the sentence is still in that document. It should be, because the **Ctrl** key means you are copying the text, not moving it.

## PASTE SPECIAL

Paste Special is a little different. When you use this feature, the text you are pasting into a document becomes an object—like a graphics image, a Text box, or a chart. It has sizing handles, and when you double click to edit the image, you will be returned to the document from which it was copied.

In addition, when you use Paste Special, you can establish a link between the two documents. If you make a change in the original document, that change will be reflected in the document where it was pasted as an object. Let's try it. Remember, Judy's number is 5.

1. Go to **Judy xxx** and click only once in the left margin to select the second sentence. (Do not include the line space following the sentence.) Copy the sentence to the Clipboard.

2. Go to **Anne xxx** and position the insertion point a double space below the final paragraph.

3. Open the **Edit** menu and choose **Paste Special**. Click the **Paste Link** button. (The dialog box will tell you that you are working with a Corel WordPerfect 8 document.) Click **OK**.

4.  The *Judy* sentence should appear, and it will have sizing handles. The font face may appear to be a little different, too.

5.  Return to **Judy xxx**. Change her number in the second paragraph from 5 to **55**.

6.  Go to **Anne xxx**. The number in the "linked object" should now reflect that change of number. Does it say 55?

7.  Point to the *Judy* object in the **Anne xxx** document and double click. It should return you to **Judy xxx**.

8.  Close all documents without saving them. Delete **Anne xxx, David xxx,** and **Judy xxx** from your solutions.

9.  Put the disk containing your integrated solutions in a safe place. You will need it again for the next set of integrated exercises following the Quattro Pro segment.

## CRITICAL THINKING ACTIVITY

**SCANS**

You saved your pages of labels in Exercise INT1.14 because you were told to do so. On the job you probably wouldn't have saved those two pages of labels. What are a couple of reasons why you wouldn't save a completed merge?

Why did you have to delete the odd pets from the customer list manually instead of using Extract to separate out the dogs and cats?

# COREL® QUATTRO® PRO 8

# CREATING A NOTEBOOK

## OBJECTIVES

**Upon completion of this lesson, you will be able to:**

- Start Corel® Quattro® Pro.
- Create a new notebook.
- Move around in a sheet.
- Select cells.
- Distinguish between labels and values.
- Edit notebook entries.
- Use the QuickFill feature.
- Copy and move text.
- Adjust the width of columns.
- Print a notebook.

**🕐 Estimated Time: 1¹/₂ hours**

A *spreadsheet* is a grid into which you can enter data that you want to organize, calculate, and analyze. Corel® Quattro® Pro is a spreadsheet program. *Spreadsheet programs* allow you to easily manage large quantities of data. You can perform complex mathematical operations in seconds and modify and update numbers with the touch of a key. In this lesson you will learn how to create a new Quattro Pro document and move around the spreadsheet. You will also learn to edit entries, change the width of the spreadsheet's columns, and print a spreadsheet.

## *Examining the Corel® Quattro® Pro Screen*

One way of starting (or *launching*) Quattro Pro is to click the Quattro Pro icon on the Desktop Application Director (DAD) which usually appears at the lower right corner of the screen. When you start Quattro Pro, a new spreadsheet document appears on the screen. You then can enter data into this spreadsheet. The opening Quattro Pro screen looks similar to Figure 1-1. In Quattro Pro a spreadsheet file is called a *notebook*. A notebook can contain many spreadsheets and each individual spreadsheet is referred to as a *sheet*. Each sheet is designated by a lettered tab at the bottom of the notebook. To move to a specific sheet, you click that sheet's tab. All of the sheets in a specific notebook are typically related to one another. For instance, the financial information for a high school drama club might be contained in a single notebook. One sheet might contain data on income from performances, another on expenses involved in productions, and so forth.

A spreadsheet is made up of horizontal *rows* and vertical *columns*. As shown in Figure 1-1, the rows are identified sequentially by numbers and the columns are identified by letters of the alphabet. The intersection of a row and a column is called a *cell*. The *active cell* is the cell that you can currently manipulate, for example, by entering new data into it or editing data that it already contains. The active cell is identified by the bordered rectangle surrounding this cell. This bordered rectangle is called the *selector*. Later you will see that more than one cell can be selected at a time.

Every cell on a spreadsheet has a specific *address* (also called a *coordinate* or *reference*). A cell's address contains the name of its sheet followed by the cell's column letter and row number. This address can be used to locate that cell. In Figure 1-1 the address of the active cell is A:A1. The first "A" indicates the current sheet, the letter "A" after the colon indicates the column, and the number "1" indicates the row. As you can see in Figure 1-1, the active cell's address appears in the input line, which is immediately above the spreadsheet grid.

When specifying the address of a cell, users often will not include the name of the sheet in the address. In this case it is assumed that the address refers to the current sheet. For example, the address B14 refers to column B, row 14 of the current sheet.

**FIGURE 1-1**
Quattro Pro Opening Screen

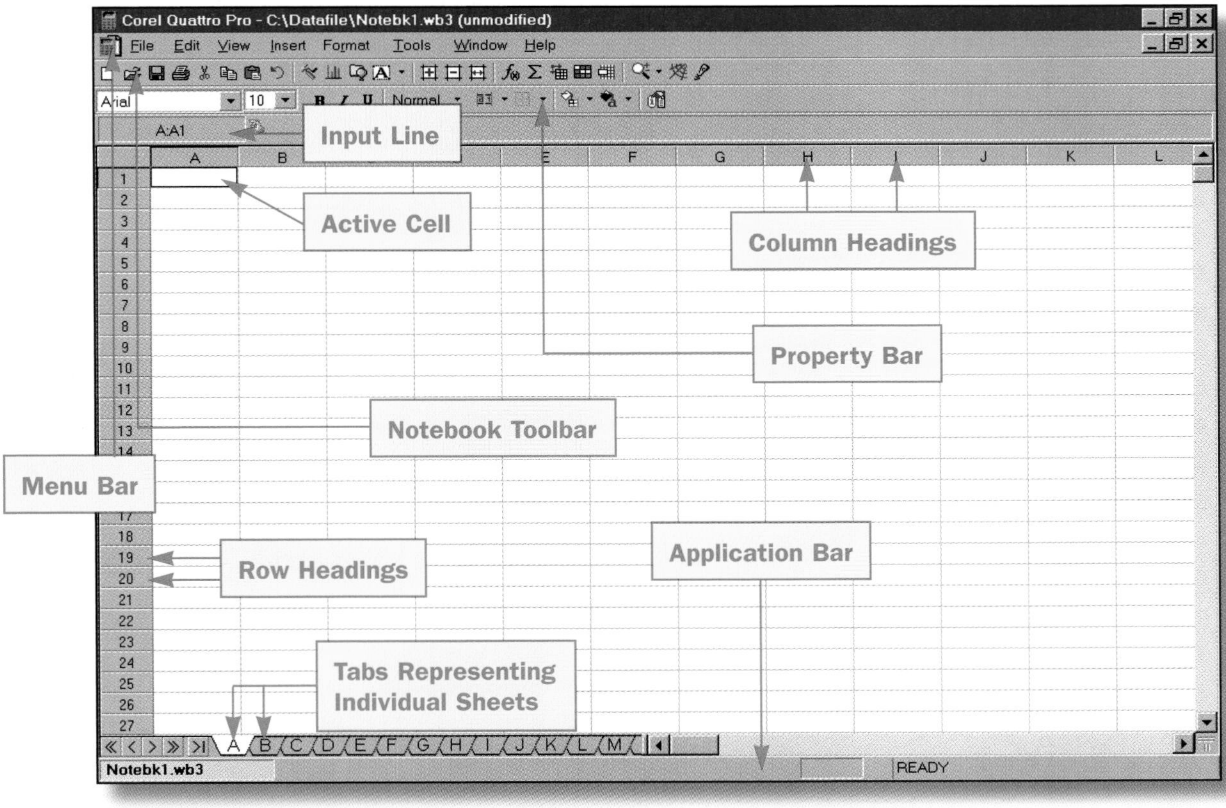

Quattro Pro has several different Toolbars. In Figure 1-1 the Notebook Toolbar is displayed. It contains buttons that are useful when performing general tasks such as saving a notebook file or copying the contents of a cell. To see the other available Toolbars, position the mouse pointer on the Notebook Toolbar and right click to display a QuickMenu containing a list of Toolbars. You can then choose the ones you want displayed.

The Property Bar is immediately below the Notebook Toolbar. Property Bars automatically appear when you are performing specific tasks. In Figure 1-1 the Property Bar contains options that are helpful in formatting a spreadsheet, such as placing text in italic or using different fonts. If you were creating a chart, the Property Bar would contain buttons that were useful for that task.

# *Moving Around a Spreadsheet*

To move from cell to cell on a sheet, you can use either the mouse or the keyboard. To use the mouse, position the mouse pointer on the cell you want to make active, and click. Pressing Tab will move you to the next cell. You also can use the arrow/directional keys to move from one cell to another. Table 1-1 explains some of the keyboard shortcuts that can be used to move around a notebook.

**TABLE 1-1**
Keyboard Shortcuts

| Keystroke | Movement |
| --- | --- |
| Tab | Moves one cell to the right |
| Shift+Tab | Moves one cell to the left |
| right arrow → | Moves one cell to the right |
| left arrow ← | Moves one cell to the left |
| up arrow ↑ | Moves one cell up |
| down arrow ↓ | Moves one cell down |
| Home | Moves to cell A1 on the current sheet |
| Ctrl+Home | Moves to cell A1 on sheet A |
| End+Home | Moves to lower right corner of the non-blank part of the current sheet |
| Page Up | Moves one windowful up |
| Page Down | Moves one windowful down |
| Ctrl+left arrow ← | Moves one windowful to the left |
| Ctrl+right arrow → | Moves one windowful to the right |
| F5 (Go To) | Moves to any cell you specify in the Go To dialog box |

# *Selecting Cells*

$\mathrm{Y}$ou enter data in a cell. Data can be entered into a cell when that cell is selected. As you already know, you can select a single cell by clicking it. To select more than one cell—called a *range* or *block*—click and drag to highlight the entire group. A range is identified by the address of the cell in its upper left corner and the address in its lower right corner, such as A1..C4. Notice the two dots (..) between the first and second cell addresses. These dots mean that all of the cells from A1 through C4 are included in this range. In Figure 1-2 the range B2..D5 has been selected.

## NOTE:

When a range is selected, only the address of the first cell selected appears on the input line. In addition, the first cell in the range appears as though it is not selected, even though it is; this allows you to easily see where the first cell is located.

**FIGURE 1-2**
The Selected Range B2..D5

You can select an entire row of cells by clicking the row's number on the spreadsheet's border. To select an entire column, click the column's letter. You can select an entire sheet by clicking the empty border button at the upper left corner or by choosing Select All from the Edit menu. Figure 1-3 shows the different selection methods.

**INTERNET**

An Internet address is a set of numbers or words that identifies a unique user or computer. Every user and computer on the Internet must have a different address so that the system knows where to send electronic mail and other data.

**FIGURE 1-3**
Selection Methods

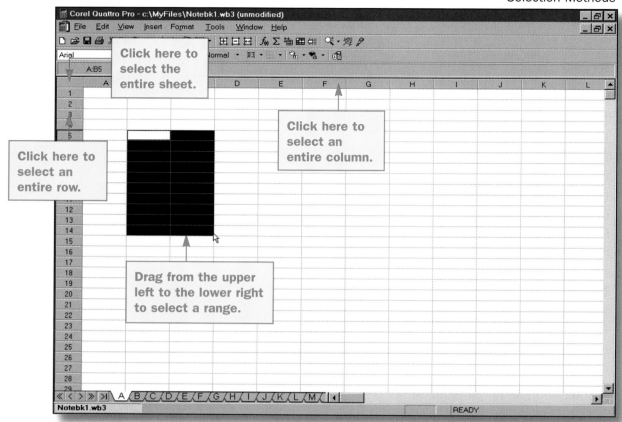

Click here to select the entire sheet.

Click here to select an entire column.

Click here to select an entire row.

Drag from the upper left to the lower right to select a range.

# EXERCISE ▭▷ QP1.1

SCANS

1.  Start Quattro Pro by clicking the **Quattro Pro** icon on the DAD on the Windows taskbar. In the new window practice clicking the various menus to see the options available in each of them.

2.  Practice clicking the **down arrow** on the scroll bar to move downward. Notice how the numbers on the rows change. Then hold down the **up arrow** to move back to the top of the spreadsheet. Hold down the **right arrow** to move to the right—new letters appear at the top of the sheet. Hold down the **left arrow** to move back to the beginning of the sheet.

3.  Click cell **D6** to select it. Notice the bordered rectangle, called the selector, that appears around it.

4.  Press the **right arrow** to move to cell E6, one cell to the right. Press **Tab** to move to cell F6.

5.  Press the **left arrow** to move back to cell E6. Press **Home** to move to cell A1.

6.  Press **F5**. The Go To dialog box appears, as shown in Figure 1-4. In the *Reference* text box key **B10**. Click **OK.** Cell B10 becomes the active cell.

**7.** Use the mouse to select the range **B2..D7**.

**8.** Position your mouse pointer over Column E. When the pointer becomes a down arrow with a small box above it, click once. The entire column is selected.

**9.** Click on the number *5* to the left of the fifth row. The entire row is selected. Notice that the first cell, A1, is white with a black border.

Whenever you select a range of cells, the first cell will be white with a black border and the remaining selected cells will be black.

**10.** Open the **Edit** menu and choose **Select All**. The entire sheet is selected. Click on any cell. The sheet is deselected.

**11.** Press **Page Up.** Return to cell A1 for the next exercise.

**FIGURE 1-4**
The Go To Dialog Box

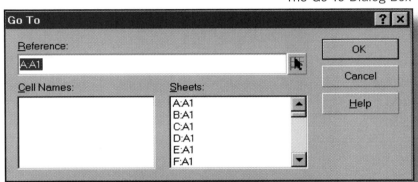

# *Understanding Labels and Values*

Two types of data can be entered into a spreadsheet: *labels* and *values*. Labels are text entries that can contain alphabetic or numeric characters that will not be used in calculations. Values are numbers, dates, and formulas. The purpose of a label is to identify the contents of the spreadsheet.

When you enter data, Quattro Pro automatically determines whether the entry is a label or a value. Labels are aligned at the left of the cell and values are aligned at the right. You will notice that sometimes your entries are longer than the width of the cell. You can make cells wider or narrower, depending on the width needed to be able to view the entire contents of the cell. You will learn how to change the width of columns later in this lesson. In the following exercise you will get a chance to enter labels and values into a spreadsheet.

**1.** In this sheet you are going to be entering data on pet grooming income for Pet Paradise, a small pet shop. Pet Paradise sells pet products and provides a variety of services, including pet grooming and boarding. In cell A1 key **Grooming Income for August 13-18**. Press **Enter**.

**2.** Key the following labels in the cells indicated. (Don't worry if the data appears to not fit in the cell.) Remember to use **Backspace** and **Delete** to correct errors as you key, and check your input line to make sure you are in the correct cell.

A4  **Complete Grooming**
A5  **Bathing Only**
A6  **Nail Clipping Only**
A7  **Brush-Out Only**
A8  **Flea Dip**
A9  **Total**

**NOTE:**

Even though the labels in column A run into column B, you can still enter values into column B. Just click in the cell in column B that you want to enter data into and begin keying. The part of the label that extends into column B will become hidden.

**NOTE:**

You can confirm an entry by pressing Tab, Enter, or the arrow keys or by moving to or selecting another cell.

**3.** Key the values in cells B4..G8 as shown below. (You will learn how to format the values with currency symbols, decimals, etc., in the next lesson.)

**NOTE:**

Notice that the labels are aligned at the left edge of the cell and the values are aligned at the right edge of the cell.

**4.** Open the **File** menu and choose **Save As**.

**NOTE:**

Your instructor will tell you where you will be saving your exercises. For example, you may be instructed to save your files on a disk in Drive A.

**5.** In the Save File dialog box open the *Save in* drop-down list box and select the location where you will be saving your files. If you are saving your files on Drive A, you would select **(A:)**.

**TABLE 1-1**
Values in Cells

|   | A | B | C | D | E | F | G |
|---|---|---|---|---|---|---|---|
| 1 | Grooming Income for August 13-18 | | | | | | |
| 2 | | | | | | | |
| 3 | | | | | | | |
| 4 | Complete | 256 | 192 | 320 | 256 | 192 | 288 |
| 5 | Bathing Or | 30 | 30 | 45 | 75 | 15 | 30 |
| 6 | Nail Clippi | 4 | 0 | 4 | 0 | 8 | 4 |
| 7 | Brush-Out | 25 | 25 | 12.5 | 37.5 | 50 | 62.5 |
| 8 | Flea Dip | 0 | 30 | 40 | 10 | 0 | 20 |
| 9 | Total | | | | | | |

**6.** Key **grooming 1-2 xxx** in the *File name* text box. Replace the "xxx" part of the filename with your initials. Then click the **Save** button.

**7.** Close the notebook by opening the **File** menu and choosing **Close**.

# *Editing Data*

When you select a single cell, that cell's contents appear in the input line, as shown in Figure 1-5. You can edit the contents in the input line by clicking on the entry. The insertion point will be positioned in the input line, and you can then edit the entry just as you would when using a word processor. After making any needed changes, you can confirm the entry either by clicking the check mark button or by pressing Enter or an arrow key. Another way of editing the contents of a cell is to double click the cell. The insertion point appears in the cell and you can make any changes you wish. If you wish to replace the entire contents of the cell, click the cell and enter the new data. This new data will replace the previous entry.

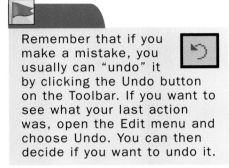

Remember that if you make a mistake, you usually can "undo" it by clicking the Undo button on the Toolbar. If you want to see what your last action was, open the Edit menu and choose Undo. You can then decide if you want to undo it.

**FIGURE 1-5**
Editing in the Input Line

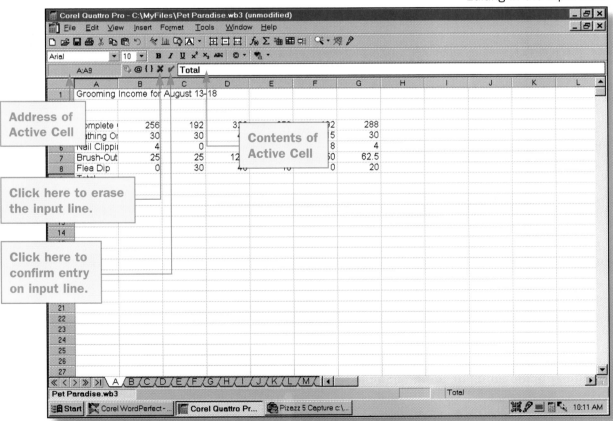

**SCANS**

**1.** Click the **Open** button on the Toolbar.

✓ **NOTE:**

Depending on your system's configuration, a *.wb3* extension may or may not appear as part of the filename in the Open File dialog box.

**2.** In the Open File dialog box select the student **Datafile** folder. Highlight **grooming 1-2 xxx** and then click **Open**.

**3.** Save the notebook as **grooming 1-3 xxx**.

**4.** Click cell **A9**. The cells's contents appear on the input line, as shown in Figure 1-5.

**5.** Click **Total** in the input line. If necessary, position the insertion point at the end of the word *Total*. Press the **space bar** once and key

the word **Income**. Click the **check mark** button to confirm the entry. If you wanted to erase the contents of the input line, you could click the **X** button.

**6.** Double click cell **D5** and change its contents to **60**. Double clicking allows you to change the contents of a cell directly in the cell, rather than on the input line. Press **Enter** to confirm this entry.

**7.** Click cell **E8** and overwrite the data with the entry **14**. Press **Enter** to confirm this entry.

Remember that many commands can be executed by using shortcut keys rather than buttons or menu commands. The shortcut key for saving a file is Ctrl+S.

**8.** Save the notebook and keep it open for the next exercise.

## *Using QuickFill*

Quattro Pro has a number of features that make data entry quicker and more efficient. One of these features is QuickFill. The QuickFill feature can be used to automatically fill a range or block of cells with a sequential series of entries, such as days of the week, months of the year, or numbers.

One way to use QuickFill is to select the range of cells you want to fill and then click the QuickFill button on the Toolbar. A QuickFill Rows or QuickFill Columns dialog box appears, as shown

**FIGURE 1-6**
QuickFill Rows Dialog Box

in Figure 1-6. Click the *Series Name* drop-down list box arrow to display a list of the QuickFill series that are available. You can then choose the one you want.

A second method of using QuickFill is to enter a *seed value*, or starting value, and then ask QuickFill to enter the rest of the values. This is the method you will be using in the next exercise.

## EXERCISE ▷ QP1.4

**1.** Save the notebook as **grooming 1-4 xxx**.

**2.** Click cell **B3**. Key **Mon** into this cell. *Mon* is the seed value.

**3.** Select range **B3..G3**.

**4.** Click the **QuickFill** button. The short versions of the days of the week should appear in cells C3 through G3.

**TIP**

Another way of accessing the QuickFill feature is to right click on the selected range. A QuickMenu appears and you can select QuickFill from it.

**5.** Save the notebook again and keep it open for the next exercise.

# Cutting, Copying, and Pasting Entries

You can modify data in the spreadsheet by using the Cut, Copy, and Paste commands in the Edit menu. Alternatively, you can use the Cut, Copy, and Paste buttons on the Toolbar. If you *cut* the contents of a cell or a range of cells, the data is removed and placed on the *Clipboard*—a special temporary storage place in Quattro Pro—until you are ready to paste it in a new location. When you *copy* the contents of a cell or range of cells, Quattro Pro makes a copy of the cell contents and places this copy on the Clipboard until you are ready to paste it. Unlike cutting, however, the original data is not removed from the spreadsheet when it is copied.

## IMPORTANT:

When pasting data to a new location, be very careful not to select cells that already contain data. Pasting will overwrite the existing contents of the cell.

## EXERCISE ▷ QP1.5

**1.** Save the notebook as **grooming 1-5 xxx**.

**2.** Select cell **A9** and then click the **Cut** button. The words *Total Income* are removed from the cell and placed on the Clipboard.

**3.** Select cell **A10** and then click the **Paste** button on the Toolbar. The words *Total Income* are moved to cell A10. Leaving a blank row between the rest of the spreadsheet and the total line makes the data more readable.

(continued on next page)

**4.** Select the range **A3..G10** and then click the **Copy** button on the Toolbar. A copy of the contents of these cells is placed on the Clipboard.

**5.** Select the range **A15..G22** and then click the **Paste** button on the Toolbar. The labels and values now appear in two places.

An easy way to cut and paste data is to select the cells, right click on the selected cells, and then choose the needed command from the QuickMenu.

**NOTE:**

As you start keying text, Quattro Pro may try to guess what you are trying to enter. If it enters something you do not want, just keep keying. Your text will be entered into the cell.

**6.** Pet Paradise has two locations: Pet Paradise I and Pet Paradise II. In cell A2 key **Pet Paradise I**. In cell A14 key **Pet Paradise II**. You now can store the grooming services income for each branch in a separate table.

**7.** Notice that the data in the cells for Pet Paradise II is the same as for Pet Paradise I. To delete the data in the second table so that it can be filled in with the correct data at a later time, select cells **B16..G20**. Open the **Edit** menu, choose **Clear**, and then choose **Values** from the submenu. The contents of this block of cells should be erased.

You can also erase the contents of selected cells by pressing the Delete key.

**8.** Click anywhere to deselect the cells.

**9.** Save the notebook again and keep it open.

# Adjusting Column Width

As you have probably noticed, some of the labels in the spreadsheet you have been creating are partially hidden. You can quickly adjust column width by using the QuickFit button on the Toolbar. Simply select any cell in the column and click the QuickFit button. The column width adjusts to accommodate the longest entry in the column. Another way to adjust the width is to position the pointer on the border between column letters. When the pointer turns into a double-headed arrow, drag the border until the column is the desired width.

**NOTE:**

Even though a column may be too narrow to completely display its contents, it is important to realize that the entire contents are still stored in the cell. Part of it is simply hidden from view.

**E X E R C I S E  QP1.6**

1. Save the notebook as **grooming 1-6 xxx**.

2. Select the range **A3..G22**.

3. Click the **QuickFit** button on the Toolbar.

4. Key the data given below for Pet Paradise II.

5. Save the notebook and keep it open for the next exercise.

**NOTE:**

When you click the QuickFit button, Column A becomes wider so that all of the labels can be seen. The remaining columns become narrower because they were wider than needed to display their contents.

**TABLE 1-2**
Grooming Data for Pet Paradise II

| Pet Paradise II | | | | | | |
|---|---|---|---|---|---|---|
| | Mon | Tue | Wed | Thu | Fri | Sat |
| Complete Grooming | 192 | 160 | 192 | 224 | 160 | 224 |
| Bathing Only | 0 | 15 | 45 | 15 | 30 | 45 |
| Nail Clipping Only | 8 | 0 | 0 | 4 | 0 | 4 |
| Brush-Out Only | 0 | 25 | 12.5 | 0 | 37.5 | 25 |
| Flea Dip | 10 | 0 | 20 | 10 | 30 | 10 |
| | | | | | | |
| Total Income | | | | | | |

# *Printing a Notebook*

There will be times when you want to print a hard copy of your spreadsheets. To print a notebook, choose the Print command on the File menu, or click the Print button on the Toolbar. The Spreadsheet Print dialog box appears, similar to that shown in Figure 1-7. The exact appearance of this dialog box will vary depending on the printer being used. Click the Print button to print the spreadsheet.

If you want to change the way the notebook sheets will print, click the Page Setup button in the Spreadsheet Print dialog box. The Spreadsheet Page Setup dialog box appears (see Figure 1-8). You can then specify whether the sheet will print in *Portrait orientation* or *Landscape orientation*. The Portrait option causes the sheet to be printed so that it is taller than it is wide. The Landscape option prints the sheet sideways, so that the sheet is wider than it is tall.

**FIGURE 1-7**
Spreadsheet Print Dialog Box

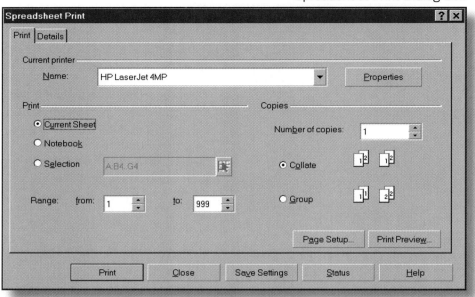

# EXERCISE ⟩ QP1.7

SCANS

1. Save the notebook as **grooming 1-7 xxx**.

2. Click the **Print** button on the Toolbar. Notice that the name of the printer that is connected to your computer is listed in the Spreadsheet Print dialog box.

3. Click **Page Setup**. The Spreadsheet Page Setup dialog box appears, as shown in Figure 1-8. The default paper size is **Letter 8$^1$/$_2$ by 11 inch**. This dialog box allows you to change this default, if you wish. You will learn more about Quattro Pro's printing options in Lesson 6,

**✓ NOTE:**

Depending on your installation of Quattro Pro, you might see a check box at the bottom of the Spreadsheet Print dialog box labeled *Adjust image to print black and white.*

*Exploring Print Options.* Click **OK** to return to the Spreadsheet Print dialog box.

4. In the Spreadsheet Print dialog box make certain that the **Current Sheet** option is selected and click **Print**. The Current Sheet option is selected by default. If Notebook is selected, the entire notebook, which in some cases may contain many sheets, is printed. If Selection is selected, only the highlighted cells will be printed.

5. Open the **File** menu and choose **Close** to close the notebook. If you are asked whether you want to save the changes in your file before closing, click **Yes**. Then exit Quattro Pro.

**FIGURE 1-8**
The Spreadsheet Page Setup Dialog Box

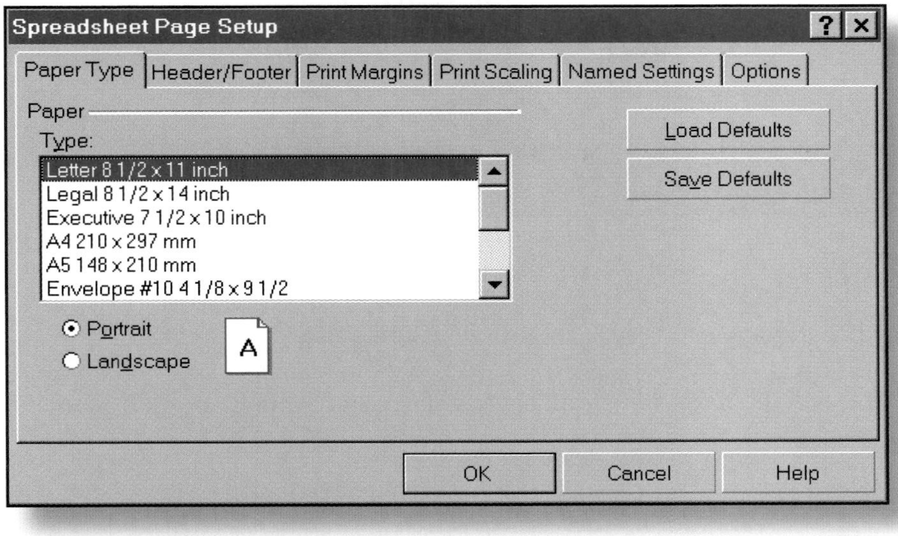

# *Summary*

This lesson introduced you to some of the basics of spreadsheets. You learned:

- a spreadsheet is a grid of lettered columns and numbered rows. Spreadsheet software allows you to manipulate and analyze data stored in spreadsheets.

- spreadsheet files are called notebooks and are made up of a group of sheets.

- each cell on a sheet has an address which consists of its sheet letter, column letter, and row number.

- to move around in a sheet in a number of ways, including using the mouse, the arrow keys, the Go To dialog box, and the scroll bars.

- to click a cell to select it. To select a column, click its letter; to select a row, click its number. Drag to select cell ranges.

- labels are text entries that are used to identify the values stored in the sheet. Values can be numbers, dates, and formulas.

- when a cell is selected, its contents appear on the input line, where they can be edited. You also can edit directly in a cell by double clicking the cell.

- to use the QuickFill feature to enter a series of labels, such as the months of the year.

- to copy a cell or range of cells by selecting the data, clicking the Copy button, selecting where the data is to be placed, and clicking the Paste button. The data appears in both the original location and the new location. Cutting is similar, except that the data is removed from its original location.

- to adjust a column or row's width to accommodate its longest entry by using the QuickFit button.

- to print a single sheet, a selection, or an entire notebook. You also can print sheets in either Landscape or Portrait orientation.

## LESSON 1 REVIEW QUESTIONS

### TRUE/FALSE

**Circle the T if the statement is true. Circle the F if it is false.**

T  F  **1.** The address of the active cell always appears at the bottom of the current sheet, on the sheet tabs.

T  F  **2.** A notebook consists of a collection of sheets that are stored in a single file.

T  F  **3.** You can copy a range of selected cells by clicking the QuickFill button on the Toolbar.

T  F  **4.** A number, a date, and a formula are all examples of labels.

T  F  **5.** The Spreadsheet Page Setup dialog box lets you tell Quattro Pro to print a sheet in Landscape orientation.

### WRITTEN QUESTIONS

**Write your answers to the following questions.**

**6.** Assume that you are currently in cell B4. List three ways you could move to cell B5.

**7.** How many cells are contained in the range B2..G4?

**8.** What is the purpose of the Clipboard?

**9.** Describe how you could quickly enter the months January through June across the top of a sheet, without keying them.

**10.** You have entered a label into each of the cells A4, B4, and C4. However, the columns are too narrow to display the entire labels. What can you do to make the entire labels visible?

## LESSON 1 PROJECT

### PROJECT 1A

Create a notebook for Pet Paradise that contains the fees for the different boarding services.

1.  Start Quattro Pro, if necessary. A new, empty notebook should be on the screen.

2.  Key **Boarding Fees** in cell A1.

3.  Key the labels in the following cells:

    | | |
    |----|----|
    | A3 | **Type of Pet** |
    | A4 | **Cat** |
    | A5 | **Small Dog** |
    | A6 | **Medium Dog** |
    | A7 | **Large Dog** |

4.  Key the following data:

    | | |
    |----|----|
    | B3 | **Per Day** |
    | B4 | **$6** |
    | B5 | **$8** |
    | B6 | **$10** |
    | B7 | **$12.5** |

5.  Adjust the width of column A so that all of the labels are visible.

6.  Save the notebook as **boarding fees proj1a xxx**.

7.  Print the Current Sheet in Portrait orientation and close the notebook.

### PROJECT 1B

Modify the sales data for Morrison Used Cars.

1.  Open the **car sales** notebook in the student **Datafile** folder. The first sheet contains the sales figures for each salesperson for three months.

2.  Save the notebook as **car sales proj1b xxx**.

3.  Move the subheading *Quarterly Sales* from cell A3 to A2.

4.  Key **Salesperson** in cell A5.

5.  Use **QuickFill** to enter **January**, **February**, and **March** in cells B5..D5.

(continued on next page)

6. Adjust the width of the columns so that all of the labels can be seen.

7. Change the value in cell B6 to **29,108**. Change the value in cell D9 to **90,504**.

8. Add the following data for a new salesperson:

   A12    **Lomez, V.**
   B12    **88,302**
   C12    **93,148**
   D12    **81,769**

9. Save the notebook and print the Current Sheet in Landscape orientation.

10. Close the notebook.

## CRITICAL THINKING ACTIVITY

SCANS

You have started a small business in which you provide a variety of services for your neighbors. Create a notebook that will contain a sheet listing each of your services. The name of each service should be listed, plus its hourly rate. Make up your own services. Some examples might include pet walking, babysitting, and yard work. What additional items might you include in your notebook? Choose a name for your business and place it at the top of the sheet. The name should describe your business. What name did you choose?

# MODIFYING THE NOTEBOOK

## OBJECTIVES

**Upon completion of this lesson, you will be able to:**

- Add a title to a spreadsheet.
- Format numbers.
- Insert, delete, and move blocks of cells.
- Change the font, font size, and font style of data.
- Change the alignment of contents of cells.
- Apply borders, shading, colors, and other special formats.
- Change the height of rows and the width of columns.
- Use the SpeedFormat feature.

⏱ **Estimated Time: 1½ hours**

Quattro Pro has many formatting options that allow you to transform your notebooks from the standard grid to attractive, professional-looking documents. In this lesson you will learn how to enhance the appearance of your notebook sheets. You will use various formatting options to change fonts and the appearance of an entire notebook sheet. You will also learn how to use Quattro Pro's timesaving SpeedFormat feature.

## Adding a Title to a Spreadsheet

Having a title on a spreadsheet allows the reader to quickly determine the spreadsheet's purpose. A title is actually a label you enter in a cell to identify the contents of the spreadsheet. You can have a single title and a number of subtitles, if you wish. They can be formatted in a variety of creative ways.

## Formatting Values

As you've probably noticed, the values that you have entered so far have not been formatted. For example, the dollar amounts haven't had a standard format, such as two decimal places. Quattro Pro makes it easy to format an entire range of values with only a few simple commands. That way, you don't have to spend lots of time keying characters like dollar signs, commands, and dates. Let's add a title to a notebook and apply a numeric format.

1. Open the **boarding** notebook in the student **Datafile** folder. The first sheet of this notebook lists Pet Paradise's daily income for boarding cats and dogs. Save the notebook as **boarding 2-1 xxx**.

2. In cell A1 key the title **Pet Paradise**. In cell A2, key the subtitle **Boarding Income**.

3. Select the range **B4..E10**. Open the **Format** menu and choose **Selection**. The Active Cells dialog box appears, as shown in Figure 2-1. Notice that this dialog box has many different tabs, each allowing you to perform a different type of formatting. You will be learning how to use these different options throughout this lesson.

4. Click the **Numeric Format** tab.

5. In the Numeric Format tab click **Currency**. Accept the default settings of two decimal places and United States currency. Click **OK.**

**NOTE:**

If a series of asterisks appears in a cell instead of a value, it simply means the entry is longer than the column width. Widen the column so that the numbers can be displayed.

6. Key the following dates in the cells indicated:

| A4: | **9/2** | A8: | **9/6** |
| A5: | **9/3** | A9: | **9/7** |
| A6: | **9/4** | A10: | **9/8** |
| A7: | **9/5** | | |

**NOTE:**

Quattro Pro may automatically format the values you enter in Step 6 as dates (for example, as 09/02).

**FIGURE 2-1**
Active Cells Dialog Box

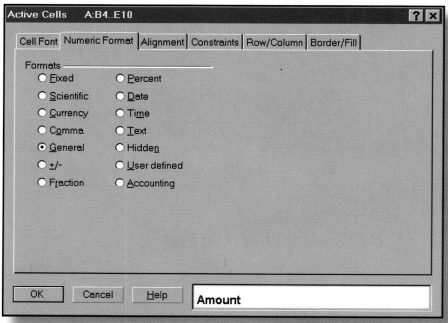

7. A fast way to open the Active Cells dialog box is to right click on a cell and use the QuickMenu. Select cell **A4**. Right click to open the QuickMenu and select **Cell Properties**.

8. In the Numeric Format tab click **Date**. For *Date Formats*, click **DD-MMM** and then click **OK**. Cell A4 appears in the specified format.

**TIP**

If you do not need to format an entire row or column, select only the portion that you need to format. Formatting more cells than are needed makes the file size larger than necessary.

9. Save the notebook and keep it open for the next exercise.

# Using QuickFormat

Quattro Pro has a useful feature called QuickFormat that allows you to copy the formatting from one cell to other cells. It can be used to copy the formatting of the cell's contents or any other formatting, such as the background color of the cell. In the next exercise you will see how easy it is to copy numeric formatting from one cell to an entire group of cells.

**EXERCISE ⇒ QP2.2**

1. Save the notebook as **boarding 2-2 xxx**.

2. Make certain that cell **A4** is still selected. Click the **QuickFormat** button on the Toolbar. The mouse pointer turns into a paint roller.

3. Drag the paint roller down cells **A5..A10**.

4. Click the **QuickFormat** button to deselect it.

5. If necessary, adjust the column widths so that all of the cells' contents are visible.

**IMPORTANT:**

As long as the QuickFormat button is depressed, you can continue copying the formatting to other locations. As soon as you are done, click the button. The mouse pointer will return to its normal appearance.

6. Save the notebook again and keep it open.

# Manipulating Blocks of Cells

The structure of a sheet in a notebook can be changed by inserting or deleting columns, rows, or ranges of cells. You also can move the contents of cells to different locations on the sheet.

## Inserting Blocks of Cells

To insert a column or row, position the pointer in the column or row that will *follow* the one you are inserting. To insert a column, open the Insert menu and choose Column. To insert a row, open the Insert menu and choose Row. You also can click the Insert button on the Toolbar. The Insert Cells dialog box appears, as shown in Figure 2-2. Regardless of which method you use, column letters and row numbers are adjusted to reflect the insertion.

**FIGURE 2-2**
Insert Cells Dialog Box

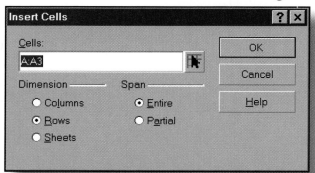

## Deleting and Moving Blocks of Cells

You can delete a selected column or row by using the Delete command in the Edit menu. The remaining columns or rows are renumbered accordingly. If you select a cell or a block of cells and press the Delete key, the cells' contents are erased.

You can reposition entries on a notebook sheet by selecting them and then dragging them to a new location. You will practice moving blocks of cells in Exercise QP2.3. When you drag a block of cells to a new location, it will overwrite any data that was previously in that location. Therefore, be very careful when moving blocks of cells so that you do not accidentally overwrite data that you need.

## E X E R C I S E ▷ QP2.3

**1.** Save the notebook as **boarding 2-3 xxx**.

**2.** Select any cell in row 3 and then open the **Insert** menu and choose **Row**. Notice that a new, blank row 3 is inserted. The data that was previously in row 3 is now in row 4.

**3.** Select any cell in column B and then open the **Insert** menu and choose **Column**. A new, blank column B is inserted.

**4.** Reposition column F (*Cats*) so that it becomes column B:
   **a.** Click in the heading for column F to select the entire column.
   **b.** Position the mouse pointer near the right edge of column F. It should turn into a four-way arrow.

### IMPORTANT:

If you drag cells to a location that already contains data, the previous data will be overwritten.

   **c.** Drag column F to the left until it is directly over column B. The colored border will help to guide you.
   **d.** Release the mouse button. The data that was in column F should now be in column B.

**5.** Save the notebook again and keep it open.

# *Changing the Appearance of Data*

The appearance of data in a notebook is characterized by various attributes that you can change to enhance the look of your spreadsheet and make it more readable. Text attributes include font (also called typeface), font size, and font style.

- *Font* or *typeface* refers to all the characters in a particular design of type. Times New Roman and Arial are examples of fonts.

- *Font size* refers to the height of characters measured in points. There are 72 points in an inch, so 72-point text measures 1 inch in height.

- *Font style* refers to attributes such as bold, italic, and underlining, which change the appearance of a font.

You can change attributes by first selecting the data you want to format and then choosing Selection from the Format menu. Select the Cell Font tab in the Active Cells dialog box. Or you can select a font or font size from the drop-down lists on the Property Bar. The Property Bar also contains Bold, Italic, and Underline buttons that you can use to change the style of data. In the next exercise you will change the fonts and font sizes used in a spreadsheet.

## E X E R C I S E ▭⟩ QP2.4

1. Save the notebook as **boarding 2-4 xxx**.

2. Select cell **A1** and then right click and then click **Cell Properties**. The Active Cells dialog box appears, as shown in Figure 2-3. Click the **Cell Font** tab.

3. In the *Font face* list box, select **Impact**. (If Impact is not available, select a similar font as directed by your instructor.)

    `Arial ▼`

**TIP**

You will probably need to scroll down in the *Font face* list box to locate the font named Impact.

4. Open the *Font size* drop-down list box and select **14**. Click **OK**.

    `10 ▼`

5. Select cell **A2**. Change the font of the subheading *Boarding Income* by clicking the

font drop-down list box on the Property Bar and selecting **Impact**.

6. Make certain that cell **A2** is still selected. Change the font size of the subheading by clicking the *Font size* drop-down list box and selecting **12**.

7. Select cells **B4..E4** and click the **Bold** button on the Property Bar to make the text boldface.

8. Select the dates in the range **A5..A11** and click the **Italic** button on the Property Bar to place the dates in italic.

9. Select the range **B5..E11**. Choose a different font; you can use any one that you wish.

10. Save the notebook and keep it open.

**FIGURE 2-3**
Cell Font Tab in the Active Cells Dialog Box

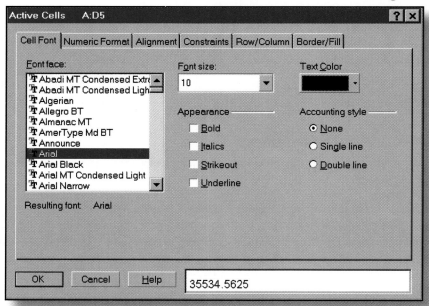

# Changing the Alignment of Data

Alignment refers to how data is positioned within a cell. As previously mentioned, Quattro Pro automatically aligns labels at the left of a cell and values at the right. You can change the vertical and horizontal alignment of data by selecting the Alignment tab in the Active Cells dialog box shown in Figure 2-4. You can see the Alignment tab by opening the Format menu, choosing Selection, and then clicking the Alignment tab.

**FIGURE 2-4**
Alignment Tab in the Active Cells Dialog Box

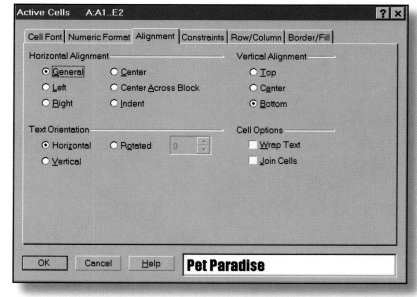

You also can change the horizontal alignment of a cell's contents by clicking the Alignment button on the Property Bar. A drop-down list box appears, allowing you to select the type of alignment you wish to use.

# EXERCISE ⟹ QP2.5

1. Save the notebook as **boarding 2-5 xxx**.

2. Select the range **A1..E2**. Right click and then click **Cell Properties**. In the Active Cells dialog box click the **Alignment** tab.

3. In the Horizontal Alignment options, General is the default alignment. If you select the Center Across Block option, the text is centered across a selected block of cells. The Wrap Text option wraps a long entry on multiple lines so it fits within a cell. The Vertical Alignment options align data within cells at the top, center, or bottom. The Text Orientation options let you determine whether entries read across the cell or up and down in the cell.

    Under *Horizontal Alignment*, click **Center Across Block** and click **OK**. The heading and subheading will be centered above the data columns.

4. Select the range **A5..A11**. Click the **Alignment** button on the Property Bar. In the drop-down menu click the **Center** option.

Click here for Center Alignment.

5. Select cells **B4..E4**. Right click and then click **Cell Properties**. The Alignment tab should appear in the Active Cells dialog box. Under *Horizontal Alignment*, click **Center** and click **OK**. The column headings will be centered.

6. Save the notebook and keep it open.

# Adding Colors and Borders to Spreadsheets

If you are using a color monitor and/or a color printer, you can dramatically enhance the appearance of your notebooks by adding color and other graphic elements such as borders. You can add color to the background of a cell or make the text within a cell colored. You also can draw borders around selected cells or around an entire sheet.

The Border/Fill tab in the Active Cells dialog box lets you add color to cells (see Figure 2-5). You can open the *Fill Color* drop-down list box and click the color you want. If you wish, click the More button at

**FIGURE 2-5**
The Border/Fill Tab in the Active Cells Dialog Box

the bottom of the *Fill Color* drop-down list box to mix your own custom color. When the More button is clicked, the Shading dialog box appears (see Figure 2-6). You can select a color from the Color 1 selections and another color from the Color 2 selections. The resulting blends appear at the bottom of the dialog box.

Borders and dividing lines add a distinctive appearance to spreadsheets and can be used to draw attention to important data. The Border/Fill tab in the Active Cells dialog box lets you select from one of a list of options (All, Outline, or Inside), or click a line segment to specify where you want a border to appear. To select more than one segment, hold down Shift as you click. Then select a border type and a border color.

**FIGURE 2-6**
The Shading Dialog Box

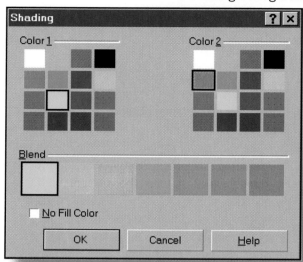

## EXERCISE ⇨ QP2.6

**1.** Save the notebook as **boarding 2-6 xxx**.

**2.** Select the range **A1..E2**. This range contains the sheet's headings. In the Active Cells dialog box click the **Cell Font** tab.

**3.** Open the *Text Color* drop-down list box and click **red**. Red is in the first column, second row. Click **OK**. Click anywhere in the spreadsheet to deselect the headings. The headings are placed in red type.

**4.** Select the range **A5..E11**. Right click and click **Cell Properties**, and then click the **Border/Fill** tab.

**5.** Open the *Fill Color* drop-down list box and click **yellow** (sixth column, fourth row). Click **OK**. The background for this range becomes yellow.

**6.** Make certain that the range **A5..E11** is still selected. Right click and click **Cell Properties**, and then click the **Border/Fill** tab.

**7.** Click the **All** button. This option will cause a grid to be placed around each cell in the range. (Remember that the grid you see on-screen does not print. This border that you are inserting will be printed.)

**8.** Open the *Border Type* drop-down list box and select the last option (the widest line). Click **OK**. The border will be applied to the range.

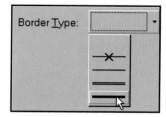

**9.** Save the notebook. When you are done with this exercise, this sheet should look like the one shown in Figure 2-8. Keep the notebook open.

**FIGURE 2-7**
The Text Color List Box in the Active Cells Dialog Box

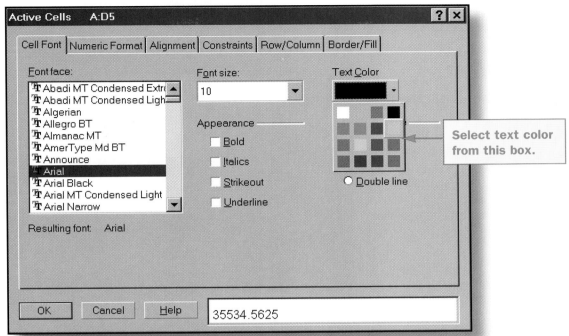

**FIGURE 2-8**
The Pet Paradise Boarding Income Sheet As It Appears at the End of Exercise QP2.6

|    | A       | B       | C          | D           | E          | F |
|----|---------|---------|------------|-------------|------------|---|
| 1  |         |         | **Pet Paradise** |       |            |   |
| 2  |         |         | **Boarding Income** |    |            |   |
| 3  |         |         |            |             |            |   |
| 4  |         | **Cats** | **Small Dogs** | **Medium Dogs** | **Large Dogs** |   |
| 5  | 02-Sep  | $24.00  | $88.00     | $90.00      | $87.50     |   |
| 6  | 03-Sep  | $12.00  | $56.00     | $60.00      | $50.00     |   |
| 7  | 04-Sep  | $12.00  | $56.00     | $50.00      | $50.00     |   |
| 8  | 05-Sep  | $12.00  | $64.00     | $50.00      | $62.50     |   |
| 9  | 06-Sep  | $6.00   | $56.00     | $40.00      | $50.00     |   |
| 10 | 07-Sep  | $36.00  | $88.00     | $60.00      | $75.00     |   |
| 11 | 08-Sep  | $36.00  | $104.00    | $80.00      | $87.50     |   |
| 12 |         |         |            |             |            |   |

# *Adjusting Row Height and Column Width*

You have already used the QuickFit button to adjust column width. The Row/Column tab in the Active Cells dialog box (see Figure 2-9) gives you even more options for changing the width of columns. It also lets you specify the height of the rows.

The width of a column can be measured in several different ways. The default measurement is in characters. To change the current width, click Reset width and then enter the new width.

You can also adjust the height of rows in the Row/ Column tab. The default measurement for row height is points. (Remember that there are 72 points in an inch.) To change the row height, click Reset height and then enter the new height.

**FIGURE 2-9**
The Row/Column Tab in the Active Cells Dialog Box

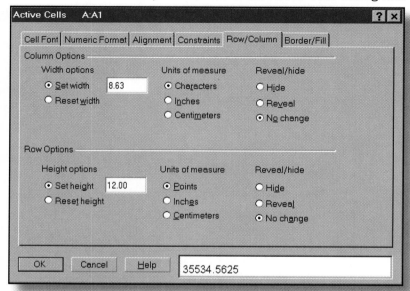

EXERCISE ⇒ QP2.7

1. Save the notebook as **boarding 2-7 xxx**.

2. Select cells **A4..E11**. Right click and then click **Cell Properties**. Click the **Row/Column** tab.

3. Click **Reset width**. In the text box to the right of *Set width*, key **14**. Click **OK**. The selected columns are made wider.

4. Select cells **A1..E2**. Right click and then click **Cell Properties**. The Row/Column tab should appear.

5. Click **Reset height**. In the text box to the right of *Set height*, key **20**. Click **OK**. Click anywhere to deselect the cells. The first two rows should become taller than the remaining rows.

6. Save the notebook. Open the **File** menu and choose **Print**. Click **Current Sheet**, if necessary. Click **Print**.

 NOTE:

Remember that while a spreadsheet may appear in color on the display screen, it will not print in color unless you are using a color printer.

7. Keep this notebook open for the next exercise.

**INTERNET**

Users of the Internet include schools, government agencies, businesses, libraries, colleges and universities, military bases, and more. Every year, in addition, more and more people can access the Internet from their homes.

# *Using SpeedFormat*

SpeedFormat is a useful feature because you can choose a predefined format and apply it to an entire notebook. SpeedFormat automatically applies the many formatting options you've learned about in this lesson, including using different fonts, font sizes, alignments, shading, text color, and borders. You will be trying out SpeedFormat in Exercise QP2.8.

**IMPORTANT:**

When you apply SpeedFormat to a range of cells, any previous formatting is removed. For example, if you had previously formatted a heading in bold type, that formatting will be removed and the SpeedFormat option you have chosen will be applied.

## EXERCISE ⟹ QP2.8

1. Save the notebook as **boarding 2-8 xxx**.

2. Select the range **A4..E11**. Open the **Format** menu and choose **SpeedFormat**. The SpeedFormat dialog box appears, as shown in Figure 2-10.

3. Spend a minute browsing through the various formats. Click several of them and see how they appear in the *Example* box. Click **Primary Colors** to select it. (You will need to scroll down to see it.)

**FIGURE 2-10**
SpeedFormat Dialog Box

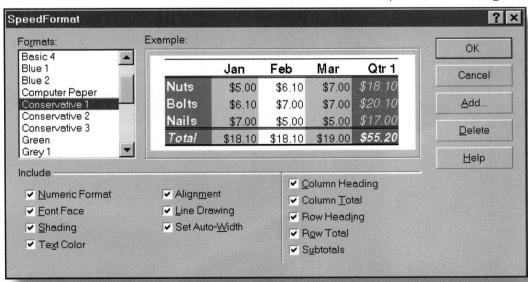

(continued on next page)

**4.** Spend a minute looking at the *Include* section at the bottom of the dialog box. This section allows you to choose the formatting options you want applied. For example, if your data does not include a totals row at the bottom, you would deselect the Column Total option because you would not want the bottom row to be formatted differently from the rest of the rows.

In the *Include* section:
- **a.** Click **Alignment** to deselect it (you want to leave the alignment as you have already specified it).
- **b.** Click **Column Total** to deselect it.
- **c.** Click **Row Total** to deselect it.
- **d.** Click **OK**.

**5.** Click anywhere on the page so that you can see the new format.

**6.** Notice that the dollar values are no longer formatted as currency. You will need to reformat them as currency. Select the range **B5..E11**. Right click and then click **Cell Properties**. Click the **Numeric Format** tab and click **Currency**. Accept the default settings of two decimal places and United States currency. Click **OK**.

**7.** If necessary, resize the columns so that all of the data in the cells is visible.

**8.** Save the notebook and then print the current sheet. The sheet should appear as shown in Figure 2-11.

**9.** Close the notebook and then exit Quattro Pro.

**TIP**

A quick way to close a notebook and leave Quattro Pro is to right click the Application Bar at the bottom of the window and click Close All.

**FIGURE 2-11**
After SpeedFormat Is Applied to Boarding Income Sheet

| | A | B | C | D | E | F |
|---|---|---|---|---|---|---|
| 1 | | | **Pet Paradise** | | | |
| 2 | | | **Boarding Income** | | | |
| 3 | | | | | | |
| 4 | | Cats | Small Dogs | Medium Dogs | Large Dogs | |
| 5 | 02-Sep | | $88.00 | $90.00 | $87.50 | |
| 6 | 03-Sep | $12.00 | $56.00 | $60.00 | $50.00 | |
| 7 | 04-Sep | $12.00 | $56.00 | $50.00 | $50.00 | |
| 8 | 05-Sep | $12.00 | $64.00 | $50.00 | $62.50 | |
| 9 | 06-Sep | $6.00 | $56.00 | $40.00 | $50.00 | |
| 10 | 07-Sep | $36.00 | $88.00 | $60.00 | $75.00 | |
| 11 | 08-Sep | $36.00 | $104.00 | $80.00 | $87.50 | |
| 12 | | | | | | |

# *Summary*

In this lesson you learned to make your spreadsheets more attractive and easier to read. You learned that:

- you can use the Numeric Format tab in the Active Cells dialog box to format numbers, currency, or dates.

- the QuickFormat button on the Toolbar lets you copy the formatting of one cell to other cells.

- the Insert menu allows you to insert new columns and rows into a sheet; the lettering and numbering is automatically adjusted.

- you can move selected columns, rows, or cells by dragging them to a new spot.

- you can use the Property Bar to change the font, font size, and font style of cell contents.

- the Border/Fill tab in the Active Cells dialog box allows you to change the background color and the color of text used in cells. In addition, borders can be added.

- the Alignment tab lets you align the contents of cells in a number of ways, including left, right, and centered. Labels can be centered across a selected block of cells.

- on the Row/Column tab, you can specify the exact width of columns and height of rows.

- the SpeedFormat feature contains a number of predefined formats that you can apply to a specific section of a sheet, an entire sheet, or even an entire notebook.

## LESSON 2 REVIEW QUESTIONS

### TRUE/FALSE

**Circle the T if the statement is true. Circle the F if it is false.**

**T  F  1.** The purpose of SpeedFormat is to allow you to adjust the horizontal width and vertical height of cells.

**T  F  2.** Quattro Pro has no easy way to center headings across a block of columns; you must center the headings manually.

**T  F  3.** When you move a column, any data previously in the new location is overwritten.

**T  F  4.** All of the text in a specific spreadsheet must use the same font.

**T  F  5.** You can place text in color or make the background of a block of cells a specific color.

(continued on next page)

## FILL IN THE BLANKS

**Complete each of the following statements by writing your answer in the blank provided.**

6. You can format numbers as currency by using the _____ tab in the Active Cells dialog box.

7. Quattro Pro's _____ feature lets you apply a predefined format to a sheet.

8. To add a new row to an existing sheet, choose Row in the _____ menu.

9. Bold, italic, and underline are all examples of font _____.

10. To change the color of the text in cells, go to the _____ tab in the Active Cells dialog box.

## LESSON 2 PROJECT

SCANS

### PROJECT 2A

You need to format a customer's bill for Pet Paradise so that it will be easy to read and professional looking.

1. Open the **bill** notebook in the student **Datafile** folder and save it as **bill proj2a xxx**.

2. Select cells **A1..D4** and center these headings across the block.

3. Select cell **A1** and change the font size to **16**. Select cells **A2..A4** and change the font size to **14**.

4. Format all of the numeric values as Currency with two decimal places.

5. Select cells **A1..D4** and place a wide navy-blue border around the outer edge of this block of cells.

6. Make the background of cells **A1..D4** light blue.

7. Select cell **A6** and make the cell's contents bold.

8. Select cells **A8..A13** and place their contents in italics.

9. Select cells **A13..D13** and make the cell's contents bold. Change the text in these cells to navy blue.

10. Select cells **A8..D8** and center the contents of these cells. Also change the font size to **12**.

11. If necessary, widen the columns so that all of their contents are visible.

12. Save the notebook and print a copy of the current sheet. Close the notebook.

## PROJECT 2B

1. Open the **morrison sale** notebook in the student **Datafile** folder and save it as **morrison sale proj2b xxx**.

2. Center the headings in rows 1 and 2 across the columns containing data.

3. Place the headings in rows 1 and 2 in a color of your own choice. Change their font size to **18**.

4. Select cells **A4..C20**. Open the SpeedFormat dialog box. Under *Formats*, select **Conservative 2**. In the *Include* section deselect **Column Total** and **Row Total**. Click **OK** to apply the format.

5. Notice that the *Year* column is now formatted with decimal places and commas. To correct this problem, select cells **B5..B20**. Open the **Format** menu and choose **Selection**. Click the **Numeric Format** tab and under *Formats*, select **Fixed**. Enter **0** for the number of decimal places. Click **OK**.

6. Format the values in the *Sale Price* column as currency with no decimal places.

7. Make certain that all of the columns are wide enough to display their values.

8. Print the current sheet.

9. Select cells **A4..C20** again. Open the SpeedFormat dialog box. Under *Formats*, select **Yellow 4**. In the *Include* section deselect **Column Total** and **Row Total**. Click **OK** to apply the format.

10. Because the formatting was removed from the *Sale Price* column, reformat these numbers as currency.

11. Print the current sheet and save it again. Close the notebook and exit Quattro Pro.

## CRITICAL THINKING ACTIVITY

SCANS

Spend some time examining the different ways a notebook can be formatted. You may wish to apply different formatting to a notebook you worked on in this lesson, such as **boarding 2-6 xxx**. Try using different colors, vertical dividing lines, and so forth, to separate the different parts of the notebook. See how different border widths and border colors affect the sheet's appearance. Also, practice applying different options in the SpeedFormat dialog box. As you try these different formatting options, compare them with one another. Print at least two examples of formatting that you think are attractive and make the sheet easier to read. Ask other people which of your formats they find easiest to read and why.

# USING FORMULAS AND FUNCTIONS

## OBJECTIVES

**Upon completion of this lesson, you will be able to:**

■ Identify the different components of a formula.

■ Reference cells in formulas.

■ Use the QuickSum feature.

■ Copy formulas.

■ Apply the rules of operator precedence to a formula.

■ Use both relative references and absolute references in formulas.

■ Examine several of the functions available in Quattro Pro.

■ Assign names to ranges of cells.

■ Use the Formula Composer to perform financial calculations.

🕐 **Estimated Time: 2 hours**

So far you have entered labels and values into spreadsheet cells and formatted them in a variety of ways. However, the true power of spreadsheet software such as Quattro Pro lies in its ability to perform calculations on data. Quattro Pro can easily find the sum of a column, determine the average of a hundred numbers, or even calculate the payments on an automobile loan. In this lesson you will learn how to create formulas to perform a variety of calculations. You also will be introduced to Quattro Pro's various predefined formulas that make your work easier.

## *The Components of a Formula*

A *formula* is any mathematical operation you perform on data. There are three types of formulas: text formulas, where the result is textual; logical formulas, where the result is either yes or no, or true or false; and arithmetic formulas, where the result is the calculation of numeric values. Arithmetic formulas are the most commonly used.

An arithmetic formula is composed of values and operators. Values can include numbers, cell references (also called addresses), or cell ranges. *Operators* indicate the type of mathematical operation you will perform. Table 3-1 lists the most commonly used operators.

To enter a formula into a cell, key a plus sign (+). The plus sign tells Quattro Pro that this cell will contain a formula. Then enter a value or a cell reference. You can reference a cell by entering the cell's address or by simply clicking the cell. Then enter an operator followed by another value or cell reference. When you press Enter or click the check mark on the input line to confirm the formula, the result appears in the cell. If the selected cell contains a formula, the result of that formula will always appear in the cell, whereas the actual formula will appear in the input line.

**TABLE 3-1**
Operators

| Operator | Operation It Performs |
| --- | --- |
| + | Addition |
| – | Subtraction |
| * | Multiplication |
| / | Division |

**TIP**

If you wish, you can enter spaces between the different parts of a formula. However, when you click the check mark to confirm the formula, Quattro Pro will automatically remove any of these spaces.

**E X E R C I S E QP3.1**

SCANS

1. Open the **grooming 1-6 xxx** notebook that you created in Lesson 1. It should be stored in the student **Datafile** folder. Save the notebook as **grooming 3-1 xxx**.

2. Format cells **B4..G10** as currency with two decimal places. Format cells **B16..G22** as currency with two decimal places.

3. Resize the cells if necessary, so that the values can be seen.

4. Insert a blank row after row 2 to separate the spreadsheet's title from the column headings.

5. Find the total for the *Mon* column for Pet Paradise I:
   a. Click cell **B11**. This is where the total will appear.
   b. Key **+** to start the formula.
   c. Click cell **B5** to enter it into the formula. Notice that it appears in the input line.
   d. Key **+** to add cell B5 to the next value.
   e. Click cell **B6** to enter it into the formula and key **+**.
   f. Click cell **B7** and key **+**.
   g. Click cell **B8** and key **+**.
   h. Click cell **B9**.
   i. Press **Enter** to confirm the formula. The total appears in cell B11.

6. Save the notebook and keep it open.

## Using QuickSum

Keying a formula that contains a number of operators and cell references is tedious, especially if all you need to do is add the values together. Fortunately, Quattro Pro has a special QuickSum feature that allows you to add the values in a column or row with the click of a button. To use QuickSum, select the range of cells to be added, including a blank cell following the range that will contain the total. Then click the QuickSum button on the Toolbar. The sum appears in the blank cell.

QuickSum adds together only the values in the selected range. It ignores any labels.

# Copying Formulas

Many times you may want to use the same formula on several different rows or columns. You can copy formulas by using the Copy button just as you would copy text. Another easy way to copy formulas is to use the QuickFill button on the Toolbar. Drag to select the cell whose formula you want copied, along with the cell or cells into which the formula should be copied. Click the QuickFill button and the formula is placed in the selected cells.

You may be wondering what happens when you copy a formula that contains one or more cell references. What's neat about Quattro Pro is that unless you specify otherwise, cell references in a formula are *relative*. A *relative cell reference* changes in relation to the cell containing the formula. For example, assume that cell A3 contains the formula A1+A2; that is, cell A3 has the sum of the two cells above it. If you copy the formula in cell A3 into cell B3, Quattro Pro automatically alters the cell references so that the formula in cell B3 is B1+B2. This makes it easy for you to use the same formula in different locations.

## EXERCISE ⇨ QP3.2

SCANS

1. Save the notebook as **grooming 3-2 xxx**.

2. Select cells **C5..C11**.

3. Click the **QuickSum** button on the Toolbar. The sum appears in cell C11.

4. Select cells **C11..G11**.

5. Click the **QuickFill** button on the Toolbar. Columns D through G are totaled.

6. Select cell **G11**. Click the **Copy** button to place the formula in this cell on the Clipboard.

7. Select cell **B23**. Click the **Paste** button to copy the formula from the Clipboard to this cell.

8. Select cells **B23..G23.**

9. Click the **QuickFill** button on the Toolbar to total cells C23..G23.

10. Make certain that all of the numeric values are formatted as currency and that the contents of all of the cells are visible.

11. Save the notebook, print it, and close it.

**NOTE:**

Numeric formatting does not affect the values themselves, just the way that they are displayed. For example, if you have the number 17.653 stored in a cell and you format it as currency with two decimal places, it will appear on the screen as $17.65. However, the value 17.653 is stored in the cell.

# *Understanding Rules of Operator Precedence*

Frequently you will want to enter more complex formulas than ones that simply total values. For example, you might want to add two values and then multiply the result by a third value. Quattro Pro carries out mathematical operations in *order of operator precedence*. For the most commonly used operators, the order of precedence is multiplication, division, addition, and subtraction.

**NOTE:**

An easy way to remember the order of precedence for the common operators is to think of the phrase **M**y **D**ear **A**unt **S**ally.

For example, in the formula +20-5*3, Quattro Pro would multiply 5 by 3 and then subtract this value from 20. The result would be 5. If Quattro Pro were to subtract 5 from 20 first, and then multiply that value by 3, the result would be 45, a very different answer. As you can see, it's important to understand the rules of precedence or you could end up with results you do not want!

You can control the order in which operations are carried out by using parentheses in formulas. Enclosing a portion of a formula in parentheses tells Quattro Pro to perform that operation first. For example, the formula +(20-5)*3 equals 45. As we have already determined, the result without the parentheses is 5. You can even nest parentheses inside other parentheses and Quattro Pro computes the operation in the innermost set of parentheses first.

EXERCISE ⟶ QP3.3

SCANS

1. Open the **weekly** notebook in the student **Datafile** folder. This notebook contains the weekly payroll spreadsheet for Pet Paradise I. Save the notebook as **weekly 3-3 xxx**.

2. Compute the gross pay for Robert Greene by multiplying the hourly rate by the hours worked.
   a. Select cell **D5**. Key **+**.
   b. Click cell **B5**. Key **\***.
   c. Click cell **C5**.
   d. Press **Enter**. The gross pay appears in cell D5.

(continued on next page)

**NOTE:**

Quattro Pro calculates results to 16 significant digits (any digit that is not a leading zero) but rounds numbers to the specified decimal place. For that reason, some results may differ slightly if they are computed on a calculator.

3. Compute the deductions for Robert Greene. This requires the FICA tax (which is 7.65%) and the federal tax (which will be computed at 15%) to be subtracted from the gross pay.
   a. Select cell **E5**. Key **+**.
   b. Click cell **D5**. Key **\***. Key **.0765** (for the FICA tax). Key **+**.
   c. Click cell **D5**. Key **\***. Key **.15** (for the federal tax).
   d. Press **Enter**.

4. Calculate the net pay.
   a. Select cell **F5**. Key **+**.
   b. Click cell **D5**. Key **-**.
   c. Click cell **E5**. Press **Enter**.

5. Use the **QuickFill** button to copy the formula in cell D5 to cells D6..D11.

6. Copy the formula in cell E5 to cells E6..E11.

7. Copy the formula in cell F5 to cells F6..F11.

8. Make certain that all of the dollar amounts are formatted as currency.

9. Save the notebook.

10. Print the current sheet and close the notebook.

# *Using Absolute Cell References*

So far we have been using relative cell references. If we copied a formula to another cell, Quattro Pro would alter the formula to refer to the corresponding cells in the new location. However, there will be times when you do not want Quattro Pro to use relative cell references. In these situations an absolute cell reference must be used. An *absolute cell reference* does not change when a formula is copied from one cell to another. You designate an absolute reference by inserting a dollar sign ($) before the column letter and row number in the cell address. For example, if you want to specify that a cell's contents should always be multiplied by the value in cell B5, regardless of where the formula was used in the spreadsheet, you would use the absolute reference $B$5.

**NOTE:**

Using a dollar sign ($) before both the column and the row means that the cell references will never change when the formula is copied to another cell. However, if you place a dollar sign before only the column (for example, $B5), the column reference will always be the same while the row reference will "float." Likewise, placing a dollar sign before the row (B$5) will cause the column reference to "float", but the row reference to remain unchanged.

# EXERCISE ▷ QP3.4

**1.** Open the **quarterly grooming** notebook in the student **Datafile** folder. This notebook contains information on Pet Paradise's grooming income by quarter. Save the file as **quarterly grooming 3-4 xxx**.

**2.** Find the total income for Complete Grooming for the first quarter and place it in cell G6.
   **a.** Select cell **G6**. Key **+**.
   **b.** Key **$B$6**. Key **\***.
   **c.** Click cell **C6**. Examine the input line. Notice that the address for cell B6 is absolute while the address for cell C6 is relative.
   **d.** Press **Enter** to confirm the entry. The total income appears in cell G6.

**3.** Use **QuickFill** to copy the formula in cell G6 to cells H6..J6.
   **a.** Select cells **G6..J6**.
   **b.** Click the **QuickFill** button.

**4.** Insert the needed formulas in Row 7.
   **a.** Click cell **G6**. Click the **Copy** button on the Toolbar.
   **b.** Click cell **G7**. Click the **Paste** button on the Toolbar. The sum appears in cell G7.

**c.** Click cell **G7**. Go to the input line and change the reference *$B$6* to **$B$7**. Press **Enter**. Now the formula will use the cost for *Bathing Only* in calculating these values.
   **d.** Use the **QuickFill** button to copy the formula in cell G7 to cells H7..J7.

**5.** Repeat Step 4 for Rows 8, 9, and 10. Be sure in each case to change the formula so that it uses the correct fee for each service.

**NOTE:**

You are using absolute addressing for the fee for each service, because the location of the cell containing the fee will not change, regardless of which quarter is being calculated.

**6.** Format cells **G6..J10** as currency. Make certain that all of the values can be seen in the sheet.

**7.** Save the notebook and keep it open.

# *Understanding Functions*

Quattro Pro provides numerous predefined formulas—called *@functions* (or simply *functions*) because they begin with the @ sign. These functions automatically perform calculations on selected data. A function can be entered alone or as part of a larger formula. In fact, the QuickSum feature we used earlier in this lesson is really just a speedy way to apply Quattro Pro's SUM function. If you select a cell on which you have used QuickSum, you will see the SUM function displayed in the input line.

The structure of a function is referred to as its syntax, or the rules that determine how it should be created. Most functions consist of a function name followed by one or more arguments in parentheses. The *argument* is the data on which the function is performed, such as a numeric value or a range of cells. If you wanted to find the sum of the values in cells B1..B10, the argument of the SUM function would be B1..B10.

Quattro Pro contains hundreds of built-in functions for performing a wide range of mathematical, financial, engineering, and statistical calculations. Table 3-2 lists some of the more commonly used functions.

TABLE 3-2
Commonly Used Functions

| Function | Calculation It Performs |
| --- | --- |
| @SUM(A1..A5) | Adds the contents of cells A1 through A5 |
| @AVG(A1..A5) | Finds the average of the contents of cells A1 through A5 |
| @COUNT(A1..A5) | Counts the number of nonblank values in the range A1..A5 |
| @MIN(A1..A5) | Finds the smallest value in cells A1 through A5 |
| @MAX(A1..A5) | Finds the largest value in cells A1 through A5 |
| @ROUND(A1,2) | Rounds the contents of cell A1 to two decimal places |

E X E R C I S E   QP3.5

**SCANS**

1. Save the notebook as **quarterly grooming 3-5 xxx**.

2. Select cell **K6**.

3. Open the **Insert** menu and choose **Function**. The Functions dialog box appears, as shown in Figure 3-1. The left side of the dialog box displays a list of the categories of functions. The right side shows the functions available for the chosen category. When you click a particular function, a description appears at the bottom of the dialog box.

4. In the Functions dialog box select **ALL** under *Function Category*.
   a. In the *Function* list select **AVG**. You will need to scroll down to see the AVG function. Click **OK**.
   b. For the argument, key **G6..J6)**. Press **Enter**. The result should be *18792*.

**TIP**

When entering the arguments into the cells to calculate the average, be sure not only to enter the cell addresses, but also to enter the closing parenthesis.

5. Copy the formula in cell K6 to cells K7..K10.

6. Complete the following steps to place the total grooming income for all four quarters in cell L6. (Make certain that you do not add the average income into the total income.)
   a. Select cell **L6**. Key **+**.
   b. Click cell **G6**. Key **+**.
   c. Click cell **H6**. Key **+**.
   d. Click cell **I6**. Key **+**.
   e. Click cell **J6**. Press **Enter**. The sum *75168* appears in cell L6.

7. Copy the formula in cell L6 to cells L7..L10.

8. Format the dollar values as currency with no decimal places.

**FIGURE 3-1**
Functions Dialog Box

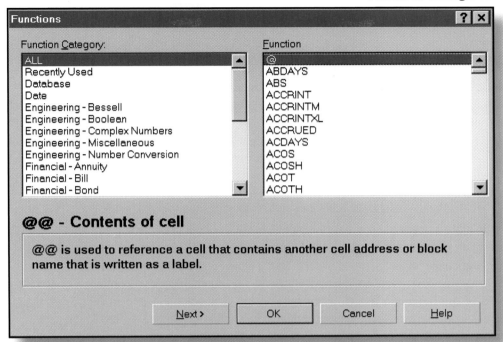

9. When you are done, the spreadsheet should appear as shown in Figure 3-2. Save the spreadsheet.

10. Print the spreadsheet in Landscape orientation and keep it open for the next exercise.

**FIGURE 3-2**
The Quarterly Grooming Income Sheet

**Pet Paradise**
**Quarterly Grooming Income**

| | Fee | Quantity Per Quarter | | | | Total Income Per Quarter | | | | Average Income | Total Income |
| | | First | Second | Third | Fourth | First | Second | Third | Fourth | | |
|---|---|---|---|---|---|---|---|---|---|---|---|
| Complete Grooming | $32.00 | 585 | 541 | 602 | 621 | $18,720 | $17,312 | $19,264 | $19,872 | $18,792 | $75,168 |
| Bathing Only | $15.00 | 221 | 230 | 248 | 205 | $3,315 | $3,450 | $3,720 | $3,075 | $3,390 | $13,560 |
| Nail Clipping Only | $4.00 | 104 | 118 | 93 | 98 | $416 | $472 | $372 | $392 | $413 | $1,652 |
| Brush-Out Only | $12.50 | 208 | 211 | 194 | 217 | $2,600 | $2,638 | $2,425 | $2,713 | $2,594 | $10,375 |
| Flea Dip | $10.00 | 179 | 162 | 112 | 128 | $1,790 | $1,620 | $1,120 | $1,280 | $1,453 | $5,810 |

# *Naming Ranges of Cells*

$Q$uattro Pro has a feature that allows you to name a range of cells. In order to assign a name to a range of cells, the cells must be contiguous. You can then reference this range by its name, rather than the addresses of its cells. For example, assume that you want to find the average of cells G6..J6. You could assign these cells the name *Grooming*. Then, if you wanted to use these cells in the AVG function, you would enter *@AVG(Grooming)*. The average of cells G6 through J6 would then be calculated. Naming ranges of cells can make spreadsheet operations easier to understand.

## EXERCISE ⟶ QP3.6

**1.** Save the notebook as **quarterly grooming 3-6 xxx**.

**2.** Select cell **K6** and press **Delete**. The contents of this cell are erased.

**3.** You are going to calculate the average income from complete groomings. However, instead of inserting the range of cells (which would be G6..J6) in the function, you are going to use the name of the range. To assign a name to the range G6..J6, perform the following steps:

    **a.** Select cells **G6..J6**.

    **b.** Open the **Insert** menu, choose **Name**, and then choose **Cells**.

    **c.** In the Cell Name dialog box, in the *Name* text box, key **Complete**.

    **d.** Click **Add** and then click **Close**.

**4.** Click cell **K6.** In the input line key **@AVG(Complete)**. Press **Enter**. The value *$18,792* should appear in the cell. This is the same result you obtained when calculating the average in Exercise QP3.5.

**5.** Save the notebook and close it.

# Using the Formula Composer to Perform Financial Computations

Quattro Pro provides a number of predefined functions that perform advanced financial calculations for you—calculations such as the accumulated interest paid on a loan after a specified number of payments (@AMAINT) or the periodic payments needed to pay off a loan over a given period of time at a specified interest rate (@PMT). If you're like most people, you leave this kind of calculating up to banks and accountants! But with Quattro Pro's Formula Composer, all you have to do is plug in a few numbers and the calculation is done for you in a matter of seconds.

## ✓ NOTE:

If the result of a formula is enclosed in parentheses, that means that it is a negative number.

The Outline pane features the formula in an outline structure. When you click each level of the outline, the calculation or value used for that level appears in the *Expression* box. This lets you view a formula in logical and understandable parts. When you are done building a formula, click OK and the result appears in the selected cell.

Formula Composer makes it easy to build and edit formulas. These formulas may or may not contain functions. Click the Formula Composer button and the Formula Composer dialog box appears. Click the @ button at the top of the dialog box and the Functions dialog box appears. After the needed function is chosen, the Formula Composer dialog box reappears, as shown in Figure 3-3. You can then create the needed formula.

**INTERNET** Many banks and lending institutions have Web sites that allow you to shop for the best loan rates from home.

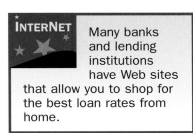

**FIGURE 3-3**
The Formula Composer Dialog Box

**Formula Composer - A:B13**

Function
Show All Panes
Show Outline and Argument Panes
Show Outline Pane Only

Cell Reference   Expression
@PMT()

? **@PMT - Amortized payment**
@PMT calculates the fully amortized periodic payment needed to repay a loan with a principal of Pv dollars at Rate percent

⦿ Periodic Payment   ○ Monthly Payment

? P̲v̲
? R̲ate (Periodic)
? N̲per (Periods)

**Function Description Pane**

Results

Outline Pane

OK   Cancel   He̲lp

Argument Pane

---

## EXERCISE ⟹ QP3.7

**SCANS**

Pet Paradise wants to purchase a van so that the business can provide pick-up and delivery service for the pets being groomed or boarded. The accountant wants to figure out how much the monthly van payments will be. Pet Paradise would like to borrow $21,000 on the $26,000 van. The loan interest rate will be 9.5%, and the loan should last for four years.

1. In the student **Datafile** folder, open the **expenses** notebook. This notebook contains the monthly expenses for Pet Paradise. Save the notebook as **expenses 3-7 xxx**.

2. Select cell **A13** and key **Van Payment**.

3. Select cell **B13** and then click the **Formula Composer** button on the Toolbar.

4. In the Formula Composer dialog box click the @ button to open the Functions dialog box. Select the **ALL** category of functions. Under *Function* select **PMT**. Click **OK**. The Formula Composer dialog box reappears. Notice that an explanation of the PMT function appears in the Function Description pane. By clicking the question mark in front of the function's description, you can receive a detailed description of the function's argument.

5. In the Argument pane click **Monthly Payment**.

6. Click the question mark before *Pv* and read the argument description. (*Pv* stands for principal.) Key **21000** in the text box as the amount to be borrowed. Notice that as you enter the number, it is inserted in the Outline pane.

(continued on next page)

**7.** Click the question mark before *Rate* and read the argument description. Key **.095** (representing the 9.5% interest rate).

**8.** Click the question mark before *Nper* and read the argument description. (*Nper* stands for the total number of payment periods.) Then key **4** in the *Nper* box because the payment should extend over four years.

**9.** Look at the Outline pane. Click each level of the formula and review it in the *Expression* box. Click the top level to redisplay all the panes.

**10.** Click **OK**. Because cell B13 has been selected, the amount of this payment, *$527.59*, should appear in this cell.

**11.** In cell A15 key **Total**.

**12.** Use **QuickSum** to place the total expenses in cell B15.

**13.** Save the notebook and print the current sheet.

**14.** Close the notebook and exit Quattro Pro.

# *Summary*

This lesson explained how to perform arithmetic operations on data. You learned that:

- formulas are entered into cells to perform mathematical operations on values. Arithmetic formulas contain operators, such as addition, subtraction, multiplication, and division, and values. The values can be numbers or cell addresses.

- QuickSum can be used to add a selected row or column of cells.

- you can cut, copy, and paste formulas from one cell to another just as you would text. The QuickFill button allows you to copy a formula to a group of cells in the same column or row.

- when a formula uses a relative cell reference, the cell addresses change when the formula is copied to another location.

- the order of operator precedence determines the order in which arithmetic is performed. The order is multiplication, division, addition, and subtraction. You can control the order by using parentheses in formulas.

- absolute cell references are indicated by placing a dollar sign in front of the column or row in the cell's address in the formula. If a dollar sign is placed in front of both the column and the row, the formula will always refer to the same cell, regardless of where the formula might be copied.

- functions (or @functions) are predefined formulas which you can select from a list.

- you can assign a name to a range of cells. This name can then be used in formulas and functions.

- the Formula Composer allows you to create your own functions and can be helpful in performing complex calculations.

## LESSON 3 REVIEW QUESTIONS

### MULTIPLE CHOICE

**Circle the best answer to each of the following statements.**

1. A formula can contain _____.
   - **A.** only operators
   - **B.** only operators and cell addresses
   - **C.** operators, cell addresses, and values
   - **D.** operators, cell addresses, values, and text describing the formula's purpose

2. What is the result of the formula +34-8*B3? (Assume cell B3 contains the number 3.)
   - **A.** 0
   - **B.** 10
   - **C.** 26
   - **D.** 78

3. Which of the following formulas will always reference cell B5, regardless of where the formula is copied in a spreadsheet?
   - **A.** +A4-B5
   - **B.** @B@5+B6
   - **C.** +$B$5* B2
   - **D.** +A5/$B5

4. Which of the following would be most useful in helping you create a complex financial function that you could use whenever you needed it?
   - **A.** Copy button
   - **B.** Formula Composer
   - **C.** QuickFill
   - **D.** QuickSum

5. When a cell is selected that contains a formula, the _____ appears in the input line while the _____ appears in the cell.
   - **A.** formula's result; formula itself
   - **B.** formula itself; formula's result
   - **C.** function's result; @function
   - **D.** formula's name; formula itself

### WRITTEN QUESTIONS

**Write your answers to the following questions.**

6  Give an example of a formula in which you would want to use a relative cell reference.

7. What is the order of operator precedence?

(continued on next page)

8. Describe two commonly used functions.

9. How does Quattro Pro recognize that you want to use an absolute cell reference in a formula?

10. What is the Formula Composer?

## LESSON 3 PROJECT

### PROJECT 3A

The owners of Pet Paradise are considering purchasing a building at a new location. The purchase price of the building would be $245,000. They would have a down payment of $60,000, requiring them to obtain a mortgage of $185,000. Calculate the monthly mortgage payments on this building with a 30-year loan. The bank has agreed to give them an interest rate of 8.5%.

1. A new, empty notebook should be on the screen. Save the notebook as **mortgage proj3a xxx**.

2. Click cell **A2** and key **Mortgage Payment**.

3. Select cell **A3** and then click the **Formula Composer** button on the Toolbar.

4. In the Formula Composer dialog box click the **@** button. In the Functions dialog box, under *Function Category*, select the **ALL** category. Under *Function* select **PMT**. Click **OK**. The Financial Composer dialog box reappears.

5. In the Argument pane click **Monthly Payment**.

6. Key **185000** in the *Pv* text box as the amount to be borrowed.

7. Key **.085** in the *Rate* text box because the interest rate will be 8.5%.

8. Key **30** in the *Nper* box because the mortgage will be for 30 years.

9. Click **OK**. The amount of the monthly mortgage payment appears in cell A3. Format it as currency with two decimal places.

10. Save the notebook and print it. Close the notebook.

### PROJECT 3B

Morrison Car Dealership needs to calculate the amount of commission owed to a sales associate. Sales associates are paid a 15% commission based on the profits from all of the sales. To determine the profit, the vehicle's cost is subtracted from the selling price. The cost includes not only what the dealership paid for the vehicle, but also any costs involved in getting it ready for sale, such as repairs and clean-up.

1. Open the **commission** notebook in the student **Datafile** folder and save it as **commission proj3b xxx**.

2. Center the headings in rows 1 and 2 across the columns containing data. Enlarge the size of the fonts used in the headings to **16** pt.

3. In cell D7 calculate the profit made on the first car. The profit is determined by subtracting the cost from the selling price.

4. Copy the formula in cell D7 to cells D8..D23.

5. In cell E7 calculate the commission earned on the first car. The commission is found by multiplying the profit by **0.15** (the commission rate is 15%).

6. Copy the formula in cell E7 to cells E8..E23.

7. In cell A25 key **Total** so that row 25 will contain the totals for each column.

8. In cell B25 place the total for all of the sales. Copy this formula to cells C25, D25, and E25.

9. Format cells B7..E25 as currency with no decimal places.

10. If necessary, widen the columns so that all of the contents can be seen.

11. Place a double-line border around the totals in row 25.

12. Make the background of cell E25 **yellow** so that the total amount of commissions will stand out from the rest of the sheet.

13. Save the notebook and print the current sheet. Close the notebook and exit Quattro Pro.

## CRITICAL THINKING ACTIVITY

**SCANS**

In the days before spreadsheet software, businesses hired employees who spent many hours using calculators to add up columns of numbers. These numbers were kept in large *ledger books* where results were written by hand. If more sophisticated formulas needed to be applied to numbers, the process was even more cumbersome, often involving many steps with a calculator. Can you think of at least two disadvantages that this method would have over using the electronic spreadsheets available today? What would be the disadvantages to the employer? What would be the disadvantages to the employee?

# CONTROLLING THE WAY DATA IS DISPLAYED

## OBJECTIVES

**Upon completion of this lesson, you will be able to:**

■ Change the way a sheet is viewed.

■ Use the Zoom feature.

■ Lock column and row titles so that they are always visible.

■ Split the display screen into panes so that data in different parts of a sheet or several different sheets can be viewed at the same time.

■ View more than one notebook at a time.

■ Hide and reveal data.

■ Protect and unprotect cells.

🕐 **Estimated Time: 1¹/₂ hours**

In this lesson you will learn a number of ways to change the way that data appears on your screen. You will learn to zoom in and out of a sheet so that it appears larger or smaller on the screen. You also will learn how to split the window so you can view different parts of a single sheet or several different sheets at the same time. In addition, you will learn how to hide and protect data so that it cannot be changed or viewed by unauthorized individuals.

## *Changing Views*

So far, you have been viewing your notebooks in Draft view. Draft view is the default view in Quattro Pro and it allows you to quickly enter data and move around the sheet. You also can choose Page view, which allows you to see how a document will appear when printed, where the page breaks will appear, and so forth. To switch to Page view, choose Page from the View menu. Figure 4-1 shows how the Income Statement for Pet Paradise appears in Page view. When in Page view, you can change the size of the page's margins by positioning the mouse pointer on a margin. When the mouse pointer turns into a double-headed arrow, drag the margin to where you want it.

**FIGURE 4-1**
The Income Statement in Page View

|  | A | B | C | D | E | F | G | H | I | J | K | L | No |
|---|---|---|---|---|---|---|---|---|---|---|---|---|---|
| 1 | | | | | | | Pet Paradise | | | | | | |
| 2 | | | | | | | Income Statement | | | | | | |
| 3 | | | | | | | | | | | | | |
| 4 | | | | | | | For the Months Ended Jan.-Dec. | | | | | | |
| 5 | | | Jan | Feb | Mar | Apr | May | Jun | Jul | Aug | Sep | Oct | No |
| 6 | Income | | | | | | | | | | | | |
| 7 | | Sales of Merchandise | $39,650 | $39,056 | $38,911 | $39,447 | $40,843 | $41,752 | $40,095 | $41,144 | $43,361 | $42,487 | $4 |
| 8 | | Sales of Services | $15,141 | $15,943 | $15,085 | $13,903 | $14,825 | $15,004 | $14,142 | $14,739 | $14,541 | $15,306 | $1 |
| 9 | Total Income | | $54,791 | $54,999 | $53,996 | $53,350 | $55,668 | $56,756 | $54,237 | $55,883 | $57,902 | $57,793 | $5 |
| 10 | | | | | | | | | | | | | |
| 11 | Expenses | | | | | | | | | | | | |
| 12 | | Cost of Sales of Merchandis | $21,038 | $20,630 | $21,066 | $20,188 | $21,238 | $21,711 | $19,246 | $20,366 | $21,464 | $20,925 | $2 |
| 13 | | Overhead | $5,202 | $5,020 | $4,845 | $4,635 | $4,510 | $4,658 | $4,749 | $4,850 | $4,725 | $4,845 | $ |
| 14 | | General & Administrative | $1,123 | $1,180 | $1,235 | $1,218 | $1,126 | $1,219 | $1,361 | $1,172 | $1,211 | $1,244 | $ |
| 15 | | Human Resources | $14,870 | $15,200 | $14,985 | $14,855 | $15,160 | $14,790 | $15,285 | $14,510 | $14,920 | $15,235 | $1 |
| 16 | | Marketing | $150 | $164 | $175 | $168 | $160 | $153 | $149 | $165 | $187 | $224 | |
| 17 | Total Expenses | | $42,383 | $42,194 | $42,306 | $41,064 | $42,194 | $42,531 | $40,790 | $41,063 | $42,507 | $42,473 | $4 |
| 18 | | | | | | | | | | | | | |
| 19 | | | | | | | | | | | | | |
| 20 | | | | | | | | | | | | | |

|  | M | N | O | P | Q | R | S | T | U | V | W | X | Y | Z | AA |
|---|---|---|---|---|---|---|---|---|---|---|---|---|---|---|---|
| 1 | | | | | | | | | | | | | | | |
| 2 | | | | | | | | | | | | | | | |
| 3 | | | | | | | | | | | | | | | |
| 4 | | | | | | | | | | | | | | | |
| 5 | Nov | Dec | TOTAL | | | | | | | | | | | | |
| 6 | | | | | | | | | | | | | | | |
| 7 | $43,094 | $44,875 | $494,715 | | | | | | | | | | | | |
| 8 | $16,698 | $17,043 | $182,370 | | | | | | | | | | | | |
| 9 | $59,792 | $61,918 | $677,085 | | | | | | | | | | | | |
| 10 | | | | | | | | | | | | | | | |
| 11 | | | | | | | | | | | | | | | |
| 12 | $21,633 | $22,886 | $252,391 | | | | | | | | | | | | |
| 13 | $4,986 | $5,025 | $58,050 | | | | | | | | | | | | |
| 14 | $1,350 | $1,310 | $14,749 | | | | | | | | | | | | |
| 15 | $16,150 | $16,575 | $182,535 | | | | | | | | | | | | |
| 16 | $297 | $310 | $2,302 | | | | | | | | | | | | |
| 17 | $44,416 | $46,106 | $510,027 | | | | | | | | | | | | |
| 18 | | | | | | | | | | | | | | | |
| 19 | | | | | | | | | | | | | | | |
| 20 | | | | | | | | | | | | | | | |

# EXERCISE ⇨ QP4.1

**1.** Open the **income** notebook in the student **Datafile** folder. This file contains the Income Statement for January through December for Pet Paradise. Save the notebook as **income 4-1 xxx**.

**2.** Open the **View** menu and choose **Page**.

**✓ NOTE:**

The solid blue borders represent the edges of the pages and the dashed blue borders represent the margins.

**3.** Increase the size of the top margin to $1/2$ inch.

**a.** Position the mouse pointer on the dashed blue border that runs across the top of the sheet. It should turn into a two-way arrow.

**b.** Hold down the mouse button and drag this border downward about $1/4$ inch and release the mouse button. When you are done, the margin should be about $1/2$ inch in size.

(continued on next page)

c. Position the mouse pointer on the border. A note appears telling you the border's size. It should say *Top Margin: 0.50 in.* If it does not, readjust the border to make the margin $1/2$ inch.

4. Save the notebook and keep it open for the next exercise.

# Using the Zoom Feature

You can enlarge or reduce the view of a sheet or a selected block of cells by opening the View menu and choosing Zoom or by clicking the Zoom button on the Toolbar. The Zoom dialog box appears, as shown in Figure 4-2.

The Zoom drop-down list on the Toolbar contains the same options, or *zoom factors*, as the Zoom dialog box. The default zoom factor is 100%, which means the display will be pretty close to the actual size of the printed page. It is often useful to select a smaller zoom factor, such as 75%, because this allows you to see more of a sheet at a time. Selecting a factor greater than 100% magnifies the sheet. The Selection option allows you to zoom in on a selected block of cells. The Custom option allows you to set your own zoom factor. You can apply a zoom factor to a single sheet or to an entire notebook.

**FIGURE 4-2**
The Zoom Dialog Box

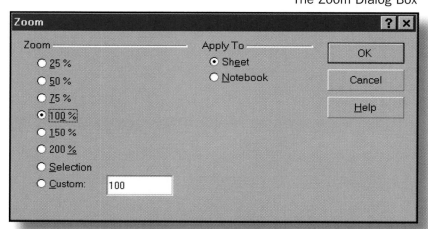

1. Save the notebook as **income 4-2 xxx**.

2. If necessary, scroll to the right so that you view the columns at the far right of the sheet. Notice that several columns will be printed on the second sheet of paper.

NOTE:

This page is set up in Landscape orientation, which means that it is wider than it is long.

3. You would like the entire spreadsheet to print on a single page, if possible. Select cells **B5..017**. Change the font size to **8**. Then click the **QuickFit** button on the Toolbar. The columns will be made narrower. Check the spreadsheet to make certain that it now fits on a single page. If it still does not, you may need to make some of the columns narrower. To make a column narrower, position the mouse pointer on the column heading's right border; it will turn into a two-way arrow. Then drag the border to the left until the column is the width that you want.

4. Open the **View** menu and choose **Zoom**. The Zoom dialog box appears. Under *Zoom* click **75%** and click **OK**. You will be able to see a larger portion of the spreadsheet at the same time.

5. Click the **Zoom** button on the Toolbar. In the drop-down menu click **Other**. Under *Zoom* select **Custom** and key **80**. Click **OK**. The spreadsheet will appear at 80% of full size.

6. Save the notebook and close it.

# *Locking Titles*

U sing the Zoom feature allows you to display more columns on a screen. However, there are many times when a sheet is too long or too wide to be seen on a single screen. To handle this problem, you can "freeze" labels (also called locking the titles) so that they are always visible, regardless of your current position in a spreadsheet.

**NOTE:**

You can lock a spreadsheet's titles when you are in Page view or Draft View.

**EXERCISE ▷ QP4.3**

1. Open the **income** notebook in the student **Datafile** folder.

2. Select column **C**.

3. Open the **View** menu and choose **Locked Titles**. A vertical blue line appears between columns B and C showing that the columns left of the blue line are locked.

4. Practice scrolling horizontally across the spreadsheet. Notice that the labels in columns A and B always remain visible, regardless of where you are in the spreadsheet.

**NOTE:**

Locked titles do not appear when a sheet is printed; they appear only in their original location.

5. Unlock the labels by deselecting **Locked Titles** in the **View** menu. Keep this notebook open for the next exercise.

# Splitting a Window

Often it is useful to be able to see two different parts of the same sheet at the same time. One way of doing this is by splitting a window horizontally or vertically. To split a window, click either the horizontal line or vertical line in the pane splitter in the lower right corner of the window. Then drag the line to the location where you want the split to occur. Or you can use the Split Window dialog box, which is shown in Figure 4-3. This second method is the one you will be using in Exercise QP4.4. Figure 4-4 shows a window that is split horizontally. The window in Figure 4-5 is split vertically.

**FIGURE 4-3**
The Split Window Dialog Box

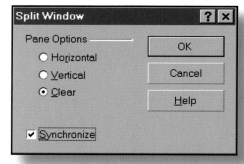

**INTERNET**

*Netiquette* is an Internet phrase that refers to the rules of conduct and behavior on the Net. For example, don't send unwanted advertising, do keep your messages brief and to the point, and don't use ALL CAPS unless you mean to shout.

**FIGURE 4-4**
A Window Split Horizontally

|  | A | B | C | D | E | F | G | H | I |
|---|---|---|---|---|---|---|---|---|---|
| 1 |  |  |  | Pet Paradise |  |  |  |  |  |
| 2 |  |  |  | Income Statement |  |  |  |  |  |
| 3 |  |  |  |  |  |  |  |  |  |
| 4 |  |  |  |  | *For the Months Ended Jan.-Dec.* |  |  |  |  |
| 5 |  |  | Jan | Feb | Mar | Apr | May | Jun | Jul | Aug |
| 6 | **Income** |  |  |  |  |  |  |  |  |  |
| 7 |  | Sales of Merchandise | $39,650 | $39,056 | $38,911 | $39,447 | $40,843 | $41,752 | $40,095 | $4 |
| 8 |  | Sales of Services | $15,141 | $15,943 | $15,085 | $13,903 | $14,825 | $15,004 | $14,142 | $14 |
| 9 | **Total Income** |  | **$54,791** | **$54,999** | **$53,996** | **$53,350** | **$55,668** | **$56,756** | **$54,237** | **$5** |
| 10 |  |  |  |  |  |  |  |  |  |
| 11 | **Expenses** |  |  |  |  |  |  |  |  |  |
| 12 |  | Cost of Sales of Merchandise | $21,038 | $20,630 | $21,066 | $20,188 | $21,238 | $21,711 | $19,246 | $20 |
| 13 |  | Overhead | $5,202 | $5,020 | $4,845 | $4,635 | $4,510 | $4,658 | $4,749 | $4 |
| 14 |  | General & Administrative | $1,123 | $1,180 | $1,235 | $1,218 | $1,126 | $1,219 | $1,361 | $1 |
| 15 |  | Human Resources | $14,870 | $15,200 | $14,985 | $14,855 | $15,160 | $14,790 | $15,285 | $14 |
| 16 |  | Marketing | $150 | $164 | $175 | $168 | $160 | $153 | $149 |  |

A B C D E F G H I J K L M

|  | A | B | C | D | E | F | G | H | I |
|---|---|---|---|---|---|---|---|---|---|
| 11 | **Expenses** |  |  |  |  |  |  |  |  |  |
| 12 |  | Cost of Sales of Merchandise | $21,038 | $20,630 | $21,066 | $20,188 | $21,238 | $21,711 | $19,246 | $20 |
| 13 |  | Overhead | $5,202 | $5,020 | $4,845 | $4,635 | $4,510 | $4,658 | $4,749 | $4 |
| 14 |  | General & Administrative | $1,123 | $1,180 | $1,235 | $1,218 | $1,126 | $1,219 | $1,361 | $1 |
| 15 |  | Human Resources | $14,870 | $15,200 | $14,985 | $14,855 | $15,160 | $14,790 | $15,285 | $14 |
| 16 |  | Marketing | $150 | $164 | $175 | $168 | $160 | $153 | $149 |  |
| 17 | **Total Expenses** |  | **$42,383** | **$42,194** | **$42,306** | **$41,064** | **$42,194** | **$42,531** | **$40,790** | **$4** |

A B C D E F G H I J K L M

**FIGURE 4-5**
A Window Split Vertically

| | C | D | E | F | G | H |
|---|---|---|---|---|---|---|
| 1 | | | **Pet Paradise** | | | |
| 2 | | | **Income Statement** | | | |
| 3 | | | | | | |
| 4 | | | | *For the Months Ended Jan.-Dec* | | |
| 5 | Jan | Feb | Mar | Apr | May | Jun |
| 6 | | | | | | |
| 7 | $39,650 | $39,056 | $38,911 | $39,447 | $40,843 | $41,75 |
| 8 | $15,141 | $15,943 | $15,085 | $13,903 | $14,825 | $15,00 |
| 9 | **$54,791** | **$54,999** | **$53,996** | **$53,350** | **$55,668** | **$56,75** |
| 10 | | | | | | |
| 11 | | | | | | |
| 12 | $21,038 | $20,630 | $21,066 | $20,188 | $21,238 | $21,71 |
| 13 | $5,202 | $5,020 | $4,845 | $4,635 | $4,510 | $4,65 |
| 14 | $1,123 | $1,180 | $1,235 | $1,218 | $1,126 | $1,21 |
| 15 | $14,870 | $15,200 | $14,985 | $14,855 | $15,160 | $14,79 |
| 16 | $150 | $164 | $175 | $168 | $160 | $15 |
| 17 | **$42,383** | **$42,194** | **$42,306** | **$41,064** | **$42,194** | **$42,53** |

| | J | K | L | M | N |
|---|---|---|---|---|---|
| 1 | | | | | |
| 2 | | | | | |
| 3 | | | | | |
| 4 | | | | | |
| 5 | Aug | Sep | Oct | Nov | Dec |
| 6 | | | | | |
| 7 | $41,144 | $43,361 | $42,487 | $43,094 | $44,875 |
| 8 | $14,739 | $14,541 | $15,306 | $16,698 | $17,043 |
| 9 | **$55,883** | **$57,902** | **$57,793** | **$59,792** | **$61,918** |
| 10 | | | | | |
| 11 | | | | | |
| 12 | $20,366 | $21,464 | $20,925 | $21,633 | $22,886 |
| 13 | $4,850 | $4,725 | $4,845 | $4,986 | $5,025 |
| 14 | $1,172 | $1,211 | $1,244 | $1,350 | $1,310 |
| 15 | $14,510 | $14,920 | $15,235 | $16,150 | $16,575 |
| 16 | $165 | $187 | $224 | $297 | $310 |
| 17 | **$41,063** | **$42,507** | **$42,473** | **$44,416** | **$46,106** |

## EXERCISE ▷ QP4.4

**SCANS**

1. Save the **income** notebook as **income 4-4 xxx**.

2. Select any cell in column E of the sheet. Open the **View** menu and choose **Split Window**.

3. In the Split Window dialog box click **Vertical**. Make certain that the **Synchronize** option is selected and click **OK**. When the Synchronize option is selected, you can scroll both panes simultaneously.

4. Click in the left pane and then click the down scroll arrow. Notice that both panes move simultaneously.

5. Open the **View** menu and choose **Split Window**. Click **Synchronize** to deselect it. Click **OK**.

6. Click in the right pane. Scroll down and back up again in this pane. Notice that the left pane no longer scrolls with the right one. Scroll back to the left so that column A is visible.

7. You can enter and edit data in a pane just as you would in a full window. In the right pane scroll to the last column of data. Click in cell **P5** and key **LOWEST**. Click in cell **Q5** and key **HIGHEST**.

8. Use the **QuickFormat** button to copy the format of cell O5 to cells P5 and Q5.

 **TIP**

Remember when you are done using QuickFormat, click the QuickFormat button to turn it off.

(continued on next page)

**9.** In cell P7 key the function **@MIN(C7..N7)**. Press **Enter**. The lowest value in this row should appear in column P.

**10.** Copy the formula in cell P7 to cells P8..P9 and P12..P17.

**11.** In cell Q7 key the function **@MAX(C7..N7)**. Press **Enter**. The highest value in this row should appear in column Q.

**12.** Copy the formula in cell Q7 to cells Q8..Q9 and Q12..Q17.

**13.** Make certain that all of the dollar values are formatted as currency. Also make certain that the columns are wide enough to display all of the values.

**14.** Remove the split screen by choosing **Split Window** in the **View** menu and **Clear** in the dialog box. Click **OK**.

**15.** Save the notebook and print it. Keep it open.

# *Viewing Several Notebooks at Once*

There will be times when you want to examine several spreadsheets at the same time, perhaps to compare their contents or to copy data among them. To do this, first open all of the notebooks you wish to view. Each opened notebook will be listed at the bottom of the Window menu. To switch to one not currently in view, click its name on the Window menu. To view all opened notebooks side by side, click Tile Side by Side on the Window menu (see Figure 4-6). To view the notebooks in separate horizontal

**FIGURE 4-6**
Notebook Windows Tiled Side By Side

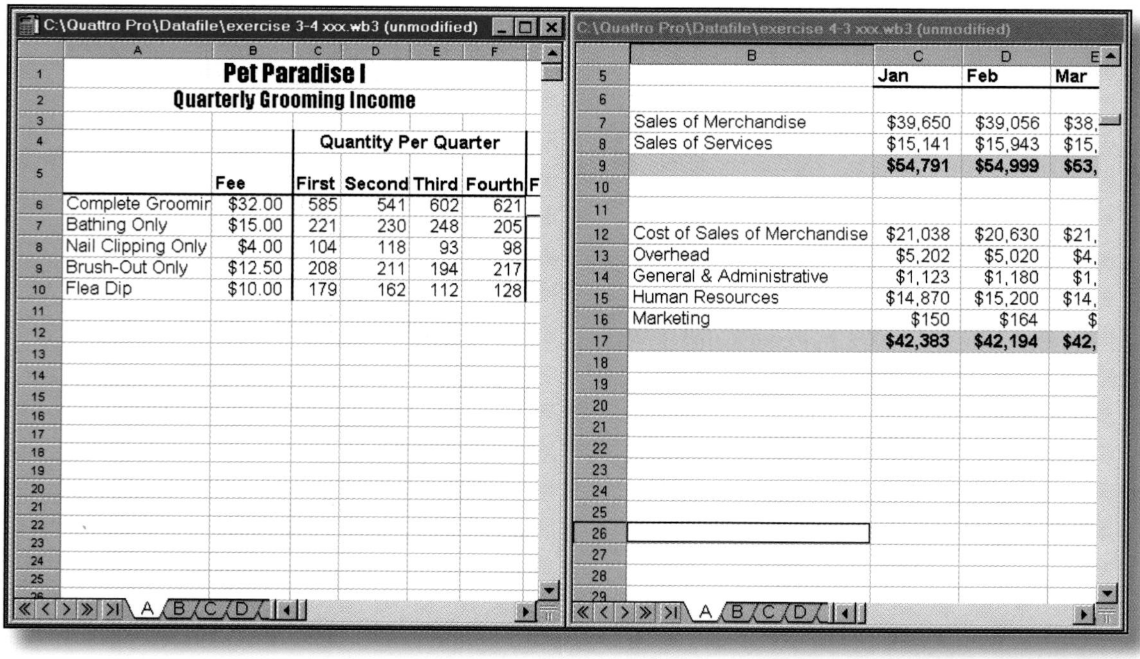

windows, click Tile Top to Bottom (see Figure 4-7). If you later want to view a single notebook, click anywhere in that notebook to select it, and then click its Maximize button in the upper right corner. The notebook's window will enlarge to fill the available space.

**FIGURE 4-7**
Notebook Windows Tiled Top to Bottom

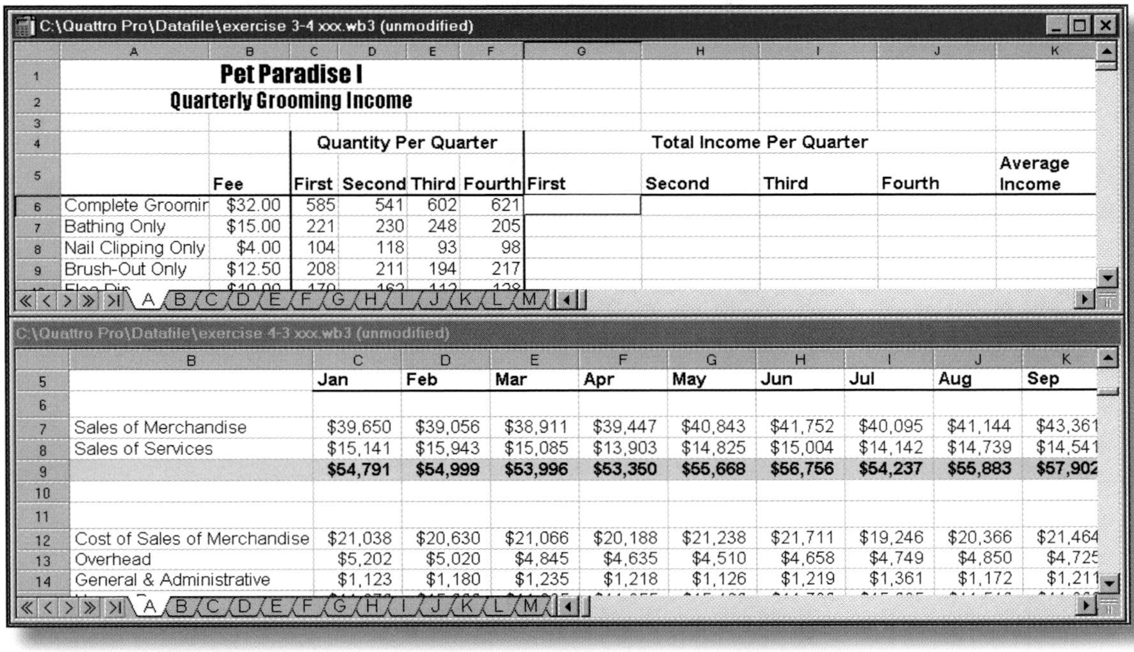

---

## EXERCISE QP4.5

**SCANS**

1. The **income 4-4 xxx** notebook should already be on the screen. Save it as **income 4-5 xxx**. Open **quarterly grooming 3-4 xxx** in the student **Datafile** folder.

2. Open the **Window** menu and choose **Tile Top to Bottom**. Both **income 4-5 xxx** and **quarterly grooming 3-4 xxx** should appear on the screen.

3. Open the **Window** menu and choose **Tile Side by Side**. The notebook windows should now be split down the center of the screen.

4. Click anywhere in **income 4-5 xxx** to make that window active. Click the **Maximize** button. The window containing **income 4-5 xxx** should fill the screen.

5. Open the **Window** menu and choose **quarterly grooming 3-4 xxx**. The screen switches to the **quarterly grooming 3-4 xxx** notebook.

6. Close **quarterly grooming 3-4 xxx**. Now **income 4-5 xxx** appears on the screen. Close **income 4-5 xxx**.

# Hiding Data

In business there are many times when people may want to hide data. An example might be when a notebook contains employee salaries. Only certain people may be authorized to see this type of information. You can temporarily remove data from view and from printouts by selecting the row or column you want to hide, right clicking on it, and then selecting Hide.

**TIP**

Even though a row or column is temporarily hidden, its contents will still be used in formulas.

### EXERCISE ▷ QP4.6

**SCANS**

1. Open **weekly 3-3 xxx** in the student **Datafile** folder.

2. Save this notebook as **weekly 4-6 xxx**.

3. Select column B. Right click on the column and click **Hide**. Column B disappears, along with its column letter.

4. Position the mouse pointer slightly to the right of the border between columns B and C. Drag to the right and column B should reappear.

5. Save the notebook and keep it open.

# Protecting Data

Quattro Pro allows you to lock, or protect, selected cells, which means that they cannot be edited, changed, or deleted. Further, any column or row containing a protected cell cannot be deleted. This prevents unauthorized people from altering data or formulas. The Protection tab in the Active Sheet dialog box allows you to protect an entire sheet. If you then wish to unprotect a part of the sheet, you can use the Constraints tab in the Active Cells dialog box. In the next exercise you will practice protecting an entire sheet and then unprotecting specific cells within it.

### EXERCISE ▷ QP4.7

**SCANS**

1. Save the notebook as **weekly 4-7 xxx**.

2. Right click Tab **A** at the bottom of the sheet. Click **Sheet Properties**.

3. In the Active Sheet dialog box click the **Protection** tab. The dialog box should look like Figure 4-8. Click **Enable Cell Locking** and then click **OK**. The entire sheet is now protected.

**NOTE:**

The Protect and Unprotect cell protection options in the Constraints tab are only effective if the Enable Cell Locking option is turned on in the Protection tab in the Active Sheet dialog box.

**TIP**

Holding down Ctrl while making selections allows you to select cells that are not contiguous.

**FIGURE 4-8**
The Protection Tab in the Active Sheet Dialog Box

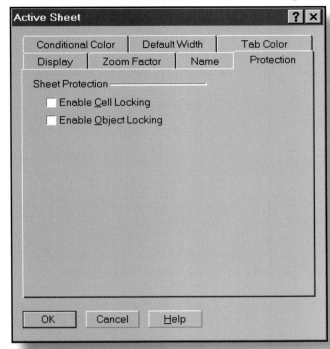

**4.** Try changing the values in several of the cells in this sheet. When you try, a message stating *Protected cell or block* should appear. Click **OK** to close this message.

**5.** You are now going to unprotect columns A, C, D, E, and F, but leave column B protected. Select column **A**. Hold down **Ctrl** and then drag to select columns **C** through **F**. When you are done, columns A, C, D, E, and F should be selected, but column B should not be selected.

**6.** Right click anywhere in the selected columns and click **Cell Properties**.

**7.** Click the **Constraints** tab and then click **Unprotect**. Click **OK**.

**8.** Try making a change to a cell in one of the columns you just unprotected. You should be able to make changes.

**9.** Try making a change to a cell in column B. You should not be able to make a change as this column is still protected.

**10.** Close the notebook. If you are asked whether you want to save any changes, click **No**.

# *Summary*

The data contained in spreadsheets can be displayed in a number of different ways. This lesson taught you that:

■ the Zoom button can be used to make the contents of a spreadsheet appear larger or smaller on the screen.

■ the Locked Titles command in the View menu can "freeze" titles so that they are always on the screen, regardless of where you are in a spreadsheet.

■ more than one notebook window can be opened at once. You can place the windows side by side or top to bottom.

■ sometimes users will want to hide data so that unauthorized users cannot view it. Select the data to be hidden and then click Hide on the Row/Column tab in the Active Cells dialog box.

■ you can protect an entire sheet or specific cells so that data cannot be deleted or altered.

### TRUE/FALSE

**Circle the T if the statement is true. Circle the F if it is false.**

**T  F**  **1.** When you have two windows open at the same time, you can place them side by side or above one another.

**T  F**  **2.** The purpose of freezing sheet titles is so that you can see labels regardless of where you are on a spreadsheet.

**T  F**  **3.** Using the Zoom button to enlarge the contents of a sheet on the screen will also make it larger when you print it.

**T  F**  **4.** In Quattro Pro you can view several sheets of the same notebook at once, but you can only have one notebook open at a time.

**T  F**  **5.** While you can protect selected cells within a spreadsheet, it is impossible to protect the entire sheet.

### MATCHING

**Write the letter of the term in Column 2 that best matches the description in Column 1.**

| Column 1 | Column 2 |
|---|---|
| \_\_\_\_ **6.** The labels of specified rows or columns are always visible, no matter where you are in the sheet. | **A.**  Protecting cells |
| \_\_\_\_ **7.** Enlarging or reducing the size at which a sheet is viewed. | **B.**  Hiding cells |
| \_\_\_\_ **8.** Making it so that you can see more than one part of a sheet at the same time. | **C.**  Locking titles |
| \_\_\_\_ **9.** Specified cells cannot be viewed on the screen. | **D.**  Splitting the screen |
| \_\_\_\_ **10.** The contents of specific cells cannot be altered. | **E.**  Zooming |

SCANS

## LESSON 4 PROJECT

### PROJECT 4A

1.   Open the **january inventory** notebook in the student **Datafile** folder and save the notebook as **january inventory proj4a xxx**.

2.   Split the window vertically. Click in the left pane and try scrolling to view the data.

3.   Open the Split Window dialog box and deselect **Synchronize**. Scroll through each window again. Notice that the windows no longer scroll together.

4.   Make the window so that it is no longer split.

5.   Lock the titles in the first four rows. Practice scrolling down the sheet. Notice that the labels at the top of the sheet are always visible.

6.   Undo the locked titles.

7.   Select a zoom factor of **75%** and see how it changes the screen's appearance. Try selecting several other zoom factors. Choose a zoom factor of **50%** and leave the notebook at this setting.

8.   Save the notebook and print it. Close the notebook.

### PROJECT 4B

1.   Open the **morrison payroll** notebook in the student **Datafile** folder and save the notebook as **morrison payroll proj4b xxx**.

2.   Open the **morrison sale** notebook in the student **Datafile** folder. Make it so that the windows containing the two notebooks are tiled side by side.

3.   Close the window containing the **morrison sale** notebook. Enlarge the **morrison payroll proj4b xxx** window so that it takes up all of the available space.

4.   The accountant for the Morrison Car Dealership wants to keep the hourly rate for employees confidential. Hide the data in column F.

5.   The accountant also does not want anyone accidentally changing the information in this sheet. Protect the entire sheet so that its data cannot be changed.

6.   The accountant has decided that the employees' addresses in column C do not need to be protected. Unprotect column C.

(continued on next page)

7. Switch to **Page** view. Make the size of the top margin about twice as large as it is currently.
   a. Position the mouse pointer on the dashed blue line that represents the top margin. The pointer should turn into a two-way arrow.
   b. Drag the arrow downward until the margin is about twice its previous size. Release the mouse button.

8. Save the notebook and print it. Close the notebook and exit Quattro Pro.

## CRITICAL THINKING ACTIVITY

SCANS

In Exercise QP4.4, you used the @MIN and @MAX functions to determine the smallest and largest values in a group of values. Functions such as these are often used in keeping track of statistics for sports such as baseball and basketball. Pick a sport with which you are familiar. Determine what statistics are commonly used in this sport. Make a list of these statistics. If necessary, obtain help from someone, such as a coach, who could help you in creating the list. Determine whether a built-in function could be used to calculate these statistics. Remember that you can go to the Functions dialog box and click on the name of a particular function in order to get a description of it. If no built-in function is available, create your own formula to calculate the statistic. When you are done, you should have a list of statistics along with a description of how each statistic can be calculated.

# SORTING DATA AND WORKING WITH MULTIPLE PAGES

## OBJECTIVES

**Upon completion of this lesson, you will be able to:**

■ Sort a spreadsheet.

■ Understand the usefulness of having multiple sheets in a notebook.

■ Move to different sheets in a notebook.

■ Move, insert, and delete sheets in a notebook.

■ Rename sheet tabs.

■ Group sheets within a notebook so that you can perform formatting and editing on the entire group.

■ Use formulas on grouped sheets.

■ Create a summary sheet in a notebook.

🕐 **Estimated Time: 2 hours**

Often you may enter data into a spreadsheet in the order you receive it. Later, you may want to sort it. For example, a spreadsheet containing employee names may need to be sorted alphabetically by name. The first part of this lesson discusses sorting data.

So far, you have been working with single notebook sheets. Now you will begin to discover how easy it is to organize the data in a notebook into multiple sheets. Usually, all of the sheets in a specific notebook will be related to one another. For example, you might have each of the quarterly statements for a business on four separate sheets followed by a summary sheet of the quarterly statements.

You will learn how to assign meaningful names to the sheets in a notebook so that you can easily locate a particular sheet. You also will learn how to group sheets so that you can save time copying and formatting data and applying formulas.

## *Sorting Data In a Spreadsheet*

Quattro Pro allows you to quickly arrange data in alphabetical or numeric order in a spreadsheet. This process is called *sorting*. You can perform an *ascending sort* (letters go from a-z and numbers from 0-9) or a *descending sort* (letters go from z-a and numbers from 9-0). In addition, you can sort by more than one column. For example, if you were sorting a list of names, you could tell Quattro Pro to first sort by the last name column and then sort by the first name column.

# EXERCISE ▷ QP5.1

**1.** Start Quattro Pro, if necessary. Open the **sort** notebook in the student **Datafile** folder and save the notebook as **sort 5-1 xxx**.

**2.** Select cells **A4..D11**.

**3.** Open the **Tools** menu and choose **Sort**. The Data Sort dialog box appears, as shown in Figure 5-1. Notice that *A:A4..D11* appears in the *Cells* text box. These are the cells that you selected.

**4.** Make certain that the **Selection contains a heading** option at the bottom of the dialog box is selected. This option must be selected since you included the headings row in your selection; otherwise, Quattro Pro would also sort the headings.

**FIGURE 5-1**
The Data Sort Dialog Box

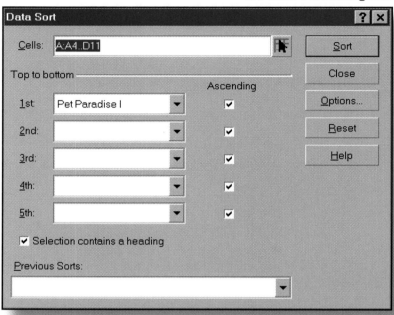

**5.** Notice that **Ascending** is selected by default for each sort key. In the *1st* drop-down list box, **Last Name** should be selected. Click **Sort**. The data should be sorted by last name. However, notice that *Sarah Greene* comes before *Robert Greene*.

**6.** Open the **Tools** menu and choose **Sort**. Open the *2nd* drop-down list box. Select **First Name**.

**7.** Click **Sort**. The data should now be sorted by both first and last name.

**8.** Reopen the Data Sort dialog box and deselect **Ascending** by the *1st* and *2nd* list boxes. Click **Sort**. The names should now be in reverse alphabetical order.

**9.** Reopen the dialog box, make certain that **Ascending** is selected by both boxes, and sort the records again. They should return to ascending alphabetical order.

**10.** Save the notebook and print the spreadsheet.

**11.** Close the notebook.

INTERNET

Gopher is a program that uses a series of menus to lead users to files of information. Gopher is named for the Golden Gophers of the University of Minnesota, where the program was developed.

# *Moving Around the Notebook*

As you know, a spreadsheet file is referred to as a notebook. A notebook is a collection of 256 sheets. Like a spiral-bound notebook that you might use to organize notes for a specific class, a Quattro Pro notebook is ideal for organizing related spreadsheets into a single file.

Notebook sheets are designated by tabs at the bottom of the window. To move to a different sheet, click its tab. You also can use the keyboard to move around the notebook. Press Ctrl+Page Down to move to the next sheet; press Ctrl+Page Up to move to the previous page. Pressing Ctrl+Home moves you to the first sheet.

If the tab of the sheet you want to move to is not visible, use the tab scroll controls to display more tabs (see Figure 5-2). These controls work similarly to the controls on a VCR and allow you to view additional tabs in both directions. The QuickTab button moves you to the Objects sheet. The Objects sheet contains icons representing the various objects, such as charts and dialog boxes, that you may have inserted into a notebook. You will learn more about the Objects sheet when you create charts.

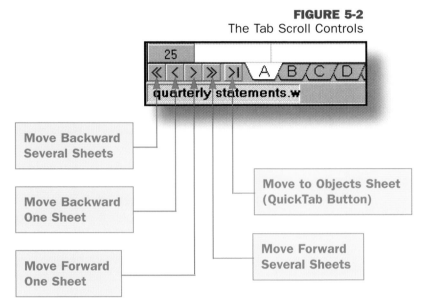

**FIGURE 5-2**
The Tab Scroll Controls

Move Backward Several Sheets

Move Backward One Sheet

Move Forward One Sheet

Move to Objects Sheet (QuickTab Button)

Move Forward Several Sheets

 **IMPORTANT:**

The tab scroll controls do *not* move you to a different sheet in the notebook—they simply bring more sheet tabs into view.

## EXERCISE ▷ QP5.2

1. Open the **quarter** notebook in the student **Datafile** folder.

2. Notice that sheet A contains the first quarter data for Pet Paradise. Click the tab for sheet **B**. The second quarter data should appear.

3. Click Tab **C**. The fourth quarter data appears.

4. Click Tab **D**. The third quarter data appears. As you can see, the third and fourth quarter statements are out of order. You will be fixing this problem in Exercise QP5.3.

5. Press **Ctrl+Page Up**. Sheet C appears.

(continued on next page)

**6.** You can only move to a sheet whose tab appears at the bottom of the window, and only a limited number of tabs can be seen at once. So, if you wanted to move to a sheet whose tab is not currently visible, you would have to use the tab scroll control to display that tab. Click the tab scroll control that allows you to move forward one tab (refer to Figure 5-2). Watch the tabs at the bottom of the screen when you click this control. One more tab appears on the screen. Click Tab **M**. You should move to sheet M, which is currently empty.

**7.** Press **Ctrl+Home** to move to sheet A.

**8.** Remain in this screen for the next exercise.

# Moving, Inserting, and Deleting Notebook Sheets

As you work on a notebook, you may realize that you want the sheets in a different order, perhaps in alphabetical order by title or arranged by date. Fortunately, sheets can easily be rearranged within a notebook. You can also insert a new blank sheet into a notebook by clicking the tab of the sheet you want to *follow* the new sheet. Then open the Insert menu and choose Sheet. The new sheet appears.

To delete a sheet that you no longer need, click the sheet tab and then open the Edit menu and choose Select All. Reopen the Edit menu and choose Delete Sheet(s). The chosen sheet is removed from the notebook.

**SCANS**

**1.** Save this notebook as **quarter 5-3 xxx**.

**2.** You are going to switch sheets C and D. Position the mouse pointer on Tab C. Drag Tab C until it is slightly to the left of Tab E. Release 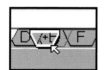 the mouse button. The Fourth Quarter sheet should now be sheet D.

**3.** Go through sheets A through D to make certain that the quarters are now in order.

**4.** Save the notebook and keep it open.

# Renaming Sheet Tabs

The problem with having the sheet tabs labeled with letters of the alphabet is that these letters have little meaning. Fortunately, it is easy to change the tabs to names that clearly identify the sheets. Any references to the sheet in formulas or dialog boxes that use cell addresses will be automatically changed to reflect the new sheet name. In the next exercise you will learn to relabel a sheet.

 **TIP**

Sheet names can contain up to 64 characters and can include spaces and special characters such as * and &.

## EXERCISE ⟩ QP5.4

1. Save the notebook as **quarter 5-4 xxx**.

2. Double click Tab **A**. The insertion point appears in the tab, as shown in Figure 5-3. Key **First Quarter** as the new name. Press **Enter**.

3. Double click Tab **B** and key **Second Quarter** as the new name. Press **Enter**.

4. Double click Tab **C** and key **Third Quarter** as the new name. Press **Enter**.

5. Double click Tab **D** and key **Fourth Quarter** as the new name. Press **Enter**.

6. When you are done changing the tab names, part (or all) of the tab for the Fourth Quarter sheet may be hidden. You can view this tab by clicking the tab scroll control that moves you forward several sheets.

**FIGURE 5-3**
Renaming a Sheet

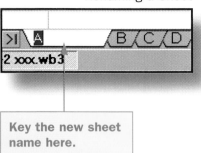

Key the new sheet name here.

7. Click the tab scroll control that moves you backward several sheets. The tab for the First Quarter sheet should reappear.

8. Save the notebook and keep it open for the next exercise.

## Creating a Group

Consider what you might have to do to insert a total column into the First Quarter sheet. Inserting the total would be a simple job that you could easily do by using the QuickSum button. But what if you wanted to place these totals on all four of the sheets in this notebook? You could copy the formula from one sheet and then paste it in another. However, this method would be time-consuming and could lead to mistakes. An easier way would be to group the sheets. When sheets are grouped, anything you do to one sheet can be done to all of the sheets in the group. For example, if you add a title to one sheet, the same title will appear in the same location on each sheet in the group. This feature is a major advantage to working with notebooks.

A group can consist of any number of sheets in a notebook. However, the sheets must be consecutive; that is, they must be one after the other. The Define/Modify Group dialog box is used to create a group and allows you to assign a name to the group. It is a good idea to assign a name that describes the grouped sheets. Before you can apply any actions to the entire group, you must activate the group. To activate the group, open the View menu and choose Group Mode. Unless the group is activated, the entire group will not be affected by any actions you take; only the current sheet will. A blue line appears under the sheet tabs that are included in the group. If you want to deactivate the group, open the View menu and choose Group Mode again.

SCANS

1. Save the notebook as **quarter 5-5 xxx**.

2. Open the **Insert** menu, choose **Name**, and then choose **Group of Sheets** in the submenu. The Define/Modify Group dialog box appears, as shown in Figure 5-4.

3. In the *Group Name* text box key **quarters**.

4. In the *First Sheet* text box key **First Quarter**.

**FIGURE 5-4**
Define/Modify Group Dialog Box

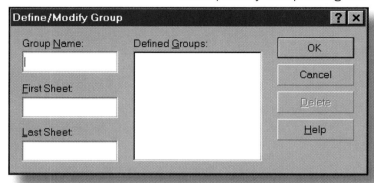

 **TIP**

You can press Tab to move from the *Group Name* text box to the *First Sheet* text box and then to the *Last Sheet* text box.

5. In the *Last Sheet* text box key **Fourth Quarter**.

6. Click **OK**.

7. Open the **View** menu and choose **Group Mode**. A blue line should appear under the tabs of the four sheets that have been grouped.

8. Save the notebook again and keep it open.

 **NOTE:**

When Group Mode is turned on, you can be on any page to perform certain tasks.

# Working in Group Mode

When Group Mode is selected, any formatting you apply to a cell in one sheet is automatically reflected in the corresponding cell in the other sheets. If you do not want to apply formatting to the entire group, you must first turn off Group Mode.

If you want to copy values, labels, and formulas to all sheets in the group, you must confirm the entry by pressing Ctrl+Enter instead of just Enter. This "drills" the entry through all of the sheets in the group. If you want to enter data on a single sheet, you can leave Group Mode on but simply press Enter to confirm the entry.

# EXERCISE ➯ QP5.6

1. Save the notebook as **quarter 5-6 xxx**.

2. Make certain that the First Quarter sheet is on the screen. Click cell **F5** and key **Total**. Press **Ctrl+Enter**. Make the *Total* label bold. Check your other sheets. Is the Total column there?

**IMPORTANT:**

It is important to always know whether Group Mode is currently activated. Remember, when it is not active, any action you take will apply only to the current sheet.

3. Copy the borders in cell E5 to cell F5.
   a. Click cell **E5**.
   b. Click the **QuickFormat** button on the Toolbar.
   c. Click cell **F5**. The upper and lower borders appear in cell F5.
   d. Click the **QuickFormat** button again to turn it off.

4. Go through the first four sheets in the notebook. Notice that they all now have the Total column with borders. Return to the First Quarter sheet.

5. Use the **QuickSum** button to place the total of the values in cells C7..E7 into cell F7.

6. Copy the formula in cell F7 to cells F8..F9. Copy the formula in cell F7 to cells F12..F17.

7. Format the values in column F as currency with no decimal places.

8. Make certain that the values in cells **F9** and **F17** are bolded and that the column is wide enough to display all of the values.

9. Once again, examine the first four sheets in the notebook and notice that the totals appear on all of these sheets. Return to the First Quarter sheet.

10. Open the **View** menu and click **Group Mode** to deselect it. Notice that the blue line no longer appears across the tabs at the bottom of the window.

11. Select cells **A9..F9**. Right click and select **Cell Properties**.

12. Click the **Border/Fill** tab. Open the *Fill Color* drop-down list and select **yellow**. Click **OK**.

13. Go to the Second, Third, and Fourth Quarter sheets. Notice that they have not been changed by this new formatting because you were not in Group Mode when you performed it. Go back to the First Quarter sheet.

14. Click the **Undo** button on the Toolbar to remove the yellow background from the cells.

15. Open the **View** menu and choose **Group Mode**. Once again make the background of cells A9..F9 yellow.

16. Select cells **A17..F17** and give them a yellow background also.

17. Examine the first four sheets in the notebook. Notice that the yellow formatting appears on all of the sheets.

18. Save the notebook. Print the First Quarter sheet. It should look similar to Figure 5-5. Keep the notebook open for the next exercise.

**FIGURE 5-5**
The First Quarter Sheet for Exercise QP5.6

|  | A | B | C | D | E | F | G | H | I | J |
|---|---|---|---|---|---|---|---|---|---|---|
| 1 |  | **PET PARADISE** |  |  |  |  |  |  |  |  |
| 2 |  | **Income Statement** |  |  |  |  |  |  |  |  |
| 3 |  |  |  |  |  |  |  |  |  |  |
| 4 |  | *First Quarter* |  |  |  |  |  |  |  |  |
| 5 |  |  | Jan | Feb | Mar | Total |  |  |  |  |
| 6 | Income |  |  |  |  |  |  |  |  |  |
| 7 |  | Sales of Merchandise | $39,650 | $39,056 | $38,911 | $117,617 |  |  |  |  |
| 8 |  | Sales of Services | $15,141 | $15,943 | $15,085 | $46,169 |  |  |  |  |
| 9 | **Total Income** |  | **$54,791** | **$54,999** | **$53,996** | **$163,786** |  |  |  |  |
| 10 |  |  |  |  |  |  |  |  |  |  |
| 11 | **Expenses** |  |  |  |  |  |  |  |  |  |
| 12 |  | Cost of Sales of Merchandise | $21,038 | $20,630 | $21,066 | $62,734 |  |  |  |  |
| 13 |  | Overhead | $5,202 | $5,020 | $4,845 | $15,067 |  |  |  |  |
| 14 |  | General & Administrative | $1,123 | $1,180 | $1,235 | $3,538 |  |  |  |  |
| 15 |  | Human Resources | $14,870 | $15,200 | $14,985 | $45,055 |  |  |  |  |
| 16 |  | Marketing | $150 | $164 | $175 | $489 |  |  |  |  |
| 17 | **Total Expenses** |  | **$42,383** | **$42,194** | **$42,306** | **$126,883** |  |  |  |  |
| 18 |  |  |  |  |  |  |  |  |  |  |
| 19 |  |  |  |  |  |  |  |  |  |  |
| 20 |  |  |  |  |  |  |  |  |  |  |
| 21 |  |  |  |  |  |  |  |  |  |  |
| 22 |  |  |  |  |  |  |  |  |  |  |
| 23 |  |  |  |  |  |  |  |  |  |  |
| 24 |  |  |  |  |  |  |  |  |  |  |
| 25 |  |  |  |  |  |  |  |  |  |  |

First Quarter / Second Quarter / Third Quarter /

# Cutting and Copying Data Among Notebook Sheets

Sometimes you may want to place data on one sheet into another. For example, you might want to make a summary sheet for the quarterly statements notebook. To do this, you could copy the Total columns from each of the four quarterly sheets onto a summary sheet. Quattro Pro lets you cut, copy, and paste data among sheets just as you would on the same sheet. Just select the cells, cut or copy them, move to the destination sheet, and paste the data into its new spot.

# Creating a Summary Sheet

Placing a summary sheet at the end of a notebook or a group of pages can help people to better understand the data. For example, the summary sheet might contain the grand total of the totals on the previous sheets. If the structure of your summary page differs from that of the individual sheets, you can use the SUM function to place a formula on the summary sheet that adds together the values from the previous sheets. The argument must contain the range of the sheets or the group name of the sheets that are to be added together. For example, if you wanted to add together the values in cell F9 on pages A and B, you would enter the formula @SUM(A..B:F9). This process is shown in Figure 5-6.

**FIGURE 5-6**
Adding Together Values on Different Sheets

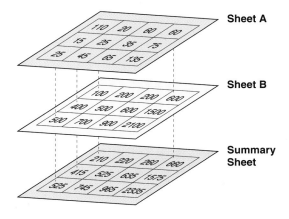

Sheet A

Sheet B

Summary Sheet

# EXERCISE ▷ QP5.7

**SCANS**

1. The **exercise 5-6 xxx** notebook should still be on the screen. Save the notebook as **quarter 5-7 xxx**.

2. Open the **View** menu and click **Group Mode** to deselect it.

3. Make certain that you are at the First Quarter sheet. Select cells **A1..F2**. Click the **Copy** button on the Toolbar.

**NOTE:**

Remember that when you cut data, you remove it from its original location; copying leaves the original data unchanged and makes a duplicate to paste in the new location.

4. Click the tab scroll control that allows you to move forward several sheets. The tab for sheet E should be visible. Double click Tab **E** and key **Summary**. Press **Enter**. You should be at the blank sheet named *Summary*.

5. Select cells **A1..F2**. Click the **Paste** button. The two headings you copied should appear on the Summary sheet.

6. Go to the First Quarter sheet and select cells **A6..B17**. Click the **Copy** button.

7. Go to the Summary sheet and select cells **A6..B17**. Click the **Paste** button. The labels appear. Click the **QuickFit** button. The columns should be adjusted to the proper width for the labels.

**FIGURE 5-7**
The Summary Sheet of Exercise QP5.7

| | A | B | C | D | E | F | G | H | I |
|---|---|---|---|---|---|---|---|---|---|
| 1 | | PET PARADISE | | | | | | | |
| 2 | | Income Statement | | | | | | | |
| 3 | | | | | | | | | |
| 4 | | | | | | | | | |
| 5 | | | Total | | | | | | |
| 6 | Income | | | | | | | | |
| 7 | | Sales of Merchandise | $494,715 | | | | | | |
| 8 | | Sales of Services | $182,370 | | | | | | |
| 9 | Total Income | | $677,085 | | | | | | |
| 10 | | | | | | | | | |
| 11 | Expenses | | | | | | | | |
| 12 | | Cost of Sales of Merchandise | $252,391 | | | | | | |
| 13 | | Overhead | $58,050 | | | | | | |
| 14 | | General & Administrative | $14,749 | | | | | | |
| 15 | | Human Resources | $182,535 | | | | | | |
| 16 | | Marketing | $2,302 | | | | | | |
| 17 | Total Expenses | | $510,027 | | | | | | |
| 18 | | | | | | | | | |
| 19 | | | | | | | | | |
| 20 | | | | | | | | | |
| 21 | | | | | | | | | |
| 22 | | | | | | | | | |
| 23 | | | | | | | | | |
| 24 | | | | | | | | | |
| 25 | | | | | | | | | |

《 〈 〉 》 ▷| \ Summary / F / G / H / I / J / K / L / M / N / O / F ◀

(continued on next page)

**8.** Key **Total** in cell C5 and press **Enter**.

**IMPORTANT:**

Be very careful when entering the SUM formula. Any keying mistakes or incorrect spacing may make the formula invalid.

**9.** In each of the four quarter income statements, the total for Sales of Merchandise appears in cell F7. Therefore, a SUM function can be used to total these values. In cell C7 key the formula **@SUM(First Quarter..Fourth Quarter: F7)**. Press **Enter**. The sum of the values in cell

F7 in each of the four previous sheets appears in cell C7.

**10.** Copy the formula in cell C7 to cells C8..C9. Copy the formula in cell C7 to cells C12..C17.

**11.** Format the values in column C as currency with no decimal places.

**12.** Save the notebook.

**13.** Make certain that you are at the Summary sheet and print it. It should appear as shown in Figure 5-7. Close the notebook and exit Quattro Pro.

# *Summary*

This lesson explained how to sort data and work with several sheets at the same time. You learned that:

■ you can use the Sort command in the Tools menu to sort spreadsheet data. Either alphabetical or numeric data can be sorted in either ascending or descending order.

■ you can click a sheet's tab to move to that sheet. The tab scroll controls allow you to see the different sheet tabs so that you can click them.

■ notebook sheets can be inserted, deleted, or moved to different locations. Use the Insert menu to insert a sheet and the Edit menu to delete a sheet. To move a sheet, drag its tab to the new spot.

■ a sheet can be renamed by double clicking its tab, keying the name, and pressing Enter.

■ Group Mode allows you to edit, format, and apply formulas to an entire group of sheets.

■ if you want to copy values, labels, and formulas to the entire group, you must press Ctrl+Enter (instead of just Enter) after performing the task.

■ data can be cut, copied, and pasted between sheets just as it can be in a single sheet.

## LESSON 5 REVIEW QUESTIONS

### MATCHING

**Write the letter of the term in Column 2 that best matches the description in Column 1.**

**Column 1**

_____ 1. Lets you define a group of sheets.

_____ 2. Allows you to alphabetize data.

_____ 3. Lets you copy values, labels, and formulas to all of the sheets in a group.

_____ 4. Allows you to rename a sheet.

_____ 5. Moves you to the first sheet in a notebook.

**Column 2**

A. Pressing Ctrl+Home

B. Doubling click a sheet's tab

C. Data Sort dialog box

D. Going to the Define/Modify Group dialog box

E. Pressing Ctrl+Enter

### WRITTEN QUESTIONS

**Write your answers to the following questions.**

6. Explain the difference between an ascending sort and a descending sort.

7. List the steps in creating a group.

8. What is the advantage of renaming the sheets in a notebook?

9. Give an example of a situation in which you might want to group some of the sheets in a notebook.

10. What is the purpose of a summary sheet?

## LESSON 5 PROJECT

SCANS

### PROJECT 5A

The accountant at Pet Paradise would like you to determine the payroll totals for the months January through March.

1. Open the **payroll** notebook in the student **Datafile** folder and save the notebook as **payroll proj5a xxx**.

2. Rename Tabs A through C as **January** through **March**, respectively.

(continued on next page)

3. Group the three sheets and find out the total hours worked and the total payroll for each month for both stores. You may need to widen the columns in order for the totals to be displayed.

4. Create a summary sheet and place the appropriate headings at the top of the sheet.

5. The summary sheet should contain the following:
   a. Column B should contain the total hours worked over the three-month period for each store.
   b. Column C should contain the total amount of the payroll over the three-month period for each store.
   c. Cell B10 should contain the total hours worked at both stores for the three-month period.
   d. Cell C10 should contain the total amount of the payroll for the three-month period.

6. Make certain that all of the values on the summary sheet are correctly labeled.

7. Save the notebook and print it.

8. Close the notebook.


## PROJECT 5B

   The West College Computer Lab keeps track of the number of students using the lab during each hour of the day. The lab supervisor would like this information summarized so that it can be used to determine how the lab can better meet the needs of its users.

1. Open the **computers** notebook in the student **Datafile** folder and save the notebook as **computers proj5b xxx**.

2. Rename Tabs A through D as **Week 1** through **Week 4**, respectively.

3. Group the four sheets, Week 1 through Week 4. Switch to **Group Mode**.

4. Find the total usage for each day on each sheet.

5. Find the total usage for each one-hour period on each sheet.

6. Place the total usage for each week in cell G23 on each of the four sheets.

7. Create a summary sheet. Name it **Summary**. Copy the headings from rows 1 and 2 from the Week 1 sheet to the Summary sheet.

8. Key **Total** in cell B4 of the Summary sheet. Make it bold.

9. Key the following (make them bold):

   | A5 | **Monday** | A8 | **Thursday** |
   |----|-----------|-----|-------------|
   | A6 | **Tuesday** | A9 | **Friday** |
   | A7 | **Wednesday** | A11 | **Grand Total** |

10. Widen column A so that all of the labels are visible.

11. Use the SUM function to calculate the total number of students using the computer lab per hour for each day of the week for the four-week period. For example, to find this value for Monday, you would add together the value in cell B23 for all four weeks. Place these totals in cells B5..B9.

12. Total the values in column B and place the sum in cell B11.

13. Format the notebook as you wish to make it attractive to read.

14. Save and print the notebook.

15. Close the notebook and exit Quattro Pro.

## CRITICAL THINKING ACTIVITY

SCANS

Assume that you are the manager of a real estate sales office. At any given time, the office has about 80 to 90 homes for sale. There are seven real estate agents who are paid a commission based on how many properties they sell.

Divide into groups and determine what kinds of spreadsheets would be helpful in determining the commissions for the real estate agents. How might you set up a notebook to keep track of their commissions? How would Quattro Pro's Group Mode be useful in keeping track of sales and sales commissions? What kinds of totals does the group think might be helpful for the managers in making business decisions? Draw a basic sketch of the types of data such a notebook might contain. Assume that the notebook would have a summary sheet. What kinds of figures would probably be included on the summary sheet?

## LESSON 6

# EXPLORING PRINT OPTIONS

## OBJECTIVES

**Upon completion of this lesson, you will be able to:**

- Use Print Preview to see how a notebook will appear when printed.
- Print different selections within a notebook.
- Insert page breaks.
- Insert headers and footers into a notebook.
- Change page margins.
- Change the print size.
- Print cell formulas.
- Print gridlines and row and column borders.

⏱ **Estimated Time: 1¹/₂ hours**

So far, you have simply been printing single notebook sheets by using Quattro Pro's basic print settings. Quattro Pro provides many more options that allow you to view, change, and enhance your printed output. In this lesson you will learn how to adjust print settings and add enhancements to your spreadsheet printouts to give them a more professional look.

## Using Print Preview

The Print Preview feature allows you to view a notebook as it will appear when printed. You also can make many page layout changes while in Print Preview. There are several ways that you can access Print Preview. One method is to open the File menu and choose Print. In the *Print* section of the Spreadsheet Print dialog box select how much of the current notebook you want to view. If you only want to see the current sheet, click Sheet. To see the entire notebook, click

**FIGURE 6-1**
A Notebook in Print Preview

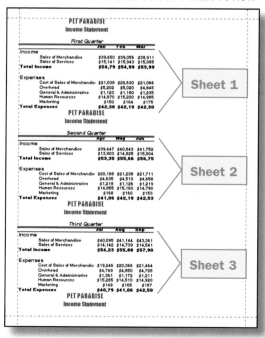

Notebook. Then click Print Preview. The Print Preview screen will appear. In Figure 6-1, Notebook was selected in the Spreadsheet Print dialog box. This means that as many sheets as possible will be printed on a single page. You can move from sheet to sheet and zoom in to see more detail or zoom out to get a better overall view of the document. When you are ready to print the document, click the Print button. If you decide to leave Print Preview without printing, click the button with the letter X over the printer.

Following are brief descriptions of some of the tools available in Print Preview:

*Page 1 of 1:*    If you select Current Sheet as the print area, this will always show only one page. When you select Notebook, this will tell you how many pages it will take to print the entire notebook.

*Page Movement Buttons:*  If you can only use these buttons when Notebook is selected as the print area. The left arrow moves you to the preceding page in the printout, while the right arrow moves to the next page.

*Zoom Factor Buttons:*  Click the button with the plus sign to increase the size, or click the button with the minus sign to decrease it. Click on the part of the page you wish to zoom in on.

*Black-and-White and Color Buttons:*  Click the Black-and-White button to change the preview to black and white, and click the Color button to change it to color.

*Margin Indicator:*  Click this button to display dashed lines representing page margins. You can drag the lines to adjust margins.

NOTE:

Changing margins on one page affects margins on all pages in the notebook.

*Change Page Setup Options:*  Click this button to open the Spreadsheet Page Setup dialog box. You will learn more about this dialog box later in this lesson.

*Set Print Options:*  Click this button to print a hard copy of the document.

*Print:*  Allows you to print without leaving Print Preview.

*Close Print Preview:*  Click this button to return to the regular spreadsheet window.

1. Open the notebook **quarter 5-3 xxx** in the student **Datafile** folder. Save the notebook as **quarter 6-1 xxx**.

2. Open the **File** menu and choose **Print**. The Spreadsheet Print dialog box appears. In the *Print* section select **Current Sheet**.

3. Click the **Print Preview** button. Notice that *Page 1 of 1* appears in the upper left corner of the Property Bar (see page QP-75 for an illustration of this button). Only a single page appears on the screen because **Current Sheet** was selected in the Spreadsheet Print dialog box.

4. Click the button with the large *X* over the printer (it's the rightmost button) to leave Print Preview.

5. In the Spreadsheet Print dialog box click **Notebook**. Click **Print Preview**. The first page of notebook sheets appears on the screen, as shown in Figure 6-1.

6. Click the **Increase Zoom** button. The Zoom factor is now 200% and the page is more readable. Practice increasing and decreasing the Zoom factor. When you are done, make certain that the Zoom factor is at 100%.

**TIP**

You can also zoom out by clicking the right mouse button.

7. Use the page movement buttons to move to the second page and then back to the first page.

8. Click the **Color** button to see the sheet in color. Click the **Black-and-White** button to see the sheet in black and white.

9. Click the **Margin** button to hide and display the margins, which appear as dashed lines.

10. Click the **Print** button. The notebook sheets will be printed on two pages.

**TIP**

You can leave Print Preview by clicking the rightmost button on the Toolbar or by pressing Esc.

11. Leave Print Preview and close the Spreadsheet Print dialog box. Keep this notebook open for the next exercise.

# Selecting a Print Area

So far, you have printed a single sheet or an entire notebook. You also can select a specific area and then tell Quattro Pro to print only that area by clicking Selection in the Spreadsheet Print dialog box. For example, you might want to print only the Total row of a spreadsheet.

You also can choose to print the same block on a number of sheets in a notebook. This is referred to as a *3D block*. In the following exercise you will learn to print a 3D block.

**INTERNET**

The most efficient form of Internet connection is a direct connection. With communications hardware physically connecting you to the Net, data is transferred between hosts and your computer at the highest possible speeds and with the highest reliability.

## EXERCISE ▷ QP6.2

1. Save the current notebook as **quarter 6-2 xxx**.

2. Make certain that you are on sheet A. Select the range **A5..E17**. Hold down **Shift** and click the sheet tabs **B**, **C**, and **D**.

3. Open the **File** menu and choose **Print**. Make certain that **Selection** is chosen in the Spreadsheet Print dialog box.

4. Click **Print Preview**. The portions of the sheets that you selected should appear one after the other on the page.

5. Click the **Print** button. A single page should be printed with the selections.

6. Leave Print Preview and close the Spreadsheet Print dialog box.

7. Click anywhere to deselect the selected areas. Keep this notebook open for the next exercise.

# Inserting a Page Break

When a page is filled, Quattro Pro automatically inserts a special type of page break, called a *soft page break*. These soft page breaks determine where a new page will begin. You also can manually specify where a new page should begin. To do this, you can insert *hard page breaks* into your notebook. When you are in Draft view, hard page breaks are shown as heavy black lines between rows or columns. You can also insert horizontal page breaks. Horizontal page breaks are useful when a spreadsheet contains too many columns to be printed across a single page. If you manually insert a horizontal page break, you can often make the spreadsheet more attractive and easier to understand. In the following exercise you will insert a hard page break.

## EXERCISE ▷ QP6.3

**SCANS**

1. Save the current notebook as **quarter 6-3 xxx**.

2. Select column **D**.

3. Open the **Insert** menu, choose **Page Break**, and then choose **Create**. Notice that a heavy line appears between columns C and D. This line indicates that there will be a page break at this point.

4. Print the spreadsheet. The left portion of the sheet should print on the first page and the right portion (columns D and E) should print on the second page.

5. Open the **Insert** menu, choose **Page Break**, and then choose **Delete**. The page break is removed.

# Inserting Headers And Footers

Many documents that contain more than one page contain headers and footers. A *header* is text that appears at the top of a printed page, while a *footer* appears at the bottom. Headers and footers often contain the title of a document, the current chapter number (in large documents that are subdivided), the date the document was produced, or the current page number. Headers and footers cannot be seen in Draft view. However, you can switch to Page view or Print Preview to see how they will look in the printed spreadsheet.

Quattro Pro provides special codes that you can place in headers or footers to specify how they should be aligned on the page or the information they should contain. For example, entering the code #d causes the current date to be inserted into the header or footer. Table 6-1 explains some of the codes that can be used.

**TABLE 6-1**
Codes for Use in
Headers and Footers

| Purpose | Code |
| --- | --- |
| Center | Shift+\ |
| Right Align | Shift+\\ |
| Page Number | #p |
| Date | #d |
| Time | #t |

**FIGURE 6-2**
The Header/Footer Tab in the Spreadsheet Page Setup Dialog Box

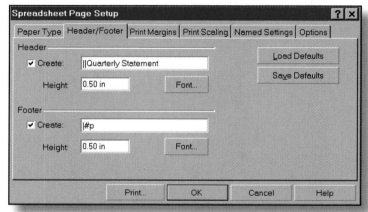

## EXERCISE ⇒ QP6.4

1. Save the current notebook as **quarter 6-4 xxx**.

2. Open the **File** menu and choose **Page Setup**. The Spreadsheet Page Setup dialog box appears. Click the **Header/Footer** tab (see Figure 6-2 above).

3. In the *Header* section select **Create**. In the *Create* text box key **||Quarterly Statement**. Be sure to key the two vertical bars before the header *Quarterly Statement*; this will make the header right-aligned. Click **Font** in the *Header* section. Under *Typeface* choose **Times New Roman** and click **OK**.

4. In the *Footer* section select **Create**. In the *Create* text box key **|#p**. The code *#p* will cause the current page number to be placed in the footer. The vertical bar will cause the page number to be centered at the bottom of each page. Click **Font** in the *Footer* section. Under *Typeface* choose **Times New Roman** and click **OK**.

5. Click **OK** to close the Spreadsheet Page Setup dialog box.

SCANS

6. Open the **View** menu and choose **Page**. You will be able to see the headers and footers by scrolling through the document.

7. Open the **View** menu and choose **Draft**. Save the notebook and keep it open.

# *Controlling How a Spreadsheet Prints*

The Spreadsheet Page Setup dialog box allows you to perform a number of other tasks besides inserting headers and footers. Following are some of the other tabs available in this dialog box:

*Paper Type Tab:*    Allows you to select the type of paper on which you want to print and to change the orientation of the page (see Figure 6-3).

**FIGURE 6-3**
The Paper Type Tab in the Spreadsheet Page Setup Dialog Box

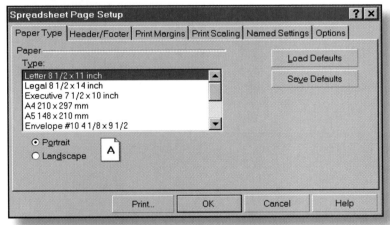

*Print Margins Tab:*    Allows you to set the exact margins instead of just eyeballing them as you can in Print Preview (see Figure 6-4).

**FIGURE 6-4**
The Print Margins Tab in the Spreadsheet Page Setup Dialog Box

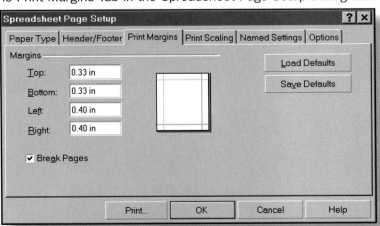

*Print Scaling Tab:*        Gives you options for proportionately adjusting the size of the area that prints on a page (see Figure 6-5). To enlarge the output, select a value of more than 100% in the *Scaling* text box; to reduce the size of the output, enter a value less than 100%.

**FIGURE 6-5**
The Print Scaling Tab in the Spreadsheet Page Setup Dialog Box

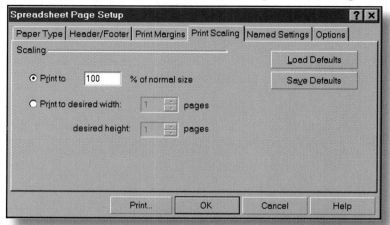

# EXERCISE ▷ QP6.5

1. Save the notebook as **quarter 6-5 xxx**.

2. Open the **File** menu and choose **Page Setup**. In the Spreadsheet Page Setup dialog box click the **Print Margins** tab.
   a. Change the *Top* text box to **1**.
   b. Change the *Bottom* text box to **1**.
   c. Change the *Left* text box to **1.5**.
   d. Change the *Right* text box to **1.5**.

3. Click the **Print Scaling** tab. In the *Print to* text box key **75**.

4. Click **OK** to close the Spreadsheet Page Setup dialog box.

5. Open the **File** menu and choose **Print**. Under *Print* select **Notebook**.

6. Click **Print Preview**. Make certain that everything looks correct. Click the **Print** button.

7. Leave Print Preview and close the Spreadsheet Print dialog box. Save the notebook and keep it open.

# The Options Tab in the Spreadsheet Page Setup Dialog Box

The Options tab in the Spreadsheet Page Setup dialog box allows you to control how your document will be printed in a number of ways (see Figure 6-6). Exercise QP6.6 lets you practice using several of these options.

**FIGURE 6-6**
The Options Tab in the Spreadsheet Page Setup Dialog Box

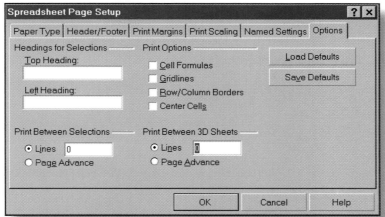

E X E R C I S E ⟹ QP6.6

**1.** Save the notebook as **quarter 6-6**.

**2.** Open the **File** menu and choose **Print**. In the *Print* section of the Spreadsheet Print dialog box, select **Notebook**.

**3.** Click **Page Setup**. In the Spreadsheet Page Setup dialog box click the **Options** tab.

**4.** Under *Print Options* select the following:
   **a.** **Gridlines** (Prints the gridlines that appear on the screen.)
   **b.** **Row/Column Borders** (Prints the row numbers and column letters as they appear on the screen.)
   **c.** **Center Cells** (Centers data on the page between the left and right margins of the printed page.)

**5.** Under *Print Between 3D Sheets* select **Page Advance**. The Page Advance option causes each sheet to be printed on a separate page. The Lines option allows you to specify the number of blank lines that should be placed between each printed sheet.

**6.** Click **OK** to close the dialog box and return to the Spreadsheet Print dialog box.

**7.** Click **Print**. The spreadsheet should print with the row numbers and column labels showing.

**8.** Open the Spreadsheet Print dialog box and click **Page Setup** to return to the Spreadsheet Page Setup dialog box.

**9.** The **Options** tab should be selected. Click **Cell Formulas** to select it. This causes any cell formulas, rather than their results, to be printed. Click **OK**.

**TIP**

If you are having problems obtaining correct formula results, you may wish to print the formulas. You can then study the printed sheets to try to locate any errors in the way that the formulas are stated.

**10.** Print the spreadsheet. The sheets should print with the formulas showing.

(continued on next page)

**11.** Open the Spreadsheet Page Setup dialog box. The **Options** tab should be selected. Under *Print Options* click **Cell Formulas** to deselect and close it.

**12.** Save the notebook. Close the notebook and exit Quattro Pro.

# Summary

This lesson taught you how to change the way in which your spreadsheets can be printed. You learned that:

- Print Preview allows you to see your notebook as it will look when printed. You can perform many tasks while in Print Preview, including zooming into parts of a sheet, moving from one page to another, and changing the printed margins.

- you can specify that only a specific part of a spreadsheet be printed. It is also possible to print the same selection on several sheets.

- manual page breaks can be inserted into spreadsheets. Page breaks can be either horizontal or vertical.

- headers and footers can be placed on each page of a notebook. Headers and footers often contain page numbers and the current date.

- you can use the Spreadsheet Page Setup dialog box to specify a notebook's margins, how it should be scaled, and the type of paper that will be used.

- the Options tab in the Spreadsheet Page Setup dialog box lets you print formulas, gridlines, and row and column borders. It also lets you center data horizontally on the page and specify that each sheet should be printed on a separate page.

## LESSON 6 REVIEW QUESTIONS

### TRUE/FALSE

**Circle the T if the statement is true. Circle the F if it is false.**

**T  F**  **1.** Another name for Print Preview is Page view.

**T  F**  **2.** A header is text that appears at the top of each page in a notebook when it is printed.

**T  F**  **3.** If you want to print all of the pages in a notebook, make certain that Sheet is selected in the Spreadsheet Print dialog box.

**T  F  4.** You can see headers and footers when you are in Page view, but not when you are in Draft view.

**T  F  5.** There is no way that you can print only a section of a sheet; you must either print the entire notebook or an entire sheet within the notebook.

## MULTIPLE CHOICE

**Circle the best answer to each of the following statements.**

**6.** Which of the following is *not* a button that appears when you are in Print Preview?
 **A.** Close Print Preview
 **B.** Color
 **C.** Margin Indicator
 **D.** Open

**7.** Which of the following will insert the current page number into a footer?
 **A.** @page
 **B.** #p
 **C.** <insert page>
 **D.** ‖n

**8.** What is the purpose of the Print Scaling tab?
 **A.** To make each sheet in a notebook print on a separate page.
 **B.** To allow you to enlarge or reduce the size of the printed output.
 **C.** To make more room on a page so that headers and footers can be inserted.
 **D.** To center data horizontally on a printed page.

**9.** Which of the following is a selection on the Options tab in the Spreadsheet Page Setup dialog box?
 **A.** Cell Formulas
 **B.** Print
 **C.** Print Preview
 **D.** Zoom

**10.** What is the purpose of a hard page break?
 **A.** It causes the on-screen gridlines to be printed.
 **B.** It saves paper by making certain that a notebook's sheets are printed one after another on the same page until that page is filled.
 **C.** It lets you specify where a new page should begin when a notebook is printed.
 **D.** It makes certain that data will be horizontally centered on the printed page.

### PROJECT 6A

Format the income statement for Pet Paradise. Also add headers and footers to it.

1. Open the notebook **income** in the student **Datafile** folder. Save the notebook as **income proj6a xxx**.

2. In cell A19 key **Profit**. In cell C19 enter a formula that will subtract the total expenses for January from the total income (subtract cell C17 from cell C9).

3. Copy the formula in cell C19 to cells D19..O19.

4. Make certain that the dollar values in Row 19 are formatted as currency with no decimal places.

5. Place the data in row 19 in brown type.

6. Go to **Page** view. Notice that this spreadsheet prints on two pages. Change the headings in the first four rows on the first page so that they are left-aligned. (They currently are centered over the entire sheet.)

7. Insert two new blank columns at the beginning of the second page. These columns will be J and K.

8. Copy the headings in cells A1..A4 to cells J1..J4. The headings will now appear on both pages when this spreadsheet is printed.

9. Select column **J**. Open the **Insert** menu and choose **Page Break**. In the submenu click **Create**. This will force the second page to begin with column J.

10. Click cell **J2**. The heading *Income Statement* should appear in the input line. Place the insertion point at the end of the heading and press the space bar to insert a blank space. Then key **(Cont.)**. This will tell the reader that this page is a continuation of the first page.

11. Select cells **A6..B19**. Copy these cells and paste them to cells **J6..K19**. Widen the cells so that all of their contents are visible.

12. Open the **File** menu and choose **Page Setup**. In the Spreadsheet Page Setup dialog box click the **Options** tab. In the *Print Options* section select **Gridlines** and **Center Cells**.

13. Click the **Header/Footer** tab to insert a header and footer.
    a. Create a header that will place your name at the top of each page. Your name should be right-aligned.
    b. Create a footer that will place the current page number at the bottom center of each page.

14. Click **OK** to close the Spreadsheet Page Setup dialog box.

15. Save the notebook and print it. Close the notebook.

## PROJECT 6B

Format the West College computer lab usage notebook. Also add headers and footers to the sheets and print each sheet on a separate page.

1.  Open the notebook **computers proj5b xxx** in the student **Datafile** folder. Save the notebook as **computers proj6b xxx**.

2.  If the first four sheets are not already in Group mode, open the **View** menu and select **Group Mode**. There should be a blue line below Week 1 through Week 4.

3.  Change the three headings at the top of each of the sheets in the group so that they are in a different font, such as Century Schoolbook. Go to the Summary sheet and change the font used in its headings to match the other sheets.

4.  Open the **File** menu and select **Print**. In the *Print* section select **Notebook**.

5.  Click **Page Setup** to open the Spreadsheet Page Setup dialog box. Click the **Options** tab. In the *Print Options* section select **Row/Column Borders**. In the *Print Between 3D Sheets* section click **Page Advance**.

6.  Click the **Header/Footer** tab to insert a header and footer.
    a.  Create a header that will place the current date at the top of each page. It should be right-aligned.
    b.  Create a footer that will place the current page number at the bottom center of each page.

7.  Close the Spreadsheet Page Setup dialog box.

8.  Go to **Print Preview** and make certain that the sheets look correct. Print the entire notebook.

9.  Leave Print Preview and save the notebook. Close the notebook and exit Quattro Pro.

## CRITICAL THINKING ACTIVITY

SCANS

This lesson discussed how you could insert page numbers and the current date into notebooks. Notebook headers and footers sometimes contain information such as the current time, the name of the person who developed it, or the name of the file in which it is stored. For example, you can insert the current time by using the code *#t*. The format will be HH:MM:SS PM/AM.

Give some examples of situations in which it might be useful to place each of these types of data into a header or footer. Can you think of any other information that might be useful? What is the advantage of using the code *#d* to enter the current date rather than just keying in today's date? What are some of the advantages of placing this information in a header or footer rather than into the spreadsheet itself, for example, as a heading? Can you think of any disadvantages?

# ANALYZING DATA

**Upon completion of this lesson, you will be able to:**

- Use the Scenario Expert to create scenarios.

- Use the What-If Expert to create tables to show the effects of changing a range of values.

- Use the Optimizer tool to find values that produce a specified result.

- Be able to determine which of the data analysis tools discussed in this lesson would be most appropriate in a given situation.

**⏱ Estimated Time: 1 hour**

So far, you have been entering data into spreadsheets and performing calculations. For example, you know how to find the average of a column of numbers or determine the amount of the monthly payments on a four-year loan. However, the true power of Quattro Pro becomes evident when you begin to use its data analysis tools. Data analysis tools can help managers in making decisions. For example, what would happen if we decreased Pet Paradise's grooming fees by 10%, but this led to an 8% rise in customer business? Would this be a good or a bad business decision? This is the kind of situation in which data analysis tools are helpful. In this lesson you will learn how to change values to produce the most desirable results, and you will discover how to pose questions to generate viable solutions.

## Creating a Scenario

A scenario is generally defined as an outline or a depiction of a course of events. In Quattro Pro a *scenario* depicts an activity in which a calculation is performed on specific data. When you entered formulas and functions to perform calculations on data in Lesson 3, you were actually creating a scenario. You can create several scenarios of the same activity by plugging in variable values to produce different results. Let's assume that the manager of Pet Paradise has the sales figures for the month of January. She knows that over the last six months sales of merchandise have increased from .5% to 2% each month, and sales of services have increased from 1% to 3% each month. From this information she would like to estimate the lowest and highest sales that are likely for February.

The Scenario Expert is well-suited to this type of analysis. First you create a baseline like the one shown in Figure 7-1. The baseline specifies the starting values that will be used when creating the scenarios. Notice that the sales for January and February are identical—no increase has been figured into the February sales. Once the baseline is set, you can start the Scenario Expert. As you will see in the following exercise, the Scenario Expert contains four steps that lead you through the process of developing a scenario.

**FIGURE 7-1**
The Scenario Baseline

| | A | B | C | D | E |
|---|---|---|---|---|---|
| 2 | | | | | |
| 3 | | | Jan | Feb | |
| 4 | **Income** | | | | |
| 5 | | Sales of Merchandise | $39,650 | $39,650 | |
| 6 | | Sales of Services | $15,141 | $15,141 | |
| 7 | **Total Income** | | **$54,791** | **$54,791** | |
| 8 | | | | | |
| 9 | | | | | |
| 10 | **Growth:** | | | | |
| 11 | | Sales of Merchandise | | | |
| 12 | | Sales of Services | | | |
| 13 | | | | | |

## E X E R C I S E ▷ QP7.1

1. Open the notebook **projected** in the student **Datafile** folder. Save the notebook as **projected 7-1 xxx**.

2. Open the **Tools** menu and choose **Scenario**. In the submenu choose **New**.

3. The Scenario Expert - Step 1 of 4 dialog box appears (see Figure 7-2). In the *Changing cells* text box, enter **C11,C12**. These are the cells that you want the Scenario Expert to manipulate.

**TIP**

As you are going through the steps in the Scenario Expert, you can always back up and change a previous entry. Just click the Back button.

**FIGURE 7-2**
The Scenario Expert - Step 1 of 4 Dialog Box

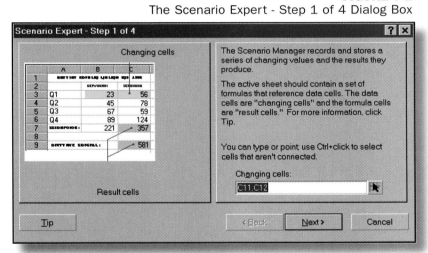

4. In the Scenario Expert - Step 2 of 4 dialog box, shown in Figure 7-3, you enter the scenario's name. You also key each of the scenarios as follows:

   a. Key **Best Case** as the Scenario name and press **Tab**. In the text box next to *C11* key **.02**. In the text box next to *C12* key **.03**. Click **Add Scenario**.

(continued on next page)

b. Key **Worst Case** as the second Scenario name and press **Tab**. In the text box next to *C11* key **.005**. In *C12* key **.01**. Click **Add Scenario**.

c. Click **Next**.

**TIP**

If you have created an incorrect scenario, you can delete it in the Scenario Expert - Step 3 of 4 dialog box. Just select that scenario and click the Delete scenario button.

5. The Scenario Expert - Step 3 of 4 dialog box, shown in Figure 7-4, lets you select the scenarios you want to view. Click **Best Case** and then click **Show Scenario**. You can then examine the scenario's results. (You may need to drag the dialog box out of your way.) Repeat this process for Worst Case. Click **Next**.

6. In the Scenario Expert - Step 4 of 4 dialog box, shown in Figure 7-5, click **Create Report**. A Scenarios sheet should appear in your notebook. It should look like Figure 7-6; it lists the results of each scenario. Note that the first sheet remains unchanged.

**FIGURE 7-3**
The Scenario Expert - Step 2 of 4 Dialog Box

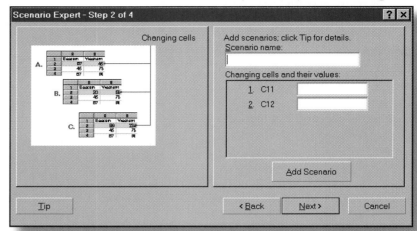

**FIGURE 7-4**
The Scenario Expert - Step 3 of 4 Dialog Box

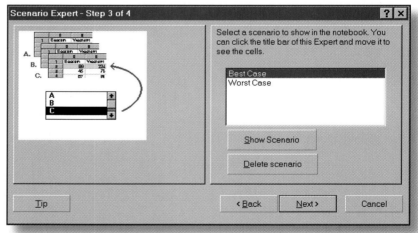

7. Save the notebook. Print the Scenarios sheet and close the notebook. Remain in Quattro Pro for the next exercise.

**INTERNET**

Sports statistics are widely available on the Web. You can locate data on a sport in which you are interested and then use Quattro Pro to analyze it.

**FIGURE 7-5**
The Scenario Expert - Step 4 of 4 Dialog Box

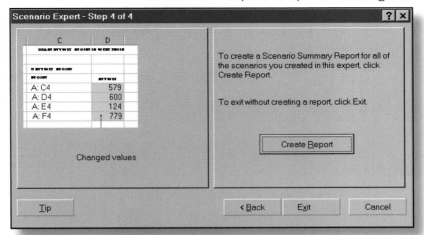

**FIGURE 7-6**
Scenarios Sheet

| | A | B | C | D | E | F |
|---|---|---|---|---|---|---|
| 1 | | Scenario Summary Report for Group3 | | | | |
| 2 | | | | | | |
| 3 | **Scenarios** | **Changing Cells** | | **Result Cells** | | |
| 4 | | Cells | Values | Cells | Values | |
| 5 | Best Case | A:C11 | 0.02 | A:D5 | $40,443 | |
| 6 | | A:C12 | 0.03 | A:D6 | $15,595 | |
| 7 | | | | A:D7 | $56,038 | |
| 8 | | | | | | |
| 9 | Worst Case | A:C11 | 0.005 | A:D5 | $39,848 | |
| 10 | | A:C12 | 0.01 | A:D6 | $15,292 | |
| 11 | | | | A:D7 | $55,141 | |
| 12 | | | | | | |

# *Creating a What-If Table*

Sometimes you may want to see how changes in variables affect an entire range of values. Quattro Pro allows you to use *What-If* tables to substitute a range of values that generates a range of results. For example, you might want to figure out the cost of a mortgage at varying loan amounts and varying interest rates. As with scenarios, Quattro Pro provides you with an expert to guide you through the process. The baseline data shown in Figure 7-7 will be used for creating the What-If table in Exercise QP7.2.

**FIGURE 7-7**
Baseline Data for What-If Table

| | A | B | C |
|---|---|---|---|
| 1 | | | |
| 2 | | | |
| 3 | **Payment** | $185,000.00 | |
| 4 | **Interest** | 8.50% | |
| 5 | **Years** | 20 | |
| 6 | | | |
| 7 | **Monthly Payment** | $1,605 | |
| 8 | **Total Payment** | $385,314 | |
| 9 | | | |

1. Open the notebook **payments** in the student **Datafile** folder. Save the notebook as **payments 7-2 xxx**.

2. Open the **Tools** menu and choose **Numeric Tools**. In the submenu choose **What-If**. In the What-If dialog box click **Expert**. Now the What-If Expert - Step 1 of 7 dialog box appears, as shown in Figure 7-8.

3. Click **Vary two cells against one formula**. Click **Next**.

4. The What-If Expert - Step 2 of 7 dialog box (see Figure 7-9) allows you to specify the cell containing the formula. In the *Formula Cell* text box key **B7** (this cell contains the @PMT formula). Click **Next**.

5. The What-If Expert - Step 3 of 7 Dialog Box, shown in Figure 7-10, lets you enter the address of the Input Cell, or the cell that is referenced in the formula that contains the value for which you want to enter substitute values. In the *Input Cell* text box key **B3** (the cell containing the loan principle). Click **Next**.

6. The What-If Expert - Step 4 of 7 Dialog Box, shown in Figure 7-11, lets you select the values that will be plugged into the cells. Click **Calculate Different Values**. In the *Start* text box key **170000**. In the *Step* text box key **5000**. In the *Stop* text box key **240000**. Click **Rebuild List** and then click **Next**.

**FIGURE 7-8**
The What-If Expert - Step 1 of 7 Dialog Box

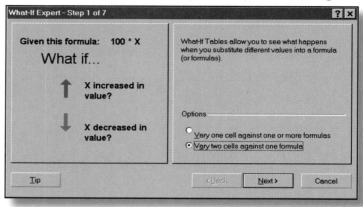

**FIGURE 7-9**
The What-If Expert - Step 2 of 7 Dialog Box

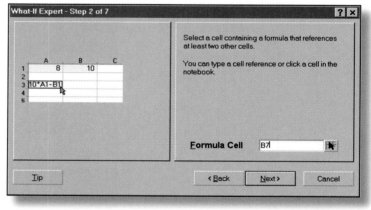

**FIGURE 7-10**
The What-If Expert - Step 3 of 7 Dialog Box

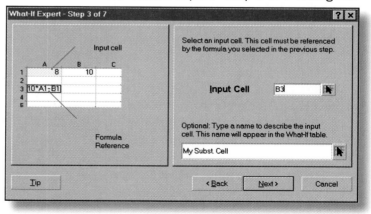

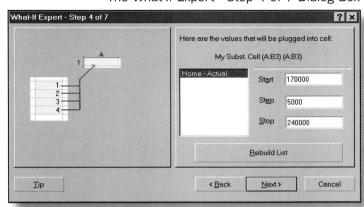
**FIGURE 7-11**
The What-If Expert - Step 4 of 7 Dialog Box

**7.** Because you are using two variables, the What-If Expert - Step 5 of 7 Dialog Box, shown in Figure 7-12, lets you select a second variable. In the *2nd Input Cell* text box key **B4** (the cell containing the interest rate) and click **Next**.

**8.** In the What-If Expert - Step 6 of 7 Dialog Box, shown in Figure 7-13, click **Calculate Different Values**. In the *Start* text box key **0.07**. In the *Step* text box key **0.0025**. In the *Stop* text box key **0.1**. Click **Rebuild List** and then click **Next**.

**9.** In the What-If Expert - Step 7 of 7 Dialog Box, key **A10** in the *Table Cells* text box. Click **Make Table**.

**FIGURE 7-12**
The What-If Expert - Step 5 of 7 Dialog Box

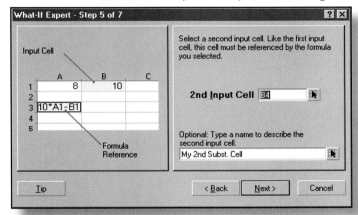

**10.** Change the contents of cell C10 to **Interest Rate**. Make it bold.

**11.** Delete the text in cells A12..A15. In cell A12 key **Loan Amount**. Make it bold.

**12.** Bold the values in row 11 and column B (rows 11-26) of the What-If table.

**13.** The table should appear as shown in Figure 7-14. Save the notebook.

**TIP**

You can format What-If tables as you would any other data in a notebook.

**14.** Print the current sheet in Landscape orientation. Close the notebook and remain in Quattro Pro for the next exercise.

**FIGURE 7-13**
The What-If Expert - Step 6 of 7 Dialog Box

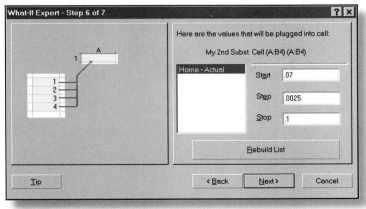

**FIGURE 7-14**

Table Showing Effects of Varying Loan Amounts and Interest Rates

| | A | B | | | | | | | | | | | | |
|---|---|---|---|---|---|---|---|---|---|---|---|---|---|---|
| 3 | Payment | $185,000.00 | | | | | | | | | | | | |
| 4 | Interest | 8.50% | | | | | | | | | | | | |
| 5 | Years | 20 | | | | | | | | | | | | |
| 7 | Monthly Payment | $1,605 | | | | | | | | | | | | |
| 8 | Total Payment | $385,314 | | | | | | | | | | | | |
| 10 | | Interest Rate | | | | | | | | | | | | |
| 11 | | $1,605 | 7.00% | 7.25% | 7.50% | 7.75% | 8.00% | 8.25% | 8.50% | 8.75% | 9.00% | 9.25% | 9.50% | 9.75% |
| 12 | Loan Amount | $170,000.00 | $1,318 | $1,344 | $1,370 | $1,396 | $1,422 | $1,449 | $1,475 | $1,502 | $1,530 | $1,557 | $1,585 | $1,612 |
| 13 | | $175,000.00 | $1,357 | $1,383 | $1,410 | $1,437 | $1,464 | $1,491 | $1,519 | $1,546 | $1,575 | $1,603 | $1,631 | $1,660 |
| 14 | | $180,000.00 | $1,396 | $1,423 | $1,450 | $1,478 | $1,506 | $1,534 | $1,562 | $1,591 | $1,620 | $1,649 | $1,678 | $1,707 |
| 15 | | $185,000.00 | $1,434 | $1,462 | $1,490 | $1,519 | $1,547 | $1,576 | $1,605 | $1,635 | $1,664 | $1,694 | $1,724 | $1,755 |
| 16 | | $190,000.00 | $1,473 | $1,502 | $1,531 | $1,560 | $1,589 | $1,619 | $1,649 | $1,679 | $1,709 | $1,740 | $1,771 | $1,802 |
| 17 | | $195,000.00 | $1,512 | $1,541 | $1,571 | $1,601 | $1,631 | $1,662 | $1,692 | $1,723 | $1,754 | $1,786 | $1,818 | $1,850 |
| 18 | | $200,000.00 | $1,551 | $1,581 | $1,611 | $1,642 | $1,673 | $1,704 | $1,736 | $1,767 | $1,799 | $1,832 | $1,864 | $1,897 |
| 19 | | $205,000.00 | $1,589 | $1,620 | $1,651 | $1,683 | $1,715 | $1,747 | $1,779 | $1,812 | $1,844 | $1,878 | $1,911 | $1,944 |
| 20 | | $210,000.00 | $1,628 | $1,660 | $1,692 | $1,724 | $1,757 | $1,789 | $1,822 | $1,856 | $1,889 | $1,923 | $1,957 | $1,992 |
| 21 | | $215,000.00 | $1,667 | $1,699 | $1,732 | $1,765 | $1,798 | $1,832 | $1,866 | $1,900 | $1,934 | $1,969 | $2,004 | $2,039 |
| 22 | | $220,000.00 | $1,706 | $1,739 | $1,772 | $1,806 | $1,840 | $1,875 | $1,909 | $1,944 | $1,979 | $2,015 | $2,051 | $2,087 |
| 23 | | $225,000.00 | $1,744 | $1,778 | $1,813 | $1,847 | $1,882 | $1,917 | $1,953 | $1,988 | $2,024 | $2,061 | $2,097 | $2,134 |
| 24 | | $230,000.00 | $1,783 | $1,818 | $1,853 | $1,888 | $1,924 | $1,960 | $1,996 | $2,033 | $2,069 | $2,106 | $2,144 | $2,182 |
| 25 | | $235,000.00 | $1,822 | $1,857 | $1,893 | $1,929 | $1,966 | $2,002 | $2,039 | $2,077 | $2,114 | $2,152 | $2,191 | $2,229 |
| 26 | | $240,000.00 | $1,861 | $1,897 | $1,933 | $1,970 | $2,007 | $2,045 | $2,083 | $2,121 | $2,159 | $2,198 | $2,237 | $2,276 |

# *Using the Optimizer Tool*

O ccasionally, you may be in a situation where you want to find the values that are needed to produce a known result. For example, let's say that you can afford to pay $140 a month for a used car and you want the loan to run a maximum of three years at ten percent interest. What would be the maximum amount you could pay for a car under these conditions? Quattro Pro's Optimizer can determine this amount for you. In essence, it lets you perform a calculation backward; that is, you know the result and Optimizer lets you insert values or cell references that produce that result. In Exercise QP7.3 you will determine the maximum amount the owners of Pet Paradise can borrow to purchase a building if they want the monthly mortgage payment to be $1,600.

EXERCISE ▷ QP7.3

**SCANS**

1. Open the notebook **mortgage** in the student **Datafile** folder. Save the notebook as **mortgage 7-3 xxx**.

✓ NOTE:

The interest rate must be divided by 12 because the PMT formula uses a monthly interest rate. The length of time for the loan must be stated in months, so the number of years has been multiplied by 12.

2. In cell B10 key **@PMT(B3,B4/12, B5*12)**. Press **Enter**. A zero appears in the cell.

3. Open the **Tools** menu and choose **Numeric Tools** and then **Optimizer**. The Optimizer dialog box appears, as shown in Figure 7-15.

4. In the *Solution Cell* text box key **B10**.

NOTE:

When inserting values into the *Solution Cell* and *Variable Cell(s)* text boxes, you can use actual values, cell addresses, or a formula containing both.

5. Click **Target Value** and key **1600** in the text box next to it.

6. In the *Variable Cell(s)* text box key **B3**. Optimizer will place the solution in cell B3.

TIP

If you wish, you can go back and modify some of your entries to see how the changes affect the result. For example, you could change the target value to 2000 to see how much more could be borrowed by increasing the monthly payment.

7. Click **Solve**. The maximum amount of the mortgage ($184,369.34) appears in cell B3. Notice also that the amount of the payment

**FIGURE 7-15**
Optimizer Dialog Box

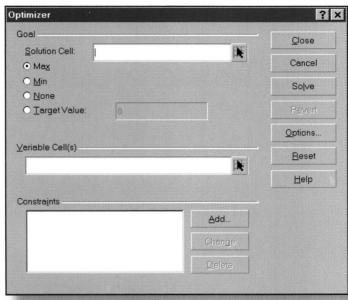

(1600) appears in cell B10. This is because it used this value in reaching the solution.

8. Click **Close** to close the Optimizer dialog box.

9. Save the notebook and print this sheet. Close the notebook.

# *Summary*

In this lesson you learned how the data contained in spreadsheets could be analyzed in several different ways. You learned that:

■ data analysis tools are useful in solving problems and making business decisions.

■ the Scenario Expert leads you through the process of creating scenarios and then determines the results of these specifications.

■ when using the Scenario Expert, you must indicate the cell whose value will change in each scenario and its current value.

■ you can use the What-If Expert to generate a table that contains results based on the values of one or two variables.

■ when creating a What-If table, you must specify the variable or variables to be varied, the starting and ending point, and the step value which determines the increments that will appear in the table.

■ the Optimizer tool takes an opposite approach. You use a formula to specify the results you want to achieve and the variables that can vary. Optimizer then solves the formula.

## LESSON 7 REVIEW QUESTIONS

### TRUE/FALSE

**Circle the T if the statement is true. Circle the F if it is false.**

**T  F  1.** The Scenario Expert places its results on a separate sheet in the notebook.

**T  F  2.** Data analysis can be used to provide information that managers can use in making business decisions.

**T  F  3.** In Step 1 of the Scenario Expert, you specify the changing cell(s), which contains a formula.

**T  F  4.** If you know how much you can make in monthly payments on a sailboat over a three-year period and you want to determine the most you can afford to pay for the boat, the fastest solution would be to create a scenario.

**T  F  5.** A What-If table would be useful for a real estate agent who needed to help clients determine what their monthly payments would be based on the cost of a house, length of time for the loan, and the interest rate.

### WRITTEN QUESTIONS

**Write your answers to the following questions.**

6. How might data analysis tools such as the ones discussed in this lesson help someone who runs a restaurant? Give at least two ways that you think data analysis might be useful.

7. What is a scenario?

8. How is the Optimizer tool different from the What-If tool?

9. Give an example of a situation in which a two-variable What-If table would be useful.

10. How might a salesperson use the Scenario Expert to determine how much merchandise she must sell to increase her commission by 5% over last month?

# LESSON 7 PROJECT

## PROJECT 7A

Calculate how much merchandise Pet Paradise would have to sell to have a 1%, 2%, and 3% increase in profit on merchandise sold for the next month.

1.  Open the notebook **increases** in the student **Datafile** folder. Save the notebook as **increases proj7a xxx**.

2.  The top part of the table contains the merchandise sales and the cost of goods sold for October. Click cell **B3**. Notice that it contains the formula *+B2 \* 1/1.9*. This formula is used to calculate the cost of goods sold based on the actual sales. Pet Paradise marks up their retail items 90%, so multiplying the retail sales by 1/1.9 will give us the cost of goods sold.

3.  Examine cell B4. It contains the total merchandise sales minus the cost of goods sold. Cell B6 will contain the amount of increased retail sales.

4.  Use the Scenario Expert to determine how much merchandise will have to be sold in November to generate a 1% increase in profit, a 2% increase, and a 3% increase. Cell B7 will be the variable cell; that is, the amount of profit that will actually be earned based on the percent of increase. Name the scenarios **1% Increase**, **2% Increase**, and **3% Increase**. The values of cell B7 for each of the scenarios will be **0.01**, **0.02**, and **0.03**, respectively.

5.  Examine each of the scenarios to determine if they appear to have obtained correct results.

6.  Create a report. This report will be placed on a new Scenarios sheet and will show the projected profits, depending on whether there is a 1%, 2%, or 3% increase.

7.  Save the notebook. Print the Scenarios sheet and close the notebook.

## PROJECT 7B

Morrison Car Dealership needs to upgrade the equipment in the service department. The manager wants to obtain a bank loan to purchase this new electronic equipment. He has determined that with the projected increase in service business, the dealership can afford to make monthly payments of approximately $2,500 on the loan. The loan would be for ten years at a 9% yearly interest rate. Use the Optimizer to determine how much money the dealership could safely borrow.

1.  Open a new notebook, if necessary.

2.  Key the following labels:
    a.  In cell A3 key **Interest**.
    b.  In cell A4 key **Years**.
    c.  In cell A5 key **Monthly Payment**.
    d.  In cell A7 key **Mortgage Amount**.

(continued on next page)

3. Widen Cclumn A so that all of the labels can be seen.

4. Key the following values:
   a. In cell B3 key **0.09**.
   b. In cell B4 key **10**.
   c. In cell B5 key **2500**.

5. In cell B2 key **@PMT(B7,B3/12, B4\*12)**. Press **Enter**. A zero appears in the cell.

6. Open the **Tools** menu and choose **Numeric Tools** and then **Optimizer**.

7. In the *Solution Cell* text box key **B2**.

8. Click **Target Value** and key **2500** in the text box next to it.

9. In the *Variable Cell(s)* text box key **B7**.

10. Click **Solve**. The maximum amount that can be borrowed should appear in cell B7.

11. Click **Close** to close the Optimizer dialog box.

12. Save the notebook as **purchase proj7b xxx** and print this sheet. Close the notebook and exit Quattro Pro.

## CRITICAL THINKING ACTIVITY

SCANS

Restaurant managers must be resourceful in keeping their businesses efficient and current because the restaurant business is very competitive. Divide into small groups and think of ways the manager of a restaurant might use each of the three data analysis tools discussed in this chapter. You might want to consider some of the many tasks the manager must perform. For example, he or she must make efficient use of staff, having the most workers present when there are also the most customers. The manager must also determine which menu items are selling the best and remove the ones that don't appeal to customers. They also must keep an eye on profits and try to keep costs down. From these ideas, and any others that the group can think of, create a list indicating how each of the three data analysis tools discussed in the chapter could be useful.

# CREATING CHARTS

## OBJECTIVES

**Upon completion of this lesson, you will be able to:**

- Identify different types of charts, including bar charts, line charts, and pie charts.

- Create a chart using the QuickChart button on the Toolbar.

- Move and resize a chart.

- Change data in an existing chart.

- Create a chart with the Chart Expert.

- Change the appearance of an existing chart.

- Add annotations to charts.

🕐 **Estimated Time: 1¹/₂ hours**

Quattro Pro notebooks can contain more than just data on a grid. As you'll learn in the next four lessons, you can do some creative, exciting things to spice up your data and make it simpler to understand. In this lesson you will learn how to use spreadsheet data to create charts. You will also learn to edit and format chart data.

## *Types of Charts*

A *chart* is a graphic representation of data. For example, you might want to create a chart that shows how sales have increased over the last six months. A line chart (see Figure 8-1A) would be good to represent this type of data. Bar charts, as shown in Figure 8-1B, compare values, such as the number and type of pets boarding on each day of the week at Pet Paradise. Pie charts are useful for items such as budgets where you might want to see what percentage of the total budget goes to a certain item, such as rent. Figure 8-1C contains a pie chart. Most charts have certain standard components. Figure 8-2 contains a typical bar chart with its components labeled. The *x-axis* is the horizontal segment of the chart and normally represents categories of data or time periods, referred to as the *data series*. The *y-axis* is the vertical segment of a chart and normally represents numeric data, such as dollar amounts or other quantities.

**FIGURE 8-1A**
Line Chart

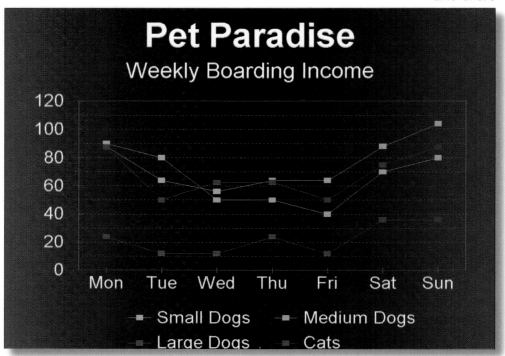

**FIGURE 8-1B**
Three-Dimensional Bar Chart

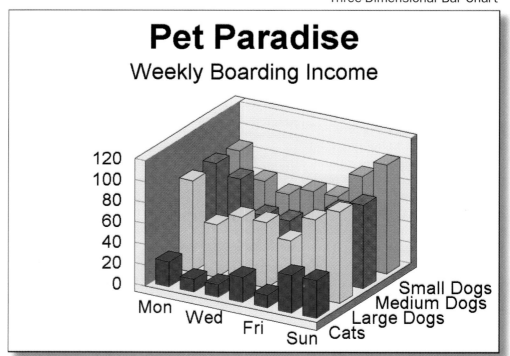

**FIGURE 8-1C**
Pie Chart

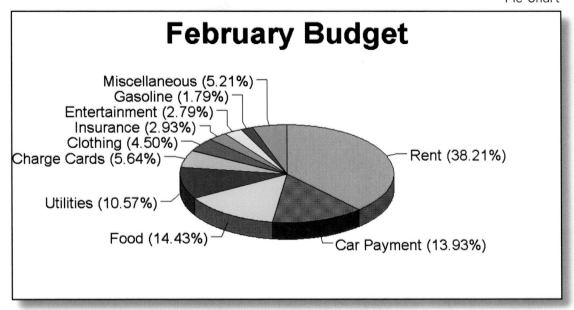

**February Budget**

Miscellaneous (5.21%)
Gasoline (1.79%)
Entertainment (2.79%)
Insurance (2.93%)
Clothing (4.50%)
Charge Cards (5.64%)
Utilities (10.57%)
Food (14.43%)
Rent (38.21%)
Car Payment (13.93%)

**FIGURE 8-2**
A Bar Chart with Its Components Labeled

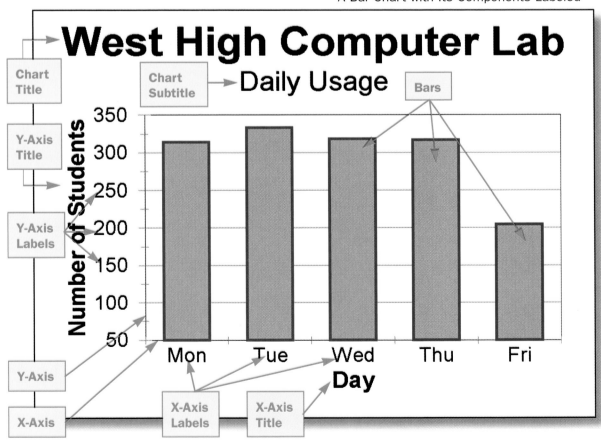

**West High Computer Lab**

Chart Title

Chart Subtitle → Daily Usage

Bars

Y-Axis Title

Y-Axis Labels

Number of Students

350
300
250
200
150
100
50

Mon    Tue    Wed    Thu    Fri
**Day**

Y-Axis

X-Axis

X-Axis Labels

X-Axis Title

# *Using the QuickChart Button*

A fast way to create a chart right on the current sheet is to use the QuickChart button. First, you select the data you want charted. If you want headings that identify data on the notebook sheet to appear in your chart as well, include them as part of the selected block. Then click the QuickChart button on the Toolbar. The mouse pointer turns into a crossbar and you drag to select the area where the chart is to be displayed. A floating chart appears on the sheet. A *floating chart* is one that is contained on a spreadsheet rather than in a separate chart window. In addition, chart buttons appear below the Notebook Toolbar. Each of these buttons is described below.

| | | |
|---|---|---|
| *Chart Types:* | | This drop-down list allows you to select from available chart types. |
| *Fill Style Button:* | | Allows you to select from a variety of fill patterns. |
| *Background Fill Color Button:* | | Lets you select a color for the chart background. |
| *Foreground Fill Color Button:* | | Lets you select a color for the chart foreground. |
| *Border Line Style Button:* | | Lets you pick a style for the chart's border. |
| *Border Color Button:* | | Lets you pick a color for the chart's border. |
| *Edit Chart Button:* | | Displays the chart in an edit window so that you can make modifications to it. |
| *Revise Data Button:* | | Lets you revise or add to the data that is charted. |
| *Add Titles Button:* | | Allows you to add a title, subtitle, or axis titles to the chart. |
| *Display Full Screen Button:* | | Places the chart in a full screen so that it can be viewed more clearly. |
| *Predefined Templates Button:* | | Allows you to apply predefined templates or color schemes to a chart. |
| *Move in Front Button:* | | Moves the selected object in front of an overlapping object. |
| *Move in Back Button:* | | Moves the selected object in back of an overlapping object. |
| *Move to Front of All Objects Button:* | | Moves the selected object in front of all overlapping objects. |
| *Move to Back of All Objects Button:* | | Moves the selected object in back of all overlapping objects. |
| *Properties Button:* | | Displays the properties of the selected object. |

# EXERCISE ⟹ QP8.1

1. Open the **pet boarding** notebook in the student **Datafile** folder. Save the notebook as **pet boarding 8-1 xxx**.

2. Select cells **A3..E10**. Click the **QuickChart** button on the Notebook Toolbar. The pointer turns into a miniature chart with a crossbar attached to it. Drag the pointer to select cells **B12..F25**.

3. Open the **Chart Type** drop-down list box at the left side of the Chart Toolbar and click the option in the first row, first column. A two-dimensional bar chart appears.

### TIP

The chart must be selected in order for the chart buttons to appear on the screen. When the spreadsheet is selected, the Property Bar appears on the screen.

4. Open the **Chart Type** drop-down list box again and select the option in the second row, fifth column. A line chart appears.

5. Open the **Chart Type** drop-down list box again and select the option in the fifth row, fourth column. A three-dimensional pie chart appears.

6. Open the **Chart Type** drop-down list box again and select the option in the first row, sixth column, which was the original chart.

7. Make certain that the chart is still selected. Click the **Border Color** button on the Chart Toolbar to see the available colors. Choose navy blue (it's in the second row, second column).

8. Click the **Border Line Style** button on the Chart Toolbar and select the widest border.

9. Click the **Display Full Screen** button on the Chart Toolbar. The chart expands to fill the entire screen. Press **Esc** to return to the sheet.

10. Click the **Add Title** button on the Chart Toolbar. The Chart Titles dialog box appears. In the *Main Title* text box key **Pet Paradise**. In the *Subtitle* text box key **Weekly Boarding Income**. Click **OK**.

11. Save the notebook and keep it open.

# *Editing the Data in a Chart*

You can move a floating chart by positioning the mouse pointer on its border and holding down the mouse button. When the pointer turns into a four-way arrow, drag the chart to a new location. To resize a chart, click on its edge to select it. Small square handles appear on the border. You can then drag these handles to resize the chart.

One of the neat features of Quattro Pro's charts is that when any changes are made to the data on a sheet, those changes are automatically reflected in the chart, regardless of whether it's a floating chart or it's in its own window. Simply select the cell whose data you want to edit and enter your changes. Quattro Pro takes care of the rest.

**1.** Save the current notebook as **pet boarding 8-2 xxx**.

**2.** Select the chart by clicking on its border. Handles should appear on its borders. Place the pointer on the middle handle on the right edge. The pointer should turn into a two-way arrow. Hold down the mouse button and drag to the right two columns. Release the mouse button. The chart should be wider. Drag the chart border back to the left until the chart is back to its original size.

> **TIP**
>
> Dragging by a corner handle helps the object being resized to maintain its original perspective.

**3.** Make certain that the chart is still selected. Place the pointer on the handle in the lower right corner of the chart. Hold down the mouse button and drag downward and to the right. Release the mouse button. The chart should be both higher and wider.

**4.** Position the mouse pointer on the chart (but not on a handle). The pointer should turn into a four-way arrow. Drag the chart two columns to the right.

> **TIP**
>
> Remember that you can alter the contents of a cell either by clicking in the cell and changing the value in the input line or by double-clicking the cell and entering the new value directly into the cell.

**5.** Spend a minute looking at the chart. Examine the size of the bar for the number of cats boarded on Friday. You are going to increase this amount. Double-click in cell **E8**. Change the value of this cell to **$48.00**. Notice that the corresponding bar in the chart becomes larger.

**6.** Save the notebook.

**7.** Click in the chart to select it. From the **File** menu, choose **Print**. In the Chart Print dialog box click **Selected Chart**. Click **Print**. Only the chart should print.

**8.** Close the notebook and remain in this screen for the next exercise.

# Using the Chart Expert

The QuickChart button is useful when you want to quickly create a chart on a spreadsheet. However, there will be times when you will want to be more specific in the way the chart appears. Quattro Pro's Chart Expert guides you through the process of creating a chart. The first step is to select the data that will be contained in the chart, just as you would when using the QuickChart button. Open the Insert menu and choose Chart. The Chart Expert will then lead you through the chart creation process.

E X E R C I S E  QP8.3

1. Open the **income** notebook in the student **Datafile** folder. Save the notebook as **income 8-3 xxx**.

2. Select cells **B5..N8**. Open the **Insert** menu and choose **Chart**. The Chart Expert - Step 1 of 5 dialog box appears (see Figure 8-3). Notice that the range you selected appears in the *Chart data* text box. The Chart Expert has already determined what chart might be most appropriate for this data and the chart appears at the left side of the box. You will be able to change this chart type in the next step. Click **Next**.

**FIGURE 8-3**
The Chart Expert - Step 1 of 5 Dialog Box

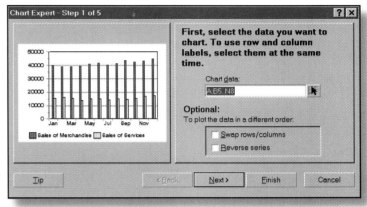

 NOTE:

If you choose a chart type that cannot accommodate the data you've selected, an error message appears in the left pane.

**FIGURE 8-4**
The Chart Expert - Step 2 of 5 Dialog Box

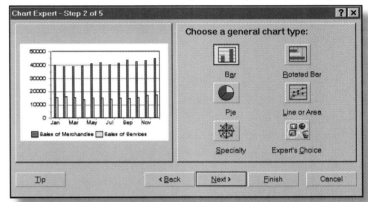

3. The Chart Expert - Step 2 of 5 dialog box shows samples of the different types of charts from which you can choose (see Figure 8-4). Under *Choose a general chart type* select **Line or Area**. Click **Next**.

4. The Chart Expert - Step 3 of 5 dialog box (shown in Figure 8-5) shows variations on the chart type you've selected. Under *Choose a specific chart type* select the second option in the 3-D row. Click **Next**.

**FIGURE 8-5**
The Chart Expert - Step 3 of 5 Dialog Box

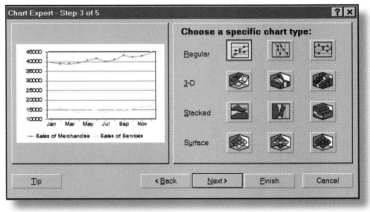

(continued on next page)

**5.** The Chart Expert - Step 4 of 5 dialog box (see Figure 8-6) lets you choose from a selection of color schemes. Under *Choose a color scheme* select **Fire and Ice**. Click **Next**.

**6.** In the Chart Expert - Step 5 of 5 dialog box, shown in Figure 8-7, perform the following steps:
   **a.** In the *Title* text box key **Pet Paradise**.
   **b.** In the *Subtitle* text box key **Monthly Sales**.
   **c.** In the *X-axis* text box key **Month**.
   **d.** In the *Y-axis* text box key **Dollar Amount**.
   **e.** Under *Destination* select **Chart Window**.
   **f.** Click **Finish**.

**7.** The chart appears in a separate window. Notice that some of the labels are hard to read because they are overlapping one another. We will fix this problem later.

**8.** Open the **Window** menu and select **income 8-3 xxx** to return to the spreadsheet window. Practice switching back and forth between the chart and the spreadsheet.

**FIGURE 8-6**
The Chart Expert - Step 4 of 5 Dialog Box

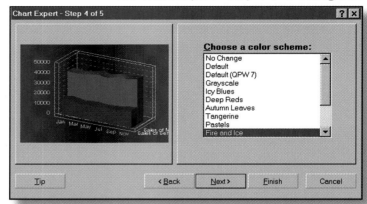

**FIGURE 8-7**
The Chart Expert - Step 5 of 5 Dialog Box

**9.** Save the notebook and keep it open.

# Displaying the Objects Sheet

To close a chart window, you click its Close button, which returns you to the current notebook sheet. The chart is saved to the Objects sheet in the notebook. Quattro Pro considers each chart or graphic, such as a map or drawing, an object. The *Objects sheet* contains an icon for each object you create in a notebook. The Objects sheet is always the last sheet in a notebook. You can go to the Objects sheet by clicking the QuickTab button at the bottom left of the window.

**EXERCISE ▷ QP8.4**

1. Save the notebook on the screen as **income 8-4 xxx**. If the chart window is currently open, click its **Close** button to close it.

2. Click the **QuickTab** button that's at the right side of the tab scroll controls in the bottom left corner of the screen.

The Objects sheet appears. It should be similar to Figure 8-8. Notice that it contains an icon representing the chart you created in Exercise QP8.3.

3. Quattro Pro assigns a default name to each object, but you can rename a chart to give it a more meaningful name. Click the icon **Chart1** with the right mouse button. A QuickMenu appears. Select **Icon Properties**. In the *Name* text box key **Income Chart** and click **OK**.

4. Click the **QuickTab** button to return to the spreadsheet.

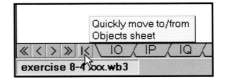

5. Save the notebook and keep it open.

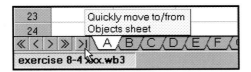
NOTE:

An object name can have a maximum of 15 characters.

**FIGURE 8-8**
The Objects Sheet

# Formatting and Enhancing Charts

$A$s we've already discussed, charts can consist of numerous elements, including axis labels, main titles, subtitles, and so forth. You can edit and format individual parts of a chart in a number of ways, depending on whether it's a floating chart or it's in its own window.

With floating charts, you can double click the chart and a blue hatched line appears around it. Right click an element of the chart, such as its title, a label, or the chart's background, and a QuickMenu appears with the related properties options at the bottom. Select the properties option to open a Properties dialog box that allows you to make changes to the chart's appearance.

When a chart is in its own window, you can modify it by going to the Objects sheet and double clicking the chart's icon. Right click the chart element you want to change and, from the QuickMenu, select the Properties option. The dialog box that opens is called the Object Inspector and it allows you to make formatting changes.

## E X E R C I S E ▭⟩ QP8.5

1. Save the current notebook as **income 8-5 xxx**.

2. Click the **QuickTab** button to go to the Objects sheet. Double click the **Income Chart** icon. The chart window opens.

 **TIP**

> Take your time when selecting the part of the chart you want to modify. It is important that the mouse pointer be properly positioned before opening the QuickMenu.

3. Position the mouse pointer on the chart edge immediately above the legend at the right side. Right click to open the QuickMenu and select **Legend Properties**.

 **TIP**

> The position of your pointer is described in the Application Bar at the bottom of the screen.

4. The Legend dialog box appears and the **Text Font** tab should be selected. Under *Point Size* select **12**. Click the **Text Settings** tab. Under

*Color* select red. Click **OK**. The labels are changed to red and reduced in size.

5. Position the mouse pointer on the x-axis. Right click to open the QuickMenu and select **X-Axis Properties**.

The X-Axis dialog box appears. Click the **Text Font** tab. Under *Point Size* select **12**. Click the **Text Settings** tab. Under *Color* select red. Click **OK**. The labels are changed to red and reduced in size.

6. Repeat Step 5 for the y-axis labels. All three sets of labels should now be red and in 12-pt. type.

7. Right click on the y-axis again and select **Y-Axis Properties** in the QuickMenu.

8. Click the **Numeric Format** tab. Under *Formats* select **Currency**. Set the number of decimal places to **0**. Click **OK**.

9. Save the notebook. The chart should now look like the one in Figure 8-9.

10. Make certain that you are still in the chart window. From the **File** menu choose **Print**. In the Chart Print dialog box click **Selected Chart**. Click **Print**.

11. Close the chart and then close the notebook.

**FIGURE 8-9**
Chart at End of Exercise QP8.5

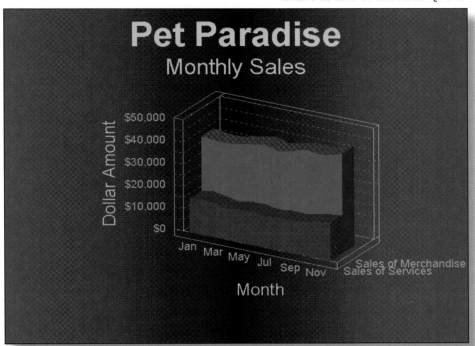

# *Adding Annotations to Charts*

Quattro Pro comes with a variety of drawing tools that you can use to enhance your charts. When you open a chart in its own window, these drawing tools appear at the top of the screen. Figure 8-10 identifies these tools.

**FIGURE 8-10**
Drawing Tools in the Chart Window

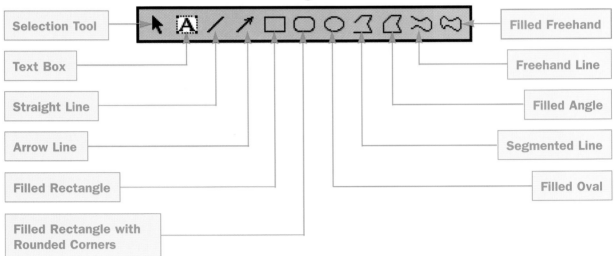

Click a tool to use it and drag to create a shape. To resize an object, select the object and drag a handle outward to enlarge it, or inward to make it smaller. To move it, hold down the mouse button until the pointer turns into a four-way arrow and then drag the object to the new location.

**EXERCISE ▷ QP8.6**

1. Open the notebook **pet boarding 8-2 xxx** in the student **Datafile** folder. Save the notebook as **pet boarding 8-6 xxx**.

2. Select the chart. Open the **Chart Type** drop-down list. Select the option in the fifth row, fourth column. The chart is changed to a three-dimensional pie chart.

3. Explode the slice labeled *Sun*.
   a. Click on the *Sun* (short for Sunday) slice. Right click on the slice to open the QuickMenu. Select **Pie Chart Properties**.
   b. Click the **Explode slice** tab. Under *Explode Distance (% of the Radius)* key **20**. Click **OK**. The chart should appear with the chosen slice pulled away from the rest of the chart.

**NOTE:**

Exploding a slice in a pie chart allows you to draw attention to that slice.

4. Add a text box and arrow line to the exploded slice as shown in Figure 8-11.
   a. Make certain that the Drawing Toolbar is open. If it is not, open the **View** menu and select **Toolbars**. In the Toolbar Settings dialog box select **Chart and Drawing Tools**.

**FIGURE 8-11**
Chart at End of Exercise QP8.6

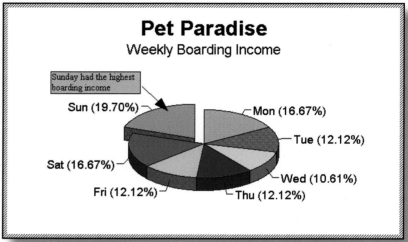

b. Click the **Text Box** tool on the Drawing Toolbar. Position the pointer above the *Sun* slice and drag to create a text box (refer to Figure 8-11 for its size and position).

c. The blinking insertion point should appear in the box. Key **Sunday had the highest boarding income**.

d. The text box should still be selected. Highlight the text you just entered. Open the **Font Size** drop-down list in the Property Bar and change the font size to **8**.

e. Resize and reposition the text box as shown in Figure 8-11.

f. Click outside the text box to deselect it.

g. Select the **Arrow Line** tool and draw an arrow in about the same position as shown in Figure 8-11.

5. Save the notebook. Print only the chart. Close the notebook.

# *Summary*

This lesson taught you how to create and modify several different types of charts. You learned that:

- common types of charts include bar charts, pie charts, and line charts. A chart's horizontal axis is called the x-axis and its vertical axis is called the y-axis.

- you can use the QuickChart button to quickly create a floating chart on a sheet. A variety of options are available in the Chart Type drop-down list.

- if you edit the data in a spreadsheet, any corresponding charts will be automatically updated. You can resize and move charts by dragging.

- the Chart Expert leads you through the steps in creating a chart and supplies more options than using the QuickChart button. You can create a floating chart or place the chart in a separate window. In addition to chart styles, the Chart Expert lets you pick a color scheme and enter titles.

- Quattro Pro considers each chart or graphic an object. These objects are represented by icons on the Objects sheet. Double click an object's icon to open it.

- you can change the formatting of a chart by right clicking on the part you want to alter and selecting the Properties option in the QuickMenu. You then can change any properties that are listed in the dialog box.

- you can use the drawing tools to add illustrations and text to your chart. The Text Box tool allows you to add an annotation. You can then draw an arrow to the part of the chart you are annotating.

## LESSON 8 REVIEW QUESTIONS

### MULTIPLE CHOICE

**Circle the best answer to each of the following statements.**

1. Charts are used for which of the following?
   A. To create formulas to analyze financial data.
   B. To graphically display data.
   C. To perform computations on numeric data.
   D. To sort data.

2. The _____ allows you to choose from a number of premade color schemes that can be applied to your chart.
   A. Chart Expert
   B. QuickTab button
   C. Selection tool
   D. Text Font tab

(continued on next page)

3. Which of the following will take you to the Objects sheet?
   **A.** Clicking the full screen button.
   **B.** Choosing Insert from the Chart menu.
   **C.** Clicking the QuickChart button.
   **D.** Clicking the QuickTab button.

4. You can resize a chart by selecting it and dragging it by one of its _____.
   **A.** axes
   **B.** handles
   **C.** labels
   **D.** text boxes

5. What is the horizontal axis of a chart called?
   **A.** The data series
   **B.** The handle
   **C.** The x-axis
   **D.** The y-axis

## MATCHING

**Write the letter of the term in Column 2 that best matches the description in Column 1.**

| Column 1 | Column 2 |
|---|---|
| _____ **6.** A chart that is contained on a spreadsheet. | **A.** Exploded slice |
| _____ **7.** Uses selected data to automatically generate a chart on the same sheet. | **B.** Objects sheet |
| _____ **8.** Contains icons that represent charts contained in a notebook. | **C.** QuickChart button |
| _____ **9.** A piece of a pie chart that is pulled away from the rest of the chart. | **D.** Text Box tool |
| _____ **10.** Can be used to add an annotation to a chart. | **E.** Floating chart |

## LESSON 8 PROJECT

SCANS

### PROJECT 8A

A chart is needed to graphically illustrate Pet Paradise's estimated monthly expenses. A pie chart will be used because it makes it easy to see what portion of the total goes for each expenditure.

1. Open the **expenses** notebook in the student **Datafile** folder. Save the notebook as **expenses proj8a xxx**.

2. Select cells A4..B12. Click the **QuickChart** button on the Notebook Toolbar.

3.   Place the chart in cells C3..J18. If necessary, enlarge the chart so that all of the labels are visible.

4.   Double click the chart to open the Pie Chart dialog box. Go to the **Text Font** tab and change the point size to **16**. Close the dialog box.

5.   Right click on the chart and select **Titles** from the QuickMenu. In the *Main Title* text box key **Estimated Monthly Expenses**. Click **OK**.

6.   Right click on the slice labeled *Human Resources* to open the QuickMenu. Select **Pie Chart Properties**.

7.   Click the **Explode slice** tab. Under *Explode Distance (% of the Radius)* key **15**. Click **OK**.

8.   Click to deselect the chart.

9.   Save the notebook. Print the chart in landscape view and close the notebook.


## PROJECT 8B

The manager of Morrison Car Dealership would like a graph that shows each salesperson's monthly sales over the last four months.

1.   Open the notebook **car sales** in the student **Datafile** folder. Save it as **car sales proj8b xxx**.

2.   Widen the columns so that you can see all of their contents. Key **Jan** in cell B5, **Feb** in cell C5, and **Mar** in cell D5. (You may not have to key Feb and Mar—Quattro Pro's QuickFill feature may enter them for you.)

3.   Select cells A5..D11. Open the **Insert** menu and choose **Chart**.

4.   In Step 1 click **Next**.

5.   In Step 2 under *Choose a general chart type*, click **Bar**. Click **Next**.

6.   In Step 3 click **Next**.

7.   In Step 4 under *Choose a color scheme*, click **Tangerine**. Click **Next**.

8.   In Step 5 perform the following steps:
     a.   In the *Title* text box key **Morrison Car Dealership**.
     b.   In the *Subtitle* text box key **Quarterly Sales**.
     c.   In the *X-Axis* text box key **Salesperson**.
     d.   In the *Y-Axis* text box key **Dollar Amount**.
     e.   Under *Destination* click **Chart Window**.
     f.   Click **Finish**.

(continued on next page)

9. Notice that in the x-axis, the font is too large to allow all of the salespeople's names to be displayed. Change the font size of the x-axis labels to **8** pt.

10. Format the labels for the y-axis as currency with no decimal places. Change the font size used in the y-axis labels to **14** pt.

11. Go to the Objects sheet and rename the chart icon **Quarterly Sales**.

12. Save the notebook. Go back to the chart window and print the chart. Close the notebook.

## CRITICAL THINKING ACTIVITY

Divide into small groups. Each group member should bring in six to eight charts obtained from different sources, such as magazines, newspapers, company reports, etc. The group should categorize the charts by type and then discuss each chart's appearance. What kinds of titles and subtitles are on the charts? Are color and different fonts and font styles used in an interesting way? Are the components clearly labeled? What factors do you think make some charts more understandable than others? What factors do you think give some charts a more attractive appearance than others? Can you think of any items on these charts that could be changed to make them more attractive and readable?

# CREATING MAPS AND INSERTING GRAPHICS

LESSON 9

## OBJECTIVES

**Upon completion of this lesson, you will be able to:**

- Identify the types of maps available in Quattro Pro.
- Create maps using the Map Expert.
- Edit and format data in a map.
- Work with map icons on the Objects sheet.
- Add overlays to maps.
- Add a graphic to a map.

🕐 **Estimated Time: 1 hour**

Quattro Pro allows you to add maps of just about any region in the world to your notebooks. You can then visually illustrate data by geographical region. In this lesson you will become familiar with the maps available in Quattro Pro. You will learn how to place them on a notebook sheet and then edit and format them. You also will learn how to customize maps by adding overlays and graphics.

## *Understanding Corel® Quattro® Pro's Mapping Capabilities*

Maps are handy tools for presenting geographical data. For example, you could show the population of each of the countries of Europe or illustrate a company's annual sales by region or state within the U.S.

Quattro Pro comes with many maps already created for you. Those available will vary, depending on your computer setup and installation, but some of the commonly used maps include the following:

- World by Country
- USA by State
- Europe by Country
- Africa by Country
- Asia by Country

- Canada by Province
- Mexico by Estado (state)
- South America by Country
- Australia by State

# Creating a Map

Adding a map to a notebook is similar to adding a chart. You can use the Map Expert to guide you through the process step by step. As with charts, you can create a floating map (one that appears on the same page in the notebook as the data you are mapping), or you can create a map in its own window so that it can be printed separately from the data. An icon representing each map in the notebook appears on the Objects sheet.

## E X E R C I S E ⟫ QP9.1

1. Start Quattro Pro, if necessary. Open the notebook **map** in the student **Datafile** folder. Save the notebook as **map 9-1 xxx**.

2. Select cells **A2..B49**. These two columns contain the name of each state, along with the percentage of households owning dogs.

3. Open the **Insert** menu and choose **Graphics**. In the submenu choose **Map**.

**FIGURE 9-1**
The Map Expert - Step 1 of 5 Dialog Box

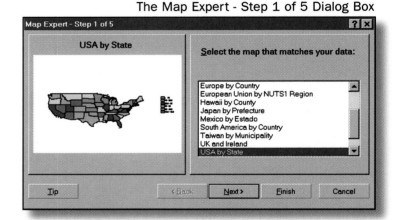

 **NOTE:**

If the mapping feature is not available to you, it is probably because it has not been installed on your computer system. The WordPerfect Suite installation program will need to be run in order to install it.

4. The Map Expert - Step 1 of 5 dialog box appears (see Figure 9-1).

Since you selected a block of data for mapping before opening the Map Expert, Quattro Pro determines which of its maps is most appropriate for plotting the data. It recognizes enough of the region names to know that they are the contiguous 48 states. Under *Select the* map that matches your data **USA by State** should already be chosen. Click **Next**.

5. The Map Expert - Step 2 of 5 dialog box appears (see Figure 9-2). This dialog box allows you to specify the columns that contain the labels and the ones that contain the data.

### ⚑ TIP

If you wanted to plot a second column of data, you would click the arrow at the end of the *Pattern data* text box. Quattro Pro would assign one of six patterns to each range of values and add that to the legend.

You can click the arrow at the end of the *Color data* text box to select the column of data you want plotted in the map. Because you selected the data before starting the Map Expert, Quattro Pro automatically determines how to break down the data into six categories, or ranges of values. Then it builds a legend by assigning one of six colors to each range of values. Click **Next.**

6. The Map Expert - Step 3 of 5 dialog box, shown in Figure 9-3, allows you to select a color scheme for your map. Try selecting several of them to see how they appear. When you are done, select **Yellows-Standard**. Click **Next**.

7. The Map Expert - Step 4 of 5 dialog box allows you to add overlays to the map (see Figure 9-4). For now, we won't worry about overlays. Click **Next**.

8. In the Map Expert - Step 5 of 5 dialog box, shown in Figure 9-5, you can add a title, subtitle, and title for a legend. In addition, you can determine whether the map will be on the notebook sheet or in its own window.
   a. In the *Title* text box key **Dog Ownership in U.S.**
   b. In the *Legend* text box key **Percent of Households**.
   c. Under *Destination* select **Map Window**.
   d. Click **Finish**. A map appears in its own window.

**FIGURE 9-2**
The Map Expert - Step 2 of 5 Dialog Box

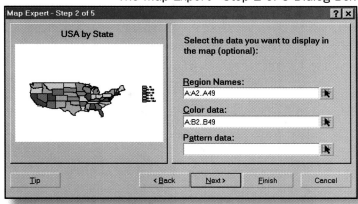

**FIGURE 9-3**
The Map Expert - Step 3 of 5 Dialog Box

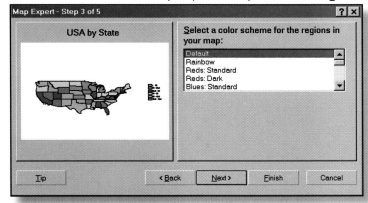

**FIGURE 9-4**
The Map Expert - Step 4 of 5 Dialog Box

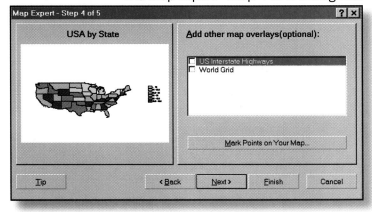

(continued on next page)

9. Notice that the legend is positioned on top of the map. Click anywhere in the legend to select it. Drag the legend to the lower right corner of the map. Click anywhere in the map to select the entire map. The map should look like the one shown in Figure 9-6.

10. Save the notebook. Open the **File** menu and choose **Print**. The Chart Print dialog box appears. Click **Selected Chart** and click **Print**. Keep this notebook open for the next exercise.

**FIGURE 9-5**
The Map Expert - Step 5 of 5 Dialog Box

**FIGURE 9-6**
Dog Ownership Map

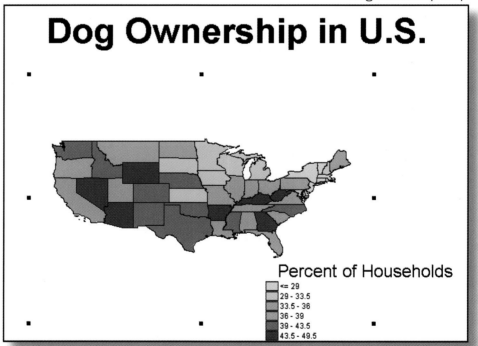

In the 1980s, the National Science Foundation (NSF) created the NSFNET. The NSFNET connected several supercomputers from around the country and allowed scientists to access the network from remote locations. Later, the ARPANET was connected to NSFNET.

# *Modifying Maps*

Many of the techniques and features you have learned about Quattro Pro charts apply to maps as well. Like charts and other graphic objects, maps are represented on the Objects sheet by a map icon and a default map name. You can rename them as you would any other object. Double clicking a map icon on the Objects sheet displays the map so that you can easily edit and format it. Right click on the map and a QuickMenu appears. Select the Data option to change the data in the map. As you will see in the next exercise, the QuickMenu's three Zoom options let you change the way you view your map.

## EXERCISE ⇨ QP9.2

SCANS

1. Save the notebook as **map 9-2 xxx**. Open the **Window** menu and choose the spreadsheet window. Click the **QuickTab** button to move to the Objects sheet.

2. Right click the **Map1** icon. The QuickMenu appears, as shown in Figure 9-7. Select **Icon Properties**.

**FIGURE 9-7**
Map Data
QuickMenu

Cut
Copy
Paste
Clear

Icon Properties...

3. In the *Name* text box key **Dog Ownership**. Click **OK**.

4. Open the **Window** menu and switch back to the map. Double click the map's title. In the Chart Title Properties dialog box click the **Text Font** tab. Under *Typeface* select a font, such as **Britannic Bold** or another font of your choosing. Click the **Text Settings** tab. Under *Color* select the reddish-brown color. (It's in the second column, fifth row.) Click **OK**.

5. Double click the legend. In the Legend dialog box click the **Title** tab. Under *Color* select the reddish-brown color (second column, fifth row). Open the **Point Size** drop-down list box and click **14**. Click **OK**.

6. The map is somewhat out of proportion. Click the map to select it. Position the pointer on the top center handle and drag upward about 1/2 inch. Position the pointer on the bottom center handle and drag downward about 1/2 inch. The map should be better proportioned.

7. Notice the color of the state of California. It should be olive green, representing 33.5-36 percent. Open the **Window** menu and return to the spreadsheet window. You should be at the Objects sheet. Click the **QuickTab** button to return to the sheet containing the data.

8. Click cell **B5**. It contains *35.5*, the percentage of California households owning dogs. Change the value in cell B5 to **37** and press **Enter**. Use the **Window** menu to return to the map. California has been changed to an orange color, indicating that it is now in a new range.

9. Position the mouse pointer on Texas and right click. In the QuickMenu click **Zoom In**. The portion of the map containing Texas is enlarged. Right click again and click **Zoom Out**. The map returns to normal. Practice zooming in and zooming out several times. When you are done, right click to open the QuickMenu and click **Zoom to Normal**.

10. Save the notebook and keep it open for the next exercise.

# Using Overlays

Quattro Pro allows you to add overlays to a map. An *overlay* is comparable to an overhead transparency. It represents additional information that you can place on the map, such as major cities or transportation routes. The available overlays depend on the map you are using. Following are the three basic types:

- Region overlays which show regional (such as state or country) boundaries.

- Static overlays which show the world grid or highways. They cannot be changed or altered.

- Pin overlays which show specific locations. They are linked to data in a series of special Quattro Pro notebooks created specifically for mapping purposes. These notebooks are typically stored in the folder **Corel\Suite8\Programs\DataMaps**. When you open the notebook containing the data you need, you will notice that it is write-protected. You can copy all or part of the data to a new Quattro Pro notebook, where you edit, format, chart, or map it. In the notebook you have been working with, the information for displaying each state capital has been copied from the Quattro Pro map containing this information. Notice that columns C through E contain each capital, along with its latitude and longitude. This is the information Quattro Pro needs to properly position the cities on the map.

NOTE:

The exact location of the Quattro Pro data maps will depend on how the Quattro Pro files have been installed on your system.

## EXERCISE ▷ QP9.3

1. Save the notebook as **map 9-3 xxx**. Make certain that you have the map open on the screen.

2. Right click on the map and select **Data** in the QuickMenu. In the Map Data dialog box click **Add Overlay**. Click the **Static** tab. Click **World Grid** and click **OK**. Click **OK** again to close the Map Data dialog box. A grid appears on the map.

3. Reopen the Map Data dialog box and click **Delete Overlay**. Click **Delete Overlay** again and click **OK**. The world grid overlay should be removed.

4. Right click the map and select **Data** in the QuickMenu. Click **Add Overlay** and then click the **Pin** tab. Click **U.S. State Capitals** and click **OK**. The Map Data dialog box appears (see Figure 9-8).

5. In the *Pin ID Cells* text box key **C2..C49**. Click **Use pin names as labels** and click **OK**.

6. Right click the map and select **Map Properties** in the QuickMenu. Click the **Pin Symbol** tab and select **Wingdings** as the typeface. Click the **Font** tab and select **Times New Roman**. Key **4** for the point size. Click **OK**.

7. Save the notebook and keep it open for the next exercise.

# *Inserting a Graphic*

Graphics, such as company logos, help make documents look attractive and professional. If you have a premade graphic stored in a file on disk, you can insert it into a document by opening the Insert menu, choosing Graphics, and then choosing From File. You can then enter the name of the file and it will be placed in the opened document, where you can resize it and move it around as needed.

**FIGURE 9-8**
The Map Data Dialog Box

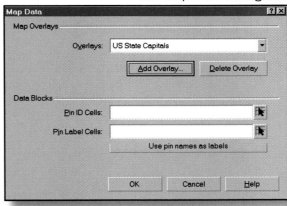

---

**E X E R C I S E** ▭▷ QP9.4

**1.** Save the notebook as **map 9-4 xxx**. Make certain that you have the map open on the screen.

**2.** You are going to insert Pet Paradise's logo onto the map. Open the **Insert** menu, choose **Graphics**, and then choose **From File**.

**3.** In the Insert Image dialog box open your student **Datafile** folder. It contains a file named **logo.wpg**. Double click on **logo.wpg** to place it on the map. Resize the graphic so that it is about $1^1/2$ inches wide and 1 inch high. Place it in the upper left corner of the map, immediately below the title. If necessary, reposition the parts of the map so that it looks similar to Figure 9-9.

**FIGURE 9-9**
The Map with the Logo Inserted

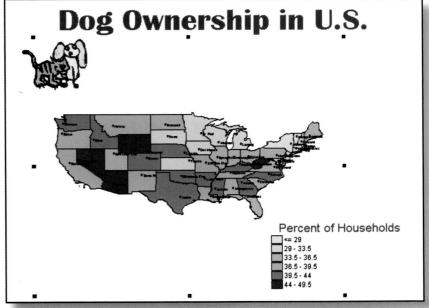

**4.** Save the notebook and print the map. Close the notebook.

# Summary

This lesson led you through the steps in creating and labeling a map and inserting graphics. You learned that:

■ you can use the Map Expert to guide you through creating a map, entering its title, and choosing its colors. Quattro Pro contains premade maps of countries that you can select from when creating a map.

■ maps can be on a separate page or they can float on the sheet containing the corresponding data.

■ you can resize and move map components just as you would any other graphic.

■ the Map Data dialog box allows you to add and delete overlays. Overlays can be used to display data such as major cities and highways.

■ a map can be edited by double clicking its icon on the Objects sheet. You can then right click the component you want to change.

■ you can insert a premade graphic stored in a file.

## LESSON 9 REVIEW QUESTIONS

### FILL IN THE BLANKS

**Complete each of the following statements by writing your answer in the blank provided.**

1. To create a new map, open the _____ menu and choose Graphics.

2. If you want to insert a graphic that has previously been saved in a file, open the Insert menu, choose Graphics, and then choose _____.

3. You can change the name of a map's icon by going to the _____ sheet and double clicking its icon.

4. Step _____ of the Map Expert allows you to specify whether or not you want the chart in its own window.

5. You can magnify part of a map by right clicking it and then selecting the _____ option.

## MATCHING

**Write the letter of the term in Column 2 that best matches the description in Column 1.**

**Column 1**

\_\_\_\_ **6.** Similar to an overhead transparency.

\_\_\_\_ **7.** Useful in illustrating data by geographical regions.

\_\_\_\_ **8.** Premade maps that come with Quattro Pro, each containing specific information such as the populations of different countries or the information required to correctly position capital cities on a map.

\_\_\_\_ **9.** Contains five steps that lead you through the process of creating a new map.

\_\_\_\_ **10.** Allow you to identify specific locations on a map, such as major cities.

**Column 2**

**A.** Map

**B.** Pins

**C.** Overlay

**D.** Map Expert

**E.** Data maps

## LESSON 9 PROJECT

**SCANS**

Morrison Car Dealership is a franchise of Bourgman Automotive, International. Bourgman has dealerships in many Western European countries. Create a map that indicates the number of dealerships in these countries.

1. Open the notebook **dealerships** in the student **Datafile** folder. Save the notebook as **dealerships proj9a xxx** in the student **Datafile** folder.

2. Sort the list alphabetically by the names of the countries.

3. Select cells **A2..B15**. Open the **Insert** menu, choose **Graphics**, and then choose **Map** in the submenu. The Map Expert - Step 1 of 5 dialog box appears. Click **Europe by Country**. Click **Next**.

4. In the Map Expert - Step 2 of 5 dialog box the data to be mapped should already be selected. Click **Next**.

5. In the Map Expert - Step 3 of 5 dialog box under *Select a color scheme for the regions in your map*, click **Reds: Dark**. Click **Next**.

6. In the Map Expert - Step 4 of 5 dialog box under *Add other map overlays(optional)*, click **World Grid**. Click **Next**.

7. In the Map Expert - Step 5 of 5 dialog box in the *Title* text box, key **Bourgman Automotive**. In the *Subtitle* text box key **Dealerships**. For *Destination*, make certain that **Current Sheet** is selected. Click **Finish**.

(continued on next page)

8. Position the mouse pointer in cell **D10** and drag to cell **I25**. Release the mouse pointer. The map should appear on the sheet.

9. Go to the Objects sheet and rename the map's icon **Dealerships Map**.

10. Return to the sheet and double click the title to edit it. Change the title's font to **Times New Roman** and its color to red.

11. Double click the subtitle. Change its font to **Times New Roman** and its color to red.

12. Double click the legend to edit it. In the Legend dialog box click the **Title** tab. In the *Title text* box key **Number per Country**. The font size for the legend's title should be **10 pt**.

13. Save the notebook and print the sheet containing the map.

14. Close the notebook and exit Quattro Pro.

## CRITICAL THINKING ACTIVITY

SCANS

In Touch Corporation provides telecommunications for companies around the world. Its salespeople help companies in 82 countries meet their information needs by providing high-speed communications lines and Internet access. Name at least three different maps that managers might create to illustrate their sales figures. Be creative in thinking of types of maps that might be generated.

# USING FILTERS AND QUERYING DATABASES

## OBJECTIVES

**Upon completion of this lesson, you will be able to:**

- Use QuickFilter to sort records according to specified fields.

- Use QuickFilter to locate records that meet specific criteria.

- Define the term *database* and identify components of a database.

- Search for specified data in a database and create tables containing that data.

- Use search formulas and wildcards to locate specific data.

**⏱ Estimated Time: 2 hours**

Quattro Pro's QuickFilter feature allows you to easily sort data and search for data items that meet specific conditions. Quattro Pro also contains database features that let you sort data or locate specific data and place it in a separate sheet so that it can be permanently stored and formatted however needed.

## *Using QuickFilter*

Quattro Pro allows you to easily sort and filter data by any column in a sheet. When you *filter* a column, only the rows that meet the conditions you specify are displayed. To use QuickFilter, open the Tools menu and choose QuickFilter. Filter buttons appear above each column, as shown in Figure 10-1. These buttons allow you to choose the way you want that column sorted or filtered. To see a list of sorting and filtering options for a particular column, click its button and the list opens. Figure 10-2 shows the list that is displayed for the Item column. Some of the tasks that you can perform include sorting in ascending or descending order by column, locating a single item within the sheet, and creating a custom filter. Let's begin by applying a few simple filters in the next exercise.

**INTERNET** Links are specially highlighted words or graphics on World Wide Web (WWW) documents. Attached to links are instructions to jump automatically to another location that is either in the same document or in a new document on a distant computer.

| | A | B | C | D | E | F | H | |
|---|---|---|---|---|---|---|---|---|
| 1 | | Pet Paradise II | | | | | | |
| 2 | | Weekly Sales | | | | | | |
| 3 | | | | | | | | |
| 4 | Item Number ▼ | Item ▼ | Quantity Sol ▼ | Wholesale Cc ▼ | Price ▼ | Profit ▼ | | |
| 5 | CA5406 | Tick & flea collar | 2 | $1.60 | $3.20 | $36.20 | | |
| 6 | CA4200 | Nylon cat collar | 12 | $1.84 | $3.68 | $22.08 | | |
| 7 | CA1056 | Cat safety collar | 4 | $2.08 | $4.16 | $8.32 | | |
| 8 | CA1069 | Nylon dog collar (small) | 9 | $1.49 | $2.98 | $13.41 | | |
| 9 | CA1070 | Nylon dog collar (medium) | 14 | $1.63 | $3.26 | $22.82 | | |
| 10 | CA1071 | Nylon dog collar (large) | 3 | $1.90 | $3.80 | $5.70 | | |
| 11 | CA8065 | Leather lead (4 foot) | 17 | $6.20 | $12.40 | $105.40 | | |
| 12 | CA8298 | Leather lead (6 fc | | $7.50 | $15.00 | $60.00 | | |
| 13 | CH5089 | Tie-out cable | | $8.90 | $17.80 | $80.10 | | |
| 14 | CH4201 | 4-foot chain | | $2.49 | $4.98 | $19.92 | | |
| 15 | CH59393 | 8-foot chain | 5 | $3.75 | $7.50 | $18.75 | | |
| 16 | TY1141 | Tug toy | 7 | $2.84 | $5.68 | $19.88 | | |
| 17 | TY3090 | Cloth pull-toy | 5 | $2.10 | $4.20 | $10.50 | | |
| 18 | TY4057 | Rubber flying disk | 12 | $3.65 | $7.30 | $43.80 | | |
| 19 | TY3175 | Large rubber bone | 2 | $1.49 | $2.98 | $2.98 | | |
| 20 | TY8274 | Play mouse | 16 | $1.25 | $2.50 | $20.00 | | |

Filter Buttons

‹ ‹ › › › ›› \ Sales / B / C / D / E / F / G / H / I / J / K / L / M ◄

**Item** ▼

(Show All)
(Top 10...)
(Custom...)
(Blanks)
(Non Blanks)

(Sort A-Z)
(Sort Z-A)

4-foot chain
8-foot chain
Burger & cheese bits
Cat bed
Cat carrier
Cat climbing tree
Cat pom-poms
Cat safety collar
Cat scratching post
Cat window perch
Chewable cat vitamins
Chewable dog vitamins
Chewable senior dog vitamins
Cloth pull-toy
Crunchy bits
Dog travel kennel (large)
Dog travel kennel (medium)
Dog travel kennel (small)
Double untippable bowl
Dr. Pet's cedar spray

# EXERCISE ⇒ QP10.1

**SCANS**

1. Open the notebook **sales** in the student **Datafile** folder and save the notebook as **sales 10-1 xxx**.

2. Click cell **A4**. Open the **Tools** menu and choose **QuickFilter**. Click the **Filter** button for the Item Number column. Select (**Sort A-Z**). The sheet's rows are sorted by item number.

3. Click the **Filter** button for the Wholesale Cost column. Select (**Sort Z-A**). The rows are sorted from highest to lowest price.

4. Click the **Filter** button for the Item column. Select **4-foot chain**. Only the data on the 4-foot chain appears.

   Notice that the Filter button for the Item column is now blue. This indicates that a filter has been applied to the column. Remove the filter by clicking the Item column **Filter** button and selecting (**Show All**). All of the data should again be displayed.

5. Click the **Filter** button for the Quantity Sold column. Select (**Top 10...**). Click **OK**. Only the ten items with the highest number of sales are displayed. Click the Quantity Sold column **Filter** button and select (**Show All**) to remove the filter.

**NOTE:**

You cannot apply the Top 10 filter to a column containing text. It works only with numeric data.

6. Save the notebook and keep it open for the next exercise.

Simple filters are helpful, but there may be times when you want the filter's results to be determined by more complex conditions. For example, you might want to see a list of all the dog food products or a list of all the combs and brushes. Custom filters can supply these results. When creating custom filters, you can perform *And* and *Or* searches. If you are looking for a list of items that are either combs or brushes, you would use an Or search. The resulting list would contain all the items that are either combs or brushes. An And search requires that each item meet both criteria. For example, if you wanted a list of all the items whose retail price was between $5.00 and $10.00, you would use

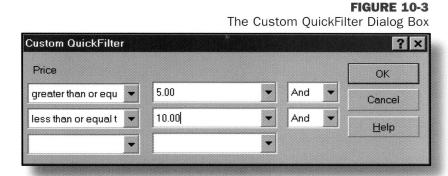

**FIGURE 10-3**
The Custom QuickFilter Dialog Box

an And search, as shown in Figure 10-3. You can also specify search criteria for more than one column. For example, if you specified that Item Number must contain *PF* and Retail Price must be greater than 8, you would get a list of all the pet food that sold for more than $8.00. (Notice that you could conduct this search because all of the pet food item numbers start with the letters PF.) Once you get the hang of it, creating more complex searches is fun, and it is easy to see how useful this feature would be in business.

**EXERCISE** ⟹ **QP10.2**

SCANS

1. Save the notebook as **sales 10-2 xxx**. The Filter buttons should appear at the top of each column.

2. Click the **Filter** button for the Item column and select **(Custom...)**. The Custom QuickFilter dialog box appears. Open the first text box and select **contains**.

3. In the first text box in the second column key **brush**. Click **OK**. Two records containing information on brushes should appear.

4. Click the Item column **Filter** button and select **(Show All)**. All of the records reappear.

⚑ **TIP**

You must first display all of the records before applying a different filter. Otherwise, Quattro Pro will apply the new filter to only those items currently on the screen.

5. Click the Item column **Filter** button and select **(Custom...)** again.

 **NOTE:**

You can create custom filters that specify up to three search conditions.

(continued on next page)

6. Perform the following steps for the first row:
   a. In column 1 select **contains**.
   b. In column 2 key **comb**.
   c. Open the text box in column 3 (it currently contains *And*) and select **Or**.

7. Perform the following steps for the second row:
   a. In column 1 select **contains**.
   b. In column 2 key **brush**.

8. Click **OK**. Only those items that are either brushes or combs should appear. Print this sheet.

9. Click the **Filter** button for the Item column and select **(Show All)**. Open the **Tools** menu and select **QuickFilter**. This will turn off QuickFilter and the Filter buttons will no longer appear on the screen.

10. Keep this notebook open for the next exercise.

# *Understanding Databases*

A *database* is an organized collection of information. Databases differ from spreadsheets, in that you can extract certain data through searches or queries and then present that data in its own table. This ability to create a new table by pulling data from an existing one is what makes searching databases different from using QuickFilter on a spreadsheet. Quattro Pro provides you with the tools you need to structure spreadsheet data as database tables.

A *database table* is made up of one or more *records* that contain related information. For example, a college's database might contain a record on each individual student. The different categories of information about the students (like their names, addresses, phone numbers, and Social Security numbers) are *fields*. In a Quattro Pro database each row represents a record and each column represents a field. The label that identifies a column of data is referred to as a *field name*. The block of cells that contains the records, fields, and field names is the *database block*. The different components of a Quattro Pro database are labeled in Figure 10-4.

## Setting Up a Database

Most of the spreadsheets and notebooks you've been working with so far are already set up so that you can perform database operations such as sorts and searches on them. Following are some rules that should be followed with databases:

■ The database block must be contiguous and confined to a single notebook sheet.

■ The block must be rectangular.

■ The top row of the database block should contain the field names. Field names must be labels (text characters) and cannot have blank spaces at the beginning or end.

■ There should be no blank rows in a database block.

■ Each column in the block must contain the same type of data—labels or values.

The QuickFilter feature allows you to locate specific records or groups of records quickly. However, it is not suitable when you want to save a search's results on its own sheet. Quattro Pro provides a more advanced feature called *querying*, that lets you extract data that meets specified criteria from a database block. This extracted data can be placed in its own table on the same notebook sheet or on a different sheet, where it can be sorted, formatted, and printed separately. You can use the Notebook Query dialog box to query a database. The simplest type of query involves locating one or more records that contain specific values.

FIGURE 10-4
A Database Block with a Criteria Table

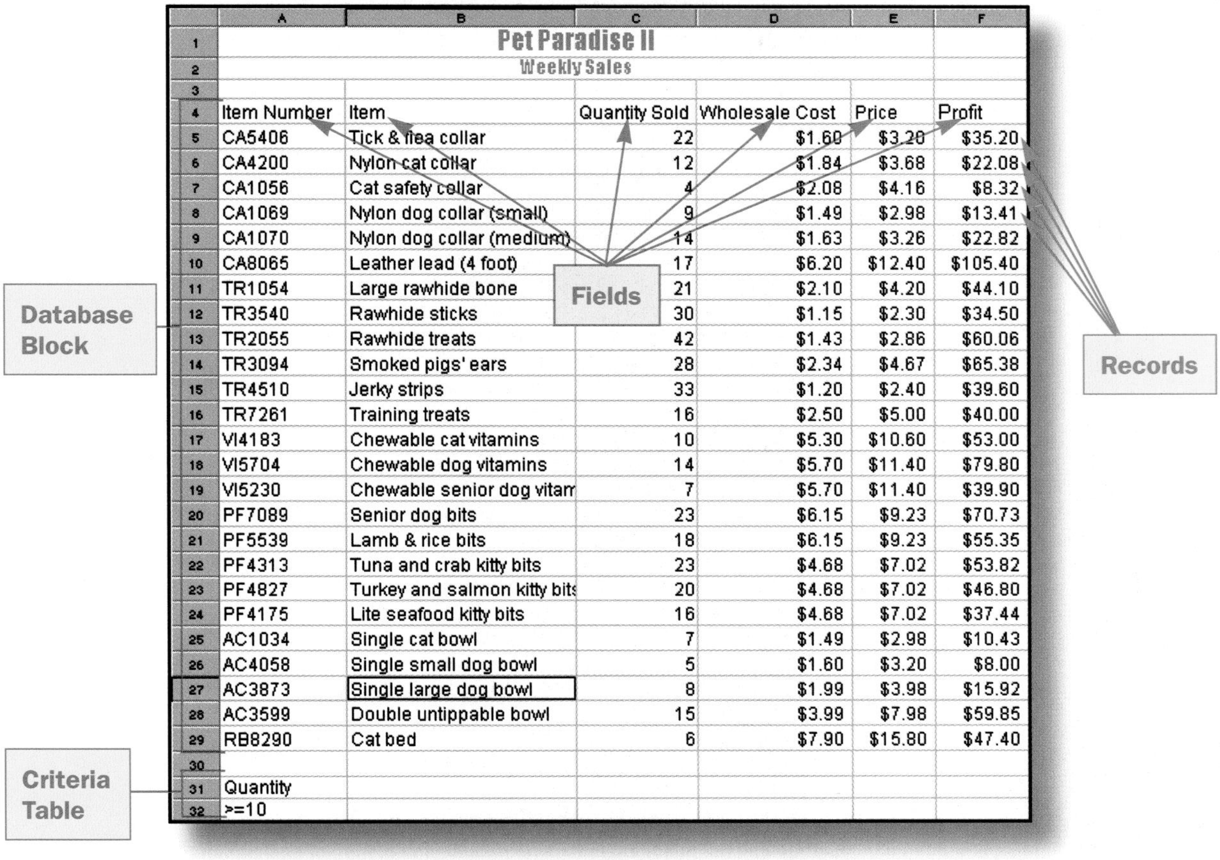

| | A | B | C | D | E | F |
|---|---|---|---|---|---|---|
| 1 | | Pet Paradise II | | | | |
| 2 | | Weekly Sales | | | | |
| 3 | | | | | | |
| 4 | Item Number | Item | Quantity Sold | Wholesale Cost | Price | Profit |
| 5 | CA5406 | Tick & flea collar | 22 | $1.60 | $3.20 | $35.20 |
| 6 | CA4200 | Nylon cat collar | 12 | $1.84 | $3.68 | $22.08 |
| 7 | CA1056 | Cat safety collar | 4 | $2.08 | $4.16 | $8.32 |
| 8 | CA1069 | Nylon dog collar (small) | 9 | $1.49 | $2.98 | $13.41 |
| 9 | CA1070 | Nylon dog collar (medium) | 14 | $1.63 | $3.26 | $22.82 |
| 10 | CA8065 | Leather lead (4 foot) | 17 | $6.20 | $12.40 | $105.40 |
| 11 | TR1054 | Large rawhide bone | 21 | $2.10 | $4.20 | $44.10 |
| 12 | TR3540 | Rawhide sticks | 30 | $1.15 | $2.30 | $34.50 |
| 13 | TR2055 | Rawhide treats | 42 | $1.43 | $2.86 | $60.06 |
| 14 | TR3094 | Smoked pigs' ears | 28 | $2.34 | $4.67 | $65.38 |
| 15 | TR4510 | Jerky strips | 33 | $1.20 | $2.40 | $39.60 |
| 16 | TR7261 | Training treats | 16 | $2.50 | $5.00 | $40.00 |
| 17 | VI4183 | Chewable cat vitamins | 10 | $5.30 | $10.60 | $53.00 |
| 18 | VI5704 | Chewable dog vitamins | 14 | $5.70 | $11.40 | $79.80 |
| 19 | VI5230 | Chewable senior dog vitam | 7 | $5.70 | $11.40 | $39.90 |
| 20 | PF7089 | Senior dog bits | 23 | $6.15 | $9.23 | $70.73 |
| 21 | PF5539 | Lamb & rice bits | 18 | $6.15 | $9.23 | $55.35 |
| 22 | PF4313 | Tuna and crab kitty bits | 23 | $4.68 | $7.02 | $53.82 |
| 23 | PF4827 | Turkey and salmon kitty bits | 20 | $4.68 | $7.02 | $46.80 |
| 24 | PF4175 | Lite seafood kitty bits | 16 | $4.68 | $7.02 | $37.44 |
| 25 | AC1034 | Single cat bowl | 7 | $1.49 | $2.98 | $10.43 |
| 26 | AC4058 | Single small dog bowl | 5 | $1.60 | $3.20 | $8.00 |
| 27 | AC3873 | Single large dog bowl | 8 | $1.99 | $3.98 | $15.92 |
| 28 | AC3599 | Double untippable bowl | 15 | $3.99 | $7.98 | $59.85 |
| 29 | RB8290 | Cat bed | 6 | $7.90 | $15.80 | $47.40 |
| 30 | | | | | | |
| 31 | Quantity | | | | | |
| 32 | >=10 | | | | | |

**Database Block** (label pointing to rows 11–13 area)

**Fields** (label)

**Records** (label)

**Criteria Table** (label pointing to rows 31–32)

# EXERCISE ⇨ QP10.3

SCANS

1. Save the notebook as **sales 10-3 xxx**.

2. Copy the contents of cells A1..F4 to Sheet B. Make certain that the titles are centered above the column headings. Switch back to the Sales Sheet.

3. In cell A77 key **Item**. Copy the contents of cell B15 to cell A78. When you are done, cell A78 should contain *Tie-out cable*.

4. From the **Tools** menu choose **Data Tools** and then choose **Notebook Query**. The Notebook Data Query dialog box appears, as shown in Figure 10-5.

5. Click the arrow to the right of the *Database Cells* text box. The dialog box should be hidden except for its Title Bar. Drag the mouse pointer to select cells **A4..F75**. These will be the cells that will be searched to locate the specified value.

(continued on next page)

**FIGURE 10-5**
The Notebook Data Query Dialog Box

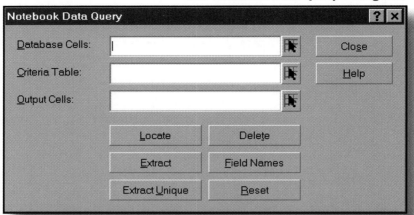

6. Click the dialog box's **Maximize** button to reopen the dialog box. Click the arrow to the right of the *Criteria Table* text box. Select cells **A77..A78**. These are the cells that specify the records to be extracted.

7. Reopen the dialog box. Click in the *Output Cells* text box. Key **B:A4..F75**. The results of the query will be placed in cells A4..F75 on Sheet B. The first record will be placed in row 4, the second will be placed in row 5, and so forth, until all of the records have been displayed.

8. Click **Extract** and then click **Close**. Click the tab for Sheet B. Sheet B should contain only

the record for the tie-out cable because it was the only one that matched the stated criteria.

**NOTE:**

The Extract button pulls any matches from the database block and places them in the output block.

9. Go back to the Sales Sheet. Save the notebook and keep it open for the next exercise.

# *Creating More Complex Searches*

The Notebook Data Query dialog box contains several query buttons. Each is explained below:

■ *Locate:* Highlights the first match in the database block. Press the down arrow key to move to the next match. When there are no more matches, you will hear a beep. Press Esc to return to the Notebook Data Query dialog box.

■ *Extract:* Pulls the matches from the database block and places them in the output block.

- *Extract Unique:* Pulls all unique matches from the database block; that is, any duplicates will not appear in the output block.

- *Delete:* Deletes all the records that match the search criteria.

- *Field Names:* Allows for the field names to be used in search formulas.

- *Reset:* Removes the current dialog box settings so that you can enter new ones.

Quattro Pro allows you to use operators to enter search formulas. Table 10-1 contains some of the operators that can be used when specifying search conditions. For example, if you wanted to find all items selling for more than $10.00, you could create a criteria table like the one shown in Figure 10-6. As with the QuickFilter feature, you can create And and Or searches. You will learn to do this in the next exercise.

**FIGURE 10-6**
A Criteria Table to Find All Items with a Price of More Than $10.00

| Price |
|-------|
| >10 |

**TABLE 10-1**

| Operator | Operation |
|----------|-----------|
| = | Finds values that are equal to criteria |
| < | Finds values that are less than criteria |
| <= | Finds values that are less than or equal to criteria |
| > | Finds values that are greater than criteria |
| >= | Finds values that are greater than or equal to criteria |
| <> | Finds values that are not equal to criteria |

## E X E R C I S E ▷ QP10.4

SCANS

1. Save the notebook as **sales 10-4 xxx**. You should be at the Sales Sheet.

**NOTE:**

The > (greater than) symbol is on the same key as the period. It is in the lower right portion of your keyboard.

2. Delete the contents of cells A77.. A78. In cell A77 key **Price**. In cell A78 key **>10**. Press **Enter**.

**IMPORTANT:**

If you do not press Enter after keying the criteria table values, the selections in the Tools menu may be "grayed out."

3. From the **Tools** menu choose **Data Tools** and then choose **Notebook Query**. Click **Reset**. Click the arrow to the right of the *Database Cells* text box. Only the dialog box's Title Bar is now visible. Drag the mouse pointer to select cells **A4..F75**.

(continued on next page)

**4.** Click the dialog box's **Maximize** button to reopen the dialog box. Click the *Criteria Table* text box and key **Sales:A77..A78**.

**5.** Click the *Output Cells* text box. Key **B:A4..F75**. The results of the query will begin in row 4 on Sheet B.

**6.** Click **Extract** and then click **Close.** Go to Sheet B. All of the records with a price of more than $10.00 should appear.

**TIP**

Be careful not to insert any spaces into the formula in the criteria table. For example, if you enter "> 10" rather than ">10," you will not obtain the correct results.

**7.** Return to the Sales Sheet. In cell B77 key **Quantity Sold**. In cell B78 key **>5**. Press **Enter**. The resulting criteria table should look like Figure 10-7. It contains an And query.

**FIGURE 10-7**
A Criteria Table for an And Query

| Price | Quantity Sold |
|-------|---------------|
| >10   | >5            |

**NOTE:**

You need to change the contents of the *Criteria Table* text box because the size of the criteria table has increased from two cells to four cells.

**8.** Reopen the Notebook Data Query dialog box. The contents from the previous query should still be stored in it. You are only going to change the *Criteria Table* text box; the other text box should remain unchanged. In the *Criteria Table* text box key **Sales:A77..B78**.

**9.** Click **Extract** and then click **Close.** Go to Sheet B. Only those records with a price of more than $10.00 *and* a quantity of more than 5 should appear. Sheet B should contain ten records.

**10.** Return to the Sales Sheet. Move the formula *>5* from cell B78 to cell B79. The criteria table should look like Figure 10-8. You have now created an Or query. In an Or criteria table the second search value is in the row below the first search value. Only one of the search conditions will need to be true for a particular record to appear in the output sheet.

**FIGURE 10-8**
A Criteria Table for an Or Query

| Price | Quantity Sold |
|-------|---------------|
| >10   |               |
|       | >5            |

**11.** Open the Notebook Data Query dialog box. The *Criteria Table* text box should now contain *Sales:A77..B79*. Click **Extract** and click **Close.** Go to Sheet B. Any record with a price of more than $10.00 *or* a quantity of more than 5 will appear on the sheet. There should be 60 records on Sheet B.

**12.** Widen the columns in Sheet B so all of their contents are visible and print Sheet B. Return to the Sales Sheet. Save the notebook and keep it open for the next exercise.

# Using Wildcards in Searches

**FIGURE 10-9**
A Search Using a
Wildcard Symbol

So far, when searching text, you have searched for exact matches. Frequently, though, you might not know exactly what you're looking for, or you might want to find records in which only part of the text is a match. For example, let's say you want to find all of the pet food records. Since these items contain "PF" in the Item Number field, you could use a wildcard in the search criteria. The *wildcard* "stands in" for missing characters. Two commonly used wildcard symbols are:

| | |
|---|---|
| **Item Number** | |
| PF* | |

?     Represents a single character. For example, *Sm?th* finds Smith, Smyth, etc.

\*     Represents any number of characters. For example, *Sm\** finds Smith, Smiley, Smack, etc.

Figure 10-9 shows a wildcard search that will locate all of the records containing item numbers that start with the letters PF.

## EXERCISE ▷ QP10.5

**SCANS**

1. Save the notebook as **sales 10-5 xxx**. If necessary, go to the Sales Sheet.

2. Delete the criteria table from the Sales Sheet. It is contained in cells A77..B79.

3. In cell A77 key **Item Number**. In cell A78 key **PF\***. Press **Enter**.

4. Open the Notebook Data Query dialog box. You will only be changing the contents of the *Criteria Table* text box. In the *Criteria Table* text box key **Sales:A77..A78**. Click **Extract** and **Close**.

5. Go to Sheet B. Only those items with item numbers starting with *PF* should appear.

6. Double click the tab for Sheet B and key **Pet Food Sales**. Press **Enter**. The sheet's name should be changed. Replace the subtitle in cell A2 with **Pet Food Sales**.

7. Print the Pet Food Sales sheet. Save the notebook and close it.

# Summary

In this lesson you learned to create filters and queries. You learned that:

■   you can use QuickFilter to sort data by the value in a specified row or to locate specific data.

■   you can create custom filters that allow you to locate specific data, such as all of the records containing a specified value.

■   more complex filters can contain And and Or searches. In an And search, both conditions must be true in order for the data to be selected. In an Or search, only one condition needs to be true.

- a database is an organized collection of data that is made up of records. All of the records in a database table contain the same fields.

- when you query a database, you extract records that meet specific criteria.

- the Notebook Data Query dialog box allows you to establish a query. You specify the records to be searched, the criteria table, and where the output should be placed.

- you can use operators such as less than (<) and greater than or equal to (>=) to create complex searches. Criteria tables can also use And and Or searches.

- wildcard symbols can be used in criteria tables to stand for missing characters.

## LESSON 10 REVIEW QUESTIONS

### TRUE/FALSE

**Circle the T if the statement is true. Circle the F if it is false.**

**T  F   1.** In a Quattro Pro database a row represents a record and a column represents a field.

**T  F   2.** You can use the QuickFilter feature to search for data that meets two conditions.

**T  F   3.** When using an And search, a record must meet both of the conditions in order to be included in the result.

**T  F   4.** You can use the QuickFilter feature to sort a sheet in ascending order, but not in descending order.

**T  F   5.** You can store the results of a filter on a separate sheet where they can be formatted, printed, etc.

### WRITTEN QUESTIONS

**Write your answers to the following questions.**

**6.** Assume that an employee database contains each employee's telephone number. How might you use QuickFilter to locate all of the records containing the area code "319" in the phone number?

**7.** Explain the difference between a field and a record in a database.

**8.** What is an advantage of using the QuickFilter feature instead of the Notebook Query command? What is a disadvantage?

9. A baseball team's database contains a record on each player. Assume that each record contains a field named Batting Average and a field named Position. How could you create a criteria table that would display all records in which the Position is Shortstop and Batting Average is greater than 2.5?

10. What is the meaning of the term *database block*?

## LESSON 10 PROJECT

SCANS

### PROJECT 10A

The Pet Paradise accountant would like the employees database to be queried for specific employee records.

1. Open the **employees** notebook in the student **Datafile** folder and save it as **employees proj10a xxx**.

2. Open the **Tools** menu and choose **QuickFilter**. Click the Last Name column **Filter** button and select (**Sort A..Z**). Open the **Tools** menu and deselect **QuickFilter**.

3. Create a criteria table that will locate all records that have a 78746 ZIP code. Copy the headings in cells B4..J4 of Sheet A to cells B4..J4 of Sheet B. Use the Notebook Data Query dialog box to perform a query based on this criteria table. Place the results of this query on Sheet B. Key the title **Employees with 78746 ZIP Code** at the top of Sheet B.

4. Copy the headings in cells B4..J4 of Sheet A to cells B4..J4 of Sheet C. Erase the previous criteria table on Sheet A and create a new one which will locate all records in which the employee is part time or makes less than $13.00 an hour. Reopen the Notebook Data Query dialog box and perform the new query. The result should be placed on Sheet C. Key the title **Employees Who Are Part Time or Have an Hourly Wage of Less Than $13.00**.

5. Copy the headings in cells B4..J4 of Sheet A to cells B4..J4 of Sheet D. Change the criteria table so that it will locate all employees who are full time and make at least $13.00 an hour. Use the Notebook Data Query dialog box to perform the query. Place the result on Sheet D. Key the title **Employees Who Are Full Time and Have an Hourly Wage of at Least $13.00**.

6. Resave the notebook and print all four sheets. Print each sheet on a separate page. Close the notebook.

(continued on next page)

## PROJECT 10B

You need to perform several queries on the Morrison Car Dealership car database. The results of each query should be placed on a separate notebook sheet.

1.  Open the **cars** notebook in the student **Datafile** folder and save it as **cars proj10b xxx**.

2.  Create a query that will locate all of the Fords and place these records on Sheet B. Sort these results alphabetically from A to Z by the name of the model. Place an appropriate title at the top of Sheet B.

3.  Create a query that locates all cars that are 1995 models or newer. Place the results on Sheet C and sort them in descending order by year. Enter an appropriate title at the top of Sheet C.

4.  Create a query that locates all cars that are 1996 models or newer *or* have fewer than 60,000 miles. The query's results should be placed on Sheet D. Sort these results in descending order by mileage. Give Sheet D an appropriate title.

5.  Create a query that places all of the cars that are in excellent condition on Sheet E. Give Sheet E an appropriate title.

6.  Go through the sheets and make certain that they are properly formatted and that all columns are wide enough to display their entire contents.

7.  Save the notebook and print all of its sheets. Each sheet should be printed on a separate page.

8.  Close the notebook.

## CRITICAL THINKING ACTIVITY

SCANS

Divide into small groups and consider a database that might be created by a restaurant. Assume that it contains a listing of the different menu items that the restaurant sells and the number of items that were sold for each lunch period and each dinner period for each day of the week. In addition, it would contain the price of each item. How might the restaurant's manager query this database to obtain information that would be useful in making decisions? Give at least three examples. Can the group think of any additional fields that it might be useful for the database to contain? How could these additional fields be used?

# CREATING REPORTS

## OBJECTIVES

**Upon completion of this lesson, you will be able to:**

■ Use Quattro Pro's Cross Tabs feature to summarize data in reports.

■ Send data to Data Modeling Desktop.

■ Rearrange data to create different reports.

■ Create labels for the reports.

■ Format reports.

■ Copy a report created in the Data Modeling Desktop to a notebook sheet.

🕐 **Estimated Time: 1¹/₂ hours**

$S$preadsheets let you display data, calculate values such as totals and averages, and analyze general trends. However, ideas generally can be presented even more effectively by using reports. A *report* generally is a printed document that summarizes data in an easy-to-understand fashion. In this lesson you will learn to create and format reports.

## *Understanding the Cross Tabs Feature*

$T$he Cross Tabs command in the Tools menu lets you select data from a notebook and specify how it should be organized, summarized, and formatted. You specify the values that should be placed in rows along the left edge of the report and in columns across the top, and also what data should be placed in the body of the report. Quattro Pro then generates the report. In the next exercise you will create a report that contains the total sales for each item at both stores for the entire three-month period.

 **INTERNET** The federal government and most of the states have Web sites that can be useful in locating income tax and sales tax rates and general tax information.

SCANS

1. Open the **report** notebook in the student **Datafile** folder and save it as **report 11-1 xxx**.

2. Select cells **A1..H109**.

3. Open the **Tools** menu, choose **Data Tools**, and then choose **Cross Tabs**. The Cross Tabs dialog box appears, as shown in Figure 11-1.

4. In the *Cells to use for the Cross Tab* text box cells **A:A1..H109** should already be selected. This range contains all of the data the report needs to use.

5. In the *Destination Cell for the Result* text box *B:A1* should appear. The resulting report will begin in the first cell of Sheet B.

6. Under *Fields* click **Item Number** and then click the button containing the vertical red bar. A red column appears at the left edge of the report,

indicating that the item numbers will appear in the first column of the report.

**TIP**

If you have placed a field in a report and want to remove it, just click on that button. The field will be removed from the report and placed back in the *Fields* list box.

7. Under *Fields* click **Item** and then click the button containing the vertical yellow bar. Each item's name will appear in the second column of the report, next to its item number.

8. Under *Fields* click **Total** and then click the button in the first column, fourth row (it contains two vertical green bars). The totals for each item sold at both stores will be placed in the body of the report.

**FIGURE 11-1**
Cross Tabs Dialog Box

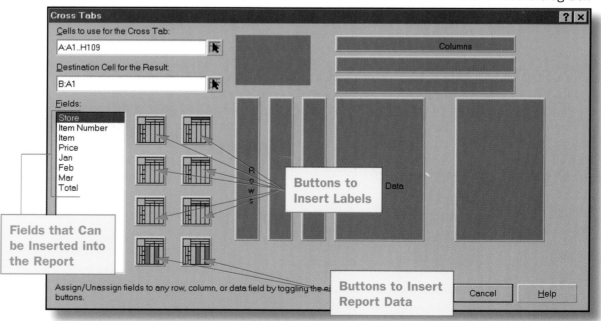

9. Click **OK**. It will take several seconds for Quattro Pro to generate the report. Sheet B appears on the screen.

10. Format the numeric values in the third column as currency with two decimal places.

11. Insert three blank lines at the top of the report. Key the title **Pet Paradise** in the first row. Key the title **Quarterly Sales Totals** in the second row. Format the titles however you wish.

12. In cell A4 key **Item Number**. In cell B4 key **Item**. Place the labels in row 4 in bold type. Widen the columns as necessary so that all of the data is visible. When you are done, your report should look similar to the one in Figure 11-2.

13. Save the notebook and print the report on Sheet B.

**FIGURE 11-2**
Pet Paradise Quarterly Sales Totals Report

| | A | B | C | D |
|---|---|---|---|---|
| 1 | Pet Paradise | | | |
| 2 | Quarterly Sales Totals | | | |
| 3 | | | | |
| 4 | **Item Number** | **Item** | **Total** | |
| 5 | AC1034 | Single Cat Bowl | $733.08 | |
| 6 | AC3599 | Double Untippable Bowl | $3,255.84 | |
| 7 | AC3873 | Single Large Dog Bowl | $895.50 | |
| 8 | AC4058 | Single Small Dog Bowl | $537.60 | |
| 9 | BF1082 | Shedding Comb | $963.16 | |
| 10 | BF9302 | Small Wire Brush | $1,189.32 | |
| 11 | BR1593 | Super-Gentle Comb | $1,102.60 | |
| 12 | BR3258 | Mat Remover | $2,263.80 | |
| 13 | BR6518 | Pet Electric Clippers | $4,623.00 | |
| 14 | BR7302 | Pet Hair Remover | $3,045.00 | |
| 15 | BR9175 | Large Wire Brush | $938.40 | |
| 16 | CA1056 | Cat Safety Collar | $848.64 | |
| 17 | CA1069 | Nylon Dog Collar (Small) | $572.16 | |
| 18 | CA1070 | Nylon Dog Collar (Medium) | $925.84 | |
| 19 | CA1071 | Nylon Dog Collar (Large) | $801.80 | |
| 20 | CA4200 | Nylon Cat Collar | $964.16 | |
| 21 | CA5406 | Tick & Flea Collar | $1,366.40 | |
| 22 | CA8065 | Leather Lead (4 Foot) | $4,414.40 | |
| 23 | CA8298 | Leather Lead (6 Foot) | $4,890.00 | |
| 24 | CH4201 | 4-Foot Chain | $1,050.78 | |
| 25 | CH5089 | Tie-Out Cable | $4,877.20 | |
| 26 | CH5939 | 8-Foot Chain | $1,327.50 | |
| 27 | EF5044 | Dog Travel Kennel (Small) | $4,606.00 | |
| 28 | EF5162 | Dog Travel Kennel (Large) | $3,534.00 | |
| 29 | EF5726 | Dog Travel Kennel (Medium) | $3,737.50 | |
| 30 | EF5903 | Cat Carrier | $5,502.40 | |
| 31 | MI3629 | No-Tears Dog Shampoo | $912.60 | |
| 32 | MI3918 | Hypoallergenic Dog Shampoo | $1,488.00 | |
| 33 | MI4308 | Tick & Flea Spray | $2,333.50 | |
| 34 | MI4721 | Hypoallergenic Cat Shampoo | $2,140.80 | |
| 35 | MI5328 | Wondercoat Shampoo | $2,155.20 | |
| 36 | MI7873 | Herbal Pet Shampoo | $994.50 | |

# *Understanding the Data Modeling Desktop*

Cross Tabs makes it easy to create reports that summarize data. Another useful feature of WordPerfect Suite 8 is Data Modeling Desktop. With Data Modeling Desktop you can reorganize the same data block in many different ways, and each depiction, or model, of the data tells a different story. Figure 11-3 shows several different models, or reports, that were generated using the data in the **report** notebook. The data must be in a single contiguous block and all of the records must contain the same fields.

Before opening Data Modeling Desktop, you select the spreadsheet data to be copied to it. Data Modeling Desktop can be thought of as its own separate "mini-program" within WordPerfect Suite 8. To access it, open the Start menu, select WordPerfect Suite 8, then select Tools, and finally Data Modeling Desktop. The window that appears looks a little different than what you're used to working in! You can use the Paste command in the Edit menu to copy the data to the source window. Figure 11-4 shows how Data Modeling Desktop would look with the Pet Paradise report data copied to the source window.

**FIGURE 11-3**

Examples of Data Models

| | | Total | |
|---|---|---|---|
| AC1034 | Single Cat Bowl | 733.08 | ▲ |
| AC3599 | Double Untippable Bowl | 3255.84 | |
| AC3873 | Single Large Dog Bowl | 895.50 | |
| AC4058 | Single Small Dog Bowl | 537.60 | |
| BF1082 | Shedding Comb | 963.16 | |
| BF9302 | Small Wire Brush | 1189.32 | |
| BR1593 | Super-Gentle Comb | 1102.60 | |
| BR3258 | Mat Remover | 2263.80 | |
| BR6518 | Pet Electric Clippers | 4623.00 | |
| BR7302 | Pet Hair Remover | 3045.00 | |
| BR9175 | Large Wire Brush | 938.40 | |
| CA1056 | Cat Safety Collar | 848.64 | |
| CA1069 | Nylon Dog Collar (Small) | 572.16 | |
| CA1070 | Nylon Dog Collar (Medium) | 925.84 | |
| CA1071 | Nylon Dog Collar (Large) | 801.80 | |
| CA4200 | Nylon Cat Collar | 964.16 | |
| CA5406 | Tick & Flea Collar | 1366.40 | |
| CA8065 | Leather Lead (4 Foot) | 4414.40 | |

| | | 1 | 2 | |
|---|---|---|---|---|
| | | Total | Total | |
| AC1034 | Single Cat Bowl | 447.00 | 286.08 | ▲ |
| AC3599 | Double Untippable Bowl | 1875.30 | 1380.54 | |
| AC3873 | Single Large Dog Bowl | 581.08 | 314.42 | |
| AC4058 | Single Small Dog Bowl | 323.20 | 214.40 | |
| BF1082 | Shedding Comb | 545.26 | 417.90 | |
| BF9302 | Small Wire Brush | 779.10 | 410.22 | |
| BR1593 | Super-Gentle Comb | 636.40 | 466.20 | |
| BR3258 | Mat Remover | 1499.40 | 764.40 | |
| BR6518 | Pet Electric Clippers | 2725.50 | 1897.50 | |
| BR7302 | Pet Hair Remover | 1737.00 | 1308.00 | |
| BR9175 | Large Wire Brush | 565.80 | 372.60 | |
| CA1056 | Cat Safety Collar | 395.20 | 453.44 | |
| CA1069 | Nylon Dog Collar (Small) | 309.92 | 262.24 | |
| CA1070 | Nylon Dog Collar (Medium) | 495.52 | 430.32 | |
| CA1071 | Nylon Dog Collar (Large) | 235.60 | 566.20 | |
| CA4200 | Nylon Cat Collar | 599.84 | 364.32 | |
| CA5406 | Tick & Flea Collar | 768.00 | 598.40 | |

| | | Jan | Feb | Mar | |
|---|---|---|---|---|---|
| AC1034 | Single Cat Bowl | 85.00 | 72.00 | 89.00 | ▲ |
| AC3599 | Double Untippable Bowl | 147.00 | 125.00 | 136.00 | |
| AC3873 | Single Large Dog Bowl | 67.00 | 73.00 | 85.00 | |
| AC4058 | Single Small Dog Bowl | 65.00 | 63.00 | 40.00 | |
| BF1082 | Shedding Comb | 76.00 | 53.00 | 113.00 | |
| BF9302 | Small Wire Brush | 119.00 | 96.00 | 159.00 | |
| BR1593 | Super-Gentle Comb | 90.00 | 84.00 | 124.00 | |
| BR3258 | Mat Remover | 68.00 | 56.00 | 107.00 | |
| BR6518 | Pet Electric Clippers | 35.00 | 37.00 | 62.00 | |
| BR7302 | Pet Hair Remover | 314.00 | 311.00 | 390.00 | |
| BR9175 | Large Wire Brush | 60.00 | 68.00 | 76.00 | |
| CA1056 | Cat Safety Collar | 52.00 | 76.00 | 76.00 | |
| CA1069 | Nylon Dog Collar (Small) | 68.00 | 44.00 | 80.00 | |
| CA1070 | Nylon Dog Collar (Medium) | 100.00 | 104.00 | 80.00 | |
| CA1071 | Nylon Dog Collar (Large) | 53.00 | 80.00 | 78.00 | |
| CA4200 | Nylon Cat Collar | 100.00 | 76.00 | 86.00 | |

NOTE:

Only part of the data can be seen in the source window. If you wish, you can enlarge the window to see more of it.

**FIGURE 11-4**
Data Modeling Desktop Window

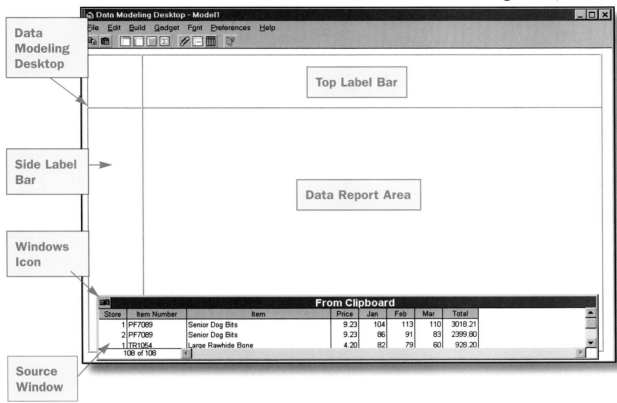

You can select a column of data in the source window and then specify that it be used to create a Top Label Bar, Side Label Bar, or be placed in the report data area. You normally place columns that contain labels in the label bars. Columns containing values are usually placed in the data area. Figure 11-5 explains the Data Modeling Desktop buttons. In the next exercise you will use Data Modeling Desktop to create a sales report for Pet Paradise.

**FIGURE 11-5**
The Data Modeling Desktop Toolbar

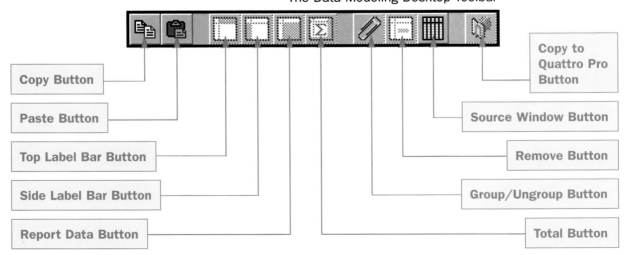

1. Save the notebook as **report 11-2 xxx**.

2. Make certain that Sheet A is displayed on the screen. Select cells **A1..H109** and click the **Copy** button.

3. Open the Windows **Start** menu, select **WordPerfect Suite 8**, then select **Tools** and **Data Modeling Desktop**.

4. Notice that the source window at the bottom of the screen is active. Open the **Edit** menu in Data Modeling Desktop and choose **Paste**. The selected cells appear in the window at the bottom of the screen, as shown in Figure 11-4.

5. In the source window click anywhere in the **Store** column. The column will be selected. Click the **Top Label Bar** button on the Toolbar. The Store column appears in the upper left corner of the window.

6. In the source window click the **Item Number** column. Click the **Side Label Bar** button on the Toolbar.

7. In the source window click the **Item** column. Click the **Side Label Bar** button on the Toolbar.

**NOTE:**

The quantities of the items sold are currently listed with two decimal places (for example, *49.00*). They should be listed as whole numbers, such as *49*. You will be fixing this problem later.

8. You are now going to place the data into the report. Click the **Jan** column. Hold down the **Shift** key and select the **Feb** and **Mar** columns. All three columns should now be selected. Click the **Report Data** button on the Toolbar. Spend a minute examining the report. Notice that both stores are listed across the top with the quantity of sales for each of the three months in separate columns.

9. Keep the report open for the next exercise.

**NOTE:**

The source window now has the title *From Clipboard*, indicating that you pasted the data from the Clipboard. It may take a few moments for this new title to appear on the screen.

## Saving, Opening, and Closing Reports

You can save a report just as you would save a notebook, by using the Save As command in the Data Modeling Desktop File menu and assigning a name to the report. To open an existing report, choose Open in the File menu. Double click the file's name in the *File name* list box.

EXERCISE QP11.3

1. In the Data Modeling Desktop window open the **File** menu and choose **Save As**.

**TIP**

Be careful to open the File menu in the Data Modeling Desktop window, not in the Quattro Pro window.

2. Make certain that you will be saving the report to the student **Datafile** folder. In the *File name* text box key **report1**. Click **OK**.

3. Open the **File** menu and choose **Close**.

4. Reopen the report by choosing **Open** in the Data Modeling Desktop **File** menu.

5. If necessary, open the student **Datafile** folder. Double click **report1.dmd** to open the file. Keep the report open for the next exercise.

**NOTE:**

The Data Modeling Desktop automatically adds the extension *.dmd* to the filename.

## Rearranging Report Data

One of the nicest features of Data Modeling Desktop is that you can easily rearrange the way data is represented just by adding, deleting, or moving label bars and the data in the data area. You insert columns simply by selecting them in the source window and clicking the appropriate label bar button. To rearrange the order of columns, position the pointer on the column's handle (see Figure 11-6). The pointer turns into a hand icon. Hold down the mouse button and a dotted line appears around the column. Drag it to a new position in the bar. You can move a column from a Side Label Bar to a Top Label Bar, or vice versa by selecting it and then pivoting, or swinging, the column upward or downward, depending on where you want it to end up.

**FIGURE 11-6**
Column Handles

| | | 1 | | | 2 | | |
|---|---|---|---|---|---|---|---|
| | | Jan | Feb | Mar | Jan | Feb | Mar |
| AC1034 | Single Cat Bowl | 4 | | 5 | | 29.00 | 31.00 |
| AC3599 | Double Untippable Bowl | 8 | | | .00 | 51.00 | 57.00 |
| AC3873 | Single Large Dog Bowl | 40.00 | 44.00 | 62.00 | 27.00 | 29.00 | 23.00 |
| AC4058 | Single Small Dog Bowl | 37.00 | 41.00 | 23.00 | 28.00 | 22.00 | 17.00 |
| BF1082 | Shedding Comb | 44.00 | 28.00 | 65.00 | 32.00 | 25.00 | 48.00 |
| BF9302 | Small Wire Brush | 84.00 | 68.00 | 93.00 | 35.00 | 28.00 | 66.00 |
| BR1593 | Super-Gentle Comb | 56.00 | 48.00 | 68.00 | 34.00 | 36.00 | 56.00 |
| BR3258 | Mat Remover | 44.00 | 37.00 | 72.00 | 24.00 | 19.00 | 35.00 |
| BR6518 | Pet Electric Clippers | 24.00 | 17.00 | 38.00 | 11.00 | 20.00 | 24.00 |
| BR7302 | Pet Hair Remover | 192.00 | 163.00 | 224.00 | 122.00 | 148.00 | 166.00 |
| BR9175 | Large Wire Brush | 40.00 | 31.00 | 52.00 | 20.00 | 37.00 | 24.00 |
| CA1056 | Cat Safety Collar | 31.00 | 40.00 | 24.00 | 21.00 | 36.00 | 52.00 |
| CA1069 | Nylon Dog Collar (Small) | 36.00 | 24.00 | 44.00 | 32.00 | 20.00 | 36.00 |
| CA1070 | Nylon Dog Collar (Medium) | 60.00 | 48.00 | 44.00 | 40.00 | 56.00 | 36.00 |

Column Handles

Column Handles

1. In the source window select the **Price** column. Click the **Side Label Bar** button on the Toolbar. Notice that the Price column is to the right of the Item column in the report.

2. Move the months columns (Jan, Feb, and Mar) from the Top Label Bar to the Side Label Bar.
   a. Select the months columns' handle at the right side of the labels for Jan, Feb, and Mar. The pointer turns into a hand.
   b. Pivot the columns down and to the left until they are immediately to the right of the Price column. This procedure can be tricky. You have to pivot in just the right direction to actually move the columns. Don't release the mouse button until you see that the dotted border is in the correct location. When it is, release the mouse button. Now the list has a completely different look.

3. Remove the Store column.
   a. Position the pointer on the Store column handle until it turns into a hand icon. Click to select it.

   b. Click the **Remove** button on the Toolbar. Now the totals for both stores appear in the data column in the report.

4. Pivot the rows for Jan, Feb, and Mar so that they are turned back into columns at the top of the report.
   a. Close the Source window by clicking its **Windows** icon and choosing **Close**.
   b. Position the pointer on the handle for the months (it's at the bottom of the window).
   c. Pivot the months up and to the right until they are back at the top of the report. Release the mouse button. Now the months columns should list the total sales for *both* stores as shown in Figure 11-7.

5. Save the report. Keep the report open for the next exercise.

# Formatting Report Data

You've probably noticed that data you send to the Data Modeling Desktop does not retain the formatting that was applied to it in the notebook sheet. You can apply numeric formatting and change the font size of the data in the report itself. To apply any formatting, the data first must be selected. You can select a column of data in the Report Data area by clicking the column when the pointer turns into a vertical arrow. To select a row, click the row when the pointer turns into a horizontal arrow. If the Report Data Labels are in the Top Label Bar, selecting a column selects all the columns in the report that contain data from the same column in the source window. If the Report Data Labels are in the Side Label Bar, selecting a row selects all the rows that contain data from the same column in the source window. To select a column or row of data in a Side Label Bar or Top Label Bar, click its handle. To select individual labels in the bars, just click the label. To select all the data in the report, click the area in the upper left corner of the report.

Once the data to be formatted is selected, open the Gadget menu and choose Format. You can then apply formatting as you would in Quattro Pro.

**FIGURE 11-7**
The Report Showing Quantities Sold per Month

| | | | Jan | Feb | Mar |
|---|---|---|---|---|---|
| AC1034 | Single Cat Bowl | 2.98 | 85.00 | 72.00 | 89.00 |
| AC3599 | Double Untippable Bowl | 7.98 | 147.00 | 125.00 | 136.00 |
| AC3873 | Single Large Dog Bowl | 3.98 | 67.00 | 73.00 | 85.00 |
| AC4058 | Single Small Dog Bowl | 3.20 | 65.00 | 63.00 | 40.00 |
| BF1082 | Shedding Comb | 3.98 | 76.00 | 53.00 | 113.00 |
| BF9302 | Small Wire Brush | 3.18 | 119.00 | 96.00 | 159.00 |
| BR1593 | Super-Gentle Comb | 3.70 | 90.00 | 84.00 | 124.00 |
| BR3258 | Mat Remover | 9.80 | 68.00 | 56.00 | 107.00 |
| BR6518 | Pet Electric Clippers | 34.50 | 35.00 | 37.00 | 62.00 |
| BR7302 | Pet Hair Remover | 3 | 314.00 | 311.00 | 390.00 |
| BR9175 | Large Wire Brush | 4.60 | 60.00 | 68.00 | 76.00 |
| CA1056 | Cat Safety Collar | 4.16 | 52.00 | 76.00 | 76.00 |
| CA1069 | Nylon Dog Collar (Small) | 2.98 | 68.00 | 44.00 | 80.00 |
| CA1070 | Nylon Dog Collar (Medium) | 3.26 | 100.00 | 104.00 | 80.00 |
| CA1071 | Nylon Dog Collar (Large) | 3.80 | 53.00 | 80.00 | 78.00 |
| CA4200 | Nylon Cat Collar | 3.68 | 100.00 | 76.00 | 86.00 |
| CA5406 | Tick & Flea Collar | 3.20 | 125.00 | 139.00 | 163.00 |
| CA8065 | Leather Lead (4 Foot) | 12.40 | 116.00 | 124.00 | 116.00 |
| CA8298 | Leather Lead (6 Foot) | 15 | 112.00 | 91.00 | 123.00 |
| CH4201 | 4-Foot Chain | 4.98 | 56.00 | 90.00 | 65.00 |
| CH5089 | Tie-Out Cable | 17.80 | 81.00 | 96.00 | 97.00 |
| CH5939 | 8-Foot Chain | 7.50 | 60.00 | 56.00 | 61.00 |
| EF5044 | Dog Travel Kennel (Small) | 24.50 | 62.00 | 71.00 | 55.00 |
| EF5162 | Dog Travel Kennel (Large) | 38 | 25.00 | 31.00 | 37.00 |
| EF5726 | Dog Travel Kennel (Medium) | 32.50 | 31.00 | 40.00 | 44.00 |
| EF5903 | Cat Carrier | 28.96 | 65.00 | 62.00 | 63.00 |

EXERCISE QP11.5

1. Position the pointer anywhere in the **Jan** column. When it turns into a vertical arrow, click the mouse button. The entire column is selected. Hold down **Shift** and use the same method to select columns **Feb** and **Mar**. When you are done, all three columns should be selected.

2. The values in the months columns should be formatted as integers. Open the **Gadget** menu and select **Format**. Select **nnn0** and then click

**Apply**. Click the **Windows** icon in the Format dialog box and click **Close**.

**TIP**

If you have closed the source window and need to reopen it, open the Build menu and choose Source Window.

3. Save the report and keep it open for the next exercise.

# Copying Data to a Notebook Sheet and Printing the Report

While you can format a report, you cannot print from the Data Modeling Desktop. To print a report, you must copy it to a notebook sheet. If you wish, you can then add titles and format it further before printing it.

**EXERCISE ⟹ QP11.6**

1. Open the **Preferences** menu and choose **Copy to Quattro Pro Options**. The Copy to Quattro Pro Options dialog box appears, as shown in Figure 11-8. Select **Always do ordinary copy**. Under *After Copy to Quattro Pro* select **Exit Data Modeling Desktop**. Click **OK**.

 **NOTE:**

The Copy to Quattro Pro Options dialog box allows you to determine whether the Data Modeling Desktop should be closed, minimized, or left unchanged when you copy a model to Quattro Pro. The default is to minimize the Data Modeling Desktop.

2. Click anywhere in the report to make certain that it is selected.

3. Click the **Copy to Quattro Pro** button on the Toolbar.

4. When the Missing Result Cell dialog box appears, enter **A:A4** in the text box. This will cause the report to be placed on Sheet A, starting in cell A4. Click **OK**.

5. The report appears on a notebook sheet. In row 1 key the title **Pet Paradise**. In row 2 key the title **Sales By Month**. Place the titles in a larger font size.

6. Format the Price column as currency with two decimal places.

7. Fix the column headings for the report.
   a. In cell **A4** key **Item Number**.
   b. In cell **B4** key **Item**.
   c. In cell **C4** key **Price**.
   d. Make the headings in row 4 bold and center the headings above the columns.

8. Widen the columns, if necessary, so that all of their contents are visible.

9. Save the notebook as **report 11-6 xxx**.

10. Print Sheet A and close the notebook.

**FIGURE 11-8**
The Copy to Quattro Pro Options Dialog Box

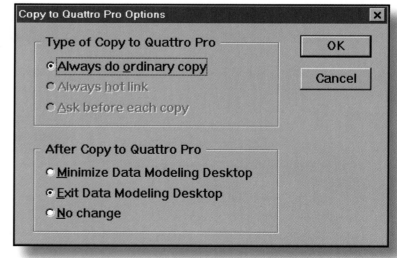

# *Summary*

In this lesson you learned how data could be organized in different ways and summarized by using reports. You learned that:

- Quattro Pro's Cross Tabs feature lets you position top and side labels and data to be contained within the report. The data will be summarized based on the labels chosen.

- you can tell Cross Tabs where to place the table containing its results. These results can be formatted as you would any other spreadsheet.

- Data Modeling Desktop is a separate mini-program that is accessed through the Windows Start menu. You select the data from a notebook that you wish to send to the Data Modeling Desktop.

- you specify which labels should be placed in the report and whether they should be side or top labels. The specified data is summarized based on the chosen labels.

- labels can be added, removed, and reordered. You can switch a side label to a top label (and vice versa) by using its handle to drag and pivot it.

- the resulting models can be saved, closed, and opened just like other documents. In order to be printed, they must be copied to a Quattro Pro spreadsheet.

## LESSON 11 REVIEW QUESTIONS

### MULTIPLE CHOICE

**Circle the best answer to each of the following statements.**

1. A _____ is generally a printed document that summarizes data in an easy-to-understand fashion.
   **A.** Cross Tab
   **B.** label
   **C.** report
   **D.** pivot

2. Cross Tabs knows where to place the results because _____.
   **A.** before you open the Cross Tabs dialog box, you must click the sheet that is to contain the results
   **B.** in the Cross Tabs dialog box you indicate where the results should be placed
   **C.** it always creates a new notebook and inserts them into it
   **D.** the results are always placed on the same sheet that contains the original data

3. When spreadsheet data is copied to the Data Modeling Desktop, it appears in _____.
   **A.** a Side Label Bar
   **B.** a Top Label Bar
   **C.** the Source Window
   **D.** the Start menu

(continued on next page)

4. When using the Data Modeling Desktop, you can switch a side label to a top label by _____ it.
   A. cross tabbing
   B. pivoting
   C. printing
   D. summarizing

5. To access the Data Modeling Desktop, you must open _____.
   A. the Help menu
   B. the Quattro Pro Edit menu
   C. the Quattro Pro Tools menu
   D. the Windows Start menu

## WRITTEN QUESTIONS

**Write your answers to the following questions.**

6. What are some of the advantages of using reports?

7. Explain how you determine what fields will be used as labels when using Cross Tabs.

8. Why is Data Modeling Desktop considered a "mini-program"?

9. When using Data Modeling Desktop, how can you turn a side label into a top label?

10. How do you send a report from the Data Modeling Desktop to a Quattro Pro notebook sheet?

## LESSON 11 PROJECT

SCANS

### PROJECT 11A

1. Open the notebook **car report** in the student **Datafile** folder and save it as **car report proj11a xxx**.

2. Select cells **A1..F24**.

3. Open the **Tools** menu, choose **Data Tools**, and then choose **Cross Tabs**.

4. Make certain that the results of the Cross Tabs feature will appear on Sheet B in the notebook.

5. Under *Fields* click **Make** and then click the button containing the vertical red bar.

6. Under *Fields* click **Model** and then click the button containing the vertical yellow bar.

7. Under *Fields* click **Sale Price** and then click the button in the first column, fourth row (it contains two vertical green bars). Click **OK**. The total sales for each model of car will appear in the report.

8. After Quattro Pro generates the Cross Tabs results, Sheet B should appear on the screen. In cell A1 key **Make**. In cell B1 key **Model**. Format the numerical values in column C as currency with no decimal places. Widen the cells so that all of their contents are visible.

9. Save the notebook and print Sheet B. Close the notebook.

## PROJECT 11B

1. Open the notebook **car report** in the student **Datafile** folder.

2. Make certain that Sheet A is displayed on the screen. Select cells **A1..F24** and click the **Copy** button.

3. Open the Windows **Start** menu, select **WordPerfect Suite 8**, then select **Tools** and **Data Modeling Desktop**.

4. Open the **Edit** menu in Data Modeling Desktop and choose **Paste**. The selected cells appear in the source window.

5. In the source window click anywhere in the **Name** column. The column will be selected. Click the **Side Label Bar** button on the Toolbar.

6. In the source window click anywhere in the **Date** column. Click the **Side Label Bar** button on the Toolbar.

7. Click the **Sale Price** column. Click the **Report Data** button on the Toolbar. The total amount of sales for each salesperson should be displayed.

8. Save this report as **report2**. Click anywhere in the report. Copy it to a Quattro Pro notebook. Make certain that you specify that Data Modeling Desktop should be closed after the report is copied to Quattro Pro. Tell Quattro Pro to copy the report to the first sheet of the notebook.

9. Insert appropriate column headings at the top of the Quattro Pro sheet. Format the Sale Price column as Currency with no decimal places.

10. Save the notebook containing the report as **car report proj11b xxx**.

11. Print the report and close the notebook.

# CRITICAL THINKING ACTIVITY

Imagine that you have created a spreadsheet that keeps track of all of your personal expenditures over the period of a year. How might creating a report help you in understanding how your money is spent? List at least two different ways that the expenditures might be categorized.

# USING COREL® QUATTRO® PRO'S PRODUCTIVITY TOOLS

## OBJECTIVES

**Upon completion of this lesson, you will be able to:**

- Run Spell Checker.

- Create and apply macros.

- Define new styles and apply styles to spreadsheet cells.

- Create a project.

**⏱ Estimated Time: 1 hour**

Now that you know how to create, enhance, and manage spreadsheet data, we'll wrap up the course by covering many of Quattro Pro's features that are designed to let you work even more efficiently. In this lesson you will learn about tools that will speed up your work and help you be more efficient.

## Spell Checking Spreadsheet Data

Although spreadsheets are generally used to enter and crunch numbers, they can contain a lot of words, too. Frequently you might find yourself so busy calculating data and tabulating results that you don't notice when labels have been misspelled. That's when Quattro Pro's Spell Checker comes in handy. Quattro Pro checks text against its built-in dictionary. Any word it doesn't recognize is displayed in the Writing Tools dialog box. Following is an explanation of the buttons that are available in the Writing Tools dialog box:

- *Replace:*       Replaces the word in the *Not found* box with the suggested replacement.

- *Skip Once:*    Skips the word once but displays other occurrences of it in the Spell Checker.

- *Skip Always:*  Skips the word on all occurrences of it in the current file.

- *Add:*            Adds the word to the built-in dictionary. This option allows you to customize the dictionary to your needs, for example, by adding last names that you frequently use.

- *QuickCorrect*: Automatically corrects commonly misspelled or miskeyed words. Allows you to add your own words to the QuickCorrect list. The next time you key the word in its incorrect form, QuickCorrect automatically corrects it with the replacement.

- *Undo:* Undoes the replacement.

- *Suggest:* Lists in the *Not found* box the number of possible replacements that Spell Checker finds and displays all of them in the *Replacements* list box.

- *Customize:* Provides options for customizing Spell Checker. For example, you can choose to have Spell Checker beep each time it finds a new word.

- *Check:* Selects portions of the document you want to spell check. Select the range to spell check before starting Spell Checker.

Using Spell Checker can locate many incorrectly spelled words. However, it will not locate every type of error. For example, if you use the word *there* when you should have used *their*, Spell Checker will not find the mistake. Therefore, it is still very important to carefully proofread your work.

## EXERCISE ⟹ QP12.1

SCANS

1. Open the notebook **new sales** in the student **Datafile** folder. Save it as **new sales 12-1 xxx**.

2. Open the **Tools** menu and choose **Spell Check**. The Writing Tools dialog box appears, as shown in Figure 12-1. Notice that it has found *Cst*, which is a misspelling of the word *Cost*. In the *Replacements* list box click **Cost** and click the **Replace** button. The word is corrected.

3. Next, cell B10 is highlighted because the word *collar* has been spelled *coller*. In the *Replacements* list box click **collar** and click **Replace**.

4. In cell B25 *Hypoallergenic* is located. Even though it is flagged, the word is correctly spelled; it simply isn't in the dictionary. Click **Skip All** so that Spell Checker will skip over the word whenever it is found.

**FIGURE 12-1**
The Writing Tools Dialog Box

5. Next, the word *Wondercoat* is found in cell B29. This word is part of a brand name and is correctly spelled, so click **Skip Once**.

6. In cell B46 *dog* has been spelled *dgo*. Click **dog** in the *Replacements* list box and click **Replace**.

7. Cell B59 contains the word *untippable*. Click **Skip Once** to leave this word as is.

8. The message *Spell check completed. Close Spell Checker?* appears. Click **Yes**. You are done spell checking the spreadsheet.

9. Save the notebook. Keep this notebook open for the next exercise.

# *Creating and Applying Macros*

In Quattro Pro you can automate repetitive tasks by creating a macro. A *macro* is a recording of the actions (commands, keystrokes, and mouse movements) you perform to complete a task. Once a macro is recorded, you save it under a name of your choosing. You then can "play back" the macro, causing all of the recorded steps to be performed automatically. For example, suppose you always want to apply the same page setup options to all of the notebooks you print. You could record the actions you go through to complete this function, save the actions under their own macro name, and then play back the macro each time you were ready to print a notebook. In the next exercise you will create a macro that inserts a header into a notebook.

**EXERCISE** QP12.2

SCANS

1. Save the notebook as **new sales 12-2 xxx**.

2. Open the **Tools** menu, choose **Macro**, and then choose **Record**. The Record Macro dialog box appears, as shown in Figure 12-2.

3. In the Record Macro dialog box click the arrow on the right side of the *Location* box. The dialog box is minimized so that you can select the cell where the macro is to be stored. On the notebook sheet click cell **A76**. The macro will be stored in this cell. Click the **Maximize** button in the Record Macro Title Bar to reopen the dialog box. The notebook **new sales 12-2 xxx** should be listed in the *Macro Library* text box. Click **OK**.

**FIGURE 12-2**
Record Macro Dialog Box

(continued on next page)

**QP-151**

**4.** The record indicator should appear in the Application Bar. (It looks like a miniature cassette tape.) From now on, until you stop the recording, every action you make will be stored in the macro. Open the **File** menu and choose **Print**. In the Spreadsheet Print dialog box click **Page Setup** and then click the **Header/Footer** tab.

The vertical bars are formed by pressing Shift + \.

**5.** Under *Header* click **Create**. In the *Header* text box key **Pet Paradise||#d**. (Remember that in headers and footers, two vertical bars indicate that the text following them will be right-aligned. Also, the code *#d* causes the current date to be inserted into the header.) Click **Font** and then select **Times New Roman** as the font, **10** for the point size, and **Italic**. Click **OK**. Click **OK** again to close the Spreadsheet Page Setup dialog box and click **Close** in the Spreadsheet Print dialog box.

 **NOTE:**

As you record a macro, the commands, keystrokes, and mouse movements you execute are being carried out on the current document as well.

**6.** Open the **Tools** menu, choose **Macro**, and choose **Record** again to stop recording the macro.

**7.** Click cell **A76**. Spend a minute examining the macro. All of the instructions contained in this macro appear on the sheet.

**8.** Name the macro by opening the **Insert** menu and choosing **Name** and then **Cells**. The Cell Names dialog box appears, as shown in Figure 12-3. Key **Paradise Header** as the name and then click **Add**. Click **Close**.

**NOTE:**

You can assign keyboard shortcuts and buttons (just like those on a Toolbar) to macros so that all you have to do to play them back is enter the keyboard command or click the button. For more information, look up *Macros: 1-2-3* in the Quattro Pro Help feature. This Help topic contains subsections on creating keyboard shortcuts and QuickButtons.

**9.** Open the **File** menu and choose **Print Preview**. Notice that the header was added to the current notebook. Close the Print Preview dialog box.

**10.** Save the notebook. Print the notebook at 70% its normal size. Leave it open for the next exercise.

 **TIP**

To make the spreadsheet print at 70% its normal size, go to the Spreadsheet Page Setup dialog box and click the Print Scaling tab. Under *Print to* key 70. Click OK.

**FIGURE 12-3**
Cell Names Dialog Box

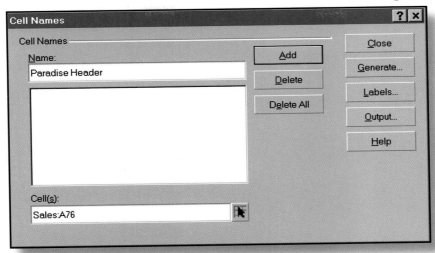

# *Defining and Applying Styles*

**FIGURE 12-4**
List of Currently
Available Styles

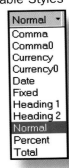

As you have learned, spreadsheet data can be formatted in a variety of ways. With SpeedFormat, you can give your spreadsheets a professional look. Quattro Pro also lets you create styles that you can use to quickly apply specified formats to selected cells. For example, if you always wanted the company name *Pet Paradise* to appear in the same font, font size, and color, you could create a style for it. Styles not only speed up the formatting process, but they also help you achieve continuity and consistency in the appearance of data.

You can see the available styles by opening the Style drop-down list on the Property Bar (see Figure 12-4). So far, you have been using the Normal style in your notebooks. The Normal style uses the Arial font and a 10-pt. font size. If you wish, you can use the Styles command in the Format menu to modify these previously defined styles or create new ones. In the next exercise you will create two new styles: The first style will be used for the main title on all Pet Paradise spreadsheets, and the second style will be used for subtitles.

**EXERCISE** ⟹ **QP12.3**

1. Save the notebook as **new sales 12-3 xxx**.

2. Define the following style for the main title for Pet Paradise spreadsheets:
   a. Open the **Format** menu and choose **Styles**. The Styles dialog box appears, as shown in Figure 12-5.

   b. In the *Define Style For* text box enter **Paradise Title**.

   c. Under *Included Properties* click **Font**. In the *Typeface* list box scroll down and select **Impact**. In the *Point Size* list box click **14**. Click **OK** to close the Font dialog box.

(continued on next page)

**FIGURE 12-5**
Styles Dialog Box

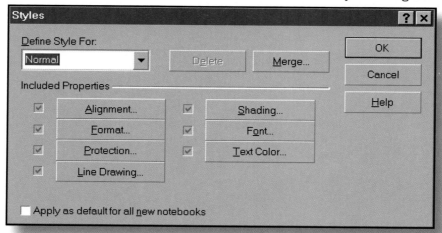

d. Under *Included Properties* click **Text Color**. Select red and then click **OK** to close the Text Color dialog box. Click **OK** again to close the Styles dialog box.

 **TIP**

If you redefine an existing style, all of the cells in the current notebook that contain that style will automatically be changed to the modified style.

3. Define the following style for any subtitles used in Pet Paradise spreadsheets:
   a. Open the **Format** menu and choose **Styles**.
   b. In the *Define Style For* text box enter **Paradise Subtitle**.
   c. Under *Included Properties* click **Font**. In the *Typeface* list box select **Impact**. In the *Point Size* list box select **12**. Click **OK** to close the Font dialog box.
   d. Under *Included Properties* click **Text Color**. Select red and then click **OK**. Click **OK** again to close the Styles dialog box.

4. Select the title *Pet Paradise II* in the current sheet. Open the **Style** drop-down list box and click **Paradise Title**. The title should be formatted in 14-pt. red type, with the Impact font.

 **TIP**

If you want to delete an existing style, open the Styles dialog box, select that style, and click Delete. Any cells in the current notebook that were formatted using that style will revert to the Normal style.

5. Select the subtitle *Weekly Sales* on the current sheet. Open the **Style** drop-down list box and click **Paradise Subtitle**. It should be formatted in the same way as the title, except with 12-pt. type.

6. Center the title and subtitle across columns A-F. If necessary, widen the columns so that their entire contents are visible.

7. Save the notebook and print the current sheet. Close the notebook.

# Understanding Projects

Quattro Pro comes with a group of predefined *projects*. A project is a predesigned notebook template you can use to serve as the basis for a new notebook. Many of the projects that come with Corel Quattro Pro provide the formatting and structural skeleton for common spreadsheets and data entry tasks used in business and at home. For example, there are projects for budgets (see Figure 12-6), expense reports, and loan payments. You also can create your own customized projects. When you open the File menu and choose New, you see a listing of the available projects. You then can select the project you wish to use, enter your own data, and modify it as you wish. Then you can save it under a new name and print it as you would any other notebook.

In the next exercise you will see how an employee could use the Expense Report project to quickly create a professional-looking expense report.

**FIGURE 12-6**
A Budget Project with Sample Data Inserted

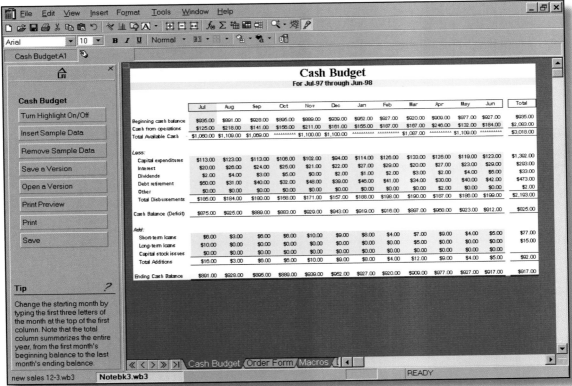

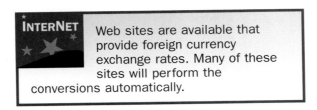

INTERNET Web sites are available that provide foreign currency exchange rates. Many of these sites will perform the conversions automatically.

## EXERCISE ⟩ QP12.4

SCANS

1. A blank notebook should currently be on the screen. In order to use the Quattro Pro projects, they must be enabled. To make certain projects are enabled, open the **Tools** menu and choose **Settings**. Click the **File Options** tab. Make certain that **Enable QuickTemplates** is selected and click **OK**.

2. Open the **File** menu and choose **New**. The New dialog box opens, as shown in Figure 12-7. It contains a listing of available projects.

3. Scroll down the box and select **Expense Report**. Click **Create**. The Expense Report project appears. In addition, PerfectExpert appears at the left side of the screen. PerfectExpert provides help in using various Quattro Pro features. Click the **X** in the upper right corner of the PerfectExpert box to close it. Reopen the **Help** menu and click **PerfectExpert** to display it again.

4. Open the **File** menu and choose **Save As**. Save the notebook as **expense report 12-4 xxx**.

**NOTE:**

Quattro Pro will not allow you to use the Save command to overwrite a project. If you click the Save button when a project is open, you will be asked to assign a name to the notebook so that the original project will not be overwritten.

5. Examine the list of buttons at the left side of the screen. Click the **Turn Highlight On/Off** button to remove the yellow highlighting. Click the button again to turn the highlighting back on.

**FIGURE 12-7**
New Dialog Box

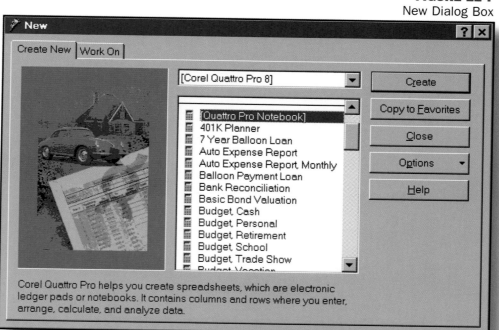

**6.** Click the **Insert Sample Data** button to see what the sheet looks like with sample data in it. Click the **Remove Sample Data** button to erase the data.

**7.** You are now going to insert the company name into the expense report. Click immediately above *NAME* at the upper left side of the report, key **Pet Paradise**, and press **Enter**. Notice that *Pet Paradise* replaced the text that was previously on this line.

**8.** Click the line to the right of *NAME* and key **Alma Alvaro**. Press **Enter**.

**9.** Key **31-Oct** for *PERIOD ENDING*. Press **Enter**.

**10.** For the rest of the sheet, key the following data: (Be careful to leave blank any fields that are not listed below.)

|  | 25-Oct | 26-Oct |
|---|---|---|
| Miles Driven | 12.00 | 14.00 |
| Parking And Tolls |  | 40.00 |
| Auto Rental | 56.00 | 56.00 |
| Airfare | 640.00 |  |
| Lodging | 113.49 | 113.49 |
| Breakfast | 8.74 |  |
| Lunch | 11.19 | 13.42 |
| Dinner | 21.57 | 25.05 |

**11.** Save the notebook. It should look like the one in Figure 12-8.

**12.** Print the expense report. Close the notebook.

**IMPORTANT:**

Do not key values into any other parts of the spreadsheet. Quattro Pro will automatically calculate these values.

**FIGURE 12-8**
The Expense Report

**Expense Report**

Pet Paradise

| NAME | Alma Alvaro | | | PERIOD ENDING | 31-Oct-98 |

| | 25-Oct-98 | 26-Oct-98 | 27-Oct-98 | 28-Oct-98 | 29-Oct-98 | 30-Oct-98 | 31-Oct-98 | Total |
|---|---|---|---|---|---|---|---|---|
| Miles Driven | 12.00 | 14.00 | | | | | | 26.00 |
| Reimbursement | $0.30 | $3.60 | $4.20 | | | | | $7.80 |
| Parking And Tolls | | | $40.00 | | | | | $40.00 |
| Auto Rental | | $56.00 | $56.00 | | | | | $112.00 |
| Taxi/Limo | | | | | | | | |
| Other (Rail Or Bus) | | | | | | | | |
| Airfare | | $640.00 | | | | | | $640.00 |
| **TRANSPORTATION TOTAL** | | $699.60 | $100.20 | | | | | $799.80 |
| Lodging | | $113.49 | $113.49 | | | | | $226.98 |
| Breakfast | | $8.74 | | | | | | $8.74 |
| Lunch | | $11.19 | $13.42 | | | | | $24.61 |
| Dinner | | $21.57 | $25.05 | | | | | $46.62 |
| SUB-TOTAL MEALS | | $41.50 | $38.47 | | | | | $79.97 |
| **LODGING & MEALS SUBTOTAL** | | $154.99 | $151.96 | | | | | $306.95 |
| Supplies/ Equipment | | | | | | | | |
| Phone, Fax | | | | | | | | |
| ENTERTAINMENT | | | | | | | | |
| **TOTAL PER DAY** | | $854.59 | $252.16 | | | | | $1,106.75 |

**DETAILED ENTERTAINMENT RECORD**

| DATE | ITEM | PERSONS ENTERTAINED BUSINESS RELATIONSHIP | PLACE NAME & LOCATION | BUSINESS PURPOSE | AMOUNT |
|---|---|---|---|---|---|
| | | | | | |
| | | | | | |
| | | | | | |
| | | | | | |

| **PURPOSE OF TRIP** | **SUMMARY** | |
|---|---|---|
| | TOTAL EXPENSES | $1,106.75 |
| | LESS CASH ADVANCE | |
| | LESS COMPANY CHARGES | |
| | AMOUNT DUE EMPLOYEE | $1,106.75 |
| | AMOUNT DUE COMPANY | $0.00 |

| PREPARED BY | DATE | APPROVED BY | DATE |

# Summary

This lesson presented a number of Quattro Pro features that can help you work more efficiently. You learned that:

- the Spell Checker will compare each word in a document to its built-in dictionary, flagging any words it does not find.

- macros allow you to save a series of steps and then play them back whenever they are needed.

- you can create your own styles that can be applied to spreadsheet cells to speed up and standardize formatting.

- projects are predefined notebook templates into which you can insert your own data. You then save them under a new name. Projects are available for many common tasks, such as keeping track of savings and budgets.

## LESSON 12 REVIEW QUESTIONS

### TRUE/FALSE

**Circle the T if the statement is true. Circle the F if it is false.**

**T F** 1. Styles are premade notebook templates for performing tasks such as keeping track of budgets and loan payments.

**T F** 2. In order to make a macro available to notebooks other than the one in which it was created, you must place it in the Macro Library.

**T F** 3. You can add more words to the Spell Checker's built-in dictionary, if you wish.

**T F** 4. You can tell when a macro is being recorded because a red light appears at the bottom of the screen.

**T F** 5. You can see a list of available projects by opening the Insert menu and choosing Sheet.

## MATCHING

**Write the letter of the term in Column 2 that best matches the description in Column 1.**

**Column 1**

_____ **6.** A prerecorded series of steps.

_____ **7.** Compares each word to a built-in dictionary.

_____ **8.** Automatically corrects any words that are contained in its list of common misspellings.

_____ **9** Used to assign specified formats, such as font type, size, etc., to selected text.

_____ **10.** The skeleton of a notebook that you can complete.

**Column 2**

**A.** Macro

**B.** Project

**C.** Style

**D.** Spell Check

**E.** QuickCorrect

## LESSON 12 PROJECT

SCANS

### PROJECT 12A

1. Open the **west computers** notebook in the student **Datafile** folder. Save it as **west computers proj12a xxx**.

2. Spell check all four sheets in the notebook, correcting any errors.

3. Create a new style named **Lab Title**. This style should use the **Times New Roman** font and have a point size of **16**. The text color should be navy blue. The style should also specify that the title be centered across the columns containing data.

4. Apply the Lab Title style to the first two lines of the four sheets in this notebook.

5. Create a macro that will place your name in a footer on each sheet of this notebook. Your name should be at the lower right corner of each sheet. In addition, the current page number should be at the lower left corner. (Remember that the code for the page number is #p.)

6. Go to **Page** view and make certain that the footer has been properly inserted into the sheets.

7. Save the notebook and print all four sheets, each on a separate piece of paper. Close the notebook.

(continued on next page)

## PROJECT 12B

1.  Open the **File** menu and choose **New** to display a list of available projects. Open the **Budget, Personal** project. Save it as **budget proj12b xxx**.

2.  Create a listing of all of your income and expenses. Enter an amount for each of your expenses and income items in the ANNUAL column. Quattro Pro will calculate the monthly amounts, along with the percent of the entire budget taken up by each item.

3.  Save the notebook and print it.

4.  Close the notebook and exit Quattro Pro.

## CRITICAL THINKING ACTIVITY

SCANS

    Imagine that you are treasurer for your community's computer club. Examine the list of projects that are available in Quattro Pro. Pick at least two of them and explain how you might be able to use them in your job as treasurer. Give specific examples of how these projects might be useful.

# INTEGRATING COREL® WORDPERFECT® AND COREL® QUATTRO® PRO

## OBJECTIVES

**Upon completion of Integration 2, you will be able to:**

■ Use Copy and Paste to transfer information between WordPerfect and Quattro Pro.

■ Share information between WordPerfect and Quattro Pro using linking and embedding.

■ Explain the uses and advantages of linking and embedding.

■ Copy a map created in Quattro Pro to WordPerfect.

🕐 **Estimated Time: 4 hours**

A big advantage of using a suite of applications such as Corel® WordPerfect® Suite 8 is the ability to transfer or share information between the applications in the suite, which is referred to as *integration*. Using each application to do what it is best suited to do and then sharing or transferring information between each application to create a document will maximize your efficiency during the integration process. In this lesson you will learn how to integrate between WordPerfect and Quattro Pro by combining elements created in both applications to create various documents.

Shown in Figure INT2-1 are three different integration procedures and their advantages and disadvantages.

Two terms often associated with the above procedures are *OLE* and *DDE*. OLE stands for Object Linking and Embedding. DDE stands for Dynamic Data Exchange. The main difference between these two terms is an OLE object can be linked or embedded, while DDE objects can only be linked.

| Method | Task | Advantages and Disadvantages |
|---|---|---|
| *Pasting* | Using Copy and Paste commands, the information that is pasted from the source application takes on the format of the destination application. This can result in a loss or change of formatting if the destination application is a different type of software. For example, information copied from Quattro Pro and pasted into WordPerfect becomes text, or more specifically a table, and loses formatting and formulas. | Copying and pasting between applications is an easy process. The size of a file is not as large when information is pasted as when it is embedded. A disadvantage is that if changes need to be made to the pasted object, the original object may need to be edited and then pasted again. Often information that is pasted is inserted as simple text and the formatting is lost. |
| *Embedding* | Using the Paste Special command when pasting embeds an object. An embedded object is a separate object within the document in which it is embedded. When editing changes occur, the source application's features of the embedded object are used. The embedded copy has no connection to the source file, so changes only affect the copy in the destination document. Using Insert and Object results in an embedded object also. | Using the source application to edit the object often makes the job easier than trying to use the destination application. Another advantage is that all the information that belongs to a document is in one file. The original program must be available for editing the edited object. A main disadvantage is that an embedded file can be very large in size. |
| *Linking* | Using the Paste Link option in Paste Special links an object. A linked object has a direct connection, or link, to the original file. When changes are made in the original file, the changes also occur in the linked object. | Having a link with the original document makes updating the linked object easy. The original file must be on the same server or disk drive and the application used to create the linked object must be available. A disadvantage is that a link can be broken if you move or rename the source file. |

# *Embedding a Quattro Pro Object into a WordPerfect Document*

The procedure for embedding an object includes copying the information from the source application and then choosing Paste Special and Paste in the target application. Dr. Paradeis has received information from the Licensing Department in the city of Austin regarding the number of cats and dogs that have been licensed in the past three years and the number of pets that have been spayed or neutered. He thought this information would help him identify trends and perhaps would be good information to share with potential customers.

First of all, you are going to create the charts in Quattro Pro that will be embedded in the WordPerfect document.

SCANS

1. Start Quattro Pro. Then open **licenses.wb3** from your student **Datafile** folder. Save the file as **licenses xxx** to your integration disk that you started using in the first integration lesson.

2. Click the *Dogs* sheet, if necessary.

3. Select cells **A4...D7**. Open the **Insert** menu and choose **Chart**. The Chart Expert appears. Answer the prompts as follows:
   a. Step 1—Click **Next**.
   b. Step 2—Choose **Rotated Bar** as the type of chart. Click **Next**.
   c. Step 3—Choose the first chart in the Regular row. Click **Next**.
   d. Step 4—Choose **Grayscale** as the color scheme. Click **Next**.
   e. Step 5—Key the following information in the text boxes:

   | | |
   |---|---|
   | Title: | **Dog Licenses** |
   | Subtitle: | **City of Austin** |
   | X-Axis: | (leave blank) |
   | Y-Axis: | **Number of Dogs** |

   f. Leave the Current Sheet chosen as the destination.

4. Click **Finish** and draw the chart box starting at approximately cell A9 and continuing through cell F22.

5. Double click the chart to see the hatched line which indicates that you are in Edit mode. Make the following changes:
   a. Click the **View** menu and choose **Floating Chart**.
   b. Click the **Chart** menu and choose **Series**. In the Series dialog box key the following range in the *Legend* text box: **(Dogs:B3..D3)**.

6. Your chart should look like Figure INT2-2.

7. Switch to the *Cats* sheet and repeat the process for creating the same chart for the cats, except for keying the following information in Step 5:

   | | |
   |---|---|
   | Title: | **Cat Licenses** |
   | Subtitle: | **City of Austin** |
   | X-Axis Title: | (leave blank) |
   | Y-Axis Title: | **Number of Cats** |

8. Save the file as **licenses xxx** to your integration disk and print the entire notebook (it will all print on one page). Leave it open.

**FIGURE INT2-2**
Chart for Exercise INT2.1

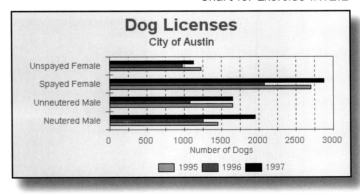

Now that you have created the charts, you will embed them in the following WordPerfect document.

## EXERCISE ▷ INT2.2

**1.** Start a new WordPerfect document. Save it as **animal licenses xxx** to your integration disk.

**2.** Retrieve the **Vet Letterhead** style. If you cannot remember how to do this, refer to the first integration lesson.

**3.** Center the following title using **14** pt., **Bold**, and **Arial**:

**Animal Licensing**
**1995-1997**

**4.** Change the justification to **Left**. Change the font back to **12** pt., **Regular**, and **Times New Roman**.

**5.** Press **Enter** twice and key the paragraph in the box at the right:

**6.** Press **Enter** two times.

**7.** Switch to the Corel Quattro Pro document **licenses xxx** using the Taskbar and click the chart in the *Dogs* sheet to select it so there are handles—not a hatched line.

**8.** Click **Edit** and **Copy**, and then switch back to the Corel WordPerfect document using the Taskbar.

**9.** Click **Edit** and **Paste Special**. Choose **Paste** and make sure **Corel Quattro Pro 8 Chart** is selected. Click **OK**. Your dialog box should look like the one in Figure INT2-3.

> Getting dogs and cats licensed is a law in Austin. The cost of a license for a male dog or cat that has been neutered and a female dog or cat that has been spayed is less expensive than a license for a male dog or cat that is not neutered as well as a female dog or cat that is not spayed. The reason for this is that the animals that have been altered are less likely to roam, are less aggressive toward people, and just make nicer pets. The chart below shows how many licenses were issued for dogs from 1995 through 1997.

**10.** Click below the chart you just added so there appears to be a couple of blank lines and key the following paragraph:

**FIGURE INT2-3**
Paste Special Dialog Box

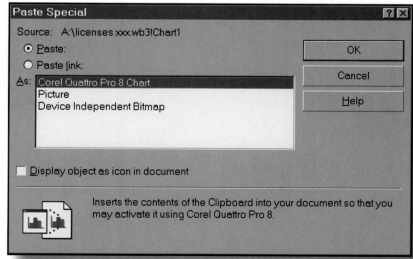

> Not all cities require cats to be licensed. Austin requires it because of health regulations. The chart below shows how many licenses were issued for cats from 1995 through 1997.

**11.** Press **Enter** two times.

**12.** Switch to **licenses xxx** using the Taskbar and click the chart in the *Cats* sheet to select it so there are handles—not a hatched line.

**13.** Click **Edit** and **Copy**, and then switch back to the Corel WordPerfect document using the Taskbar.

**14.** Click **Edit** and **Paste Special**. Choose **Paste** and make sure **Corel Quattro Pro 8 Chart** is selected. Click **OK**. Your finished document should look similar to Figure INT2-4.

**15.** Press **Enter** to move your insertion point below the second chart, and play the **pf** macro.

**16.** Save the file again as **animal licenses xxx**, but keep it open for the next exercise.

**FIGURE INT2-4**
Completed Document for Exercise INT2.2

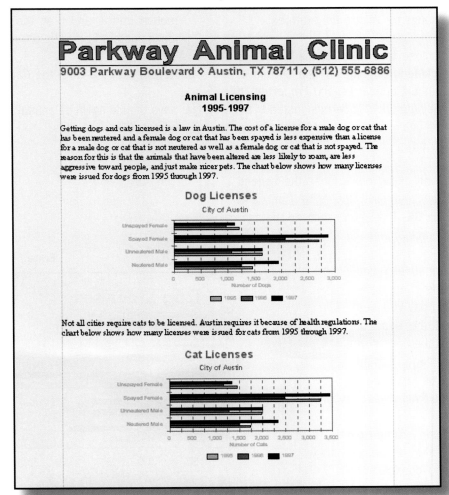

# Editing an Embedded Object

$N$ow you are going to see what happens when you edit an embedded object. When you double click the object, you will see the features of the source application appear, which in this case is Quattro Pro.

## EXERCISE ⟹ INT2.3

1. You are going to edit the embedded charts to change the position of the legend and to change the formatting of the values on the y-axis.

2. Double click the *Dogs* chart. The hatched line appears and you see the Menu Bar and Toolbars change to Quattro Pro features.

3. Right click close to the left of the legend so that a QuickMenu appears. At the bottom of the menu should appear *Legend Properties*. If you see *Background Properties* instead, try right clicking again. Click **Legend Properties** in the QuickMenu.

4. In the Legend dialog box choose the **Legend Position** tab and click the third (far right) choice. Click **OK**. The legend shifts to the right side of the chart.

5. Right click the y-axis where the numbers appear so that you see handles at the ends of the axis. At the bottom of the QuickMenu should appear *Y-Axis Properties*. Click **Y-Axis Properties**.

6. Click the **Numeric Format** tab. Choose **Comma** and change the number of decimals to **zero**. Click **OK**.

7. Click away from the chart to get out of Edit mode. There should still be handles on the chart but no hatched line. The results of your formatting should resemble Figure INT2-5.

8. Center the chart by moving the pointer over the chart until you see four arrows. Hold down the mouse button and drag the chart so that it looks centered between the margins.

9. Repeat Steps 2–8 for the *Cats* chart.

10. Save the file again as **animal licenses xxx** and print it. Close the files.

**FIGURE INT2-5**
Edited Chart for INT2.3

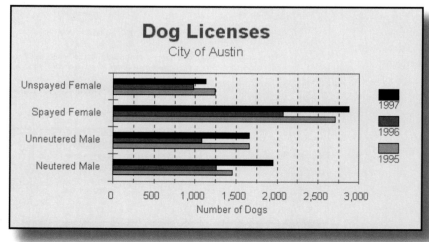

Do you think it was easy to embed the chart and to edit the embedded chart? If you do, then you are ready to try the last procedure for integration, which is linking.

Dr. Paradeis decides it is necessary to prepare information telling potential clients of the clinic's fees. These fees will be kept in a notebook you will create in Quattro Pro. The information will be copied to a WordPerfect file. Copying between applications is the same as copying between documents within one application. Basically, the information in the source application is selected and copied. In the destination document the Paste button is clicked and the data is copied. Modifications may have to be made after pasting.

## EXERCISE ▷ INT2.4

**SCANS**

1. Start a new WordPerfect document and save the file as **fees xxx** to your integration disk.

2. Retrieve the **Vet Letterhead** style.

3. Key the following paragraph:

> Thank you for calling Parkway Animal Clinic. Listed below are the fees for services provided for dogs and cats. All surgery fees include the charges for anesthesia, surgery, antibiotic injection, hospitalization, and recheck visit for suture removal, if required. If you have any questions, please feel free to call us at (512) 555-6886. We would like to help you to ensure the health and happiness of your cat and/or dog.

4. Press **Enter** twice after keying the paragraph.

5. Open Quattro Pro and open the notebook named **fees1998.wb3** from the student **Datafile** folder. Save the file as **fees1998 xxx** to your integration disk.

6. Click the **Both** sheet tab.

7. Turn off the grid lines by clicking **Format** and **Sheet**. Turn off both the Vertical and Horizontal Grid Lines because these will show in the object when it is pasted in WordPerfect.

8. Select the data from cells **A1:B33** and click the **Copy** button.

9. Switch back to WordPerfect by clicking the **Corel WordPerfect...** button on the Taskbar.

10. With the insertion point still two lines below the paragraph, click the **Paste** button or choose **Paste** from the **Edit** menu.

11. Notice that the information from Quattro Pro has been converted into a WordPerfect table. Some of the formatting has been lost and the first column may not be wide enough to show all of the text. Your document should look like Figure INT2-6.

12. Leave the file open and read on to continue with this document in Exercise INT2.5.

# Parkway Animal Clinic

9003 Parkway Boulevard ◇ Austin, TX 78711 ◇ 512-555-6886

Thank you for calling Parkway Animal Clinic. Listed below are the fees for services provided for dogs and cats. All surgery fees include the charges for anesthesia, surgery, antibiotic injection, hospitalization, and recheck visit for suture removal, if required. If you have any questions, please feel free to call us at (512) 555-6886. We would like to help you ensure the health and happiness of your cat and/or dog.

### Parkway Animal Clinic Fees 1998

**Services for Dogs**

| Description | Fee |
| --- | --- |
| Office Visit | $12.00 |
| Dist-Hep-Lept-Pi-Parvo-Coro | $15.00 |
| Heartworm Check | $12.00 |
| Deworm | $5.00 |
| Lyme Vaccination | $17.00 |
| Bordetella Vaccination | $16.00 |
| Flea Prevention | $18.00 |
| Fecal Exam | $16.00 |
| Castration | $90.00 |
| Spay | $101.00 |
| Rabies Vaccination | $10.00 |
| Heartworm Pills | $5.00 |

**Services for Cats**

| Description | Fee |
| --- | --- |
| Office Visit | $12.00 |
| Pan-Rhino-Chlamy-Caliciv | $10.00 |
| Deworm | $5.00 |
| Feline Leukemia/FIV Test | $24.00 |
| Feline Leukemia Vaccination | $20.00 |
| Feline Infectious Peritonitis Vaccination | $9.00 |
| Flea Prevention | $18.00 |
| Fecal Exam | $16.00 |
| Castration | $55.00 |
| Spay | $85.00 |
| Rabies Vaccination | $10.00 |
| Heartworm Pills | $5.00 |
| Front Declaw | $65.00 |
| Sumed Declaw | $72.00 |
| Four Paw Declaw | $105.00 |

# *Linking Information*

While you know you could work on the table to align it and format the columns, you decide instead to try linking.

## EXERCISE ▷ INT2.5

**SCANS**

1. Undo the Paste command you just carried out by clicking the **Undo** button. If this does not work, then select the entire table, click the **Table** menu, and choose **Delete...Entire table**.

2. With the insertion point still two lines below the paragraph, choose **Edit** and the **Paste Special** button. The selected data that was copied in Quattro Pro should still be in the Clipboard.

**3.** Click **Paste link** and make sure that **Corel Quattro Pro 8 Notebook** is selected. Click **OK**.

**4.** The data from Quattro Pro is linked.

**5.** Make sure the linked data is still selected and has handles. Move the mouse pointer onto the data until you see four arrows. Drag the linked data so that it is centered between the margins.

**6.** Move your insertion point to the end of the document and play your **pf** macro.

**7.** Save the file as **fees xxx** to your integration disk and print the document. Leave the files open for Exercise INT2.6.

The next time you open **fees xxx**, you will see a dialog box like the one showing in Figure INT2-7, asking you if you want to update the information in the linked object. If you had made changes in **fees1998 xxx** since saving it last, then the information would be updated in the WordPerfect file containing the link.

To have your linked file update automatically when opening the file, select Spreadsheet/Database from the Insert menu and click Options. Then turn on the Update on Retrieve option.

You can view information about the links in your document by clicking Edit and Links. You will see the dialog box shown in Figure INT2-8. Notice that you can see where the source data is located, and what type of update is turned on. You can change the update from automatic to manual so that you always have to open this dialog box to update the link. Links are updated automatically unless you specify manual updating in Link Options. This is useful if you want more control over what information appears in your document. You can also break the link. When a link is broken, you then are left with the information but no link.

Just as you changed the embedded chart to see how the Quattro Pro features appeared, you will now edit the linked notebook. When you double click the notebook object, you will be taken back to the original notebook.

**FIGURE INT2-7**
Update Links Dialog Box

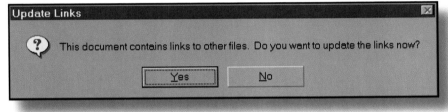

**FIGURE INT2-8**
Links Dialog Box

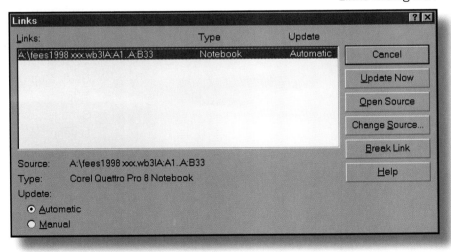

SCANS

1. Double click the linked data in **fees xxx**. You should now be in the source document **(fees1998 xxx)** in Quattro Pro.

2. Change the fee for the Dist-Hep-Lept-Pi-Parvo-Corn charge from *$15.00* to $23.00 by clicking in cell **B5** and keying **23**. Then press **Enter**. You do not have to key the dollar sign or two decimal places because the cell is formatted for currency.

3. Now switch to the WordPerfect file by clicking the Taskbar. Do you see that the figure in the linked object is also $23.00?

4. Print the **fees xxx** document and exit WordPerfect, but do not save the changes.

# Creating a Map in Quattro Pro

Dr. Paradeis has received statistics in a Quattro Pro file from a colleague on the number of heartworm disease cases in the United States. He decides he wants to make a map chart of the statistics and then display this map on a flyer he wants created in WordPerfect to alert customers of the prevalence of this disease.

SCANS

1. Open a file in Quattro Pro named **heartworm** from the student **Datafile** folder. Save the file as **heartworm xxx** to your integration disk.

2. Select cells **A2..B52**.

3. Choose **Graphics** from the **Insert** menu. Click **Map**.

4. The Map Expert begins. Complete the information in each window as follows:

| | |
|---|---|
| Map: | **USA by State (AK and HI insets)** Click **Next**. |
| Region names: | **A:A2..A52** |
| Color data: | **A:B2..B52** |
| Pattern data: | **Blank** Click **Next**. |
| Color scheme: | **Blues: Dark** Click **Next**. |
| Other Map Overlays: | **None** Click **Next**. |
| Title: | **Heartworm Disease** |
| Subtitle: | **United States - 1997** |
| Legend: | **Blank** |
| Destination: | **Current Sheet** Click **Finish**. |

5. Click **Finish**. Draw the map from approximately cells D2..I17. Your file should resemble Figure INT2-9.

6. Save the file as **heartworm2 xxx**. Print the file and leave it open for the next exercise.

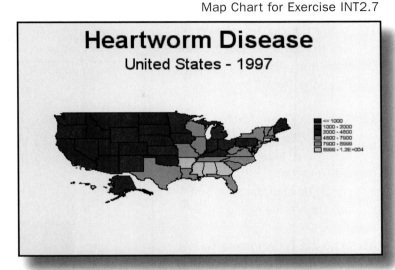

# Linking the Map to a WordPerfect File

Now that the map is completed, you will link it to a WordPerfect file and add a TextArt box that includes text that should stand out.

## EXERCISE ⟹ INT2.8

SCANS

1. Start a new WordPerfect file.

2. Switch to or open **heartworm2 xxx** from your integration disk.

3. Click the map and click the **Copy** button.

4. Switch back to the new WordPerfect file and choose **Edit** and **Paste Special**. Choose **Corel Quattro Pro 8 Notebook** and click **Paste link**.

5. Click **OK**. The map should appear in the WordPerfect file.

6. With the map selected, resize the map graphic using the lower right handle so that it is approximately two-thirds of the page (inside the margins). Click away to deselect the map.

7. If the Graphics Toolbar is not on, choose **View** and **Toolbars**. Turn on **Graphics**.

8. From the Graphics Toolbar, click the **TextArt** button. Key the following text:
**Protect Your Pet From This Disease!**

9. Choose the **Shadow** button on the 2-D tab and choose a **dark blue** for the text color and a **light gray** for the shadow color.

(continued on next page)

**10.** In the General tab change the font to **Arial** and choose **Center** from the Alignment button. Close the TextArt dialog box.

**11.** Right click the TextArt frame and choose **Size**. In the Size dialog box leave the width at the default setting, which should be approximately 6.88", and change the height to **.80"**.

**12.** Move the TextArt frame so that it is centered between the margins at the bottom of the page. Your finished document should look similar to Figure INT2-10.

**13.** Move your insertion point so it is at the end of your file and play your **pf** macro.

**14.** Save the file as **heartworm flyer xxx** to your integration disk and print it. Close the document. Exit WordPerfect and exit Quattro Pro.

**FIGURE INT2-10**
Completed Exercise INT2.7

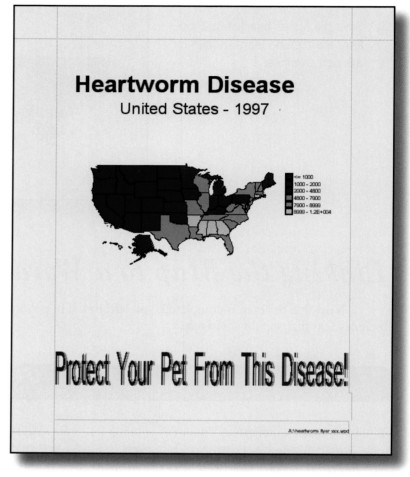

# *Summary*

This lesson contains procedures for integrating information between WordPerfect and Quattro Pro. You learned that:

- there are three basic procedures for integrating between applications.

- embedding can be done through the use of the Insert menu.

- embedding can also be done by using the Paste Special command in the Edit menu.

- double clicking on an embedded object brings up the features of the source application but does not change the original or source document.

- linking can be done by using the Paste Special command in the Edit menu and choosing the Paste link option.

- double clicking a linked object actually opens the source document for editing.

- changes made in the source document directly change the linked object.

- a link can be automatic or manual and a link can be broken.

- copying and pasting may have its drawbacks because the pasted data takes on the formatting of the destination application.

## INTEGRATION 2 REVIEW QUESTIONS

### FILL IN THE BLANKS

**Complete each of the following statements by writing your answer in the blank provided.**

1. The ability to transfer or share information between software applications is referred to as
_____.

2. Information that is selected and copied is kept in the _____, which is a temporary memory in Windows.

3. The integration procedure that directly affects the destination document when changes are made in the source document is called _____.

4. Besides copying and pasting using Paste Special, _____ can also be done by opening the Insert menu and choosing the object.

5. Two terms often associated with integration are _____ and _____.

### TRUE / FALSE

**Circle the T if the statement is true. Circle the F if it is false.**

**T    F    6.** To embed data from the source document to the destination document, you use the Copy and Paste commands.

**T    F    7.** Double clicking an object that is linked opens the source document in its original application.

**T    F    8.** Breaking a link will cause the object to be deleted.

**T    F    9.** It is not necessary for the linked file to be stored on the same drive as the file containing the linked object.

**T    F    10.** The application in which the embedded object was created must be available on the same computer as the destination file for editing.

Dr. Paradeis is an active member of the Friends of the Shelter Humane Society in Austin. As a member of the Society, he has volunteered to head the education committee that informs the public of the services of the Parkway Animal Shelter. Because Animal Appreciation Week is coming up on November 2 – 8, the committee decided to sponsor an open house at the Parkway Animal Shelter on November 8. Dr. Paradeis needs a flyer created that will be posted in public buildings. He has given you his go-ahead to be creative, but certain items need to be included in the flyer. One of the items is a pie chart that shows the outtake status of the animals in 199X.

## PROJECT INT2A

1. Open the **outtake199X** file from your student **Datafile** folder. Save it as **outtake199X xxx** to your integration disk.

2. Figure the totals for cells B7..F7 using the **Sum** button.

3. Select cells **C7..F7** because when you want to make a pie chart, you should select contents in only one row or one column.

4. Choose **Chart** from the **Insert** menu and answer the prompts as follows:
   Confirm the range (cells C7..F7).
   Select the Pie type.
   Select the second pie in the Regular shape row (3-D pie).
   Leave the color scheme as the default.
   Title the chart          **Parkway Animal Shelter**.
   Subtitle the chart        **199X Annual Outtake Report**.
   Click **Finish** and draw the chart from approximately cells B9..E26.

5. Double click to edit the chart.

6. Right click directly on the pie and choose **Pie Chart Properties** from the QuickMenu.

   In the *Label Options* section key **(A:C4..F4)** and choose **None**.

   In the *Text Font* section change to a point size of **14**. The chart should look like Figure INT2-11.

7. Save the file, print it, and leave the file open.

**FIGURE INT2-11**
Completed Project INT2A

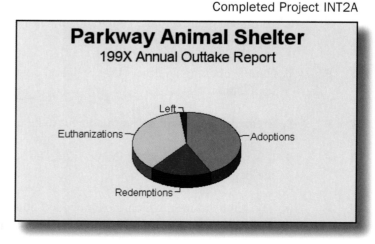

Now that you have that part completed, you will link this chart to the flyer that you will create.

## PROJECT INT2B

1. Start a new WordPerfect file and save it as **animal shelter xxx**.

2. At the top of the page, embed a TextArt object by choosing the **Insert** menu and then choosing **Graphics** and **TextArt**.

3. Key **Open House**.

4. You make the choices on the formatting of the TextArt object.

5. Press **Enter** twice to leave two blank lines below the TextArt object.

6. Change the font to **32 pt.**, **Arial**, **Bold** and change the paragraph format to **Center** justification. Then key the following lines:
**Parkway Animal Shelter**
**November 8, 199X**
**10 a.m. - 4 p.m.**

7. Press **Enter** twice and key the following bullet list, making sure that the justification is **Left**, the font is **Arial**, and the size is **16** pt.
**Tour the shelter**
**Talk to our staff**
**Meet our animals**
**Find out about our services**
**Learn about our Adopt-A-Friend program**

8. Press Enter twice and key the following line centered, keeping the same font:
**Sponsored by**

9. Press Enter, change the font to **Comic Sans MS**, and center the following lines:
**friends of the**
**shelter**

10. Link the pie chart you created in the **outtake199X xxx** file to the **animal shelter xxx** file using the **Copy**, **Paste Special**, and **Paste link** commands.

 **NOTE:**

Don't be alarmed that you cannot view all of the pie slice labels. You will correct that in the following steps.

11. Move the pie to where you think it is most appropriate. Size the pie to be about 3" wide by 3" tall. You can do this by right clicking the chart after it is linked and choosing **Size** from the QuickMenu. Check the dimensions in the Size dialog box.

12. Insert the following two graphics from your disk: **cartoon dog** and **cartoon cat**, which are in your student **Datafile** folder. Move these two graphics where you think they fit the best.

13. Right click each graphic (one at a time) and choose **Size**. Size each graphic to about 1.5" to 2" wide and turn on **Maintain proportions under Height**.

14. Right click each graphic again and choose **Wrap**. Choose **In front of text** for the Wrap type.

15. Double click the chart and change the data in the notebook to the following:
    D6 = 220
    E6 = 276

**FIGURE INT2-12**
Possible Solution for Project INT2B

16. Right click the slice representing the adoptions and choose **Pie Chart Properties**. In the **Explode Slice** tab set the distance in the Explode Slice to **20**.

17. Return to the **animal shelter xxx** file. Do you see the changes in the chart?

18. Move your insertion point to the end of the document and play your **pf** macro.

19. Save the file with the same name and print it. A sample of how it could look is showing in Figure INT2-12.

SCANS

You want a chart to appear in your WordPerfect document. A chart can be created from a table in WordPerfect, and a chart can be created from data in a Quattro Pro file and then be embedded or linked in a WordPerfect file. What would be the advantages and/or disadvantages of both methods?

# COREL®
# PRESENTATIONS™ 8

# CREATING YOUR FIRST PRESENTATION

## *Introduction*

This lesson will teach you how to plan and create a Corel® Presentations™ slide show. You are probably quite excited about learning to use Presentations and are ready to start keying and clicking. Remember, though, that Presentations is the *tool* you will use to create your slide show. Before you can use this tool effectively, you need to plan and organize your presentation.

## *Planning Your Slide Show*

Following is a list of steps you can follow to plan your slide show:

1. **Define the presentation's purpose.** Every presentation should have a purpose, and you should know that purpose before creating slides. Defining your purpose will help you to convey your message clearly to your audience. For example, some presentation purposes might be:

   - Selling a product
   - Teaching a concept
   - Kicking off a group project

2. **Gather and organize the necessary materials.** Collect the materials you need, such as reports, articles, product literature, spreadsheets, or schedules. Next, organize these materials and write a rough outline for the slide show.

3. **Prepare the slides.** When you create slides, keep the wording concise. Use the slides to display key thoughts that you, as the speaker, can explain in more detail to the audience.

4. **Review the presentation.** Check your presentation to make sure it is professional in appearance. Check the spelling and grammar of the text, and the consistency of the slides' appearance. For example, does each slide's title use the same font face, size, and color? If not, is there a good reason why they are different?

## Grammatically Parallel Headings

You should structure your titles and subtitles so they are grammatically parallel; that is, they use the same grammatical structure. For example, if you use a command verb to begin the title of the first slide, all slide titles should begin with a command verb. Look at the following chart for examples of grammatically parallel and nonparallel headings:

| Parallel Headings | Nonparallel Headings |
| --- | --- |
| Listen to the Problem | Listen to the Problem |
| Ask Questions | Next, Ask Questions |
| Plan a Solution | Planning the Solution |

Subtitles should also be grammatically parallel to one another, but they may have a different grammatical structure from the titles. For example:

**Title:**       Writing Screenplays for Fun and Profit
**Subtitle:**   Your Ticket to a New Career

# *Creating a New Presentation*

Before you can create slides, you must decide what type of slide show to create and what you want the slide background to look like. The New dialog box and the Master Gallery dialog box offer you several options to start and design your slide show.

## The New Dialog Box

When you start Presentations, the New dialog box appears. If necessary, you can click on the Create New tab to display it, as shown in Figure 1-1.

In this dialog box you can make the following choices:

■ Create a new Presentations slide show.

■ Create a new Presentations slide show using a predesigned template, such as Annual Report Slide Show or Team Meeting Slide Show. When you choose such an option, the

**FIGURE 1-1**
The New Dialog Box

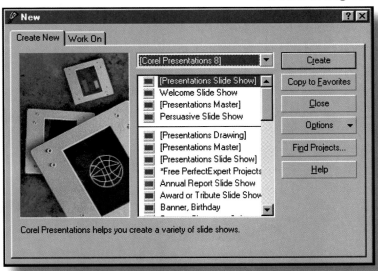

Corel Presentations helps you create a variety of slide shows.

PerfectExpert appears. The PerfectExpert is a Presentations tool that guides you through the creation process.

- Create a new Presentations *master*, the combination of a predesigned graphic *background* and a *layout*, the way text is formatted and positioned on the slide.

- Create a new drawing using Presentations' drawing tools.

- Edit an existing slide show.

- Open a slide show from a list of files you have worked on recently.

## The Startup Master Gallery Dialog Box

If you choose to create a new Presentations slide show, the Startup Master Gallery dialog box appears as shown in Figure 1-2.

Depending on how you or your instructor has installed Corel Presentations 8, not all of the masters that come with the program may be available. You will still have several masters to choose from.

**FIGURE 1-2**
The Startup Master Gallery Dialog Box

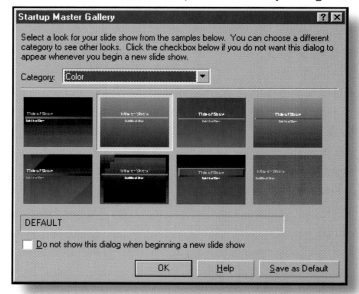

The Startup Master Gallery is a collection of professionally designed backgrounds for your slides. The *Category* drop-down list box enables you to select from the following categories:

- 35mm (for 35mm slides)

- Business

- Color

- Design

- Nature

- Printout (black-and-white options that print well on standard printers)

- Theme

To choose a master from the Startup Master Gallery:

■ Choose the category desired and then click on one of the master samples to select it. Click OK to apply it to the new slide show.

■ If you do not choose a master, Presentations will select the *DEFAULT* master, a green background from the Color category.

E X E R C I S E ⇨ PR1.1

1. To start Presentations, click the **Start** menu and select **Corel WordPerfect Suite 8**, then select **Corel Presentations 8**. The New dialog box appears.

2. In the New dialog box make sure the **[Presentations Slide Show]** option is highlighted. Click **Create**. The Startup Master Gallery dialog box appears.

3. In the Startup Master Gallery dialog box notice that the text below the master samples reads *DEFAULT*. Click **OK**. The Presentations working screen appears with the new slide's background and layout displayed, as shown in Figure 1-3.

4. Leave this on the screen for the next exercise.

**FIGURE 1-3**
The Presentations Working Screen

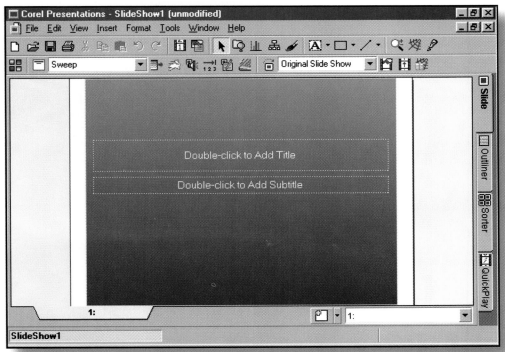

## Understanding The Presentations Working Screen

Your screen displays the new slide show, titled *SlideShow1*, with the *DEFAULT* master and the Title template displayed. The Title template provides a box for a title and a box for a subtitle. As you will learn in later lessons, other templates provide different kinds of boxes where you can insert information for your slide.

Notice that the Presentations working screen gives you access to a number of different tools to help you prepare your slide show: a Menu Bar, Toolbar, Property Bar, and View tabs. You will learn about more tools as you progress through the lessons.

# *Entering Text on a Slide*

Presentations has automated the process of entering text and other data on a slide. All layouts display one or more dotted boxes on the slide that tell you how to enter text into the box. The title slide, for example, has a box that tells you to *Double-click to Add Title*.

When you double click in a box, the dotted outline changes to a heavy blue-hatched border, as shown in Figure 1-4. This box is called the *text editor*. It contains an *insertion point* (the blinking vertical line) that indicates where your text will begin when you start keying. The box automatically changes depth to contain the text you enter. When you have finished entering text, click elsewhere on the screen to close the text editor. You can then enter text in another box, if desired.

**FIGURE 1-4**
The Text Editor

Even though your layout may show a number of boxes, you do not have to enter text in all of them. You can leave a box blank. The outline and the prompt will not appear in your final presentation.

If you need to make a correction to your text after you have closed the text editor, double click the text to reopen the text editor. Correct your text and then close the text editor.

INTERNET

A host is a computer that is attached directly to the Internet and that provides services to users. Host computers are also called "servers".

## EXERCISE ⇨ PR1.2

**1.** Insert the slide's title.

    **a.** Double click in the box that reads *Double-click to Add Title*. The dotted outline changes to a heavy blue-hatched border with a blinking insertion point in the center.

    **b.** Key the following title: **Proper Pet Care**.

    **c.** Click outside of the box to close the text editor.

**2.** Insert the slide's subtitle.

    **a.** Double click in the box that reads *Double-click to Add Subtitle*.

    **b.** Key the following subtitle: **Important Information for New Pet Owners**.

    **c.** Click outside of the box to close the text editor.

**3.** Leave the slide on the screen for the next exercise.

# Saving a Slide Show

As with most all computer applications, it is important to save your work. Frequent saving prevents loss of work due to a power failure or a system problem that shuts down your program.

There are two commands on the File menu used for saving: Save and Save As. There is also a Save button on the Toolbar. When you save a slide show, Presentations automatically assigns the extension *.shw* to the file.

**NOTE:**

Depending on how you have set up your Windows95 folder View properties, you may not be able to see the MS-DOS extensions such as *.shw* at the end of your file names. For information on how to display these extensions, see the topic *extensions, filename* in your Windows 95® Help file.

For more information on saving, please see the Getting Started section at the beginning of this book.

Before you attempt Exercise PR1.3, ask your instructor for more information about where you will save your files.

## EXERCISE ⇨ PR1.3

**SCANS**

**1.** Insert your data disk into the appropriate drive.

**2.** Click the **File** menu and select **Save**. The Save As dialog box appears, as shown in Figure 1-5.

**3.** Click the *Save in* drop-down list box. Select the drive name, then the folder, if necessary, where you will store your files.

(continued on next page)

**4.** In the *File name* text box at the bottom of the dialog box, key the file name **pet care 1-3 xxx** (use your initials in place of *xxx*).

**5.** Click **Save**. You will see a graphic representation of the file-saving process, then Presentations returns you to the working screen.

**6.** Notice that the title bar now displays the new filename.

**7.** Click the **File** menu and select **Close**.

**FIGURE 1-5**
The Save As Dialog Box

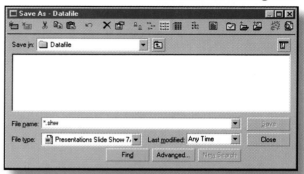

 **NOTE:**

Before keying a long filename, consider where your slide show file might end up. If it is used on a system that does not support this feature, the long filename will be shortened to eight characters, potentially making it hard to identify.

# *Summary*

In this lesson you learned that:

■ you must plan to create a successful, coherent presentation. Once you have a plan, you can use Corel Presentations as a tool to create your slide show.

■ before you create slides, you need to start a new presentation and choose a master.

■ Presentations provides several different slide layouts with varied numbers and placements of text boxes. These boxes provide you with instructions on how to enter text.

■ it is important to save your work frequently. You can use the Save or Save As command from the File menu, or the Save button on the Toolbar.

## LESSON 1 REVIEW QUESTIONS

### TRUE/FALSE

**Circle the T if the statement is true. Circle the F if the statement is false.**

**T  F  1.** You should define the purpose of a slide show after you create the slides.

**T  F  2.** **Tying Your Shoe** and **Buckle Your Belt** are parallel headings.

**T  F   3.** The Master Gallery enables you to choose different slide backgrounds.

**T  F   4.** If a slide has an empty text box, you must fill it with text.

**T  F   5.** When you save a slide show, you must key the extension *.shw* at the end of each filename.

## WRITTEN QUESTIONS

**Write your answers to the following questions.**

**6.** List the steps necessary to plan and organize a presentation.

**7.** Give examples of two parallel titles with parallel subtitles.

**8.** Name three of the different Master Gallery categories.

**9.** Explain what the term *default* means.

**10.** Give at least five different purposes for giving a presentation.

## LESSON 1 PROJECT

SCANS

### PROJECT 1A

You have just been hired as a consultant by Pet Paradise, a successful pet store chain in Austin, Texas, to create several slide shows. These slide shows will help Pet Paradise present a more organized and professional image to its customers, employees, and the surrounding community.

Your first assignment is to start a slide show for a presentation that Pet Paradise will make to prospective employees.

**1.** Start a new slide show.

**2.** In the Startup Master Gallery dialog box click the *Category* drop-down list box. Select **Theme**.

**3.** Select the master named *ROAD*.

**4.** Key the following title: **Working for Pet Paradise**.

**5.** Key the following subtitle: **Your Road to Success**.

**6.** Save the new slide show as **prospective employee 1a xxx**.

**7.** Close the slide show.

## PROJECT 1B

Create a slide show that will explain "Pet Perks," Pet Paradise's new customer rewards program.

1.  Start a new slide show.

2.  In the Startup Master Gallery dialog box choose the *ICE* master from the Color category.

3.  Key the following title: **Pet Perks**.

4.  Key the following subtitle: **Pet Paradise's Customer Rewards Programs**.

5.  Save the new slide show as **pet perks 1b xxx**.

6.  Close the slide show.

## PROJECT 1C

Paul and Polly Paradeis, the co-owners of Pet Paradise, are teaching a job preparation class at a local community center. Create a presentation for them that will teach people job interviewing techniques.

1.  Start a new slide show.

2.  In the Startup Master Gallery dialog box choose the *BUMPBAR* master from the Business category.

3.  Key the following title: **Winning First Impressions**.

4.  Key the following subtitle: **How to Interview Successfully**.

5.  Save the new slide show as **first impressions 1c xxx**.

6.  Close the slide show.

## CRITICAL THINKING ACTIVITY

**SCANS**

Think about different presentations, meetings, or lectures you have attended. What were the strengths that the speakers displayed? What, if any, were their obvious shortcomings? How could they have made their presentations more clear?

Discuss this with at least one other person. Make a list of five to ten things that a speaker needs to do to give a successful presentation.

# WORKING WITH TEXT SLIDES

## OBJECTIVES

**Upon completion of this lesson, you will be able to:**

■ Open an existing slide show.

■ Add and delete slides.

■ Switch between different slide views.

■ Add and delete text boxes.

■ Play a slide show.

■ Print the slides in a slide show.

 **Estimated Time: 1¹/₂ hours**

## *Introduction*

The first type of slide you will learn to create is a *text slide*. The Text Slide layout provides boxes for a title, subtitle, and a block of text. You may key one line or an entire paragraph. Remember, though, that you should keep your text as clear and concise as possible.

You can also add blocks of text to any slide, regardless of its layout, by inserting a *text box* onto it.

This lesson will also teach you to add and delete slides. You will also learn how to take advantage of the different views that Presentations offers.

Finally, you will learn how to play a slide show on your monitor and how to print copies of the slides.

## *Opening an Existing Presentation*

There are three common ways to open an existing slide show. Exercise PR2.1 will teach you all three methods.

# EXERCISE ⟩ PR2.1

1. Click the **File** menu and select **Open**, or click the **Open** button on the Toolbar.

2. Click the **Work On** tab of the New dialog box (see Figure 2-1).

3. Look for the name of the **pet care 1-3 xxx** presentation in the list box. If you see it listed, select it and click **Open**.

**FIGURE 2-1**
The Work On Tab

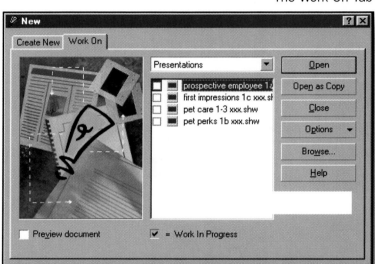

 **NOTE:**

If you do not see a file listed in the Work on tab of the New dialog box, you can click the Browse button to access the Open File dialog box.

4. Open another file using the Open File dialog box.
   a. Click the **File** menu and select **Open**, or click the **Open** button on the Toolbar. The Open File dialog box appears (see Figure 2-2).

   b. Select **prospective employee 1a xxx** and click **OK**. Presentations opens the file on the screen.
   c. Close this file so that you may practice opening it using another method.

**5.** Open a file using the files list at the bottom of the **File** menu.

    **a.** Click the **File** menu and locate the list of most recently used files at the bottom of the menu.

    **b.** Select **prospective employee 1a xxx**. Presentations opens the file on the screen.

    **c.** Close this file.

**6.** Leave the **pet care 1-3 xxx** slide show on the screen for the next exercise.

**FIGURE 2-2**
The Open File Dialog Box

---

### TIP

You can open up to nine slide shows at the same time in Presentations. Switch between them by clicking the Window menu and selecting the file name of the desired slide show.

# *Adding Slides*

You can add slides as you create your presentation, as well as insert new slides in between existing slides while editing. New slides have the same background as the existing slides, but you can apply predesigned page layouts called *templates*. Templates automatically format titles and text to ensure consistency from slide to slide.

To add a slide to your slide show, open the New Slide dialog box and select the desired template (Text or Bulleted List, for example). Key a number or click the spin arrows to select the number of desired slides.

## EXERCISE ⟹ PR2.2

**1.** Click the **Insert** menu and select **New Slide**. The New Slide dialog box appears (see Figure 2-3), displaying different slide type icons. You have a choice of Title, Bulleted List, Organization Chart, Data Chart, Combination, and None.

**2.** Select the desired slide layout and number of new slides.

    **a.** Click the third icon from the left in the first row. The Layout description should read *Text*.

    **b.** In the *Number to add* spin box, click the up spin arrow once to display the number *2*.

(continued on next page)

**FIGURE 2-3**
The New Slide Dialog Box

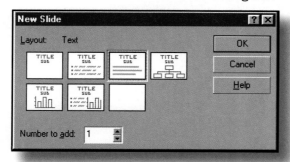

**NOTE:**

A *spin box* is a text box that has adjacent up and down, or spin, arrows. Spin boxes are generally used for numeric values. You can either key the value in the box or click on the up or down arrow to increase or decrease the value, respectively.

c. Click **OK**. Two new blank slides appear in the working area.

3. Enter text on Slide 2.
   a. Key the following title: **Your Pet and You**.
   b. Key the following subtitle: **The Start of a Beautiful Relationship**.
   c. In the *Double-click to Add Text* box, key the following sentences. Notice how the box expands to accommodate the text.

**Congratulations on choosing your newest friend. Whether he or she is a cat or dog, bird or fish, gerbil or turtle, your new pet will provide you with companionship and warm feelings.**

4. Close the text editor.

5. Key the following information on Slide 3:
   a. Title: **Your Friend in Need**
   b. Subtitle: **The Responsibilities of Pet Ownership**
   c. Text:

**As you look forward to many years with your pet, realize that they need much more than love. Pets require a proper diet, exercise, shelter, and a safe and stable environment.**

6. Add a new slide using the **New Slide** button.
   a. Find the **New Slide** button, located just to the right of the last slide tab. It is divided into two pieces, one with a picture and the other with an arrow.
   b. To select what type of slide you want to add, click the arrow button. Select **Insert Text Slide** from the pop-up menu. A new blank text slide appears on the screen.

7. Key the following information on Slide 4:
   a. Title: **Your Companion for Life**
   b. Subtitle: **The Everchanging Relationship**
   c. Text:

**Your pet will relate to you differently as he or she grows. The fact that your dog, for example, is less playful as she gets older, does not mean she cares for you any less.**

8. Close the text editor.

9. Save your changes in a new file so that you can keep the old version of the file intact.
   a. Click the **File** menu and select **Save As**. The Save As dialog box appears.
   b. Make sure that your student **Datafile** folder is the current folder.
   c. Key **pet care 2-2 xxx** in the *File name* text box and click **Save**.

10. Leave this slide on the screen for the next exercise.

# Deleting Slides

You can delete a slide or slides at any time from a slide show. Remember, once you delete a slide, it disappears permanently!

**E X E R C I S E ⇒ PR2.3**

**1.** Click the **Insert** menu and select **New Slide**.

**2.** Add a new title slide to the presentation.

**3.** Oops! You decide you don't need another slide, after all. Click the **Edit** menu and select **Delete Slides**.

**4.** The Delete Slide warning box appears. Click **Yes** to delete Slide 5 permanently.

**5.** Slide 4 reappears. Leave this slide on the screen for the next exercise.

# Viewing Slides

**FIGURE 2-4**
View Tabs

Presentations provides you with View tabs, as shown in Figure 2-4. These are three quick ways to access different views of your slides.

- The *Slide Editor view* is the view that appears on your screen now. It shows the slide as it will appear when presented or printed.

- The *Outliner view* shows the slides in outline form.

- The *Slide Sorter view* displays thumbnails of the slides in the order in which you have arranged them and gives the title of each. This view also provides additional information about transitions between slides. More on this topic will be covered in Lesson 11.

    To access any of these views, simply click its corresponding tab.

1.  Click the **View** menu and select **Slide Outliner**. Notice how the contents are listed as an outline, with each type of text (Title, Subtitle, and Text) indicated in the left margin.

2.  Also notice that for each slide, there is a slide icon in the left margin. Double click the icon for Slide 3. (You may have to scroll up to see Slide 3.) Slide 3 appears in Slide Editor view.

3.  Click the **Slide Sorter** tab on the right side of the working area. The slides appear as thumbnails on the screen, with information listed below.

4.  Add a slide in Slide Sorter view.
    a.  Click the arrow next to the New Slide button. A list of slide types appears. Select **Insert Title Slide**. A new blank slide appears.
    b.  Switch to Slide Editor view by clicking the **Slide Editor** tab on the right side of the working area.

5.  Insert the following text:
    a.  Title: **Presented by Pet Paradise**
    b.  Subtitle: **Serving Austin's Pet Owners Since 1988**

6.  Close the text editor and return to **Slide Sorter** view.

7.  Change the order of the slides.
    a.  Make sure that Slide 4 is selected. (The *Slide Select* drop-down list box will indicate *4: Presented by Pet Paradise*, and the entire slide will be outlined.)
    b.  Click anywhere on Slide 4 and hold down the mouse button as you drag to the left. The pointer changes to a slide attached to an arrow.
    c.  When a red vertical rule appears to the left of Slide 2, release the mouse button. Slide 4 should now be Slide 2.

8.  Change to **Slide Editor** view. Click the **Slide 1** tab at the bottom of the working area. Leave Slide 1 on the screen.

9.  Save your changes as **pet care 2-4 xxx**. Leave Slide 1 on the screen.

# Using Text Boxes

In addition to the template boxes, Presentations enables you to add your own text boxes. This may prove useful when customizing a slide show for a particular group. If you no longer want a text box, you can also delete it.

Exercise PR2.5 will teach you to add and delete text boxes to and from a slide.

# EXERCISE ⟹ PR2.5

1. Click the **Text Object Tools** icon (the letter A) on the Toolbar. When you click the tool, the pointer changes to a hand holding a box.

2. Position the pointer in the upper left corner of the slide, approximately one-quarter of an inch from the top and left edges. Hold down the mouse button and drag the box the entire width of the slide. Release the mouse button. Your screen should look like Figure 2-5.

3. In the text editor box key the following: **Presented to the Seniors & Pets Pairing Program**.

4. Close the text editor.

5. Add another text box to the bottom of the slide.

6. In the text editor box key the following: **Sample Text**. Close the text editor.

7. Delete the new text box.
   a. Click the text box once. A series of six small squares called *handles* appear around the box, indicating it is selected.
   b. Press **Backspace** or **Delete** to delete the box.

8. Save the slide show as **pet care 2-5 xxx** and leave Slide 1 on the screen for the next exercise.

**FIGURE 2-5**
The New Text Box

**Proper Pet Care**

Important Information for New Pet Owners

# *Playing a Slide Show*

While you will ultimately play the slide show when you present it to others, you will want to play it while you are working on it, too. This enables you to view the show as it will appear to your audience, without the text boxes, toolbars, and other program tools.

**INTERNET**

A browser is a software program that gives access to most Internet services. A browser is required to connect to the multimedia documents on the World Wide Web.

**E X E R C I S E** ⟹ **PR2.6**

1. Click the **View** menu and select **Play Slide Show**, or click the **Play Slide Show** button on the Property Bar. The Play Slide Show dialog box appears, as shown in Figure 2-6.

2. Accept the current settings in the Play Slide Show dialog box and click **Play**.

3. Wait for the first slide to appear. Click the left mouse button to advance through the slides. When you have reached the end of the slide show, Presentations redisplays the working screen.

4. Leave the working screen as is for the next exercise.

**FIGURE 2-6**
The Play Slide Show Dialog Box

# Printing a Slide Show

Presentations provides you with different printing options. To print a slide show, you can click the File menu and select Print, or click the Print button on the Toolbar. To print an entire copy of the slide show, click Print.

If you want to see how the slides will appear when printed, click the Print Preview button. Click anywhere on the preview screen to return to the Print dialog box.

You can also choose to print slide shows in other formats:

■ Click *Current view* to print only the slide currently on the screen.

■ Click *Slides* to print selected individual slides or a range of slides.

■ Click *Handouts* to print a designated number of slides as thumbnails on one page.

■ Click *Speaker notes* to print a slide as a thumbnail with your notes in a text box below it.

■ Click *Audience notes* to print a slide as a thumbnail with ruled lines beneath it for note taking.

## EXERCISE PR2.7

1. Click the **File** menu and select **Print**. The Print dialog box appears (see Figure 2-7).

2. In the *Print group* box, click the **Handouts** radio button.

3. In the *Number of slides per page* spin box, key **4**, if necessary.

4. Click the **Print Preview** button to preview your handouts. When finished, click anywhere on the preview screen to return to the Print dialog box.

5. Click **Print** to print the handouts.

6. Close this file without saving it.

**FIGURE 2-7**
The Print Dialog Box

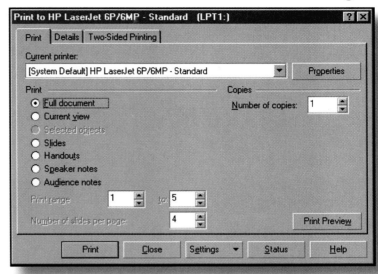

### Adjusting an Image to Black And White

By default, Presentations places a check mark in the *Adjust image to black and white* check box. This means that the printer will not attempt to print the color background of the slide. If you deselect this check box, it may take a long time to print each slide. Unless your printer can print at least 600 dpi resolution, your backgrounds will look very grainy. To save time and frustration, you are advised to print your slide shows adjusted for black and white.

# *Summary*

In this lesson you learned that:

- you can open an existing presentation and add and delete slides to and from it at any time.

- Presentations offers you three different views for looking at slides: Slide Editor view, Outline view, and Slide Sorter view.

- in addition to the large text block that appears when you create a new text slide, you can also add text boxes and position them wherever you want on the slide.

- you can print a slide show in several formats: as full-page slides or multiple thumbnails per page (called handouts). If desired, you can print speaker notes underneath the slides or blank lines for audience members to take notes.

## LESSON 2 REVIEW QUESTIONS

### MATCHING

**Write the letter of the term in Column 2 that best matches the description in Column 1.**

| Column 1 | Column 2 |
|---|---|
| _____ 1. Displays thumbnails of slides in order. | **A.** Outliner view |
| _____ 2. Paper printouts of slide thumbnails. | **B.** Handles |
| _____ 3. Displays slide title, subtitles, and text in outline form. | **C.** Slide Sorter view |
| _____ 4. Displays the slide visibly for editing. | **D.** Handouts |
| _____ 5. Small black boxes used as sizing tools. | **E.** Slide Editor view |

### WRITTEN QUESTIONS

**Write your answers to the following questions.**

6. Give a reason why you might want to insert a text box on a slide.

7. List at least three ways you can print slides.

8. How do you add a text slide to an existing presentation?

9. Why is it advisable to adjust your slides for black and white when printing?

10. When you play a slide show on your computer monitor, how do you advance to the next slide?

## LESSON 2 PROJECT

### PROJECT 2A

Add text slides to an existing slide show.

1. Start Presentations. Open **pet perks 1b xxx**.

2. Add text slides, inserting the titles, subtitles, and text listed below.

Slide 2
| | |
|---|---|
| Title: | **Repeat Rewards** |
| Subtitle: | **Get a Free Gift** |
| Text: | **Pet Paradise is grateful to you, our loyal customers. After all, you helped make us Austin's top-rated pet store! That is why we are giving all repeat customers the choice of a free Pet Paradise water dish, leash, or tote bag.** |

Slide 3
| | |
|---|---|
| Title: | **Bonus Bucks** |
| Subtitle: | **Buy Now and Save Later** |
| Text: | **For every $50 you spend, we will give you coupons called "Bonus Bucks," worth $25 off select merchandise.** |

Slide 4
| | |
|---|---|
| Title: | **Dog Days** |
| Subtitle: | **Check Out Our Summer Savings** |
| Text: | **Look for our annual summer promotion, the "Dog Days of Summer," which brings big discounts on our products and services.** |

Slide 5
| | |
|---|---|
| Title: | **Kredit Kickbacks** |
| Subtitle: | **Earn Points Every Time You Charge** |
| Text: | **For every dollar of every credit card purchase you make, we will give you one point. Accumulate 500 points and we will "kickback" $50.** |

3. Save the slide show as **pet perks 2a xxx**, then play it.

4. Print the slide show as slides, then close it.

(continued on next page)

## PROJECT 2B

Add, delete, and move text slides in a slide show.

**1.** Open **prospective employee 1a xxx**.

**2.** Add text slides, inserting the titles, subtitles, and text listed below.

Slide 2
Title:      **Introduction**
Subtitle:   **Hiring Immediately!**
Text:       **Pet Paradise is currently hiring. Thanks to tremendous growth, we are looking to fill several part- and full-time positions. This presentation will provide you with information about our growing company and our employment philosophy.**

Slide 3
Title:      **Company Overview**
Subtitle:   **Serving Pet Owners Since 1988**
Text:       **Founded in 1988, Pet Paradise is a full-service pet store chain. Currently, we have two locations in Austin, and we are planning to open a third store next year.**

Slide 4
Title:      **Products & Services**
Subtitle:   **Providing One-Stop Shopping**
Text:       **We sell pets and pet supplies, and we provide a full array of related services, including grooming, training, pet sitting, short- and long-term lodging, and owner education.**

Slide 5
Title:      **Employment Drive**
Subtitle:   **Seeking Animal Lovers**
Text:       **We need people to support our rapidly growing clientele. You do not need any previous pet store experience--just a love and respect for animals.**

Slide 6
Title:      **On-the-Job Training**
Subtitle:   **Offering Paid Cross-Training**
Text:       **All new hires receive on-the-job training in Animal Care and Customer Service. We also cross-train our employees on at least two positions.**

Slide 7
Title:      **Part- and Full-Time Positions**
Subtitle:   **Molding Our Schedule to Fit Yours**
Text:       **Our part-time positions are perfect for high school and college students, as well as for people looking for supplemental income. There are also full-time positions for people seeking to begin a career.**

Slide 8
Title:      **Benefits Package**
Subtitle:   **Caring for Our Employees**
Text:       **Our benefits package includes a competitive hourly wage, semi-annual raise reviews, two weeks paid vacation, health insurance, and free uniforms.**

Slide 9
Title:          **Pre-Employment Tour**
Subtitle:       **Inviting Prospective Employees**
Text:           **Come to one of our two locations and ask the manager for a tour.  He or she will be happy to show you our business in action.**

Slide 10
Title:          **Conclusion**
Subtitle:       **Seeking All Interested Applicants**
Text:           **Fill out an application, and ask the presenter any questions you might have. Thank you for attending today's presentation!**

3.  Save the slide show as **prospective employee 2b xxx**.

4.  The logical order of the slide show flows better if the information about part- and full-time positions precedes the information about free training. Move Slide 7 in front of Slide 6.

5.  Because so many people have been attending the prospective employee presentations, the managers have decided to limit tours to applicants who pass the first interview. Delete Slide 9 from the slide show.

6.  Save the slide show under the same name, then play it.

7.  Print the slide show as handouts with four slides per page.

8.  Close the slide show.

## CRITICAL THINKING ACTIVITY

SCANS

    Your U.S. Government instructor heard that you are learning Corel Presentations, and has asked you to prepare a slide show for her class lecture on the Bill of Rights. Prepare the show with a title slide, a text slide that introduces the Bill of Rights, and subsequent text slides summarizing each right.

# EDITING, FORMATTING, AND CUSTOMIZING TEXT SLIDES

## *Introduction*

Once you create a slide show, you will want to improve its appearance so that it grabs the attention of your audience. Presentations offers you a number of tools to edit and format your text. You can also change the master for a slide show to achieve a different look.

## *Changing Masters in an Existing Slide Show*

You can change the master at any time after you have begun the slide show. Remember, though, that some masters have different layouts, and this will affect the appearance of your text. For example, some masters automatically center-justify text, while others left-justify it. If you modify text properties using the format commands, your text will retain its new formatting, but it may not look as good on some backgrounds. You are advised to establish your master before formatting text.

Exercise PR3.1 will teach you how to change a master.

E X E R C I S E ▷ PR3.1

1. Open **pet care 2-5 xxx**.

2. Select **Slide Sorter** view. Note how all the slides currently have the *DEFAULT* master applied.

3. Apply a new master to the project.
   a. Click the **Format** menu and select **Master Gallery**.

   b. Click the *Category* drop-down list box and select *THEME*.
   c. Select the *PARCHMENT* master and click **OK**. Note how all the slides take on the properties of the *PARCHMENT* master.

4. Save the slide show as **pet care 3-1 xxx**. Switch back to Slide Editor view and leave the slide show on the screen for the next exercise.

# Editing a Text Slide

To change, delete, or add text in an existing text block, open the text editor by double clicking on the text block. When the text editor is activated, the pointer becomes an *I-beam* you can use to make changes.

- To highlight text (select individual characters or phrases) for editing, click and drag the I-beam to highlight the appropriate text. To deselect text, click outside the selected text.

- To insert text, position the I-beam where you want the new text to begin, then key the text.

- To delete text, highlight the text you want to delete and then press Backspace or Delete.

   You need to make a few changes to the text on the *Pet Care* show slides. Make the changes given in Exercise PR3.2.

E X E R C I S E ▷ PR3.2

SCANS

1. On Slide 2 you need to delete a word from the subtitle.
   a. Double click the subtitle to open the text editor.
   b. Click to position the I-beam after the word *Serving*. Press the **Delete** key to remove the word *Austin's*.
   c. Close the text editor.

2. On Slide 4 you need to add a sentence to the text.
   a. Double click the text to open the text editor.

   b. Add the following sentence to the end of the text: **In many ways, your pet relies on you as a child relies on a parent.**
   c. Close the text editor.

3. Save the slide show as **pet care 3-2 xxx**. Print the slide show. Leave it on the screen for the next exercise.

# Moving Text Boxes

Before you can move a text box, you must first select it with the pointer. Exercise PR3.3 will teach you how to move a box to a new location.

## EXERCISE ▷ PR3.3

1. Display Slide 1. Click once on the text box at the top of the slide that contains the text *Presented to the Seniors & Pets Pairing Program.* Handles appear, indicating the box is selected (see Figure 3-1).

2. With the pointer inside the text box, hold down the mouse button and drag the box to the bottom of the slide. A dashed line shows the outline of the text box so you can easily position it.

**FIGURE 3-1**
Handles

Presented to the Seniors & Pets Pairing Program

3. Release the mouse button. Click outside of the box to deselect it.

4. Save the file as **pet care 3-3 xxx**, and print Slide 1. Then, close the slide show.

# Inserting Symbols

The Symbols dialog box (see Figure 3-2) enables you to insert special symbols that are not on the keyboard, such as typographic symbols (©, $^1/_2$, –), mathematical and scientific characters ($\Sigma$, Å, $\infty$), and multinational characters (ü, ç, ñ).

Exercise PR3.4 will teach you how to insert a symbol into a text box.

## EXERCISE ▷ PR3.4

1. Open **prospective employee 2b xxx**. Select **Slide 5**.

2. Double click the text box to open the text editor.

3. Place the cursor after the word *experience*. Delete the two hyphens.

4. Click the **Insert** menu and select **Symbol.** The Symbols dialog box appears (see Figure 3-2).

5. Click the Set list and select **Typographic Symbols**.

6. Click the scroll bar until you see the dash shown in Figure 3-2. Select the dash and click **Insert and Close**.

7. Close the text editor. Save the file as **prospective employee 3-4 xxx** and print Slide 5. Then, close the slide show.

Notice that the Symbols dialog box has a *Numbers* text box. Each symbol has a two-number code, such as *4,34* for an em dash. You can memorize these for the characters you use frequently to save yourself time.

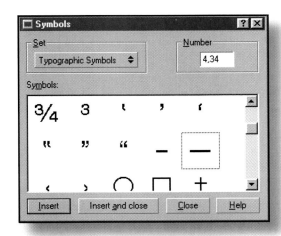

**FIGURE 3-2**
The Symbols Dialog Box

## *Inserting the Date and Time*

The Date/Time dialog box (see Figure 3-3) enables you to insert the date and/or time into a text box in a variety of formats.

### EXERCISE ⇒ PR3.5

1. Open **pet care 3-3 xxx**. Select **Slide 1**.

2. Double click the text box at the bottom of the slide to open the text editor. Position the I-beam at the end of the text. Press **Enter** to start a new line.

3. Click the **Insert** menu and select **Date/Time**. The Date/Time dialog box appears (see Figure 3-3).

4. Select the date format that shows the day of the week and the date, such as *Thursday, January 1, 1998*.

5. Click the **Keep the inserted date current** check box to make the date always appear current when you open the file. Click **Insert**.

6. Close the text editor.

7. Save the file as **pet care 3-5 xxx** and print Slide 1. Then, close the slide show.

**FIGURE 3-3**
The Date/Time Dialog Box

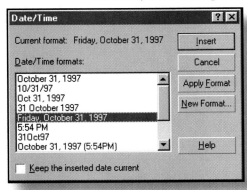

# Spell Checking

Nothing is more unprofessional than spelling errors in a slide show. Always spell check every presentation you create.

**NOTE:**

The Spell Checker cannot identify errors in word selection, such as "Your the Boss." Proofread your work carefully!

You can select and spell check individual text boxes in Slide Editor view. The easiest way to spell check, however, is to check the entire presentation at once in Outliner view. To begin your spell check:

- Switch to Outliner view.

- Click the Tools menu and select Spell Check. The Writing Tools dialog box appears, opened to the Spell Checker tab.

When the Spell Checker finds a possible error, it highlights the word in the outline and offers a list of suggested corrections, as shown in Figure 3-4.

**FIGURE 3-4**

The Spell Checker

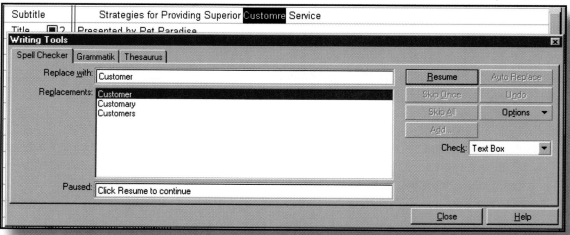

You have the following options:

- Skip the suggestion, once or always.

- Select a word from the list and choose Replace.

- Key the correct word in the *Replace with* text box, then choose Replace.

- In the case of a repeated word, you can delete one of the words, skip the word to retain both instances, or exit the spell check by selecting Close.

- Continue until the document has been checked completely. To exit the spell check before it is complete, click Close.

**NOTE:**

If the Writing Tools dialog box is blocking the highlighted words, you can move it by clicking on its title bar, holding down the mouse button, and dragging it out of the way.

**SCANS**

## EXERCISE ⟹ PR3.6

**1.** Open the **customer service** presentation from the student **Datafile** folder.

**2.** Switch to **Slide Outliner** view to check the spelling of the entire show.

**3.** Click the **Tools** menu and select **Spell Check**. The Writing Tools dialog box appears, opened to the Spell Checker tab.

**4.** The Spell Checker highlights *Customre*. The correct spelling, *Customer*, is highlighted in the Replacements list. Click **Replace** to insert the correct spelling.

**5.** Next, the Spell Checker highlights the word *Seely*. Since this is a surname, you do not need to replace it. Click **Skip Once**.

**6.** Next, the Spell Checker highlights *agrue*. Look at the list of possible replacements carefully! The highlighted replacement word is *agree*. This word would completely change the meaning of the sentence. The word you want is *argue*. Select it from the list and click **Replace**.

**7.** Finally, the Spell Checker highlights *in in*. You want to correct this double word occurrence. The *Replace with* text box already contains one occurrence of *in*. Click **Replace**.

**8.** A message box informs you that the spell check is complete. Choose **Yes** to close the Spell Checker.

**9.** Save the file as **customer service 3-6 xxx** and print the entire slide show. Leave it on the screen for the next exercise.

# *Changing Text Appearance*

Y ou can change the text's appearance by selecting a specific font, style, size, pattern, and color. You can also change the text's *justification*; that is, the alignment relative to the edges of the slide.

## Changing Font Properties

Corel® WordPerfect® Suite 8 comes with a set of fonts that should meet your needs. The fonts available on your system are listed in the Font Properties dialog box shown in Figure 3-5.

You can change the following font properties in the Font Properties dialog box:

■ **Font face**. The current font face is highlighted in the Font face list (for example, Times New Roman or Arial). Select the font that you want. (**NOTE:** You can also select fonts for your text by clicking the Font Selection button on the Property Bar and selecting a font face from the drop-down list.)

- **Font size.** The current font size, measured in points, is highlighted in the Font size list. (There are 72 points to one inch, so 12-point type is one-sixth of an inch high.) Select the desired point size.

- **Style**. The current font style is highlighted in the Font style list. Select Regular, Italic, Bold, or Bold Italic.

- **Appearance.** Appearance refers to character enhancements similar to font styles that are useful when a particular font does not offer any styles. The Appearance area has three check boxes: Bold, Underline, and Italic. Check any individual box or combination of boxes.

**FIGURE 3-5**
The Font Properties Dialog Box

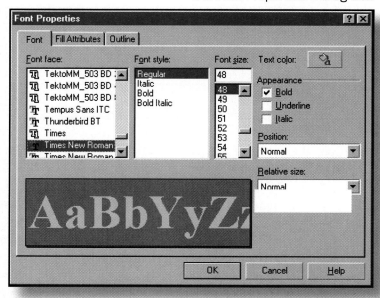

Exercise PR3.7 will teach you how to make changes to font properties, using the **customer service 3-6 xxx** slide show.

## EXERCISE ⟩ PR3.7

1. To make the title and subtitle stand out more clearly on the slides, change their fonts, sizes, and styles. First, change the font for the title on the first slide.
   a. Switch to **Slide Editor** view. On Slide 1 double click the title to open the text editor. Click and drag to select the title text.
   b. Click the **Format** menu and select **Font**. The Font Properties dialog box appears (see Figure 3-5).
   c. Select **Arial** from the Font face list and **Bold** from the Font style list, then click **OK**.

2. Close the text editor and observe the changes to the title.

3. Next, change the subtitle.
   a. Double click the subtitle to open the text editor. Select the text.
   b. Click the **Format** menu and select **Font** to display the Font Properties dialog box.
   c. Select **Arial** from the Font face list, **Bold** from the Font style list, and **32** from the Font size list. Click **OK**.

4. Close the text editor and observe the changes to the subtitle.

5. Save the file as **customer service 3-7 xxx** and print Slide 1. Leave the slide show on the screen for the next exercise.

## Using Quickfonts

Presentations enables you to select the most recently used font face and properties using the QuickFonts button.

### EXERCISE ▷ PR3.8

1. Use **QuickFonts** to apply the new title and subtitle styles to the other slides in the slide show.
   a. Display Slide 2. Open the title's text editor and select the text.
   b. Click the **QuickFonts** button on the Property Bar. A drop-down list of the fonts and sizes you have most recently used appears. Select **Arial 48**. The highlighted text changes to show the new font.
   c. Using this same process, select the subtitle text and click the **QuickFonts** button. Select **Arial 32** to change the subtitle format.
   e. Make the same changes to the title and subtitles on Slides 3 through 7.

2. Display Slide 3. Make the following change in the text area of the slide:
   a. Open the text editor box and select the last sentence (do not highlight the period).

   b. Click the **Bold** and **Underline** buttons on the Toolbar.
   c. Close the text editor.

3. Display Slide 1. Change the color of the text in the *May I Help You?* box.
   a. Open the text editor for this title box and select the text.
   b. Access the Font Properties dialog box. Click the text color box to display the color palette.
   c. Choose the bright yellow color by clicking the sixth color box in the fourth row of the palette. Click **OK**.
   d. Close the text editor.

4. Save your changes as **customer service 3-8 xxx** and print Slides 2 and 3. (In the Print dialog box, the *Print range* should read **2** to **3**.) Then, close the slide show.

## Changing Text Justification

*Justification* refers to how text aligns relative to the edge of the text box. You have three options: Left, Right, and Center.

**INTERNET** In certain browsers and other Internet programs, a bookmark or hotlist is a special file used to save addresses and locations. By saving and recalling addresses, it is easy for you to visit your favorite sites over and over.

1. Open **pet care 3-5 xxx** and display Slide 1.

2. Double click the text box at the bottom of the slide to select it.

3. Click the **Format** menu and select **Justification**. Choose **Center** from the cascade menu. The text appears centered in the box.

4. Close the text box.

5. Experiment by right-justifying the title and subtitle.
   a. Double click the title. Click the right mouse button once and select **Justification** from the pop-up menu. Choose **Right** from the cascade menu.
   b. Make the same change to the subtitle.

6. Notice that in this case, Right justification is not as aesthetically pleasing as Center justification. Change the title and subtitle back to **Center** justification.

7. Save your changes as **pet care 3-9 xxx** and print Slide 1. Leave the slide show on the screen for the next exercise.

## Changing Font Fill And Outline

The Font Properties dialog box has two additional tabs, Fill Attributes and Outline, that enable you to make further font changes. The Fill Attributes tab (see Figure 3-6) enables you to choose no fill, a patterned fill, or a gradient (color gradation) fill.

The Outline tab (see Figure 3-7) of the Font Properties dialog box enables you to add a colored outline of a particular thickness around each letter of your text.

**FIGURE 3-6**
The Fill Attributes Tab

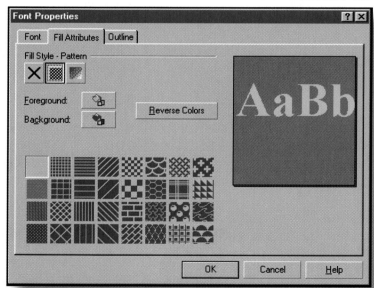

**FIGURE 3-7**
The Outline Tab

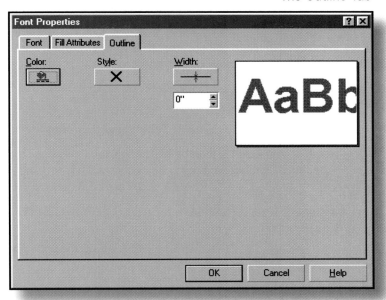

EXERCISE ⟹ PR3.10

1. Display Slide 1. Change the fill attribute of the title text to a gradient.
   a. Select the title text. Access the Font Properties dialog box and click the **Fill Attributes** tab.
   b. Click the **Gradient** button. Click the first gradient in the first row of the palette.

2. Add an outline around the title text.
   a. With the Font Properties dialog box still open, click the **Outline** tab.
   b. Click the **Color** button. Select the color **Black** from the palette that appears.
   c. Click the **Style** button to produce a palette. Select the first option in the second column.
   d. Click the **Width** button to produce a palette. Select the first option in the second column. The spin box below should indicate the width of the line is *0.010".* Click **OK**.

3. Close the text editor and observe the way color grades from light to dark.

4. To make the gradient more obvious, change the title text to **66** pt.

5. Save the slide show as **pet care 3-10 xxx** and then play it.

6. When you have finished viewing the slides, print the slide show as handouts with two slides per page.

7. Close the slide show.

# Summary

In this lesson you learned that:

- you can change a slide show's master, the combination of background and layout, at any time. Presentations provides you with a number of preformatted masters to choose from.

- Presentations enables you to add, edit, and delete text on an existing slide. Simply open the text editor and make the desired changes.

- once you create a text box, you can move it by clicking and dragging it elsewhere on the slide.

- the Symbols dialog box lets you insert special characters into a slide, such as typographic symbols (©, $^1/_2$, —), mathematical and scientific characters ($\Sigma$, Å, $\infty$), and multinational characters (ü, ç, ñ).

- you can insert the date and/or time on a slide in a variety of formats. If desired, you can have the date and time automatically update whenever you open the slide show.

- Presentations' Spell Check feature searches for and notifies you about potential errors, such as misspelled and duplicate words. You can accept the Spell Checker's suggestions, make your own changes, or skip the error.

- you can change the font face, size, style, and appearance of text in the Font Properties dialog box. In addition, you can apply a pattern or gradient to text.

- the QuickFonts feature lets you quickly select a font face and size combination from a list of those most recently used.

- Presentations lets you change the alignment, or justification, of text to Left, Center, or Right.

## LESSON 3 REVIEW QUESTIONS

### FILL IN THE BLANKS

**Complete each of the following statements by writing your answer in the blank provided.**

1. The _____ view is the best view for spell checking the slide show.

2. Font size is measured in _____.

3. A master is composed of a background and a _____.

4. _____ is the alignment of text relative to the edge of the text box.

5. ®, ¢, and ñ are examples of _____.

## WRITTEN QUESTIONS

**Write your answers to the following questions.**

**6.** Explain why it is better to change a slide show's master before formatting text.

**7.** Why would you check the Automatic update check box on the Date/Time dialog box?

**8.** When the Spell Checker highlights a possible error in your slide show text, what are your options?

**9.** List at least four different ways to change the appearance of text.

**10.** How would you apply a red checkered pattern to text?

## LESSON 3 PROJECT

**SCANS**

### PROJECT 3A

Edit an existing slide show.

**1.** Start Presentations and open **pet perks 2a xxx**.

**2.** Apply the *POLO* master from the Design category to the slide show. Move through the slides to see how they look with this master.

**3.** The subtitles are somewhat hard to see. Change all the subtitles to **32** pt. and bold and italicize them. (**TIP:** Use QuickFonts to change the subtitles quickly.)

**4.** Slide 3 has the wrong discount listed. Delete the words *twenty-five dollars* and insert $\frac{1}{2}$ **to** $\frac{1}{3}$. You can find the $\frac{1}{2}$ and $\frac{1}{3}$ symbols in the Typographic Symbols set of the Symbol dialog box.

**5.** On Slide 2 insert a new text box at the bottom of the slide. Key the following text: **Offer valid while supplies last**. Change the color of the text to yellow and change the size to **24** pt. Center the text in the box.

**6.** Spell check the slide show. Skip the word *Kredit*, as it is deliberately misspelled.

**7.** Save the slide show as **pet perks 3a xxx**.

**8.** Print the slide show as handouts with three slides per page. Close the slide show.

## PROJECT 3B

Edit an existing slide show.

1. Open **pet care 3-10 xxx** and display Slide 1.

2. Select the text box at the bottom of the screen. Reduce the font size on all the text so that the text *Presented to the Seniors & Pets Pairing Program* fits on one line.

3. Change all titles, subtitles, and text blocks to **Left** justification.

4. Change all subtitles to **32** pt. and **bold**.

5. Spell check the slide show.

6. Save the slide show as **pet care 3b xxx**.

7. Print the slide show as handouts with four slides per page.

8. Close the slide show.

## CRITICAL THINKING ACTIVITY

SCANS

Imagine that you are giving a successful presentation, when suddenly an audience member points out that the word *average* is misspelled on the screen as *averege*. It is merely a typographical error on your part, as you know the proper spelling of the word. Regardless, the person has brought it to the attention of the other audience members. You thank this person for pointing out the error, and move on to the next slide, only to have the same person point out that the word *the* has been miskeyed as *hte*. Now the audience seems distracted, and you are slightly annoyed with this person for making such a fuss over two small typos. You have worked hard on this presentation, and do not see why someone should interrupt you for such a small reason.

Now imagine that you are in the audience and you see several typographical errors throughout someone else's presentation. How would you react to this? What might you assume about this person?

What conclusions can you draw from these scenarios?

# CREATING BULLETED LISTS AND TABLES

## OBJECTIVES

**Upon completion of this lesson, you will be able to:**

■ Create a bulleted list slide.

■ Insert bulleted text.

■ Change bulleted list properties.

■ Create and customize a table.

■ Format data in a table.

**🕐 Estimated Time: 1¹/₂ hours**

## *Introduction*

In addition to adding text slides to your slide shows, Presentations enables you to create *bulleted list* slides. Bullets are small symbols (•, ■, ➤, etc.) that mark the beginning of a line of text. They are best used to clearly mark each point in a list of entries. Presentations has a Bulleted List template that you can use to create a new bullet chart, as well as apply to an existing slide.

Presentations also lets you add *tables* to your slides. Tables are sets of data arranged into rows and columns.

## *Creating Bullet Charts*

Following are two ways to create a new bulleted list slide:

■ Click the Insert menu and select New Slide to access the New slide dialog box. Select the Bulleted List sample and enter the number of new bulleted list slides you want to add. Click OK.

■ A second way to create a bulleted list slide is to click the Insert New Slide icon, located at the right bottom edge of the slide. This button has a small down-pointing arrow attached to it. Click the arrow to produce a pop-up menu of layout choices (see Figure 4-1), and select Insert Bulleted List Slide. The layout pictured on the face of the button changes to a bulleted list, which you can click to insert a new bulleted list slide.

**FIGURE 4-1**
Pop-Up List of Slide Layouts

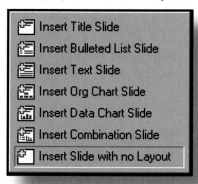

**EXERCISE ⇨ PR4.1**

**1.** Create a new Presentations slide show.

**2.** In the Master Gallery dialog box select the **Nature** category and choose the *SUMMER* master.

**3.** Create the title slide.
   **a.** In the title box key **Dog Days of Summer**.
   **b.** In the subtitle box key **Pet Paradise's Summer Promotion**.

**4.** Click the **Insert** menu and select **New Slide**. Select the **Bulleted List** slide (top row, second icon) from the New Slide dialog box. Click **OK**.

**5.** On the new slide key the title **Discounts by Category** and the subtitle **Products & Services**.

**6.** Leave the slide show on the screen for the next exercise.

## Inserting Bulleted Text

When you double click the text box on a bulleted list slide, the text editor opens with a bullet character located at the beginning of the line (see Figure 4-2). Simply key the line of text, then press Enter to begin a new bulleted line.

**FIGURE 4-2**
The Bullet Character

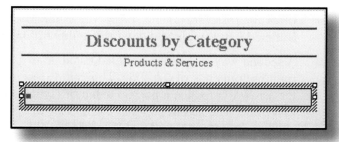

## EXERCISE ⇨ PR4.2

1. Double click the text box to open the text editor. The text editor should display a bullet, as in Figure 4-2.

2. Key the first bullet entry: **Products**.

3. Press **Enter**. Notice that a new bullet appears, ready for another Level 1 entry.

4. Press **Tab** to insert a Level 2 bullet. Key the entry: **Chew Toys—25% off**. Notice that the Level 2 entry is indented to the right, is a different color, and has a different bullet symbol.

5. Press **Enter** and key another Level 2 entry: **Dog Houses**.

6. Press **Enter** to start a new line, then press **Shift+Tab** to move back to Level 1.

7. Using the same process for Level 1 and Level 2 entries, key the remaining bullet entries shown in Figure 4-3.

8. Save the file as **dog days 4-2 xxx** and print Slide 2. Leave the slide show on the screen for the next exercise.

**FIGURE 4-3**
The Completed Bulleted List

## *Changing Bulleted List Properties*

You can use the Bulleted List Properties dialog box to change the font of the bullet text, the bullet style and color, and bullet text spacing. You can also draw a box around the bullet text and animate the text, if desired.

## EXERCISE ⇨ PR4.3

1. Click the bulleted list once to select it.

2. Click the **Format** menu and select **Bulleted List Properties**. The Bulleted List Properties dialog box appears. Click the **Bullets** tab to see a dialog box like the one in Figure 4-4.

3. Change the color of the Level 1 bullet to match the Level 1 text.
   a. If necessary, click the Level 1 bullet entry in the box displaying different bullet types.

(continued on next page)

b. Click the **Bullet Properties** button. The Bullet Properties dialog box appears.

c. Click the **Foreground** button. The color palette appears. Select the second color in the third row, **Teal**. Click **OK**. Notice that the sample box shows the bullet is now the same color as the text.

4. Change the bullet style of the Level 2 entries to stars.

a. Click the Level 2 entry to select it. The bullet style is currently a triangle.

b. Click on the *Bullet shape* drop-down list box and select **Small Star**.

c. Click **Apply to All**. Your changes appear on the slide. Click outside of the bullet chart to deselect it.

**FIGURE 4-4**
The Bulleted List Properties Dialog Box

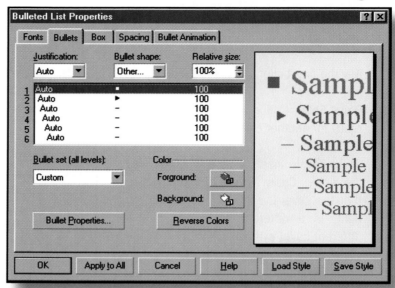

5. Save the file as **dog days 4-3 xxx** and print Slide 2. Leave the slide show on the screen for the next exercise.

# Creating a Table

The Presentations Data Chart template enables you to insert a table into a slide. When you select this template, Presentations displays a screen like the one shown in Figure 4-5.

**FIGURE 4-5**
The Data Chart Template Screen

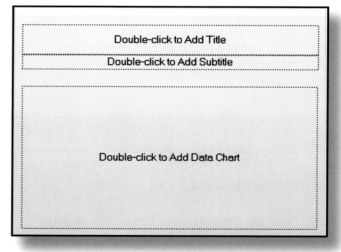

**INTERNET**

The World Wide Web is a subnetwork of computers that display multimedia information, including text, graphics, sound, and video clips. Web documents also contain special connections that allow users to switch to other documents that could be on computers anywhere in the world.

## EXERCISE ▭⟩ PR4.4

1. Add a slide to your slide show with the Data Chart template.

2. Insert a title and subtitle for the new slide.
   a. Title:
      **Projected Sales**
   b. Subtitle:
      **June, July, and August 1998**

3. Double click the data chart box. The Data Chart Gallery dialog box appears, as shown in Figure 4-6.

4. Select **Table** from the *Chart type* list box. Several table templates appear.

5. Click on the first table type (the top left table in the gallery), then click **OK**. The datasheet appears on your screen, along with the Range Highlighter dialog box.

**FIGURE 4-6**
The Data Chart Gallery Dialog Box

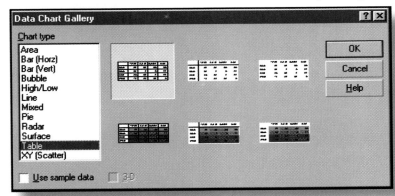

6. You may need to resize the datasheet so that you can view the entire chart. Point to the lower right corner of the datasheet until the double-headed arrow appears. Click and drag until you can see at least rows 1 through 4 and columns A through D.

7. Leave the chart on the screen for the next exercise.

# *Working with the Datasheet*

The datasheet (see Figure 4-7) has numbered *rows* and lettered *columns*. The boxes where rows and columns intersect are called *cells*, designated by combining the column letters and row numbers (A1, B3, etc.). To move around on the datasheet, move the mouse pointer, use the arrow keys on the keyboard, or press Tab.

 **NOTE:**

You can click and drag the edges of the datasheet to enlarge it and show more data.

The datasheet contains four rows and columns of sample data that will help you to set up your own table. If you need more than four rows and/or columns, you can add the additional data in the subsequent rows and columns. Click the desired cell and begin keying the data. Press Enter to insert the new data.

**FIGURE 4-7**
The Datasheet

| Legend | A | B | C | D |
|--------|---|---|---|---|
| Labels | 1st Qtr | 2nd Qtr | 3rd Qtr | 4th Qtr |
| 1 North | 90 | 50 | 65 | 85 |
| 2 South | 50 | 40 | 45 | 70 |
| 3 East | 25 | 30 | 40 | 20 |
| 4 West | 10 | 20 | 30 | 45 |

**NOTE:**

To display the datasheet without sample data, deselect the Use sample data check box at the bottom left side of the Data Chart Gallery dialog box.

If your table requires fewer rows and/or columns than shown in the sample, you can delete the extra entries. To delete columns or rows:

- Click the column letter or row number to select the entire column or row.

- Click the Edit menu and select Delete. A dialog box asks you to confirm the deletion. Click Yes to delete the cells or No to cancel the deletion.

## EXERCISE ▷ PR4.5

SCANS

1. In the datasheet click the cell that currently contains the text *1st Qtr.* Key **June**, then press **Tab**.

2. In the cell labeled *2nd Qtr*, key **July** and press **Tab**.

3. In the cell labeled *3rd Qtr*, key **August** and press **Enter**.

4. Click the cell currently labeled *North*. Key **Chew Toys** and press **Tab**.

5. Now fill in the data for this row.
   a. Key **1,750** and press **Tab**.
   b. Key **3,500** and press **Tab**.
   c. Key **2,250** and press **Enter**. Your datasheet should look similar to Figure 4-8.

**FIGURE 4-8**
The First Entries in the Datasheet

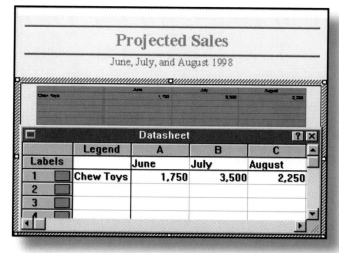

**6.** Enter the remaining data in the datasheet, following the above instructions. Key the following data:

|  | June | July | August |
|---|---|---|---|
| Dog Houses | 3,500 | 7,800 | 11,000 |
| Boarding | 6,400 | 15,300 | 8,400 |
| Classes | 1,750 | 2,800 | 2,100 |
| Grooming | 5,000 | 10,000 | 11,000 |

**7.** Remove the sample data from column D.
   **a.** Click the letter *D* to select the entire column.
   **b.** Click the **Edit** menu and select **Delete**.

   **c.** When the warning message appears, click **Yes** to confirm the deletion.

**8.** The datasheet is now complete. Close the datasheet by clicking the **X** in the upper right corner.

**9.** The slide shows the data in place. Click outside the chart to close the chart editor.

**10.** You will no doubt notice that the text is too small. You will enlarge it in the next exercise. For now, save your changes as **dog days 4-5 xxx** and print Slide 3. Leave the slide show on the screen for the next exercise.

# *Customizing the Table*

After entering the data, you can change the appearance of the table using the Table Properties dialog box, as shown in Figure 4-9.

- The Layout tab enables you to assign colors for data ranges, if desired, and to change the fill and line colors of the current table. The Font tab enables you to change font properties.

- This dialog box also includes a handy Preview button that enables you to view your changes as you make them.

**FIGURE 4-9**
The Table Properties Dialog Box

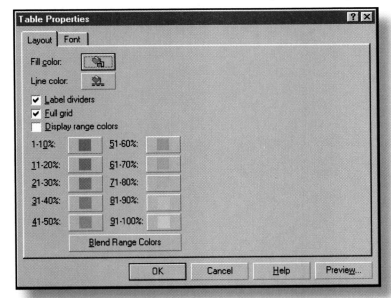

1. Double click the table on Slide 3 to open the chart editor.

2. Click the **Chart** menu and select **Layout/Type**. The Table Properties dialog box appears.

3. The text is hard to read on the current fill color. Change both the fill and line color.
   a. Click the **Fill color** button to display a color palette.
   b. Choose the fourth color in the first row, **White**.
   c. Click the **Line color** button and choose the second color in the third row, **Teal**.

   d. To see the changes so far, click the **Preview** button. When you are finished previewing, click **Back** to return to the Table Properties dialog box.

4. Change the text appearance.
   a. Click the **Font** tab.
   b. Choose **Times New Roman**, **Bold**, and **24** pt. Use **Teal** for the text color.
   c. Preview your changes. Click **OK** to accept the changes and return to the slide.

5. Close the chart editor. Save your changes as **dog days 4-6 xxx** and print Slide 3. Leave the slide show on the screen for the next exercise.

# Formatting Numeric Data

The Format dialog box (see Figure 4-10) provides a variety of formatting options, including currency, comma separator, floating or decimal numbers, and so on. These formats are the same as those used in spreadsheets.

In the following exercise you will change the format of numbers.

**FIGURE 4-10**
The Format Dialog Box

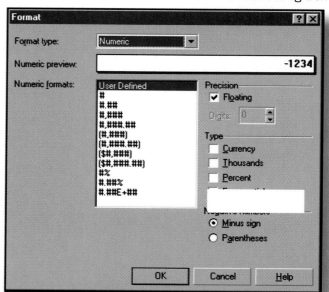

## EXERCISE ▭⟩ PR4.7

SCANS

1. Open the chart editor. Click the **View** menu and select **Datasheet** to display the datasheet.

2. Select the cells containing numbers in the datasheet by clicking in cell A1 and dragging to cell C5.

3. Click the **Data** menu and select **Format**. The Format dialog box appears.

4. Click the **Currency** check box in the *Type* section of the dialog box. Click **OK**.

5. Close the datasheet and observe the change on the slide. Close the chart editor.

6. Save the slide show as **dog days 4-7 xxx**. Print the slide show in handout form with four slides per page.

7. Close the slide show.

## *Summary*

In this lesson you learned that:

■ bullets are best used to set off multiple points about one topic. You can create a bulleted list by applying the Bulleted List template to a slide.

■ pressing Tab in a bulleted list moves to the next bullet level; pressing Shift+Tab returns you to the previous level.

■ Presentations enables you to change bullet attributes such as type, size, and color, using the Bulleted List Properties dialog box.

■ a table is one of the many data charts Presentations offers. You can enter numeric data into the table, then apply a numeric format such as currency. You can also customize the table's line color and width, fill color, and text font.

## LESSON 4 REVIEW QUESTIONS

### TRUE/FALSE

**Circle the T if the statement is true. Circle the F if the statement is false.**

**T  F  1.** You can apply the Bulleted List template to an existing slide.

**T  F  2.** Bullets are mainly used to introduce large, single paragraphs.

**T  F  3.** You can have only two levels of bullets on one slide.

**T  F  4.** A datasheet is similar to a spreadsheet.

**T  F  5.** Rows are the intersection of columns and cells.

## WRITTEN QUESTIONS

**Write your answers to the following questions.**

6. When would you use a bulleted list slide rather than a text slide?

7. Explain how to delete a column or row in a datasheet.

8. How do you create a second level bullet in a bulleted list?

9. List the four numeric format types.

10. Describe the procedure for editing the datasheet.

## LESSON 4 PROJECT

### PROJECT 4A

Add bullets to an existing slide show.

1. Open **first impressions 1c xxx**.

2. Add three slides with the Bulleted List template. Insert the following information on the slides, as indicated:

Slide 2
| | |
|---|---|
| Title: | **Preparation** |
| Subtitle: | **How to Prepare Yourself for the Interview** |
| Bullet 1: | **Prepare your materials and plan your transportation the night before.** |
| Bullet 2: | **Get enough sleep the night before.** |
| Bullet 3: | **Eat a good breakfast.** |
| Bullet 4: | **Dress conservatively and professionally.** |
| Bullet 5: | **Get to the interview site 15 to 30 minutes early.** |

Slide 3
| | |
|---|---|
| Title: | **Execution** |
| Subtitle: | **How to Conduct Yourself in the Interview** |
| Bullet 1: | **Greet the interviewer with a smile and a firm handshake.** |
| Bullet 2: | **Always maintain eye contact.** |
| Bullet 3: | **Sit up straight and keep nervous movements to a minimum.** |
| Bullet 4: | **Answer questions directly and with examples.** |
| Bullet 5: | **Express keen interest in the company and position.** |

Slide 4
| | |
|---|---|
| Title: | **Follow-Up** |
| Subtitle: | **How to Represent Yourself After the Interview** |
| Bullet 1: | **Write and mail a thank-you note the same day of the interview.** |
| Bullet 2: | **Wait to hear from the interviewer by mail or telephone, unless otherwise instructed.** |
| Bullet 3: | **Telephone the interviewer if you have not heard from him or her after two weeks.** |

3. Switch to **Outliner** view and spell check the presentation.

4. Switch back to **Slide Editor** view and play the slide show.

5. Print the slide show as handouts with four slides per page.

6. Save the slide show as **first impressions 4a xxx**. Close the slide show.

## PROJECT 4B

Add bullets to an existing slide show.

1. Open **pet classes**.

2. Add three slides with the Bulleted List template. Insert the following information on the slides, as indicated:

Slide 2
| | |
|---|---|
| Title: | **Beginner Classes** |
| Subtitle: | **For the New Pet Owner** |
| Level 1 Bullet: | **Proper Pet Care** |
| Level 2 Bullet: | **Meets every Monday, Wednesday, and Friday** |
| Level 1 Bullet: | **Choosing the Right Pet Food** |
| Level 2 Bullet: | **Meets every Tuesday and Thursday** |
| Level 1 Bullet: | **Pet First Aid** |
| Level 2 Bullet: | **Meets every Saturday** |

Slide 3
| | |
|---|---|
| Title: | **Intermediate Classes** |
| Subtitle: | **For the Experienced Pet Owner** |
| Level 1 Bullet: | **Ask the Veterinarian** |
| Level 2 Bullet: | **Meets the first Saturday of every month** |
| Level 1 Bullet: | **Teach Your Pet Tricks** |
| Level 2 Bullet: | **Meets the second Saturday of every month** |
| Level 1 Bullet: | **Build a Pet Playground** |
| Level 2 Bullet: | **Meets the third Saturday of every month** |

Slide 4
Title:           **Expert Classes**
Subtitle:        **For the Advanced Pet Owner**
Level 1 Bullet:  **Breeding & Pedigrees**
Level 2 Bullet:  **Meets the fourth Saturday of every month**
Level 1 Bullet:  **Pet Psychology**
Level 2 Bullet:  **Meets the second Friday of every month**

3. Switch to **Outliner** view and spell check the presentation

4. Switch back to **Slide Editor** view and play the slide show.

5. Print the slide show as handouts with four slides per page.

6. Save the slide show as **pet classes 4b xxx**. Leave it on the screen for the next project.

## PROJECT 4C

Add a table to an existing slide show.

1. Add a slide at the end of the show with the Data Chart template.

2. Insert the following title and subtitle:

   Title:       **Course Fees**
   Subtitle:    **Payable the First Day of Class**

3. Double click the data chart area to display the Data Chart Gallery. Choose a table style and click the **Use sample data** check box to deselect it. Click **OK**.

4. The datasheet appears. Resize the datasheet, if necessary, for better viewing.

5. Insert the following data in the datasheet:

|                                | Fee   |
|--------------------------------|-------|
| Proper Pet Care                | 5.00  |
| How to Choose the Right Pet Food | 5.00  |
| Pet First Aid                  | 10.00 |
| Ask the Veterinarian           | 12.50 |
| Teach Your Pet Tricks          | 15.00 |
| Build a Pet Playground         | 27.50 |
| Breeding & Pedigrees           | 35.00 |
| Pet Psychology                 | 35.00 |

6. While still in the datasheet, select the entire Fee column. Access the Format dialog box.

    a. In the *Precision* section of the dialog box, click the **Floating** check box to remove the check mark. The *Digits* spin box becomes active.

    b. Click the up spin arrow to display *2* in the *Digits* spin box.

    c. Click the **Currency** check box, then click **OK**.

7. In order to view the long course name titles in the chart, you need to widen the first column.

    a. Click in any cell in the first column.

    b. Click the **Data** menu and select **Column Width**. The Column Width dialog box appears.

    c. Key **20** and click **OK**. The column widens.

8. Close the datasheet. With the chart editor still open, access the Table Properties dialog box and change the appearance of the table as desired. You can change the fill and line color and the font, style, size, and color of text. Use the **Preview** button to check your changes.

9. Spell check the slide show.

10. Save the slide show as **pet classes 4c xxx**. Print only Slide 5.

11. Close the slide show.

## CRITICAL THINKING ACTIVITY

SCANS

    Create a presentation that teaches a skill you are good at, such as making a pizza, parallel parking a car, or shooting a hockey puck. Include a title slide and at least three bulleted list slides. You can make each bulleted list slide a step in the process or general areas of concern. Create at least three bullets per page, and include Level 2 bullets to further describe your Level 1 bullet text. For example, if a Level 1 bullet item reads *Adjust your rearview mirror*, the Level 2 bullet might read *Another driver may have moved it since you last used the car.*

    Save and print the slide show. Present it to the class.

# PRESENTATION TIME-SAVERS

## OBJECTIVES

**Upon completion of this lesson, you will be able to:**

■ Use a PerfectExpert project to create a slide show.

■ Import outlines into Presentations.

■ Use QuickMenus.

**⏱ Estimated Time: 1¹/₂ hours**

## *Introduction*

Presentations offers several ways to automate or speed the slide show creation and editing process. The PerfectExpert feature can assist you in creating a slide show by providing different preformatted slide shows that you can individually edit.

You will learn to import an outline from a word processing program into Presentations. The headings on the text outline become titles, subtitles, and text on the slides.

Finally, you will learn how to use QuickMenus, menus that contain commonly used commands. You access the menus by right clicking the current view; this saves you the time of having to click a menu from the Menu Bar and select a command.

## *Using PerfectExpert Projects*

Presentations contains several predesigned slide shows, called PerfectExpert projects. These shows are designed for specific purposes, as their names imply (*Business Plan Slide Show, Market Research Slide Show,* etc.). You can select one of these shows and enter your own data. This saves you the time of choosing a master and slide layouts, and provides you with prompts on what type of information belongs on each slide.

# EXERCISE ⟹ PR5.1

1. Click the **File** menu and select **New** to access the New dialog box. Click the **Create New** tab, if necessary.

2. Scroll to the bottom of the list of available projects and select **Welcome Slide Show**. Click **Create**. The new slide show appears,

with the PerfectExpert on the left side of the screen, as shown in Figure 5-1.

3. Leave the slide show on the screen for the next exercise.

**FIGURE 5-1**
A PerfectExpert Project

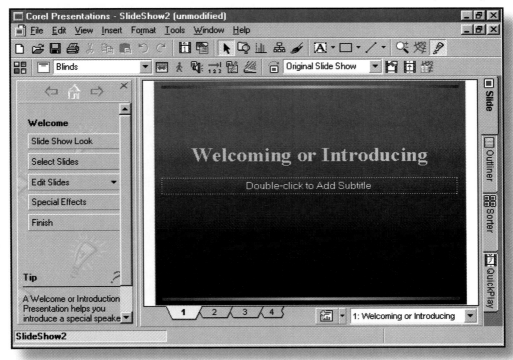

# *Keying Text and Changing Templates*

The easiest way to add your own text to this slide show is to switch to Outliner view. This saves you the time and effort involved in switching from slide to slide and opening the text editor for each text box.

The PerfectExpert project's settings are merely guidelines. If you want to change the layout of a slide, you can apply another template. You can also delete or reorder slides, if desired.

1. Switch to **Outliner** view.

2 Key a title on the first title slide in the outline.
   a. Select the first title line, *Welcoming or Introducing*.
   b. Key **Welcome Aboard!** and press **Enter**. Notice that Presentations inserts a blank subtitle line.
   c. Key the subtitle as follows: **New Employee Orientation Meeting**.

3. Click the title for Slide 2. Look at the **Select Layout** button on the Property Bar and observe that it is a bulleted list slide, which is just what you want. Select the existing title and key a new title: **Overview**.

4. Below this title line are text lines. Replace these text lines with the following lines:
   Bullet 1: **We want to welcome you to the staff of Pet Paradise.**
   Bullet 2: **This meeting will serve as an orientation to our employee benefits and policies.**

5. Add the following to Slide 3:
   Title: **Orientation Materials**
   Bullet 1: **Pet Paradise Employee Handbook**
   Bullet 2: **Pet Paradise Employee Benefits Kit**

6. Click the title for Slide 4. Notice that this, too, is a bulleted list slide. You need to change it to a text slide.
   a. Click the **Select Layout** button on the Property Bar and select **Text**.
   b. Key the following information for the slide (note that you will skip the subtitle).

Title: **Today's Speaker: Polly Paradeis**
Text Line 1: **Polly Paradeis is the co-owner and General Manager of the Pet Paradise chain. She began the business in 1988, working as the sole employee! Today, she and her husband, Paul, employ 20 people, own 2 stores, and are looking to expand the chain.**
Text Line 2: **Polly visits both stores every day and knows all her employees by name. She is here to welcome you to her growing business.**

7. Slides 5 and 6 are unnecessary, and so you should delete them. You can delete them both simultaneously in the Slide Sorter view.
   a. Switch to **Slide Sorter** view.
   b. Hold down the **Ctrl** key and click on both **Slide 5** and **Slide 6**.
   c. Click the **Edit** menu and select **Delete Slides**.
   d. Click **Yes** to confirm the deletion.

8. Switch back to **Outliner** view and spell check the slide show.

9. Switch back to **Slide Editor** view and flip through each slide. Notice that Slides 2, 3, and 4 have unnecessary subtitles. Click once on each box to select it, then press **Delete** to remove it.

10. Save the slide show as **orientation 5-2 xxx**. Print the slide show as handouts with four slides per page.

11. Close the PerfectExpert by clicking its **Close** button. Then close the slide show.

# *Importing Outlines into Presentations*

Another Presentations time-saver is the ability to import outlines from word processing programs such as Corel WordPerfect. Each heading in these outlines converts to a slide title. You can change the levels of these titles in Outliner view. Press Tab to change a title to a subtitle, and press Tab twice to change a title to a text or bullet entry.

## EXERCISE ⟹ PR5.3

SCANS

1. Start a new Presentations slide show and accept the *DEFAULT* master. Switch to **Outliner** view.

2. Click the **Insert** menu and then click **File**. The Insert Outline dialog box appears (see Figure 5-2). If necessary, access the drive where your student **Datafile** folder is located. Notice that only files with the *.wpd* (WordPerfect document) extension appear in the file area of the dialog box.

**FIGURE 5-2**
The Insert Outline Dialog Box

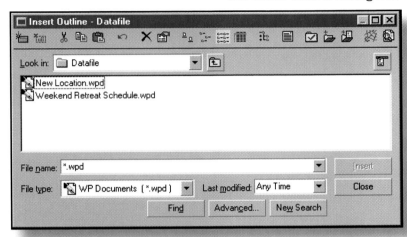

3. Select *Weekend Retreat Schedule* and click **Insert**. Presentations displays the outline in Outliner view. Your screen should appear similar to Figure 5-3.

4. Insert a new slide in Outliner view to serve as the title for the slide show.
   a. Position the insertion point to the left of the first slide's title. Press **Enter** twice.
   b. The title is now on a text line. Press **Shift+Tab** to make it a title again.
   c. Press the up arrow key twice to return to the top of the outline. Change the new Slide 1 to a Title template. Key the following title and subtitle:

   Title:  **Pet Paradise Employee Retreat**
   Subtitle: **August 7-9, 1998, Oasis Corporate Retreat Center**

5. Switch to **Slide Editor** view and move through the slides. Delete any empty text boxes.

6. Leave the slide show on the screen for the next exercise.

**INTERNET**

The Internet's Online Career Center is an employment database to which job hunters can submit personal data via email (occinfo@occ.com). There are more than 30,000 résumés stored there.

**FIGURE 5-3**
The Imported Outline in Outliner View

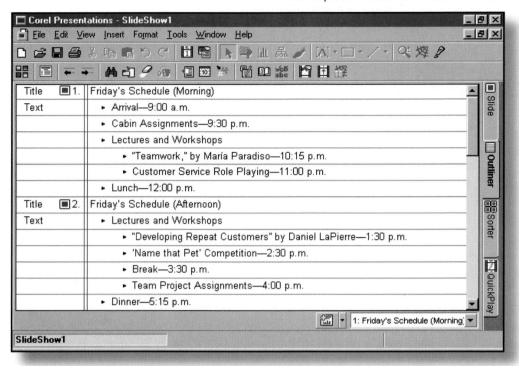

# *Using QuickMenus*

Presentations offers *QuickMenus* to help you modify your slide show without having to maneuver through numerous menu options. To display a QuickMenu, right click the screen.

These QuickMenus vary in appearance depending on where you click the screen. For example, right clicking in Outliner view with text selected produces the QuickMenu shown in Figure 5-4.

**FIGURE 5-4**
The Outliner View
QuickMenu

**EXERCISE ⟹ PR5.4**

SCANS

1. Change the master using a QuickMenu.
   a. With Slide 1 on the screen, right click anywhere in the slide background, outside of the title and subtitle text boxes. A QuickMenu appears.
   b. Click **Master Gallery**. The Master Gallery dialog box appears.
   c. Select the *GREEN MARBLE* master from the Design category. Click **Apply**.

2. Someone points out that the retreat facilitator, Maria Gomez, spells her first name *María*. Make this change on Slide 2. (Note: On your copy of the file, the accent mark on *María* may already be present.)
   a. Double click the bulleted entries on Slide 2 to open the text editor.
   b. Position the insertion point after the *i* in *Maria* and press **Backspace**.
   c. Right click to display a QuickMenu. Click **Characters** to display the Symbols dialog box.
   d. Select the Multinational character set and choose the *í* character. Click **Insert and Close** and deselect the text box.

3. The slide is not dynamic enough. Use a QuickMenu to change the appearance of Slide 1.
   a. Display Slide 1. Though it displays the show's title, it is not technically a title slide. Right click to display the QuickMenu and select **Appearance**. The Slide Properties dialog box appears.
   b. Click the **Appearance** tab, if necessary.
   c. The background could use a bit more pizzazz. Click the *Backgrounds* drop-down list box and select **From nature masters**. A set of backgrounds with nature themes appears.
   d. Click the third background from the left. It displays a serene coastline, appropriate to the theme of this retreat. Click **OK**. Note how the appearance of the title slide changes.

4. Save the slide show as **weekend retreat 5-4 xxx** and print the entire slide show.

5. Close the slide show.

# *Summary*

In this lesson you learned that:

■ Presentations has predesigned slide shows, called PerfectExpert projects, that you can use to save time when creating a presentation. You can pick the type of show that matches your needs, enter text and data, and customize the slides.

■ Presentations enables you to import outlines from Corel WordPerfect and other word processing programs. It converts each heading into a slide.

■ you can right click any slide to produce a QuickMenu, which saves you the time of navigating through several menu options. These QuickMenus contain the most frequently used commands, and vary in appearance depending on what view you are in and what item you have selected.

## FILL IN THE BLANK

**Complete each of the following statements by writing your answer in the blank provided.**

1. You can import _____ from word processing programs to save time.

2. In order to display a QuickMenu, you must _____ with the mouse.

3. Press _____ in order to change a title to a subtitle in Outliner view.

4. Press _____ + _____ to change a text line to a title line in Outliner view.

5. _____ projects are predefined slide shows.

## WRITTEN QUESTIONS

**Write your answers to the following questions.**

6. List at least five types of predefined slide shows.

7. Explain why using a QuickMenu saves time.

8. Describe how to import an outline into a slide show.

9. Why is it easier to add text to a predefined slide show in Outliner view than in Slide Editor view?

10. What steps do you save by selecting a predefined slide show?

## LESSON 5 PROJECT

SCANS

### PROJECT 5A

The management of Pet Paradise is considering opening a new store. They have scouted several locations, and now need to compare the information. Import an outline to create a slide show they can use at their next management meeting to make a decision.

1. Create a new slide show using the master of your choice.

2. Switch to **Outliner** view and insert the **new location** file.

3. Change slide templates as necessary. Add a subtitle to Slide 1 that contains the date, keeping it current.

4. You already have an annual lease price for the Waterford Mall location. As you are preparing this slide show, the lease prices from the other property owners come in. Following the Waterford Mall slide as a model, add a Level 1 bullet with the appropriate lease price to the remaining slides:

**Camptown Shopping Plaza:** $25,000 per year
**Main Street Storefront:** $50,000 per year
**Industrial Park Warehouse:** $41,500 per year

5. You have received additional information regarding the leases. Some of the store owners offer discounts on multiyear deals, while others do not. Add the following information as Level 2 bullet entries beneath the lease prices. (**TIP:** To add the Level 2 bullet entries, position the insertion point at the end of the Level 1 entry, press Enter, and then press Tab.)

**Waterford Mall:** Offers a discount for a three-year lease
**Camptown Shopping Plaza:** Offers no discount
**Main Street Storefront:** Offers a discount for a four-year lease
**Industrial Park Warehouse:** Offers no discount

6. Switch to **Slide Editor** view and remove any unused text boxes. Make any formatting changes desired using QuickMenus.

7. Save the slide show as **new location 5a xxx**. Print the slide show as audience notes with five slides per page. Close the slide show.

## PROJECT 5B

Create a slide show using the PerfectExpert.

1. Prepare a slide show on the subject of your choice, using the following steps:

   a. Using the information you learned in Lesson 1, decide what type of presentation you want to make. Rough out the text you might use in the presentation.
   b. Create a new presentation, selecting a predefined slide show that best matches your idea. Select the desired master.
   c. Switch to **Outliner** view. Replace text in the sample outline with your own. Add or delete slides and change slide layouts, as necessary. Your slide show should include at least five slides using several different layouts.

2. As always, spell check the slide show.

3. Play the slide show to see if you think it is effective. Make any necessary adjustments to the text and format.

4. Save the slide show with an appropriate name.

5. Play the slide show for someone else (friend, relative, fellow student, or instructor). Ask them for their feedback. If you think they have made some good suggestions, make the changes and save them.

6. Print the slide show, then close it.

SCANS

Based on your answers to the Critical Thinking Activity for Lesson 1, create an outline in Corel WordPerfect (or another word processing program) detailing how to give a good presentation. Save the outline and import it into Presentations. Add a title slide and edit the slides, as necessary.

Play the slide show for a classmate, making sure to follow your own advice.

# USING DRAWING TOOLS AND CLIPART

## OBJECTIVES

**Upon completion of this lesson, you will be able to:**

■ Use Presentations' drawing tools.

■ Create graphics for your presentation.

■ Edit graphic objects you have created.

■ Insert clipart images.

■ Transform graphic objects.

**⏱ Estimated Time: 1¹/₂ hours**

Pictures can help you get your message across to an audience. By placing an image of a jack-o'-lantern on a slide, for example, you immediately start the audience thinking about Halloween.

Presentations enables you to create your own pictures using its drawing tools. You can also add *clipart*, or predesigned graphic images, that comes with *Corel® WordPerfect® Suite 8*.

## Creating a Drawing

You can create, color, and pattern a drawing on any slide template using Presentations' drawing tools. To access the drawing tools, click the Insert menu and select Shape, or select drawing tools from the Toolbar or Tool Palette.

 **TIP**

The Tool Palette is an additional toolbar that offers all the drawing tools in one location. To access it, click the View menu, select Toolbars, check the Tool Palette check box, and click OK.

## EXERCISE ▷ PR6.1

1. Open **bonus bucks** from the student **Datafile** folder and display Slide 4.

2. Click the **Insert** menu and select **Shape**. A cascade menu appears, listing the available shape tools. Leave it on the screen for the next exercise.

## Selecting Drawing Tools

**FIGURE 6-1**
The Shape Cascade Menu

The Shape cascade menu shown in Figure 6-1 lists the available drawing tools. Each of these drawing tools is also available on the Toolbar.

The drawing tools on the Toolbar are organized within the following two icons:

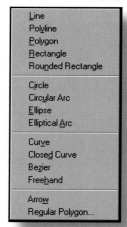

■ The Closed Object Tools icon lets you create squares, rectangles, circles, ellipses, polygons, and so on.

■ The Line Object Tools icon lets you create straight, diagonal, and curved lines of various kinds.

Only the current object appears on the face of the icon at any given time. To display the palette of all available objects, click the arrow portion of the icon.

To use a drawing tool:

■ Select it from the menu or from the Toolbar. The pointer changes to crosshairs.

■ Position the crosshairs where you want to begin drawing the figure.

■ As a general rule, click to begin drawing and double click to complete the object. The object will be surrounded by handles, indicating you can move or resize the object (you saw these earlier when you worked with text boxes). The inside handles allow you to resize either the height or width of the object. The corner handles let you resize both the height and width simultaneously. Click outside the object to leave it in place.

**TIP**

If you are not satisfied with a figure you have drawn, delete it immediately (while it is still surrounded by handles) by pressing Delete.

As part of their Bonus Bucks employee rewards program, Pet Paradise will throw a party annually. Draw balloons on an existing slide to illustrate this.

## EXERCISE ➤ PR6.2

1. Create the first balloon.
   a. Click **Ellipse** on the **Drawing Tools** cascade menu.
   b. The pointer changes to crosshairs. Position the crosshairs just below the subtitle and about 2 inches from the left edge of the slide. Drag to form an ellipse about 1.5 inches high to represent a balloon. By default, Presentations fills the ellipse with the color Teal.

2. Draw two more ellipses roughly in the positions shown in Figure 6-2. You'll need to select the Ellipse tool again for each ellipse.

3. Draw the balloon strings.
   a. Click the arrow on the **Line Object Tools** icon to display the palette. Select the curved line.
   b. Position the crosshairs at the bottom of one of the balloons and click to begin drawing the line.

c. Hold down the mouse button and drag the line to the left to create a small curve. Click the mouse button to change direction. Drag the crosshairs to the right to create another small curve. Click the mouse button to change direction again. Double click to complete the line, stopping short of the bottom of the slide to give the impression the balloons are floating. The finished product should look something like the line in Figure 6-2.

d. Draw lines for the other two balloons.

4. Leave the slide show on the screen for the next exercise.

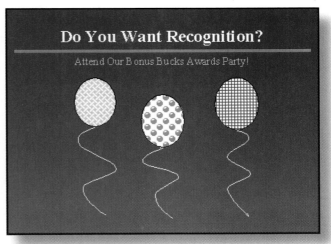

**FIGURE 6-2**
The Completed Drawing

## Changing Line And Fill Choices

You can change the lines and fill styles of the objects you draw. *Line*, in this case, refers not only to the lines you draw, but also to the outlines of the objects you draw. *Fill* refers to the pattern or color within a closed figure such as a rectangle or closed curve.

E X E R C I S E ⟹ PR6.3

SCANS

1. Change the colors and patterns of the balloons.
   a. Right click the first balloon, and select **Object Properties** from the pop-up menu. The Object Properties dialog box appears, opened to the Fill tab (see Figure 6-3).
   b. Click the **Foreground** button and select a yellow color from the palette.
   c. Select any pattern from the Pattern palette. Click **OK**.
   d. Using this process, change the colors and patterns of the remaining balloons.

2. Because of the dark background of the slide, the balloon strings are practically invisible. Make them thicker and color them white.
   a. Right click the line and select **Object Properties**. The Object Properties dialog box appears, opened to the Line tab.
   b. Click the **Color** button and select **White** from the palette.
   c. Click the **Width** button and select a slightly wider line from the palette. Click **OK**.
   d. Repeat this process for the remaining two balloon strings.

(continued on next page)

**3.** Save the slide show as **bonus bucks 6-3 xxx** and print Slide 4. Leave the slide show on the screen for the next exercise.

FAQs stands for Frequently Asked Questions. Many Internet hosts provide files containing answers to FAQs about their services.

**FIGURE 6-3**
The Object Properties Dialog Box

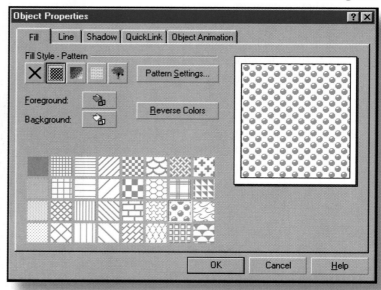

## Editing a Drawing

Presentations enables you to resize, move, and delete objects. You can also copy any object and paste copies of it elsewhere in the drawing.

**To resize an object and retain the same proportions:**

■ Select the object. Click and drag on a corner handle (dragging an inside handle stretches the object horizontally or vertically).

**To move an object:**

■ Select the object. Click inside the object, then drag it to its new location.

**To delete an object:**

■ Select the object, then press the Delete key.

**To *undelete* (restore) the last object you deleted:**

■ Click the Edit menu and select Undo, or click the Undo button on the Toolbar. Presentations remembers your last ten deletions from the current work session. You can continue to click Undo to reverse a whole series of changes.

**To group objects together so they can be moved or sized as a single unit:**

■ Click the first object. Next, hold down Ctrl and click any additional objects.

■ Click the Group button on the Property Bar.

**To copy and paste an object:**

- Select an object and click the Copy button on the Toolbar.

- Click the Paste button on the Toolbar. The copied object appears directly on top of the original object. To reposition the copy, drag it to the desired location on the slide.

## EXERCISE ⇨ PR6.4

1. Increase the size of the balloons.
   a. Select the first balloon by clicking it.
   b. Drag the top right handle upward to increase the width and height of the balloon slightly.
   c. Repeat this procedure for the remaining two balloons.

2. Add more balloons by copying an existing one.
   a. Click the center balloon to select it. Next, hold down the **Ctrl** key and click the string. Click the **Group** button on the Property Bar.
   b. Click the **Copy** button on the Toolbar. Next, click the **Paste** button on the Toolbar. Although you do not see a change on the screen, a copy of the selected balloon is now on top of the original balloon. Drag the selected balloon and position it as desired on the screen.
   c. Click **Paste** once more to create another balloon. Drag and position this balloon, then change the fill colors and patterns of both new balloons.

3. Move the balloons as far apart as possible.

4. Save the slide show as **bonus bucks 6-4 xxx**. Print the current slide as a handout with two slides per page.

5. Close the slide show.

# Adding Clipart to Your Slides

Presentations comes with preformatted graphics called *clipart* that you can add to enhance your slides. You can use many of the skills you learned for using the drawing tools with clipart images as well.

When you select clipart, the Scrapbook window appears (see Figure 6-4). The Scrapbook window also has a CD Clipart tab, which requires the *Corel® WordPerfect® Suite 8* CD-ROM. To use the additional clipart images that are stored on the disk, insert the CD-ROM in the CD-ROM drive.

## NOTE:

Inserting the *Corel® WordPerfect® Suite 8* CD-ROM may start the AutoRun program, which produces a setup screen. If this happens, it is not a problem. Simply click the Exit prompt.

**FIGURE 6-4**
The Scrapbook Window

EXERCISE ▷ PR6.5

SCANS

1. Open **pet care 3b xxx**. Display Slide 1.

2. Add a clipart image to the slide.
   a. Click the **Insert** menu and select **Graphics**, and then select **Clipart** from the cascade menu. (Alternatively, you can click the **Clipart** button on the Toolbar.)
   b. The Scrapbook window appears. If necessary, click the **Clipart** tab. Note that the first image in the first row of the window is a picture of a dog holding a newspaper, entitled *dogholdi*.
   c. Click this image and drag it outside of the window, onto the slide. You will see a rectangular outline once you drag the pointer image over the slide. (Do not worry about the position of the picture on the slide now. You will move it in a moment.)
   d. Minimize the Scrapbook window for now. You will access it again in the next exercise.

3. The image appears selected on the slide. Click and drag the image somewhere between the subtitle and the text box at the bottom of the slide. Make sure that it does not overlap either.

4. Still pointing to the image, click the right mouse button once. A pop-up menu appears. Select **Align**.

5. A cascade menu appears. Select **Center Left/Right**. The image appears centered horizontally.

6. Click outside the image to deselect it. The slide should resemble Figure 6-5.

7. Save the slide show as **pet care 6-5 xxx** and print Slide 1. Leave the slide show on the screen for the next exercise.

**FIGURE 6-5**
The Clipart Image in Place

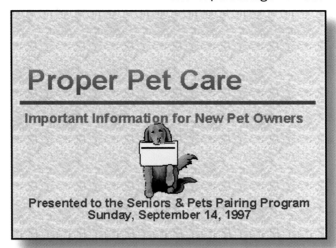

# *Transforming Objects*

Presentations offers you several ways to transform the look of drawn or clipart images, including rotating, skewing, flipping, and blending.

- *Rotating* means turning the object from its original position around an invisible axis in the center of the object.

- *Skewing* means distorting the graphic so it appears stretched.

- *Flipping* means reversing an object from left to right or top to bottom.

- *Blending* means creating mixed images between two objects, making it appear that one object is transforming into another.

✓ **NOTE:**

This next exercise requires clipart stored on the *Corel® WordPerfect® Suite 8* CD. If you do not have access to the CD, substitute clipart from the Clipart tab of the Scrapbook window.

**E X E R C I S E ⬛⟩ PR6.6**

SCANS

1. Move to Slide 2 and add two new clipart images.
   a. Open the clipart Scrapbook window, and click the **CD Clipart** tab. Double click the **Animals** folder. Next, double click the **Pets** subfolder.

   b. Click and drag the **doghappy** image onto the slide.
   c. Click and drag the **cat3** image onto the slide. Close the Scrapbook window.

(continued on next page)

2. Move the images to place them more attractively, leaving some space between them.

3. Change the angle at which the dog appears.
   a. Right click the dog image and select **Rotate** from the QuickMenu. The rotate and skew handles appear (see Figure 6-6).
   b. Click the upper left corner rotate handle and drag it upward until the dog is horizontal. When you are satisfied with the dog's position, release the handle.

4. With the dog image still selected, access the QuickMenu. Select **Flip**, then select **Left/Right** from the cascade menu.

5. Flip the cat so it is looking at the dog.

6. Skew the cat slightly to make the cat look as if it is recoiling from the dog.
   a. With the cat still selected, access the QuickMenu. Select **Rotate**. The rotate and skew handles appear.

**FIGURE 6-6**
The Rotate and Skew Handles

   b. Click and drag the bottom center handle and drag to the right until the cat appears slightly skewed. When you are satisfied with the cat's appearance, release the mouse button.
   c. Click outside the image to deselect it.

7. Save the slide show as **pet care 6-6 xxx** and print Slide 2. Leave the slide show on the screen for the next exercise.

## EXERCISE ⟫ PR6.7

**SCANS**

1. Display Slide 5 and insert the **puppy** graphic from the CD Clipart tab of the Scrapbook.

2. Move the puppy to the lower left corner of the slide.

3. Resize the graphic so it is approximately an inch tall.

4. Copy the graphic and paste it. Move the new copy of the puppy to the lower right corner of the screen. Resize the new graphic (on the right) so that it is about two inches tall.

5. Click one copy of the puppy to select it, then hold down the **Ctrl** key and click the other. Both graphics should be surrounded by the same set of handles.

6. Blend the images.
  a. Click the **Tools** menu and select **Blend**. The Blend dialog box appears.
  b. Enter the number **8** in the dialog box and click **OK**. Presentations inserts the images, which get larger as they progress right. The images give the appearance that the dog is growing larger (see Figure 6-7).
  c. Click outside of the images to deselect them.

7. Save the slide show as **pet care 6-7 xxx**. Print the show as handouts with two slides per page.

8. Close the slide show.

**FIGURE 6-7**
Blended Images

# *Summary*

In this lesson you learned that:

- you can draw line objects, like straight lines and curves, and closed objects, like circles and ellipses. You can change the line and fill colors and styles of these objects, as well as move, resize, or delete them.

- you can group drawn objects together in order to resize, move, or delete them as a single unit.

- Presentations comes with clipart, preformatted graphics that you can add to a slide show to enhance it. You can change the appearance of these graphics by rotating, skewing, flipping, and blending.

## LESSON 6 REVIEW QUESTIONS

### FILL IN THE BLANKS

**Complete each of the following statements by writing your answer in the blank provided.**

1. Presentations comes with preformatted graphics called _____.

2. You can draw ellipses, triangles, and rectangles using Presentations' _____ tools.

3. _____ means distorting a graphic so it appears stretched.

4. _____ means reversing a graphic from left to right or top to bottom.

5. _____ means creating mixed images between two objects.

## WRITTEN QUESTIONS

**Write your answers to the following questions.**

**6.** Define the word *fill* as it relates to the drawing tools.

**7.** Describe how to group objects together.

**8.** Explain why you do not see a second object when you copy and paste a graphic.

**9.** How do you resize an object so it retains the same proportions?

**10.** Describe how to blend two objects.

## LESSON 6 PROJECT

SCANS

### PROJECT 6A

Add clipart to a presentation.

**1.** Open **pet perks 3a xxx** from the student **Datafile** folder. Display Slide 1 on the screen.

**2.** Click the **Clipart** button on the Toolbar. The Scrapbook window appears.

**3.** Locate the **celebrat.wpg** icon, a picture of a champagne bottle. Click and drag a copy of the image onto the slide. Minimize the Scrapbook window.

**4.** Enlarge the image by clicking and dragging on one of the corner handles.

**5.** Right click the image to produce the QuickMenu. Click **Align**, then select **Center Left/Right** from the cascade menu. Presentations centers the image horizontally.

**6.** Click outside the image to deselect it.

**7.** Add the following pieces of clipart to the designated slides:

Slide 2:    **giftshp1.wpg**
Slide 3:    **fistocsh.wpg**
Slide 4:    **dogholdi.wpg**
Slide 5:    **crdtcr2.wpg**

**8.** Align and resize the clipart as desired.

**9.** Save the file as **pet perks 6a xxx**. Print the slide show.

**10.** Close the slide show.

## PROJECT 6B

Draw an object and edit it.

1. Open **bonus bucks 6-4 xxx** and display Slide 1.

2. Draw a triangle below the title and resize it so it is about 1.5 inches tall.

3. Set the triangle for **Center Left/Right** justification.

4. Fill the triangle with a texture.

   a. Right click the triangle and select **Object Properties**.
   b. In the Fill tab of the Object Properties dialog box click the **Texture** button in the *Fill Style* section. Click the **Category** drop-down list box and select **Objects**. Select the **US Coins** texture from the palette. Click **OK**.

5. Rotate the triangle so it appears like an upside-down pyramid. Move it downward slightly to improve the vertical spacing, if necessary.

6. Save the file as **bonus bucks 6b xxx** and print Slide 1. Leave the slide show on the screen for the next exercise.

## PROJECT 6C

Add two clipart graphics and blend them.

1. Display Slide 3. Add the **lighbul** graphic to the lower left corner of the slide. Add the **fistocsh** graphic to the lower right corner of the screen. Resize them so they are approximately the same size, if desired.

2. Move the fist graphic up, so that it is slightly higher from the bottom of the slide than the lightbulb graphic.

3. Blend the two graphics, inserting six objects between them.

4. Save the file as **bonus bucks 6c xxx** and print Slide 3. Then, close the slide show.

## CRITICAL THINKING ACTIVITY

SCANS

Open the **good communication** slide show from the student **Datafile** folder. Add three pieces of clipart and at least one drawing to the slide show. These graphics should be pertinent to the slide text. When you are finished, print the slides (one per page) and show them to your instructor. Save the file as **good communication xxx**.

# PRESENTING STATISTICS WITH CHARTS

## OBJECTIVES

**Upon completion of this lesson, you will be able to:**

- Identify the different charts available in Presentations.

- Create a statistical chart.

- Edit a chart with the chart editor.

**Estimated Time: 1¹/₂ hours**

In the business world, converting information into charts and graphs and interpreting information from charts and graphs is an essential part of many jobs. These statistical representations are particularly important because they illustrate data and help viewers form conclusions.

Because charts and graphs send such a powerful message, you must be certain that they provide accurate information. Avoid using visuals that do not accurately convey the message, that mislead, or that show insignificant statistics. For example, it would be very misleading to show a graph showing the rise in bicycle thefts next to a graph illustrating the rise in coffee consumption.

## *Types of Charts*

You have already learned about one type of chart available in Presentations: a table. The remaining chart types include the following:

- **Pie chart.** A pie chart represents an entire group of data as a circle divided into proportional sections based on some type of distinguishing characteristic. Pie charts always add up to 100%. Figure 7-1 shows a pie chart.

**FIGURE 7-1**
A Pie Chart

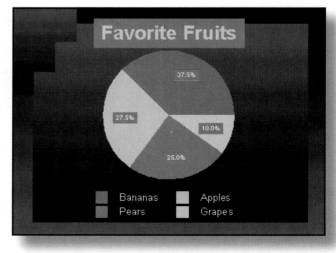

■ **XY chart.** An XY chart uses a grid with horizontal (X) and vertical (Y) axes to determine placement of the data points. XY charts include bar charts, line charts, scatter charts, and area charts. Figure 7-2 shows a vertical bar chart.

■ **Organization chart.** An organization chart (see Figure 7-3) indicates the relationship of individuals in an organization.

   This lesson will cover statistical charts. Other chart types will be discussed in later lessons.

   Table 7-1 helps you determine which type of chart to use in a given situation.

   If you select a chart form and find that the data representation would be better in a different form, Presentations makes it easy to switch to another type of chart.

## Inserting the Statistical Chart into a Slide

   For your first statistical chart, you will create one of the most common types of statistical charts: a *bar chart*. A bar chart is particularly good for comparing quantities. For example, if an ice cream company adds a new flavor to its product line, the marketing department might want to find out how well the new flavor is selling compared to flavors already in the product line. A bar chart can graphically illustrate these differences.

**FIGURE 7-2**
A Vertical Bar Chart

**FIGURE 7-3**
An Organization Chart

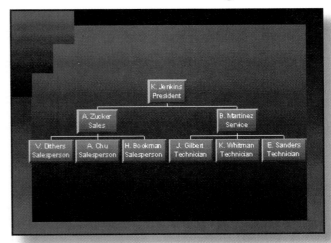

**INTERNET**

Gopher is a program that uses a series of menus to lead users to files of information. Gopher is named for the Golden Gophers of the University of Minnesota, where the program was developed.

**TABLE 7-1**
Gallery of Charts in Presentations

## CHARTS

| Use this kind of chart . . . | . . . when you want to: |
| --- | --- |
| Table | list data in columns and rows. |
| Organization | show hierarchical relationships in an organization. |
| Pie | show proportions and relationships of parts to the whole. |
| Bar | show variations between components, but not in relation to the whole. |
| Line | show trends and rate of change over time. |
| Area | show trends and amount of change over time. |
| Surface | show three-dimensional representations of data, with connected data points forming a surface. |
| Radar | compare data over time and show variations and trends. |
| Mixed | use different series types to compare data. |
| High/Low | show high, low, open, and close quotes for stocks. |
| Bubble | plot three different values on the x and y axes. |

## EXERCISE ▷ PR7.1

**SCANS**

1. Start Presentations. Create a new slide show and select the *ELEGANT* master from the **Design** category. Click **OK**.

2. Key the following information on the title slide:
   Title: **Pet Food Sales Analysis**
   Subtitle: **A Comparison of the Three Leading Brands**

3. Add a new slide with no layout.

4. Click the **Insert** menu and select **Chart**, or click the **Chart** button on the Toolbar. The pointer changes to a hand holding a box.

5. Click the working screen. The Data Chart Gallery dialog box appears.

**6.** Choose the chart type.

   **a.** In the Chart type list box select **Bar (Vert)**. Notice that a gallery of available chart styles appears.

   **b.** Select the first chart in the top row of example bar charts.

   **c.** Click the **Use sample data** and **3-D** check boxes to remove the checks, if necessary. Click **OK**.

**7.** The datasheet appears. Leave the datasheet on the screen for the next exercise.

## Entering the Data

When you enter data into your chart, you should consider what aspects of the data you want to emphasize. If you want to stress the highest values, arrange the data in *descending order*, from highest to lowest. If you want to stress the lowest values, arrange the data in *ascending order*, from lowest to highest. If you want to compare data for a specific city to data for all cities in the same general geographic region, you might show the data for that city first, followed by the data for the other cities.

You enter the data directly into the datasheet that appears on the screen when you choose a chart type. The datasheet now on your screen differs from the one that you worked with in Lesson 4. First, note that the datasheet does not contain sample data. Next, note the Legend column and the Labels row, shown in Figure 7-4.

**FIGURE 7-4**
The Legend Column and Labels Row

| | Legend | A | B | C |
|---|---|---|---|---|
| Labels | | Dog | Cat | Bird |
| 1 | Friendly | | | |
| 2 | Chow-Chow | | | |
| 3 | Health-Mix | | | |
| 4 | | | | |
| 5 | | | | |

Entries that you make in the Legend column, such as *Health-Mix*, will appear at the bottom of your chart as the *legend*. The color box next to each entry in this column indicates what color the bar will be on the chart. Entries that you make in the Labels row, such as *Cat*, become the labels for the data in the columns below them.

 **NOTE:**

Remember that you can move and resize the datasheet as needed to make data entry easier.

# EXERCISE ⟹ PR7.2

1. Enter the following data into the datasheet. Begin the label entries (*Dog, Cat, Bird*) in column A. Begin the legend entries (*Friendly, Chow-Chow, Health-Mix*) in row 1.

|   |            | A        | B        | C        |
|---|------------|----------|----------|----------|
|   |            | Dog      | Cat      | Bird     |
| 1 | Friendly   | 23,000   | 18,000   | 9,000    |
| 2 | Chow-Chow  | 15,000   | 52,000   | 19,000   |
| 3 | Health-Mix | 49,000   | 23,000   | 37,000   |

2. As you insert data, notice how Presentations places it in the new chart below the spreadsheet.

3. When you have finished entering the data, close the datasheet, then close the chart editor. Your new chart appears on the slide.

4. Save the slide show as **pet food 7-2 xxx** and print Slide 2. Leave the slide show on the screen for the next exercise.

## Adding Titles and Subtitles

The title of your chart should describe what the data shows. You can add a title and subtitle to your chart.

# EXERCISE ⟹ PR7.3

1. Double click the chart to open the chart editor. Select the pointer tool from the Toolbar, if necessary.

2. Click the **Chart** menu and select **Title** to open the Title Properties dialog box (see Figure 7-5).

3. In the *Display chart title* text box key **Pet Food Sales by Brand**.

4. The current text color for the title is White, which does not show up well on the *ELEGANT* master. Click the **Text color** button to display the color palette. Select **Royal Blue**, the last color in the second row. Click **OK**.

**FIGURE 7-5**
The Title Properties Dialog Box

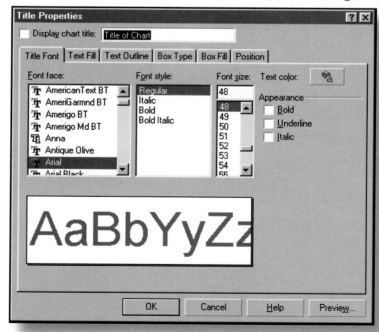

**5.** With the chart editor open, click the **Chart** menu and select **Subtitle** to open the Subtitle Properties dialog box.

**6.** In the *Display chart subtitle* text box key **Comparative Analysis**.

**7.** Change the color of the subtitle to **Royal Blue**.

**8.** Close the chart editor. Save your changes as **pet food 7-3 xxx** and print Slide 2. Leave the slide show on the screen for the next exercise.

# *Editing a Statistical Chart*

Some editing features that you have already learned can also be used to edit statistical charts. Presentations also offers other editing features that can be used for any chart type.

## Moving and Resizing a Chart

To move or resize a chart:

■ Select the pointer tool from the Toolbar.

■ Click the chart to select it (handles will appear around the edges of the chart).

■ To move the chart, place the pointer inside the selected chart and drag the chart to the new position.

■ To resize the chart, place the pointer on one of the handles and drag. Dragging a corner handle changes both height and width at the same time.

## Adding New Data to the Chart

You can add new data to a chart at any time by redisplaying the datasheet and inserting the data. You can also add a new row or column before, in between, or after existing rows and columns. When you close the datasheet, the new data appears.

## Changing the Chart Type

Once you have created a chart, you can easily change it to another chart type without having to re-enter data. You can also change the chart from two-dimensional to three-dimensional with the click of the mouse.

---

## EXERCISE ▷ PR7.4

SCANS

**1.** You need to add another pet food manufacturer to the data chart. Add the data for Vitality.

    **a.** Double click the chart to open the chart editor.

**b.** Click the **View** menu and select **Datasheet**, or click the **View Datasheet** button on the Toolbar to redisplay the datasheet.

(continued on next page)

c. To insert a row above the Health-Mix row, click row number **3** to select the entire row, then click the **Edit** menu and select **Insert**. A blank row appears as the new row 3.

d. Insert the following data in row 3:

**Vitality**     **6,000**     **9,000**     **8,000**

2. Close the datasheet.

3. Change the chart to a horizontal, three-dimensional bar chart.

a. With the chart editor still open, click the **Chart** menu and select **Gallery**. In the *Chart type* list choose **Bar (Horz)** and select the third chart type in the top row.

b. To make the chart three-dimensional, click the **3-D** check box at the bottom of the dialog box, or click the **3-D Chart** button on the Toolbar. Click **OK**.

c. With the chart displayed on the screen, click the **3-D Chart** button on the Toolbar to toggle back to two-dimensional view. This button toggles the chart between the two- and three-dimensional views.

d. Close the chart editor. Leave the slide show on the screen for the next exercise.

## Editing Data Series Properties

Each row of data in a chart is called a *series*. Presentations assigns default colors, shapes, and other attributes to the data series in the chart.

# EXERCISE ⟹ PR7.5

SCANS

1. Double click the chart to open the chart editor.

2. Edit the title.
   a. Double click the title to open the Title Properties dialog box.
   b. Change the font of the title to **Bold** and **44** pt.
   c. Change the position of the title by clicking the **Position** tab and clicking the leftmost option button.
   d. Click the **Box Type** tab. Click the **No box** check box to deselect it and display a palette of box choices.
   e. Choose the second box type from the right on the top row of the palette.

   f. Click the **No border** check box to deselect it. Change the color of the box border by clicking the **Border color** button to display a color palette. Choose the last color in the second row. Click **OK**.

3. Change the colors of the bars representing the data series.
   a. At the bottom of the chart, double click the color marker next to *Friendly*. The Series Properties dialog box appears (see Figure 7-6). You can use this dialog box to change the shape used to represent the series, as well as select a color, pattern, line width, and style for the shape.

FIGURE 7-6

**b.** Notice that *Series 1: Friendly* displays at the top of the dialog box. The Sample box displays the current shape and color of the bar for this series of data.

**c.** Click the **Fill** tab, then click the **Foreground** button to display a color palette. Choose a bright yellow color for the bar color. Use the **Preview** button to make sure that you like this color. Then click **Back** to return to the Fill Attributes tab.

**d.** Click the large, right-pointing arrow at the top of the dialog box to display *Series 2: Chow-Chow*. Choose a new color for this bar.

**e.** Using this process, select new colors for the remaining two series. You can return to a previous series by clicking the large, left-pointing arrow at the top of the dialog box.

**4.** When you are satisfied with your changes, click **OK** to close the Series Properties dialog box. Close the chart editor.

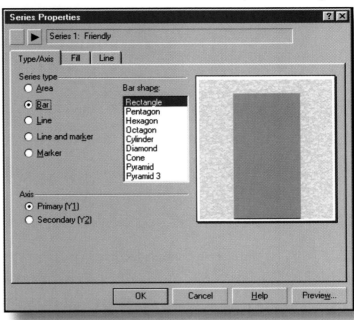

The Series Properties Dialog Box

**5.** Based on the information in the chart on your screen, what brand of pet food seems to be least popular in the Bird category? What brand is most popular in the Cat category? What brands are most and least popular overall?

**6.** Save the slide show as **pet food 7-5 xxx** and print it as a handout with two slides per page.

**7.** Close the slide show.

# *Summary*

In this lesson you learned that:

- Presentations offers many different chart types that enable you to graphically represent data. The major chart types include tables, as well as pie, XY, and organization charts.

- in order to create a statistical chart, you access the Data Chart Gallery dialog box, which lets you choose the chart type, as well as a predesigned chart style.

- you enter the data into the datasheet, where you also designate legends and labels identifying what the data represents. Once you have created the chart, you can edit its values and appearance. You can also change the chart type.

- you can change the data series properties–default colors, shapes, and other attributes which make it easy to identify and track different data series.

### TRUE OR FALSE

**Circle the T if the statement is true. Circle the F if the statement is false.**

**T    F    1.** A bar chart is an example of an XY chart.

**T    F    2.** You can create a chart using one chart type, then apply a different chart type later.

**T    F    3.** To stress the lowest values in the data you are presenting, arrange the data in ascending order.

**T    F    4.** Each column in a chart is called a data series.

**T    F    5.** A pie chart represents the relationship between the parts and the whole.

### WRITTEN QUESTIONS

**Write your answers to the following questions.**

**6.** How do you think color has an impact on how an audience views a chart?

**7.** Describe how to insert a vertical bar chart onto a slide.

**8.** What is a statistical chart?

**9.** Name four types of XY charts.

**10.** Describe how to add a title to a chart.

## LESSON 7 PROJECT

SCANS

### PROJECT 7A

Add a bar chart to an existing slide show.

**1.** Open **dog days 4-7 xxx**. Display Slide 3.

**2.** Pet Paradise's management would like to see the data in Slide 3 in a bar chart. Double click the chart to display the chart editor. Click the **View** menu and select **Datasheet**. The datasheet appears.

**3.** You will copy the data from this datasheet to the Windows clipboard. With the datasheet still open, click the **Edit** menu and select **Select All**. The entire datasheet is highlighted. Click the **Copy** button.

4. Close the datasheet and the chart editor. Add a new slide with no layout.

5. Click the **Insert** menu and select **Chart**. The pointer changes to a hand holding a box. Click the slide once to access the Data Chart Gallery dialog box. Choose a vertical bar chart from the examples. If necessary, click the **3-D** box to deselect it. Click **OK**.

6. The datasheet appears. Click the **Paste** button. The data from the chart on Slide 3 fills the datasheet.

7. Close the datasheet. The chart appears.

8. Add a title to the chart: **"Dog Days" Projected Sales**. Change the title font to **Red**, **48** pt, and **Bold**. If desired, change the colors of the bars in the chart.

9. Save the slide show as **dog days 7a xxx**. Print only Slide 4 as a handout with one slide per page. Close the slide show.

## PROJECT 7B

The owners of Pet Paradise are preparing a customer satisfaction report, and they want to include a chart which details the results of a customer satisfaction survey for each of the two store locations. Open the report and insert a slide with a vertical bar chart illustrating the results.

1. Open **customer survey** from the student **Datafile** folder.

2. Add a data chart slide to the end of the show.

3. Insert a vertical bar chart and enter the following information into the datasheet:

| | Customer Service | Store Appearance | Products & Services | Pricing |
|---|---|---|---|---|
| Pet Paradise | 96 | 98 | 88 | 91 |
| Pet Paradise II | 94 | 63 | 89 | 87 |

4. Insert the title **1996 - 1997 Customer Satisfaction Survey Results** in 44 pt. Bold type.

5. Insert the subtitle **Satisfied Customers Per 100**.

6. Change the fill color of the data series to a bright color of your choice.

7. Place a single-lined box around the legend.

8. Save the file as **customer survey 7b xxx** and print Slide 6. Then, close the slide show.

Open **acme annual sales** from the student **Datafile** folder, and display Slide 2. Look at the bar chart and draw some conclusions. What did you assume?

One reasonable conclusion you might draw is that Store 3 is the most profitable store Acme, Inc. has. After all, Store 3 sold about twice as much as Store 1 and Store 2.

What would you then think, however, if you discovered that Store 3 is a warehouse store, physically much larger than the other two stores?

What would you think if you discovered that Store 3 is the least profitable of all the stores in the chain, barely making any net profit (profit after expenses and taxes)?

Draw some overall conclusions. Is it possible that some charts can "lie"?

# CREATING AND ENHANCING PIE CHARTS

## OBJECTIVES

**Upon completion of this lesson, you will be able to:**

- Create a pie chart.

- Edit and enhance a pie chart.

- Explode a slice of the pie.

- Create multiple pies on one chart.

- Create proportional multiple slices.

- Create linked pie charts.

🕐 **Estimated Time: 2 hours**

Pie charts pictorially illustrate the relation of the parts to the whole. When statistics add up to 100 percent of the whole, a pie chart often best depicts the data. For example, you may want to show, in percentages, how many students out of an entire class received an A, B, C, and so forth on a test.

Presentations enables you to enhance a pie chart by changing the color of a slice to emphasize it, as well as distinguish it from an adjacent slide. You can also separate one or more slices to emphasize an important part of the pie.

## *Creating a Pie Chart*

Key words to look for when choosing a pie chart to represent your data are *share*, *percentage of total*, *market share*, *proportion*, or *specified percent*. When you plan your pie chart, try not to use more than six segments, as it will crowd the chart and reduce its impact. If you have more than six groupings of data, choose the five largest and group the rest together as *Others*.

SCANS

1. Open **pet food 7-5 xxx**.

2. Add a new slide with no layout after Slide 2.

3. Click the **Insert** menu and select **Chart**, or click the **Chart** button on the Toolbar. Click the new slide with the hand icon to access the Data Chart Gallery dialog box.

4. Choose **Pie** from the Chart type list, and select the first pie in the top row of choices. Make sure the **3-D** check box is deselected. Click **OK**. The datasheet appears.

5. Leave the datasheet on the screen for the next exercise.

## Entering Data

The datasheet for a pie chart differs from that for a bar chart, as shown in Figure 8-1. The pie chart datasheet lets you enter data and specify labels for more than one pie. You can also specify entries for more than one pie in the Legend column. Use a legend or labels to indicate what the slices represent.

**FIGURE 8-1**
The Datasheet for a Pie Chart

| | Legend | Labels 1 | Pie 1 | Labels 2 |
|---|---|---|---|---|
| 1 | | | | |
| 2 | | | | |
| 3 | | | | |
| 4 | | | | |
| 5 | | | | |

SCANS

1. The data for the datasheet is listed below. Enter the text in the Legend column. Enter the numbers in the column headed *Pie 1*.

| Friendly | 50,000 |
|---|---|
| **Chow-Chow** | **76,000** |
| **Vitality** | **23,000** |
| **Health-Mix** | **109,000** |

2. Your screen should resemble Figure 8-2. Close the datasheet.

**FIGURE 8-2**
The Completed Datasheet

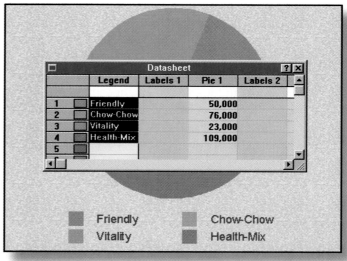

3. Click the **Chart** menu and select **Title** to open the Title Properties dialog box. Insert a title: **Total Sales by Brand**.

4. Close the data chart editor. Leave the slide show on the screen for the next exercise.

## Displaying Labels

You can choose what type of label to display, as well as make formatting changes to it in the Data Labels (Pie) dialog box (see Figure 8-3).

The Position tab of the Data Labels (Pie) dialog box enables you to display text, value, or percentage labels inside or outside the slices. You can choose between two orientations for labels: One line and Stacked.

The Font tab lets you choose a font, style, size, appearance, and color for the labels. The Box Type tab enables you to select a box style to surround the labels. Use the Box Fill tab to specify a pattern or color for the label boxes.

**FIGURE 8-3**
Data Labels (Pie) Dialog Box

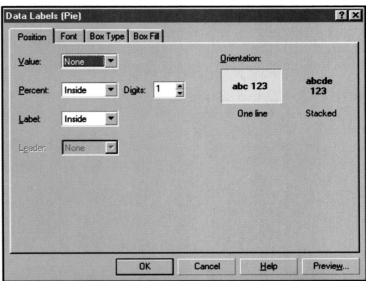

EXERCISE ⟩ PR8.3

SCANS

1. Double click anywhere on the pie to open the chart editor.

2. Click the **Chart** menu and select **Data Labels**, or click the **Labels** button on the Toolbar. The Data Labels (Pie) dialog box appears (see Figure 8-3). Select the **Position** tab, if necessary.

3. Click the **Percent** drop-down list box and select **Inside**. Preview the change, then click **OK**.

4. Close the chart editor and leave the slide show on the screen for the next exercise.

# *Editing and Enhancing a Pie Chart*

You can use skills you have already learned in previous lessons to edit a pie chart:

■ To *move* a pie chart, select it and drag it to a new location, as for any other object.

■ To *resize* a pie chart, select it and drag handles to enlarge or shrink the chart. Dragging a corner handle will change both height and width.

- To *edit* any part of a pie chart, such as a slice or label, double click the object while in the chart editor.

- To change the pie chart from two-dimensional to three-dimensional, access the Data Chart Gallery dialog box and click the 3-D check box, or click the 3-D Chart button on the Toolbar.

Presentations also enables you to enhance pie charts using the Layout/Type Properties dialog box, as shown in Figure 8-4.

## Exploding a Pie Slice

You can separate a pie slice from the whole pie to emphasize it, which is called *exploding* a slice. You can use the Layout/Type Properties dialog box to explode a slice, but there is an even easier way to do it: click the pie slice to select it, and drag the slide to a new position.

**FIGURE 8-4**
The Layout/Type Properties Dialog Box

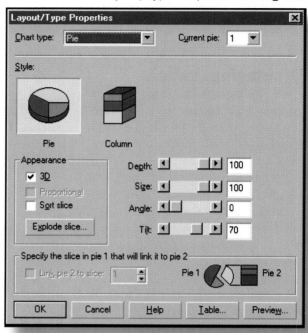

---

E X E R C I S E ⟹ PR8.4

**SCANS**

1. Open the chart editor, if necessary.

2. Emphasize the Health-Mix portion of the pie by exploding the slice.
   a. Click the Health-Mix slice to select it.
   b. Click the slice and drag it about a quarter of an inch from the rest of the pie chart.
   c. Click elsewhere on the pie chart to deselect the slice.

3. Click the **3-D Chart** button on the Toolbar to make the pie chart three-dimensional.

4. Change the slice colors.
   a. Double click the slice to open the Series Properties dialog box. Click the **Fill** tab.
   b. Click the **Foreground** button and choose a new color for the slice on the color palette. Use the arrows at the top of the dialog box to move to the other slices and change their colors as desired.
   c. Click **OK** to return to the chart editor.

5. Save your changes as **pet food 8-4 xxx** and print Slide 3. Leave the slide show on the screen for the next exercise.

# Creating Multiple Pies on The Same Chart

You can display several pies on a single chart. This enables you to compare wholes to wholes, such as two fiscal years. To add data for multiples pies:

■ Retrieve the datasheet. Insert the new data in the Pie 2 column, and insert new labels, if necessary.

■ If you want the new pie to share the same legend colors with the existing pie, use the same rows used by the existing pie. If you want to use new legend colors, begin your new data in rows below those already used.

Presentations lets you make changes to each pie in a multiple pie chart using the Layout/Type Properties dialog box. For example, you can adjust the sizes of each pie on the chart. To access this dialog box:

■ Click the Chart menu and select Layout/Type, or click the Layout button on the Toolbar. The Layout/Type Properties dialog box appears.

■ Select a pie number in the Current pie drop-down list box to change layout options for that pie. To change the size of a pie, for example, make sure the correct pie number is shown in the Current pie box, then key a new percent value in the Size box.

Pet Paradise's managers want to compare the pet food sales by brand at Pet Paradise and Pet Paradise II. Add a second pie to the chart to illustrate the comparison.

## EXERCISE ⟹ PR8.5

**SCANS**

1. Open the chart editor.

2. Insert an explanatory subtitle.
   a. Click the **Chart** menu and select **Subtitle**. The Subtitle Properties dialog box appears.
   b. Key the following subtitle: **Pet Paradise vs. Pet Paradise II**. Click **OK**.

3. Add data for the Pet Paradise II location.
   a. Open the datasheet.
   b. The second pie uses the same legend as the first pie, so you just need to fill in the Pet Paradise II location sales figures. In the Pie 2 column key only the figures below (you may need to scroll right):

   **36,000**
   **58,000**
   **17,000**
   **89,000**

4. Close the datasheet and observe the second pie in place on the slide. Notice that the label style is the same as that created for the first pie.

5. Explode the Health-Mix slice as you did for the first pie.

6. Save your changes as **pet food 8-5 xxx** and print Slide 3. Leave the slide show on the screen for the next exercise.

## Creating Proportional Pies

When you display several pies on one slide, you can make the pies *proportional*. Presentations sizes the pies according to the numbers in the datasheet. For example, the total sales from Pet Paradise are greater than those at the Pet Paradise II location on the current slide. The location with greater sales will result in a larger pie.

## EXERCISE ▷ PR8.6

1. Open the chart editor for the pies.

2. Click the **Chart** menu and select **Layout/Type**. The Layout/Type Properties dialog box appears.

3. In the *Appearance* section of the dialog box click the **Proportional** check box, then click **OK**. Notice that Pie 1 is larger than Pie 2.

4. Leave the slide show on the screen for the next exercise.

## Changing Text Font And Attributes

You can change the font and attributes of any text or box on the chart, including titles, labels, and legends. To change text or box attributes:

■ In the chart editor, double click the text you want to edit.

■ For a title (or subtitle), change font, style, size, appearance, and color of text in the Title Font tab of the Title (or Subtitle) Properties dialog box. Click the Box Type or Box Fill tab to change box attributes.

■ For labels, click the Font tab of the Data Labels dialog box to change text. Click the Box Type or Box Fill tab to change box attributes.

■ For a legend, click the Text Font tab of the Legend Properties dialog box to change text. Click the Box Type or Box Fill tab to change box attributes.

## EXERCISE ▷ PR8.7

1. With the chart editor open, double click any of the percent labels. The Data Labels (Pie) dialog box appears.

2. Choose the **Box Type** tab and click the **No box** check box to remove the boxes around the percentages.

3. Choose the **Font** tab. Change the font style to **Bold** and the font size to **20** pt. If desired, choose a font color that contrasts well with your pie slice colors. Click **OK**.

4. Double click the subtitle and change its font style to **Bold**.

5. Save your changes as **pet food 8-7 xxx** and print Slide 3. Leave the slide show on the screen for the next exercise.

# *Linking Pies*

You can *link* a slice of the pie to a breakdown of the contents of the slice. For example, you might want to link a slice in one pie representing chocolate ice cream to a second pie illustrating which flavor of chocolate is most popular. Your underlying message for that slide might be that because Dutch chocolate has such a small share of the market, it does not pay to produce it. You are comparing one slice of the pie to the entire second pie.

**EXERCISE ▭▷ PR8.8**

**SCANS**

1. Use the existing data for Pie 1 to create the linked pie chart. Copy the data in the datasheet for Pie 1 to be used for a new pie chart.
   a. Open the chart editor for the current pie chart. Display the datasheet.
   b. Click and drag to select the data for the legend and Pie 1 column, as shown in Figure 8-5.

**FIGURE 8-5**
Highlighted Datasheet Entries

   c. Click the **Copy** button on the Toolbar.
   d. Close the datasheet and the chart editor.

2. Add a new slide with no layout. Click the **Chart** button on the Toolbar, then click the new slide with the hand-shaped pointer to open the Data Chart Gallery dialog box.

3. Select the first pie chart in the sample area and click **OK** to display the datasheet.

4. Click the first cell in row 1. Click the **Paste** button to insert the data you copied from Pie 1 on the previous slide. The data appears in the datasheet and a pie appears on the new slide.

5. Insert the labels for the three types of Vitality brand pet food (Dog, Cat, Bird) in the Labels 2 column of the datasheet, beginning in row 5 (this will ensure that the new pie slices will have different colors from those in Pie 1). Insert the numbers for these items in the Pie 2 column. Use the following entries:

   **Dog 6,000**
   **Cat 9,000**
   **Bird 8,000**

6. Your datasheet should resemble Figure 8-6. Close the datasheet.

7. Link the Vitality slice in Pie 1 to the breakdown in Pie 2.
   a. Click the **Chart** menu and select **Layout/Type**.
   b. Click the **Current Pie** drop-down list box. Select **1**.
   c. Click the **Link pie 2 to slice** check box to check it. Use the spin box arrows to select slice **3**. Click **OK**.

(continued on next page)

8. Enhance the appearance of the linked pies.
   a. Make the pies three-dimensional by clicking the **3-D Chart** button on the Toolbar.
   b. Select options from the Data Labels (Pie) dialog box to make the Pie 2 labels more readable and attractive.
   c. If desired, change the slice colors for both pies.

9. Make the second pie slightly smaller.
   a. Click the **Layout** button on the Toolbar to display the Layout/Type Properties dialog box.
   b. Make sure that the *2* appears in the Current pie drop-down list box.
   c. In the Size box key **90**. Click **OK**.

10. Insert the following title for the chart: **Vitality Sales by Type**. Close the chart editor.

**FIGURE 8-6**
The Second Pie Figures

| | Legend | Labels 1 | Pie 1 | Labels 2 | Pie 2 | |
|---|---|---|---|---|---|---|
| | | | Total Sales | | | |
| 1 | Friendly | | 50,000 | | | |
| 2 | Chow-Chow | | 76,000 | | | |
| 3 | Vitality | | 23,000 | | | |
| 4 | Health-Mix | | 109,000 | | | |
| 5 | | | | Dog | 6,000 | |
| 6 | | | | Cat | 9,000 | |
| 7 | | | | Bird | 8,000 | |
| 8 | | | | | | |
| 9 | | | | | | |
| 10 | | | | | | |
| 11 | | | | | | |

11. Save your changes as **pet food 8-8 xxx**. Print only Slides 3 and 4 as handouts with two slides per page.

12. Close the slide show.

# *Summary*

In this lesson you learned that:

- a pie chart illustrates the relationship of the parts to the whole, and that pie charts are best used when statistics add up to 100 percent of the whole.

- you can enter data for more than one pie chart into the datasheet, meaning you can display more than one pie chart per slide.

- Presentations enables you to emphasize a particular slice of a pie by exploding it.

- you can make multiple pie charts proportional, meaning the greater of the two pies appears larger than the other.

- you can link a slice of one pie to a whole other pie chart, allowing you to illustrate the elements that make up the slice.

## LESSON 8 REVIEW QUESTIONS

### TRUE OR FALSE

**Circle T if the statement is true. Circle F if the statement is false.**

**T  F   1.** Presentations lets you "explode" a pie slice to emphasize the data that the slice represents.

**T  F   2.** You are limited to one pie chart per slide.

**T  F   3.** Legends is another term for labels.

**T  F   4.** Pie charts are best used to track data over a period of time.

**T  F   5.** Making pie charts proportional means that you can make the chart with the greater values larger.

### WRITTEN QUESTIONS

**Write your answers to the following questions.**

**6.** Describe how to display percent labels within pie chart slices.

**7.** Give one example of when creating a pie chart would be appropriate.

**8.** Explain how to link one slice of a pie chart to another pie chart.

**9.** Why would you want to make pie charts proportional?

**10.** Explain how to change the fill color of a pie slice.

## LESSON 8 PROJECT

SCANS

### PROJECT 8A

The owners of Pet Paradise want to analyze the characteristics of the customers who participated in their customer satisfaction survey. Create a pie chart that illustrates the percentages of first time, repeat, and loyal customers.

**1.** Open **customer survey 7b xxx**.

**2.** Add a data chart slide to the end of the show. Insert a pie chart on the slide.

**3.** Enter the following data in the datasheet. Enter **Pet Paradise** in the first cell in the Labels 1 column, then insert the customer types beneath it in the Labels 1 column. Enter the corresponding values in the Pie 1 column.

| | |
|---|---|
| **Loyal** | **62** |
| **Repeat** | **23** |
| **First-Time** | **15** |

**4.** Insert another pie to show the results for the Pet Paradise II store location. Enter **Pet Paradise II** in the first cell in the Labels 2 column, then insert the customer types beneath it in the Labels 2 column. Enter the corresponding values in the Pie 2 column.

| | |
|---|---|
| **Loyal** | **45** |
| **Repeat** | **33** |
| **First-Time** | **22** |

**5.** Insert a title: **Customer Participation by Type**.

**6.** Position the Labels on the outside. Insert Percent labels on the inside.

**7.** Enhance the pies, titles, and labels as desired.

**8.** Save the file as **customer survey 8a xxx** and print Slide 7. Then, close the slide show.

## PROJECT 8B

Polly, co-owner of Pet Paradise, is considering which cat toys to continue purchasing and which ones to discontinue based on sales. Create a pie chart to help management make a decision.

**1.** Open **cat toys** from the student **Datafile** folder.

**2.** Add a slide with no layout to the end of the slide show. Insert a pie chart of your choice on the slide.

**3.** Insert the following data in the datasheet:

| | |
|---|---|
| **Whimsy** | **27,000** |
| **Tailspin** | **45,000** |
| **Cat Charms** | **36,000** |
| **Pet Pals** | **4,000** |
| **Paw Patch** | **19,000** |

**4.** Insert another pie to show the following items that make up the Pet Pals slice:

| | |
|---|---|
| **Squeeze Mouse** | **750** |
| **Bell Ball** | **2500** |
| **Chew Stick** | **250** |
| **Scratch Block** | **500** |

5. Link Pie 2 to slice 4 of Pie 1.

6. Change the size of Pie 2.

   a. In the Layout/Type Properties dialog box click **2** in the Current pie drop-down list box.
   b. Change the number in the Size box to **75**. Click **OK**.

7. Insert the following title: **Pet Pals: A Poor Peformer**.

8. Enhance the pies as desired.

9. Save the file as **cat toys 8b xxx**. Print Slide 3 as a handout with one slide per page.

10. Close the slide show.

## CRITICAL THINKING ACTIVITY

SCANS

Create a questionnaire for your classmates using Corel WordPerfect (or another word processing program). List five colors and ask people to choose their favorite. Next, indicate whether the participants are male or female.

Create one pie that illustrates the results of the favorite colors. Choose the most popular color, then tally the male/female results for the color and create a second pie using the results. Link the two pies.

Change their appearances, add titles, etc., as desired.

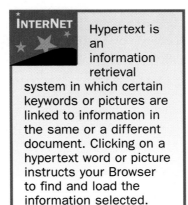

**INTERNET**

Hypertext is an information retrieval system in which certain keywords or pictures are linked to information in the same or a different document. Clicking on a hypertext word or picture instructs your Browser to find and load the information selected.

# CREATING AND ENHANCING XY CHARTS

## OBJECTIVES

**Upon completion of this lesson, you will be able to:**

- Create a line chart.
- Edit and enhance a line chart.
- Change a line style.
- Add axis labels.
- Change frame options.
- Format tick marks and grid lines.

**⏱ Estimated Time: 1 hour**

XY charts show relationships between two variables. The *dependent variable* (a quantity that can change based on another value) is plotted on the *x-axis*. The x-axis is a horizontal line divided into segments. The *independent variable* is plotted on the *y-axis*. The y-axis is a vertical line, also divided into segments.

The most commonly used XY charts are bar charts and *line charts*. Since you have already learned how to create bar charts in Lesson 7, you will now focus on line charts.

## *Creating a Line Chart*

Line charts are particularly useful for showing *trends*—that is, how something changes over time.

Paul and Polly Paradeis, the owners of Pet Paradise, want to examine how sales of pets have increased over the last three years. Create a line chart that shows the number of pets Pet Paradise has sold.

# EXERCISE ⟶ PR9.1

1.  Open **pet sales** from the student **Datafile** folder.

2.  Add a slide with no layout to the end of the slide show. Insert a chart.

3.  In the Data Chart Gallery select **Line** and choose the first chart in the top row of chart types. Click **OK**. The datasheet appears.

4.  Leave the datasheet on the screen for the next exercise.

## Entering the Data

The datasheet for a line chart is similar to the bar chart datasheet. Note that you can enter labels and legends only for one set of data. Also, note that the line chart does not specify colors for legend entries. Rather, the lines appear with differing patterns. You can, however, change line colors when you edit the data chart.

# EXERCISE ⟶ PR9.2

1.  Enter the following data in the datasheet. Key the pet types in the Legend column and begin the year labels in column A.

|        | 1995 | 1996 | 1997  |
|--------|------|------|-------|
| Birds  | 108  | 242  | 379   |
| Cats   | 614  | 863  | 1,014 |
| Dogs   | 827  | 615  | 940   |
| Fish   | 445  | 467  | 453   |

2.  Notice that the line chart appears on the screen as you enter the data. Close the datasheet.

3.  Add the following title: **Pet Sales by Year**.

4.  Leave the slide show on the screen for the next exercise.

## Changing Line Styles and Colors

By default, Presentations chooses line patterns and a single color—black—to represent your data. You can change a line's pattern, thickness, and color.

# EXERCISE ⟶ PR9.3

1.  Double click the chart to open the chart editor, if necessary.

2.  Double click any line in the chart. The Series Properties dialog box appears (see Figure 9-1).

3.  Click the **Line** tab. If *Series 1: Birds* does not appear at the top of the dialog box, click the large left or right arrow until it appears.

(continued on next page)

4. Click the **Width** button to display the Line width palette. Select the third option in the second column to produce a heavier line.

5. Click the **Color** button to display a color palette. Choose a color for the line. Preview your choice to make sure the color is visible on the slide.

6. Click the large right-pointing arrow at the top of the dialog box to bring up Series 2. Change the line width as you did for Series 1. Click the **Style** button and select the first choice in the second column, the solid line. Choose an appropriate color.

7. Using the process in Step 6, change the line width, style, and color for the remaining two series.

**FIGURE 9-1**
The Series Properties Dialog Box

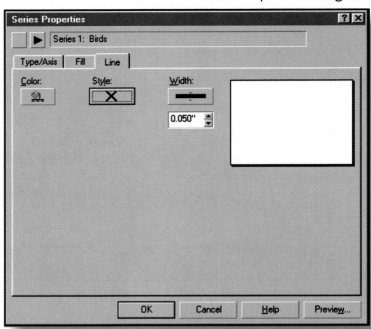

8. Save your changes as **pet sales 9-3 xxx** and print Slide 2. Leave the slide show on the screen for the next exercise.

# Editing and Enhancing an XY Chart

You can use the skills you have already learned to edit a line chart. Moving and resizing are the same for a line chart as for a pie chart. You can also change font and attributes for title and labels in the same way as for any other chart type.

Presentations also offers special editing and enhancing features for XY charts. Although you will use a line chart to explore these options, they are available for bar charts and other types of XY charts.

## Adding Axis Titles

You can add *axis titles* to give further information about the x and y axes. In the chart on your screen the x-axis represents time in years, and the y-axis represents a range of numbers. While the x-axis year labels are self-explanatory, the numbers are not. This is a good example of the need for an axis title to explain to the viewer what the numbers mean.

To add an axis title:

■ In the chart editor click the **Chart** menu and select **Axis**, and then choose **X** or **Primary Y** from the cascade menu. The X Axis Properties or Primary Y Axis Properties dialog box appears. Figure 9-2 shows the Primary Y Axis Properties dialog box.

■ In this dialog box you can insert and format an axis title and choose an orientation for the title. You can change the appearance of the axis labels, as well as change the maximum and minimum values displayed to focus the chart more precisely on reported data.

**FIGURE 9-2**
The Primary Y Axis Properties Dialog Box

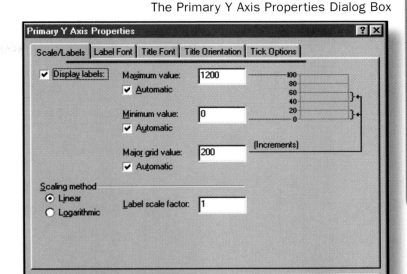

# EXERCISE ⟹ PR9.4

1. With the chart editor open, click the **Chart** menu and select **Axis**, and then choose **Primary Y** from the cascade menu. The Primary Y Axis Properties dialog box appears, as seen in Figure 9-2.

2. Click the **Title Font** tab. In the *Display title* text box key the axis title: **Pets Sold**. Make the title font **Bold** and change its size to **20** pt. Preview the change, then click **Back**.

3. The axis labels (the numbers on the y-axis) now look large in comparison to the axis title.

Change them as follows:
   a. Click the **Label Font** tab.
   b. Make the axis labels **Bold** and **18** pt. Preview the change and click **OK**.

4. Change the x-axis labels.
   a. Click the **Chart** menu and select **Axis**, and then select **X** from the cascade menu.
   b. Click the **Label Font** tab and make the labels **Bold** and **18** pt. Click **OK**.

5. Save your changes as **pet sales 9-4 xxx** and print Slide 2. Leave the slide show on the screen for the next exercise.

## Changing the Frame and the Grid

The *frame* of an XY chart consists of the y-axis line, the x-axis line, the top line, and the right line (if the chart type has a right line) that enclose the chart. The frame also includes a fill color or pattern that appears behind the chart elements. You can change the color of these frame elements, or eliminate them to give your chart a more customized look.

To change a frame element:

- In the chart editor click the Chart menu and select Frame, or double click any area of the frame fill. The Frame Properties dialog box appears, as shown in Figure 9-3.

- In the Display Options tab click the Border Width or Border Color button and select a line width or color from the palette. Click check boxes to display or remove frame lines. In the Fill tab change the pattern and color for the frame fill area.

The *grid* is the series of horizontal and vertical lines that mark increments on the x and y axes. Some Presentations charts have only horizontal grid lines, while others have both horizontal and vertical grid lines.

To change the grid:

- In the chart editor click the Chart menu and select Grids, or double click a grid line. The Grid Properties dialog box appears.

- In this dialog box you can change color and style for both vertical and horizontal lines. You can also use this dialog box to add grid lines if they do not automatically appear in your chart.

**FIGURE 9-3**
The Frame Properties Dialog Box

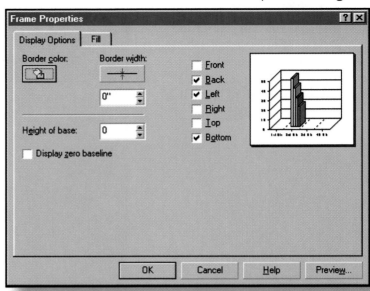

**FIGURE 9-4**
The Grid Properties Dialog Box

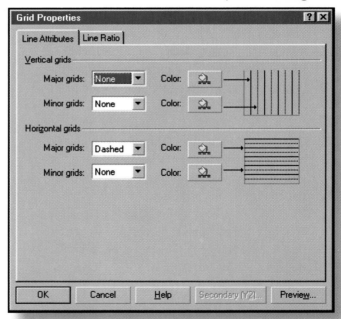

## EXERCISE ▷ PR9.5

1. With the chart editor open, click the **Chart** menu and select **Frame**. The Frame Properties dialog box appears.

2. Change the frame properties.
   a. In the Display Options tab click the **Back**, **Left**, **Right**, **Top**, and **Bottom** check boxes, if necessary.
   b. Select the **Fill** tab.
   c. Click the **Pattern** button. The Pattern palette appears with the solid gradient already selected.
   d. Click the **Foreground** button to display the color palette. Select the third color in the first row, **Light Gray**.
   e. Click **OK**. Note the change to the frame border and fill on the chart.

3. Change the grid lines.
   a. Double click any grid line. The Grid Properties dialog box appears.
   b. In the Horizontal grids area of the dialog box click the **Major grids** drop-down list box and select **Dashed**. Click **OK**.

4. Leave the slide show on the screen for the next exercise.

## Editing The Legend

Legends are available with all types of charts. You can customize a chart's legends in much the same way you edit titles and labels.

## EXERCISE ▷ PR9.6

1. In the chart editor double click the legend to display the Legend Properties dialog box (see Figure 9-5).

2. Select the **Type/Position** tab, if necessary. In the *Position* section of the dialog box click the right-center option button. This places the legend on the right side of the chart, centered from top to bottom.

3. Change the text font properties.
   a. Select the **Text Font** tab. Change the text font to **Bold** and **30** pt.
   b. Click the **Text color** button to display the color palette. Select the second color in the second row, **Dark Blue**. Click **OK**.

4. Save the slide show as **pet sales 9-6 xxx**. Print the slide show.

5. Close the slide show.

(continued on next page)

FIGURE 9-5
The Legend Properties Dialog Box

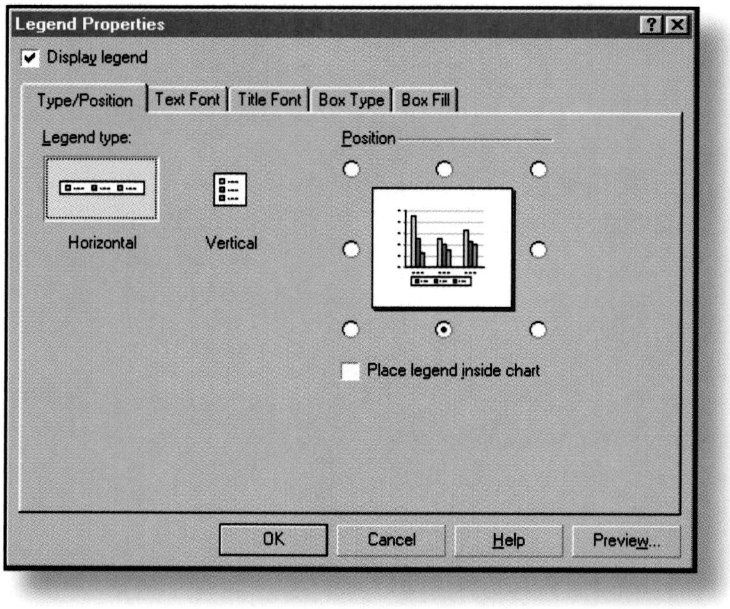

# Summary

In this lesson you learned that:

■ XY charts show relationships between two variables. The most common XY charts are bar charts and line charts. Line charts are particularly useful for showing trends.

■ you create and edit a line chart much the same way you create a bar chart.

■ Presentations enables you to change the appearance of line types, thicknesses, and colors, as well as the chart's frame, fill, and grid lines.

■ you are encouraged to add x- and y-axis titles, as well as a legend, to make it clear to the reader what the data represents. You can position the legend where you like in relation to the chart.

## LESSON 9 REVIEW QUESTIONS

### FILL IN THE BLANKS

**Complete each of the following statements by writing your answer in the blank provided.**

1. The _____ variable is plotted on the x-axis.

2. The two most common XY charts are _____ and _____.

3. The _____ of an XY chart consists of the y-axis line, the x-axis line, the top line, and the right line that enclose the chart.

4. The _____ is the series of horizontal and vertical lines that mark increments on the x and y axes.

5. The _____ dialog box enables you to change the fill color of a line chart.

### WRITTEN QUESTIONS

**Write your answers to the following questions.**

6. For what purpose are line charts particularly useful?

7. What types of data get plotted on the x-axis?

8. What types of data get plotted on the y-axis?

9. Describe how to position a legend to the right of a chart.

10. Explain how to add a y-axis title to a line chart.

## LESSON 9 PROJECT

SCANS

### PROJECT 9A

Pet Paradise's management wants to view how their "Dog Days of Summer" promotion has affected sales at the two stores over the past three years.

1. Open **dog days 7a xxx**.

2. Add a slide with no layout to the end of the show. Insert a line chart of your choice.

3. Insert the following information into the datasheet:

|  | 1995 | 1996 | 1997 |
|---|---|---|---|
| Chew Toys | 5,600 | 5,000 | 5,500 |
| Dog Houses | 13,500 | 16,800 | 18,300 |
| Boarding | 15,000 | 24,000 | 29,000 |
| Classes | 7,000 | 7,500 | 8,500 |
| Grooming | 14,000 | 19,000 | 22,000 |

4. Enhance the chart as follows:
   a. Change the colors, widths, and styles of the lines, as desired.
   b. Insert a 20-pt. Bold y-axis title: **In Dollars**.
   c. Change the x- and y-axis label fonts to **18** pt. and **Bold**.
   d. Insert a title: **"Dog Days" Trends**. Change the text color as desired.
   e. Change the legend text to **20** pt. and **Bold** and enclose it in a box with a light fill.

5. Notice that the charts include values from 0 to 30,000, even though there are no values less than 5,000. Change the scale of the y-axis to set a minimum value of 5,000.

   a. Access the Primary Y Axis Properties dialog box. Click the **Scale/Labels** tab, if necessary.
   b. In the *Minimum value* text box key **5,000**. Click **OK**.
   c. Notice that the chart now shows values from 5,000 to 30,000.

6. Based on the information on the screen, which products and/or services do not appear significantly affected by the promotional discounts?

7. Save the file as **dog days 9a xxx** and print the current slide as a handout with one slide per page. Close the slide show.


## PROJECT 9B

Polly Paradeis, the co-owner of Pet Paradise, wants to make a big impression on her new employees. Add a slide to the **orientation** slide show that shows the booming sales growth the two Pet Paradise stores have experienced over the last three years.

1. Open **orientation 5-2 xxx**.

2. Add a slide with no layout at the end of the slide show. Insert a line chart.

3. Key the following data in the datasheet:

|  | 1995 | 1996 | 1997 |
|---|---|---|---|
| Pet Paradise | 350 | 475 | 600 |
| Pet Paradise II | 195 | 375 | 525 |

4. Enhance the chart as follows:

   a. Insert a title: **Growth in Total Annual Sales**
   b. Change the line width, style, and color as desired.
   c. Add a Primary y-axis title: **In Thousands**. Change the font, style, and size of the axis labels as desired.

   d.  Change the frame to display lines on all four sides, and add a light-colored fill.
   e.  Change the legend font, style, size, and position as desired. Insert a legend title by clicking the **Title Font** tab in the Legend Properties dialog box. Click in the **Display title** check box and key **Stores** in the text box. Format the title as desired.
   f.  Add dashed vertical grid lines.

5. Save your changes as **orientation 9b xxx** and print the current slide as a handout with one slide per page.

6. Close the slide show.

## CRITICAL THINKING ACTIVITY

SCANS

   Use the evening news or daily newspaper to record the high and low temperatures. Create a line chart that tracks the high and low temperatures for this week.

   If you are feeling resourceful, try to find the high and low temperatures for the same days for the last five years. Chart all the highs in one chart, and the lows in another. Change the appearance of the chart as desired.

INTERNET

FTP stands for File Transfer Protocol. FTP software transfers files of data from one computer to another.

# CREATING AND ENHANCING ORGANIZATION CHARTS

**Upon completion of this lesson, you will be able to:**

■ Create an organization chart.

■ Understand organizational structure.

■ Add entries to the organization chart.

■ Change the orientation of an organization chart.

🕐 **Estimated Time: 1¹/₂ hours**

An organization chart (see Figure 10-1) shows the chain of command in a company or other organization. Typically, an organization chart begins with a single box at the top of a pyramid, representing the president or CEO (Chief Executive Officer). Entries below the top box are *subordinate* to it. In turn, subordinate entries can be *superior* to other entries. In Figure 10-1, for example, Manager A is subordinate to the President, but superior to Employees 1, 2, and 3.

You can also use the organization chart to show the structure of a unit or department, to depict a flow of activity in a work system, or to design a family tree.

**FIGURE 10-1**
An Organization Chart

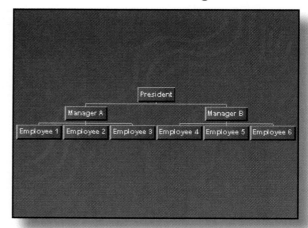

# *Creating an Organization Chart*

A chart that starts at the top and flows downward is usually easiest to follow. Although most charts are laid out from top to bottom, Presentations enables you to display an organization chart from bottom to top, left to right, or right to left.

 **NOTE:** You cannot place more than one organization chart on a slide.

Now that Pet Paradise's owners are considering expansion, they are trying to create a clearer picture of their organizational structure. Prepare an organization chart they can use for planning.

 **EXERCISE** ▷ **PR10.1**

**SCANS**

1. Open **expansion plan** from the student **Datafile** folder.

2. Add a slide with no layout to the end of the slide show. Click the **Insert** menu and select **Organization Chart**, or click the **Organization Chart** button on the Toolbar. Click the new slide with the hand pointer to open the Layout dialog box (see Figure 10-2).

**FIGURE 10-2**
The Layout Dialog Box

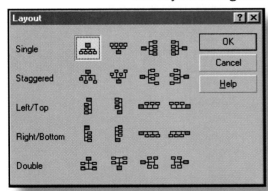

3. The Layout dialog box displays a palette of chart styles. Click **OK** to accept the default organization chart style (first style, top row).

**NOTE:**

You can also select the **Org Chart** template to create an organization chart. Doing so opens a working screen with boxes for a title, subtitle, and the organization chart.

4. An organization chart with placeholders for names and titles appears in the chart editor, as shown in Figure 10-3.

**FIGURE 10-3**
The Sample Organization Chart

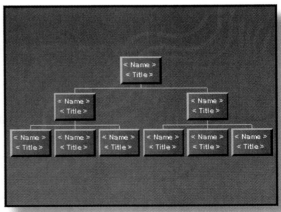

5. Leave the slide show on the screen for the next exercise.

## Entering the Data

Before you enter data in the sample organization chart, you must decide what kind of information you want to display in each box of the chart. By default, Presentations supplies placeholders for a name and a title. These placeholders are called *box fields*. You can choose to insert both of these fields, only one of them, or add your own.

To change the fields in the organization chart boxes:

■ In the chart editor select a box or boxes. Next, click the Format menu and select Box Fields, or click the Box Fields button on the Toolbar. The Box Fields dialog box appears, as shown in Figure 10-4.

**FIGURE 10-4**
The Box Fields Dialog Box

■ To remove a field from each box in the organization chart, click its check box to remove the *X*. To add a new field, key the field name in the *Add new fields* text box and click Add. Click OK when finished.

Clicking any box in the organization chart selects it and any boxes directly subordinate to it. You can use a QuickMenu to select more than one box at a time:

■ To select a box and all boxes that branch from it, right click the box and click Select Branch on the QuickMenu.

■ To select a box and all other boxes on the same level, right click the box and click Select Level on the QuickMenu.

Once you have selected the fields you want, enter text in each box. Simply double click the field name enclosed in angle brackets (<>) and begin keying. To move to the next field, press Tab.

## EXERCISE ▷ PR10.2

1. Enter the first name and title in the top position box.
   a. Double click the *<Name>* placeholder. It disappears and leaves a blinking insertion point in place.
   b. Key **Polly and Paul Paradeis**.
   c. Press **Tab**. The insertion point replaces the *<Title>* placeholder. Key **Owners/ Operators**.

2. In the left box below the top position box key **Alma Alvaro** and **Manager**. In the right box below the top position box key **Daniel LaPierre** and **Manager**.

3. There are two assistant managers subordinate to each manager. Key **Albert Hapner** and **Reynaldo Nuert** under Alma Alvaro and **Betsy**

> **TIP**
>
> To key an ñ, access the Symbols dialog box. It is number *1,57* in the Multinational set.

Johnson and **Vera Seely** under Daniel LaPierre. Be sure to key **Assistant Manager** under each of their names.

4. Notice that the organization chart changes in size to accommodate the third-level boxes. Also notice that there are two empty third-level boxes. Leave them for now. You will deal with them in the next exercise.

5. Save the slide show as **expansion plan 10-2 xxx** and print the organization chart slide. Leave the organization chart on the screen for the next exercise.

# *Editing and Enhancing an Organization Chart*

You can edit an organization chart by adding or deleting boxes, changing the level of subordination of entries, and adding staff positions. You can also switch the overall layout of the chart.

To enhance an organization chart, you can change the color of the box fill and the color of the *connector* lines, as well as line thickness, box style, and font.

## Deleting, Adding, and Changing Subordination of Entries

To delete any entry on the organization chart:

■ Click the desired box. If the box has subordinate entries, they will also be selected.

■ Click the Edit menu and select Delete. The selected box and its subordinates are deleted.

When you add a box to an organization chart, you can add it as a subordinate or as a coworker. Adding a subordinate inserts a new box subordinate to the selected box. Adding a coworker inserts a new box on the same level as the selected box.

To add a subordinate:

■ Select the box that you want the new box to be subordinate to.

■ Click the Insert menu and select Subordinates. The Insert Subordinate dialog box appears. Choose how many subordinates to add and click OK.

To add a coworker:

■ Select a box on the same level as the box you want to add.

■ Click the Insert menu and select Coworkers. The Insert Coworker dialog box appears. Choose how many coworkers to add, and whether their boxes should appear to the left or right of the selected box. Click OK.

You can change levels for any box except the top position box. If a person in the organization chart is promoted, for example, you can move the person up a level.

To change subordination of an entry:

■ Click the desired box.

■ Drag the box onto a box at the level you want your selected box to appear until you see a solid red outline on the box. Release the mouse button. The selected box should appear at the new level.

## EXERCISE ⬚ PR10.3

SCANS

1. First, remove the unused boxes in the organization chart.
   a. Click the empty box subordinate to Alma Alvaro's box.
   b. Press **Delete**. The box disappears.
   c. Delete the box subordinate to Daniel LaPierre's box using the same procedure.

2. With the expansion to a new store, Vera Seely will become manager of the store where she currently works. Daniel LaPierre will manage the new store. Make Vera a coworker of Daniel's.
   a. Click Daniel's box to select it. Click the **Insert** menu and select **Coworkers**. The Insert Coworkers dialog box appears, set to add 1 coworker to the left of Daniel's box. Click **OK**. A new second-level box

(continued on next page)

appears directly underneath Paul and Polly's box.

b. With Daniel's box still selected, click the **Copy** button. Click the new box to select it, and click the **Paste** button. Daniel's name and title appear in the new box.

c. Click Vera's box to select it. Click the **Edit** menu and select **Replace Manager**. Vera's box replaces Daniel's, while Betsy remains as Vera's subordinate. Edit Vera's title so it says **Manager**.

d. A blank box replaces Vera's old box. Delete it.

3. Polly and Paul have decided that each store will only have one assistant manager until Polly has time to select some new assistant manager candidates. She is sending Reynaldo to work for Daniel. Move Reynaldo's box to reflect this change.

a. Click Reynaldo's box to select it.

b. Move the pointer inside Reynaldo's box until the four-headed arrow appears. Drag

it on top of Daniel's box until it is highlighted, then release. Reynaldo's box now appears subordinate to Daniel's.

4. Because the original store has unused storage space, it will serve as a warehouse and distribution center for the other two stores. Paul and Polly want to promote someone from within the company to order goods for all three stores, manage the inventory, and ship the goods to the other two stores. This person will be subordinate to Alma Alvaro.

a. Click Alma's box to select it.

b. Click the **Insert** menu and select **Subordinates**. The Insert Subordinate dialog box appears, set to insert 1 subordinate. Click **OK**.

c. Insert the name and title: **Miguel Flores** and **Inventory Manager**.

5. Save the file as **expansion plan 10-3 xxx** and print the organization chart slide. Leave the slide show on the screen for the next exercise.

## Adding a Staff Position

*Staff* positions are not considered part of the formal structure of an organization, so Presentations sets them off in a special way with a dashed or dotted line extending from the box of the staff person to the connector of the staff person's superior.

EXERCISE ⟶ PR10.4

SCANS

1. Because the operation is getting significantly larger, Polly and Paul will no longer handle the books themselves. Polly is hiring a bookkeeper who will report only to her. Add a staff position.

a. Click Polly and Paul's box to select it.

b. Click the **Insert** menu and select **Staff**. The Insert Staff dialog box appears, set to insert 1 new position. Click **OK**. A position subordinate to Polly and Paul, but unrelated to the managers, appears.

c. Insert the following name and title in the new box: **Jill Jefferies** and **Bookkeeper**.

2. Using the above procedure, add another staff position. Insert the name **Calvin Banks** and the title **Administrative Assistant**.

3. Leave the slide show on the screen for the next exercise.

✓ NOTE:

You can also find formatting commands on QuickMenus. Right click any box to see these commands.

## Changing the Appearance of the Organization Chart

To change the appearance of the boxes on the organization chart, click the Format menu and select Box Properties, or click the Box Properties button on the Toolbar. The Box Properties dialog box appears, as shown in Figure 10-5. In this dialog box you can change the box style, border color, fill color, and box size.

You can also change box size by simply clicking to select the box and then dragging a corner handle to increase or decrease the box size.

Presentations will not apply a font size if the size prevents proper layout of boxes on the slide. If you change a font size and nothing happens on the screen, you have chosen too large a size for your current layout of boxes. To change the appearance of the connectors, click the Format menu and select Connectors, or click the Connectors button on the Toolbar. The Connectors dialog box appears, as shown in Figure 10-6. In this dialog box you can change the width, style, and color for both subordinate and staff lines.

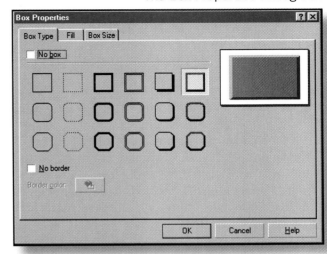

**FIGURE 10-5**
The Box Properties Dialog Box

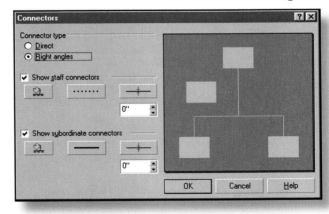

**FIGURE 10-6**
The Connectors Dialog Box

### EXERCISE ⟹ PR10.5

1. In the chart editor right click on Paul and Polly's box and choose **Select Branch** to select all the branches in the chart.

2. Right click again on Paul and Polly's box and select **Box Properties**. The Box Properties dialog box appears.

3. Chose the third box style in the first row. Change the border color, if desired. Click **OK**.

4. With all boxes still selected, right click and select **Font Properties**. The Font Properties dialog box appears. Change the text font to **Bold**, **24** pt. **Arial**. Click **OK**.

5. With all boxes still selected, click the **Format** menu and select **Connectors**. Change the width of the subordinate and staff lines to a heavier weight. If desired, change the color of the connectors to match the color of the border.

6. Leave the slide show on the screen for the next exercise.

## Changing the Structure of the Organization Chart

To change the structure of the boxes in the organization chart, select the branch you want. Click the Format menu and select Branch Structure, or click the Branch Structure button on the Toolbar. The Branch Layout dialog box appears with the Structure tab selected, as shown in Figure 10-7a. Choose a style for the box display.

To change the orientation of the chart, select Orientation, or click the Orientation button on the Toolbar. The Branch Layout dialog box appears, with the Orientation tab selected, as shown in Figure 10-7b. Choose a direction for the organization chart to display.

**FIGURE 10-7A**
The Branch Layout
Dialog Box
Structure Tab

**FIGURE 10-7B**
The Branch Layout
Dialog Box
Orientation Tab

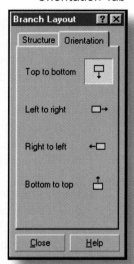

## EXERCISE ⟹ PR10.6

**SCANS**

**1.** In the chart editor right click Paul and Polly's box and click **Select Branch** to select all the boxes in the chart.

**2.** Right click again and select **Orientation**. The Branch Layout dialog box appears, with the Orientation tab selected. Click **Left to right**, then click **Close**. Observe how the chart has changed.

**3.** Save the slide show as **expansion plan 10-6 xxx**. Print the current slide as a handout with one slide per page.

**4.** Close the slide show.

## *Summary*

In this lesson you learned that:

■ an organization chart illustrates the hierarchical relationships among members of an organization, such as a business. You can also use an organization chart to create a family tree.

■ organization charts typically begin with a single box at the top. Boxes below the top box are subordinate to it. These subordinate boxes are also superior to boxes beneath them.

■ before you enter data, you need to decide which box fields to have. You can use the default *Name* and *Title* fields that Presentations supplies, or add your own.

■ you can add and delete boxes to and from an existing chart, as well as change the level of subordination of a box.

- Presentations enables you to add staff positions: boxes that are not part of the formal organizational structure. They are set off by dotted or dashed lines.

- you can change the appearance of an existing organization chart, including the box style and fill, and font size, style, and color.

## LESSON 10 REVIEW QUESTIONS

### TRUE OR FALSE

**Circle the T if the statement is true.  Circle the F if it is false.**

**T    F    1.**  A box that is subordinate can also be superior.

**T    F    2.**  You must use the default box fields that Presentations supplies.

**T    F    3.**  Organization charts are always displayed from top to bottom.

**T    F    4.**  Once you position a box in an organization chart, its level of subordination is fixed.

**T    F    5.**  If you delete a box that has subordinate boxes attached, the subordinate boxes are not affected.

### WRITTEN QUESTIONS

**Write your answers to the following questions.**

**6.**  Aside from charting business hierarchies, what else can you use an organization chart for?

**7.**  Describe how to add your own box fields to an organization chart.

**8.**  How does Presentations differentiate a staff position box from a regular subordinate box?

**9.**  Explain how to change a box's level of subordination.

**10.**  How do you change the thickness of connectors for subordinate boxes?

## LESSON 10 PROJECT

SCANS

### PROJECT 10A

Paul Paradeis has joined a local community improvement organization, and he has volunteered to make an organization chart for the group. He has, in turn, given you his notes and asked you to create the chart using Presentations.

**1.**  Open **community action** from the student **Datafile** folder.

2. Add a slide with no layout to the end of the slide show. Insert an organization chart on the new slide. Choose the default chart style.

3. Add another field to the chart.

   a. Right click the top box and select **Select Branch**.
   b. Right click the top box again and select **Box Fields**.
   c. Add a new field called **Organization** between the Name and Title fields. Click **OK**.

4. Insert the following information in the organization chart. Remember, to move from one field to the next in a box, press **Tab**.

   Level 1
   **Roger Pikes**
   **Starlight Diner**
   **President**

   Level 2
   **Paul Paradeis**                          **Midori Yoshino**
   **Pet Paradise**                           **Flowers by Midori**
   **Chairperson, Business Committee**        **Chairperson, Community Affairs Committee**

   Level 3—Subordinate to Paul Paradeis
   **Peter Cooper**                           **Eleanor Drake**
   **PC Rentals, Inc.**                       **Drake's Rare Books**
   **Treasurer**                              **Secretary**

   Level 3—Subordinate to Midori Yoshino
   **Gloria Delgado**                         **Ofc. Ken Noonan**
   **Watkins Bank & Trust**                   **Austin P.D.**
   **Treasurer**                              **Secretary**

5. Add a staff position for Roger Pikes. The staff name should be **Kay Dunlap** and the title should be **Assistant to the President**. Remove the Organization field.

6. Increase the size of the text so that the chart is more readable.

7. Save your changes as **community action 10a xxx**. Print the slide as a handout with one slide per page.

8. Close the slide show.


## PROJECT 10B

Polly and Paul Paradeis envision expanding even further next year. They plan to open a small manufacturing plant to make specialty pet supplies. Create a chart that will display the organization's structure by job title.

1. Open **paradise pet supplies** from the student **Datafile** folder.

2. Add a slide with no layout to the end of the slide show. Insert an organization chart on the new slide.

3. Insert the following information in the organization chart:

Level 1
**President**
Staff Position
**Assistant to the President**

Level 2
**Director of Operations**
Staff Position
**Assistant to the DOO**
Staff Position
**Accountant**

Level 3
**R & D Manager  Production Manager  Sales & Marketing Manager  Customer Service Manager**

Level 4–Subordinate to R & D Manager
**R & D Specialists**

Level 4–Subordinate to Production Manager
**Shop Foreperson  Shipping Foreperson**

Level 4–Subordinate to Sales & Marketing Manager
**Salespeople  Marketing Specialists**

Level 4–Subordinate to Customer Service Manager
**Customer Service Specialists**

Level 5–Subordinate to Shop Foreperson
**Production Specialists**

Level 5–Subordinate to Shipping Foreperson
**Shipping Clerks  Delivery Drivers**

4. Change the chart's orientation to **Left to right**.

5. Increase the size of the font and make it bold to make the chart more readable. If desired, change the box style.

6. Change the color of the boxes for the different branches of the company as follows:
   a. Click the Research & Development Manager's box to select it. Right click and choose **Select Branch** to select all the boxes in the R & D branch. Choose a bright orange fill for the box.
   b. Select the Production Manager branch and choose a yellow color.
   c. Select the Marketing & Sales Manager branch and choose a bright blue color.
   d. Select the Customer Service Manager branch and choose a purple color.

7. Change the line width of all the connectors to a heavier weight.

8. Polly and Paul have decided to split the Sales & Marketing departments. Create a Marketing Manager position equal to the Sales Manager, and make the Marketing Specialists box subordinate to the new manager.

9. Save your changes as **paradise pet supplies 10b xxx**. Print the current slide as a handout with one slide per page.

10. Close the slide show.

### PROJECT 10C

Create a family tree for Paul Paradeis.

1. Open **paradeis family tree** from the student **Datafile** folder. Insert a slide with no layout.

2. Add an organizational chart. In the Layout dialog box select the second layout in the Single row. Click **OK**.

3. There are six boxes in the first row. Delete two (one per set of three).

4. Enter the names of Paul Paradeis' grandparents in the top row.

| | |
|---|---|
| Name: | **Francis Paradeis** |
| Title: | **Paternal Grandfather** |
| Name: | **Moira Sullivan** |
| Title: | **Paternal Grandmother** |
| Name: | **Roger Parker** |
| Title: | **Maternal Grandfather** |
| Name: | **Fay Wallace** |
| Title: | **Maternal Grandmother** |

5. Enter the names of Paul's parents.

| | |
|---|---|
| Name: | **Sean Paradeis** |
| Title: | **Father** |
| Name: | **Patricia Parker** |
| Title: | **Mother** |

6. Enter **Paul Paradeis** in the final box. Right click the box and select **Box Fields**. Deselect the Title field for this box and click **OK**.

7. Save the file as **paradeis family tree 10c xxx** and print Slide 2. Then, close the slide show.

## CRITICAL THINKING ACTIVITY

SCANS

Create your own family tree, trying to begin with your great-grandparents. Think about how you would add multiple children under one set of parents.

# ADDING TRANSITIONS AND SPECIAL EFFECTS

## OBJECTIVES

**Upon completion of this lesson, you will be able to:**

■ Choose transition options for your slide show.

■ Add object animation.

■ Advance your slides automatically.

■ Add sound effects to your slides.

⏱ **Estimated Time: 1 hour**

When you have finished preparing your slides, you can put the finishing touches on your work. Adding a visual and/or sound effects to your slides can add emphasis, as well as grab your audience's attention.

## Adding Transitions to a Slide Show

A *transition* is the way one slide changes to another. In the slide shows you have played up to now, the transition has been *Normal*–that is, one slide displays, disappears from view, and is replaced by another. Presentations provides many more transitions, as well as the option of directing the movement for some of them (left to right, top to bottom, clockwise, right and up, vertical etc.). You can also choose from three transition speeds: slow, medium, and fast.

To add transitions to your slides:

■ Display the desired slide. Click the Format menu and select Slide Properties, and then select Transition from the cascade menu. The Slide Properties dialog box appears with the Transition tab open, as shown in Figure 11-1.

■ The text box at the top of the dialog box shows which slide is on-screen. The

**FIGURE 11-1**
The Transition Tab

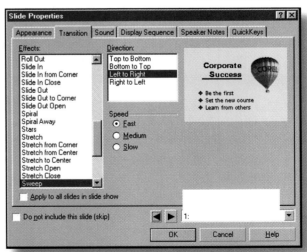

Effects list box displays a list of all available transition effects. When you choose a transition, the Sample slide demonstrates how the transition will appear when the slide show is played.

■ Depending on the transition effect, you may have a choice of direction in the Direction list box. Click to choose a direction, click a speed, then click OK.

## EXERCISE ⟹ PR11.1

1. Open **prospective employee 3-4 xxx**.

2. Review the slide show to determine what kind of visual effects might be appropriate.

3. Add transitions to the first two slides.
   a. Display Slide 1 on the screen. Click the **Format** menu and select **Slide Properties**, and then select **Transition** from the cascade menu. The Slide Properties dialog box appears.
   b. Click on the **Spiral** in the Effects list box. Observe the effect on the Sample slide.
   c. Click **Counter Clockwise** in the Direction list box. Observe the effect on the Sample slide.

   d. Locate the drop-down list box at the bottom of the dialog box that says *1: Working for Pet Paradise*. Click the right-pointing arrow next to the list box. The list box now displays *2: Introduction*.
   e. Click on each transition in the Effects list box. Observe the effect on the Sample slide. Pick one you like for Slide 2. If the transition you choose offers a choice of directions, choose one. Click **OK** to close the dialog box.

4. Play the slide show to view the visual effects of the first two slides. Remember to click the mouse button to move to the next slide.

5. Leave the slide show on the screen for the next exercise.

## Adding Transitions Using the Property Bar

You can also add transitions using the Slide Transitions drop-down list box on the Property Bar. This enables you to quickly change a slide's transition without having to open and close the Slide Properties dialog box. You can choose available directions by clicking the adjacent Direction button and selecting the desired option.

## EXERCISE ⟹ PR11.2

1. Display Slide 3. Click the **Slide Transitions** drop-down list box on the Property Bar. A list of available transition effects appears, with an adjacent Sample slide.

2. Choose a transition effect.

3. Click the **Direction** button and select your desired direction, if any.

4. Display the next slide. Continue with this procedure until you have assigned transitions to all the slides.

5. Play the slide show and observe your transitions.

6. Save the slide show as **prospective employee 11-2 xxx** and close the slide show.

# *Adding Object Animation*

Presentations also has an Object Animation feature. This lets you animate bullet and text entries, charts, and clipart, so they "fly" onto the screen or appear piece by piece.

To animate an object on the slide:

■ Select the object to animate, such as a bulleted list, chart, or piece of clipart, by clicking it *once*. Black selection handles surround the object.

■ Click the Format menu and select Object Properties. Select Object Animation from the cascade menu. An animation properties dialog box appears, similar to the one in Figure 11-2.

■ For bullet charts, you can specify three additional effects. You can display the bullet entries one at a time, highlight them, or reverse their display order.

**FIGURE 11-2**
The Object Animation Tab

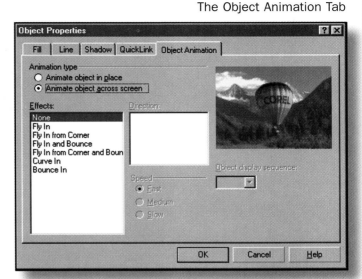

## EXERCISE ▭▷ PR11.3

SCANS

**1.** Open **pet classes 4b xxx**. Display Slide 2 on the screen.

**2.** Click once on the bulleted list to select it. Handles appear.

**3.** Click the **Format** menu and select **Object Properties**, and then select **Object Animation** from the cascade menu. The Bulleted List Properties dialog box appears, opened to the Bullet Animation tab.

**4.** Accept the default **Fly In** effect. Click **Right to Left** in the Direction list box. Make sure the **Display one at a time** check box is checked.

**5.** Click the **Apply to All** button to apply this effect to all bulleted list slides in the chart.

**6.** Play the slide show to view your visual effects. Remember to press the left mouse button to move to the next slide.

**7.** Save the slide show as **pet classes 11-3 xxx** and leave it on the screen for the next exercise.

**INTERNET**
Instead of sending and reading written documents as e-mail, in the future you will use the Internet for video and voice mail. If the person you want to reach is not available, you will be able to leave a message for video playback later.

## Controlling Slide Advance

The Display Sequence tab of the Slide Properties dialog box (see Figure 11-3) lets you choose and configure manual or time-delay slide advance options.

Thus far, you have only used manual advance—manually advancing the next slide by clicking the mouse button. If you use the time-delay option, Presentations automatically advances to the next slide after a preset delay (in seconds). You can set this delay option to apply to bulleted lists, as well.

**FIGURE 11-3**
The Display Sequence Tab

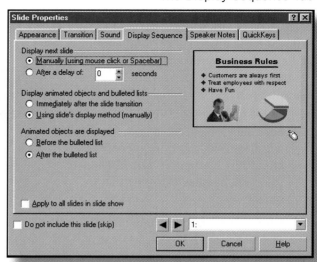

---

EXERCISE ➤ **PR11.4**

SCANS

1. Display Slide 1 on the screen. Click the **Format** menu and select **Slide Properties**, and then select **Display Sequence** from the cascade menu.

2. In the *Display next slide* section of the dialog box, click the **After a delay of** option button. Click the spin box arrow so that the spin box is set for **3** seconds.

3. Click the **Apply to all slides** check box near the bottom and click **OK**.

4. Play the slide show again and observe how Presentations advances the slides and cascades the bullets automatically.

5. Save the slide show as **pet classes 11-4 xxx** and leave it on the screen for the next exercise.

## The Slide Sorter View

You will find the Slide Sorter view helpful at this stage of preparing your slide show. It displays all the slides in your presentation with the type of transition (if any) and how you propose to advance through your slides (see Figure 11-4).

**FIGURE 11-4**
The Slide Sorter View

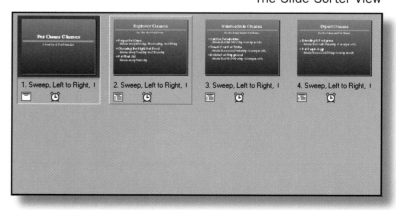

# Adding Sound to Your Slide Show

The Sound tab of the Slide Properties dialog box (see Figure 11-5) lets you add sound effects to your slide show, if your system is set up for sound. Presentations provides 15 Wave (*.wav*) sound files and 12 MIDI (*.mid*) sound files you can use. You can also add sounds from a CD.

To add sound effects to your slides:

■ Click the Format menu and select Slide Properties, and then select the Sound option from the cascade menu, or click the Sound button on the Property Bar. The Slide Properties dialog box appears, opened to the Sound tab.

■ Select a Wave or MIDI sound by clicking the Browse folder button in the text box next to each sound type. The Open File dialog box appears. Select the desired file and click Open.

**FIGURE 11-5**
The Sound Tab

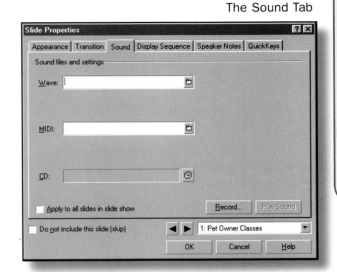

■ To select a CD file, click the CD button in the *CD section* text box. The Slide-CD Audio dialog box appears. Make selections regarding track number and starting and ending times, if desired. Click OK.

■ Click the Play Sound button if you want to listen to what the effect will sound like when you play the slide show. Click the Loop Sound check box, Apply this Sound to All Slides check box, or Do Not Include this Slide (Skip) check box, if appropriate. Click OK.

## EXERCISE ⇨ PR11.5

**SCANS**

**1.** Display Slide 1 on the screen. Click the **Sound** button on the Property Bar to access the Sound tab of the Slide Properties dialog box.

**2.** Click the folder icon in the *MIDI* section's text box. The Open File-Sounds dialog box appears.

**3.** Select **inds_06.mid** and click **Open**. The full pathname of the MIDI file appears in the text box. The *Save within slide show* document and *Loop sound* check boxes should appear checked.

**4.** Click the **Play Sound** button to listen to the sound. You can click the **Stop Sound** button at any time thereafter.

**5.** Play the slide show. Save it as **pet classes 11-5 xxx**.

**6.** Close the slide show.

# Summary

In this lesson you learned that:

- a transition is the way that one slide advances to the next. Presentations offers you numerous dynamic transitions that will grab an audience's attention.

- you can select the transition type, as well as the direction and speed, in the Slide Properties dialog box.

- you can set a slide show to automatically advance the slides after a fixed number of seconds.

- Presentations lets you animate objects such as text bullets, clipart, and drawings. These animation effects are also another way to grab an audience's attention.

- Presentations comes with prerecorded Wave and MIDI sounds that you can add to enhance your slide show.

## LESSON 11 REVIEW QUESTIONS

### FILL IN THE BLANKS

**Complete each of the following statements by writing your answer in the blank provided.**

1. The visual effect that changes from one slide to the next is called a _____.

2. There are two types of slide advances: _____ and _____.

3. You can add three types of sounds to your slide show: _____, _____, and _____.

4. The _____ view displays transition, advance, and sound information about each slide.

5. You can use the _____ feature to make bullets, charts, and clipart "fly" across the screen.

### WRITTEN QUESTIONS

**Write your answers to the following questions.**

6. Describe how to change a transition effect and its direction from the Property Bar.

7. Name the three additional effects you can add to a bullet animation.

8. Explain the procedure for creating a slide show that runs automatically.

9. How do you add a Wave file to a slide show?

10. Describe how to animate bullets.

## LESSON 11 PROJECT

### PROJECT 11A

Add transitions and special effects to an existing slide show.

1. Open **bonus bucks 6c xxx** and display Slide 1.

2. Access the Slide Properties dialog box. Add the **Lines Skip** transition to the slide. Add transitions of your choice to each remaining slide using the Property Bar.

3. Display Slide 2 and add the **lightbul** graphic to the slide. Align the graphic as desired.

4. Right click the lightbulb and select **Object Animation**. Animate the object across the screen by having it bounce in at medium speed.

5. Assign the in-place object animation effect of your choice to the triangle on Slide 1.

6. Display Slide 3. Select all of the objects and assign the **Roll In** animation from **Left to Right**.

7. Display Slide 4. From left to right, set each balloon to fly in from **Bottom to Top**.

8. Play the slide show. When Slides 3 and 4 appear, note that you have to click the left mouse button to get each individual object to roll in. (It takes several mousestrokes, but it is a neat effect.) Did your effects work the way you wanted? Make any changes, if desired.

9. Add a sound of your choice to the slide show. Set the sound to loop while the slide show is playing.

10. Save your change as **bonus bucks 11a xxx**. Close the slide show.

### PROJECT 11B

Add object animation and time advances to an existing slide show.

1. Open **first impressions 4a xxx**. Display Slide 2.

2. Right click the bulleted list and select **Object Animation**. Set the bulleted items to bounce in one at a time.

3. Apply different animation effects to the remaining slides. Experiment and choose your favorite.

4. Set the slides and bulleted items to automatically advance every **2** seconds.

5. Add a sound, if desired, to the slide show.

6. Save the slide show as **first impressions 11b xxx**. Close the slide show.

## CRITICAL THINKING ACTIVITY

This lesson has taught you how to use visual and audio effects to help you emphasize certain points in your presentation, as well as to make them fun. Do you think, however, that you should use them in all presentations? What types of slide shows do you think would benefit from these effects, and which would not?

Establish criteria for determining when you should and should not use visual and audio effects. For those presentations you think would benefit from these effects, create guidelines for using them appropriately. Review your findings with your fellow students.

<table>
<tr><td>LESSON<br>12</td><td># MAKING PROFESSIONAL PRESENTATIONS</td></tr>
</table>

## OBJECTIVES

**Upon completion of this lesson, you will be able to:**

- Create and print speaker notes.
- Use the Custom Audiences feature.
- Create a Show on the Go.
- Assign and use QuickKeys.
- Create and use QuickLinks.
- Use the QuickMenu tool during the slide show.
- Highlight slide show text.

**⏱ Estimated Time: 1 hour**

You have learned how to create and emphasize your slide shows. This final lesson will teach you how to use features that help you look professional when you play your slide shows for an audience.

# *Creating and Printing Speaker Notes*

In addition to the slide text that the audience sees, you can create notes for each slide in your presentation. Then you can print them and use them when you give your presentation.

EXERCISE ▷ PR12.1

**SCANS**

1. Open **first impressions 4a xxx** and display the first slide you want to write notes for, Slide 1.

2. Click the **Format** menu and select **Slide Properties**, and then select **Speaker Notes** from the Cascade menu. The Slide Properties dialog box appears, opened to the Speaker Notes tab (see Figure 12-1).

3. Click the **Insert Text from Slide** button. The slide's title and subtitle should appear in the text box. Press **Enter** twice.

4. Key the following notes in the large text box:

**Welcome the participants to the presentation. State your name and credentials. Ask each participant to state his or her name and expectations of the seminar.**

**5.** Click the right-pointing arrow next to the drop-down list box displaying the slide's name. It should now display *2: Preparation*. Insert the text from the slide and add the following notes:

**Before discussing the slide, ask the participants what they think is necessary to prepare for an interview. Next, explain the slide points. Finally, ask them if their idea of proper preparation has changed.**

**6.** Switch to Slide 3. Do not add any notes to this slide.

**7.** Switch to Slide 4. Insert the text from the slide and key the following notes:

**After discussing this slide, present good and bad examples of interviewing behavior. Ask the participants to state whether the examples are good or bad, and why.**

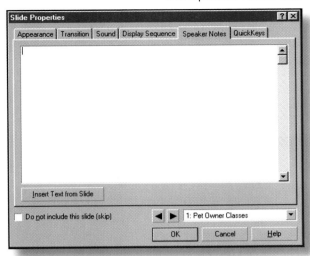

**FIGURE 12-1**
The Speaker Notes Tab

**8.** Click **OK**. Save the presentation as **first impressions 12-1 xxx**. Leave the slide show on the screen for the next exercise.

## Printing Speaker Notes

You have already learned how to print a slide show in various formats. To print speaker notes, simply access the Print dialog box and click the Speaker notes option button. Select how many slides you want per page, then click OK. The notes print underneath the slide thumbnails.

### EXERCISE PR12.2

**1.** Click the **File** menu and select **Print**. The Print dialog box appears.

**2.** Click the **Speaker notes** button. Make sure the dialog box is set to print four slides per page.

**3.** Click the **Print Preview** button to view how the page will print. Click anywhere to return to the Print dialog box.

**4.** Click **OK**. The slide show prints with the speaker notes underneath each slide thumbnail. Note that there is still blank space underneath Slide 3 where you can jot notes.

**5.** Close the slide show.

# Using the Custom Audiences Feature

You may, at some point, want to give the same presentation with minor differences to different groups. Rather than create separate slide shows, you can use Presentations' Custom Audiences feature to create alternative versions of the same slide show.

Once you have defined your custom version, you can play the original slide show or the alternative version. Simply click the drop-down list on the Property Bar and select either Original Slide Show or the name of the new version, then play the show.

## EXERCISE ⟩ PR12.3

**SCANS**

1. Open **prospective employee 3-4 xxx**. Click **Custom Presentations** from the drop-down list box on the Property Bar. The Custom Audiences dialog box appears (see Figure 12-2).

2. In the Custom Audiences dialog box click **New**. Key the name **Experience Required** and click **OK**.

**FIGURE 12-2**
The Custom Audiences Dialog Box

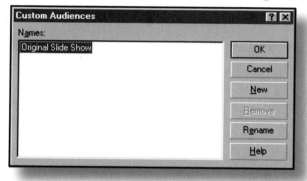

3. Switch to **Slide Sorter** view and select Slide 5. Click the **Skip** button on the Property Bar. The slide appears grayed out.

4. Save the slide show as **prospective employee 12-3 xxx**.

5. Click the drop-down list on the Property Bar and select **Original Slide Show**. Play the slide show.

6. Click the drop-down list on the Property Bar and select **Experience Required**. Play the slide show. Did you notice the difference? Does it affect the show significantly?

7. Leave the slide show on the screen for the next exercise.

# Creating a Show on the Go

Presentations has a feature called Show on the Go, which enables you to create portable slide shows, then play them without the Corel Presentations software. This is useful in the following situations:

■ You may need to send a slide show to a client or coworker who does not have the Corel Presentations software.

■ You may need to present a slide show at a location that does not have Corel Presentations.

  To create a Show on the Go:

■ Open the desired slide show. Click the File menu and select Show on the Go. If you have not recently saved the slide show, a dialog box informs you the show must be saved before proceeding. Click Yes. The Show on the Go dialog box appears.

- Click Change. The Show on the Go dialog box changes in appearance, offering options on where you want the show saved. Select the destination, then click Next.

- The Show on the Go dialog box now offers you options on what operating system Presentations should create the show for (see Figure 12-3). Make the appropriate selection and click Next.

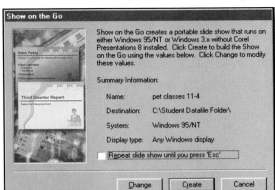

**FIGURE 12-3**
The Show on the Go Dialog Box

- The Show on the Go dialog box offers you choices on the Windows displays. If you are not sure about this option, use the default option Any Windows display. Click Finish. The original Show on the Go dialog box appears.

- Click Create. Presentations displays message boxes indicating that it is creating and compressing the Show on the Go file.

NOTE:

- To play a Show on the Go, exit Presentations and click the Windows Start button, then select Run. The Run dialog box appears. Key the full pathname of the file, or click Browse to find and select it. Click Run. Windows runs the portable show, which automatically shuts off when it is complete.

Choosing the correct operating system is crucial. If you select On Windows95/NT but need to play the show on a PC that runs Windows 3.1, it will not work.

## EXERCISE ➡ PR12.4

SCANS

1. Click the **File** menu and select **Show on the Go**. (You may get a dialog box instructing you to save your slide show. If you do, save the slide show as directed.) The Show on the Go dialog box appears.

2. Click the **Change** button. The dialog box changes in appearance. If necessary, click the **Other destination** option button and enter the pathname of the student **Datafile** folder.

3. Assume for this exercise that the operating system and Windows display options are correct. Click **Finish**, then click **Create**. Presentations displays two message dialog

boxes informing you that the show is being created.

4. When the message boxes disappear, the show is complete. Exit Presentations.

5. Click the Windows **Start** menu button and select **Run**. The Run dialog box appears. Key the full pathname of the Show on the Go file, or browse for the file. Once the file is listed in the text box, click **Run**.

6. Watch the show. When it is complete, it disappears automatically. Start Presentations again.

# Assigning QuickKeys

QuickKeys are keystrokes that you assign to perform various tasks quickly while playing a slide show. The tasks you can assign to QuickKeys include the following:

- Accessing the next, previous, first, or last slide.
- Advancing to a particular slide.
- Advancing bulleted list items one at a time.
- Advancing charts, clipart, or other animated objects.
- Starting and stopping sound clips.
- Quitting the slide show.

To use the QuickKeys, play the slide show and press the appropriate keystroke for the slides you assigned them to.

**NOTE:**

Enter your QuickKeys in the speaker notes and print them. That way, you will have a list to refer to when you play the slide show.

## EXERCISE ▷ PR12.5

**1.** Open **pet classes 11-5 xxx** and display Slide 2.

**2.** Click the **Format** menu and select **Slide Properties**, and then select **QuickKeys** from the cascade menu. The Slide Properties dialog box appears, opened to the QuickKeys tab (see Figure 12-4).

**3.** Select the letter **S** in the Keystrokes list box.

**4.** Click the **Action** button, then click the adjacent drop-down list box. Select **Stop Sound**. The action *Stop Sound* should now appear next to the *S* key in the Keystrokes list box.

**5.** Click the **Apply to all slides in slide show** check box. Click **OK**.

**6.** Save the slide show as **pet classes 12-5 xxx**.

**7.** Play the show, allowing at least two slides to advance. Then press the **S** key. Did the sound stop playing? Play the show again and try to stop the sound on a different slide. Did it work?

**8.** Close the slide show.

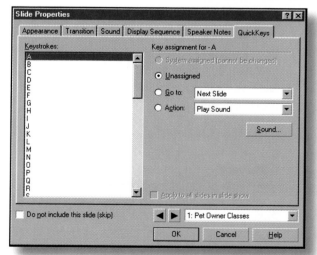

**FIGURE 12-4**
The QuickKeys Tab

# *Creating and Using QuickLinks*

You can assign the same types of tasks to QuickLinks that you did to QuickKeys. The difference between them, however, is that instead of assigning a task to a key, you assign it to an object that is not part of the slide's layout layer, such as a piece of clipart. When you click the clipart, for example, the task executes. QuickLinks proves convenient when you want to run the slide show exclusively with the mouse.

To use the QuickLink, simply play the slide show. When the appropriate slide appears, click the designated object.

## E X E R C I S E ⇒ PR12.6

SCANS

1. Open **pet perks 6a xxx** and display Slide 2. Right click the picture of the present and select **QuickLink**. The Object Properties dialog box appears, opened to the QuickLink tab (see Figure 12-5).

2. Click the **Go to** option button and select **Previous Slide** from the adjacent drop-down list box. Click **OK**.

3. Create the same QuickLink for each piece of clipart on Slides 3, 4, and 5.

4. Save the slide show as **pet perks 12-6 xxx**.

5. Play the slide show. Click on each piece of clipart. Do the QuickLinks work?

6. Close the slide show.

**FIGURE 12-5**
The QuickLink Tab

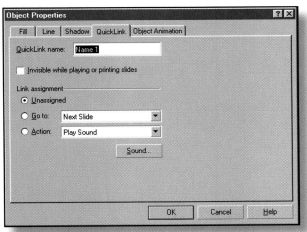

# *Using QuickMenu Tools*

When you play a slide show, Presentations provides you with a QuickMenu filled with valuable tools. Simply play the show, then right click on any slide. The QuickMenu appears, as shown in Figure 12-6.

**FIGURE 12-6**
The QuickMenu Tools

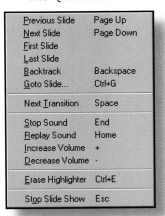

| | |
|---|---|
| Previous Slide | Page Up |
| Next Slide | Page Down |
| First Slide | |
| Last Slide | |
| Backtrack | Backspace |
| Goto Slide... | Ctrl+G |
| Next Transition | Space |
| Stop Sound | End |
| Replay Sound | Home |
| Increase Volume | + |
| Decrease Volume | - |
| Erase Highlighter | Ctrl+E |
| Stop Slide Show | Esc |

1. Open **prospective employee 12-3 xxx**. Play the slide show.

2. When the slide titled *Intoduction* appears, right click the slide. The QuickMenu appears.

3. Click **Next Slide**. The next slide should appear.

4. Bring up the QuickMenu again. This time, click **Last Slide**. The last slide appears.

5. Experiment with several other QuickMenu options.

6. Leave the slide show on the screen for the next exercise.

# Highlighting Slide Show Text

When you play a slide show, Presentations enables you to highlight the text on the screen, much the same way you would highlight text in a book.

1. Access the Play Slide Show dialog box. Click the **Highlighter color** button and select a color from the palette.

2. Click **Play**. When the slide show starts, use the QuickMenu to advance quickly to Slide 3, titled *Company Overview*.

3. Click and drag to use the highlighter to underline the words *third store next year*.

4. Access the QuickMenu and select **Erase Highlighter**.

5. Press **Esc** to stop the slide show. Close the slide show.

# Summary

In this lesson you learned that:

■ you can create speaker notes using the Slide Properties dialog box, then print them to assist you in delivering your presentation.

■ you can create alternative versions of the same slide show by omitting particular slides using the Custom Audiences feature.

■ the Show on the Go feature lets you create portable slide shows. This enables you or someone you know to play the slide show on a Windows-based PC that does not have Corel Presentations software.

■ QuickKeys, QuickLinks, and QuickMenus are all ways to quickly perform tasks while playing a slide show.

■ Presentations enables you to emphasize points on a slide show using a colored highlighter.

## LESSON 12 REVIEW QUESTIONS

### TRUE OR FALSE

**Circle T if the statement is true. Circle F if the statement is false.**

**T  F  1.** When you print speaker notes, Presentations prints blank lines underneath each slide thumbnail.

**T  F  2.** You do not need Corel Presentations software to play a Presentations slide show on another Windows-based PC.

**T  F  3.** A QuickLink enables you to assign a task, such as advancing to the next slide, to an individual keystroke.

**T  F  4.** When playing a slide show, you can access a QuickMenu by clicking the left mouse button once.

**T  F  5.** You can emphasize text while playing a slide show with a colored highlighter, as well as erase the highlighting.

### WRITTEN QUESTIONS

**Write your answers to the following questions.**

**6.** Why do you need speaker notes for a slide, when the slide already contains text?

**7.** Name two reasons why you might need to create a Show on the Go.

**8.** Describe how to use the Custom Audiences feature.

**9.** Give one reason why you might prefer to use a QuickKey instead of a QuickMenu tool when giving a presentation.

**10.** What should you consider when choosing a highlighter color?

## LESSON 12 PROJECT

SCANS

### PROJECT 12A

Pet Paradise has a presentation that details each of the pet owner education classes it offers. Use the Custom Audiences feature to create a version of this slide show for the Beginner, Intermediate, and Expert level courses.

**1.** Open **course catalog** from the student **Datafile** folder. Play the slide show to get a feel for it.

**2.** Switch to **Slide Sorter** view.

**3.** Access the Custom Audiences dialog box. Create a version of the show titled **Beginner**. Skip all the Intermediate and Expert level class slides for this version.

**4.** Using the same procedure, create two more versions of the show, entitled **Intermediate** and **Expert**. Skip the appropriate slides in each.

**5.** Play each version of the slide show. Return to the original version.

**6.** Save the slide show as **course catalog 12a xxx**. Leave the slide show on the screen for the next exercise.

## PROJECT 12B

Assign QuickKeys and QuickLinks to an existing slide show.

1. Assign a QuickKey to the slide show that stops the sound from playing. Assign another that plays the same sound already assigned to the show.

2. Add a clipart arrow to the lower right corner of Slide 2. Copy, paste, and move it next to the original arrow. Flip it so each arrow points in the opposite direction.

3. Assign a QuickLink to the left-pointing arrow that moves to the previous slide. Assign a QuickLink to the right-pointing arrow that advances to the next slide.

4. Select both arrows simultaneously and copy them. Display each subsequent slide and paste them. This copies the QuickLinks with the arrows.

5. Play the slide show. Use the QuickKeys and QuickLinks.

6. Save the slide show as **course catalog 12b xxx**. Leave it on the screen for the next exercise.

## PROJECT 12C

Create a Show on the Go, play it, and use the QuickMenu tools and highlighter.

1. Create a Show on the Go. Set it up to loop until you press **Esc**.

2. Play the Show on the Go. Use the QuickMenu tools to decrease the volume.

3. Use the arrows to advance to the *Teach Your Pet Tricks* slide. Use the highlighter to underline *Hollywood*. Then use the QuickMenu to erase the highlighter.

4. Experiment with the QuickKeys, QuickLinks, QuickMenu tools, and the Highlighter.

5. Press **Esc** to end the show. Close the slide show.

6. Return to Presentations and exit the program.

## CRITICAL THINKING ACTIVITY

SCANS

At this point, you have learned a great deal about Presentations. Create a slide show that provides an overview of the skills you learned. Use your accumulated knowledge, creating different types of slides, drawing objects and adding clipart, creating charts, applying transitions and special effects, and using the special features you learned in this chapter.

Give your presentation to the class.

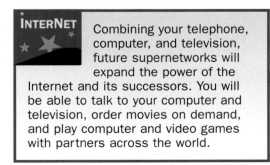

INTERNET

Combining your telephone, computer, and television, future supernetworks will expand the power of the Internet and its successors. You will be able to talk to your computer and television, order movies on demand, and play computer and video games with partners across the world.

# INTEGRATING COREL® WORDPERFECT®, COREL® QUATTRO® PRO, AND COREL® PRESENTATIONS™

INTEGRATION

3

## OBJECTIVES

**Upon completion of Integration 3, you will be able to:**

- Create bullet slides in Presentations directly from a WordPerfect outline.

- Embed a notebook from Quattro Pro into Presentations.

- Copy and paste charts from Quattro Pro into Presentations.

- Create a watermark in Presentations and open it as an image to use as a watermark in WordPerfect.

- Import a WordPerfect outline to create a Presentations organization chart.

- Create a Presentations handout in WordPerfect.

- Copy and paste an organization chart into WordPerfect from Presentations.

⏱ **Estimated Time: 4 hours**

$M$ost of the procedures you have learned in Integration 1 and 2 can be applied in Presentations. This section will help you learn the typical types of information sharing that can occur among the three applications. Transferring information between Presentations and WordPerfect and Quattro Pro is possible using the same methods of copy and paste, embedding, and linking. Basically, you want to be efficient in your use of the three programs and use each one for its intended purpose. Then the information can be shared from the source application rather than recreating it in the destination applications.

## Importing an Outline from WordPerfect into Presentations

$D$r. Paradeis has been asked to make a presentation to the third grade class at a nearby elementary school about the care of pets. He knows that children are easily distracted and bored, so he decides to create a computer presentation to help explain the care of pets. With minor modifications, he could use it for other presentations he may be asked to make in the future.

He has prepared an outline using WordPerfect and would like you to use this outline as the text for the presentation. You learned how to do this in Lesson 5 of Presentations, so this will be a review for you.

## EXERCISE ▷ INT3.1

1. Start a new Presentations Slide Show and accept the **DEFAULT** master. Switch **to Slide Outliner** view.

2. Click the **Insert** menu and click **File**. The Insert Outline dialog box appears. If necessary, access the drive where your data disk is located.

3. Select **pet care outline** from the student **Datafile** folder and click **Insert**. Presentations displays the outline in Slide Outliner view.

4. You should have 11 slides in your presentation. Save the presentation as **pet care xxx** on your integration disk.

5. Now that you have the text inserted, you can get busy formatting the presentation and inserting objects from different applications.

6. Change to **Slide Editor** view and select the title slide. Double click the *Subtitle* text box. Key the following: **Presented by Dr. Glen Paradeis, DVM**

7. Click the empty text frame to select it. Press the **Delete** key to delete it.

8. In the area of the deleted text box, insert two graphics from the student **Datafile** folder: **square dog** and **square cat**. If one is on top of the other, move one so it is next to the other, as shown in Figure INT3-1.

9. Click the dog graphic to select it. While holding down the **Shift** key, click the cat graphic. Now both graphics are selected.

 **TIP**

You can also select multiple objects that are close to each other by pointing to a spot above the left corner of the upper left-most object and drawing a *marquee* around both objects. A marquee is a dotted box that is formed as you drag to select all objects. When all objects are inside the marquee, release the mouse button and all objects are selected.

10. Align the two selected graphics so that they are even at the bottom part of each graphic by right clicking on an area inside the selected graphics and choosing **Align**. In the submenu select **Bottom**. While they are still selected, choose **Align** again and this time choose **Center Left/Right**. Now they are also centered between the right and left margins of the slide.

**FIGURE INT3-1**
Title Slide for Exercise INT3.1

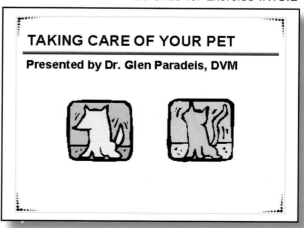

**11.** One more time right click the two selected graphics and choose **Group**. Now they are one object rather than two separate objects. Your slide should look like Figure INT3-1.

**12.** Save the file again with the same name, **pet care xxx**.

Now you are going to make some simple changes to the overall format of the presentation by going to the Slide Layout feature.

SCANS

**EXERCISE ▷ INT3.2**

**1.** Change the slide show master to another design. Click **Format** and choose **Master Gallery**.

**2.** Choose the **Printout** category and select the design to the far right. (It's named Corners.) Click **OK**.

**3.** Choose **Layout Layer** from the **Edit** menu. Click the **Bulleted List** tab, if necessary.

**4.** Select the *Subtitle* text box and delete it by clicking **Delete**.

**5.** Move the text box containing the bulleted items up to where the *Subtitle* text box was before deleting it.

**6.** Click the **Edit** menu and click **Slide Layer**. Save the file again.

# Copying and Pasting Between Applications

The first opportunity for sharing between applications will be adding an existing Quattro Pro notebook and then adding two charts from a different Quattro Pro notebook. The process is nothing new to you. You will open the source application and select the range of cells or the chart and choose Copy. Then you will switch back to the destination application using the Taskbar and use Paste or Paste special.

**EXERCISE ▷ INT3.3**

SCANS

**1.** In your slide show, click Slide 6 (Training Your Pet). Click the **Insert** menu and choose **New Slide**. The New Slide dialog box appears.

**2.** Select the first slide in the first row. Click **OK**.

**3.** Double click the *Title* text box and key the following text: **Vaccinations**

**4.** Drag the *Title* text box to the top of the slide and delete the *Subtitle* text box, if necessary.

**5.** Open Quattro Pro either from the **Start** menu or from the Taskbar. Open the file **vac schedule** from the student **Datafile** folder.

(continued on next page)

**6.** Select the range **A1..F12** and click the **Copy** button on the Toolbar.

**7.** Click the **Corel Presentations** button on the Taskbar and, with the new slide showing, click the **Edit** menu and choose **Paste Special**. Make sure **Corel Quattro Pro 8 Notebook** and **Paste** are selected. Click **OK**.

**8.** You can resize the pasted object to fill out the slide, if necessary. Your new slide should look like Figure INT3-2.

**9.** Save the presentation again as **pet care xxx**.

**10.** Switch back to Quattro Pro and close **vac schedule**.

**FIGURE INT3-2**
Pasted Notebook

Now you will edit an existing notebook to include a new pie chart in the presentation.

**EXERCISE ➡ INT3.4**

**1.** Open **licenses xxx** from the student integration disk.

**2.** Click cell **D8** in the *Dogs* sheet and total the number of licenses for dogs for 1997 by clicking the **QuickSum** button. Be sure you don't include the year in cell D3.

**3.** Do the same on the *Cats* sheet for the total number of licenses for cats. Be sure you don't include the year in cell D3.

**4.** You are now going to create a pie chart based on these two new cells. Right click sheet C and rename it **Pie Chart**.

**5.** Click the **Insert** menu and choose **Chart** to start the Chart Expert. Fill in the boxes as follows:

| | |
|---|---|
| Chart range: | **A:D8..B:D8** |
| General chart type: | **Pie** |
| Specific: | **3-D** |
| Color scheme: | **Default** |
| Title: | **Dogs and Cats Licensed** |
| Subtitle: | **Austin - 1997** |

**6.** Click **Finish** and draw the chart from approximately cells B2..G16.

**7.** Double click the chart to edit it. Turn on the Chart and Drawing Toolbar from **Toolbars** in the **View** menu.

8. Choose the Text box tool and draw a Text box over the percentage of cats (*45.37%*) and key the word **CATS**.

9. Select the word you just keyed and change the font to **Arial**, **Bold**, and **24** pt.

10. With the box still selected, click the **Format** menu and choose **Selected Object**. Click the **Fill Setting** tab and change the Pattern Color to **White**.

11. Resize the box to fit better around the word, click the **Alignment** button on the Toolbar, and choose **Center** alignment.

12. Repeat this process for the label *DOGS* over the (*54.63%*). Your finished pie chart should resemble Figure INT3-3.

13. Save the file as **licenses2 xxx**. Print the new sheet only. In the Print dialog box, choose **Sheet**.

14. Click the new pie chart so that there are handles on it. Click the **Copy** button.

**FIGURE INT3-3**
New Pie Chart

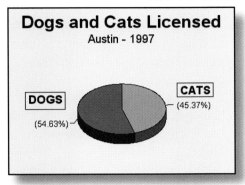

Now you will paste the new pie chart into the Presentations slide.

## EXERCISE ➡ INT3.5

1. Switch back to Presentations using the Taskbar and click Slide 10 (Lost Pets).

2. Click **Insert** and **New Slide** and choose a title slide.

3. Delete both the *Title* text box and the *Subtitle* text box using the **Delete** key.

4. Click **Paste** and you should see the pie chart. Resize it so it fits well in the slide. Check with Figure INT3-4 to see if your slide is accurate.

5. Save the presentation again under the same name of **pet care xxx**.

**FIGURE INT3-4**
Pasted Pie Chart

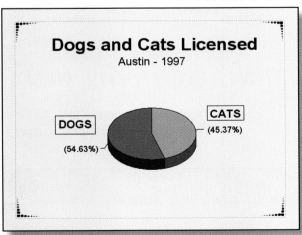

Since that went so well, now you will paste a map chart from Quattro Pro into Presentations.

## EXERCISE ⟹ INT3.6

**1.** Click Slide 6 (Training Your Pet) and click the down arrow next to the **Insert a new slide after current slide** button in the lower right corner of the screen. Choose **Insert Title Slide**. Delete the *Title* and *Subtitle* text boxes, if necessary.

**2.** Switch to Quattro Pro and close the **licenses2 xxx** file, if necessary. Open the **heartworm2 xxx** file from your integration disk.

**3.** Click once inside the map to select it. Make sure you only have the black selection handles, not the blue hazy line. Click the **Copy** button.

**TIP**

Click toward the top of the map, right inside the top border. It's tricky!

**4.** Switch back to Presentations. With the new slide still showing, click the **Paste** button.

**5.** Resize the map object to stretch to the margins of the slide, keeping inside the corner borders.

**FIGURE INT3-5**
Pasted Map Chart

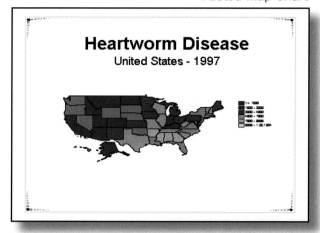

**6.** Your slide should look like Figure INT3-5.

**7.** Switch to Quattro Pro and close the file **heartworm2 xxx**. Switch back to Presentations and save the file again as **pet care xxx**. Keep the file open to add some clipart.

# Adding Clipart to Your Presentation

Adding clipart to your presentation is always fun. It helps convey the message and adds interest to the words. You will add a few clipart images to your presentation as follows.

## EXERCISE ⟹ INT3.7

**1.** Go to Slide 2 (Bringing Home a New Pet). Turn on the **Ruler** in the **View** menu. Click the bullet box so that you see handles. Resize the text box by pulling the right side in to about $7^1/2$" on the horizontal ruler.

**2.** Click the **Insert** menu, choose **Graphic**, and choose **From File**. From the student **Datafile** folder, choose the **doghouse** graphic and click **Insert**.

3. Move the graphic to the right side of the slide so the dog's head is facing the words. You may need to resize the bullet box by pulling the right side toward the left of the slide to make room for the graphic you just inserted.

4. Click Slide 5 (Health Care). Notice that there is quite a bit of room at the bottom of the slide. This would be an ideal slide to have an animated object move onto the slide from the left side. You have the perfect graphic for that on your student **Datafile** folder called **running dog**.

5. Repeat Step 2 to bring in the graphic named **running dog** and move it to the lower right corner of the slide. Right click the object and choose **Object Animation**.

6. Choose **Fly In** for effects and **Left to Right** for the direction.

7. Now go to Slide 6 (Training Your Pet) and insert the object **climbing cat** from student **Datafile** folder. Place this one in the lower right corner of the slide. Again right click and choose **Object Animation**. Choose **Fly In** for effects and **Top to Bottom** for the direction.

8. Add one more graphic on the last slide (Slide 14) showing the benefits of owning a pet. Insert the graphic named **happy dog** and move it to the lower right corner. Right click and choose **Object Animation**. Turn on **Bounce In** for effects and **Right and Down** for the direction.

9. Do you feel it needs more clipart? If so, ask your instructor if you can add more.

10. Save the file with the same name of **pet care xxx**. Run the slide show. Close the file for now but don't exit Presentations. You will return to it later and add another slide.

# Creating a Watermark Graphic in Presentations

Presentations has a drawing tool that allows you to create your own graphics and use the Tool Palette and Feature Toolbar to edit those graphics. The resulting graphics are saved as WordPerfect graphics (.wpg) which can be inserted into any Corel WordPerfect Suite 8 document. You learned about the Presentations Drawing feature earlier in the book. In the following exercise you are going to create a graphic that will be used as a watermark in WordPerfect.

## EXERCISE ▷ INT3.8

1. Start a new file in Presentations and choose **Presentations Drawing** in the Create New dialog box.

2. Make sure the Tool Palette is turned on. If it is not, choose **Toolbars** from the **View** menu and click **Tool Palette**.

3. Also turn on the grids option, which is found in the **View** menu under **Grid/Guides/Snap**. Select **Display Grids**. This tool helps you to measure and align objects. Your screen should now look like Figure INT3-6.

(continued on next page)

**NOTE:**

Your Tool Palette may be at the left side of the window and not a floating Toolbar.

**FIGURE INT3-6**
Tool Palette and Grids

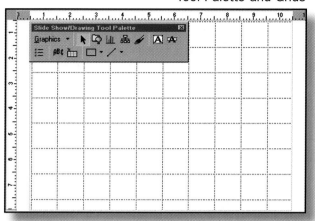

4. Insert two files from the student **Datafile** folder by clicking **Insert** and choosing **Graphics**. Choose **From File** and select **cartoon cat**. Repeat the same process for inserting **comic dog** from your student **Datafile** folder.

5. Arrange these two graphics so the animals' tails are overlapping. Select both graphics and right click to bring up the QuickMenu. Click **Align** and choose **Bottom**. (This ensures that both animals are evenly lined up at the base of the graphics.)

**FIGURE INT3-7**
Inserted Clipart

6. Right click the two selected graphics again and choose **Group**. Now these two graphics will be treated as one graphic. The two objects can be moved and resized as one.

7. The two graphics should look like Figure INT3-7. It does not matter where on the page this graphic is located.

The next step to creating this graphic to be used as a watermark is to add two text boxes identifying the name of the animal clinic. All three objects will then be grouped so that you will only have one graphic.

**EXERCISE ▭ INT3.9**

SCANS

1. Select the **Text box** tool on the Tool Palette and draw a text box approximately 6" wide above the top of the graphic. Key the following text: **Parkway Animal Clinic**

2. Change the font to **Arial**, **36 pt.**, and **Bold**. Center the text in the text box by clicking **Justification** and choosing **Center**.

3. Now create another text box below the graphic that is about 5" wide and key the following text: **Companion Animal Services**. Change the font to **Arial**, **24 pt.**, and **Bold**. Center the text in the Text box.

4. Select all three graphics and right click. Click **Align** and choose **Center Left/Right**.

5. Right click the three selected objects again and click **Group**.

6. Size the new graphic to be approximately 6" wide and $3^1/_2$" tall. You can only size from a corner handle so it stays proportionate as you resize. It still does not matter where the graphic is located on the screen. Your final graphic should look like Figure INT3-8.

**FIGURE INT3-8**
Completed Clinic Logo

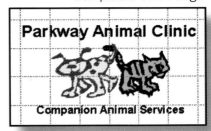

7. Select the graphic one more time and click **Save**. You will choose the option to save the **Selected item**. Choose the $3^1/_2$ *Floppy (A:)* drive and name the file **clinic logo xxx**.

8. Print the file and close it. Choose **No** to not save the Presentations file. It is saved as a .wpg file that can be opened again in Presentations if changes need to be made.

# *Inserting a Presentations Graphic into a WordPerfect Watermark*

Now that you have created your graphic, you will insert it as a graphic into a WordPerfect watermark.

## EXERCISE ▷ INT3.10

1. Open **P&P 1-3 xxx** from the student integration disk.

2. Click **Insert** and choose **Watermark**. Click **Watermark A** and **Create**.

3. In the Watermark screen, choose **Insert** and click **Graphic**. Choose **From File**. Insert **clinic logo xxx** from your student integration disk.

4. Now you need to lighten up the graphic slightly so that it doesn't stand out too much on the text page and distract from the text in the document. Click the **Shading** tool on the Toolbar (see Figure INT3-9). If you can't see this Toolbar, click away from the graphic toward the top of the page. Change the shading for both the Text and Image to **20%**.

5. Click **File** and **Close.** The top portion of the letter is shown in Figure INT3-10 with the watermark behind the text of the letter.

(continued on next page)

**FIGURE INT3-9**
Watermark Toolbar

6. Save the file as **P&P 3-10 xxx** to your integration disk and print the file. Close this file, but leave WordPerfect open for the next exercise.

**FIGURE INT3-10**
**P&P 3-10** with Watermark

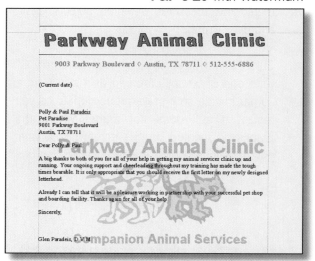

# Creating a WordPerfect Outline for an Organization Chart

One more slide needs to be created for the **pet care** slide show. It is an organization chart for Parkway Animal Clinic. It is easy to create an organization chart in Presentations, but an easier way is to key the chain of command as a WordPerfect outline and then import the information into Presentations. You are now going to create the outline showing the people working at Parkway Animal Clinic.

SCANS

1. Create a new file in WordPerfect.

2. Select **Outline/Bullets & Numbering** from the **Insert** menu.

3. Click the **Numbers** tab and choose the paragraph style of outlining—**1. a. i. (1)**.

4. Enter the name **Dr. Glen Paradeis** as the top executive and press **Shift+Enter**. This action puts you on the next line without numbering it. Press **F7** to indent the line. Key **Owner** on the second line. Putting the word *Owner* on the second line will insert it as a separate line in the first box in the organization chart. This

makes the box less wide and makes the text easier to read.

5. Enter subordinate levels as indented paragraphs, using **Tab** to move down a level and **Shift+Tab** to move up. Continue to key the outline so that it appears as shown in Figure INT3-11.

6. Save the document as **organization chart outline xxx** to your integration disk.

**FIGURE INT3-11**
Subordinate Levels

| | |
|---|---|
| 1. | Dr. Glen Paradeis<br>Owner |
| 2. | Dr. James Johnson<br>Associate |
| | a.    Cindy Grant<br>      Vet Assistant |
| | b.    Kerry Mason<br>      Vet Assistant |
| 3. | Perri Fredrickson<br>Office Manager |
| | a.    Abby Hunt<br>      Receptionist |
| | b.    Billie Jo Hill<br>      Receptionist |

Now that you have created the outline for the organization chart, your next step is to import the outline into Presentations to create a graphic organization chart.

# Importing a WordPerfect Outline to Create a Presentations Organization Chart

## EXERCISE ⇨ INT3.12

**SCANS**

1. Switch to or open the **pet care xxx** Presentations file.

2. Click Slide 14, which should be the last slide in the show. Click the down arrow next to the **New Slide** button at the lower right corner of the screen. Choose **Insert Text Slide**.

3. Key **Parkway Animal Clinic** in the *Title* text box. Change the font to **Arial** and **Bold** (if necessary).

4. Delete the *Subtitle* box by clicking it so that the handles show and pressing **Delete**.

5. Move the Text box to the bottom of the slide for now.

6. Click **Organization Chart** from the **Insert** menu and drag to draw the chart so that the marquee fills most of the blank area on the slide.

7. Choose the first option for the Single Layout. Click **OK**.

8. Select **Import Outline** from the **Chart** menu.

9. Choose the **organization chart outline xxx** file and click **Insert**.

10. Resize the organization chart, if necessary, to fill most of the remaining part of the slide below the title.

(continued on next page)

**11.** Add the following text to the text box at the bottom of the slide: **Visit us anytime!** Make sure the text is centered inside the box and that the box is centered horizontally at the bottom of the page. Change the font to **Arial** and **Bold** (if necessary). Your new slide should look like the one in Figure INT3-12.

**12.** Switch to **Slide Sorter** View. Choose **Select** and **All** from the **Edit** menu. Choose the transition called **Photo Lens Out**. Play the slide show and see how you like it!

**13.** Save the Presentations file again as **pet care xxx**. Keep the file open to prepare handouts.

**FIGURE INT3-12**
Organization Chart Slide

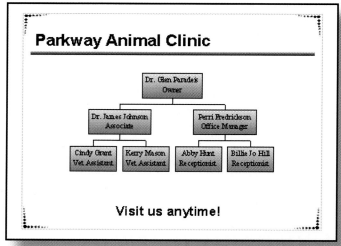

# *Creating a Presentations Handout in WordPerfect*

You can use the Send to command in WordPerfect to send or export slides and speaker notes from Presentations to WordPerfect. In WordPerfect you can format the information in your speaker notes, audience notes, and handouts as you would in any WordPerfect document. You can position the slides above or beside the note text or blank lines.

EXERCISE ⇒ INT3.13

SCANS

**1.** Make sure **pet care xxx** is still open in Presentations.

**2.** Click the **File** menu and choose **Send To**. Choose **Corel WordPerfect**. You may be prompted to save the Presentations file again. Save it as **pet care xxx** and choose **Yes** if asked to replace the previous version.

**3.** A dialog box will appear, as shown in Figure INT3-13. Fill in the choices as follows:

Page layout:  **Multiple slides per page**
Page options: **(Header Information)**
　　　　　　　 **Pet Care Presentation**
Notes options: **Print lines for audience notes**

**4.** Click **Finish**. The document in WordPerfect is created and it is opened. It should resemble the page shown in Figure INT3-14.

**5.** Save the file as **pet care handout xxx** and print it. Switch back to Presentations.

**FIGURE INT3-13**
Send to Corel WordPerfect Dialog Box

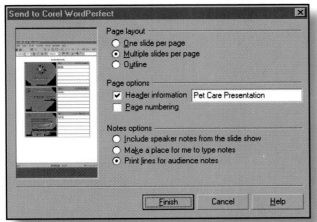

**FIGURE INT3-14**
Presentations Handout

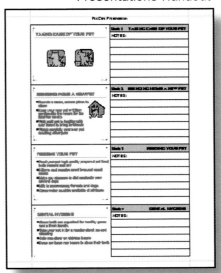

# Pasting a Presentations Object into WordPerfect

You have learned how to insert a Presentations drawing into WordPerfect when you created the watermark for the Parkway Animal Clinic. You also learned how to embed and paste a Quattro Pro notebook and chart onto a Presentations slide. It is possible to export objects through copying and pasting from Presentations to other applications. You will now copy and paste the organization chart created in Exercises INT3.11 and INT3.12 into WordPerfect. You will find out that using the Paste button in this activity defaults to the embedding mode.

## EXERCISE ▷ INT3.14

SCANS

**1.** Click Slide 15, which contains the organization chart.

**2.** Click the organization chart to see the selection handles and click the **Copy** button.

**3.** Open a new document in WordPerfect. Change the orientation of the page to **Landscape** through the Page Setup dialog box accessed from the **File** menu.

**4.** Click the **Paste** button. You will see that the chart is a very small object in the upper left corner of the page. Zoom to **Full Page** to see the entire layout.

**5.** All you can do is move the object at this point. Select the chart and right click the object. Select **Edit Image**. Notice that the object now has a hatched border and handles are appearing.

(continued on next page)

**6.** Drag the lower right handle until the image of the box outlines the margins. You should see rulers and grid lines. You are in the Presentations Drawing object window. The organization chart will stay small.

**7.** There should be one handle at the lower right corner of the little organization chart object. Drag that handle until the sides are touching the right and left margins. Now you should be able to read the chart boxes better. You may need to resize the Drawing window and the chart inside a few times to come up with the right size.

**8.** With the Drawing window selected, you will see at the left end of the Toolbar two OLE buttons—one for updating the object and the other for closing the Presentations Drawing editor window. Click the second button. In the WordPerfect window try clicking the object once to select it. Nothing happens.

**9.** Double click the organization chart and you are back in the Presentations Drawing object window. Click away from the Presentations Drawing object to deselect it. Add a TextArt object at the top of the page containing the following words: **Parkway Animal Clinic**. (If you

**FIGURE INT3-15**
Organization Chart in WordPerfect

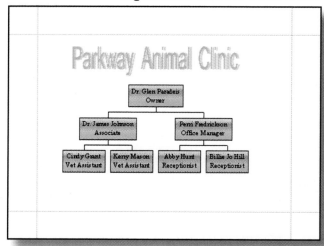

don't see the Tool Palette containing the TextArt button, you may have to turn it on through the Tools dialog box, which can be selected in the View menu.

**10.** Check your screen at this time with Figure INT3-15. Close the Presentations Drawing editor window and in the WordPerfect document window, save the file as **org chart xxx** and print it.

**11.** Exit WordPerfect and Presentations.

# *Summary*

In this section you learned that:

■ the text for the bullet slides can be created in WordPerfect and inserted into Presentations.

■ notebooks and charts can be embedded or pasted into Presentations.

■ graphics used for watermarks in WordPerfect can be created in Presentations.

■ a WordPerfect outline can be used to create a Presentations organization chart.

■ Presentations handouts can be created in WordPerfect.

## TRUE / FALSE

**Circle the T if the statement is true. Circle the F if it is false.**

**T   F   1.** The results from embedding data using Paste Special in Presentations are different from embedding using the other Corel Suite applications.

**T   F   2.** For text created in WordPerfect to convert to bullet slides in Presentations, it must also be created in bullet format in WordPerfect.

**T   F   3.** The Send To command in Presentations is only used for sending a file through e-mail.

**T   F   4.** Switching between applications for transferring information requires closing the source application and opening the destination application.

**T   F   5.** WordPerfect is the Corel WordPerfect Suite 8 Suite application best suited to create graphics-intensive layouts.

## WRITTEN QUESTIONS

**Write your answers to the following questions.**

**6.** Explain the two methods for selecting more than one object at a time in Presentations Drawing.

**7.** What menu and command do you select to convert a Presentations slide show to a WordPerfect file to prepare handouts?

**8.** How does a WordPerfect document have to be formatted in order for the text to be inserted as text for an organization chart?

**9.** What is the purpose and what are the advantages of the Group command in Presentations Drawing?

**10.** What file format does Presentations use when it saves a graphic created in Presentations Drawing?

## INTEGRATION 3 PROJECT

SCANS

In anticipation of the upcoming Animal Appreciation Week starting on November 2, Dr. Paradeis has volunteered to prepare a Presentations slide show to run at the Parkside Animal Shelter at their open house on November 8. He intends to make *Pet Overpopulation* the theme of the slide show.

### PROJECT INT3A

**1.** Create a new Presentations file. Choose **Presentations Slide Show** and click **Create**.

**2.** In the Startup Mastery Gallery choose **Business** as the category and choose the **Arrows** design.

**3.** On the one slide showing, key **Animal Overpopulation** in the *Title* text box and **Why Spay/Neuter?** in the *Subtitle* text box.

(continued on next page)

4. In the title slide click the **Edit** menu and choose **Layout Layer**.

5. Select and change the title font to **Arial** and the subtitle font to **Arial** and **Bold**. Click the **Slide Layer** in the **Edit** menu.

6. Click the down arrow next to the new slide button in the lower right corner and choose the **Insert Bulleted List** slide. Again choose **Edit** and **Layout Layer** as follows:
   a. Change the title font to **Arial**.
   b. Delete the *Subtitle* text box.
   c. Change the bullet list font to **Arial**.
   d. Move the bullet box up closer to the *Title* text box.

7. After returning to the Slide Layer, choose the **Insert** menu and click **File**.

8. Select the file named **overpopulation** from the student **Datafile** folder. You should have an additional six slides. Read each slide and look for any layout problems.

## PROJECT INT3B

1. Create a new slide at the end using the **Insert a new slide** button and choose the **Insert Data Chart** slide. Delete the chart box and delete the subtitle.

2. In the *Title* text box, key **Dog Population Control**. Change the font to **Arial**.

3. Open the Quattro Pro file **licenses2 xxx**.

4. Click the *Dogs* sheet. Click the bar chart so that the handles are showing.

5. Click the **Copy** button and switch to the Presentations file.

6. In the new slide click the **Paste** button. Resize the chart so that it fills up most of the portion of the slide under the *Title* text box. Be careful not to distort it as you resize it.

7. Now repeat the same process for the bar chart for cats. The title in the new slide should be **Cat Population Control**. Change the font to **Arial** (if necessary).

8. Save the Presentations file as **pet overpopulation xxx**.

9. Add any clipart that you feel will enhance the slide show and turn on suitable transitions and bullet build features.

10. Print the slide show as handouts from Presentations and run it for your instructor to view.

## CRITICAL THINKING ACTIVITY

SCANS

Assume that you are a volunteer at the local humane society in your area. The director knows that you have excellent computer skills and asks you to create a presentation that the director can take to various civic organizations to promote being a volunteer at the humane society. The director wants to make a computer presentation at meetings and also wants a document describing the possible volunteer positions. Write out a brief plan on how you would create the presentation and the document.

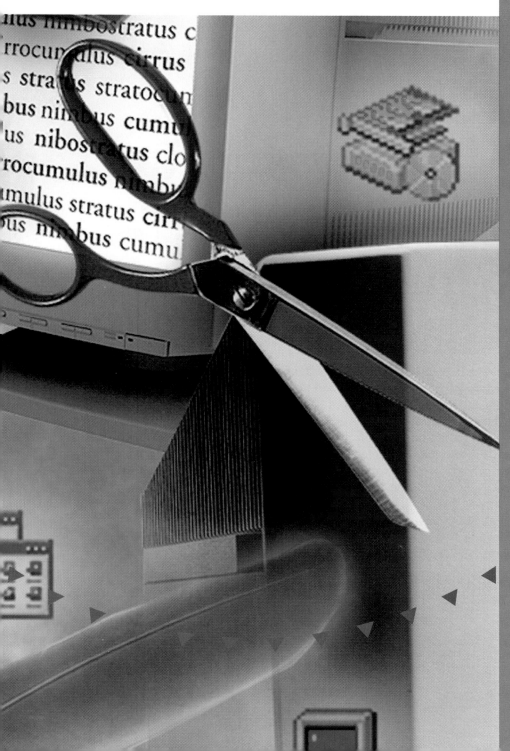

# COREL®
# PARADOX® 8

# CREATING A DATABASE

## OBJECTIVES

**Upon completion of this lesson, you will be able to:**

- Identify the basic parts of a database.
- Set a working directory for database files.
- Define fields in a database table.
- Save a database.

**⏱ Estimated Time: 1 hour**

In this lesson you will learn how to plan, create, and save a Paradox database. You will learn the basic components of a database, as well as what makes Paradox a relational database.

## *Understanding Databases*

You encounter data every day: telephone numbers, street addresses, birth dates, prices, and checking account numbers (to name a very few). Individually, these pieces of data do not mean much. When you organize data into a *database*, however, it becomes valuable information. For example, a name, street address, city, state, or ZIP code by itself is not enough information to send a letter. Organize them together in the proper format, though, and you can mail the letter.

A database, then, is simply an organized collection of data. You probably encounter databases on a daily basis. For example, when you call Directory Assistance for a telephone number or look up a book at your local library, you are getting information from a database.

In Corel® Paradox® data is organized into tables. The database can consist of one table or many tables. In many cases, you will want to break down the data into smaller, more manageable tables that are linked by a common field. This is referred to as a *relational database* (see Lesson 6 for more information).

Each database table is made up of *fields* and *records*. A field is a category, such as name, address, or phone number. A record is a collection of all the fields on a single subject, such as the name, address, and telephone number of one person. The following is the overall relationship:

**field ➡ record ➡ table ➡ database**

# Starting Paradox

When you start Paradox, the Paradox Startup Expert appears (see Figure 1-1). The Paradox Startup Expert provides the following options:

- *Use the Paradox Database Expert to choose a predefined database structure, where I can begin storing my data.* Paradox comes with a number of predesigned databases that you can customize to suit your needs.

- *Give a name to a database that I want to create myself.* Select this option to create a database from scratch.

- *Name a database I've already created.* This lets you rename an existing database.

- *Open a database.* Select this option to display a list of existing Paradox databases in the list box. Select the one you want to open.

You can exit the Startup Expert by clicking its close button, and proceed directly to the Project Viewer (see Figure 1-2). In the Project Viewer you can quickly create new tables, forms, queries, and reports, as well as access existing ones. These are referred to as Paradox *objects*. Each category of objects is identified by an icon in the Project Viewer.

Before you create new tables in Paradox, you should establish a *working directory*. This is the location on the hard or floppy disk to which you will save your files. It will also display in the Project Viewer when you start Paradox. (The default directory name *WORKING* might appear in the Project Viewer.)

To determine a working directory, click the File menu and select Working Directory. The Set Working Directory dialog box appears (see Figure 1-3).

Click the Browse button to select the disk and folder you want to set as your working directory. You can also assign an

**FIGURE 1-1**
The Paradox Startup Expert
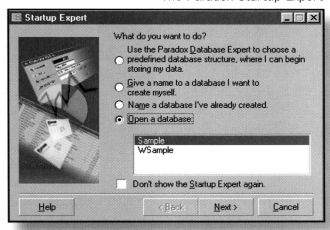

**FIGURE 1-2**
The Project Viewer
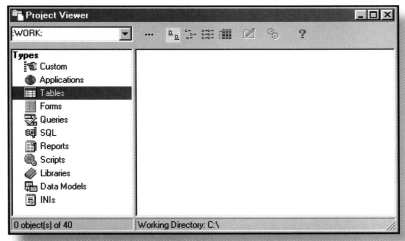

**FIGURE 1-3**
The Set Working Directory Dialog Box
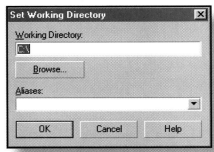

**P A - 3**

alias to the working directory; instead of keying the path and name of the working directory, you can simply enter the alias.

In Exercise PA1.1 you will practice starting Paradox and setting up a working directory for your database files.

EXERCISE ⟶ PA1.1

1.  Start Paradox. The Paradox Startup Expert appears. Click **Cancel** to access the Project Viewer window.

2.  Set a working directory.
    a.  Click the **File** menu and select **Working Directory**. The Set Working Directory dialog box appears.

    b.  In the Set Working Directory dialog box click the **Browse** button and select the disk and folder to which you want to save your database files. (Your instructor will tell you where to save your files.)

    c.  Click **OK**. Remain in this screen for the next exercise.

# Creating a Database Table

■ In the Project Viewer, right click Tables in the *Types* list box and select New.

■ The New Table dialog box appears. Click Blank. A dialog box asks you to verify that you want to create a Paradox 7 & 8 table. Click OK. The Create Paradox 7 & 8 Table dialog box appears (see Figure 1-4).

Exercise PA1.2 will teach you how to create a database table.

EXERCISE ⟶ PA1.2

1.  Click the **File** menu and select **New**. The New dialog box appears, opened to the Create New tab.

2.  Click the drop-down list box, if necessary, to select **Corel Paradox 8**. Select **[New Table]** and click **Create**. The New Table dialog box appears.

3.  Click **Blank**. The Create Table dialog box appears.

4.  The *Table type* drop-down list box is currently set to *Paradox 7 & 8*. Click **OK**.

5.  The Create Paradox 7 & 8 Table dialog box appears (see Figure 1-4). Leave it on the screen for the next exercise.

**FIGURE 1-4**
The Create Paradox 7 & 8 Table Dialog Box

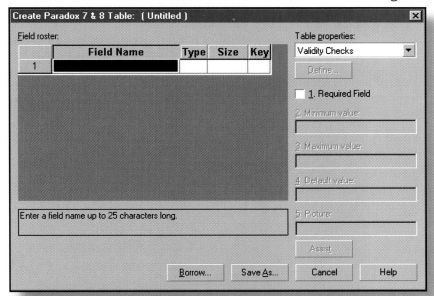

## Creating Fields

In the Field roster you enter the fields (or categories of information) you want to include in the table, as well as their type and size. To define fields for a database table:

■ Key the name of the first field in the shaded box under *Field Name*. The field name you enter appears in the table and in queries, forms, and reports you generate using the table's data. Press the Tab key to move to the Type box.

■ Click the right mouse button or press the space bar to display a list of the different types of fields you can define (see Figure 1-5). The most common field types are Alpha, which represents alphabetic characters and numerals that cannot be added (such as ZIP codes, telephone numbers, etc.); Number, which represents numeric values that can be used in calculations; $ (Money), which represents dollar amounts; and Memo, which represents a field of any size where you can enter lengthy notes that do not appear on the screen.

**FIGURE 1-5**
Field Types

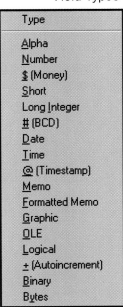

■ Select a field type by highlighting and then clicking the right mouse button, or by pressing the underscored character on the keyboard.

■ Press Tab again to move to the Size box. Enter the number of characters the field can contain. (For some field types, Paradox assigns a size.) Press Tab to move to the Key box. If you choose to establish a field as a key, Paradox arranges records in the table according to the key field.

When sizing a field, count or estimate the number of characters of the largest possible entry. Then, add one extra character for safety. For example, if the longest last name you expect to enter in a LAST NAME field is 12 characters long, make the field size 13.

 **NOTE:**

If you assign a key field, it must be the first field in the database table structure.

■ Press Tab to enter additional fields in the table. When you have defined all the fields, click Save As. The Save Table As dialog box appears, as shown in Figure 1-6.

**FIGURE 1-6**
The Save Table As Dialog Box

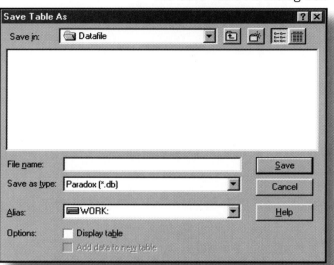

The working directory you designated in the Paradox Startup Expert should be displayed in the *Save in* text box. If it is not, click the arrow and select a location from the drop-down list box. Enter a name for the table in the *File name* text box and then click Save.

Now let's create a database table for Pet Paradise, a growing pet store business that needs to create a database for their pet owner classes.

## EXERCISE ⇨ PA1.3

**SCANS**

1. In the Create Paradox 7 & 8 Table dialog box key **Instructor Code** under *Field Name*. Press **Tab**.

2. Right click to display the types of fields. Highlight and click **Alpha**, or press the **A** key on the keyboard. Press **Tab**.

3. Under *Size* key **2**. Press **Tab**.

4. Double click the **Key** box to establish Instructor Code as a key field. Next, press **Tab** to define another field.

5. Enter **Last Name** as the Field Name. Select **Alpha** as the Type and enter **12** as the Size. Press **Tab** twice.

6. For the third field, enter **First Name** as the Field Name and select **Alpha** as the Type. Enter **10** as the Size and press **Tab** once.

7. For the final field, enter **Pay Rate** as the Field Name. Select **$ (Money)** as the Type. Paradox assigns a default size to money field types.

8. Click **Save As**. In the Save Table As dialog box, make sure your working directory is displayed in the *Save in* text box. Key **instructors xxx** as the file name (where *xxx* represents your initials), then click **Save**.

9. The new table should appear in the Project Viewer. (NOTE: If *instructors xxx* is not listed in the Project Viewer, make sure *Tables* is selected.)

10. Leave this exercise on the screen for the Lesson 1 Project.

**NOTE:**

During the save process, Paradox may display the following warning: "*No features specific to Paradox 7 & 8 have been chosen. Your table has been saved in Paradox 4 to remain compatible.*" This is not cause for concern—your table will still be saved properly.

# *Summary*

In this lesson you learned that:

■ a database is an organized collection of data. It consists of fields, categories of data such as last name or price, and records, the collection of all the fields on a single subject.

■ Corel Paradox 8 is a relational database program, meaning that its databases can consist of multiple tables linked by a common field.

■ before creating your first database in Paradox, it is a good idea to establish your working directory, the folder where you want to store your Paradox files.

■ the first step in creating a database is to define its field roster. You need to assign a name, field type, size, and, if desired, a key. Common field types include Alpha, Number, $ (Money), and Memo.

■ you must use the Save Table As dialog box to save your database table structure.

## LESSON 1 REVIEW QUESTIONS

### TRUE / FALSE

**Circle the T if the statement is true. Circle the F if it is false.**

**T  F**   1.  You can include one table per Paradox database.

**T  F**   2.  A field is the collection of all the records on one subject.

(continued on next page)

T  F  3. A telephone book is an example of a database.

T  F  4. The Memo field type lets you key free-form text.

T  F  5. A field named Telephone Number would be a Number field type.

## WRITTEN QUESTIONS

**Write your answers to the following questions.**

6. Explain the difference between data and information.

7. Define the term *relational database*.

8. Describe how to create a new table.

9. List and describe at least four field types.

10. List four examples of Paradox objects.

## LESSON 1 PROJECT

The owners of Pet Paradise want to create a database table to track their pet classes.

1. Make sure your working directory is selected in the Project Viewer. Click the **File** menu and select **New**, then select **Table**.

2. In the Create Table message box click **OK** to verify that you want to create a Paradox 7 & 8 table.

3. In the Field roster define the following fields:

| | Field Name | Type | Size | Key |
|---|---|---|---|---|
| 1. | Class Code | Alpha | 2 | * |
| 2. | Class Name | Alpha | 28 | |
| 3. | Level | Alpha | 15 | |
| 4. | Location | Alpha | 25 | |
| 5. | Instructor Code | Alpha | 2 | |
| 6. | Fee | $ (Money) | | |

4. Save the table to your working directory as **pet classes xxx**.

## CRITICAL THINKING ACTIVITY

Think of a collection you have or would like to have, such as music, books, videos, etc. Create a database table to track this collection. Include fields for the individual items' names, the artists' names (author, recording artist, etc.), price, and category (CD versus cassette tape, fiction versus nonfiction, etc.).

Save the database table as **collection xxx**.

**LESSON 2**

# ENTERING RECORDS

## OBJECTIVES

**Upon completion of this lesson, you will be able to:**

- Open an existing database table.

- Distinguish between View and Edit modes.

- Enter records in a table.

- Edit records.

- Insert and delete records.

- Print a table.

⏱ **Estimated Time: ¹/₂ hour**

O nce you have created the structure for a database table, you can enter data into it. In this lesson you will key data into the fields you defined for the tables you created in the last lesson. You will learn to make simple corrections and edit data, as well as learn how to print a copy of the table.

## *Opening an Existing Database Table*

Y ou can open existing database tables quickly and easily using the Project Viewer. Exercise PA2.1 will show you how.

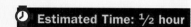

**EXERCISE ▷ PA2.1**

1. Start Paradox and set your working directory, if necessary. Click **Tables** in the Project Viewer to display your existing data tables.

2. Double click the **instructors xxx** icon. The table appears in View mode.

3. Leave the table on the screen for the next exercise.

# *Entering Records into a Data Table*

Paradox has two modes: *View* and *Edit*. In View mode you can view the table structure and the records you enter. To enter and edit records, you must switch to Edit mode. To toggle between View and Edit modes, press F9 or click the Edit Data button on the Toolbar.

Figure 2-1 shows a table in Edit mode. Notice the highlight in the first field, indicating you can enter your first record. Also notice that the Status Bar indicates that you are now in Edit mode.

**FIGURE 2-1**
Table in Edit Mode

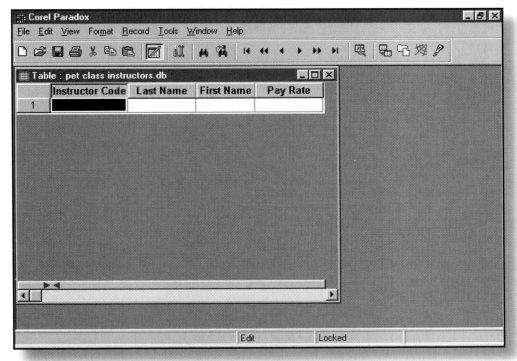

Exercise PA2.2 will teach you to enter records into the table you created for tracking Pet Paradise's class instructors.

## EXERCISE ⟹ PA2.2

1. Press **F9** to switch to Edit mode.

2. Enter the first record.
   a. Key **01** as the Instructor Code. Press **Tab** to move to the next field.
   b. Key **Harrigan** as the Last Name. Press **Tab**.

c. Key **Jeff** as the First Name. Press **Tab**.
d. Key **35** as the Pay Rate. Press **Tab** to start a new record. Notice how the $ (Money) type field format is automatically applied to the value entered in the Pay Rate field.

**P A - 1 1**

**3.** Enter the remaining records as follows:

| Instructor Code | Last Name | First Name | Pay Rate |
|---|---|---|---|
| 02 | Walters | Nancy | 35 |
| 03 | Melindez | Gloria | 35 |
| 04 | Davies | Peter | 35 |
| 05 | Chang | Kathy | 50 |
| 06 | Jackson | Mabel | 50 |
| 07 | LaPaz | Ernesto | 35 |

**4.** Switch back to View mode by pressing **F9**. Look at the Application Bar to verify that *View* is showing.

**5.** Remain in this screen for the next exercise.

 **NOTE:**

Once you save a database structure, you do not need to save it to preserve the records you enter. Paradox automatically saves any record you enter or edit.

# Editing Records

You must be in Edit mode to make changes to records. To edit a record:

- Click on a field in a record. It is highlighted, indicating you can key a new value to overwrite the existing one. Use Tab or the arrow keys to move around.

- If you do not want to replace a field completely, but only want to make changes to specific characters, you can switch to Field View by pressing F2.

- To make multiple changes to various values, you can enter Persistent Field View by pressing Ctrl+F2. Press Tab or Alt and an arrow key to move around.

## EXERCISE ▷ PA2.3

SCANS

**1.** Switch to Edit mode.

**2.** Click the **First Name** field in record **2**. Key **Alison** to overwrite the existing entry. Press **Enter**.

**3.** Press **Ctrl+F2** to enter Persistent Field View.

**4.** Press **Tab** to move to the Pay Rate field in record **4**. Change *35* to **40**.

**5.** Press **Tab** three times to move to the First Name field in record **5**. Change *Kathy* to **Cathy**. Press **Ctrl+F2** to exit Persistent Field View.

**6.** Correct any other errors you made when you keyed the table information in Exercise PA2.1. Remain in this screen for the next exercise.

# *Inserting and Deleting Records*

To add a record to a table:

- Click the last field in the last record and press Enter.
- If you want to insert a record at a particular location in the table, click any field in the record *below* where you want to insert the new record. Click the Record menu and select Insert, or press the Insert key.

To delete a record:

- Click any field in the record you want to delete. Click the Record menu and select Delete, or press Ctrl+Delete.

## EXERCISE PA2.4

SCANS

1. Click the last field in the last record. Press **Enter**.
2. In the blank record, key **08** in the Instructor Code field; **Wu** in the Last Name field; **Tsang** in the First Name field; and **35** in the Pay Rate field.
3. Click any field in record **7**. Press **Ctrl+Delete**. Remain in the screen for the next exercise.

# *Printing and Closing a Table*

You can print a table using the Print dialog box, as shown in Figure 2-2.

- The Print dialog box has an *Overflow handling* drop-down list box, which contains printing options in case the data does not fit across the page.
- The *Clip to page width* option trims all data that does not fit on the page within the margins.
- The *Create horizontal overflow pages as needed* option prints additional pages to accommodate all the data.

**FIGURE 2-2**
The Print Dialog Box

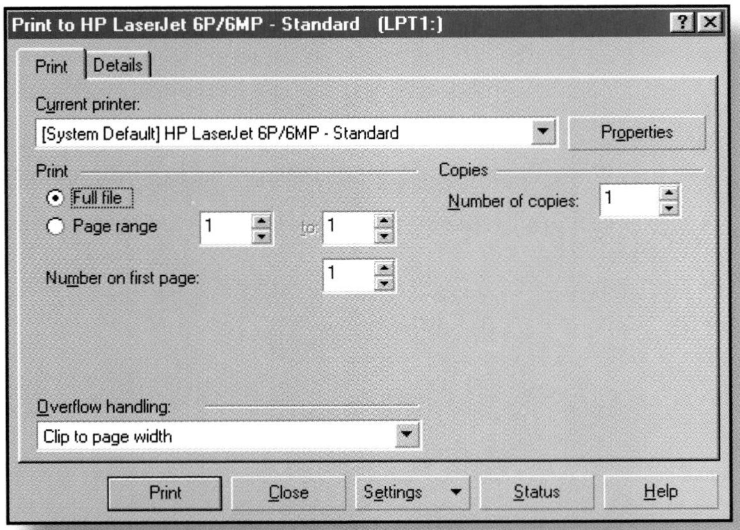

- The *Panel vertically (all possible panels)* option pertains primarily to reports.

When you print a table, Paradox automatically places a header on the page that indicates the table name, a page number, and the current date.

To close a table, click its close button or click the File menu and select Close. Paradox automatically saves your data and returns you to the Project Viewer.

## EXERCISE ⇒ PA2.5

1. Click the **File** menu and select **Print**. The Print dialog box appears.

2. Make sure that the Print box is set to **All** and that you are printing **1** copy. Leave the Overflow handling set to *Clip to page to width*. Make sure the Print option is set to **Full file**, then click **Print**.

3. Review your printout and turn it in to your instructor.

4. Close the table by clicking the **File** menu and selecting **Close**.

# Summary

In this lesson you learned that:

- you can open an existing database table from the Project Viewer. Once the table opens, you are in View mode.

- in order to enter records into a database table, you need to be in Edit mode. You toggle between View and Edit modes by pressing the F9 key.

- you can make changes to existing records in Edit mode. Field View (F2) lets you make changes to an entry without overwriting it. If you need to make changes to multiple entries, use Persistent Field View (Ctrl+F2).

- Paradox lets you insert records between existing records, as well as delete records.

- you can print a database table, and set Overflow handling in case the data does not fit across the page.

## LESSON 2 REVIEW QUESTIONS

### TRUE / FALSE

**Circle the T if the statement is true. Circle the F if it is false.**

**T  F  1.**  You can add records to a table in both View and Edit modes.

**T  F  2.**  Pressing F9 toggles between Edit and View modes.

**T  F  3.**  You can use Tab or the arrow keys to move around in a table.

**T  F  4.**  Before you close a table, you have to save it.

**T  F  5.**  When you print a table, Paradox automatically places a header on the printout.

### WRITTEN QUESTIONS

**Write your answers to the following questions.**

**6.**  Explain how to open an existing table.

**7.**  What is the difference between Field View and Persistent Field View?

**8.**  How would you add a record between the fifth and sixth records in a table?

**9.**  How can you distinguish between View and Edit modes?

**10.**  List and explain the three printing overflow options.

## LESSON 2 PROJECT

**SCANS**

### PROJECT 2A

Enter records in the Pet Paradise pet class database.

**1.**  Open **pet classes xxx** from your working directory.

**2.**  Add the following records to the table:

**NOTE:**

If you designate a key field in a database table, the records will automatically sort themselves based on that field when you enter the records.

| Class Code | Class Name | Level | Location | Instructor Code | Fee |
|---|---|---|---|---|---|
| PC | Proper Pet Care | Beginner | Pet Paradise | 03 | $5.00 |
| PF | Choosing the Right Pet Food | Beginner | Pet Paradise | 08 | $5.00 |
| FA | Pet First Aid | Beginner | Pet Paradise | 01 | $10.00 |
| WP | Washing Your Pet | Beginner | Pet Paradise | 03 | $15.00 |
| PP | Build a Pet Playground | Intermediate | Community Center | 04 | $27.50 |
| BP | Breeding & Pedigrees | Advanced | Pet Paradise | 06 | $35.00 |
| PS | Pet Psychology | Advanced | The Vet Center | 05 | $35.00 |

3. Print a copy of the table using the default settings in the Print dialog box.

4. Leave the table open for the next exercise.

## PROJECT 2B

Insert and delete records.

1. Insert the following records above the *Build a Pet Playground* record:

| AV | Ask the Veterinarian | Intermediate | Community Center | 01 | $12.50 |
|---|---|---|---|---|---|
| TT | Teach Your Pet Tricks | Intermediate | Community Center | 07 | $15.00 |

2. Delete the *Washing Your Pet* record from the database table.

3. Print a copy of the table, then close it (Paradox automatically saves your changes to the database table).

## CRITICAL THINKING ACTIVITY

Open **collection xxx** from your working directory. Enter at least ten records into it, making sure to enter at least two items by the same artist. Deliberately misspell some entries. When you are finished entering the records, go back and edit the misspelled entries.

Why do you think it is important to properly spell entries in a database table?

Delete record 5, whatever it is. Insert a new record before record 3. Print the table.

# LESSON 3

# RESTRUCTURING TABLES

## OBJECTIVES

**Upon completion of this lesson, you will be able to:**

- Change the name and order of fields in the table structure.
- Change field types.
- Change the size of the fields.
- Add and delete fields.
- Rename a table.

⏱ **Estimated Time: 1 hour**

You may need to edit the structure of a database table after you create it. In this lesson you will learn to edit, add, and delete fields, as well as to rename a table.

## Restructuring a Table

You can easily change the look and organization of a database table using the Restructure Paradox 7 & 8 Table dialog box (see Figure 3-1).

Using this dialog box, you can rename fields, rearrange the order of fields, add and delete fields, and change the field types and sizes.

 **IMPORTANT:**

Making changes to a field—such as changing the field type or deleting the field altogether—can result in the loss of data.

## Changing the Names and Order of Fields

You can change the name of a field that you have already created, as well as change its order in the table. Exercise PA3.1 will show you how to do so using the Restructure Paradox 7 & 8 Table dialog box.

**FIGURE 3-1**
The Restructure Paradox 7 & 8 Table Dialog Box

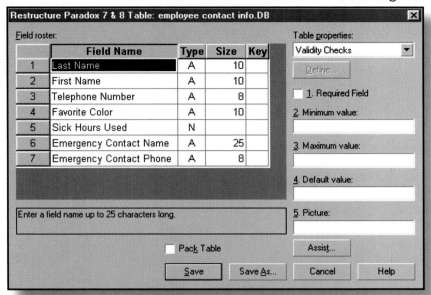

**NOTE:**

You cannot move a key field in the Restructure Paradox 7 & 8 Table dialog box because Paradox requires that it be the first field in the database table.

## EXERCISE ⟹ PA3.1

**SCANS**

1. From your working directory, open the **contact info** database table.

2. Click the **Restructure** button on the Toolbar. The Restructure Paradox 7 & 8 Table dialog box appears.

3. Rename the Telephone Number field.
   a. Click **Telephone Number** in the *Field Name* column to highlight it.
   b. Key **Phone No.**.

4. Rename the Emergency Contact Name field.
   a. Double click **Emergency Contact Name** in the *Field Name* column to produce the cursor.
   b. Press the **End** key to move the cursor to the end of the field name.
   c. Press the **Backspace** key to delete the word *Name* and the space that precedes it.

5. Using the method in Step 4, rename the Emergency Contact Phone field **Emergency Phone No.**.

6. Reorder the Emergency Contact field.
   a. Click the Emergency Contact field number (the number 6) and keep holding it down.
   b. Drag it upward until Field 4 is highlighted.
   c. Release the mouse button. *Emergency Contact* should now be Field 4.

7. Using the above method, reorder the Emergency Phone No. field so it is the fifth field in the roster.

8. Click the **Save As** button, name the restructured table **contact info xxx,** and view the results of your changes.

9. Print the table. Remain in this screen for the next exercise.

## Changing Field Types and Field Sizes

As you have already learned, you need to be careful when changing field types, as you could lose data. There may be times, however, when you want to change field types. For example, you might want to change a Number field to a Short field where decimals are not added to a number, or you might want to apply a Date format to ensure that only valid dates are entered in the field.

You may also find when you try to enter records into a database table that you did not make the field large enough to accommodate all the data. Or perhaps you allowed too much room, and the field takes up unnecessary space in the table.

Exercise PA3.2 will teach you how to change a field type and size.

### E X E R C I S E ⟹ PA3.2

SCANS

1. Click the **Restructure** button on the Toolbar.

2. Change the Sick Hours Used field type.
   a. Right click the **Type** column in the Sick Hours Used field.
   b. Select **Short** as the type. This will delete the decimal point and decimal places from the data.

3. Change the size for the Phone No. field.
   a. Click the **Size** column in the Phone No. field. The current size, *12,* appears highlighted.
   b. Key **8**.
   c. Press **Enter**.

4. Using the above method, change the size for the Emergency Phone No. field to **8**.

5. Click **Save**. In the Restructure Warning dialog box click **OK** to accept the default Trim settings for both fields.

6. View the results in the table. Notice that none of the data was lost.

7. Print the table. Remain in this screen for the next exercise.

## Adding and Deleting Fields

To add a field to the end of a table:

■ Click the Restructure button. In the Restructure Paradox 7 & 8 Table dialog box, use the arrow keys to move down until a new row appears. Enter the Field Name, Type, and Size.

To add a field between existing fields:

■ In the Restructure Paradox 7 & 8 Table dialog box, click the field you want to follow the new field and press the Insert key. Then enter the Field Name, Type, and Size.

To delete a field:

■ Click the desired field number and press Ctrl+Delete.

**IMPORTANT:**

When you delete a field, you delete it from any forms, queries, or reports that you have generated using the table, as well as all the data contained in the field.

As always, save your changes.

## EXERCISE ⟹ PA3.3

SCANS

1. Click the **Restructure** button on the Toolbar.

2. Insert a field between *Emergency Contact* and *Emergency Phone No.*.
   a. Click the **Emergency Phone No.** field.
   b. Press the **Insert** key.
   c. Enter **Relation** as the Field Name, **Alpha** as the Type, and **12** for the Size.

3. Delete the Favorite Color field by clicking the Favorite Color field number and pressing **Ctrl+Delete**.

4. Click **Save**. In the Restructure Warning dialog box click **OK** to confirm the deletion. View the results and remain in this screen for the next exercise.

# Saving a Restructured Table

Each time you click the Save button in the Restructure Paradox 7 & 8 Table dialog box, you save the changes you made to the table structure. If you want to maintain the table in its original structure and save it in its new structure as well, click the Save As button. The Save Table As dialog box appears. Select your working directory and enter a name for the table, then click Save.

## Renaming a Table

If you simply want to rename an existing table:

■ Open the Project Viewer and select the desired table. Right click the mouse and select Rename from the menu. The Rename dialog box appears, as shown in Figure 3-2.

**FIGURE 3-2**
The Rename Dialog Box

- Select your working directory, if necessary. Enter a new name for the table and click Rename.

## EXERCISE ▷ PA3.4

**SCANS**

1. Close the **contact info xxx** table by clicking its close button.

2. In the Project Viewer select **contact info xxx**. Right click the icon and select **Table Rename**.

3. In the Rename dialog box verify that your working directory is displayed. Enter **new contact info xxx**, then click **Rename**.

4. Double click the **new contact info xxx** table to open it. Click the **Print** button and select the **Panel vertically** option in the *Overflow handling* drop-down list box. Click **OK**.

5. Close the database table.

# Summary

In this lesson you learned that:

- you can use the Restructure Paradox 7 & 8 Table dialog box to edit an existing database table structure.

- you can change the name of existing fields in a database table, as well as reorder them.

- you can change field types, though you must be cautious when doing so, as you may lose data.

- if your fields do not have enough space to accommodate your data, or they have too much space that wastes room, you can change the field size.

- you can add fields to the end of a roster, as well as in between existing fields. You can also delete a field; doing so, however, deletes all other occurrences of the field in forms, queries, and reports, as well as all the data contained in the field.

- you can rename an existing table so that you may save both the old and new structures.

## LESSON 3 REVIEW QUESTIONS

### FILL IN THE BLANKS

**Complete each of the following statements by writing your answer in the blank provided.**

1. You can makes changes to the structure of an existing database table using the _____ dialog box.

2. You cannot move a _____ from its position in the field roster.

3. To delete a field from the roster, select its field number and press_____.

4. If you want to remove the decimal points from the entries in an existing Number field, change its type to_____.

5. If you delete a field from the roster, those fields also disappear in any _____ , or _____ you have created.

### WRITTEN QUESTIONS

**Write your answers to the following questions.**

6. Name two reasons why you would want to change the size of a field.

7. Explain how to insert a field between two existing fields.

8. How do you change the order of a field?

9. What could possibly happen if you change the field type of an existing field?

10. How do you rename a table?

SCANS

Modify the structure of an existing database table.

1. Open **product return** from your working directory.

2. Open the Restructure Paradox 7 & 8 Table dialog box and make the following changes:
   a. Change the Customer Last Name field to **Last Name**.
   b. Change the Customer First Name field to **First Name**.
   c. Change the Type of the Date Returned field to **Date**. Delete the entry in the Size column for this field.
   d. Change the Size of the Reason Returned field to **25**.
   e. Switch the order of the Date and Reason Returned fields.

3. Delete the Middle Initial field.

4. Save the restructured table as **product return xxx**. In the warning message boxes, accept the defaults and click **OK**.

5. View the results in the table. Print a copy of the table. Be sure to select the **Panel vertically** option.

6. Close the table.

7. In the Project Viewer rename the table **new product return xxx**.

# CRITICAL THINKING ACTIVITY

SCANS

Open **collection xxx** from your working directory. Perform the following:

■ Think of a reason why you would want to rename a field or fields. Then, based on that reason, rename at least one field.

■ Think of a reason why you might want to reorder the fields. Then reorder at least one field.

■ Think of a reason why you might want to add and delete fields. Then add one field and delete one field.

Rename the database table structure as **new collection xxx**, and print a copy.

# SORTING RECORDS

W hen you enter records into a database, they are arranged in the order you enter them in (unless you designate a key field, in which case they automatically rearrange themselves in order based on the key field).

Paradox enables you to temporarily rearrange the order of your records using indexes. It also lets you permanently rearrange their order by using sorts.

## *Understanding Key Fields*

W hen you designate a key field in a table, the records are arranged alphabetically (or from smallest to largest) according to the values in that field. The key field is also referred to as the table's *primary index.*

You can temporarily change the order of records in a keyed table—and still keep the key intact—by establishing a secondary key field, or *secondary index.*

### Creating a Secondary Index

You create a secondary index using the Define Secondary Index dialog box (see Figure 4-1). Exercise PA4.1 will show you how.

**FIGURE 4-1**
The Define Secondary Index Dialog Box

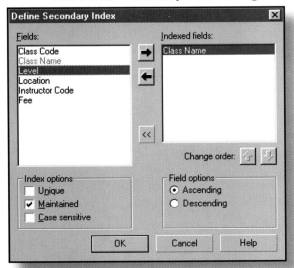

SCANS

1. Open the **pet classes xxx** database table from your working directory.

2. Click the **Restructure** button on the Toolbar.

3. In the Restructure Paradox 7 & 8 Table dialog box click the **Table properties** drop-down list box and select **Secondary Indexes**. Click **Define** to produce the Define Secondary Index dialog box.

4. Select **Class Name** in the Fields list and click the right-pointing arrow to place it in the Indexed fields box. Click **OK**. The Save Index As dialog box appears (see Figure 4-2).

5. In the Save Index As dialog box key **Class** as the Index name and click **OK**.

6. Click **Save** to close the Restructure Paradox 7 & 8 Table dialog box. Remain in this screen for the next exercise.

**FIGURE 4-2**
The Save Index As Dialog Box

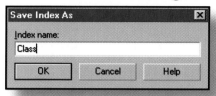

**NOTE:**

When you save a secondary index, it cannot have the same name as the field used for the index.

**FIGURE 4-3**
The Filter Tables Dialog Box

## Rearranging Records Using a Secondary Index

The Filter Tables dialog box (see Figure 4-3) lets you temporarily rearrange records in a database table.

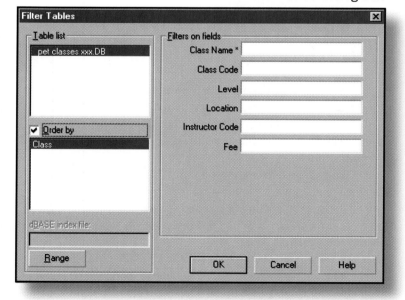

EXERCISE PA4.2

**1.** Click the **Filter** button on the Toolbar. The Filter Tables dialog box appears.

**2.** In the Filter Tables dialog box select **Class** from the Order by list. Click **OK**. The first record in the table should be *Ask the Veterinarian*.

**3.** Paradox does not allow you to print a copy of an indexed table. Instead, ask your instructor to view the indexed table on your monitor.

**4.** Return the records to their original order.
   **a.** Access the Filter Tables dialog box.
   **b.** Click the **Order by** check box to deselect it.
   **c.** Click **OK**. Notice that the records return to their original order.

**5.** Remain in this screen for the next exercise.

# Sorting Records

While secondary indexes are a quick way to manage the order of records in a table, they are only temporary, and you cannot print the records in their new order. When you close the table, the records revert to their original order. You can rearrange records permanently by using a *sort*.

## NOTE:

A new sort table can be saved to your working directory and can appear in the Project Viewer, just like the other database tables you create.

If the table has a key field, you must save the sort to a new table in order to preserve the integrity of the keyed table. If the table does not have a key field, performing a sort on it permanently changes the order of the records. If you want to maintain a copy of the unkeyed table in its original order, you can save the sorted records to a new table as well.

**FIGURE 4-4**
The Sort Table Dialog Box

To conduct a sort:

■ Click the Tools menu and select Utilities, and then select Sort from the cascade menu. The Select File dialog box appears. Open the table you wish to sort. The Sort Table dialog box appears (see Figure 4-4).

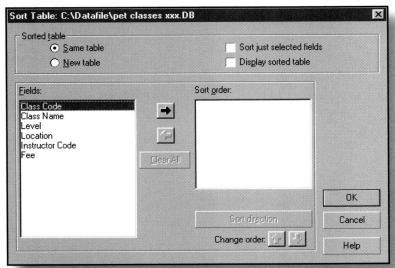

- Click the Same table or New table option button. If you choose the New table button, enter a name for the table in the *New Table* text box.

- From the Fields list, select the field you want the records sorted by. Click the right-pointing arrow to move the field to the Sort order box. The field appears in the Sort order box with a plus next to it, indicating the records will be sorted in ascending order. If you want to change the order to descending, click the Sort direction button.

- To sort by more than one field, simply add fields to the sort order. Paradox sorts records based on the order of fields in the Sort order list.

- If the Sort Just Selected Fields check box is not checked, Paradox sorts the records by the field(s) in the Sort order list; if, however, there are two records with identical values in the sort fields, then Paradox sorts them by the remaining fields in the Fields list. If you checked this option, then Paradox sorts only by the fields in the Sort fields list.

- If you select the Display sorted table check box, the sorted table opens when you click OK.

## E X E R C I S E  ⇨  PA4.3

SCANS

1. Click the **Tools** menu and select **Utilities**, and then select **Sort** from the Cascade menu.

2. From the Select File dialog box, choose **pet classes xxx**, then click **Open**.

3. In the Sort Table dialog box notice that you must save the sorted records to a new table since the table has a key field. Enter **pet classes sort xxx** as the name of the new table.

4. Click the **Display sorted table** check box to select it.

5. In the Fields list select **Fee** and click the right-pointing arrow to add it to the Sort order list.

*Fee* appears with a plus (+) in front of it, indicating an ascending sort.

6. Click the **Sort direction** button to change the sort direction from ascending to descending. A minus sign (-) should now appear in front of *Fee*.

7. Click **OK**. The new **pet classes sort xxx** table appears. *Breeding & Pedigrees* should be the first record. Print a copy of the sorted table.

8. Close the **pet classes sort xxx** table, then close the **pet classes xxx** table. Paradox automatically saves your changes.

# *Summary*

In this lesson you learned that:

■ you can temporarily change the order of records in a keyed table—and still keep the key intact—by establishing a secondary index.

■ you can permanently rearrange the order of records in a keyed table by creating a sort. Depending on whether the table has a primary key, you can save the sort results to the existing table or as a new database table.

■ you can sort a table on multiple fields, meaning if two or more records have the same entry for the first sort field, Paradox sorts them by their entries in the second sort field, and so on.

## LESSON 4 REVIEW QUESTIONS

### TRUE / FALSE

**Circle the T if the statement is true. Circle the F if it is false.**

**T   F   1.** A secondary index permanently changes the order of records in a table.

**T   F   2.** Indexing and sorting are interchangeable terms.

**T   F   3.** You can sort records by only one field.

**T   F   4.** If a database table has a primary key, you can save the table sort to the same table.

**T   F   5.** A plus (+) next to a field in the Sort order box indicates an ascending sort.

### WRITTEN QUESTIONS

**Write your answers to the following questions.**

**6.** Describe how to create a secondary index.

**7.** When would you use a secondary index versus a sort?

**8.** Explain how to change the direction of a sort.

**9.** When would you sort records to a new table?

**10.** If there are multiple fields in the Sort order box, how does Paradox sort the database table?

## PROJECT 4A

Create secondary indexes.

1. Open the **instructors xxx** database table from your working directory.

2. Click the **Restructure** button on the Toolbar.

3. In the Restructure Paradox Table 7 & 8 dialog box click the **Table properties** drop-down list box and select **Secondary Indexes**. Click the **Define** button.

4. In the Define Secondary Index dialog box select **Last Name** in the Fields list and click the right-pointing arrow. Click **OK**.

5. In the Save Index As dialog box key **Instructor Name** and click **OK**.

6. Click **Define** to create another secondary index.

7. Add **Pay Rate** to the Indexed fields list. Click **OK**.

8. Save the new index as **Instructor Pay Rate**.

9. Click **Save** to close the dialog box.

10. Click the **Filter** button on the Toolbar. In the Filter Tables dialog box click **Instructor Name** in the Order by box. Click **OK**. The first record in the table should be *Chang*. Ask your instructor to view the indexed table on your monitor.

11. Access the Filter Tables dialog box again. This time, order the table by **Instructor Pay Rate**. Click **OK**. The first record should be *Harrigan*. Ask your instructor to view the indexed table on your monitor.

12. Close the table.

## PROJECT 4B

Create a multiple sort.

1. Open **pet classes xxx** from your working directory.

2. Click the **Tools** menu and select **Utilities**, then select **Sort**.

3. In the Select File dialog box choose **pet classes xxx**, then click **Open**.

4. In the Sort Table dialog box notice that you must save the sorted records to a new table since the table has a key field. Key **pet classes sort 2 xxx**.

5. Click the **Display sorted table** check box to select it.

6. From the Fields list select **Location** and click the right-pointing arrow to add it to the Sort order list.

7. Next, add **Class Name** to the Sort order list. Click **OK**. The sorted table appears on the screen.

8. Print the sorted table. Use the default setting **Clip to page width**, then click **OK**.

9. Close the **pet classes sort 2 xxx** table. Then, close the **pet classes xxx** table and exit Paradox.

## CRITICAL THINKING ACTIVITY

SCANS

Open **collection xxx** from your working directory. How many different sorts can you perform? Which do you think would be most relevant?

Perform at least one sort and save it to a different table. Print the sorted table and show it to your instructor.

Next, create a sort based first on the Artist field and then on the Item Title field. Save this new sort to a different table. Print the sorted table.

Compare your printouts of the initial table and the sorted tables.

# LESSON 5

# QUERYING RECORDS

This lesson will teach you how to create and run queries, tools that let you search for records that meet particular criteria. In Lesson 1 you learned that the value of a database is the ability to organize information. Queries are powerful in that they help you to pull such valuable information from a database.

## *Understanding Queries*

A *query* lets you extract records that meet certain requirements from a table. Think of a query as a tool that finds the answer to a question concerning a database table. For example, how many books do you have written by Ernest Hemingway? How many mystery novels do you have? How many books did you buy in 1997?

 **NOTE:**

The table you are querying does not have to be open in order for you to create a query.

## Creating a Query

To create a query:

- Click the File menu and select New. The New dialog box appears. Select [New Query] and click Create.

or

- In the Project Viewer right click the Queries icon in the Types list, and select new.

■ The Select File dialog box appears. Select the desired database table and click Open. The Query window appears, similar to the one shown in Figure 5-1.

**FIGURE 5-1**
The Query Window

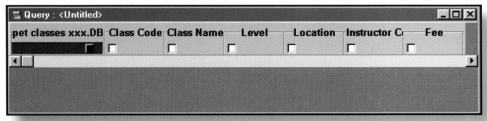

■ Click the check boxes next to the fields that you want displayed in the results. Clicking the table check box indicates you want all of the fields to appear.

■ Enter search selection conditions in the space next to the check box in the appropriate field(s). Selection conditions can include actual values—such as *Adams* or *135*—or a combination of *comparison operators* and values—such as *>1000* (all entries whose values are greater than 1000). Table 5-1 lists commonly used comparison operators.

**TABLE 5-1**
Commonly Used Comparison Operators

| Operator | Meaning |
|---|---|
| = | Equal to (optional because Paradox assumes you are looking for an exact match) |
| > | Greater than |
| < | Less than |
| >= | Greater than or equal to |
| <= | Less than or equal to |

■ Finally, you can save the query so that you can run it over and over on the table. Click the File menu and select Save As. In the Save As dialog box locate your working directory, enter a name for the query in the *File name* text box, and click Save.

To close a query:

■ Click the File menu and select Close or click the query's close button.

# EXERCISE ⟹ PA5.1

**Create a query.**

1. In the Project Viewer, right click **Queries** in the Types list and select **New**.

2. In the Select File dialog box choose your working directory. Select **pet classes xxx** and click **Open**.

3. Maximize the Query window to make it easier to view. Click the table check box so that a check mark appears next to all the fields to display them all in the results.

4. For the selection condition, key **Advanced** in the Level field. This will search for all advanced level classes.

5. Your query should now look like Figure 5-2.

6. Click the **File** menu and select **Save As**.

7. In the Save As dialog box, select your working directory. Enter **basic query xxx** as the file name and click **Save**.

8. Close the query by clicking its close button.

**FIGURE 5-2**
The Completed Query

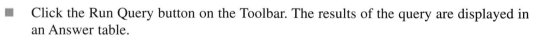

| pet classes xxx.DB | Class Code | Class Name | Level | Location | Fee | Instructor Code |
|---|---|---|---|---|---|---|
| ☐ | ☑ | ☑ | ☑ Advanced | ☑ | ☑ | ☑ |

## Running a Query

To run an open query:

■ Click the Run Query button on the Toolbar. The results of the query are displayed in an Answer table.

To open and run a query:

■ Open the Project Viewer and select Queries. Double click the desired query icon. The Query automatically runs on the table and leaves both the query and Answer table open.

By default, Paradox generates a table for the query results that it calls *answer.db* and stores in a pre-existing directory called *Priv*. The Answer table is only temporary. Every time you run a query, a new Answer table is generated that overwrites the previous one. You can edit an Answer table, but the changes are not made to the table being queried. You can also print an Answer table just as you would print any database table.

To return to the Query window:

■ Click the Window menu and select the name of the query. You can then change the selection conditions of the query and run it again, or erase them completely and save it as a new query.

## EXERCISE ➡ PA5.2

**1.** In the Project Viewer select **Queries** and then double click **basic query xxx**. The query runs automatically and both the query and Answer table open. Look at the results.

**2.** Print the Answer table by clicking the **Print** button. Click **OK** in the Print dialog box.

**3.** Click the **Window** menu and select **Query: basic query xxx**.

**4.** Create another query for the table.
   **a.** Click the database table check box to remove the checks from all the fields. Click the **Class Name**, **Location**, and **Fee** fields.

   **b.** Highlight **Advanced** in the Location field and press **Delete**.

   **c.** In the Location field, key **Pet Paradise** to search for all the classes that are held at Pet Paradise.

   **d.** Click the **File** menu and select **Save As**. Save the query in your working directory as **second query xxx**.

**5.** Click the **Run Query** button on the Toolbar.

**6.** Look at the results in the Answer table. Print the table.

**7.** Remain in this screen for the next exercise.

Exercise PA5.3 will teach you how to create a query using a comparison operator.

## EXERCISE ➡ PA5.3

**1.** Click the **Window** menu and select **Query: second query xxx**.

**2.** Create a query using comparison operators:
   **a.** Highlight **Pet Paradise** in the *Location* field and delete it. Click the **Location** check box to deselect it. Currently, the *Class Name* and *Fee* fields should appear checked.

   **b.** In the *Fee* field, key **>10.00**. This will search for the records of classes with fees of more than ten dollars.

   **c.** Click the **File** menu and select **Save As**. Save the query in your working directory as **comparison query xxx**. Your screen should look like Figure 5-3.

**3.** Click the **Run Query** button on the toolbar.

**4.** Look at the results in the Answer table. Print the table.

**5.** Close all open windows.

**FIGURE 5-3**
Query with Comparison Operator

| pet classes xxx.DB | Class Code | Class Name | Level | Location | Instructor C | Fee |
|---|---|---|---|---|---|---|
| ☐ | ☐ | ☑ | ☐ | ☐ | ☐ | ☑ >10.00 |

# Summary

In this lesson you learned that:

- a query is a tool that finds the answer to a question concerning a database table. You can save a query, then apply it to a database table over and over.

- in the Query window you designate which fields you want to display in the results, as well as enter selection conditions. Selection conditions can be actual values or a combination of comparison operators and values.

- you can run a query automatically just by opening it. Paradox opens both the Answer table and the Query window.

- once you have created and run a query, you can make changes to it and run it again or save it under a different name.

## LESSON 5 REVIEW QUESTIONS

### TRUE / FALSE

**Circle the T if the statement is true. Circle the F if it is false.**

**T  F  1.** A query is a tool you use to ask questions about the data in a database.

**T  F  2.** By default, Paradox saves each Answer table as a separate table file to your working directory.

**T  F  3.** You must have a table open to create a query for it.

**T  F  4.** Less than (<) is an example of a common comparison operator.

**T  F  5.** You can run a query automatically by opening it.

### WRITTEN QUESTIONS

**Write your answers to the following questions.**

**6.** How do you open the Query window?

**7.** Name four common comparison operators.

**8.** How do you switch between the Query window and the Answer table?

**9.** How do you select all the fields at once in the Query window?

**10.** What is the easiest way to close a query?

## LESSON 5 PROJECT

### PROJECT 5A

Create and run a query.

1.  Create a new query for the **new product return xxx** database table in your working directory.

2.  Check the **Customer Last Name**, **Customer First Name**, and **Date Returned** fields to display in the Answer table.

3.  Enter **LaSalle** as the selection condition in the Last Name field.

4.  Save the query as **return query xxx** to your working directory.

5.  Run the query.

6.  Print a copy of the Answer table.

7.  Close the table and query.

### PROJECT 5B

Create and run a query.

1.  Create a new query for the **instructors xxx** database table in your working directory.

2.  Check all fields to display in the Answer table.

3.  Set up the selection conditions to display all instructors who earn less than $50.00.

4.  Save the query as **instructor query xxx** to your working directory.

5.  Run the query and print a copy of the results.

6.  Close the table and query.

# CRITICAL THINKING ACTIVITY

What types of queries would you create for your **collection xxx** database? Think of at least three. Choose to display all fields in one query, and selected fields in the other two.

Save the three queries separately as **collection query 1 xxx**, **collection query 2 xxx**, and **collection query 3 xxx**. Print the results of each query, and turn them into your instructor.

# UNDERSTANDING RELATIONAL DATABASES

## OBJECTIVES

**Upon completion of this lesson, you will be able to:**

■ Understand relational databases.

■ Create a data model that links database tables.

■ Create a report with related tables.

**⏱ Estimated Time: 1 hour**

As you learned in Lesson 1, Paradox is a relational database program. In this lesson you will learn how to link two database tables, as well as how to create a report using information from both tables.

## *Understanding Relationships*

Although you can use queries, forms, and reports to present a table's data in different ways, there are times when one database does not suit all your needs. Because Paradox is a relational database, you can combine two separate tables together to increase the amount of information you display.

To combine two tables together, you must first establish a relationship, or *link*, between the tables. A link is based upon a common field between the tables. The common field must be the same size and of the same field type (Alpha, Number, $ (Money), etc.) in both tables. Also, the field must be the key or indexed field in at least one of the tables involved in the relationship.

You define a link between tables by creating a data model that physically shows what tables you are linking and on which field the link is based. To create a data model:

■ Click the File menu and select New. In the New dialog box select [New Report] and click Create. The New Report dialog box appears. Click Data Model to produce the Data Model dialog box (see Figure 6-1).

■ In the Data Model dialog box select the tables you want to link from the table list and click the right-pointing arrow to add them to the data model panel. In a relationship you have a *master table*, which is the primary table in the relationship. The *detail table* is secondary in the relationship. The common field in the table must be indexed.

■ To establish a link between the tables, click on the master table. The pointer turns into a linking tool. Drag the linking tool to the detail table. The Define Link dialog box appears, as shown in Figure 6-2.

**FIGURE 6-1**
The Data Model Dialog Box

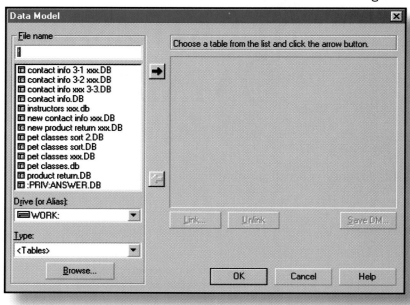

**FIGURE 6-2**
The Define Link Dialog Box

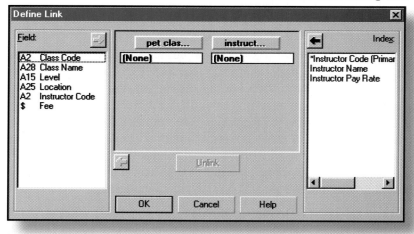

■ The master tables' files are listed in the Field box. Select the common field on which you want to base the link and then click the right-pointing arrow (which is grayed out until you select a field). The field name appears below the table name. If Paradox finds an index (or indexed field) in the table that matches the common field you selected in the master table, it displays the field name below the detail table name and completes the link. Click OK.

In the Data Model dialog box you will notice that Paradox has drawn a line between the tables to indicate the link has been established. You can save the data model by clicking Save DM and giving it a filename. Click OK. The Design Layout dialog box opens. The options in this dialog box are discussed in the next section.

It's important to understand that when you link tables, you are telling Paradox to look up values in the common field of the detail table that match values in the common field of the master table. When Paradox finds a record where the values match, it combines the record fields from both tables.

## EXERCISE ▷ PA6.1

SCANS

1. In the Project Viewer click the **File** menu and select **New**. In the New dialog box select **[New Report]** and click **Create**.

2. In the New Report dialog box click **Data Model**.

3. In the Data Model dialog box your working directory should be displayed. (If it is not, click Browse and select the disk and/or folder that represents your working directory.) Select **instructors xxx** from the tables list and click the right-pointing arrow. Then, select **pet classes xxx** from the tables list and click the right-pointing arrow.

4. Click **pet classes xxx** in the data model panel. This is the master table in the relationship. Drag the linking tool to the **instructors xxx** table.

5. In the Define Link dialog box select **A2 instructor Code** in the Field list and click the right-pointing arrow. Paradox should find the instructor code index in the detail table for you and complete the link. Click **OK**.

6. In the Data Model dialog box notice how the link has been established between the tables. Click **OK**. The Design Layout dialog box opens. Remain in this screen for the next exercise.

# Designing a Report from Related Tables

In the Design Layout dialog box (see Figure 6-3), you can determine the layout of your report. By default, the Show Layout options are displayed in the dialog box. To design a report:

■ Select a type of style from the Style options. An example of how that style looks appears in the window. Depending on the Style option you choose, you can also select from the Field layout and Multi-record layout options.

■ Select the Fields tab. Click the Reset Fields button to determine which fields are included in the report. The dialog box options change (see Figure 6-4).

■ All the fields from each of the tables in the relationship are listed in the Selected fields list. You can delete fields you don't want to appear in the report by selecting them and clicking Remove Field. You can select more than one field at a time by holding down the Ctrl key as you click each field.

■ You can also change the order of the fields in the report by using the Order buttons. When you are satisfied with the layout of the report, click OK. The report opens in the Report design window.

■ To save the report, click the File menu and select Close. You are asked if you want to save it. Click Yes. In the Save File dialog box enter a filename for the report and select the folder and/or disk representing your working directory. Click OK.

**FIGURE 6-3**
The Design Layout Dialog Box

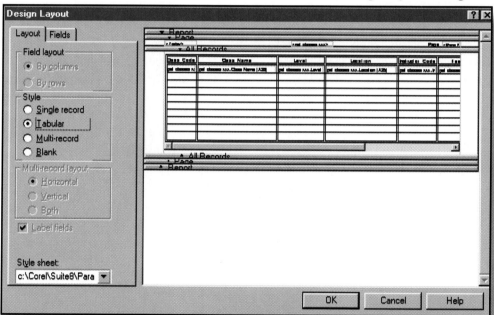

**FIGURE 6-4**
Updated Results in the Design Layout Dialog Box

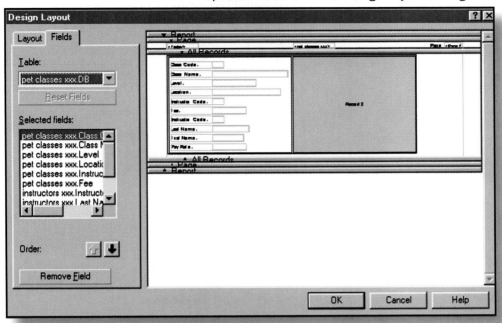

## EXERCISE ⟩ PA6.2

1. In the Design Layout dialog box select **Multi-record** as the Style of the report. In the *Multi-record layout* section click **Both**.

2. Click the **Fields** tab. In the Selected fields list select **instructors.Pay Rate** and click **Remove Field**.

3. Click **OK**.

4. Click the **View** menu and select **Run Report**. After a few seconds, the report appears on the screen (see Figure 6-5).

5. Click the **Print** button. In the Print dialog box click **OK**.

6. Click the **File** menu and select **Close**. Click **Yes** to save the report.

7. In the Save File As dialog box enter **class assignments xxx** as the name of the report and save it to your working directory. Click **Save**.

**FIGURE 6-5**
The Completed Report

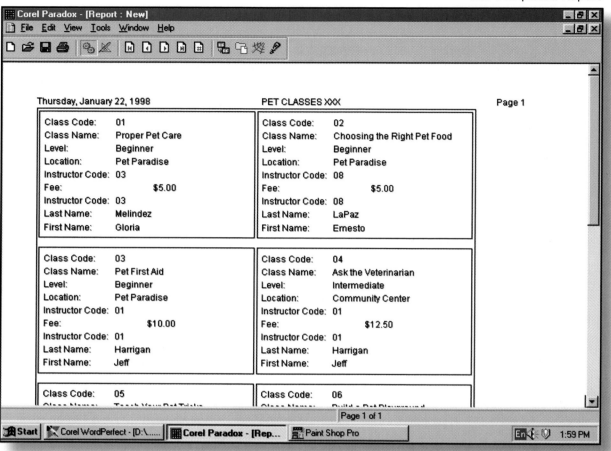

Figure 6-5 — The Completed Report (Corel Paradox - [Report : New])

Thursday, January 22, 1998          PET CLASSES XXX          Page 1

| Class Code: | 01 |
| Class Name: | Proper Pet Care |
| Level: | Beginner |
| Location: | Pet Paradise |
| Instructor Code: | 03 |
| Fee: | $5.00 |
| Instructor Code: | 03 |
| Last Name: | Melindez |
| First Name: | Gloria |

| Class Code: | 02 |
| Class Name: | Choosing the Right Pet Food |
| Level: | Beginner |
| Location: | Pet Paradise |
| Instructor Code: | 08 |
| Fee: | $5.00 |
| Instructor Code: | 08 |
| Last Name: | LaPaz |
| First Name: | Ernesto |

| Class Code: | 03 |
| Class Name: | Pet First Aid |
| Level: | Beginner |
| Location: | Pet Paradise |
| Instructor Code: | 01 |
| Fee: | $10.00 |
| Instructor Code: | 01 |
| Last Name: | Harrigan |
| First Name: | Jeff |

| Class Code: | 04 |
| Class Name: | Ask the Veterinarian |
| Level: | Intermediate |
| Location: | Community Center |
| Instructor Code: | 01 |
| Fee: | $12.50 |
| Instructor Code: | 01 |
| Last Name: | Harrigan |
| First Name: | Jeff |

Class Code: 05
Class Code: 06

Page 1 of 1

# *Summary*

In this lesson you learned that:

■ you can create a relationship, or link, between two database tables as long as they share a common field of the same size and type.

■ you define a link between tables by creating a data model that physically shows what tables you are linking and on which field the link is based.

■ in the Data Model dialog box, you create a link between the master, or primary, database table and the detail, or secondary, table.

■ once you have linked the two tables, you can generate and print a report that lists all the fields in the two tables that you desire.

## LESSON 6 REVIEW QUESTIONS

### TRUE / FALSE

**Circle the T if the statement is true.  Circle the F if it is false.**

**T  F   1.**  A link is based on a common field between tables.

**T  F   2.**  A common field has to have either the same size or be the same type to connect two tables.

**T  F   3.**  You use the Data Model dialog box to define a link between two tables.

**T  F   4.**  When designing a report from linked tables, you must use all the fields in both tables.

**T  F   5.**  You can switch the order of fields in a report from linked tables.

**Write your answers to the following questions.**

6. What is the difference between a master table and a detail table?

7. In defining a relationship between a master table and a detail table, which table's common field must be indexed?

8. Explain how you select the fields you want to display in a linked tables report.

9. How do you run a report?

10. How do you change the order of the fields in a linked table report?

## LESSON 6 PROJECT

**SCANS**

Link two tables and create a report.

1. In the Project Viewer right click the **Reports** icon and select **New**. In the New Report dialog box click **Data Model**.

2. In the Data Model dialog box select **employee location** from the tables list and click the right-pointing arrow. Next, select **new contact info xxx** from the tables list and click the right-pointing arrow.

3. Create a link in which **new contact info xxx** is the master table and **employee location** is the detail table. Use **Last Name** as the common field.

4. Click **OK** to close the Data Model dialog box.

5. In the Design Layout dialog box select **Multi-record** as the Style. In the *Multi-record layout* section, click **Both**.

6. Remove the **Sick Hours Used** field from the Selected fields list. Move the Store Location field below the First Name field.

7. Run the report and print a copy of it.

8. Save the report as **employee info xxx**.

## CRITICAL THINKING ACTIVITY

Think of a second database table you might create and link to your **collection xxx** table. Create the second database table, then link the two tables together.

Now think about a report you can create for the linked tables. Create the report and print it.

# INTEGRATING COREL® WORDPERFECT®, COREL® QUATTRO® PRO, COREL® PRESENTATIONS™, AND COREL® PARADOX®

**INTEGRATION**

**4**

## OBJECTIVES

**Upon completion of Integration 4, you will be able to:**

- Use Import to transfer information between Paradox and Quattro Pro.

- Share information between Quattro Pro and WordPerfect by using the Insert Database/Spreadsheet feature.

- Use a Paradox table to merge with WordPerfect for form documents and envelopes.

- Copy and paste Paradox data into a Presentations file.

🕐 **Estimated Time: 3 hours**

In Integration 3 you learned the basic methods of transferring information between applications through the use of copying and pasting, embedding, and linking. In this section you will learn that there are some very specific procedures for merging information between WordPerfect and Paradox and for importing data into WordPerfect, Quattro Pro, and Presentations. You have found out that Paradox is a powerful database used to keep records pertaining to customers, patients, and inventory. Those records in their entirety, or just certain fields from each record, can provide information necessary for creating inside addresses for letters, addresses for envelopes and labels, and information for various reports.

## *Merging a Paradox Database with a WordPerfect Form Document*

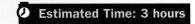

In this section you will continue to do work for Dr. Paradeis, the veterinarian. Since he is new to the area, his brother (Paul Paradeis) gave him a database of his customers. Dr. Paradeis deleted records of animals that were not dogs or cats since these are his specialties. He wants to send out a letter to his brother's customers, informing them that he has opened his office and would welcome their business for veterinarian services. You will now create a form document containing merge codes using WordPerfect and merge that form document with a Paradox database. You will see that other than selecting a Paradox table as the data file, the merging process is the same as though you were using a WordPerfect data file.

1. Insert your integration disk into the floppy disk drive. Start Paradox. Cancel the Startup Expert if it appears by clicking **Cancel**.

2. Right click **medical records.db** from the contents window in Paradox. Click **Table Copy**.

3. Select **medical records**. In the **Save in**: text box, click the down arrow and choose **3$^1$/$_2$ floppy (A:)**. Click **Copy**. The database will be copied. Close Paradox.

4. Create a new WordPerfect document and save it as **introduction letter xxx** on the integration disk you used for the last three integration sections.

5. Retrieve the **Vet Letterhead** style.

6. Put the insertion point two lines below the letterhead and change the font to **Times New Roman**, **12 pt.**, and **Black**. Key the letter shown in Figure INT4-1. The merge codes will be added in the next step, so some of the spacing, wording, or punctuation may appear incorrect.

7. Click **Merge** from the **Tools** menu. Click **Create Document** and choose the **Use file in active window** option. Click **OK**.

**FIGURE INT4-1**
Text for Form Document

```
Dear :

My name is Dr. Glen Paradeis and I am a licensed veterinarian who
recently opened up a practice at 3009 Parkway Boulevard. I share a
building with Pet Paradise, which is owned by my brother, Paul
Paradeis.  We are a family of animal lovers.

This letter is to invite you to bring in your pet, , for any
veterinarian services your pet needs. I am enclosing a sheet
explaining the rates for some of the more typical veterinarian
services as well as the times the office will be open.

If you need to bring in your pet for any services, please call ahead
and make an appointment. I hope that I will have an opportunity to
meet you and in the near future.

Sincerely,



Dr. Glen Paradeis

Enclosures
```

**8.** In the Associate Form and Data dialog box click the **Associate a data file** option. Then click the **Browse** button. Choose $3^1/_2$ **Floppy (A:)**, if necessary, in the Look in drop-down list.

**9.** In the File type list choose **All files (*.*)**. Choose the **medical records** database and click **Select**. Your dialog box should look similar to Figure INT4-2. If it does, click **OK**. The association has been made and the Merge Feature Bar now appears in the letter window.

**10.** Click the **Date** button on the Merge Feature Bar.

**11.** Press **Enter** four times after the date.

**12.** Click the **Insert Field** button. Insert the fields as shown below for the inside address and greeting:

FIELD(First name) FIELD(Last name)
FIELD(Street)
FIELD(City), FIELD(State) FIELD(ZIP Code)

Dear FIELD(First name):

Remember that you can keep the field list open as you insert fields.

**13.** Insert the Pet name field in the first line of the second paragraph between the commas. Also insert the Pet name field in the last paragraph on the last line following the word *and*.

**14.** Your letter should now look like Figure INT4-3.

**15.** Now merge the letter by clicking the **Merge** button on the Feature Bar.

**16.** Your dialog box should look like the one in Figure INT4-4. Click the **Output** button and choose **New Document** as the output.

**17.** Click the **Merge** button and you should have 53 merged letters.

**18.** Choose **Print** from the **File** menu. Print only the first letter by choosing **Current page**. Click **Print**.

**19.** Do not save the unnamed merged letter file containing the 53 letters. You can always merge the form document and data file again. Keep the form document open on your screen for the next exercise.

**FIGURE INT4-2**
Associate Form and Data Dialog Box

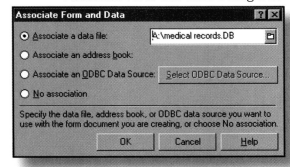

(continued on next page)

**FIGURE INT4-3**
Document with Merge Codes

```
DATE

FIELD(First name) FIELD(Last name)
FIELD(Street)
FIELD(City), FIELD(State) FIELD(ZIP Code)

Dear FIELD(First name):

My name is Dr. Glen Paradeis and I am a licensed veterinarian who
recently opened up a practice at 3009 Parkway Boulevard. I share a
building with Pet Paradise, which is owned by my brother, Paul
Paradeis.  We are a family of animal lovers.

This letter is to invite you to bring in your pet, FIELD(Pet name),
for any veterinarian services your pet needs. I am enclosing a sheet
explaining the rates for some of the more typical veterinarian
services as well as the times the office will be open.

If you need to bring in your pet for any services, please call ahead
and make an appointment. I hope that I will have an opportunity to
meet you and FIELD(Pet name), in the near future.

Sincerely,



Dr. Glen Paradeis

Enclosures
```

**FIGURE INT4-4**
Perform Merge Dialog Box

**TIP**

Check for spacing in your document, particularly around the merge codes.

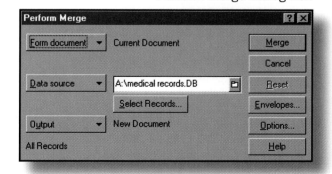

# *Merging a Paradox Database with a WordPerfect Envelope Form*

Now you will create envelopes for the letters created in the above exercise. Creating labels and envelopes using a Paradox table as the source is the same as creating labels and envelopes using a WordPerfect data file. The only difference, as you just experienced in the above exercise, is that you have to associate the main document in WordPerfect with a Paradox table.

## E X E R C I S E ⟹ INT4.2

SCANS

1. With the form document still on your screen, click the **Merge** button on the Feature Bar.

2. In the Perform Merge dialog box, click the **Envelopes** button.

3. Key the return address in the *Return Address* text box as follows:

   **Parkway Animal Clinic**
   **9003 Parkway Boulevard**
   **Austin, TX 78711**

4. Click in the *Mailing Address* text box. Insert the fields for the address by clicking the **Field** button. Your Envelope dialog box should look like Figure INT4-5. If it does, click **OK**.

5. Check the Data source in the Perform Merge dialog box. Make sure it is at **A:\medical records**. If it isn't, use the **Browse** button to find it and select it again.

6. Click **Merge**. Print only the first envelope, which is now page 54.

7. Close the document without saving. Close WordPerfect.

**FIGURE INT4-5**
Envelope  Dialog Box

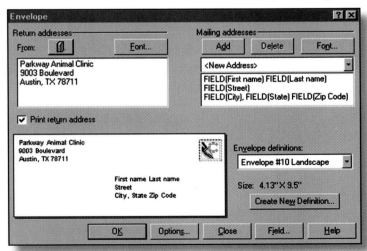

# Inserting a Paradox Database into a Quattro Pro File

Now that Dr. Paradeis has been in business for a few months, he asks you to prepare a report showing the status of the veterinarian inventory. This includes products that are used during an inspection of an animal, an operation, and products that are sold to customers. You are going to share information between Paradox and Quattro Pro for this activity. Information in a Paradox table can be imported directly into Quattro Pro by opening the Insert menu and choosing the External Data option. There are three reasons why this is a useful feature:

1.  The data from Paradox does not need to be rekeyed.

2.  Calculations can be more easily carried out in Quattro Pro.

3.  Charts can be created from the Paradox data once it is in Quattro Pro.

    As a result of the integration process, the imported information becomes "pasted." It is not linked or embedded.

## EXERCISE ▷ INT4.3

SCANS

1.  Start Paradox. Cancel the Startup Expert if it appears by clicking **Cancel**.

2.  Right click **veterinarian supplies.db** from the contents window in Paradox. Click **Table Copy**.

3.  Select **veterinarian supplies**. In the **Save in**: text box, click the down arrow and choose **3¹/₂ floppy (A:)**. The database will be copied. Close Paradox.

4.  Open Quattro Pro.

5.  Click the **Insert** menu and choose **External Data**. Then click **Import Database File** and locate the Paradox database in your student **Datafile** folder named **veterinarian supplies**. Click **Open**.

6.  The entire table is imported. Notice that many of the columns are too narrow to show all of the information and that most of the numeric data is not formatted. This is one disadvantage of importing or pasting data from Paradox.

7.  Widen all columns that are not showing all the data, and format columns E through J to be Fixed numeric format with two decimal places.

8.  Now you are going to insert a new column. The first new column will be to the right of column F. Click column G using the column indicator bar labeled *G*, and click the **Insert** menu. Choose **Column**.

9.  Click in cell **G1** and key **Used**. This column will show the difference between the beginning inventory (column E) and the number of items on hand (column F).

**10.** Click in cell **G2**; key the following formula:

+e2–f2

Now press **Enter**. You should see a figure that shows the difference of the two numbers. If you look in the formula bar however, you will see the following formula:

**+~Beg Inv-~Number on Hand**

**11.** Copy the formula down through the entire column by using the **QuickFill** feature. Click cell **G2** and point to the lower right corner of the cell until you see a crosshair. Hold down your mouse button and drag the crosshair down through the last row containing data. Did the formula copy down?

**12.** At the far right of your spreadsheet you are going to add two more new columns. In cell L1 key **Amt Tax**. In cell L2 you are going to enter a formula that will take the sales price of an item and add to it the dispensing fee (if there is any). Then you will take this sum and multiply it by the tax rate (if there is any) to determine if any tax is charged on the inventory item. Can you figure out what this formula would be? Key the following formula in cell L2:

**+(H2+I2)*K2**

Press **Enter**. Copy the formula down the column using **QuickFill**.

**13.** In cell M1 key **Expended**. In cell M2 you are going to enter a formula that will add the dispensing fee and tax rate to the sales price,

and then multiply that sum by the number of items sold or used. This formula should be keyed as follows in cell M2:

**+(H2+I2+L2)*G2**

Copy the formula down the column using **QuickFill**.

**14.** Format these two new columns as Fixed with two decimal places.

**15.** Now you are going to sort the spreadsheet by the Key of Inventory field. To do this you need to select cells **A2..M51**. Click **Tools** and choose **Sort**.

**16.** In the Sort dialog box make sure that in the *Cells* text box, the appropriate sheet and range are listed. It should be **A:A2..M51**. In the **Top to bottom** (the direction of the sort) section of the dialog box, key **A:D2** in the first, or primary, field by which to sort. Click **Sort**.

**IMPORTANT:**

If you don't select the entire range to be sorted and instead only select a single column, only the data in that column will be sorted.

**17.** Save the file to your integration disk, and name it **expended inventory xxx**, and print it. It will print on two pages. Close the file.

# *Importing a Paradox File into WordPerfect*

The above procedure can also be done from Paradox for exporting the database to a spreadsheet file. Importing a Paradox file into WordPerfect can be just as easy. You can select exactly what fields you want to import rather than the entire database, and you can use a query to set criteria for selected records. This is all done through the Import Data dialog box. Dr. Paradeis wants to put together an information sheet regarding vaccinations for dogs and cats. You will use WordPerfect and Paradox in the next exercise to create that document.

**1.** Start Paradox. Cancel the Startup Expert if it appears by clicking **Cancel**.

**2.** Right click **vaccination.db** from the contents window in Paradox. Click **Table Copy**.

**3.** Select **vaccination**. In the *Save in* text box, click the down arrow and choose **3$^1$/2 floppy (A:)**. Click **Copy**. The database will be copied. Close Paradox.

**4.** Open the WordPerfect file named **vac information** from the student **Datafile** folder. Save it as **vac information xxx** on your integration disk.

**5.** Move your insertion point to the end of the file and insert a page break.

**6.** Key the following title, using **Center**, **Bold**, **Arial**, and **14 pt.**:
Recommended Vaccination Schedule for Dogs and Cats

**7.** Press **Enter** twice. Choose the **Insert** menu and click **Spreadsheet/Database**. Click **Import**. Choose to import as a **Table**.

**8.** In the Import Data dialog box choose **Paradox** as the type of file and, using the **Browse** button, locate **vaccination.db** on the **A:\** drive and double click to select it.

**9.** Select all of the fields except Description, 1997, and 1998. Also turn on **Use field names as headings** to create the column headings in WordPerfect. See Figure INT4-6 to make sure your Import Data dialog box is filled in correctly. Click **OK**.

**10.** The data from Paradox comes in as a "pasted" table. If it needs reformatting, use the WordPerfect Table features. You may want to make the column headings containing (Weeks) and (Months) into two-line column headings, and then choose **Size to Fit** from the **Table** menu to narrow the width of each column.

**11.** Move your insertion point to the end of the document and play the **pf** macro.

**12.** Save the file as **vac information xxx** and print it. Close the file.

FIGURE INT4-6
Import Data Dialog Box

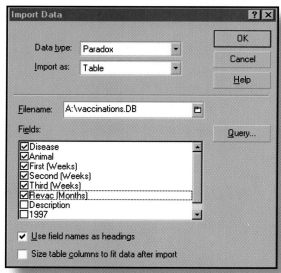

# Importing a Spreadsheet into WordPerfect

Now that you see how easy it is to import a database file into WordPerfect, you will now try the same procedure for importing a spreadsheet file. Dr. Paradeis is often asked for his opinion on what is a good breed of dog. He has his personal opinion, but he has decided to look up that information on the Internet. He found the information on the American Kennel Club site listing the 140 breeds of dogs registered in the year 1995. He copied the information into a spreadsheet, thinking he may add his own statistics for breeds of dogs seen at the Parkway Animal Clinic. For now, he would like you to import that information into a WordPerfect file and add a title and graphic, to produce an informational sheet to give to customers who ask about breeds of dogs or to use for presentations.

## EXERCISE ▭ INT4.5

**SCANS**

1. Open the file **breeds.wb3** from the **Datafile** folder. Save it to your integration disk as **breeds xxx**. Close Quattro Pro.

2. In a new WordPerfect document, change to **Arial**, **Bold**, and **16 pt.**, and center the following title:

   **Popular Dog Breeds***

3. Change your font to **12 pt**. Press **Enter** four times and change justification to **Left**.

4. Click the **Insert** menu and choose **Spreadsheet/Database**. Click **Import**.

5. In the Import Data dialog box, make the following selections:
   
   | | |
   |---|---|
   | Data type: | **Spreadsheet** |
   | Import as: | **Table** |
   | Filename: | **breeds.wb3** |
   | Range: | **A:A3..A:C43** |

6. Make sure the Import Data dialog box looks like the one in Figure INT4-7. Click **OK**.

7. You should see the imported data in the format of a WordPerfect table.

8. Click anywhere in the table and click the **Table** button.

9. Choose **Format** and then click the **Table** tab. Under the Table position on the Page drop-down list, choose **Center**. Click **OK**.

**FIGURE INT4-7**
Import Data Dialog Box

(continued on next page)

**10.** Click below the table and press **Enter** twice.

**11.** Change the font to **Arial**, and **10 pt**. (no Bold), and key the following two lines:
**\*Dog Registration Statistics January 1 through December 31, 199X**
**The above breed statistics were provided by the American Kennel Club, New York, NY**

**12.** Insert a "dog" graphic of your choice on the page where you feel it would look the best. You may have to right click the graphic to select it and change the Wrap option to **behind text**.

**13.** Move your insertion point to the end of the file and run the **pf** macro.

**14.** Make sure the document is only one page long. Save the file as **topdogs xxx** to your integration disk and print it. Close the file.

# *Pasting Data from Paradox into Presentations*

One last integration application is to see how information from Paradox can be brought into a Presentations file. The Insert, File and the Insert, Object features both look inviting for inserting a Paradox database into Presentations, but beware. The **Insert, File** feature brings up a message that the Paradox file is an incompatible format. The **Insert, Object** feature may bring in the object, but it is an unacceptable format. The best way to bring in Paradox data is to use the simple copy and paste method. Using the feature this way, data can be selected not only from a table, but also from a query.

**SCANS**

**1.** Create a new Presentations file. Choose a slide master that shows a title and a subtitle from the color category. Choose any color category you want.

**2.** In the first slide, you will insert a WordPerfect outline. Choose **Insert, File** and select **geriatric pet outline**.

**3.** In the first slide, change the slide layout to a title slide by choosing **Format, Layout Gallery**. From the **Appearance** tab, choose **Title** and click **OK**.

**4.** Still in the first slide, insert the Parkway logo by choosing **Insert, Graphics, From File**. Choose the **clinic logo xxx** file and click **Insert**. Resize the logo to fit below the title. Center the logo.

**5.** Save the slide presentation as **geriatric pet presentation**.

**6.** Go to Slide 5 and add a new slide by clicking on the down arrow in the lower right corner of the screen labeled **Insert slide after current slide**. Choose **Insert the Slide with no Layout**.

**7.** Leave the new slide showing on the screen and open Paradox.

**8.** Open the **Project Viewer** (Tools menu). Right click on the **Queries** object and choose **New**.

**9.** Choose the **vaccinations** table. The Query dialog box opens, showing the fields in the vaccinations table.

**10.** Select the **Disease**, **Animal**, and **Revac** fields. Run the query.

**11.** Select the cells in the displayed query results. You should see three columns, as shown in Figure INT4-8.

**NOTE:**

You cannot select the column or row headings.

**12.** Click the **Copy** button, switch back to Presentations, and click **Paste**.

**13.** Resize the query object to approximately 8" wide by 5" tall and position it to start at approximately $2^1/_2$" vertically.

**14.** Use the **text object** tool to create a text frame that is as wide as the query object. Key the following text:
**Keep Up With Regular Vaccinations (shown below in intervals of months)**

**15.** **Center** and **bold** the text.

**16.** You can crop away the extra white space with the query object (if needed) by double clicking the query object, which takes you to a bitmap editing screen, as shown in Figure INT4-9.

**17.** Drag the center handle on the right side until there is less white space in the third column.

**18.** Click on the **File** menu and choose **Close Bitmap Editor**. Center the query object in the slide.

**19.** Add another new slide with no layout.

**FIGURE INT4-8**
Query Results

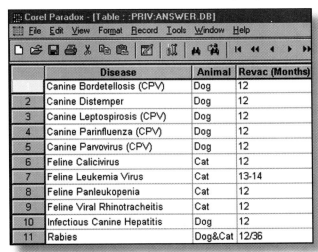

**FIGURE INT4-9**
Bitmap Editor

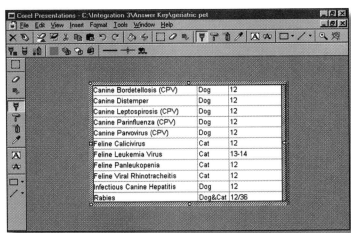

**20.** Create a text object in the center of the slide to include the following text:

**Remember: The care and love received from YOU**
**can be the most important treatment for your pet's longevity!**

**21. Center** and **bold** the text and change the point size to **36**.

**22.** Insert two graphics on the same slide. In the upper left corner above the text frame, insert **cartoon cat.** In the lower right corner below the text frame, insert **comic dog.**

**23.** Save the file again. Print out the file as handouts with four slides on a page.

# *Summary*

This lesson introduced additional procedures for transferring information between applications. You learned how to:

- associate a Paradox file as a data file in WordPerfect for a merge operation.

- insert fields from an associated Paradox file into a WordPerfect document.

- import an entire Paradox table into a Quattro Pro file.

- import only selected fields of a Paradox table into a WordPerfect file.

- import a Quattro Pro file into a WordPerfect file.

- copy and paste a Paradox query into a Presentations file.

## INTEGRATION 4 REVIEW QUESTIONS

### WRITTEN QUESTIONS

**Write your answers to the following questions.**

1. What is an advantage of using a Paradox database for inserting FIELD codes?

2. When you are merging in WordPerfect, how do the results differ when using a database as the data file rather than a data file created in WordPerfect?

3. What are the main differences in the results between importing a spreadsheet in WordPerfect and embedding a spreadsheet in WordPerfect?

4. What extra step can you take in the Import Data dialog box in WordPerfect to select certain records from a Paradox database?

5. Which method(s) do you prefer for transferring information between applications? Why?

## FILL IN THE BLANKS

**Complete each of the following statements by writing your answer in the blank provided.**

6. The dialog box used to identify a database to use in a merge operation in WordPerfect is called the _____.

7. Information in a Paradox table can be imported directly into Quattro Pro through the _____ menu.

8. The _____ feature on the Insert menu in WordPerfect allows you to then click Import to import a file from a different application.

9. The _____ feature in WordPerfect provides the ability to create envelopes and add fields from an associated database.

10. The _____ box in the Import Data dialog box in WordPerfect allows you to use the field names as column headings for the imported table from Paradox.

## INTEGRATION 4 PROJECT

SCANS

Since Dr. Paradeis is a real advocate of neutering and spaying pets, he has decided to offer a discount to his current customers for these services for their pets during Animal Appreciation Week (November 2-8). He wants a postcard created that includes the name of the customer and the name of the pet. He will also need labels printed for these selected records.

### PROJECT INT4A

1. Create a new WordPerfect document and save it as **discount letter xxx** to your integration disk.

2. Retrieve the **Vet Letterhead** style.

3. Choose **Merge** in the **Insert** menu. Click **Create Document** and choose the **Use file in active window** option. Click **OK**.

4. In the Associate Form and Data dialog box click the **Associate a data file** option. Then click the **Browse** button. Choose **3¹/₂ Floppy (A:)**, if necessary, in the Look in drop-down list.

5. In the File type list choose **All files (*.*)**. Choose the **medical records** database and click **Select** or double click the **medical records** database. Click **OK**.

6. Key the text and insert the FIELD codes as indicated in Figure INT4-10.

(continued on next page)

**7.** Save the document again as **discount letter xxx**. Leave the file open.

```
DATE

FIELD(First name) FIELD(Last name)
FIELD(Street)
FIELD(City), FIELD(State) FIELD(ZIP Code)

Dear FIELD(First name):

Animal Appreciation Week is November 2-8 this year. One of the major
concerns regarding the care of animals is the vast overpopulation of
animals in this country. This problem can be lessened if more people
would have their dogs and cats neutered or spayed.

To promote these procedures, the Parkway Animal Clinic is providing
discounted neutering and spaying rates for customers whose animals
have not yet been altered. Our records indicate that FIELD(Pet name)
is one of those animals. Our usual fee for these procedures will be
discounted at 50% for this week. The discounted rates are listed
below. Please call (512) 555-6886 for an appointment or if you have
any questions.

Dr. Glen Paradeis, DVM
```

Now you are going to embed a spreadsheet showing the discount rates.

## PROJECT INT4B

**1.** Press **Enter** twice following Dr. Paradeis's name.

**2.** Open Quattro Pro and open the **fees1998** notebook from the **Datafile** folder. Save the file as **fees1998 xxx** to your integration disk.

**3.** Click the **Discount** sheet and select the range **A1..B7**.

**4.** Click the **Copy** button.

**5.** Switch to WordPerfect using the Taskbar and choose **Paste Special** from the **Edit** menu.

**6.** Choose the **Paste** option and select **Corel Quattro Pro 8 Notebook**. Click **OK**.

7. The range showing the discounted rates should be in your WordPerfect file below the doctor's name. If it is not, just drag it to about two lines below the name.

8. Center the object horizontally by moving it to approximately the center of the page.

9. You are going to format the object to not show the grid lines. Double click the object, and you should now be viewing the **Quattro Pro** menu and Toolbar.

10. From the **Format** menu, select **Sheet**. Click the **Display** tab and turn off the Horizontal and Vertical Grid Lines. Click **OK**. Click away from the object to turn off the hatched line.

**FIGURE INT4-11**
Embedded Object

Discount Rates
Animal Appreciation Week
(November 2-8, 1998)
| Castration (male dog) | $45.00 |
| Spaying (female dog) | $50.00 |
| Castration (male cat) | $27.00 |
| Spaying (female cat) | $42.00 |

11. Click once on the embedded object so just the graphic handles appear. From the Graphics Feature Bar choose the **Border Style** button. Click the border that looks like a dotted line—the first dotted line border in the second row. Doesn't that look like a coupon?

12. Click away from the object and check the object against Figure INT4-11.

13. Save the file again as **discount letter xxx**.


## PROJECT INT4C

1. Now you are going to merge the document by clicking the **Merge** button on the Feature Bar.

2. To select just those records that contain "unneutered male" and "unspayed female," click the **Select Records** button in the Perform Merge dialog box.

3. In the Select Records dialog box add the following conditions:
   a. For Cond 1, select the Sex field from the drop-down list. Key **unneutered male** in the text box.
   b. For Cond 2, key **unspayed female** in the text box—still in column 1 under the Sex field. The Select Records dialog box should resemble the one showing in Figure INT4-12.
   c. Click **OK** and click **Merge**. You should have 29 records.

(continued on next page)

**4.** Print just the first letter. Do not save the merged document.

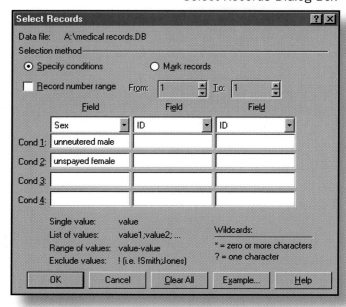

## CRITICAL THINKING ACTIVITY

SCANS

You have been given the task of presenting information in a format that contains rows and columns. Knowing that you can do that in a WordPerfect table, Paradox table, and Quattro Pro notebook, what questions should you ask yourself about the data and its output format before you decide which application to use?

# The Hardware

If you have never before had any formal training on the computer, it is important that you are comfortable with the equipment which you will be using for the duration of this course. Even if you consider yourself "computer literate," you should look through the information in this appendix so that you can see how each part of the computer will be used in your Corel WordPerfect Suite 8 training.

Turn to the Start-Up Checklist in the front of this text. Here you will see that a certain level of computer is required for your work with Corel WordPerfect Suite 8. Your instructor has made sure WordPerfect will run on your computer. You need to be familiar with the computer parts.

Look at the computer in front of you. It consists of six major hardware components: the video display terminal (VDT or screen), the central processing unit (CPU), the keyboard, the disk drives, the mouse, and the printer. In most classrooms the printer is located in a different part of the room, but it is connected to your computer with a cable. Can you identify the parts of the hardware illustrations in Figures A-1, A-2, and A-3 as they are discussed? Find them on your own computer.

1. **The VDT**. Starting at the top, the *video display terminal* (VDT) is used to show you what you are doing as you use the computer. Look at your VDT. Find the power switch and controls for brightness and contrast.

   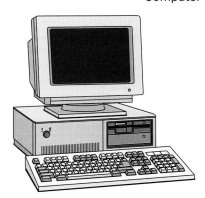

   **FIGURE A-1**
   Computer

2. **The CPU**. The brains, or logic center, of the computer is housed in the piece of equipment called the *central processing unit* (CPU). Sometimes the CPU sits on your desk under the VDT. In other cases, the CPU might be on the floor beside the desk. Inside the CPU is a hard drive where Corel WordPerfect Suite 8 has been installed if you are working on a stand-alone machine. In many cases, however, the suite is installed on the file server of a network. That means your PC will be running a program stored on the CPU of a computer in a different part of the room or even in a different room.

   In addition to the hard drive of the computer, the CPU has a temporary memory area called RAM (random access memory) where your work is remembered until you save it on your disk. Find the power switch on your CPU. When the power switch is turned off, any text in RAM is lost.

3. **The Keyboard**. Look at the keyboard. In addition to the alphabetic keys, you should find a set of function keys. The function keys are labeled with *F* and a number from 1 to 12 in a row across the top of the keyboard.

On the right is a series of miscellaneous keys. You should have a numeric keypad and some keys with arrows used to move the insertion point. (The *insertion point* is the little flashing vertical line in the window showing where you are working at any time.) You should also see keys with labels such as **Home**, **End**, **Page Down**, **Page Up**, **Insert**, and **Delete**.

4.  **The Disk Drives**. In addition to the hard drive of your computer, a number of configurations are possible for the floppy disk drives. You might have one or two drives that hold $3^1/_2$-inch disks or you might also have a drive for a CD-ROM. If you are working in a networked environment, you might not have any drives for disks.

    Your instructor will help you determine what kind of drives your computer has and what type of disk you should use for your training. If you have never before used a computer, ask your instructor to give you special instructions regarding the handling of disks and how to insert them into the computer.

5.  **The Mouse**. While it is possible to use Corel WordPerfect Suite 8 without a mouse, the use of a mouse or some other kind of pointing device is almost imperative. Many features are available only with a mouse. In addition to accessing features with the mouse, the mouse is an efficient means of selecting text, positioning the insertion point, displaying QuickMenus, and moving through your documents. If you have never before used a mouse, specific instructions in the use of a mouse are included later.

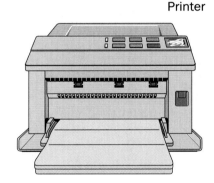

6.  **The Printer**. Literally hundreds of printers might be connected to your classroom computer. Most printers today feed cut sheets of paper from a bin or tray. These printers are either *laser printers*, *ink jet printers*, or *bubble-jet printers*, and the printed pages look like they might have come from a copy machine.

    Some classrooms have printers where the paper is connected in one long sheet. The paper is pushed or pulled through the printer by way of sprocket wheels that fit into the holes of tear strips on the sides of the paper. These are called *dot matrix printers*, and they are noisy.

# *Network*

You may be using a stand-alone version of the software, or your computer might be connected to a number of other computers by way of a network. Whether or not you are using a network won't affect your training, but it may affect how you print and how you save your work. Be sure your instructor gives you the "rules" for your particular class.

# *Using a Mouse*

You may have read articles about using a computer for extended periods of time and remaining physically healthy. One consideration is sitting properly in a good chair. Another consideration is the keyboard–whether you keep your wrists straight when your fingers are busy keying, or if you allow your wrists to rest somewhere in front of the keyboard. The third consideration, although it receives less attention, is the use of a mouse.

## Hand Position

Listed here are basic guidelines for using the mouse in such a way that it doesn't cause physical problems to your hand, arm, or shoulder. Use this list to check your hand position:

■ Align your thumb along one side of the mouse, with two or three fingers on the other side.

■ The mouse should nestle in the palm of your hand, with two or three fingers (depending on whether you have a two-button mouse or a three-button mouse) over the mouse buttons.

■ Keep your wrist straight! This means supporting at least a portion of your forearm on the surface where the mouse is positioned. With the wrist straight and the mouse in your palm, you should be able to draw a straight line from your elbow to the cord end of the mouse.

■ Position the mouse so you don't have to reach for it. Positioning the mouse beside the keyboard would be good if you have proper arm support with it in that position.

■ The mouse should be at about the same height as the keyboard.

## The Mouse Buttons

On PCs, the mouse has either two or three buttons. The button at the left is known as the *primary* mouse button. When you are told to click with the mouse button, the assumption is that you will use the left button.

The button on the right is known as the *secondary* mouse button. In some programs, using the button on the right is becoming common for certain tasks. In these learning materials, whenever you are to use the right mouse button, you are told to *right click*.

Sometimes a mouse will have three buttons. When you have a three-button mouse, the mouse driver can be configured to assign special tasks to the middle button. Most often, that assignment is a double click. In other words, when you are told to double click, click the middle button one time.

## Lefties

Left-handed people can learn to use the mouse with their right hands, if they wish. On a computer that is shared with other workers who are right-handed, this might be the better option.

If the left-handed person wishes to use the mouse with his or her left hand, a couple of options are available. One option is to learn to click the primary mouse button with the middle finger. Then the index finger is used to click the secondary mouse button.

It is a simple process to exchange the left and right mouse assignments. This is done in the Windows Control Panel. If you wish to make this change on your home or office machine and you are not familiar with the Control Panel, someone who has had Windows training can help you make this change. Your instructor would probably prefer you NOT make this change.

In the learning materials of this text it is assumed that the primary mouse button is the left button. If you have switched your mouse buttons, keep that change in mind as you proceed.

## Clicking and Dragging

When you move the mouse on its mouse pad, the mouse pointer moves in the window. The appearance of the pointer differs, depending on its location in the window. Most of the time, when the pointer is in the document portion of the window, it is a vertical line. When the line is where you want the insertion point, click the left mouse button to position it there.

When the pointer is an arrow, it helps you choose menu items or buttons from one of the many bars or dialog boxes. It also is used with the scroll bars. When the pointer is in the left margin, the fat white arrow points in the opposite direction. Following is a summary of some of the things you will do with the mouse on your computer:

- **Click** once to display a menu or to select an item from the Toolbar, the Property Bar, or a dialog box. You will also click once to position the insertion point in your document. You will always use the left mouse button for this.

- **Right Click** to display a QuickMenu or certain bar preferences.

- **Double Click** to select a word or start a program. In the Open File dialog box you may need to double click to change drives or folders. Many choices made in dialog boxes may involve clicking to select an item and then clicking OK to close the dialog box. If you double click the item you are selecting, the process often makes the selection and closes the dialog box automatically. Until you get used to working in dialog boxes, you may struggle with WHEN to click and when to double click.

- **Triple Click** to select a sentence in WordPerfect. You won't use triple clicking very often.

- **Click and Hold** for some drop-down menus in dialog boxes. If you don't hold the mouse button after pointing to the button and clicking, the menu will close before you have a chance to make your choice.

- **Drag** is the process of holding the mouse button while you drag the mouse across the mouse pad, moving the pointer from one location to another. You might use this to select or highlight a block of text. You might also use it to drag selected text from one location to another.

## Mouse Pad

It is important that you use a mouse pad under your mouse. This helps the mouse work well for you. It is frustrating when your mouse doesn't do what you want it to do! The mouse pad provides a better surface "grip" for the mouse ball. Without a mouse pad, the mouse ball picks up all kinds of dirt and needs to be cleaned more often. Also, the bottom of the mouse wears more rapidly when a mouse pad is not used.

Take good care of your mouse. Clean it regularly. With a little practice, you'll develop skill using the mouse that will serve you very well.

# APPENDIX B

## *Introduction to Windows 95*

Welcome to Microsoft Windows 95. Windows 95 provides you with an operating system that encourages you to think of your computer as your desk. It is a working area with quick access to the tools you use daily, such as your calculator, telephone, fax, and filing cabinet. It also enables you to run your favorite applications programs.

This text is dedicated to helping you learn to use Corel WordPerfect Suite 8, which runs under Windows 95. This appendix will give you a brief glimpse of your operating system and the tools that come with the system.

## *Benefits of Windows 95*

Windows 95 is a popular operating system because it provides a number of important benefits. Following is a list of some of the benefits that are important to most users:

- **Consistent Interface.** All programs that you run under Windows 95 look the same. The window is similar, the dialog boxes are similar, and the menus are similar, along with the other window parts. This makes it easier for you to go from one program to another.

- **Multitasking.** Windows 95 allows you to be running several tasks or applications at the same time, making you a better manager of your time.

- **Plug and Play.** Windows 95 comes with a number of drivers enabling you to install software or hardware in your computer, and Windows will automatically update your system.

- **Internet Access.** Microsoft Network, which comes as part of Windows 95, makes it easy for you to access the Internet, whether you wish to use it for e-mail or research purposes.

- **32-Bit Processing.** In the Windows 95 environment your programs can process data 32 bits at a time as opposed to the 16-bits-at-a-time standard in earlier Windows and DOS environments.

- **Long File Names**. In naming your documents in a Windows 95 environment, file names can be up to 255 characters or spaces long, freeing you from the DOS convention limiting you to an 8-character file name with a 3-character extension.

# The Desktop

$A$ll work in programs running Windows 95 begins at the desktop. Regardless of how your system has been customized, the desktop contains some common tools. If necessary, have your instructor help you to display the Windows 95 desktop. Then find the following tools as they are discussed:

■ **Taskbar**. The wide gray bar usually located at the bottom is known as the taskbar. Your taskbar may contain some buttons indicating that some applications are in use.

■ **Start Button**. The Start button is at the left of the taskbar.

■ **Clock**. In the lower right corner is a clock, telling you the current time (assuming your computer has been set with the time and date).

■ **Icons**. The icons on the desktop will vary. The two you are most likely to see are *Recycle Bin* and *My Computer*. In addition, a variety of other icons might appear. If the icon contains a bent black arrow in the lower left corner, that icon has been put on the desktop as a shortcut to a program or tool.

# The Taskbar

$A$s mentioned in the previous section, the default location for the taskbar is at the bottom of the window, although it can be moved to any side. When you open a program, document, or window, a button for it appears on the taskbar. You can use this button to quickly switch between the windows or programs you have open. The more programs or tools you have running, the smaller the buttons for those tools are so that they can all be displayed at one time. If necessary, you can make the taskbar deeper so it will hold more buttons.

# The Start Button

$T$he Start button opens the Start menu, from which you can choose whatever you need to do your work. Figure B-1 shows the choices in the Start menu and what you can expect from each of those choices.

The Start button always shows in the taskbar, so you can make any choices you wish, even when you have a different window open or a different application running.

**FIGURE B-1**
Choices in the Start Menu

■ **Programs.** Used to open the Programs submenu. This gives you access to the programs you use most often. An arrow to the right of an item indicates that a submenu will appear.

■ **Documents.** Displays the names of the last 15 documents you have opened. Click the document you wish to open. Windows will load the appropriate program and open the document.

■ **Settings.** Enables you to access many of the Windows environment settings.

■ **Find.** Used to search for files and folders on your computer or on a network.

■ **Help.** Opens the Windows Help feature.

■ **Run.** Used to start a program.

■ **Shut Down.** Used to shut down and restart Windows safely.

# *Accessories*

A wide variety of tools are included in the Windows 95 accessories. These tools include a calculator, two simple word processing programs, and games. If you are using a computer in the classroom, however, the games may have been removed to help you focus on your work. Figure B-2 lists most of the Windows 95 accessories and gives you a brief description of each.

Several of the accessories such as Fax, Dial-Up Networking, HyperTerminal, and Phone Dialer, require the use of a modem and communications capabilities. Others, such as Calculator, Notepad, Paint, and WordPad are ready for use. With Corel WordPerfect Suite 8, you don't need most of these accessories, because the same tools are available within the suite.

**FIGURE B-2**
Accessories that Come with Windows 95

- **Fax.** Sends and receives faxes if you have the appropriate hardware.

- **Games.** Provides miscellaneous games.

- **Internet Tools.** Contains the Internet Explorer and Internet Setup Tools.

- **Multimedia.** Provides the ability to use video and sound or other media in your work, if you have the appropriate hardware.

- **System Tools.** Includes several utilities you can use to maintain your system's performance.

- **Calculator.** Performs mathematical calculations.

- **Character Map.** Provides a utility for displaying and printing unusual characters not found on the computer keyboard.

- **Dial-Up Networking.** Allows you to connect the computer to other computers and a network by way of a modem.

- **Direct Cable Connection.** Allows you to physically connect two computers that are running Windows 95. The computers don't need to be networked.

- **HyperTerminal.** Allows you to transfer and receive data over telephone lines if you have the appropriate hardware.

- **Notepad.** Provides a simple word processing program for writing and reading text files.

- **Paint.** Provides a drawing program with tools for creating or editing graphics.

- **Phone Dialer.** Stores up to ten phone numbers and speed-dials your calls using a modem.

- **Tips and Tour.** Introduces Windows 95 and displays tips—each time you start the program, if you wish.

- **WordPad.** Provides a simple word processing program for creating and saving text files.

# *My Computer*

My Computer is used to quickly and easily see everything on your computer. Double click the My Computer icon on the desktop to display the My Computer dialog box. It will look much like Figure B-3 with differences, of course, in the type of computer and configuration.

**FIGURE B-3**
My Computer Dialog Box

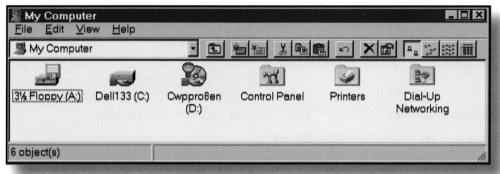

## CD-ROM Drive

An important tool in the My Computer dialog box is the CD-ROM drive. If you or your instructor has the Corel WordPerfect Suite 8 CD and your computer has a CD-ROM drive, you can access the Reference Center. This is a set of on-line "books" containing detailed instruction for using WordPerfect, Quattro Pro, Presentations, Paradox, CorelCENTRAL™, Envoy™, SGML, and a number of other utilities. Each of these references contains a Contents section to help you find what you need, and the Envoy viewer is used to display the pages of the reference. As you progress with your training, your instructor may require you to use the reference so that you become acquainted with it.

## Control Panel

Another important tool in the My Computer dialog box is the Control Panel. When you are using your own computer or you are in charge of the computer at your job, you may find the Control Panel useful for a wide variety of tasks. Your instructor will probably ask you not to make any changes in the Control Panel. Figure B-4 illustrates the icons for most of the tools in the Control Panel and describes the use of those tools.

Adds or removes fonts.

 Provides access to the **Printers** folder where you may install a printer, choose the default printer, assign ports, specify graphics resolution, connect to network printers, or choose paper size.

 Adjust the speed settings for repeating (typematic) keys, cursor blink rate, etc.

 Sends and receives electronic mail and faxes, providing your hardware is properly equipped.

 Enables you to set currency, time, date, and other settings for a number of different countries.

 Allows you to change the password you use when you log onto Windows.

 Enables you to set different sounds for different things that happen when you are using a program.

 Controls the type of video display terminal attached to your system. Allows you to change visual settings.

 Appears only if you are on a network. Is used to control network features. You may also set a user's password.

 Opens a dialog box that lets you choose a variety of options to make your system easier to use if you have a visual, dexterity, or hearing impairment.

 Helps you get everything working correctly when you install new hardware for your system.

| | |
|---|---|
|  | Installs or uninstalls parts of the Windows program or installs or removes applications programs. |
|  | Provides the tool for changing the date and time displayed by the system. |
|  | Controls the CD-ROM as well as the available variety of multimedia tools. |
|  | Displays information about CPU, memory, disk drives, monitor, and other system resources. |
|  | Provides guidance in installing and configuring a modem for transmitting data over telephone lines. |
|  | Tailors the way your mouse performs—double clicking and mouse speed. Also used to switch left and right mouse buttons. |

# *File Management*

M y Computer can be used for file management, although you will probably do most of your file management from within Corel WordPerfect Suite 8. One of the things you can't do from within the suite is format disks.

To **format a disk** using My Computer, follow these steps:

1.  In My Computer click once to select the icon for Drive A.

2.  Open the File menu.

3.  Choose Format. Follow the prompts to complete the formatting.

To **create a folder** (directory) using My Computer, follow these steps:

1.  In My Computer double click to select Drive A.

2.  Choose File and then New. Choose Folder.

3.  Key the folder name and press Enter.

To **rename a folder** using My Computer, follow these steps:

1. Point to the folder to be renamed and right click.

2. Key the new folder name.

To **copy and move folders** using My Computer, use these procedures:

1. To **copy** a folder to a different disk, drag the folder icon on top of the destination disk icon.

2. To **copy** a folder to a different location on the same disk, hold Ctrl while you drag the folder icon on top of the destination disk icon.

3. To **move** a folder to a different disk, hold Shift while you drag the folder icon on top of the destination disk icon.

4. To **move** a folder to a different location on the same disk, drag it to the new location.

As you learn file management in the Getting Started section, you may find it easier to manage your files from within the suite rather than using the Windows file management tools.

# *Explorer*

E xplorer is another way to quickly and easily list and maintain files and folders, as well as to create shortcuts. All of the same procedures listed for the handling of files in My Computer (except the formatting of disks) can be performed from the Windows 95 Explorer.

You can access Explorer in one of the following ways:

■ Click the **Start** button, choose **Programs**, and then choose **Microsoft Explorer**.

■ Point to the **Start** button and right click. Choose **Explorer**.

The Explorer window is split into two "panes" (see Figure B-5). The left pane is the *All Folders* pane. It lists the drives and the folders on those drives. In the figure the minus sign at the left of the Drive (C:) line indicates that all of the folders in Drive C are displayed below. To close that list, simply click the minus sign. It will become a plus sign which reports to the user that the folder contains files which are not displayed.

**FIGURE B-5**
Windows Explorer

The pane at the right is the *Contents* pane. At the top is a line telling you *3¹/₂ Floppy (A:)* is chosen. Because the disk in Drive A is empty, no files or folders are listed in the box. If you wish, you can use the Help feature to learn more about the Windows Explorer on your own.

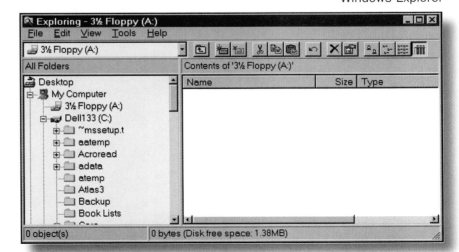

## Creating Shortcuts

Windows 95 has a number of ways for you to create shortcuts so that you can run the programs or start the desired applications from the desktop. One way is to do it from the Windows Explorer.

To create a shortcut using the Explorer, be sure you can see a portion of the desktop outside of the Explorer dialog box. Then follow these easy steps:

1. Click the **Start** button on the taskbar and choose **Programs**. Then choose **Windows Explorer**.

2. Locate the icon that starts the program to which you would like easier access.

3. Click that icon to select it.

4. Open the File menu in the Explorer and choose Create Shortcut. Windows will make a copy of the icon and drop it to the bottom of the open folder. It will still be highlighted.

5. Drag that icon to the desktop. If you wish to change the text under the icon, click it once to select it. Then right click and choose Rename. Key the new name.

6. If you wish to delete a shortcut from the desktop, click once to select it. Press the Delete key on your keyboard and confirm the deletion.

# *Summary*

This has been a quick introduction to Windows 95. In order to be proficient with this operating system, you will want to take a class or two. Windows 95 works well to get you in and out of WordPerfect. If all you use is Corel WordPerfect Suite 8, you don't have to be very skilled in the use of Windows 95. You can use this suite for most of your needs.

# File Management

Creating and saving documents (or files) is only part of what a good application can help you do. Managing those files after you've prepared them is an important part of what YOU must do. The computer can help you, but it is your responsibility to manage your files in such a way that they can be located when needed.

# Naming Files

The word *file* and the word *document* both refer to a collection of data, words, or information to be saved. Those words may be used interchangeably in these materials. A file name may consist of up to 255 characters, spaces, or punctuation marks. For example, both **appendix-c** or **appendix c for WordPerfect Suite 8 text** would be acceptable for the file name of this appendix. When naming your files, use consistency and organization. This makes both naming and locating your files easier.

Most file names have an extension. This extension is three characters at the end of the name that are separated from the name with a period. In Corel WordPerfect Suite 8 an extension is automatically added to the end of your file. The primary extensions in the suite include the following:

| | | | |
|---|---|---|---|
| WordPerfect document | .wpd | Quattro Pro worksheet | .wb1 |
| WordPerfect graphic | .wpg | Quattro Pro Data Modeling Desktop | .dmd |
| WordPerfect macro | .wcm | Presentations show | .shw |
| WordPerfect data file | .dat | Paradox database | .db |
| WordPerfect form document | .frm | Paradox database model | .dm |
| WordPerfect template | .wpt | CorelCENTRAL™ planner. | .ccp |

Whether you can see those extensions when you display your list of files in the Open File or Save As dialog boxes depends on a Windows 95 setting. When you are viewing the names of your files in either dialog box, if you don't see the extension, ask your instructor if you may display them. With permission, follow these simple steps:

1. Go to the Windows 95 desktop, choose My Computer, and open the View menu.

2. Click the View tab. The only option that should be chosen is the second round button. If other options are chosen, deselect them.

3. Finally, close the dialog box and return to your Corel application.

In any application developed previous to Windows 95, the Disk Operating System (DOS) allowed only eight characters, a period, and the three-symbol extension. If you save a file in a Windows 95 application using a long filename and later wish to open it in an earlier version, it will contain the first several letters of the long filename and a tilde (~) to indicate missing characters. Files created in WordPerfect 6, WordPerfect 7, and WordPerfect 8 are all compatible. In fact, when you save a WordPerfect 8 file, the chosen setting is WordPerfect 6/7/8.

# Organizing Files

Visualize an office with no organized paper filing system. When you open the file drawers, you find letters, memos, reports, and contracts piled into the drawers. The same thing can happen when you store files on disks and have no plan for what is stored on which disk or in which folder. File management is as important for computerized files as it is for paper files—maybe even more so because you can't see what's on a disk by looking at it. You must access each file, unless it is very clearly named, to see what that file is about.

Whether you save your files on diskettes or a hard disk, the issue of file management is critical. Let's look at some of the principles of file management. If you save on the hard drive of a computer, both your software files and your document files are stored on the same hard disk. It becomes especially important to set up a system of organizing files so they aren't mixed in with the program files and so you can find them when you need them.

Learn to group the files into *folders*, as discussed in the next section. The main folder on a hard drive is usually known as **C:**. The main folder can contain dozens of folders, and each of those folders can contain dozens of folders of their own, and so on. The same is true of diskettes. If the diskette is in Drive A, the main storage area is referred to as **A:**. You can create folders on diskettes, and those folders can contain more folders, etc.

If you are working on a network, you may have a number of drives, each named with an alphabetic letter. In a networked classroom you will be given access to a special area to save your work, and you can create folders in that area.

# Using Folders

As with paper files, a folder is a place where related files are kept together. Sometimes you will create a folder to hold a special kind of work before you begin the work. Then, as the files are created, they will be saved into that folder. (Please note that *folder* is the Windows 95 name for what was called a *directory* in DOS computing.)

Sometimes you will create the folder for related files after some of the files have been prepared and saved. At that point, you may move the files into the folder.

Figure C-1 illustrates a typical folder structure. Note that you have two levels—the original main level and a set of folders on the second level. The names of the folders on each level must be unique. In other words, you can't have two **Paradox** folders on the same level. You could, however, have a **projects** folder in each of the folders illustrated.

It is very important that you PLAN the arrangement of your folders so your work is stored logically. If it isn't, you are likely to have trouble finding a file when you need it.

**FIGURE C-1**
Sample Folders

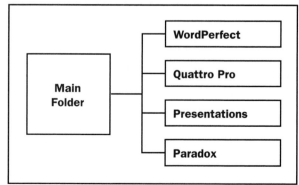

# Making Backup Files

One of the most important things you must do when you are filing documents on disk is to make backup files on a regular basis. This prevents loss of important files due to disk damage or problems with the computer. Proper backup procedures also protect your office from theft and natural disaster. Backup disks or tapes may be stored in a fireproof vault or at a different location.

Backup of your files may simply include copying all of the files created during one working day from the file disk or folder you were using that day onto another disk. This gives you two copies of everything you save.

Backups can be made from the Windows Explorer or My Computer (see Appendix B). Tape backup systems or zip drives can be used to back up entire hard drives on a regular basis. This includes files you've created as well as program files, although most systems allow you to specify which folders are to be backed up.

The method of backup your office uses might determine how you name your files. In any case, it is important that you back up your work regularly and save your backup disks in a safe place.

# Purging Files

Regular paper filing cabinets must be cleaned out regularly. A good records management program mandates the disposal of files that are old or no longer needed. Disk files need to be cleaned out on a regular basis, too. Time should be set aside each week, or preferably each day, to go through the files on your disks and "clean house." The Preview feature in the Open File dialog box of most Corel WordPerfect Suite 8 applications will help you preview files when you can't immediately remember a filename. By limiting the files stored, your retrieval time for accessing files will be improved.

Some files can simply be discarded when they have no further value to you or your firm. You can do that with the Delete option when you are in the Open File dialog box. Other files may have value but may be used only once every several months. Those files that are not needed on a regular basis might need to be archived.

*Archiving* refers to storing seldom-used files in a safe but out-of-the-way place. By copying these seldom-used files to a special disk and deleting them from your working disks, you can improve your retrieval time. In addition, your working disks or folders will have more room for your current work. You will want to have some system for archiving files so that you can find them when you need them.

# Disk Capacity

File sizes are measured in *bytes*. A byte is approximately equal to a character. The most commonly used diskette is the $3^1/2$-inch size, which holds 1,440,000 bytes (1.44 *megabytes,* or Mb). Be careful not to fill a diskette more than three-quarters full. The Open File dialog box reports the number of bytes in the files on a disk or in a folder. Sometimes file sizes are reported in kilobytes (Kb). Each *kilobyte* is 1,024 bytes.

The current capacity of hard drives is much, much greater than that of diskettes, but much of the space on today's hard drives is filled with operating system and program files. This means that you must always be careful with disk space.

In your lessons you will be asked to save some files that have no future importance. Some exercises involve deleting some files and moving others to related folders. Complete these exercises along with the others in the lessons so you continue to have room to save your files as directed.

# Selecting Files

To select a single file, display the Open File dialog box, use the mouse pointer to point to the file to be selected, and click. When a file has been selected, you may open the File menu and choose Delete, Move, Copy, Rename, or a number of other options.

To select a group of files, point to the first file to be selected with the mouse pointer and click to highlight it. Then hold the Shift key while you click the last file in the group to be selected. The first and last file will remain highlighted, and all of the files between the two will also be highlighted. If there are more files to be selected than are showing at one time in the file name box, continue to hold the Shift key and use the scroll bar to move the list so you can see the final file to be selected. Click that file and release the Shift key. The Status Bar at the bottom of the Open File dialog box will tell you how many files are selected and how many bytes are in the selected files. With the files selected, you may copy, delete, or move the highlighted files as described above.

To select scattered files, hold the Ctrl key while you click those to be selected. You may use the scroll bar (still holding Ctrl) to move through the list to find the files. When you have highlighted all of the files to be selected, open, delete, move, or copy the files as desired.

# GLOSSARY

**@functions** Predefined formulas that begin with the @ sign. They automatically perform calculations on selected data. (p. QP-39)

## A

**Absolute cell reference** A reference to a cell in a formula that does not change when a formula is copied from one cell to another. (p. QP-38)

**Active cell** The cell that you can currently manipulate, for example by entering data into it; the active cell has a heavy border around it. (p. QP-3)

**Address** The location of a specific cell, identified by its column and row (for example, B11). Also called a *coordinate* or *reference*. (pp. WP-95, QP-3)

**Alignment** The positioning of text on a page or data within a cell. (pp. WP-99, QP-24)

**AND search** A search which locates only those records that meet more than one set of criteria. (p. QP-125)

**Archiving** Moving important but seldom-used documents to a safe, out-of-the-way place. (p. C-3)

**Argument** The data on which a function is performed. (p. QP-39)

**Ascending sort** A procedure which arranges numeric data in order from smallest to largest or alphabetic data in order from A to Z. (pp. WP-127, QP-51, PA-28)

**Axis title** A label that provides information about the data plotted on the x- or y-axis of an XY chart. (pp. WP-149, QP-97, PR-94)

## B

**Background** A predesigned graphic for a master that provides a uniform look for all the slides in a slide show. (p. PR-4)

**Bar chart** A chart that represents sets of data on the x and y axes. A bar chart is particularly good for comparing quantities. (p. PR-71)

**Blend** To create mixed images between two objects, making it appear as though one object is transforming into another. (p. PR-65)

**Block** A group of selected text or contiguous cells; also called a *range*. (pp. WP-102, QP-5)

**Block Protect** The feature that enables you to keep a block or section of text together on a page. You can adjust the size of the block to make soft page breaks fall in desirable locations. (p. WP-66)

**Bookmark** A WordPerfect feature that enables you to mark a location in your document so that you can return to that location quickly. (p. WP-84)

**Boot** To start a computer or program.

**Border** A line that extends around parts of a document or sections of text. (p. WP-146)

**Box field** A placeholder for various kinds of information in an organization chart. (p. PR-104)

**Bullet** A small symbol (■, ◆, ●) that marks the beginning of a line of text. (pp. WP-48, PR-37)

**Button** A rectangular section on the Toolbar, Property Bar, or Application Bar, or in a dialog box, where you may click to accept or confirm a selection. (p. GS-3)

**Byte** The computer measurement of storage—usually representing one character, one space, or a command such as Tab or Hard Return. (p. C-3)

## C

**Case-sensitive** A feature, such as in Find, where the results vary, depending on whether the letters are uppercase or lowercase.

**Cell** The intersection of a row and a column in a table or spreadsheet. A cell can hold text, a number, or a formula. (pp. WP-95, QP-3)

**Chart** A graphic representation of data. (pp. WP-149, QP-97)

**Click** To position the mouse pointer on something and then press and quickly release the mouse button. (p. A-4)

**Clipart** Preformatted graphics used to enhance a document, such as a slide show. (pp. WP-136, PR-63)

**Clipboard** A special temporary storage area used to hold data while it is waiting to be pasted to another location. (pp. WP-23, QP-11)

**Codes** The hidden commands that cause your document to be formatted. In WordPerfect you can use the Reveal Codes feature to see what codes are formatting your document and the location of those codes. (p. WP-6)

**Column** A vertical arrangement of text on a page. (p. WP-51) A single vertical grid within a table or spreadsheet, identified by a letter of the alphabet. (pp. WP-195, QP-3)

**Comparison operator** A mathematical symbol—such as greater than (>), less than (<), or equal to (=)—used alone or combined in a query to define criteria (for example, PAY_RATE >= 13.50). (p. PA-33)

**Connector line** A line that joins two boxes on an organization chart. (p. PR-105)

**Context-sensitive** A feature that responds in different ways, depending on what you are doing when you use it. In WordPerfect the Property Bar changes to tools for formatting tables when your insertion point is in a table. (p. GS-16)

**Coordinate** The location of a specific cell, identified by its column and row (for example, B11). Also called an *address* or *reference*. (pp. WP-95, QP-3)

**Copy** To place a duplicate copy of data or text on the Clipboard. (pp. WP-23, QP-11)

**CPU** The working portion of the computer, known as the Central Processing Unit, that contains the processing and memory chips and the circuit boards that enable the computer to process your commands. (p. A-1)

**Criteria table** In a database, a table containing the field names of the fields you want to search and the criteria or conditions that the fields must meet. (p. QP-129)

**Cut** To remove data or text and place it on the Clipboard. (pp. WP-23, QP-11)

## D

**Data series** A row of data in a chart. (p. PR-76) *OR*: The data that's being charted. (p. QP-97)

**Data source** (Data file) A collection of information to be merged with a form document. Often the data source contains names, addresses, and telephone numbers of customers or clients. (p. WP-116)

**Database** An organized collection of related information, such as a collection of names and addresses of a group of people or a collection of parts in an inventory. In WordPerfect a database is referred to as a *data file*. (pp. WP-132, QP-126, PA-2)

**Database block** In a spreadsheet, the block of cells that contains records, fields, and field names. (p. QP-126)

**Datasheet** A spreadsheet-like guide used to enter text and numerical data for charts. (p. PR-41)

**DDE** (Dynamic Data Exchange) A background method of sharing information between Windows-based programs. (p. INT2-1)

**Default** A setting built into a program that takes effect unless some alternative setting is specified. For example, in WordPerfect, the default margin settings are one inch on all sides of the page. (p. GS-7)

**Dependent variable** A quantity that can change based on another value; it is plotted on the x-axis of an XY chart. (p. PR-92)

**Descending sort** A procedure which arranges numeric data in order from largest to smallest, or alphabetic data in order from Z to A. (pp. WP-127, QP-61, PA-28)

**Desktop** The opening window in a graphic environment, where the user may start a program by choosing the representative icon. (p. B-2)

**Detail table** In a relational database, the secondary table in the relationship. The common field in the detail table must be indexed. (p. PA-39)

**Dialog box** A box that appears in the window to provide you with information or to let you select options and settings. (p. GS-5)

**Document** Any collection of information stored on a disk. You create a document when you collect graphics and/or text, give the collection a name, and save it. This term is used interchangeably with *file*. (p. GS-13)

**DOS** (Disk Operating System) Software that enables your computer to communicate with your disk drives and your software. (p. C-1)

**Double click** To click the mouse button twice. Some actions can be accessed by clicking once; others must be accessed by double clicking. (p. A-4)

**Drag** The act of positioning the insertion point in the window and holding the left mouse button while you move to the end of the section to be selected. (p. WP-20)

**Drop Cap** A large letter dropped below the line of writing. It is used to call attention to the beginning of an article in a newsletter or magazine. (p. WP-143)

# E

**Em dash** A symbol that is used to join two related phrases. It is the longest dash used. In WordPerfect you can key it by pressing the hyphen key three times. (p. WP-31)

**Embed** To place a copy of an object in a different application. When editing changes occur, the source application features of the embedded objects are used. (p. INT2-2)

**Endnotes** A Reference to another work or publication. Endnotes are printed as a list on the final page of the document. (p. WP-60)

**Explode** To separate a pie slice from a whole pie chart to emphasize it. (p. PR-84)

**Extension** The part of a document name following the period. DOS restricts the extension portion of a document name to a maximum of three characters. In WordPerfect it is not imperative that a document name include an extension. Exceptions are macros, style libraries, templates, form documents, data files, and graphics. (p. C-1)

# F

**Field** A single piece of information in a data file. In WordPerfect, fields are separated by an ENDFIELD code and a hard return. (p. WP-116) In a spreadsheet or database, each column represents a field. (p. QP-126) A specific category in a database, such as name, address, or phone number. (p. PA-2)

**Field name** The label that identifies a category of information in a WordPerfect data file. (WP-116) The label that identifies a column of data in a database. (p. QP-126)

**File** Any collection of information saved on a disk. You create a file when you collect graphics and/or text, give the collection a name, and save it. This term is used interchangeably with *document*. (p. GS-13)

**File name** The first part of the name of a document to be saved on a disk. (p. WP-12)

**Filepath** The route to where a document is stored on a disk. A filepath includes the use of different levels of folders. For example, a document named *whale* in a folder named *mammals* that is in a folder named *animals* on the hard drive would have the following filepath: *C:\animals\mammals\whale*. (p. WP-12)

**Fill** The background or shading that is present in some graphics or objects. (p. WP-146)

**Filter** To locate data that meets specified conditions. (p. QP-123)

**Find** A WordPerfect feature that enables you to key a unique string of characters and then tell WordPerfect to find that text string. *Replace* is part of the feature. (p. WP-80)

**Flip** To reverse an object from left to right or top to bottom. (pp. WP-139, PR-65)

**Floating cell** A one-cell table in a WordPerfect document that is attached to a larger table in the same document. When changes are made in the table, those changes are reflected in the floating cell. (p. WP-106)

**Floating chart** A chart that is placed on the same sheet that contains the data being charted. (p. QP-100)

**Flush right** The alignment of text at the right margin, leaving the left edges of the text ragged. (p. WP-39)

**Folder** A division on your disk to hold related files. You can create folders to hold your computer documents much like you create folders for paper documents. (p. GS-13)

**Font** A set of all characters (letters, numbers, and symbols) in a particular typeface and size. When you select a font (e.g., Times New Roman 12 pt.), you are specifying typeface and size. (pp. WP-4, QP-23)

**Font size** The height of characters in a font as measured in points; each point is 1/72 of an inch. (pp. WP-4, QP-23)

**Font style** An attribute, such as bold, italic, or underlining. (pp. WP-3, QP-23)

**Footer** A piece of information printed at the bottom of the pages of a multiple-page document to tie the document together. Footers might include page numbers, chapter or unit titles, the title of the publication, or the date, depending on the kind of document being prepared. (pp. WP-56, QP-78)

**Footnotes** References to other publications or quotations taken from other publications. A footnote is usually numbered and positioned at the bottom of the page on which the quoted or referenced text is mentioned. (p. WP-60)

**Form document** (Form file) The shell or main document used in a merge. It contains the standard text to be merged with the data source. (p. WP-116)

**Formula** An equation used to perform a calculation in a spreadsheet or a table. (pp. WP-104, QP-34)

**Frame** The lines enclosing the top, bottom, front, back, and/or sides of an XY chart. It also includes a fill color or pattern that appears behind the chart elements. (p. PR-95)

**Function** A predefined formula that begins with the @ sign; it automatically performs calculations on selected data. (p. QP-39)

**Function keys** The set of twelve *F* keys on a computer keyboard. The function keys are used as an alternative to the menu system in choosing and executing WordPerfect features. (p. GS-7)

# G

**Grid** The series of horizontal and vertical lines that mark increments on the x and y axes. (p. PR-96)

# H

**Handle** A small box that is displayed on the perimeter of a graphics box when the box has been selected. Handles can be dragged to size and shape a graphics box. (p. WP-136)

**Hanging indent** A paragraph format in which the first line of the paragraph begins at the left margin and the remaining paragraph lines are indented to the level of the first tab stop. (p. WP-47)

**Hard copy** The printed copy of a document.

**Hard drive** The high-capacity storage device that is usually permanently affixed inside the CPU of the computer. Computer programs such as WordPerfect are recorded on the hard drive for easy access. (p. GS-9)

**Hard page break** A page break in a document entered manually by the person preparing the document. Hard page breaks always stay in the same position in a document, regardless of text added or deleted. A hard page break in WordPerfect is entered by holding Ctrl while pressing Enter. (pp. WP-59, QP-77)

**Hard space** A space used between two words or word parts which are not to be separated at the end of the line; (e.g., between the first name and the initial in *Gail M. Weber*). A hard space is entered in WordPerfect by holding Ctrl while pressing the space bar. (p. WP-31)

**Header** A piece of information printed at the top of the pages of a multiple-page document. Headers tie a document together and might include page numbers, chapter or unit titles, the title of the publication, or the date, depending on the kind of document being prepared. (pp. WP-56, QP-78)

**HTML** (HyperText Markup Language) The commands needed to format documents for the Internet. WordPerfect will convert documents to HTML format. (p. WP-169)

**Hyphen character** A kind of hyphen used between two word parts that are not to be separated at the end of a line. Hyphen characters might be used as minus signs in equations or between the parts of a telephone number. (p. WP-31)

# I

**Icon** A miniature graphic representing a window, a document, a program, or a feature. Icons are often used on the desktop or on buttons —like those on the Toolbar. (p. GS-1)

**Independent variable** A quantity that does not change based on another value; it is plotted on the y axis of an XY chart. (p. PR-92)

**Index** To temporarily rearrange the order of records in a database table based upon a field or fields. (p. PA-25)

**Insertion point** The blinking vertical bar indicating where you are working in a document. (p. WP-8)

## J

**Justification** The way in which text is aligned on the line of writing. The default in Word-Perfect is Left justification (text is aligned at the left margin but not at the right margin). (p. WP-38)

## K

**Key** A criterion for sorting order when working with WordPerfect Sort. (p. WP-126)

**Key field** The field in a database table on which the entire table is automatically sorted as you enter records. Also referred to as the *primary index*. (p. PA-5)

**Keyboard merge** A form document with no data source. A KEYBOARD code tells Word-Perfect to stop for you to key the required information as the merge progresses. (p. WP-125)

**Kilobyte** A unit of computer storage consisting of 1,024 bytes. (p. C-3)

## L

**Label** A text entry that can contain alphabetic or numeric characters that are used to identify a value. (p. QP-7)

**Landscape** Page orientation where the long edges of the paper are at the top and bottom and the short edges are at the left and right. (p. WP-67)

**Launch** To start a software program. (p. QP-2)

**Layout** The way text is formatted and objects are positioned. (p. PR-4)

**Leaders** Dots (periods) that direct (lead) your attention from one column on a line of text to another. (p. WP-40)

**Legend** The key at the bottom of a chart that indicates which colors or patterns in the chart represent which data series. (p. PR-73)

**Line chart** A data chart that represents data values as points on a line plotted on the x- and y- axes. (p. PR-92)

**Line spacing** The vertical distance between two lines of type, measured from baseline to baseline. (p. WP-38)

**Link** To connect a pie slice to a second pie chart in order to further break down the contents of that slice. (p. PR-87) Also, a relationship between relational database tables based upon a common field. (p. PA-39)

**Linking** Placing a copy of an object in a document in a different application by double clicking the object to open the original application and edit the source document. (p. INT2-2)

## M

**Macro** A collection of keystrokes that are recorded because they are used together frequently. Macros are used to simplify and automate repeated sets of commands. (pp. WP-86, QP-151))

**Master** A predesigned background for a Presentations slide that contains formatted layouts for text, bulleted lists, charts, etc. (p. PR-4)

**Master table** In a relational database, the primary table in the relationship between two tables. (p. PA-39)

**Masthead** The large title and date section at the top of a newspaper or newsletter identifying the document, the volume or edition, and the date. Publishers use the same layout for the masthead with each edition. (p. WP-165)

**Megabyte** A unit of computer storage consisting of 1,024 kilobytes or 1,048,576 bytes. (p. C-3)

**Menu** A list of choices. (p. GS-4)

**Menu Bar** The menus across the top of the working window from which you can choose program features and tools. (p. GS-4)

**Merge code** A code used to organize the text appropriately when two files are combined. Merge (sometimes called mail merge) is most useful for repetitive documents, such as in combining the names and addresses in a mailing list with a standard letter. (p. WP-115)

**Mnemonics** Related letters used to simplify commands, like *b* for *bold* or *u* for *underline*. In WordPerfect menus, choices may be made by keying the underlined mnemonic letter.

**Modem** A device that enables you to transmit computer (digital) information over telephone lines. (p. GS-16)

## N

**Network** A configuration of computers cabled together with one workstation designated as the file server. In a networked environment, software frequently is loaded on the server only, and individual workstations access the program from the server as needed. (p. GS-9)

**No-print zone** An area around the outside edges of a sheet of paper where the printer is incapable of printing. The size of the no-print zone varies according to the manufacturer or model of printer.

**Notebook** A spreadsheet file that contains multiple sheets. The contents of these sheets are typically related to one another. (p. QP-2)

## O

**Object animation** A feature that uses special effects to make text and graphics "fly" onto the screen in a Presentations slide show. (p. PR-115)

**Objects sheet** The sheet that contains an icon for each object (such as a chart or graphic) contained in a notebook. (p. QP-104)

**OLE** (Object Linking and Embedding) A method of merging varieties of data into one file. An icon is inserted into a file which, when double clicked will take you to the source document. (p. INT2-1)

**Operator** A symbol that represents an arithmetic operation, such as addition (+) or multiplication (∗). (p. QP-34)

**Option** A choice in a dialog box. (p. GS-11)

**OR search** A search that finds records that need only meet one of the specified criteria. (p. QP-125)

**Order of operator precedence** The order in which mathematical operations will be performed. (p. QP-37)

**Organization chart** A chart that shows the chain of command in a company or other organization. (p. PR-102)

**Orphan** The last line of a paragraph that appears by itself at the top of a page of text. (p. WP-57)

**Outliner view** The view in Presentations that shows the content of the slides in outline form. (p. PR-15)

**Overlay**  A feature comparable to an overhead transparency; it represents additional information that can be placed on a map. (p. QP-118)

# P

**Page break**  An instruction to the computer to begin a new page. A *soft page break* is inserted by WordPerfect when a page is full. A *hard page break* may be inserted wherever desired by pressing Ctrl+Enter. (p. WP-59)

**Page orientation**  The way a page is turned in relation to the printing on it. When the paper is vertical, it is said to be in *portrait orientation*. When the page is horizontal, the orientation is referred to as *landscape*. (p. WP-67)

**Paste**  To insert text or graphics that have been copied or cut from a different location in your document into place at the location of the insertion point. (pp. WP-23, QP-11, PR-63)

**Paste Special**  A command used when an object is to be embedded or linked. (pp. INT1-15, INT2-2)

**PerfectExpert**  A Corel® WordPerfect® Suite 8 tool that helps you format various types of documents and saves them as projects for when they are needed again. Some PerfectExpert projects are already prepared and available when you install your software. (p. WP-163)

**Pie chart**  A chart that represents an entire group of data as a circle divided into proportional sections based on some type of distinguishing characteristic. This type of chart resembles a pie divided into different-sized pieces, and always adds up to 100%. (p. PR-70)

**Point size**  The vertical size of a character of type. A 72-pt. character would be approximately an inch tall. A 12-pt. character would be approximately a sixth of an inch tall. The greater the number of points, the taller the letter. (p. WP-4)

**Pointing**  Using the mouse to move the pointer in the window. Normally, when you have positioned the pointer at the desired location, either the left or right mouse button is used to position the insertion point or make menu choices. (p. A-4)

**Portrait**  The page orientation where the short edges of the paper are at the top and bottom of the page and the long edges are at the sides. (p. WP-67)

**Primary index**  See *Key field.*

**Printer driver**  The software file that enables a program to communicate with the printer. (p. WP-5)

**Project**  In WordPerfect or Quattro Pro, a predesigned template, or "skeleton" of a document or notebook. In Quattro Pro, the project provides the basis for a new notebook on a specific topic. For example, projects are available for creating expense reports or keeping track of loan payments. (pp. WP-163, QP-155)

**Proportional pies**  Pie charts sized according to the numbers entered in the datasheet. The chart whose data values total the most is drawn larger than the other pie. (p. PR-86)

# Q

**Query**  To extract data that meets specified criteria from a database block. (p. QP-126) An action to find records in a database that meet certain criteria or conditions. For example, you might query an employee database file to find out how many employees have the last name *Jones*. (p. PA-32)

**QuickCorrect**  A feature that automatically replaces certain text with other specified text. It will also correct errors and capitalization and can be used to correct predetermined keying and spelling errors. (p. WP-28)

**QuickKey** A keystroke assigned to perform a task while playing a Presentations slide show. (p. PR-124)

**QuickLink** An object on a slide, such as a piece of clipart or a drawn object, that performs an action or advances to another slide when you click it. (p. PR-125)

**QuickMenu** A context-sensitive menu that appears when you click the right mouse button. (pp. GS-7, PR-54)

**QuickSelect** To select words, sentences, or paragraphs by double, triple, or quadruple clicking. (p. WP-20)

**QuickWords** Abbreviations set up by the user that expand into complete text. (p. WP-82)

# R

**RAM** (Random Access Memory) The temporary storage area or working space for the document you are creating and the program you are using. This storage area is emptied if the computer is turned off or if the electricity supplying it is interrupted. (p. A-1)

**Range** In a spreadsheet, a group of contiguous cells; also called a *block*. (p. QP-5)

**Record** All of the information about a particular customer, client, or product in a data file. It is the complete collection of data about that individual. In WordPerfect, records usually are separated by an ENDRECORD code and a Hard Page code. In Quattro Pro, each row in a database block represents a record. (pp. WP-115, QP-126, PA-2)

**Redline** A feature that enables you to mark text suggested for addition to a document. Text marked with Redline is printed with a shaded background. (p. WP-186)

**Reference** The location of a specific cell, identified by its column and row (for example,

B11). Also called an *address* or *coordinate*. (pp. WP-95, QP-3)

**Relational database** A database that consists of multiple tables linked by a common field. (p. PA-2)

**Relative cell reference** A reference to a cell in a formula that changes in relation to the cell containing the formula. (p. QP-36)

**Report** A model that can be generated using spreadsheet data; reports often summarize data and arrange it in an easy-to-understand format. (p. QP-135)

**Rotate** To turn a graphic from its original position around an invisible axis in the center of the object. (pp. WP-138, PR-65)

**Row** A single horizontal grid within a table or spreadsheet, identified by a number. (pp. WP-95, QP-3)

# S

**Save (a document)** To transfer a document from the memory of the computer to a disk so that it is available at some future time. (p. GS-8)

**Scenario** A depiction of an activity that performs a calculation on specified data; variable values are plugged into a data model, generating specific results. (p. QP-86)

**Scroll bars** The bars on the right side or bottom of the window that provide a tool for moving vertically and/or horizontally through a document or a list. You can move by clicking the scroll arrows, by dragging the scroll box, or by clicking above or below the scroll box. (p. GS-2)

**Secondary index** A second key field with which you can temporarily sort a database table. (p. PA-25)

**Seed value** A value that is used to determine the starting point in a range of values. (p. QP-11)

**Selected text** In word processing, a section of text that has been blocked or highlighted. You might select text to be moved, copied, or deleted. You might also select text to add a special kind of formatting, like bold, underline, or a new font face. (p. WP-20)

**Selector** The bordered rectangle around the active cell. (p. QP-3)

**Sheet** An individual grid, or spreadsheet within a notebook. (p. QP-2)

**Size** To change the size of an object by dragging the sizing handles that appear when the object is selected. (p. WP-136)

**Skew** To distort a graphic so that it appears stretched. (p. PR-65)

**Slide Editor view** The view in Presentations that shows the slide as it will appear when presented or printed. (p. PR-15)

**Slide Sorter view** The view in Presentations that displays thumbnails of the slides in the order in which you have arranged them and gives the title of each, as well as any special effects assigned to the slides. (p. PR-15)

**Soft page break** A page break that is automatically inserted when a page is full. (pp. WP-59, QP-77)

**Sort** To arrange information or data in a specific order, such as alphabetically or numerically. (pp. WP-127, QP-61, PA-27)

**Spreadsheet** Columns and rows forming a grid that contains data, labels, or formulas. Spreadsheets are often used for calculations and accounting purposes. (pp. WP-95, QP-2)

**Spreadsheet program** Software that allows you to easily manage large quantities of data by performing calculations on it and organizing and analyzing it. (p. QP-2)

**Staff position** On an organization chart, a support person for another position. Staff persons include administrative assistants. (p. PR-106)

**Strikeout** A feature that enables you to mark text suggested for deletion from a document. Text marked with Strikeout is printed with a line drawn through it. (p. WP-186)

**Style** A master format for a particular kind of document or document part. Styles are collections of keystrokes and menu choices used to speed up the formatting of documents when the same formats are used repeatedly. (pp. WP-165, QP-153)

**Subordinate position** On an organization chart, a position that reports to a higher position. (p. PR-102)

**Subscript** The term used to refer to the position of a character that is printed below the normal line of writing (the baseline). An example is the 2 in $H_2O$. (p. WP-31)

**Superior position** On an organization chart, a position that has other positions reporting to it. (p. PR-102)

**Superscript** The term used to refer to the position of a character that is printed above the normal line of writing. An example is the 2 in $x^2$. (p. WP-31)

**Suppress** A feature that tells WordPerfect not to include the header, footer, watermark, or page number on a specific page of a document. (p. WP-57)

# T

**Table** A set of data organized into rows and columns. (p. PR-37)

**Template** A master format for a particular kind of a document in WordPerfect, or a document part in other brands of word processing software. (p. WP-163)

**Text editor** The box on a Presentations slide that enables you to key and edit text for items such as titles and subtitles. (p. PR-6)

**Thumbnails** Reduced-size versions of slides used to display several slides on a screen, or to print several slides on a page. (p. PR-15)

**Transition** The way a slide show changes from one slide to another. (p. PR-113)

**Trend** The way a value changes over time. (p. PR-92)

**Typeface** One design of type. A typeface has a name, like Arial, Arrus, Times New Roman or Univers. It includes all characters of all sizes in the matching design. (pp. WP-4, QP-23)

# U

**URL** (Uniform Resource Locator) An address code for finding hypertext or hypermedia documents on World Wide Web (WWW) servers around the world. (p. WP-178)

# V

**Value** An entry in a spreadsheet that consists of a number, date, or formula. (p. QP-7)

**VDT** (Video Display Terminal) The screen or monitor of the computer. (p. A-1)

# W

**Widow** The first line of a paragraph that appears by itself at the bottom of a page. (p. WP-57)

**Wildcard** A character that represents unknown text in a search formula. (p. QP-131)

**Window** The area where you key a document when using a graphical user interface. (p. GS-2)

**Windows** An operating system utilizing the graphical user interface which allows a user to have several documents or programs available at any one time. It allows you to move easily from one to another without having to exit from a program. (p. B-1)

**Word wrap** The feature that causes a word that doesn't fit at the end of one line to drop to the beginning of the next line. (p. WP-2)

**Working directory** In Paradox, the location where you store your files. (p. PA-3)

# X

**X-axis** Horizontal segment of a chart. (p. QP-97, PR-92)

**XY chart** A chart that uses a grid with horizontal (X) and vertical (Y) axes to determine placement of the data points. XY charts include bar charts, line charts, scatter charts, and area charts. (p. PR-71)

# Y

**Y-axis** Vertical segment of a chart. (p. QP-97, PR-92)

# Z

**Zoom** To expand or reduce the size of the view of a document or an image in the window. (p. WP-4)

**Zoom factor** The percentage by which the contents of a screen are increased or decreased in size. (p. QP-50)

*NOTE: Some of the terms listed in this Glossary are terms used when discussing software suites, but are not used in this text.*

# INDEX

# PROGRESS RECORDS

## Corel® WordPerfect® 8

Name _____

| | | Printed | Score | Date Completed | Instructor |
|---|---|---|---|---|---|
| **Lesson 1** | pp 1-2 | . . . . . . . . . | _____ | _____ | |
| | pp 1-10 | . . . . . . . . . | _____ | _____ | |
| | Buster 1-11 | envelope | _____ | _____ | |
| | Review Questions | . . . . . . . . . | _____ | _____ | _____ |
| | Corel proj1 | . . . . . . . . . | _____ | _____ | _____ |
| | Lesson 1 Quiz | . . . . . . . . . | _____ | _____ | _____ |
| | | | | | |
| **Lesson 2** | return 2-2 | . . . . . . . . . | _____ | _____ | |
| | return 2-3 | . . . . . . . . . | _____ | _____ | |
| | welcome 2-10 | . . . . . . . . . | _____ | _____ | |
| | char 2-13 | . . . . . . . . . | _____ | _____ | |
| | sale memo 2-14 | . . . . . . . . . | _____ | _____ | |
| | Review Questions | . . . . . . . . . | _____ | _____ | _____ |
| | welcome proj2a | . . . . . . . . . | _____ | _____ | _____ |
| | welcome proj2b | . . . . . . . . . | _____ | _____ | _____ |
| | suite proj2c | . . . . . . . . . | _____ | _____ | _____ |
| | Lesson 2 Quiz | . . . . . . . . . | _____ | _____ | _____ |
| | Production Test 1&2 | . . . . . . . . . | _____ | _____ | _____ |
| | | | | | |
| **Lesson 3** | welcome 3-4 | 2 pages | _____ | _____ | |
| | welcome 3-7 | . . . . . . . . . | _____ | _____ | |
| | dog stuff 3-10 | . . . . . . . . . | _____ | _____ | |

[1] All printed exercises are one page long unless otherwise indicated.

| | Printed | Score | Date Completed | Instructor |
|---|---|---|---|---|
| prices 3-11 | . . . . . . . . | _____ | _____ | |
| form 3-12 | . . . . . . . . | _____ | _____ | |
| welcome 3-13 | . . . . . . . . | _____ | _____ | |
| bullets 3-14 | . . . . . . . . | _____ | _____ | |
| list 3-16 | . . . . . . . . | _____ | _____ | |
| welcome 3-18 | . . . . . . . . | _____ | _____ | |
| Review Questions | . . . . . . . . | _____ | _____ | _____ |
| fund proj3 | 2 pages | _____ | _____ | _____ |
| Lesson 3 Quiz | . . . . . . . . | _____ | _____ | _____ |
| | | | | |
| **Lesson 4** obedience 4-2 | 2 pages | _____ | _____ | |
| ethics 4-4 | 2 pages | _____ | _____ | |
| footnotes 4-5 | . . . . . . . . | _____ | _____ | |
| ethics 4-6 | 2 pages | _____ | _____ | |
| ethics 4-7 | endnote page | _____ | _____ | |
| fit 4-9 | . . . . . . . . | _____ | _____ | |
| ethics 4-10 | 2 pages | _____ | _____ | |
| ethics 4-13 | 3 pages | _____ | _____ | |
| Review Questions | . . . . . . . . | _____ | _____ | _____ |
| welcome proj4 | 3 pages | _____ | _____ | _____ |
| Lesson 4 Quiz | . . . . . . . . | _____ | _____ | _____ |
| Production Test 3&4 | . . . . . . . . | _____ | _____ | _____ |
| | | | | |
| **Lesson 5** psych 5-4 | . . . . . . . . | _____ | _____ | |
| summary 5-5 | . . . . . . . . | _____ | _____ | |
| advance 5-11 | . . . . . . . . | _____ | _____ | |
| fax 5-16 | . . . . . . . . | _____ | _____ | |
| Review Questions | . . . . . . . . | _____ | _____ | _____ |
| obedience proj5 | 2 pages | _____ | _____ | _____ |
| Lesson 5 Quiz | . . . . . . . . | _____ | _____ | _____ |

|  |  | Printed | Score | Date Completed | Instructor |
|---|---|---|---|---|---|
| **Lesson 6** | bones 6-4 | . . . . . . . . . | _____ | _____ | |
| | groom 6-6 | . . . . . . . . . | _____ | _____ | |
| | board 6-10 | . . . . . . . . . | _____ | _____ | |
| | message 6-11 | . . . . . . . . . | _____ | _____ | |
| | forests 6-13 | 2 pages | _____ | _____ | |
| | Review Questions | . . . . . . . . . | _____ | _____ | _____ |
| | time proj6 | . . . . . . . . . | _____ | _____ | _____ |
| | Lesson 6 Quiz | . . . . . . . . . | _____ | _____ | _____ |
| | Production Test 5&6 | . . . . . . . . . | _____ | _____ | _____ |
| | | | | | |
| **Lesson 7** | open 7-3 | 3 letters | | | |
| | open 7-5 | envelope | | | |
| | cust list 7-6 | . . . . . . . . . | _____ | _____ | |
| | cust list 7-7 | . . . . . . . . . | _____ | _____ | |
| | cust table 7-8 | . . . . . . . . . | _____ | _____ | |
| | gordon 7-9 | . . . . . . . . . | _____ | _____ | |
| | bella 7-9 | . . . . . . . . . | _____ | _____ | |
| | sort 7-10 | . . . . . . . . . | _____ | _____ | |
| | sort 7-11 | . . . . . . . . . | _____ | _____ | |
| | customers 7-12 | page 5 | _____ | _____ | |
| | terrier 7-13 | . . . . . . . . . | _____ | _____ | |
| | small pets 7-14 | 2 pages | _____ | _____ | |
| | Review Questions | . . . . . . . . . | _____ | _____ | _____ |
| | cats proj7 | . . . . . . . . . | _____ | _____ | _____ |
| | Lesson 7 Quiz | . . . . . . . . . | _____ | _____ | _____ |
| | | | | | |
| **Lesson 8** | arrow 8-3 | . . . . . . . . . | _____ | _____ | |
| | rose 8-4 | . . . . . . . . . | _____ | _____ | |
| | rose 8-5a | . . . . . . . . . | _____ | _____ | |

| | Printed | Score | Date Completed | Instructor |
|---|---|---|---|---|
| rose 8-5b | . . . . . . . . | _____ | _____ | |
| rose 8-6 | . . . . . . . . | _____ | _____ | |
| text box 8-7 | . . . . . . . . | _____ | _____ | |
| art 8-8 | . . . . . . . . | _____ | _____ | |
| drop cap 8-9 | . . . . . . . . | _____ | _____ | |
| lines 8-10 | . . . . . . . . | _____ | _____ | |
| shapes 8-11 | . . . . . . . . | _____ | _____ | |
| joining 8-11 | . . . . . . . . | _____ | _____ | |
| graphics 8-12 | . . . . . . . . | _____ | _____ | |
| flyer 8-13 | . . . . . . . . | _____ | _____ | |
| dog 8-14 | . . . . . . . . | _____ | _____ | |
| graphics 8-15 | . . . . . . . . | _____ | _____ | |
| groom 8-16 | . . . . . . . . | _____ | _____ | |
| equation 8-17 | . . . . . . . . | _____ | _____ | |
| top 8-18 | . . . . . . . . | _____ | _____ | |
| draw 8-19 | . . . . . . . . | _____ | _____ | |
| cat 8-20 | . . . . . . . . | _____ | _____ | |
| Review Questions | . . . . . . . . | _____ | _____ | _____ |
| flyer proj8 | . . . . . . . . | _____ | _____ | _____ |
| Lesson 8 Quiz | . . . . . . . . | _____ | _____ | _____ |
| Production Test 7&8 | . . . . . . . . | _____ | _____ | _____ |
| **Lesson 9** travel 9-2 | . . . . . . . . | _____ | _____ | |
| calendar 9-7 | . . . . . . . . | _____ | _____ | |
| Spring News 9-11 | 2 pages | _____ | _____ | |
| web1 | . . . . . . . . | _____ | _____ | |
| web2 | . . . . . . . . | _____ | _____ | |
| web3 | . . . . . . . . | _____ | _____ | |
| Review Questions | . . . . . . . . | _____ | _____ | _____ |
| proj9 | . . . . . . . . | _____ | _____ | _____ |
| Lesson 9 Quiz | . . . . . . . . | _____ | _____ | _____ |

|  | | Printed | Score | Date Completed | Instructor |
|---|---|---|---|---|---|
| **Lesson 10** | contents 10-2 | contents page | _____ | _____ | |
| | contents 10-3 | contents page | _____ | _____ | |
| | numbers 10-4 | page 2 | _____ | _____ | |
| | index 10-5 | index | _____ | _____ | |
| | sale memo 10-9 | . . . . . . . . | _____ | _____ | |
| | teeth 10-10 | . . . . . . . . | _____ | _____ | |
| | Review Questions | . . . . . . . . | _____ | _____ | _____ |
| | master proj10 | index & toc. | _____ | _____ | _____ |
| | Lesson 10 Quiz | . . . . . . . . | _____ | _____ | _____ |
| | Production Test 9&10 | . . . . . . . . | _____ | _____ | _____ |

# Corel® Quattro® Pro 8

Name _____

| | | Printed[1] | Score | Date Completed | Instructor |
|---|---|---|---|---|---|
| **Lesson 1** | grooming 1-7 | . . . . . . . . . | _____ | _____ | |
| | Review Questions | . . . . . . . . . | _____ | _____ | _____ |
| | boarding fees proj1a | . . . . . . . . . | _____ | _____ | _____ |
| | car sales proj1b | . . . . . . . . . | _____ | _____ | _____ |
| | Lesson 1 Quiz | . . . . . . . . . | _____ | _____ | _____ |
| **Lesson 2** | boarding 2-7 | . . . . . . . . . | _____ | _____ | |
| | boarding 2-8 | . . . . . . . . . | _____ | _____ | |
| | Review Questions | . . . . . . . . . | _____ | _____ | _____ |
| | bill proj2a | . . . . . . . . . | _____ | _____ | _____ |
| | morrison sale proj2b | 2 pages | _____ | _____ | _____ |
| | Lesson 2 Quiz | . . . . . . . . . | _____ | _____ | _____ |
| **Lesson 3** | grooming 3-2 | . . . . . . . . . | _____ | _____ | |
| | weekly 3-3 | . . . . . . . . . | _____ | _____ | |
| | quarterly grooming 3-5 | . . . . . . . . . | _____ | _____ | |
| | expenses 3-7 | . . . . . . . . . | _____ | _____ | |
| | Review Questions | . . . . . . . . . | _____ | _____ | _____ |
| | mortgage proj3a | . . . . . . . . . | _____ | _____ | _____ |
| | commission proj3b | . . . . . . . . . | _____ | _____ | _____ |
| | Lesson 3 Quiz | . . . . . . . . . | _____ | _____ | _____ |
| | Production Test 1-3 | . . . . . . . . . | _____ | _____ | _____ |
| **Lesson 4** | income 4-4 | 2 pages | _____ | _____ | _____ |
| | Review Questions | . . . . . . . . . | _____ | _____ | _____ |
| | january inventory proj4a | 2 pages | _____ | _____ | _____ |

[1] All printed exercises are one page long unless otherwise indicated.

| | | Printed | Score | Date Completed | Instructor |
|---|---|---|---|---|---|
| | morrison payroll proj4b | . . . . . . . . . | _____ | _____ | _____ |
| | Lesson 4 Quiz | . . . . . . . . . | _____ | _____ | _____ |
| **Lesson 5** | sort 5-1 | . . . . . . . . . | _____ | _____ | |
| | quarter 5-6 | . . . . . . . . . | _____ | _____ | |
| | quarter 5-7 | . . . . . . . . . | _____ | _____ | |
| | Review Questions | . . . . . . . . . | _____ | _____ | _____ |
| | payroll proj5a | . . . . . . . . . | _____ | _____ | _____ |
| | computers proj5b | 2 pages | _____ | _____ | _____ |
| | Lesson 5 Quiz | . . . . . . . . . | _____ | _____ | _____ |
| **Lesson 6** | quarter 6-1 | 2 pages | _____ | _____ | |
| | quarter 6-2 | . . . . . . . . . | _____ | _____ | |
| | quarter 6-3 | 2 pages | _____ | _____ | |
| | quarter 6-5 | 2 pages | _____ | _____ | |
| | quarter 6-6 | 8 pages | _____ | _____ | |
| | Review Questions | . . . . . . . . . | _____ | _____ | _____ |
| | income proj6a | 2 pages | _____ | _____ | _____ |
| | computers proj6b | 5 pages | _____ | _____ | _____ |
| | Lesson 6 Quiz | . . . . . . . . . | _____ | _____ | _____ |
| | Production Test 4-6 | . . . . . . . . . | _____ | _____ | _____ |
| **Lesson 7** | projected 7-1 | . . . . . . . . . | _____ | _____ | |
| | payments 7-2 | . . . . . . . . . | _____ | _____ | |
| | mortgage 7-3 | . . . . . . . . . | _____ | _____ | |
| | Review Questions | . . . . . . . . . | _____ | _____ | _____ |
| | increases proj7a | . . . . . . . . . | _____ | _____ | _____ |
| | purchase proj7b | . . . . . . . . . | _____ | _____ | _____ |
| | Lesson 7 Quiz | . . . . . . . . . | _____ | _____ | _____ |

| | | Printed | Score | Date Completed | Instructor |
|---|---|---|---|---|---|
| **Lesson 8** | pet boarding 8-2 | chart only | _____ | _____ | |
| | income 8-5 | chart only | _____ | _____ | |
| | pet boarding 8-6 | chart only | _____ | _____ | |
| | Review Questions | ......... | _____ | _____ | _____ |
| | expenses proj8a | chart only | _____ | _____ | _____ |
| | car sales proj8b | chart only | _____ | _____ | _____ |
| | Lesson 8 Quiz | ......... | _____ | _____ | _____ |
| | | | | | |
| **Lesson 9** | map 9-1 | map only | _____ | _____ | |
| | map 9-4 | map only | _____ | _____ | |
| | Review Questions | ......... | _____ | _____ | _____ |
| | dealerships proj9a | ......... | _____ | _____ | _____ |
| | Lesson 9 Quiz | ......... | _____ | _____ | _____ |
| | Production Test 7-9 | ......... | _____ | _____ | _____ |
| | | | | | |
| **Lesson 10** | sales 10-2 | ......... | _____ | _____ | |
| | sales 10-4 | 2 pages | _____ | _____ | |
| | sales 10-5 | ......... | _____ | _____ | |
| | Review Questions | ......... | _____ | _____ | _____ |
| | employees proj10a | 4 pages | _____ | _____ | _____ |
| | cars proj10b | 5 pages | _____ | _____ | _____ |
| | Lesson 10 Quiz | ......... | _____ | _____ | |
| | | | | | |
| **Lesson 11** | report 11-1 | ......... | _____ | _____ | |
| | report 11-6 | ......... | _____ | _____ | |
| | Review Questions | ......... | _____ | _____ | _____ |
| | car report proj11a | ......... | _____ | _____ | _____ |
| | car report proj11b | ......... | _____ | _____ | _____ |
| | Lesson 11 Quiz | ......... | _____ | _____ | _____ |

|  | | Printed | Score | Date Completed | Instructor |
|---|---|---|---|---|---|
| **Lesson 12** | new sales 12-2 | 2 pages | _____ | _____ | |
| | new sales 12-3 | 2 pages | _____ | _____ | |
| | expense report 12-4 | . . . . . . . . . | _____ | _____ | |
| | Review Questions | . . . . . . . . | _____ | _____ | _____ |
| | west computers proj12a | 4 pages | _____ | _____ | _____ |
| | budget proj12b | varies | _____ | _____ | _____ |
| | Lesson 12 Quiz | . . . . . . . . . | _____ | _____ | _____ |
| | Production Test 10-12 | . . . . . . . . . | _____ | _____ | _____ |

# Corel® Presentations™ 8

Name _____

| | | Printed[1] | Score | Date Completed | Instructor |
|---|---|---|---|---|---|
| **Lesson 1** | pet care 1-3 | n/a | _____ | _____ | |
| | Review Questions | n/a | _____ | _____ | _____ |
| | prospective employee 1a | n/a | _____ | _____ | _____ |
| | pet perks 1b | n/a | _____ | _____ | _____ |
| | first impressions 1c | n/a | _____ | _____ | _____ |
| | Lesson 1 Quiz | n/a | _____ | _____ | _____ |
| | | | | | |
| **Lesson 2** | pet care 2-2 | n/a | _____ | _____ | |
| | pet care 2-4 | n/a | _____ | _____ | |
| | pet care 2-5 (PR2.7) | 2 pages | _____ | _____ | |
| | Review Questions | n/a | _____ | _____ | _____ |
| | pet perks 2a | 5 pages | _____ | _____ | _____ |
| | prospective employee 2b | 3 pages | _____ | _____ | _____ |
| | Lesson 2 Quiz | n/a | _____ | _____ | _____ |
| | | | | | |
| **Lesson 3** | pet care 3-1 | n/a | _____ | _____ | |
| | pet care 3-2 | 5 pages | _____ | _____ | |
| | pet care 3-3 | . . . . . . . . . | _____ | _____ | |
| | prospective employee 3-4 | . . . . . . . . . | _____ | _____ | |
| | pet care 3-5 | . . . . . . . . . | _____ | _____ | |
| | customer service 3-6 | 7 pages | _____ | _____ | |
| | customer service 3-7 | . . . . . . . . . | _____ | _____ | |
| | customer service 3-8 | 2 pages | _____ | _____ | |
| | pet care 3-9 | . . . . . . . . . | _____ | _____ | |
| | pet care 3-10 | 2 pages | _____ | _____ | |
| | Review Questions | n/a | _____ | _____ | _____ |

[1] All printed exercises are one page long unless otherwise indicated.

| | | Printed | Score | Date Completed | Instructor |
|---|---|---|---|---|---|
| | pet perks 3a | 2 pages | _____ | _____ | _____ |
| | pet care 3b | 2 pages | _____ | _____ | _____ |
| | Lesson 3 Quiz | n/a | _____ | _____ | _____ |
| | | | | | |
| **Lesson 4** | dog days 4-2 | . . . . . . . . | _____ | _____ | |
| | dog days 4-3 | . . . . . . . . | _____ | _____ | |
| | dog days 4-5 | . . . . . . . . | _____ | _____ | |
| | dog days 4-6 | . . . . . . . . | _____ | _____ | |
| | dog days 4-7 | . . . . . . . . | _____ | _____ | |
| | Review Questions | n/a | _____ | _____ | _____ |
| | first impressions 4a | . . . . . . . . | _____ | _____ | _____ |
| | pet classes 4b | . . . . . . . . | _____ | _____ | _____ |
| | pet classes 4c | . . . . . . . . | _____ | _____ | _____ |
| | Lesson 4 Quiz | n/a | _____ | _____ | _____ |
| | Production Test 1-4 | 3 pages | _____ | _____ | _____ |
| | | | | | |
| **Lesson 5** | orientation 5-2 | . . . . . . . . | _____ | _____ | |
| | weekend retreat 5-4 | . . . . . . . . | _____ | _____ | |
| | Review Questions | n/a | _____ | _____ | _____ |
| | new location 5a | . . . . . . . . | _____ | _____ | _____ |
| | Project 5B | multiple pgs. | _____ | _____ | _____ |
| | Lesson 5 Quiz | n/a | _____ | _____ | _____ |
| | | | | | |
| **Lesson 6** | bonus bucks 6-3 | . . . . . . . . | _____ | _____ | |
| | bonus bucks 6-4 | 2 pages | _____ | _____ | |
| | pet care 6-5 | . . . . . . . . | _____ | _____ | |
| | pet care 6-6 | . . . . . . . . | _____ | _____ | |
| | pet care 6-7 | 3 pages | _____ | _____ | |
| | Review Questions | n/a | _____ | _____ | _____ |
| | pet perks 6a | 5 pages | _____ | _____ | _____ |

| | | Printed | Score | Date Completed | Instructor |
|---|---|---|---|---|---|
| | bonus bucks 6b | . . . . . . . . | _____ | _____ | _____ |
| | bonus bucks 6c | . . . . . . . . | _____ | _____ | _____ |
| | Lesson 6 Quiz | n/a | _____ | _____ | _____ |
| **Lesson 7** | pet food 7-2 | . . . . . . . . | _____ | _____ | |
| | pet food 7-3 | . . . . . . . . | _____ | _____ | |
| | pet food 7-5 | . . . . . . . . | _____ | _____ | |
| | Review Questions | n/a | _____ | _____ | _____ |
| | dog days 7a | . . . . . . . . | _____ | _____ | _____ |
| | customer survey 7b | . . . . . . . . | _____ | _____ | _____ |
| | Lesson 7 Quiz | n/a | _____ | _____ | _____ |
| **Lesson 8** | pet food 8-4 | . . . . . . . . | _____ | _____ | |
| | pet food 8-5 | . . . . . . . . | _____ | _____ | |
| | pet food 8-7 | . . . . . . . . | _____ | _____ | |
| | pet food 8-8 | . . . . . . . . | _____ | _____ | |
| | Review Questions | n/a | _____ | _____ | _____ |
| | customer survey 8a | . . . . . . . . | _____ | _____ | _____ |
| | cat toys 8b | . . . . . . . . | _____ | _____ | _____ |
| | Lesson 8 Quiz | n/a | _____ | _____ | _____ |
| | Production Test 5-8 | 5 pages | _____ | _____ | _____ |
| **Lesson 9** | pet sales 9-3 | . . . . . . . . | _____ | _____ | |
| | pet sales 9-4 | . . . . . . . . | _____ | _____ | |
| | pet sales 9-6 | . . . . . . . . | _____ | _____ | |
| | Review Questions | n/a | _____ | _____ | _____ |
| | dog days 9a | . . . . . . . . | _____ | _____ | _____ |
| | orientation 9b | . . . . . . . . | _____ | _____ | _____ |
| | Lesson 9 Quiz | n/a | _____ | _____ | _____ |

|  |  | Printed | Score | Date Completed | Instructor |
|---|---|---|---|---|---|
| **Lesson 10** | expansion plan 10-2 | 3 pages | _____ | _____ | |
| | expansion plan 10-3 | . . . . . . . . | _____ | _____ | |
| | expansion plan 10-6 | . . . . . . . . | _____ | _____ | |
| | Review Questions | n/a | _____ | _____ | _____ |
| | community action 10a | . . . . . . . . | _____ | _____ | _____ |
| | paradise pet supplies 10b | . . . . . . . . | _____ | _____ | _____ |
| | Lesson 10 Quiz | n/a | _____ | _____ | _____ |
| **Lesson 11** | prospective employee 11-2 | n/a | _____ | _____ | |
| | pet classes 11-3 | n/a | _____ | _____ | |
| | pet classes 11-4 | n/a | _____ | _____ | |
| | pet classes 11-5 | n/a | _____ | _____ | |
| | Review Questions | n/a | _____ | _____ | _____ |
| | bonus bucks 11a | n/a | _____ | _____ | _____ |
| | first impressions 11b | n/a | _____ | _____ | _____ |
| | Lesson 11 Quiz | n/a | _____ | _____ | _____ |
| **Lesson 12** | first impressions 12-1 (PR12.2) | n/a | _____ | _____ | |
| | prospective employee 12-3 | n/a | _____ | _____ | |
| | pet classes 12-5 | n/a | _____ | _____ | |
| | pet perks 12-6 | n/a | _____ | _____ | |
| | Review Questions | n/a | _____ | _____ | _____ |
| | course catalog 12a | n/a | _____ | _____ | _____ |
| | course catalog 12b | n/a | _____ | _____ | _____ |
| | Lesson 12 Quiz | n/a | _____ | _____ | _____ |
| | Production Test 9-12 | 5 pages | _____ | _____ | _____ |

# *Corel® Paradox® 8*

Name _____

| | | Printed[1] | Score | Date Completed | Instructor |
|---|---|---|---|---|---|
| **Lesson 1** | Ex. PA1.1 | n/a | _____ | _____ | |
| | Ex. PA1.2 | n/a | _____ | _____ | |
| | Ex. PA1.3 | n/a | _____ | _____ | |
| | Review Questions | n/a | _____ | _____ | _____ |
| | Lesson 1 Project | n/a | _____ | _____ | _____ |
| | Lesson 1 Quiz | n/a | _____ | _____ | _____ |
| | | | | | |
| **Lesson 2** | Ex. PA2.1 | n/a | _____ | _____ | |
| | Ex. PA2.2 | n/a | _____ | _____ | |
| | Ex. PA2.3 | n/a | _____ | _____ | |
| | Ex. PA2.4 | n/a | _____ | _____ | |
| | Ex. PA2.5 | . . . . . . . . . | _____ | _____ | |
| | Review Questions | n/a | _____ | _____ | _____ |
| | Lesson 2 Project | 2 pages | _____ | _____ | _____ |
| | Lesson 2 Quiz | n/a | _____ | _____ | _____ |
| | | | | | |
| **Lesson 3** | Ex. PA3.1 | . . . . . . . . . | _____ | _____ | |
| | Ex. PA3.2 | . . . . . . . . . | _____ | _____ | |
| | Ex. PA3.3 | n/a | _____ | _____ | |
| | Ex. PA3.4 | . . . . . . . . . | _____ | _____ | |
| | Review Questions | n/a | _____ | _____ | _____ |
| | Lesson 3 Project | . . . . . . . . . | _____ | _____ | _____ |
| | Lesson 3 Quiz | n/a | _____ | _____ | _____ |
| | | | | | |
| **Lesson 4** | Ex. PA4.1 | n/a | _____ | _____ | |
| | Ex. PA4.2 | . . . . . . . . . | _____ | _____ | |

[1] All printed exercises are one page long unless otherwise indicated.

| | Printed | Score | Date Completed | Instructor |
|---|---|---|---|---|
| Ex. PA4.3 | . . . . . . . . . | _____ | _____ | |
| Review Questions | n/a | _____ | _____ | _____ |
| Project 4A | 2 pages | _____ | _____ | _____ |
| Project 4B | . . . . . . . . . | _____ | _____ | _____ |
| Lesson 4 Quiz | n/a | _____ | _____ | _____ |
| | | | | |
| **Lesson 5** Ex. PA5.1 | n/a | _____ | _____ | |
| Ex. PA5.2 | 2 pages | _____ | _____ | |
| Ex. PA5.3 | . . . . . . . . . | _____ | _____ | |
| Review Questions | n/a | _____ | _____ | _____ |
| Lesson 5 Project | 2 pages | _____ | _____ | _____ |
| Lesson 5 Quiz | n/a | _____ | _____ | _____ |
| | | | | |
| **Lesson 6** Ex. PA6.1 | n/a | _____ | _____ | |
| Ex. PA6.2 | . . . . . . . . . | _____ | _____ | |
| Review Questions | n/a | _____ | _____ | _____ |
| Lesson 6 Project | . . . . . . . . . | _____ | _____ | _____ |
| Lesson 6 Quiz | n/a | _____ | _____ | _____ |
| Production Test 1-6 | 7 pages | _____ | _____ | _____ |

# Integration 1–4

Name _____

|  | Printed[1] | Score | Date Completed | Instructor |
|---|---|---|---|---|
| **Integration 1** (following WordPerfect section) | | | | |
| P&P 1-3 | . . . . . . . . . | _____ | _____ | |
| bus-card 1-5 | . . . . . . . . . | _____ | _____ | |
| ad-copy 1-6 | . . . . . . . . . | _____ | _____ | |
| brochure | 2 pages | _____ | _____ | |
| mailing 1-14 | 2 pages | _____ | _____ | _____ |
| Review Questions | . . . . . . . . . | _____ | _____ | _____ |
| Integration 1 Project | . . . . . . . . . | _____ | _____ | _____ |
| **Integration 2** (following Quattro Pro section) | | | | |
| licenses | . . . . . . . . . | _____ | _____ | |
| animal licenses | . . . . . . . . . | _____ | _____ | |
| fees (INT2.5) | . . . . . . . . . | _____ | _____ | |
| fees (INT2.6) | . . . . . . . . . | _____ | _____ | |
| heartworm2 | . . . . . . . . . | _____ | _____ | |
| heartworm flyer | . . . . . . . . . | _____ | _____ | |
| Review Questions | . . . . . . . . . | _____ | _____ | _____ |
| outtake199x | . . . . . . . . . | _____ | _____ | _____ |
| animal shelter | . . . . . . . . . | _____ | _____ | _____ |
| **Integration 3** (following Presentations section) | | | | |
| licenses2 | . . . . . . . . . | _____ | _____ | |
| clinic logo | . . . . . . . . . | _____ | _____ | |
| P&P 3-10 | . . . . . . . . . | _____ | _____ | |
| pet care handout | 5 pages | _____ | _____ | |
| org chart | . . . . . . . . . | _____ | _____ | |

[1] All printed exercises are one page long unless otherwise indicated.

|                  | Printed | Score | Date Completed | Instructor |
|------------------|---------|-------|----------------|------------|
| Review Questions | . . . . . . . . | _____ | _____ | _____ |
| pet overpopulation | 3 pages | _____ | _____ | _____ |

**Integration 4**  (following Paradox section)

|                  | Printed | Score | Date Completed | Instructor |
|------------------|---------|-------|----------------|------------|
| merged introduction letter (first page) | . . . . . . . . | _____ | _____ | |
| merged envelope (first envelope) | . . . . . . . . | _____ | _____ | |
| expended inventory | 2 pages | _____ | _____ | |
| vac information | . . . . . . . . | _____ | _____ | |
| topdogs | . . . . . . . . | _____ | _____ | |
| geriatric pet | 2 pages | _____ | _____ | |
| Review Questions | . . . . . . . . | _____ | _____ | _____ |
| discount letter (first letter) | . . . . . . . . | _____ | _____ | _____ |